RESTORING AMERICAN GARDENS

RESTORING AMERICAN GARDENS

An Encyclopedia of Heirloom Ornamental Plants

1640–1940

DENISE WILES ADAMS

TIMBER PRESS
Portland · Cambridge

Mention of trademark, proprietary product, or vendor does not constitute a guarantee or warranty of the product by the publisher or authors and does not imply its approval to the exclusion of other products or vendors.

While every effort has been made to trace copyright holders and obtain permission, this has not been possible in all cases; any omissions brought to our attention will be remedied in future editions.

Published in 2004 by
Timber Press, Inc.
The Haseltine Building
133 S.W. Second Avenue, Suite 450
Portland, Oregon 97204 U.S.A.

Timber Press
2 Station Road
Swavesey
Cambridge CB4 5QJ, U.K.

Printed in Hong Kong

Library of Congress Cataloging-in-Publication Data

Adams, Denise W.
    Restoring American gardens : an encyclopedia of heirloom ornamental plants, 1640–1940 / Denise Wiles Adams.
        p. cm.
    Includes bibliographical references (p.).
    ISBN 0-88192-619-1
    1. Gardening--United States. 2. Heirloom varieties (Plants)--United States. 3. Landscape plants--Heirloom varieties--United States. I. Title.

    SB453.A32 3004
    635.9'0973--dc21   2003057274

A catalog record for this book is also available from the British Library.

This book is dedicated to

John, Heather, and Jonathan.

CONTENTS

PREFACE

AMERICAN HEIRLOOM ORNAMENTAL PLANTS connect us with our family and national roots and provide lasting continuity between successive generations. They are plants to be studied, appreciated, cherished, and preserved for future generations. Historic plants and gardens are subjects of increasing interest in the United States today. The growth of regional garden history societies throughout the country is evidence of this trend, as is the plethora of popular books and articles on the subject

Garden historians, landscape architects, educators, and growers are challenged with the task of identifying and producing appropriate plant material for period landscaping, taking into account regional variations in the popularity and availability of particular plant species and cultivars for different eras. By studying the plant offerings of nurseries and design recommendations in the literature for specific regions and individual states, we can make better choices concerning plant selection and incorporation into period gardens and landscapes.

Of course, professionals are not the only people interested in heirloom plants. Heirloom gardening provides an important connection to the past. A gardener might not be interested in re-creating an entire historic garden typical of, say, 1915, but would like to know some of the plants that a grandmother living in North Dakota might have grown in her garden. Likewise, the new owner of an 1840s Greek Revival home in Ohio's Western Reserve might like to grow a few appropriate plants, combining them in a mixed period design to enhance the architecture. Heirloom plants are appropriate for both purist and eclectic approaches to landscape design.

Many historic plants have inherent properties that make them desirable for cultivation aside from, or in addition to,

their heirloom status. The sweet fragrance of an old-fashioned rose or the vigor and cheerfulness of the blue morning glory are certain inducements for culture. The stalwart reliability of the Norway spruce or the American arborvitae has allowed these heirloom plants to remain high on popularity lists consistently from the nineteenth through the twenty-first centuries. Some heirlooms emerge unbidden, but still appreciated, in the landscape—plants like the star-of-Bethlehem that studs the lawn in early spring or seedling petunias that germinate in midsummer after resting dormant in the soil. Many country people still follow the custom of lining a vegetable garden with an old gladiolus or preserving the line of peonies that marked an early pathway to a now-demolished outhouse.

This is a book about heirloom ornamental plants for gardens of the contiguous United States. Researching the components of historic gardens is both a science and an art, relying not only on hard evidence, but also on educated interpretations. I have chosen to explore the written and published documentation, realizing that it provides but one small part of the garden history story for the United States. In all parts of this country, gardeners also grew beloved plants, having obtained them from noncommercial sources, and did *not* write about them. Someone else will have to tell that story.

Few books available today emphasize *American* ornamental plant history. The history of ornamental plants immediately following their introduction, primarily in Europe, is certainly of interest but those stories have already been told very well. My research concentrated on following a plant after it reached our shores or, in some cases, from its introduction from the fields and forests of this country. This book answers questions such as: Who first cultivated the plant in America? How was it used in American garden design? Who propagated and sold the plant? Why was the plant popular?

Many landscape historians agree that the nursery plant or seed catalog is a good source for reliable information on nursery activities and plants available during a certain period. Several biases are inherent in this type of documentation, however. Catalogs typically are representative of those nurseries or seed houses that were prosperous enough to issue them for distribution. For example, evidence documents that over 1000 different nurseries existed in the state of Ohio at some time during the nineteenth century. Only about 3 percent of those firms are represented by an extant nursery or seed catalog in contemporary collections. Obviously, data based on just those catalogs is skewed toward a few representatives. Moreover, catalogs had to be of sufficient quality to survive for 100-plus years in often less than optimal conditions, and someone, somewhere, had to be motivated to save the catalogs. *Vick's Floral Guide* of 1872 reported that it issued 200,000 copies for distribution. Only a handful of these has survived.

Today, rare book and paper dealers classify trade catalogs as "ephemera," a term that states the case succinctly. An additional concern is that, without sales records, it is impossible to determine the extent of the actual exchange of any particular plants or even to prove that the listing insured availability. Plant nomenclature offers yet another challenge since there is little confirmation that the correct name was used for a particular plant, with common names providing further obstruction to verifiable identification. Still, catalogs remain one important means for studying the horticultural tastes of a previous era.

For this book, I consulted over 300 seed and nursery catalogs from all over the United States. My goal was to have at least one firm predating 1940 from each of the contiguous forty-eight states and, in addition, to have credible representation from each of six geographic regions, ranging from the New England states to the western and mountain states. The only state for which I did not find evidence of local plant commerce was Nevada. The diversity of plants in the American nursery trade was astonishing—my plant database includes over 25,000 different taxa. While the diversity was incredible, so too was the commonality, with over 100 species and varieties consistently available throughout the entire country—an All-American plant list that is discussed in Appendix A.

After determining which plants were available, I looked to the period books and magazines for confirmation and descriptions of ornamental garden cultivation. It is important to recognize a bias in this literature since many garden writers were also nursery entrepreneurs. It is easy to imagine that they wrote about the plants they hoped to sell. The bibliography provides a good representation of important American garden literature.

Growers in the nineteenth century were surprisingly consistent in their use of botanical names in their catalogs. At that time only an informal international scientific standard existed for naming plants, although most followed the binomial nomenclature established by Carl Linnaeus in *Species Plantarum* (1753). In 1867 Alphonse DeCandolle made the first attempt at standardization of plant names at the First International Botanical Congress in Paris. It was not until 1930, however, at the Fifth International Congress in Cambridge, England, that the *International Code of Botanical Nomenclature* was adopted. Standards for horticultural nomenclature came later, in 1953, with *The International Code of Nomenclature for Cultivated Plants*.

In the nineteenth century, with few exceptions, listings of ornamental plants used the Linnaean binomial system, sometimes accompanied by the common name. The common name was often a strict translation of the Latin, for example, "denticulated dragon's head" for *Dracocephalum denticulatum*, although many more descriptive or whimsical common names were used as well, such as whip-poor-will shoe for what we now call lady's slipper, *Cypripedium acaule*. The naming of seedling and horticultural varieties followed two forms: Latin descriptive phrases, for example, *Paeonia striata rosea alba* (pre-1850); and, more commonly in the second half of the century, English "fancy" names like *Paeonia* Mons. Jules Elie. In modern times, such varieties are labeled cultivars—for cultivated variety—and are indicated by the use of single quotes, for example, *Paeonia* 'Mons. Jules Elie'. I have transcribed the older Latin names to their modern synonyms. The index cross-references these names.

The first chapter in this book is aimed toward those who wish to accurately document a historic landscape as well as those searching for some historic garden details to enhance their own landscapes. From the four approaches recommended by the National Park Service to commonsense observations of extant garden relics, this section will assist the researcher in determining what might have existed in a particular garden and how best to portray those elements.

Chapter 2 attempts to synthesize the architectural and garden history of the United States. We can define four general periods of building style from the earliest years of this country to World War II: Folk or Vernacular, Colonial (Federal, Georgian, Greek Revival), Victorian (Gothic Revival, Italianate, Queen Anne), and Twentieth Century (Colonial Revival, Craftsman). Within these periods, particular elements of garden style were often used alongside specific architectural styles. I discuss these most common garden elements and give appropriate plant lists and references to American horticultural literature and garden designers.

Chapter 3 takes the descriptions of architectural garden styles one step further and places them informally into a geographic context. It became obvious in the course of research for this book that garden styles themselves do not vary much across the country. However, the plant palette changes and develops with considerations of climate and heritage. Most examples in the Gardens and Geography chapter pertain to the vernacular landscape.

The remaining chapters comprise the Encyclopedia of Heirloom Ornamental Plants, categorized by plant type: trees, shrubs, vines, roses, and herbaceous plants—annuals, biennials, perennials, and bulbs. I did not choose the species and varieties randomly, but selected those plants most representative of American taste as indicated by the frequency with which they were found in nursery catalogs. Each entry includes descriptions of how the plants were placed in the landscape and what the desired effects were, as well as the first citation I was able to find in American horticultural literature. Actual dates of introduction into American horticulture are elusive, but, as researchers continue to study the literature, I hope some of these "earliest American citations" can be verified as introduction dates for this country. I have also included observations concerning the plant's virtues as recorded by period gardeners, as well as successful plant combinations. The stunning plant images represent the best of catalog art throughout the years, augmented by antique photos of heirloom plants in actual period landscapes and superb modern photographs.

My hope is that everyone will choose to garden with heirloom plants—from the favorite niece cultivating great-aunt Lucille's beloved fragrant pink rose, to the gardeners propagating and passing along their neighborhood's own ubiquitous blue iris, to the museum curator using well-documented flowering and evergreen shrubs to depict a nineteenth-century perimeter planting. American heirloom ornamental plants are national treasures to be honored and conserved and shared.

ACKNOWLEDGMENTS

THE WRITING OF THIS BOOK simply would not have occurred but for the encouragement and support of my dear friend and the world's greatest Indomitable Spirit, Tracy DiSabato-Aust. Many thanks also to Dr. Steve Still for encouraging me early on to research the subject about which I was most passionate, namely heirloom plants.

Many gifted people shared their talents with me in the development of this manuscript. Sherry Hawley, Deb Knapke, Marlea Graham, Tracy DiSabato-Aust, and Scott Kunst read the manuscript and offered suggestions for improvement. The catalog lists in my own collection were supplemented by photocopies of original documents from Sherry Vance of the Mann Library of Cornell University; Renee Jensen at the Andersen Horticulture Library of the University of Minnesota Landscape Arboretum; and Blanche Farley, formerly of the Cherokee Garden Library in Atlanta, Georgia. Additional plant lists came from Greg Grant, Art Tucker, Flora Ann Bynum, George Stritikus, Scott Kunst, and the staffs at the National Agriculture Library in Beltsville, Maryland, and at the Albert and Shirley Small Special Collections Library of the University of Virginia. Cynde Georgen of Trail End State Historic Site of Sheridan, Wyoming, sent plant records as did Joseph Lyons of the Oregon Historic Cemeteries Association and Lenadams Dorris in Nevada. Della Barnett discussed intergenerational gardening in Utah. Susan Hitchcock of the National Park Service in Atlanta graciously forwarded to me her master's thesis on Colonial Revival garden design. Lynn Adams kindly sent information from The Historic New Orleans Collection.

In addition to those friends listed above, encouragement came from Laura Burchfield, Laura Deeter, Holly Hawkins, Pam Duthie, Michele Thomas, Carolyn Still, Janet Oberliesen, Susannah Lawson, and Carol Lawson. Thanks also to my writing colleagues: LuAnn Brandsen, former editor of *Country Gardens*; Jennifer Benner at *Fine Gardening*; and Peg St. Clair of *The Gardener's Network*.

I also am very indebted to the Heirloom Flowers e-group for information and stimulating conversation concerning heritage plants and historic gardens. Some of its members are acknowledged elsewhere, but their names bear repeating here with the rest of the "gang," past and present: leader Scott Kunst, Art Tucker, Peggy Cornett, Bill Finch, Susan Hitchcock, Thomas Brown, Chuck Gleaves, Marty Ross, Susan Schnare, Rae Chambers, Bill Welch, Anne Haines, Pam Ruch, Deb Knapke, Greg Grant, Nancy Smith, Wesley Greene, Marlea Graham, Camilla Wilcox, Jim Cochran, Flora Ann Bynum, Beate Jensen, Kent Krugh, Bobby Green, Julie Daicoff, Pam Parrish, Susan Stieve, David Tay, Caroline Stalnaker, Joe Seals, Kathy Mendelson, and Glenn Varner.

When it was time to locate images to accompany my text, the excellent photographs that people enthusiastically allowed me to use were truly, in a word, "awesome." Many, many thanks again go to Scott Kunst and his helpful staff at Old House Gardens; Roy Klehm of Klehm's Song Sparrow Farm; Pat Sherman of Fragrant Garden Nursery; Susan Schnare of Mountain Brook Primroses; Peggy Cornett of the Thomas Jefferson Foundation; Bobby Green of Green Nursery; members of The American Hemerocallis Society, especially Tim Fehr, Mark Cook, and John Pike; Brent Heath of Brent and Becky's Bulbs; Marge Garfield; Robert Herman; Marlea Graham; Mike Shoup of the Antique Rose Emporium; Greg Grant; Dr. Steve Still of The Ohio State University; and LuAnn Brandsen and Pete Krumhardt at *Country Gardens* magazine. Gracious garden owners who allowed me to photograph their historic gardens include the staff at Gunston Hall, Lucy Weller of Gwinn estate, Barbara Kelley, and

Terre Matthews. Jean Easton of Pixels in Charlottesville handled the scanning of the black-and-white period images and Bill Moretz of ProCamera created the color transparencies. Susannah Lawson also assisted in image reproduction. Unless noted otherwise, all the period images came from my ever expanding collection of illustrations and photographs of heirloom ornamental plants and American historic landscapes.

Thanks to my editors: Neal Maillet, Lynn Bey-Roode, Lisa DiDonato, and Jane Merryman, for their thoroughness and expertise—and also their graciousness no matter how many deadlines I missed.

My son, Jonathan, set up the FileMaker Pro database for studying the catalog plants and daughter Heather combined interest and encouragement in her requests for frequent progress updates. John has been the proverbial long-suffering husband who gave up vacations and endured painting the house by himself while I toiled over the computer. My sister, Melanie, was most generous with her interest and support of this project. Thanks also to my parents, Bernard and Mary Wiles. This book is for all of you!

HISTORIC AMERICAN
GARDEN DESIGN

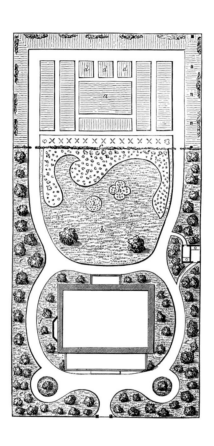

· 1 ·

READING THE HISTORIC LANDSCAPE

PERHAPS YOU JUST MOVED into a wonderful 1888 Queen Anne–style house in Iowa and would like the plantings to represent the late 1800s. Or maybe you are on the staff of a museum house and require the most detailed documentation for the management of features, both inside and out. Suppose you wish to imitate the gardening fashion of your grandmother's era in your own landscape or you may just be looking for a certain old-fashioned iris or peony that is said to be particularly fragrant. Any number of circumstances can motivate an interest in historic gardens and heirloom plants. Whatever the reason, preserving or adding

The appeal of ornamental plants transcends time. Photograph ca. 1915.

heirloom plants to modern landscapes not only honors our gardening predecessors, but also enriches our surroundings.

APPROACHES TO THE HISTORIC LANDSCAPE

Approaches to the challenge of what and how to plant can vary from well-defined treatments to more casual attitudes. The U.S. National Park Service (NPS) has taken a leadership role in the development of treatments for historic properties. *Guidelines for the Treatment of Cultural Properties* (Birnbaum 1996) describes four approaches for the treatment of historic landscapes. The Department of the Interior developed these strategies in response to increased interest and awareness of the need for accuracy and documentation in the management of historic landscapes.

Preservation seeks to identify, retain, stabilize, and provide continued maintenance of the historic features of a property. Nothing is added and little is taken away. The historic landscape is studied and measures are taken to preserve it with minimal intervention so the topography and vegetation features remain intact and are protected from future injury. A Civil War battlefield might be the object of preservation. Another good example of this treatment is Gwinn, the William Mather estate near Cleveland, Ohio, and the object of an ongoing landscape preservation effort. Robin Karson described the history and details of this landscape in the book *The Muses of Gwinn* (1995). Gwinn dates to the beginning years of the twentieth century and is distinguished by having been the object of design for several prominent landscape architects of the era, including Warren H. Manning, Charles A. Platt, and Ellen Biddle Shipman. Today, the plant-

Gwinn, the estate of William Mather, is an excellent example of landscape preservation. Photograph by author.

ings have been simplified due to economic constraints, but the overall landscape, with its atmosphere of elegance and charm, remains much the same as in its earlier days.

Restoration accurately portrays the landscape from a period of historical significance. It may be the era when the house was built or the years of residence of a famous person. Important landscape features from the significant period are identified and preserved or reconstructed, while details from subsequent or previous years are eliminated. Extensive research is necessary, often including archaeological digs. Restoration is a very exact treatment and rarely lends itself to a private residence. The gardens at George Washington's Mount Vernon exemplify this approach, with much of the documentation coming from Washington's diaries and records and landscape features preserved over time.

The goal of a restoration is "to make the landscape appear as it did at a particular—and most significant—time in its history." The NPS guidelines call for the identification and

Mature boxwoods at Gunston Hall in Virginia present a challenge to making the landscape appear exactly as it did in an earlier time. Photograph by author.

preservation of existing vegetation from the period of restoration. Fully grown trees and shrubs might appear differently than during the historically significant period, but are still considered valuable and retainable features of the past. Occasionally, the appearance of mature vegetation can interfere with the stated goals of a restoration attempt. At Gunston Hall in northern Virginia, if a decision is made to try to duplicate exactly what the colonial patriot George Mason saw when he walked out his door, then the huge, mature boxwoods that line the path to the Potomac River could interfere with that view. The original path was 12 ft. wide, but 200 years' growth of the boxwoods has greatly narrowed the passage. Whether or not to preserve those boxwoods would be a legitimate and probably highly charged debate.

Reconstruction seeks to re-create the features of a vanished site in order to depict its appearance during a period of significance. It is another treatment that requires extensive research and may use modern as well as old materials for reproduction structures. Archaeological digs can provide information ranging from the location of garden boundaries and fence posts to identification of some original plantings. The oft-cited example of a reconstructed site is the terraced vegetable garden at Thomas Jefferson's Monticello, near Charlottesville, Virginia. Aided by documentation obtained from Jefferson's letters and diaries, as well as evidence from the site itself, the major features of this garden, including planting bed lines, walls, and the pavilion that overlooks the vineyard, have been reconstructed. Reconstruction starts with little or nothing in the way of historic relics and is not attempted often in the treatment of historic properties.

Rehabilitation calls for the identification and preservation of the "historic character of a property" while adding necessary repairs or alterations so that the property might be used in a new way. This approach is appropriate to residential historic properties and multipurpose museum sites. The Ohio Historical Society's Paul Laurence Dunbar House (about 1880) in Dayton, Ohio, is in the early stages of landscape rehabilitation. The house and grounds serve as a museum to honor the African-American poet and provide a meeting place for local organizations. The aim is to rehabilitate the landscape to include as many features as possible from the years of Dunbar's residency (1903–1906). Early photographs, diaries, and existing vegetation provide documentation of the historic features of the site. Other considerations will be to make the property accessible and safe for the elderly or physically challenged without making too many drastic changes in its overall appearance.

A garden of heirloom perennials occupies the former site of a fallen oak at the author's home. Photograph by author.

In addition to the NPS guidelines, more informal perspectives exist for approaching a historic landscape. Many homeowners seek to match the landscape to the period or architecture of their house, using appropriate design features and focusing on popular period plants. As with the NPS treatments, this approach should begin with a site inventory to identify and preserve existing landscape features. Research into appropriate period styles and plants is necessary. Research strategies to obtain information concerning features of past landscapes are discussed in a later section of this chapter.

Finally, the most eclectic approach to a historic landscape might be called *making-a-new-layer*. Such was the advice that I received from another attendee at a conference of landscape historians at Old Salem, North Carolina, regarding my own eighteenth- to nineteenth-century property in Virginia. In any approach to the historic landscape, it is always important to determine what exists on the site that is historically important before adding or taking anything away. Making-a-new-layer then synthesizes the found aspects of the landscape—the mature white oaks, the grove of naturalized sweet mock orange, the August surprise lilies—with other heirloom flowers, as well as more recent cultivars. It is often helpful to separate the planting beds so the unique forms and fragrances of the heirloom favorites might be enjoyed in composition.

My individual perspective is that *all* the years preceding my residency at Gravel Hill are significant to its landscape history. During the mid-nineteenth century when the house served as a tavern and post office, few ornamental plantings graced the landscape, although the white oaks, which appear to follow an early, now-buried road, probably date from this period. It was not until the 1950s that ornamental gardens

were added to the property in a style more typical of New Orleans than central Virginia—since that was the hometown of that owner. Few herbaceous plants were used prior to 1998. The landscape at Gravel Hill could not be labeled eighteenth or nineteenth century, as are the buildings; it has evolved into the twenty-first century with as many plants of the past as I can possibly preserve or introduce.

DOCUMENTING FEATURES OF THE HISTORIC LANDSCAPE

Determining the features of a historic landscape is like working a puzzle. Details come from the site inventory, existing plants, architectural style, period books and magazines, photographs, diaries, even oral histories. Coordinating all the pieces into an accurate picture and plan is the garden researcher's challenge.

The architecture of the house can help define a period of time and provide guidance as to the shape and extent of the accompanying gardens. Whether a building is high style or of vernacular design provides information concerning the economic status of the owner—indicating how much time and money might have been invested in a garden. A stately Georgian mansion in the Virginia tidewater region obviously implies a more formal landscape than a Midwestern vernacular farmhouse.

The circulation pattern between the main structure and dependencies will reveal details about the garden. Look for remnants of roads, paths, walkways, and steps. Often layers of soil and wear obscure such permanent features. At an 1845-era house in Ohio, a row of double, white Chinese peonies lined the path between the house and the outhouse, long since dismantled—but the peonies remained 150 years later. At an 1806 Federal-style house nearby, locating the early well helped to uncover a brick pathway to the house, buried about 10 in. deep. Anyone who has edged the lawn along a walkway understands how quickly the grass will encroach on the paved surface. For primary documentation of circulation features and spatial appropriations, visit your county court house to view historic plans, old surveys, U.S. Geological Survey maps, plats, and tax maps. Aerial photographs can indicate details in the larger landscape that escape the eye at ground level.

Decorative garden features may still exist or be hidden under a trash heap or natural debris. The brick outline of a long-ago garden is apparent to visitors at the Oxford, Mississippi, home of author William Faulkner. At a garden in

The owners of this Newark, Ohio, property uncovered a fountain and lily pond, ca. 1925, buried under a trash pile. Matthews residence. Photograph by author.

This early-1900s garden has changed little over the past ninety years. Kelley residence. Photograph by author.

A modern rose bed occupies the space where once a path to the garden existed. Matthews residence. Photograph by author.

Newark, Ohio, an early twentieth-century fountain and pool were buried under trash at the rear of the property. Even the concrete lily boxes remained. At this same property, modern rose beds occupy the space formerly marking the pathways in the garden. It is important to take nothing for granted and to search every inch of the landscape for clues as to what might have existed in a previous period.

Anything that describes or depicts the property, be it old photographs, newspaper clippings, household records, letters, or diaries, is invaluable to the garden researcher. Barbara Kelley, also of Newark, Ohio, was fortunate in the rehabilitation of her heirloom garden to have planting records from the original inhabitant, an artist. Today that garden continues to project the distinctive flavor of the early 1900s. If documents do not exist for the property itself, information might be gleaned from parallel or similar sites in the region. Old

postcards and general photographs, nursery catalogs, garden magazines and books, paintings, and stereoscopic views may all provide details of garden features of a particular period. An old photograph might indicate plants, fencing, and other details of a similar landscape. In the early years of the twentieth century, it was common for an itinerant photographer to photograph a house and sell the image to the homeowner on postcards. Many of these "real-photo" postcards still exist, particularly from 1905 to 1920. A postmark supplies instant identification of place and year. Collections of old photographs reside in many historical societies and museums, not to mention the Archives of American Gardens at the Smithsonian Institution in Washington, D.C. This collection contained over 60,000 images of American gardens at the time of this writing and on-line access is available at www.si.edu/gardens/aag.htm.

Other sources for information concerning landscapes and gardens of the past are the county atlases that so many places commissioned in the mid- to late-1870s. These documents, often reprinted today by local historical societies, show drawings of many prominent residences in the county and their landscapes, frequently including features like fences, flower gardens, and trees and shrubs. Perhaps the artists embellished their landscape depiction—it is impossible to know for sure. Still the details are usually appropriate and fashionable for the period.

One additional consideration, not to put a damper on your enthusiasm, is to realize that many dwellings in former times did *not* have extensive gardens or well-developed cultivated landscapes, and photos and records that you find may convey this. Sometimes only a morning glory vine on a string and a red maple tree in the front yard composed all the ornamental plantings. Simplicity has merit, too. It is not surprising that many landscapes of the past were not so different in details from what we observe when driving through an average neighborhood. Many homes do not have elaborate gardens.

Throughout your research a tension will always exist between what might be defined as "the real" versus "the ideal." Photographs depict what was real, for that moment in that place. Paintings might be accurate or they might demonstrate a romanticized or embellished view of the landscape. Period books can go either way. Often writers discuss their personal experiences designing gardens and growing plants, but they also recommend ideas for design and plant choices based on what they deem to be tasteful—the ideal. Gardening magazines can be excellent sources of evidence for gardening activities. The letters to the editor often include brief descriptions of *real* gardens from around the country, while the main text of these volumes typically describes the most fashionable and *ideal* trends in gardening.

After the primary materials have been thoroughly scrutinized, secondary sources

Photograph from the late nineteenth century reveals garden details such as a picket fence and a Norway spruce in the yard of a Greek Revival-style house.

A real-photo postcard depicts a bottle planter and a row of Lombardy poplars, ca. 1908.

may prove helpful to identify garden features. These include books written about the period, state and local histories, theses and dissertations, National Register of Historic Places documentation, and oral histories. The books of Alice Lockwood, Rudy Favretti, and Ann Leighton are particularly useful for identifying period garden features. When using a secondary source, it is helpful to examine the bibliography to see on what basis the author has compiled information. Some books, unfortunately, merely repeat the work of other writers and other books are based on scholarly research dealing with original historical documents.

Residence of Thomas Fallon, San Jose, California. *Historical Atlas Map of Santa Clara County*, California, 1876. Reprint 1973.

DEVELOPING A PLANT LIST

The first and most important step in all treatment approaches to historic properties is to completely survey the site. Plan to record all existing plants over several seasons, if possible. It is surprising what is obvious in the early spring, as compared with late summer. Daffodils or other bulbs that have endured through many generations might emerge. Peonies, daylilies, yucca, and roses often survive many decades in a garden. If possible, *nothing should be removed* until this inventory has been completed. It might be difficult to wait, but *don't clean up* until everything is recorded. Stroll around in the neighborhood to observe plantings in local gardens. See what is growing in roadside culverts or what has naturalized in other nearby places. In the Midwest and the upper South, I have observed perennial sweet peas growing along roadsides, as well as yucca, orange daylilies, money plant, blue bearded iris, and daffodils, all escapees from past gardens.

Woody plants represent the evolution of a garden better than any other vegetative feature. The size and maturity of trees and shrubs can help determine the age of a garden. Of course, trees and shrubs may be original plantings or they might be exotic intruders that have taken over the garden—species like Norway maple in the Northeast, *Wisteria* and honeysuckle in the Middle Atlantic states, mimosa in Al-

abama and Florida, or tamarisk in the West. Sometimes these trees and woody vines must first be cleared so original plantings can be identified, but any such clearing should be done cautiously.

This is a good place to mention that not all heirloom plants are appropriate for planting in today's gardens. Plants that have proved to be invasive or particularly vigorous might threaten the environment where you live. *Lythrum salicaria* is an example of an heirloom plant found on fashionable planting plans of the early 1900s that is now on prohibited noxious weed lists in many states; Japanese honeysuckle is another. Appendix D provides lists of potentially invasive plants for regions across the United States. Always substitute for those plants that might take over, even if they have historic value to your site. The future must be protected as well as the past.

Some plants, particularly certain trees, are no longer respected, although they were extremely fashionable a century or two ago. For example, silver maple and tree-of-heaven enjoyed a popularity in the 1800s, but are much maligned today. Try to keep an open mind when conducting your plant inventory and attempt to understand what made each plant valuable or beautiful to a previous cultivator. Also, some plants of the past can be ravaged by pests of the present. The American elm and chestnut are classic examples. Sometimes substitutions are appropriate. When making a *necessary* plant substitution for a species known to have existed in the landscape, we must ask ourselves what was the purpose of that plant and why was it originally selected and cultivated. Was its form significant, as in the case of the Lombardy poplar? Or perhaps the fruit, flowers, or other ornamental feature was important to the overall design of the garden. Resolving to set aside modern biases and "getting into the head" of the original cultivator or designer can help us make appropriate substitutions.

Nursery catalogs are one of the few extant forms of period documentation for plants used in early American gar-

Springtime surveillance might reveal daffodils from long ago. Photograph by author.

Lonicera japonica, Japanese honeysuckle, may be beautiful, but it has proven to be too invasive to be introduced into landscapes over most of the country. Photograph by author.

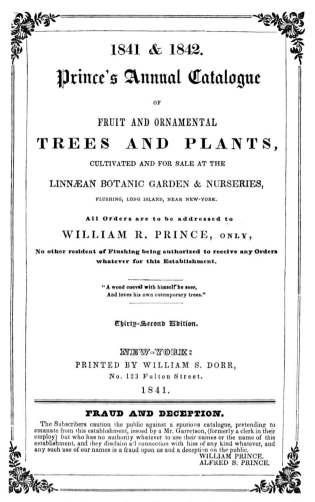

1841 & 1842 Prince's Annual Catalogue of Fruit and Ornamental Trees and Plants.

dens. Nurseries and seed houses that were located in the region of inquiry will prove most helpful, although after 1850 mail order was common. As discussed in the preface, some inherent problems arise from depending completely on the evidence of seed and nursery catalogs. Without the accompanying sales records, we cannot be sure if a particular plant was actually purchased, although inferences can be made by the frequency with which any particular plant was listed in the catalogs. No absolute assurance exists that plants actually were available or that they were identified accurately. Still, catalogs are extremely useful for the garden researcher and offer extensive insight into this country's horticultural heritage.

Besides considering the plants themselves, it also is important to think about how they arrived in the gardener's life and what they represented in the earlier landscape. Were the plants functional, sentimental, or ornamental? *Mobile Reg-*

ister environmental editor Bill Finch believes that, in addition to the plants, we must consider the entire context and functionality of the landscape:

> I think we can put too much emphasis on the specific plant material and not enough emphasis on the processes, the living context, the needs, limitations and advantages of a time and place that created a particular landscape, whether native or historic.
>
> I'd like to argue that the processes that created many historic landscapes . . . were fundamentally different than the processes that lead to the creation of modern gardens, and that's one of the reasons it's been very difficult for us to recreate accurate representations of the past. In the historic landscape, these processes might include everything from the tools (or lack thereof) for maintenance and propagation, to the sources of the plants, to the use of the landscape for things landscapes are no longer used for (grazing, cooking, laundry, fire protection). These processes may arguably be far more important to the understanding, recreation, and interpretation of historic gardens than the plants themselves. (Finch 2002)

Locating the plants that are documented on a plant list can be a challenge. Unfortunately, many cultivars of ornamental plants have been the casualties of the vagaries of fashion and are no longer available. In recent years, several nurseries and seed firms have focused on providing period plants and those names are provided in Appendix C. You might have to take steps to ensure the survival of plants that are already on your landscape. It may be necessary to take cuttings and start a new generation of a venerable tree or shrub that is in its twilight years. Maintenance interventions like pruning might improve the health of an old-timer. You might also find plants along the roadside or in early cemeteries. Of course, the rule is always to get permission from the owner of the property and then to be as noninvasive to the plant as possible, taking only a few of the seeds or a small cutting, and leaving most of the plant intact.

We each have a responsibility to assist in preserving the old varieties by planting seeds and cuttings that are important to our own families and in our neighborhoods. I have a nineteenth-century climbing rose by my back door that is called 'Seven Sisters' in my area of the country, but which actually is the rose 'Excelsa', also known as 'Red Dorothy Perkins'.

The name 'Seven Sisters' refers to the diverse shades of pink and rose included in the plant's blossoms and the fact that seven flowers compose a cluster, but my plant's name has additional significance. A dear friend, Tracy DiSabato-Aust, gave me this rose, which came from her grandmother who was one of seven sisters. Poll your own families and neighbors to find significant plants and preserve them in your landscape. Future generations will thank you for it!

If authenticity is the goal, it is important to not give in to our own ideas of how a historic garden should look. We cannot evaluate the taste or judgment of earlier gardeners in terms of our own culture and worldview. This issue frequently comes up when the appearance of the lawn is questioned at museum gardens—tall, coarsely cut grass and broad-leaf plants in keeping with the period versus a velvety emerald carpet? Is it more important to please the visitors or to accurately depict the landscape? Such decisions can be particularly difficult when financial support depends on the answer.

Using new cultivars of old-time plants in a historic garden is as anachronistic as a bench of recycled plastic. Avoid setting up cutesy scenes of rustic-looking items. For example, in one museum garden I once visited, some old tools and a wheelbarrow were set out "artistically" in the midst of a vegetable garden. No nineteenth-century gardener would have posed her tools in such a way and left them to the weather.

Maintenance is a consideration in every approach, from the detailed to the informal. If you work in a museum and wish for an authentic appearance, use period methods of maintaining the garden. Styles of pruning, mulching, and fertilization differ by time period. Another consideration is that some insect pests and diseases that might plague our contemporary plantings, for example, the Japanese beetle, did not exist in the United States in earlier times and so must be controlled with contemporary measures. In any approach for a period garden, it is important to confirm a manageable and, in the case of the four NPS approaches, a documented maintenance approach.

From restoration to making-a-new-layer, a historic landscape approach is available for anyone who wishes to document, cultivate, or otherwise venerate garden ornamentals of the past. The artistry and charm of heirloom ornamental plants are appropriate to the most highly documented historic garden as well as to an eclectic contemporary landscape. The next chapter provides details of garden styles specific to various architectural building types.

· 2 ·

GARDENS AND ARCHITECTURE
Design Styles for Historic American Building Types

It is just as well to remember that in arranging and planting around the home, it is not necessary to imitate what someone else is doing; some of the best effects can be produced by displaying individual taste, and making the grading, leveling, etc. conform to the surroundings. Don't buy expensive plants because your neighbor does; $5.00 spent in annual and perennial seeds, with a few hardy plants, will make quite a show; . . . don't try to do too much at once, but keep at it; allow no rubbish to accumulate in the corners, and you will be surprised in what a short time there is in transformation in the looks of the home grounds.

—How to beautify our home grounds, *American Gardening*, 1894

PEOPLE NOT ONLY GREW different plants in the past, they arranged them in their yards differently than we do today. This chapter describes garden styles associated with specific architectural types and provides several period designs for modern implementation. Differences in urban gardening practices versus rural, and high style versus vernacular, can be important. We must remember also that once a garden style was recognized in American gardens, it might have been used at any time thereafter--for any architectural type. This information comes from the pages of period garden magazines and books. You will notice that some descriptions record what *really* happened in a particular garden, while others promote the ideal garden that writers recommended as fashionable for the time. Specific period plants for various regions of the country can be found in Appendix B.

VERNACULAR AND FOLK HOUSES, 1600–1920

The earliest vernacular homes took different shapes and forms depending on the location, but all are similar in their simplicity and in the use of local materials for construction. Medieval-style frame houses, log cabins, sod houses, and dogtrot are some of these folk styles. Sometimes they would include some features reminiscent of the high style or fashion of the age, but economy and practicality defined both the houses and their gardens. Often these early houses were intended to be temporary structures, providing shelter just until the family had prospered in their new community and could move into a more elaborate, permanent residence. The original inhabitants typically contemplated little, if any, ornamental landscaping.

The Ideal. *Vick's Monthly Magazine*, 1880.

The selection of plants would have been limited to what the people brought with them to their new home or to what was available in the surrounding woods and meadows. However, we cannot assume that native beauties were automatically cultivated in early gardens. Throughout our gardening past, native plants often were considered so common as to be taken for granted. The emphasis in the majority of early gardens was on edible and medicinal plants: fruits, vegetables, and herbs. The establishment of nurseries selling trees—at first fruit trees—typically followed the first generation of settlers to a community, influenced by feelings of stability and permanency. In the development of the nursery industry, ornamentals were the final type of plant that was offered.

Limited evidence exists that decorative plants were cultivated in the average folk landscape. When the first settlers arrived on the shores of eastern North America, making ornamental gardens was probably the furthest thing from their minds. However, some of them did bring cuttings and seeds from their former homes to make roots in their new surroundings. I find it appeals to our own contemporary desire to bring natural beauty into our lives to believe that everyone, everywhere, has had similar instincts. People of all ages and cultures surely recognized the beauty in a rose or lily. Even in this photograph of a primitive sod house in Nebraska, the little girl appears to be gesturing to a flowering plant. As one writer explained, "As

Garden designs in the "ancient style." Leonard Meager, *The English Gardener*, 1670. Albert and Mary Small Special Collections Library, The University of Virginia, Charlottesville, Virginia.

man moves about the earth, consciously and unconsciously he takes his own landscape with him" (Anderson 1952).

For the earliest of these vernacular dwellings, we can only speculate concerning the appearance of the cultivated landscape. In the absence of American garden books for the seventeenth and eighteenth centuries, we must base our assumptions on European practices. While most ornamental plantings consisted of the simple placement of a shrub or flower next to the front door, the vegetable or kitchen garden might have taken a geometric and symmetrical form—sometimes called the "ancient style." The ancient style has been a fundamental component of American garden style from the seventeenth century to the present and follows design principles popular in Europe in the sixteenth and seventeenth centuries.

Gardens in the ancient style were composed of geometric components, originally relying mainly on right-angled forms like squares and rectangles. The ancient-style estate gardens in Europe encompassed many acres and included long straight walks, labyrinths and mazes, meticulously pruned hedges and topiary, water and rock features, and

A Nebraska sod house, 1911.

emphasis on level ground, although terracing and sloping hills were also used. Early American gardens sometimes followed an extremely simplified version with orderly square and rectangular beds and straight walkways. The beds primarily held vegetables and herbs, with perhaps a few flowers. A flowering shrub or two and perhaps a vine would be at the gate or by the doorway or a corner of the house. More formal estates followed the European antecedent, including more garden features. The ancient style has remained in favor for kitchen and ornamental gardens to the present day.

As the path of settlement extended westward

Prairie home with sweet peas and morning glories growing on wires on side of house, ca. 1900.

across North America, similar gardens and decorative plantings cropped up in the landscapes of the simple homes typical of the early communities. People tend to take their traditions in plants and garden styles with them as they move to new locations. The main difference in these later landscapes was not so much the design, but rather the plants. The number of plants available to U.S. gardeners multiplied almost exponentially throughout the nineteenth century due to plant explorations in all parts of the world, from western North America, to the Orient, to South Africa. So, by the time the farthest settlements were in progress, those settlers had more plants from which to choose.

The popular gardening periodicals were not likely to describe the "correct" landscape for a log cabin or dogtrot house, but fortunately we do have a few descriptions of how things really were. These dwellings did not have elaborate landscapes. Sometimes the only ornamental planting was a single peony or rose or a couple of annual vines on the house. A vegetable garden with some herbs and small fruits was the most important landscape feature.

A few historic descriptions of log cabins can provide a flavor of the style. A correspondent to the 1885 *Vick's Monthly Magazine*, "A. C. F.," described a traditional log cabin in Michigan: "The path to it was bordered with gay flowers, and over one side clambered a Rose bush . . . while fruit trees and flowering shrubbery otherwise added to its attractiveness. No elegance of architecture can ever make up for lack of nature." Solon Robinson described the adornment of a log cabin where he stayed as a guest near Coffeeville, Mississippi, in 1845: "From that rude, block log cabin to the front gate, extended a neat arbor for the support of twining flowers, climbing vines and roses" (Robinson 1845a).

An excellent description of plant ornamentation of the dogtrot style in 1838 central Alabama comes to us from Philip Gosse's *Letters from Alabama* (for the complete quote, see the discussion of southern gardens in chapter 3). Gosse emphasized the importance of growing vines around the doorways and on the walls of the dwelling. Some favorite climbing plants that he observed were cypress vine, native glycine, honeysuckle, and climbing roses. Gosse also related that shade trees were always planted around a southern house, whether elaborate or modest. He saw oaks and sycamores used for shade in Alabama and pride of China for ornament.

William Cobbett (1821) described flower gardens as he saw them during his travels in America: "As to the spot for flowers, the smaller kinds, and even the small shrubs, such as roses, dwarf honey-suckles, and the like, may be planted by the sides of the broad walks in the kitchen garden." Walter Elder described a similar landscape in 1850 as having two evergreen trees flanking the front walk. The primary garden was a fruit and vegetable garden, *bordered by flowering shrubs and roses.* He also advised that every house should have a "veranda" (porch) upon which to put climbing plants.

Writers throughout the nineteenth century decried the lack of verdant ornamentation on farmhouses. "Aunt Fanny" described a simple farmhouse garden in the 1883 *Vick's Monthly Magazine*—an old garden with pinks bordering the walks, roses by the door, and a sweetbriar planted by a

PLAN OF A FARMER'S GARDEN.

Plan of a farmer's garden. *The Ohio Cultivator*, March 1845.

bedroom window. Even as late as 1925, Mrs. Francis King was concerned about the state of farmhouse landscape embellishments. She suggested that the farm wife should choose a large tree that would be the focal point of her garden and then she should make a paved walk lined with lilacs to that tree. Between the lilacs, or in front of them, should be planted alternating groups of three to five pale pink peonies and irises in pinkish lavender and dark purple. She noted that the only adornments on farmhouses of her experience had been a crimson rambler or Dorothy Perkins rose and purple Jackman's clematis. She suggested that the farm wife should exercise a little more creativity in her approach to adorning the outside of her house (King 1925).

The editor of the 1857 *New England Farmer* described the attraction of a rural garden:

> If we wish to inspire our rising offspring with an enduring love of the scenes of home and an attachment to rural pursuits, our farms must not be without their flower-gardens—neat, modest and simple gardens—that do not dazzle the eyes, but present hundreds of simple and beautiful objects, to be loved in youth, and remembered ever afterwards, as the souvenirs of a happy period of life. (Brown 1857)

HIGH-STYLE ARCHITECTURE

GEORGIAN, FEDERAL, 1700–1830

The owners of fancy homes built during this period were faced with competing garden design styles: the ancient or geometric style and the fashionable English naturalistic style following Capability Brown and William Kent. Urban locations were more amenable for the ancient style, while rural mansions graced plantations that could be molded easily into the more modern English landscape style.

Bernard M'Mahon (1806) described some essential design details of the modern style. The boundary of the property was planted with clumps of trees, shrubs, and hardy herbaceous plants. Thickets and shrubberies were important. Well-shaped trees dotted the lawn. Natural-looking water features, grottoes, bridges, and other lavish structures might have been featured along with sweeping views. Shrubs were massed in shrubberies to form a natural-looking understory beneath groupings of trees. Hedgework was sometimes important.

Flowers, both annual and perennial, were interspersed throughout shrubberies or planted in geometric flower beds lined with box or other edging material. In addition to a box-edged parterre, other elements of the ancient style were allowed for contrast, for example, a terrace or an allée of trees. Washington's Mt. Vernon in northern Virginia and the William Paca house in Annapolis, Maryland, display landscape features in keeping with M'Mahon's advice.

Residence in the Greek Revival style, ca. 1885.

GREEK REVIVAL, 1820–1860

The Greek Revival style was so popular in its time that it was also known as the National Style (McAlester 1984). Luther Tucker wrote in *The Cultivator* of January 1848 that, "The stately and Formal Grecian . . . may also suit the stiff geometric style of planting." The antebellum Greek Revival plantation homes of the southern states were often surrounded by landscapes designed in the ancient style. A common garden feature of many of these homes was an elaborate boxwood garden, with beds lined with dwarf edging boxwood, constructed in intricate geometric to simple shapes. The centers of these beds were planted with flowering shrubs, lilies, bulbs such as hyacinths, or annuals such as larkspur. Pathways were lined with box and flanked by crepe myrtles, southern magnolias, or red cedars.

Lockwood (1934) vividly described the remnants of an old Georgia garden at the Greek Revival Mimosa Hall as it appeared in the 1930s:

> The ground and gardens were laid out and planted by Major Dunwody and his wife [about 1850] and the outlines of the original layout are easily seen at the present day. Mimosas, brought by Major Dunwoody from Darien, are planted in a row on each side of the path which leads from the front gate to the front door. A formal planting of cedars of Lebanon flanks this walk, and mimosas, cedars, and Osage oranges are used at other points. To the west of the house there still survives a formal garden, charming in the simplicity of design and the planting. It consists of oval beds, edged with stone curbing and filled with lily-of-the-valley. To the east of the house is another portion of the old planting, consisting of a number of wide terraces, set with deutzia, syringa, Persian lilacs, cydonia, old roses, shading from pink to red, and varieties of narcissus. In spring they all bloom in masses, although the terraces are overgrown with a tangle of honeysuckle and vinca. Against the east side of the house there survives a pink chinquapin rose, and all the ivy on the house is of the original growth, as is the large vitex, covered with a yellow Banksia rose, which shades the front portico.

ITALIANATE, 1840–1885

The Italianate architectural style, popular in this country between 1840 and 1885, was strongly emphasized in the books of Andrew Jackson Downing (1815–1852). Downing also designed for what we now call the Gothic Revival cottage. Downing's popular books, *A Treatise on the Theory and Practice of Landscape Gardening* (1841) and *Cottage Residences* (1842), described and illustrated his fashionable landscape ideals. Downing claimed to write both for the gentry and for the working person, although his ideas were likely too grandiose for the average worker. His general approach to the landscape began by distinguishing between "the Beautiful" and "the Picturesque" in nature. The

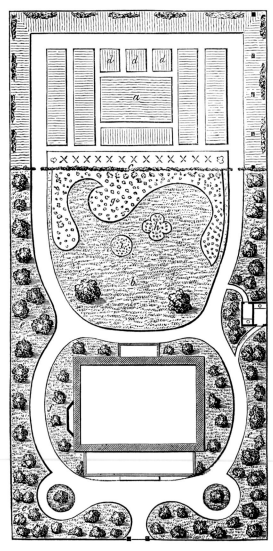

Landscape plan. Andrew Jackson Downing, *Cottage Residences*, 1844.

Trees of medium and smaller size should be so interspersed with those of larger growth, as to break up all formal sweeps in the line produced by the tops of their summits, and occasionally, low trees should be planted on the outer edge of the mass, to connect it with the humble verdure of the surrounding sward. (Downing 1859)

A detailed discussion of Downing designs for flower gardens can be found in chapter 8. Visitors to Downing's own garden in 1841 noted "arabesque beds on the lawn" for roses and greenhouse plants and circular beds for petunias and annual phlox. His flower garden was described as

A small space laid out in seven circular beds; the center one nearly twice as large as the outer ones: these were all filled with plants: a running rose in the center of the large bed, and the outer edge planted with fine phloxes, Bourbon roses, & c., the other six beds were all filled with similar plants excepting the running rose, which would be of too vigorous growth for their smaller size. (Hovey 1841)

This design was featured in Downing's 1844 edition of *Cottage Residences*, a book that featured houses in the Gothic Revival, Italianate, and Tudor Revival architectural styles. At the rear of the property is the service area as well as rectangular beds for fruits, vegetables, and herbs. This area is camouflaged by a vine-covered trellis, featuring roses, honeysuckles, and wisteria, immediately between the large flower bed and the kitchen garden. Driveways and walking paths are curvilinear. Two large circles, each containing a balsam fir, accent the curves in the front drive. Fragrant shrubs, including daphne, roses, sweet shrub, magnolia, and Missouri currant, are positioned throughout the lawn area near the house. The back lawn was to be expansive except for two flower beds cut into the turf, one for roses and the other for mignonette and shrubs.

Downing's arabesque flower border completes the scheme. It varies in width from 4 to 14 ft. Downing explained the unusual shape: "to a person looking across the lawn from any part of the walk near the house, this variety of form in the boundary increases the apparent size of the area of turf which it encloses." It is a bed for herbaceous perennial flowers, arranged by height. Downing suggested lilies, bee larkspur, hosta, phlox, peonies, pinks, penstemon, and pansies. This design could be simplified for a modern Downingesque landscape by limiting the number of trees placed in the lawn, reducing

Beautiful promoted the gentle side of nature, featuring soft and undulating outlines and harmonious composition, while the Picturesque echoed the power and violence inherent in nature, with irregular outlines and abrupt imagery.

The grouping of trees for a natural perspective was the challenge of the landscape gardener according to Downing. He wrote:

Whether the landscape is small and will only afford room for three trees or if it is a large area suitable for hundreds, great care must be taken not to place them in any regular or artificial manner . . . but to so dispose them as that the whole may exhibit the variety, connexion, and intricacy seen in nature. . . .

A landscape in "poor taste." *The Cultivator and Country Gentleman,* 1869.

Well-planted grounds. *The Cultivator and Country Gentleman,* 1869.

the size of the arabesque-style flower garden, and eliminating the service area.

Joshua Hoopes, in his 1872 article "How to Plant a Rural Home," promoted many of Downing's ideas. The essential elements of Hoopes' design for a one-acre landscape were:

Trees and shrubs: Belt of low evergreens at rear of lawn

Fruit trees behind the house

Norway spruce on southwest corner of property

Shade tree near house; other large trees positioned throughout lawn

Deciduous shrubs grouped on property line

Weeping beech is elegant feature for front lawn.

Hemlock or arborvitae hedge to screen service area

Use shrubs with ornamental flowers or fruits to accent curves in driveway, choose from forsythia, weigela, barberry, hydrangeas, and coralberry.

Flowers: Three circular flower beds in front lawn. Fill with coleus, bright annuals or roses.

In the post-Downing era, garden writers were critical of landscapes that lacked such fashionable details. *The Cultivator & Country Gentleman* of 1869 published a drawing of a landscape "in poor taste" that depicted trees and flower beds planted in straight lines perpendicular to the house and the rest of the grounds relatively unadorned. Images in county atlases confirm that this planting technique was fairly common in the 1870s. The well-planted or *ideal* landscape, according to *The Cultivator & Country Gentleman,* was in the Downing mode and featured strategically placed trees and shrubs creating a verdant frame that surrounded the property in soft undulating lines.

QUEEN ANNE, 1880–1910

The Queen Anne style of house was constructed across the country, primarily between the years of 1880 and 1910. Excessive detailing in the house architecture provided a fanciful backdrop for landscape design. During this time, a plethora of published materials inspired the gardener. Of particular importance were the many horticultural periodicals such as *Gardener's Monthly, Vick's Monthly Magazine, The Ladies' Floral Cabinet, The American Garden, American Gardening,* and *The Mayflower.* These and various local and agricultural sheets kept cultivators informed about the latest discoveries in the ornamental plant world and fashionable garden styles.

Vick's Monthly Magazine in 1880 described an ideal landscape treatment for a house with "towers and gables, and curious porches, and strange windows." The article began with the observation that for most people, "having obtained a good lawn, the usual practice is to spoil it as soon as possible, by making unnecessary walks and flower beds, and by excessive planting of tress and shrubs." Vick advised restraint. The front lawn was to be unbroken except for an occasional shade or ornamental tree. Clumps of shrubs were spaced periodically along the property line.

Flower beds were strategically positioned to be viewed from windows. These were planted in the popular carpet bedding or ribbon styles of brilliantly colored annuals. "The most magnificent of all" would be a circular bed of large subtropical plants, including castor bean in the center, followed by a ring of cannas, next a row of elephant ears, with an edging of coleus or dusty miller. (See examples of bedding designs and a subtropical bed in chapter 9.) A simple border with favorite flowers for cutting, such as China asters, zinnias, stock, and sweet peas, could be located at the back of the house on the edge of the lawn.

Nearly every Queen Anne house had a porch or veranda and the perfect addition was a trellis for flowering and foliage vines. These plants not only were decorative, but also provided privacy and shade in the heat of the day. Vines of particular importance were Boston ivy and Virginia creeper, both renowned for good fall color.

URBAN TOWN HOUSE

The gardens of the early row houses in eastern cities, including New York, Boston, and Philadelphia, featured particular efficiency in the use of space and plants. Six designs for embellishing city yards appeared in the *American Gardening* magazine in 1894. Each back garden space was 40 ft. by 20 ft., and the use of one or two simple geometric figures gave form and function to the area. The first step in the ornamentation of these properties was to cover the fence with a vine like honeysuckle, Boston ivy, or Dutchman's pipe. The designer suggested that annuals like marigolds, balsam, and zinnias be planted in all sunny spots, preferably started from seed to keep costs down. Perennials appropriate for these smaller gardens were yuccas, tall spiky plants like foxgloves, campanulas, and gladiolus. Roses were also used. Shady sites were host to native ferns such as the maidenhair or to clumps of lily-of-the-valley. The finishing touch was an urn of flowers in each front yard (R. S. B. 1894; Bresloff 1915).

Garden Vase. *Vick's Monthly Magazine*, 1880.

CRAFTSMAN, PRAIRIE, 1900–1930

The beginning of the twentieth century ushered in a new appreciation for nature and outdoor spaces. Architecturally, the Craftsman and Prairie styles demonstrated simplicity of line and emphasis on craftsmanship using natural materials. Gardens followed suit. Plantings connected the house with the natural world. Gardeners cultivated exotics, but native plants became more important, particularly in areas with water conservation issues like the Far West.

The terrace or patio became significant as a center for family outdoor activities. These areas provided new settings for planting and gardening. "As a garden the patio has certain advantages. . . . It is near the house. . . . It must be fairly small and compact, and therefore can be seen as a whole . . . it is possible to keep it always interesting by the use of pot plants and their rotation and change" (Mitchell 1934). Containers of pelargoniums and colorful annuals brightened terraces and pots of evergreens performed as portable hedges.

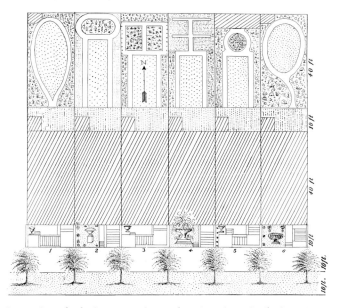

Suggestions for laying out a city garden. *American Gardening*, 1894.

A Private Residence, STOCKTON,

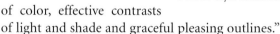
Prairie-style architecture. Stockton, California, ca. 1906.

O. C. Simonds of the Chicago School set out guidelines for the landscaping of home grounds in his book *Landscape-Gardening* (1920, reissued 1931). "The front yard . . . should be the most artistic part of the home grounds." A skyline should be formed by binding the sky with the outline of trees and shrubs judiciously placed in a natural manner. Preference should always be given to the existing plants. Simonds advised, "One's aim should be to introduce trees, shrubs and flowers that will give harmonious combinations of color, effective contrasts of light and shade and graceful pleasing outlines."

Ground covers were used in lawn areas and also for transitions. These might have included plants such as vinca, English ivy, spreading juniper, horizontal cotoneaster, Virginia creeper, or bearberry. Plantings at the foundation of the house joined the walls of the house with the landscape. These plantings typically were not the uniform belts of evergreens that we now associate with the term "foundation planting." A combination of perennials, shrubs, and vines accomplished the transition from structure to nature.

Flower gardens were placed in view of the terraces, as perimeter plantings, or to line walkways. Garden writers stressed complementary color combinations and mixed borders combining shrubs with herbaceous plants. From a maintenance perspective, the universality of the lawn mower prohibited cutting out flower beds or placing a shrub specimen in the lawn as was common in the 1800s.

COLONIAL REVIVAL, 1880–1955

The foundation of the Colonial Revival styles of architecture and landscape design stems from the 1876 Centennial Exhibition in Philadelphia. Looking to the past with a sense of nostalgia for simpler years, designers once again espoused the ancient style for inspiration for garden form and incorporated old-fashioned plants in their gardens. The Colonial Revival garden emphasized straight lines, a central axis that connected the house and garden, terracing in the case of larger estates, fountains, and box-lined parterres, along with the old-fashioned plants. White picket fences predominated. More relaxed gardens of bulbs and ground covers might be adjacent to these formal areas (Hitchcock 1998). These gardens were a romanticized version of early American gardens, with many of the virtues and few of the faults of their predecessors. Besides the colonial motifs, international influence also entered these gardens, with Italian pergolas or Japanese teahouses in evidence. By the 1930s many landscapes might have featured an herb garden. The houses of the Colonial Revival, as well as other revival styles such as Tudor and Mediterranean, were also likely candidates for foundation plantings, which became popular in the second quarter of the twentieth century.

> For a Colonial house, the good, old-fashioned plants should be used: box, lilacs, syringas, and snowberries, as shrubs; grapes, wistaria, and woodbine, as vines, or English ivy against brick. Use them not in meaningless masses so popular in modern planting, but simply, with the severity and restraint that are characteristic of the Colonial period. The planting should emphasize the dominant points of the house. Frame the entrance with clumps of lilacs, or more formally with round bushes of box. Use vines . . . to soften a hard line, to accentuate the beauty of a

chimney, to make a porch part of the house, to lend color and texture to a wall. . . .

Foundation planting must form a setting for the house. . . . The planting may take the form of a clipped hedge of one kind of shrub . . . or it may show a more informal use of shrubs of natural growth, emphasizing one or two varieties. . . . Either of these types, especially with evergreens, will be found useful to screen a porch or any part of the house that needs seclusion from the passer-by. . . .

It is a good rule to plant only what the house seems to require; to see not how much one can plant but how little and, above all, how few varieties. Restraint should be the watchword in foundation planting. (Greely 1922)

The early 1900s saw the inclusion of the herbaceous or mixed border as a prominent feature in landscapes, with much attention paid to color and harmonious plant combinations. This is discussed in more detail in chapter 8. Magazines like *The Garden Magazine*, *The House Beautiful*, and *Better Homes and Gardens* featured instructions for how to compose a garden all of gray foliage or other color schemes. Judicious use of color was the sign of a savvy gardener. As a writer exclaimed in a 1922 issue of *The House Beautiful*, concerning a combination she found particularly exciting, "Rose and purple make such a lovely color scheme for a garden, so altogether distinguished, so smart and in the spirit of our times" (Perrett 1922).

Fletcher Steele was one of many landscape designers active during this period. Steele observed that the beauty of the garden lay in its arrangement, not in the varieties of plants. Plants, according to Steele, are just part of the total of materials used, including stone, brick, wood, gravel, water, and sky. Echoing the remarks of O. C. Simonds, Steele believed that the sky was used the least intelligently of all. He urged that all elements be considered carefully. "Restraint in the use of decoration must be practiced in all gardens" (Steele 1925).

Essential points from Steele's informal design for a middle class residence, 11 Maple Cove Street, would be appropriate for urban or suburban homes of the 1920s and 1930s.

The north-facing front yard contains rhododendrons and Japanese yew.

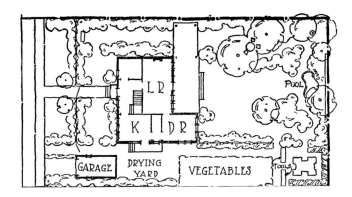

Design for 11 Maple Cove Avenue. Fletcher Steele, *Design in the Little Garden*, 1924.

"A narrow bed around the area could be filled with ferns, wild wood-flowers, and spring bulbs, . . . with a few shade-enduring shrubs."

Where grass will not grow in shade, Steele advised using *Vinca minor* or *Pachysandra terminalis*.

The garage is constructed near the street so land is not wasted in a long drive.

A hawthorn hedge and fence separate the property from the street.

The total lawn area is reduced, with many plantings including a rose bed in the corner with four standards, a small pool, and a bench in the front yard hedge, hidden from the view of the street. In the border planting, the shrubs are scattered in an irregular fashion and "the lawn is fitted to the shrubs after the planting is done."

On the east side of the house is a shady terrace with shrubs on each corner.

"The main axis of the garden, prolonged on the living room door and terrace steps, is almost disguised by unsymmetrical planting. . . . At the terminus, a small irregular pool (made to look like a natural spring) is built as part of a rock garden screen at the back."

Architectural style can be the key indicator to the type of landscape or garden that is appropriate for a house. Readers are urged to study the period garden literature and to look at examples of how other historic gardens are interpreted in their own region for additional details to apply to their own heirloom garden.

· 3 ·

GARDENS AND GEOGRAPHY
Ornamental Garden Traditions from Maine to Oregon

GARDEN STYLES TEND TO FOLLOW the architecture of the dwelling, but are obviously also influenced by the climate, topography, and cultural traditions of the region. In this section I have collected a variety of vignettes from different areas of the United States to pinpoint a little more closely just how people created their gardens and decorated their landscapes in earlier days. This is the story for the most part of vernacular gardens and what individuals actually accomplished in their gardens—whether or not it was in fashion or modern readers find their accomplishments to be tasteful. How representative are these individual stories and recommendations is open to speculation, since we cannot assume that those who took the time to record the details of their gardens were speaking for all gardeners in their locality.

The work of the many successful and prominent professional landscape architects across the country in the period before World War II is yet another tale and an exhaustively detailed regional garden history is beyond the scope of this book. I encourage interested readers to delve more deeply to the history of your region by visiting libraries and public record depositories, talking with old-timers in your neighborhood, and joining local and regional garden history societies, such as the California Garden History

Society or the Southern Garden History Society. Regional and national garden history books, such as those by Hedrick, Lockwood, Leighton, Cochran, Emmet, Welch and Grant, Padilla, and others, are resplendent with details of gardening and should form the basis of any inquiry. This chapter should be but a starting point for you to research your own regional historic garden. Some areas, such as the Middle Atlantic States, have a plethora of published information; others, like the Great Plains, are not quite so well documented. With the background information and plant lists that I have been able to gather, you have a good foundation to search for more detailed gardening practices in your particular state or region.

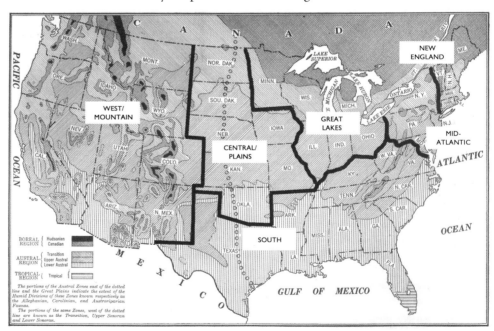

Regional map of the United States. Adapted from *The Garden Magazine,* January 1916.

Some may find my delineations of regions to be arbitrary. It is difficult to divide the country into meaningful regions with regard to gardening practices. Many states have their own diversities of climate and topography that make attempts at uniformity unreasonable, if not impossible. Therefore, I have chosen to rely on political boundaries, using state lines and topographical features like plains or mountains as my measure, except in the case of the southern region. For the South I use the boundaries set down by the Southern Garden History Society, which include West Virginia, Arkansas, and all of Texas as well as those states conventionally recognized entirely as "southern."

As I studied the gardening practices of different areas of the United States, it became increasingly clear that landscaping and garden styles remained fairly consistent and homogeneous across the continent. The main defining characteristic of each region turns out to be the palette of ornamental plants that gardeners successfully cultivated.

NEW ENGLAND REGION
Connecticut, Maine, Massachusetts, New Hampshire, Rhode Island, Vermont

The written American record of gardens and the cultivation of ornamental plants began in New England. Although utility was the order of the day, the literature abounds with references to efforts to beautify the landscape. William Wood, writing in 1634, referred to Dorchester, Massachusetts, as "well wooded and watered . . . and pleasant Gardens, with kitchen-gardens." Referring to the situation in 1641, Edward Johnson (1654) described the settlement:

> Further, the Lord hath been pleased to turn all the wigwams, huts, and hovels the English dwelt in at their first coming, into orderly, fair, and well-built houses, well-furnished many of them, together with orchards filled with goodly fruit trees, and gardens with variety of flowers: There are supposed to be in the Massachusetts Government at this day, neer a thousand acres of land planted for orchards and gardens, besides their fields are filled with garden fruit.

Daniel Slade, in his *The Evolution of Horticulture in New England* (1895), asserted that the first garden on record belonged to a Gamaliel Wayte of Boston, who planted a garden in 1642 that was renowned for its fruits and flowering plants. In 1654, Governor William Bradford

of Massachusetts described in verse some of the cultivated plants that he had observed in the landscape:

> All sorts of roots and herbes in gardens grow:
> Parsnips, carrots, turnips, or what you'll sow;
> Onions, melons, cucumbers, radishes,
> Skirrets, beets, coleworts, and fair cabbages.
> Here grow fine flowers many, and, 'mongst those,
> The fair white lily and th' sweet, fragrant rose.

Several years later, in the 1670s, English visitor John Josselyn recorded his observations of plants that were growing in gardens: "Of Such Garden Herbs, as do thrive there, and of such as do not." Among the ornamental and herbal plants that Josselyn listed (in his original spelling) were:

Marygold

French Mallowes

Time

Sage

Fennel

Housleek

Hollyhocks

Clary

Sweet Bryer, or Eglandtine

English Roses

Celandine

Spear Mint

Rew, will hardly grow,

Fetherfew prospereth exceedingly

Southernwood is no plant for this country,

Nor Rosemary,

Nor Bayes

Whitten Satten groweth pretty well, so doth Lavender Cotton,

But Lavender is not for this climate

Pennyroyal

Ground Ivy or Ale Hoof

Gilly Flowers will continue two years (Josselyn 1672)

In the eighteenth century, Boston was a busy port city and some of its wealthier citizens installed ornamental gardens surrounding their mansions. Many gardens were terraced, with the uppermost heights providing water views.

Gardens were designed around a central axis that aligned with the main house entrances, front and back. Often the front garden was enclosed, providing either an elaborate forecourt with formal plantings or, in the case of more modest residences, the archetypical New England dooryard garden. An active nursery profession, anchored by such people as the Messrs. Winthrop, Kenrick, Hovey, and Washburn, ensured that a wide selection of tress, shrubs, and herbaceous plants were available to New England gardeners at the end of the eighteenth century and into the nineteenth.

Landscape architect Arthur Shurtleff examined New England colonial gardens at the beginning of the twentieth century and wrote of the details that he discovered in gardens in the northeastern section of Massachusetts. Again, there was evidence of a central axis plan, but Shurtleff observed that in the examples he saw the main axis was not always geometrically aligned with the house, although the gardens were accessible to the house. Landscapes were

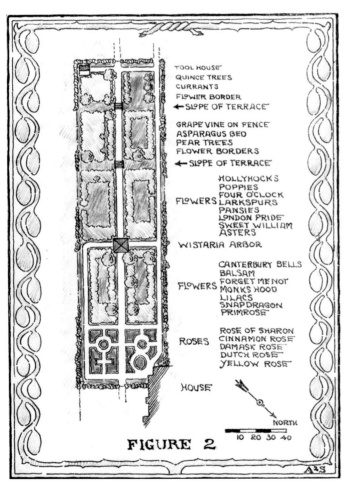

TOOL HOUSE
QUINCE TREES
CURRANTS
FLOWER BORDER
← SLOPE OF TERRACE

GRAPE VINE ON FENCE
ASPARAGUS BED
PEAR TREES
FLOWER BORDERS
← SLOPE OF TERRACE

FLOWERS
HOLLYHOCKS
POPPIES
FOUR O'CLOCK
LARKSPURS
PANSIES
LONDON PRIDE
SWEET WILLIAM
ASTERS

WISTARIA ARBOR

FLOWERS
CANTERBURY BELLS
BALSAM
FORGET ME NOT
MONKS HOOD
LILACS
SNAPDRAGON
PRIMROSE

ROSES
ROSE OF SHARON
CINNAMON ROSE
DAMASK ROSE
DUTCH ROSE
YELLOW ROSE

HOUSE

NORTH
10 20 30 40

FIGURE 2

Old formal garden. Arthur Shurtleff, *New England Magazine*, 1899.

always enclosed with fences and hedging, and flower bed layouts were obvious from an ancient edging of box. Old-fashioned flower favorites remained on many of the sites, including hollyhocks, larkspur, Canterbury bells, four-o'clocks, sweet William, rose of Sharon, lilacs, and roses.

Maine's gardens developed a little more slowly than those in the more southerly New England states. However, by the beginning of the nineteenth century, there were records of ornamental gardens. The Kennebec settlement was the setting for the diary that was the subject of the 1991 book *A Midwife's Tale* by Laurel T. Ulrich. Ulrich reported that the one fully documented ornamental garden in Kennebec in the early 1800s was that of Dr. Benjamin Vaughan of Hallowell. According to family memoirs, the doctor cultivated "a large garden of several acres tastily laid out, with broad paths and numerous alleys, whose borders were adorned with flowers shaded with currant bushes, fruit trees and shrubbery. The whole under the care of an English gardener."

Vernacular gardens were simple across the region and across the country, as a correspondent from Bethel, Maine, reported to the *New England Farmer* of 1856:

> I had a small front yard, thirty-six by eighteen feet, fenced in from a common. I spaded up the ground, manured and planted it with potatoes. . . . The next year I spaded, took out the small stones, manured and sowed with carrots, beets, and other roots, and at the same time set out a row of trees around the garden, consisting mostly of rock maples. The neat-looking beds were no mean ornament as the weeds were kept out. . . . The second year of planting my trees I had shoots eighteen inches in length. There is no tree that loves good treatment like the maple. As opportunity occurred, I introduced trees and shrubbery and diminished the space for garden vegetables, until I had a complete forest in my little front yard. (N. T. T. 1856)

Additional advice for the making of simple gardens was found in the *New England Farmer*, which suggested in 1868 that every residence, no matter how small, had the potential for horticultural ornamentation:

> Suppose you live in the city, where only a narrow strip—a few inches—of soil borders your dwelling. Even this may hold a vine, which you can train and trim, and which, climbing along the walls and drooping over the windows can curtain them with

beauty and afford you many a recess from household toil, in watching and assisting in its growth and the formation and perfection of its fruit. If, besides this, you have a small enclosed piece of ground—a "yard," you call it—where children play or rubbish accumulates, you can keep it neat, and dig and break up the soil—which is perhaps nearly as hard as the pavement—and plant there pretty shrubs and flowers. . . . But if you are fortunate enough to have the control of a rod or more land you may consider yourself rich in material for health and happiness. (Hale 1868)

Throughout the Victorian age various horticultural writers asserted that there was a moral obligation to grow flowers for the betterment of men and women alike. One such New England writer described in 1878 his perceived benefits of gardening:

Flowers are a sign of taste and culture, and we never see a flowering plant set in the window of a dwelling, however humble, but that we think better of the inmates on account of it. . . .

Nor should the cultivation of flowers be thought of as something more appropriate for girls than for boys. . . . It would be a special blessing to our boys if, from their youngest years, they were incited to sow the seeds of various plants and then to watch and assist their growth, and thus become acquainted with the laws of nature and with the beautiful and wonderful processes of vegetable life. . . . It would give us a succession of grown-up men, more intelligent, and therefore more capable of managing the affairs of husbandry and making farmlife successful . . . while it would also make them more refined and tasteful.

Husband and wife, and sons and daughters, would be in harmony of feeling, and all would delight to co-operate in embellishing their home and blessing their daily life with the beauty and cheer which flowers are capable of giving. Such a common and accordant employment would also tend to draw the family together and strengthen the bond of attachment to each other, and would do much to withstand those influences the effect of which is, too often, to loosen the ties of domestic life, and to

make the home less precious and attractive than it should be. (Egleston 1878)

Other New England gardeners, for example, Sarah Goodwin of Portsmouth, New Hampshire, created more elaborate gardens with many herbaceous plants and flowering shrubs. Sarah's garden evolved during her residence in her house from 1832 to 1896. The Goodwin house is now part of the historic museum village Strawberry Banke. Sarah Goodwin left detailed records of her gardens. She wrote of her love for old-fashioned flowers like Canterbury bells and sweet Williams and she cultivated several varieties of roses. She also experimented with the new bedding designs and was an early cultivator of new varieties of China aster, verbena, and stock (Emmet 1996).

MIDDLE ATLANTIC REGION
Delaware, Maryland, New Jersey, New York, Pennsylvania, and Washington, D.C.

The wild beauty of the Middle Atlantic region vied with any creative impulses that the settlers might have had toward building gardens. Daniel Denton described the countryside in his 1670 book:

The Herbs which the Countrey naturally afford are Purslane, white Orage, Egrimony, Violets, Penniroyal, Alicampane, besides Saxaparilla very common with many more. Yea, in May you shall see the Woods and Field, so curiously bedecke with Roses, and an innumerable multitude of delightful Flowers, not only pleasing the eye, but smell, that you may behold Nature contending with Art, and striving to equal, if not excel many Gardens in England.

Many of the earliest cultivation citations that I note elsewhere in this book originate from the gardens of horticultural collectors like John and William Bartram, William Hamilton, Humphrey Marshall, and David Hosack, who gardened, establishing botanic gardens and arboreta, in Pennsylvania and New York in the eighteenth and nineteenth centuries. Plant exploration and identification of indigenous species evolved to a fine art in this region, and it is believed that people like Bartram certainly cultivated many of the plants found in meadows and forests along the eastern coast.

Although nurseries and seed houses developed with the settlement of the colonies all along the East Coast, nowhere did they predominate as they did in the Middle Atlantic region. The Prince Nursery of Flushing, Long Island, New York, is often cited as one of the first nurseries to offer ornamental plants in the eighteenth century, following its establishment as a seller of fruit trees in 1732. After the Revolutionary War, in 1784, David Landreth started one of the first American seed houses in Philadelphia. A branch office of the Landreth firm was established in Charleston, South Carolina, in 1803. Also in Philadelphia was Bernard M'Mahon's seed business, which he established around 1802. Grant Thorburn began his seed house in New York City, also in 1802. Rochester, New York, became the epicenter of the nursery industry in the middle of the nineteenth century, earning it the nickname of "Flower City." By 1865, there were over 150 growers operating in Rochester, and by 1870, at least half the country's output in fruit and shade trees, as well as vines and other plant items, including seeds, came from the Rochester area (Aeberli and Becket 1982).

The diary of William Faris of Annapolis, Maryland, provides a view of how ordinary tradesmen constructed their ornamental gardens in the second half of the eighteenth century and dispels any notion that "ordinary" men did not know how to follow garden fashion. Situated in front of Faris's property were rectangular beds planted annually with flowers "in the Dutch tradition." Grass walkways bordered those beds. The walk to the "necessary" was "flanked by box-lined rectangular beds starring carefully trimmed holly trees (collected from the woods) surrounded by bulbs and flowers." The entire property was enclosed by a picket fence bordered by another narrow rectangular bed. "The area behind the house was dominated by a walnut tree. Nestled around its base was a circular bed divided into boxwood-lined quarters filled with tulips and bleeding hearts in May [these must have been a native *Dicentra* as the oriental bleeding heart had yet to be introduced], followed by a bright succession of perennials throughout the summer months" (Sarudy 1998).

One garden style that appeared throughout the eastern United States was that of large rectangular beds filled with vegetables, the beds lined with herbaceous plants and surrounded by borders of small fruits, fruit trees, and flowering shrubs. Another repetitive style for wealthier home owners and their gardeners was a terraced landscape, with gardens situated around a central axis, such as that discovered at the William Paca house in Annapolis.

Throughout American garden history there has been a tension between the comfortable ancient style and the newer landscape gardening style with its serpentine walks and strategically placed trees and shrubs. In addition to this quandary, later gardeners were faced with whether or not to embrace the bedding style with its brightly colored beds of annuals and tropical plants. Often, if we can follow the progression of a garden, we see the newer elements incorporated over time, although many gardens never did change from the geometric ancient style, even in the twenty-first century.

The first garden (late eighteenth century) at Sherwood Forest in Maryland was formal with terraces, boxwood-lined beds, stone walls, and small flower beds. Around 1836, the property was purchased by a Dr. Reynolds who followed the more picturesque style of a wide lawn with an 8-ft. by 100-ft. border surrounding the lawn. Dr. Reynolds also cultivated over 250 varieties of roses (Lockwood 1934).

The closely situated houses of New York City provided a special challenge to gardeners in the nineteenth century as they do today. One recommendation for getting the most visual effect from a small space came from the 1878 *Vick's Monthly Magazine*, which recommended the subtropical style of gardening as opposed to ribbon beds or a border planting of flowers. The landscape pictured was a narrow 18-ft. by 30-ft. space behind a row house. A central pathway was supported by board-lined beds. A huge urn planted with tropical-looking foliage served as a focal point. "Cannas, Ricinus, Caladiums, Coleus, Dahlias, Gladiolus & c. do all very well in a city yard, and with some care taken in planting them a very fine effect can be produced, even on a small scale" (Vick 1878e).

A New York City flower garden. *Vick's Monthly Magazine*, 1878.

Young boy in Middle-Atlantic area garden, ca. 1900.

Some gardeners filled the landscape behind their homes in the city without conforming to fashionable garden trends. Thus, the garden pictured above, surrounded by a board fence, is a floriferous setting for play or photography. Pansies and iris are recognizable and the ground obviously has been cultivated to keep weeds at bay.

In the more open areas of the city, gardeners were able to take advantage of the scenery and the lay of the land, developing extensive estates featuring shrubberies and carpet bedding, using a wide diversity of plant material. Such was the 1885 garden of W. F. Cochrane in Yonkers, New York, along the Hudson River. This landscape featured a large expanse of lawn.

> The margin of this lawn has been fringed by clumps and belts of trees, and along the road are flower beds of various shapes, some of them planted as carpet beds, others with mixed foliage, others again with a combination of flowers and foliage. . . .
>
> A large carpet bed near the gate has a star as a center, with a crescent at either end; the star is solid with Alternanthera, edged with Echeverias and dwarf Pilea; the crescents are worked out similarly with the two latter plants and the resulting spaces filled with three species of Alternanthera.

> Another simple but extremely effective bed is planted with a star of Golden Bedder Coleus, edged with Coleus Verschaffeltii. A salmon-colored Geranium (Mme. Ruthersdolf) is very effective. . . . This is immediately surrounded in one case by Mountain of Snow Geraniums, with an edging of Iresine. Summit of Perfection is a good double scarlet Geranium.
>
> Immediately in the front of the house is a large bed in which a number of Coleus plants have been successfully handled. The center is a salmon-flowered Geranium, surrounded by Mountain of Snow, then follow lines of Iresine, Coleus Verschaffeltii, Golden Bedder Coleus, Perilla and Geranium, and Lobelia speciosa. (MacPherson 1885)

Anna B. Warner wrote her book *Gardening by Myself* in 1872, when she lived on Constitution Island across from West Point in New York. Throughout that book brief vignettes illustrate the ways in which she observed people surrounding their homes, however humble, with ornamental plants. She described the low, unpretentious house of two poor brothers, which had next to each side of the front door "an immense hydrangea; with heads of bloom that can rival anything. And of the rare colour too." Another home that she observed had a decorative vine in the third floor window: "Across one of the windows, trained from side to side till the whole is covered with a network of twigs and leaves and blossoms, a honeysuckle stretches its pretty sprays, growing contentedly in a pot on that third story window-sill." Warner praised the effect of all modest efforts in cultivation saying, "Did ever Mr. Vick's twenty acres of spring bloom smell as sweet, I wonder, as a single fair little buff hyacinth that was given me long ago? When it was my only one, and not even the small amount of capital it represented could have been spent by me for such luxury."

Once gardeners planted a particular species, the ease with which it could be propagated often determined how ubiquitous it would become in the gardens of that locality. The editor of the *American Agriculturist* for August 1887 cited such a phenomenon.

> In a town in New Jersey, through which we occasionally pass, every dooryard has a perennial phlox and a chrysanthemum, all of the same variety, in singular uniformity. When the people "make garden" in the Spring, finding the clumps of these

flowers too large, they are trimmed by cutting away a portion of the roots; neighbors gladly accept these trimmings, and thus the front yards of the whole town become planted with the same plants. In a large town in Connecticut, we noticed that each door-yard had a large clump of a white-flowered Day-lily, with as much regularity as if required by law. (The day lilies— funkias 1887)

A Pennsylvania garden. *American Gardening*, 1895.

Although garden designers who wrote books and articles for publications always cautioned against overloading a landscape with too many different varieties dotted about on the lawn, enthusiastic gardeners often did just that (obviously not confined to just this region). The photograph above shows the front lawn of Mr. Charles T. Logue of Williamsport, Pennsylvania, in 1895. It featured a bed 14 ft. in diameter that held six rows of different cannas arranged by height, with the tallest-growing 'Robusta' in the center and colorful coleus forming the final edge. A clump of maiden grass grew to the front and left of the cannas and a cycad to the front and right. A tree fern and a palm were situated for best effect. Along the fence was a 50-ft. by 6-ft. bed of caladiums and more cannas. This garden was supported by the owner's conservatory where the tender plants could be placed during the winter months.

SOUTHERN REGION
Alabama, Arkansas, Florida, Georgia, Kentucky, Louisiana, Mississippi, North Carolina, South Carolina, Tennessee, Texas, Virginia, West Virginia

Mention of old-time southern gardens conjures up images of boxwood-lined parterres adjacent to antebellum Greek Revival mansions, courtyard gardens of old New Orleans, and subtropical palm trees lining Charleston streets. Even in the middle South of Tennessee and Kentucky, garden making has been an enduring pastime. Gilbert Imlay, writing from Kentucky in the 1790s, observed, "Flowers and their genera form one of the studies of our ladies, and the embellishment of their houses with those which are known to be salutary constitutes a part of their employment" (Imlay 1793). The South has a garden history that is an integration of responses to a diverse climate and the various cultural influences of immigrants from France, Spain, Germany, and England. From the moderate weather of the central Virginia piedmont, to the southern tip of Florida where it rarely freezes, to the Texas scrub area, plantings must be diverse to meet the challenges of minimal winter chilling, heavy humidity, and varying rainfall. Some writers commented that the main challenge of a gardener in the South was trying to maintain twelve-month, all-season interest in the garden. Many states included in this section have the bonus of a coastline on the Atlantic Ocean or the Gulf of Mexico. Plants for their gardens came not only from conventional nursery or people-to-people routes, but also directly from the ships that docked in their ports from exotic lands.

Tree species that functioned as street or avenue trees in the South were distinctive. One 1827 visitor to Riceborough, Georgia, noted the rows of pride-of-India trees that shaded the walks and lent a tropical air to the scene there and also in Charleston and Savannah (Basil Hall in 1827, quoted by Loudon 1838). Many historians agree that pride-of-India referred to *Melia azedarach* in this case. Live oaks abounded in the plantation-era South, lining the long drives to the Greek Revival mansions. The Spanish moss hanging from those trees made them appear to be inter-

272

"Pride-of-India" trees in front of a house in Riceborough, Georgia, 1827. John C. Loudon, *Encyclopedia of Gardening*, 1838.

woven with the landscape (Shafer 1939). Visitors to Natchez, Mississippi, in mid-nineteenth century, described avenues of *Magnolia grandiflora*, the grande dame of native southern evergreens (A Trip 1858). Species of palm functioned as street trees in south Georgia and Florida, and borders of oleander were cultivated on some Texas thoroughfares.

Many southern gardens were enclosed with walls, particularly those in the metropolitan areas of Charleston, Savannah, Mobile, and New Orleans. Favorite materials included brick, tabby (a mixture of ground seashells, pieces of oyster shells, and sand preferred on the east coast of Georgia and Florida), and wooden planks. Whatever the material, a vine or vines would commonly accent the enclosing structure creating shade and a green canvas. Early writers observed that the primary color in a southern garden was always green. The gardens within these walled enclosures might have contained geometric, formal flower beds with a crepe myrtle or a palm in the center, or sometimes there was no ornamental garden at all and the space was used for practical household tasks.

Many descriptions remain of box-lined formal gardens so popular in antebellum days, although most of the gardens themselves are long gone. Typically, the designs of these gardens were variations of the ancient style illustrated in chapter 2. Boxwood is particularly identified with the gardens of Virginia and Georgia—probably because garden histories emphasizing those pungently scented gardens were written by state garden clubs during the 1930s and remain to provide us with the details. In Georgia, between 1825 and 1860, the formal garden usually lay in front or to the side of the house with the service area separated from the ornamental garden by a picket fence. Dwarf box might have been used to edge the individual flower beds, although sometimes gardeners used herbaceous plants like iris or

violets for that purpose. Tree box might surround the greater whole. A combination of native plants, tropicals, and bedding plants would have been planted to present a picturesque and colorful pattern for visual enjoyment.

Mary Rion, in *Ladies Southern Florist* (1860), provides us with a view of what fashionable gardens were supposed to look like during her time. She recommended that the slightly elevated beds within a stylish garden should be oval, circular, or irregular in shape, but never square or rectangular. Besides box, other edging plants might be considered, including lavender, pinks, violets, and lemon or vanilla grass. Large hedges to mark boundaries could be made of wild orange, privet, French furze, euonymus, or tree box in either the green or variegated form. She advised that corresponding sides of the garden should be balanced but not identical and suggested that roses of similar size but different colors flank each side or that an English laurel be placed opposite a magnolia. Conscious of the importance of using plants with a nearby provenance, Rion exhorted, "Never import plants from a more northern clime, as the process of acclimation is difficult and always hazardous."

Roses were synonymous with southern gardens. The Cherokee rose was introduced in the eighteenth century. It quickly became so ubiquitous as to appear indigenous to future observers and was used as hedge material in Georgia and Mississippi. Noisette roses were particularly popular, with 'Chromatella' ('Cloth of Gold') and 'Lamarque' the most frequently listed roses in the catalogs of the South. The Noisette rose was the first American hybrid rose. John Champneys of Charleston, South Carolina, crossed *Rosa chinensis* with *Rosa moschata* to produce the first Noisette, 'Champneys' Pink Cluster', around 1811. Many southern growers also offered the teas 'Safrano' and 'Devoniensis', the China roses 'Cramoisi Supérieur' ('Agrippina') and 'Géant des Batailles', and the all-time favorite, hybrid perpetual 'Général Jacqueminot'.

Travelers who recorded their observations in the region in the nineteenth century give us a peek at what went on in the gardens of the wealthy and in more modest gardens as well. Harriet Martineau wrote in 1837 of her impressions of gardens at a site near the Battle of New Orleans: "Gardens of roses bewildered my imagination. I really believed at the time that I saw more roses that morning than during the whole course of my life before." She continued with a more general observation about gardens in America:

> Gardens are so rare in America, that, when they do occur, they are a precious luxury to the traveler,

especially when they are in their spring beauty. In the neighborhood of Mobile, my relative, who has a true English love of gardening, had introduced the practice; and there I saw villages and cottages surrounded with a luxuriant growth of Cherokee roses, honeysuckles, and myrtles, while groves of orange-trees appeared in the background. (Martineau, in Hedrick 1988)

Philip Gosse described the vernacular landscape of Alabama in 1838:

Of course the houses differ in their degrees of comfort and elegance . . . but in general they are built double; a set of rooms on each side of a wide passage, which is floored and ceiled in common with the rest of the house, but is entirely open at each end. . . . Various kinds of climbing plants and flowers are trained to cluster about either end of these passages, and by their wild and luxuriant beauty take away from the sordidness which the rude character of the dwellings might otherwise present. The *Glycine frutescens* with its many stems twisted tightly together like a ship's cable, hangs its beautiful bunches of lilac blossoms profusely about, like clusters of grapes; the elegant and graceful Scarlet Cypress-vine (*Ipomoea coccinea*), with hastate leaves, and long drooping vermilion flowers, shaped like those of a convolvulus; the still more elegant Crimson cypress-vine (*Ipomoea Quamoclit*), whose flowers, shaped like those of the sister species, are of the richest carmine, and whose leaves are cut, even to the mid-rib, into a multitude of long and slender fingers; our own Sweet-brier, the Trumpet honeysuckle (*Caprifolium sempervirens*) whose dark scarlet tubes are the twilight of the sounding-winged Hawkmoths. . . . These, with other favourite plants, cover the rough logs and shingles with so dense a mass of vegetation and inflorescence, as effectually hide them from view.

Gosse went on to say that shade trees were always planted around dwellings, both elaborate and modest. He most often observed oaks and sycamores used for shade and the pride of China tree for ornament. Besides the ipomoeas and honeysuckle observed in Alabama, the yellow Carolina jasmine also decorated the doorways of cottages in the South.

The desire to imitate the trendy Victorian garden style of mounded bedding was sometimes evident in the efforts of homesteaders, including the following from Ladonia, Texas, in 1878:

Sitting here, on my cool, shaded porch, enjoying the beauty and fragrance of my flowers, I feel constrained to write and tell you how I am succeeding in beautifying one of the rudest homes I ever saw. . . .

There were many unsightly objects to be gotten rid of, but soon all were removed or covered, and a delightful lawn of blue grass, with a few mounds and beds, partially shaded by native oaks and hickories, made our home a place of beauty. I had an Indian wigwam built of brush, large enough for a summer reading-room, and obtained cane from the creek bottom for Madeira vines to run on. For shade I planted roses and flowering shrubs. . . . I wish you could look down here and see my brush summer-house covered with Morning Glories; my huge Cypress cones, and arches (made of hickory poles and barrel hoops); my splendid double rose Balsam, my mounds, blazing with double Portulaca, Verbenas, Petunias, and Phlox. By every tree I have a climber—Clematis, Jasmine and Honeysuckle. I have not said anything about my magnificent Zinnias, nor my comical Pansies. (J. D. H., Mrs. 1878)

Just four years later another correspondent to *Vick's Monthly Magazine* described her home in a very different setting in Florida:

My home is in the midst of a large Orange grove. The flower garden is entered from the street through an avenue of Oleanders, is hedged with Rose geraniums, with scarlet and pink Geraniums growing on either side of the walks. I succeed well with most greenhouse plants. My verandah is wound with vines of Thunbergia and Maurandya, which are a mass of blooms continuously. I have two large Wax vines growing over the door, forming an arch, which is very much admired. ("H" 1882)

The mild temperatures in much of the Deep South, from South Carolina across and below, interfered with the cold requirements of some perennials and bulbs. An

A private residence surrounded by tropical foliage. Florida, 1919.

A photograph of a New Orleans garden for the 1886 volume of *Vick's Monthly Magazine* reveals the semi-tropical character of the vegetation of that locality (January, 1886). Vick noted that the massive live oak, with its drapery of gray moss, and the palms in the other scene, would be strange forms to northern eyes, but were picturesque and attractive. Note also the wire edging in the front bed.

At the beginning of the twentieth century, when perennial borders became more in vogue here and abroad, southern garden writers could not recommend gardens solely of perennials. They suggested mixed borders that took advantage of the wide variety of flowering shrubs, perennials, and annuals (many so-called northern annuals are perennial in the South), as well as the available evergreen canopy of trees. Hume (1929) wrote:

> The border for perennials alone is quite out of the question. . . .
>
> The problem of making a border is best solved by using such perennials as can be grown in conjunction with other plants, annuals and shrubs particularly. Shrubs, both broad-leafed and coniferous will from the permanent background.

Hume suggested that lantana, jasmines, hibiscus, gardenias, azaleas, viburnums, and nandina form the structure of those gardens. Then, in indentations in the shrubbery, the gardener could carefully place the perennials. Larger shrubs and trees were also integral to ornamentation of the landscape. In Florida, many species of plants were hardy that could not be grown elsewhere in the United States. These tropical plants created a lush scenery around Florida dwellings.

With such a compatible-for-gardening climate, we would not expect southern gardeners to feel the need to grow plants in containers as frequently as their counterparts in more northerly zones. They apparently did,

View in a New Orleans garden. *Vick's Monthly Magazine*, 1886.

Abbeville, Louisiana, gardener noted her successes and failures with Dutch bulbs:

> I live in the most southern portion of the State, not more than six miles, in a direct line, from the Gulf coast. The land is low, soil black, and very rich. I have very little space for cultivating flowers, and therefore, buy only a few at a time. I have tried Crocuses and Tulips in the house and garden, and they proved a perfect failure. . . . Scillas do well, and increase rapidly; Narcissus do finely. . . . Hyacinths succeed here to perfection. (Rice 1879)

however, and southern catalogs included many traditional standards like cast iron plant and geraniums for cultivation in tubs or smaller containers. Riley Blitch, reporting on the vernacular gardens of Florida, described his ancestral home as having a porch lined with potted plants in "every kind of container imaginable" (Blitch 1997). Geraniums of different hues were favorites in the Blitch Victorian-age household. Containers in a more formal setting defined New Orleans gardens of the nineteenth century, where an inventory of one man's home in the Vieux Carre, dated 1831, listed items found in the flower garden as "six iron flower pots, six terra cotta pots painted green, and twenty-four wooden boxes, all with plants" (Irvin 1995).

A comfortable porch with many container plantings.

Trying to envision a garden of early days is a relative activity—one that has challenged gardeners over the years. So it was that a writer for *The American Garden* in 1888, who called herself "B," reminisced about Carolina gardens that were old-fashioned to *her*:

> Among the prominent plants were camellias in endless variety, growing to small trees in favored localities; the snowy syringa, the lilacs, red and yellow woodbine (lonicera); the sweet shrub (calycanthus), its rich maroon blossoms perfuming the air; the sweet bay (*Magnolia glauca*), with its flowers so soft in texture, so milky white, so fragrant; the oleanders of varied hue; the fringe tree (chionanthus), with ethereal, almost unique white blossoms; the crape myrtle (lagerstroemia), the Cape jessamine (gardenia), with camellia-like flowers and delicious perfume; the spiraeas and snowball; the semi-tropical opopanax with most delicate foliage and fascinating, fluffy yellow balls and lasting perfume; the sweet olive, and one might add the citrina, as under favorable circumstances its height was often from 5 to 6 feet. Conspicuous in some gardens was the wild Cherokee rose, its

> ambitious white blossoms and glossy green leaves waving provokingly from the very top of neighboring trees.

> Among the useful as well as ornamental trees and shrubs of the garden one must not overlook the oranges, "sweet," and "sour" . . . there were the true myrtles, single and double, both worthy of mention . . . and a wild variety . . . which bears a small berry from which it was the custom at one time to make candles. . . . If to the above list the sweet and Ogeechee limes and olives are added, some idea of the larger growth of an old-time garden has been given.

> Among the bulbs was the snowdrop, daffodil, narcissus, jonquil, all coming into favor once more. Among geraniums the hardy varieties were favorites; the rose, whose branches sometimes grew to the length of 5 or 6 feet; the spice and ottar . . . the fish, commonly planted as a hedge, growing 4 to 5 feet high and blooming generously. No garden in city or country was considered quite complete without a protecting hedge, and the popular shrubs for this purpose were the cedar, arbor vitae, wild orange, euonymus, box and cassine (yapon).

GREAT LAKES STATES
Illinois, Indiana, Michigan, Minnesota, Ohio, Wisconsin

Concentrated settlement in the territory between the southern shores of Lakes Erie, Michigan, and Superior and the Ohio River occurred in the early years of the nineteenth century. Water transportation routes, followed by modest roadways and then the railroads by midcentury, insured that those areas were connected with the East almost from the beginning. Gardening began, as elsewhere, with the planting of fruit trees and kitchen gardens and progressed to ornamental features as the settlements became more secure and established. An emigrant's manual described the process:

> First comes the pioneer who depends for the subsistence of his family chiefly upon the natural growth of vegetation, called the "range", and the proceeds of his hunting. His implements of agriculture are rude, chiefly of his own make, and his efforts directed mainly to a crop of corn, and a "truck patch". The last is a rude garden for growing cabbages, beans, corn for roasting ears, cucumbers and potatoes. . . .

> The next class of emigrants purchase the lands, add field to field, clear out the roads, throw rough bridges over streams, put up hewn log houses, with glass windows, and brick or stone chimneys, occasionally plant orchards . . . and exhibit the picture and forms of plain, frugal, civilized life. . . .

> [Then] the men of capital and enterprise come. . . . The small village rises to a spacious town or city; substantial edifices of brick, extensive fields, (and) gardens . . . are seen. (Peck 1837)

Early travelers to Cincinnati declared that its cultivated landscape compared favorably with the eastern states. As early as in the 1820s, Frederick Marryat observed in his travel diary, "The streets have a row of trees on each side near the curbstone; and most of the houses have a small frontage filled with luxuriant flowering shrubs, of which the Althea Frutex is the most common." James Buckingham wrote in 1840, "The private dwellings of Cincinnati are in general quite as large and commodious as those of the Atlantic cities . . . a greater number of them have pretty gardens, rich grass-plats, and ornamental shrubberies and flowers surrounding them, than in any of the Eastern cities." At the end of the century, the garden of the prominent horticulturist Nicholas Longworth (1782–1863) still entranced visitors with colorful and fragrant splendor.

Southwestern Ohio had a thriving nursery industry, several horticultural publications, many privately owned greenhouses, and an active horticultural society by the 1850s. However, whether or not all cultivated space followed the dictates of fashion and taste was a debatable question. Richard Davies, the gardener at the R. P. Resor residence in trendy Clifton in Cincinnati, described in 1850 his critical impression of the town's gardens:

The garden of Nicholas Longworth. Cincinnati, Ohio, 1907.

One of the principal errors in laying out places around Cincinnati is in the disproportion of the parts. Some of the carriage roads are from fifteen to sixteen feet and more in width, and not over three hundred feet in length. . . .

Another prevailing error is the width of the garden walks—these are in some places too wide, and in others they are the reverse, miserably narrow. . . .

Another fault is in the form and disposition of the groups of trees and shrubs: they seem in some places as if they had dropped from the clouds, without any object or aim in view; you see one here and another there, and some planted as if the design of shutting out the best and most interesting points in the landscape.

Another common error is the mixed character of the grounds: here you perhaps see highly dressed ground, and proceed only ten or twelve yards from the carriage road and you see nothing but coarse, rank grasses and weeds.

Throughout Ohio there appears to have been some attention to floral residential adornment in the early years. Buckingham (1840) noted in other towns that he visited, including St. Clairsville, Cambridge, and Norwich, "We thought there was more of a substantiality, neatness, and cleanliness, than we had observed in towns of a similar size in the country. A love of flowers and an attempt to adorn the fronts of their dwellings with flowering shrubs and creepers, was more prevalent here then we had observed elsewhere."

Immigrants to the area from Europe brought slips and seeds with them for practical reasons and to remind them of home. Emigrant Liwwät Boke traveled to northwestern Ohio in 1834 from Germany. Her packing list for her trip to America, translated by her great grandson Luke Knapke, exemplified the practice of including both the practical and the ornamental:

Samen—seeds
11) Saodel 1. Soat Käorn—seed corn. 2. Haver—
oats. 3. Weissen—wheat. 4. Klööver—clover.
5. Giärst—barley. 6. Röeggen—rye.
alle in iähr Tuten—all in their bags

12) Saodel 1. Appeln—apples. 2. Kirsken—
cherries. 3. Pfiärfsig—peaches. 4. Biärne—pears.
5. Kuitte—quince. 6. Prume—plum. 7. Prume—
plum. 8. Prumkot—apricot.
alle in iähr Tuten—all in their bags
13) Saodel Blome—flowers
1. Rüen—margarita. 2. Snappen—snapdragon.
3. Pönian—peonies. 4. Holsken—lady slipper.
5. Morgen—morning glory. 6. Hulsk—tulip; crocus.
alle in iähr Tutken—all in their little bags.
(Knapke 1987)

Only rarely are we fortunate to be able to observe through the written record the evolution of a garden over a number of decades. Such records exist for the garden at Adena in Chillicothe, Ohio. Originally the home of the second governor of Ohio, Thomas Worthington, and his family and now in the twentieth-first century an Ohio State Historical Society museum, Adena's gardens have persisted in one form or another for almost two centuries.

The original 1814 layout of the gardens at Adena included three large 100-ft. by 200-ft. terraces. Karl Bernhard, Duke of Saxe-Weimar Eisenbach, recorded what he observed concerning some of the early planting details at Adena:

The Governor's house is surrounded with Lombardy poplars. It is constructed in the style of an Italian villa of freestone, with stone steps on the exterior; is two stories high; has two wings, having a court in front of the center building, containing honeysuckle and roses. On one side of the house is a terrace with flowers and vegetables. This garden was arranged by German gardeners, who keep it in very good order. (Bernhard 1826, in King 1889)

The Worthington archives reveal which types of apples grew in the orchards of Adena, but, unfortunately, complete records concerning the ornamental beds do not exist. We do know that an American arborvitae was planted prior to 1827. Other plants that flourished in that early nineteenth-century garden included lilacs, snowball, allspice, jonquils, China aster, pinks, mignonette, and dwarf iris. Mrs. Worthington grew several varieties of roses, including a wild prairie-type rose that came to be known as the "Worthington rose."

In 1902, nearly 100 years after the origin of this garden, an article appeared in *Harper's Monthly Magazine* romantically describing the Adena garden as observed on one June day:

> In the garden the Calycanthus has dropped its scented blooms, the yellow corcoris flower is withered as it climbs over the low wall on the slope above the kitchen-garden; the snowballs are dry and brown, and the June lilies are budding. The great broad leaves of the daylilies shelter the white trumpets of a coming July and shield the tansy and thyme growing against the stone flagging. Here and there an old-fashioned rose hides itself against its leaves as if mourning lost sisters. The microphylla which once grew over the trellis is dead, and the damask and cabbage roses vanished long ago. Syringa-bushes are thickly set with white stars of perfume, and gorgeous masses of peonies give color to the scene. At the root of a dead tree the star of Bethlehem makes a spotless wreath; and close at hand the yuccas lift white-green cups to heaven. Yellow Nile lilies and flaunting tiger-lilies are opening to catch the color of the sun, and the wild grape perfume is wafted from the woods. Giant fleur-de-lis shake out odor and color, and Canterbury bells ring a sweet entrancing tune. . . . It is not a modern garden. . . . There is nothing but the bulbs and bushes and shrubs of a century ago; nothing but memories and associations, and the fragrance of dead Summers. (Guthrie 1902)

Throughout the nineteenth century, savvy gardeners tried to follow the horticultural fashions of the eastern states and installed wide lawns with ribbon beds and picturesque adornments. Robert Buist in *The Gardener's Monthly* (1868) described the landscape of W. J. Gordon in Cleveland, Ohio, as having an entry lawn enhanced by artificial rocks. The background of the garden displayed clumps of *Rhododendron* and low shrubbery. Ribbon beds contained different colors of coleus and dusty miller. Other beds featured scarlet geraniums edged with *Nierembergia*, and some beds had cannas in the center or back rows. Although the property was but three acres, it also included a number of additional conceits such as old English ruins, ponds, waterfalls, a rustic bridge, a grotto, an underground passage to the stables, a rosary, a grapery, a hot house, a violet pit, and houses for camellias, cacti, orchids, and azaleas. Buist's comment was, "This rare and picturesque place is kept in the most perfect order."

Despite such examples, it is safe to say that most residential gardens in the Great Lakes region were modest in appearance throughout the nineteenth century and into the early years of the twentieth. As was the case elsewhere, it often took several decades for communities to become established enough to progress to having ornamental trees and herbaceous plants. Solon Robinson, traveling in that part of the country in 1845, described homes on the Illinois prairie without trees or shrubs, either for protection or beauty. He noted an exception was in the town of Tremont where a "multitude of shade and fruit trees" surrounded and beautified the dwellings (Robinson 1845a). One Michigan correspondent to *The Horticulturist* in June 1853 described the typical farmer's yard as containing a piece of a neighbor's blush rose, a piece of a cousin's lilac, and two flower beds along the front walkway (Scott 1853). A photograph of the grounds of an Ohio dwelling in 1907 shows a tree encircled by a ground cover of hosta, a hydrangea, and another hosta solo as a "perennial in the lawn"—all this complete

Boy mowing lawn in Twinsburg, Ohio, 1907.

Eugene Wahl residence. Minneapolis, Minnesota, ca. 1895.

with groundskeeper. Not much had changed thirty years later when *The Minnesota Horticulturist* reported concerning farmhouse gardens:

> Even renters have their obligations to keep the farmsteads neat and attractive. It is related of one farm woman tenant, who loved flowers and planted them, that the various farms the family had occupied could be easily located by the trail of hollyhocks that persisted season after season. How much better than a trail of cans and rubbish that so many leave. (Mackintosh 1936)

Urban gardens in the Great Lakes region resembled many others throughout the country at the beginning of the twentieth century. Shade trees, often a maple or an elm, predominated. Typically, a vine grew on the porch and a modest flower garden decorated the back yard along with drying lines and a vegetable garden.

Advice for improving the home grounds came from the horticultural societies in this relatively newly settled countryside. Such advice seemed almost timeless, extending over the course of the century into the 1900s. For example, a member of the Illinois Horticultural Society reminded all in the 1909 *Transactions* of that organization that the main considerations for beautifying the home landscape were utility and simplicity. Based on what this correspondent cautioned against, we can surmise just what the reality of many landscapes actually was.

> Do not plant in spots like shoe buttons all over your lawn. . . . Plant in border masses . . . with free easy flowing lines of foliage mass. Trees should be planted . . . liberally in certain parts of the border. Do not plant them in even numbered groups since this suggests formality.

> In planting shrubbery use large enough masses so that you realize the effect of your variety. Nature is not stingy. . . . Penuriousness is one of the biggest bugbears to the art of landscape gardening. If you cannot buy nursery stock you can at least collect elderberries, and nothing could be more attractive than their mass of white flowers, followed by red or black berries. (Major 1909)

Newcomers to the Great Lakes area experimentally cultivated some of the plants that they knew from the East and found them to be less than hardy in their new climate. Included in this group were different varieties of boxwood, cedar, English and Irish yew, paulownia, azalea, and Chinese arborvitae (Downing 1859, Cranefield 1912). A host of native plants drew the attention of horticulturists in Wisconsin and elsewhere as being hardier and worthy of cultivation, including bearberry, buttonbush, prince's pine, ninebark, deciduous holly, and staghorn sumac, among others (Cranefield 1912). This recommendation coincided with a greater awareness across the country in the early 1900s of the value of native plants in the landscape.

A resident of Chicago at the beginning of the twentieth century described in the book *How to Make a Flower Garden* (Bailey 1903) his attempt to landscape his new home on the banks of Lake Michigan. His report was filled with self-deprecating humor at his initial lack of understanding of the details of landscape design and was exemplary of the way in which many approached the landscape art. W. C. Egan left every stump from old oak trees previously cleared on the property in the hope that they would grow again to towering majesty. He described a rock garden situated in the middle of the lawn: "It was fearfully and wonderfully made and looked it." Flowers grew in the top of the rock heap, too far over the heads of any observers to be seen. Following the prevailing enthusiasm for a diversity of plants, Egan's next step was to litter his lawn with every imaginable exotic plant. He commented, "My man got dizzy dodging them with the lawn mower." Finally, Egan decided to research landscape theory, citing the work of Liberty H. Bailey. He removed the clutter of exotics from his lawn, opening up the center and massing shrubs and trees along the perimeter. The rocks were removed to a ravine where they were installed to imitate natural outcroppings. His final step was to incorporate perennials in the shrubbery beds so that a different species was visible in each directional view. At last satisfied with his landscape, Egan commented, "The pleasures of gardening are infinite and varied."

CENTRAL AND GREAT PLAINS REGION
Iowa, Kansas, Missouri, Nebraska, North Dakota, Oklahoma, South Dakota

When looking at early gardening practices in various areas of the country, nowhere do we see more emphasis on the use of the native flora than in the Central and Great Plains states. Professor W. D. F. Lummis, writing for the 1879 *Iowa Horticultural Society Proceedings*, described the situation for ornamental gardening as he saw it in his home state:

> The first idea presented to us is that very many of our prairie settlers of Iowa are yet poor, and hardly able to obtain the expensive exotic trees, shrubs, vines, and flowers. Fortunately for this numerous class we have enough that cost little more than the cartage and digging, to make the humblest lawn a thing of beauty. If, as the years go on, a native tree or shrub shall be rooted out and thrown over the fence to give place to something more graceful and perfect, who shall say that such changes in the lawn do not afford one of the chief delights of the owner of a leafy home.

Professor Lummis's remarks seem aimed primarily at trees, as he suggested maple, oak, hickory, black walnut, hackberry, elm, birch, the "always interesting" buckeye, catalpa, wild black cherry, ash, locust, hornbeam, juneberry, buffalo berry, and native larch. Among native shrubs, he approved of the snowberry, elder, bladder nut, false indigo, Missouri currant, dogwood, thorn, and native crabapple. When the list extended to herbaceous plants, Professor Loomis drew the line and recommended mainly exotics for homestead gardens. He listed tiger lily and day lily, larkspur, foxglove, dahlia, cannas, crocus, hyacinth, and tulips. He also included balsam, China aster, poppy, portulaca, sweet pea, cockscomb, and calliopsis, among other annuals. Obviously, it was practical and efficient to dig a partially grown, relatively slow-growing tree or shrub from the woods and plant it, but when it came to herbaceous material, seeds and bulbs were fairly inexpensive and gave quick gratification.

The challenges of gardening on the prairie encompassed extreme weather changes and temperatures, wind, soil conditions, and pests. As one prairie writer noted, "The most serious drawback to the planting of our yards and lawns has been the voracious appetite of the migratory grasshopper. They are dainty feeders, and to them, the foliage of our choicest plants seems most attractive" (Oberholtzer 1879).

The force of the wind was legendary throughout the central section of the country. To protect from the prairie wind, horticulturists recommended an L-shaped line of trees on the north and northwest of the house. Evergreens were the best plants for a windbreak, with red cedar, Scotch pine, or Austrian pine considered to be good choices. The Colorado spruce was hardy enough, but could be expensive. Deciduous trees, including maple, elm, ash, and hackberry, were planted among the ever-

The prairie home owner had to consider cold and wind tolerance in the choice of ornamental and shade trees. Nebraska, ca. 1915.

greens. Different species and types of trees were to be intermingled rather than planted in a straight line. Several writers directed that "nurse trees" should be planted also—fast growers like box elder and mulberry—to provide some shelter and weed control while the slower growers were becoming established. The nurse trees were cut down as the other trees matured and grew larger.

Wind affected herbaceous plantings as well. One gardener from Kansas wrote to *Vick's* in November 1886 to recommend some wind-resistant decorative plants.

> I see in your August number that H. W. of Scotia, Nebraska, wants to know what plants will do in that part of his state. I do not believe that the wind blows any more there than here in northern Kansas, as it can almost blow one bald-headed without half trying. Let him plant double Balsams, Zinnias, any of the double Pinks, New Japan Cockscombs and the beautiful Phlox; these will all stand hard wind. As to Perennials, first the Perennial Phlox is best of all, it will not freeze out here; next Chinese Pinks, Hibiscus moscheutos, Yucca, Aquilegia chrysantha and Paeonies. These plants all do well in Nebraska and northern Kansas, as I have tried them. (W. C. M. 1886)

Cold hardiness was another challenge for the gardeners of the Central and Great Plains states. The Nebraska State Horticultural Society published recommendations, including a few cautionary notes, for hardy trees and shrubs from its members in its *Annual Reports* for 1888:

Nebraska State Horticultural Society recommendations for hardy trees and shrubs

Abies balsamea "I have not had good success in transplanting them."

Acer negundo "Excellent for avenues."

Acer platanoides "One of the most valuable ornamental trees for the lawn."

Acer saccharinum "Desirable for immediate effect."

Acer saccharum

Betula pendula 'Laciniata' "A very handsome tree."

Cercis canadensis

Chaenomeles speciosa "The most beautiful of all the flowering shrubs for hedge plants."

Chionanthus virginicus "The most valuable shrub or small tree is the White Fringe."

Fagus sylvatica 'Atropurpurea', but "the Purple Leaf Maple is an entire failure."

Ginkgo biloba "One of the most beautiful trees we have."

Gymnocladus dioica "One of our finest ornamental trees."

Hibiscus syriacus "Are all more or less tender."

Hydrangea paniculata "Is the noblest of all autumn bloomers."

Larix decidua "Seem to be hardy along the line of the B. & M. R. Railway."

Liriodendron tulipifera

Magnolia acuminata "Has the appearance of a tropical tree."

Morus alba var. *tatarica*

Philadelphus coronarius

Picea abies

Picea engelmannii "Sometimes called the 'Blue Spruce.'"

Picea pungens

Pinus flexilis

Prunus glandulosa

Pseudotsuga menziesii "Not a spruce, nor is it a hemlock."

Robinia hispida "The finest bloomer of the whole family of shrubs is the Moss Acacia."

Salix ×*pendulina*

Spiraea prunifolia

Syringa vulgaris "Lilacs are all hardy here."

Taxodium distichum

Thuja occidentalis "It will stand our climate, but will want shading first."

Tilia americana

Tilia platyphyllos "One of the best."

Ulmus americana "One of the grandest of park or street trees."

Viburnum opulus 'Roseum' "The old Snowball is hardy in every part of the state."

Weigela florida "Needs protection."

(Barnard 1888)

Similarly, the Kansas State Horticultural Society in 1898 recommended a group of very tolerant trees as the best choices for western Kansas. Their list included the honey locust, black locust, white ash, elm, hackberry, black walnut, Russian mulberry, Osage orange, catalpa, Carolina poplar, and cottonwood. Among the conifers, they suggested red cedar and Austrian, Scotch, and bull pine (Wheeler 1899).

Writers for many horticultural publications around the country lamented the general lack of ornamental plantings in the nineteenth century, and observers from this region were no exception. Mr. J. W. Canney reported to the South Dakota Horticultural Society in 1921, "There is room for a great many more trees in the western part of the state. When I drive from here [Stamford] to Pierre I wonder how some of the farmers get along without trees or shrubbery of any kind and can bring up families on a treeless farm."

Still, the exceptions provided hope that the land would eventually be tamed. Mrs. E. D. Cowles of Vermilion, South Dakota, described her own idyllic garden:

October 20, 1919, I moved into my little brown bungalow, just west of the old home place where I had lived among the flowers for more than twenty years. I was very thankful for some old shrubs, southeast of the house, a clump of purple lilac and a clump of syringa, two nice rows of Persian lilac, a couple of clumps of spirea VanHouteii, and several clumps of variegated elder. A few steps northwest of the house is a clump of large maple trees, about a dozen. About thirteen years ago I set among them a lot of wild flowers, white and yellow violets, blood-root, Jack in the Pulpit, and Dutchman's britches. . . .

When we sold the home place we reserved shrubbery and flowers to plant the new place . . . planted the shrubbery along the fence. We put a row of peonies and a row of Liberty iris through the garden next to the everbearing strawberries. This spring I want to set out a spirea hedge along the roadside, in front of the house, to help break the dust from the road, and in a few years I expect to fill in the space east of the house with peonies. I have a row of tulips on the east edge of my brush patch in view of the road. In the northeastern corner of the yard I have a stone pile. Last summer it was covered with sweet alyssum, red geraniums,

dew plant, cypress vine, a canna on top, and I just checked all sorts of plants into and around it to get it covered as quickly as possible. (Cowles 1921)

The state of Missouri had a number of nurseries from the earliest days of settlement. Still, the decision to make an ornamental garden presented challenges in obtaining plant material. Neighbors passed among themselves the standards like lilacs, snowballs, and roses. Seeds and bulbs for herbaceous plants could be obtained from some local seed houses or ordered from eastern firms. Ann Withers of Fairville, Missouri, designed two ambitious mixed borders of shrubs, bulbs, roses, and perennials in the 1870s. Each border was 3 ft. wide and 210 ft. long. She planted a wonderful assortment for all-season bloom, including hyacinth, daffodil, tulip, salvia, larkspur, balsam, phlox, different varieties of spiraea, mock orange, hardy hydrangea, yucca, California poppy, verbena, gladiolus, tuberose, canna, geranium, petunia, carnation, selections of dianthus, and lemon verbena. She cultivated moss roses, as well as 'Géant des Batailles', 'Mme. Charles Wood', 'Duke of Wellington', and dwarf white roses. A 10-ft.- tall snowball and white peonies completed the border. On her summerhouse she planted a Queen of the Prairie rose, Japanese honeysuckle, Madeira vine, and nasturtiums. As she exclaimed, "my two long borders are a feast to the eye from June until frost" (Withers 1878).

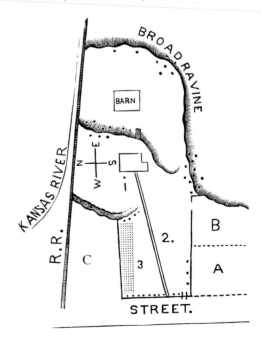

Grounds unimproved (scale 200 ft:1 in.). *Vick's Monthly Magazine*, 1882.

A man from Lawrence, Kansas, consulted with the staff of *Vick's* to assist with the landscape plan for his yard. On the plan (facing page) A and C indicate neighbors' yards and B is a foundry. The property is about 400 ft. deep from the street to the ravine and lies in two grades, with the lower back area accessible by steps. The width of the lot is 200 ft. wide where the house stands. The Atchison, Topeka, and Santa Fe Railroad track provides the property line to the left of the house. A straight 170-ft. path leads to the street and several trees are already in place: 1, Catalpa; 2, Walnut; 3, Elm. The small dots bordering the front and side fence indicate silver maple and box elder planted 10 ft. apart. A stand of native trees, including sycamore, oak, and willow, borders the back ravine.

Vick's responded to this query with a design (below) that would have made Downing proud (Vick 1882a). Naturally, coming from the pen of a grower, it emphasized the

use of an extensive variety of plants. However, Vick claimed that his design was based more on care and patience than on expense. A slight curve was added to the walk, since the gate was not aligned with the front door of the house. The path was 6 to 8 ft. wide and filled with gravel. The group of native trees (A) was to be enlarged with other natives, such as *Amelanchier*, and also with some old favorites like lilac, mock orange, and Tatarian honeysuckle. In front of the shrubbery was a perennial bed that featured *Delphinium*, *Astilbe* (Vick could have meant *Aruncus*), *Anemone japonica*, *Dicentra spectabilis*, sweet William, day lily (this might have referred to a *Hosta* or a *Hemerocallis*), iris, phlox, pansies, and violets. Vines were suggested to grow on the house.

Group (C) is hardy flowering shrubs, and the native tree planting (B) was to have flowering shrubs in the foreground. Plants for both of these areas were to be chosen from *Spiraea*, *Weigela*, *Deutzia*, *Calycanthus*, *Amorpha*, *Forsythia*, *Berberis*, *Euonymus*, *Hydrangea*, snowball, azaleas, *Mahonia*, thorns, and so on. Also to be included at (B) was a planting of roses and lilies in the foreground. Flower beds are indicated by FB.

The legend for the remainder of the trees is as follows:

1, Walnut; 2, Catalpa; 3, Elm; 4, Norway Spruce; 5, Red Cedar; 6, Austrian Pine; 7, Yellow Wood; 8, Cut-Leaved Weeping Birch; 9, Purple-leaved Beech; 10, Fern-leaved Beech; 11, Cut-leaved Alder; 12, Red Oak; 13, Austrian Pine; 14, Acer Negundo; 15, European Ash; 16, Dwarf Pine; 17, Japan Quince; 18, Magnolia Lennei; 19, Magnolia Soulangeana; 20, Siberian Arborvitae; 21, Hovey's Golden Arborvitae; 22, Thujopsis borealis [*Chamaecyparis nootkatensis*]; 23, Juniperus Sabina; 24, Double-flowering Althea; 25, Double Scarlet-flowering Thorn; 26, Double White-flowering Thorn.

Vick designed this elaborate plan for his reader's modest home, but it exudes a typical Victorian enthusiasm. Simplifying the plant choice, keeping the idea of the shrubbery of native trees and flowering shrubs to the rear, and the strategic placement of some nineteenth-century tree

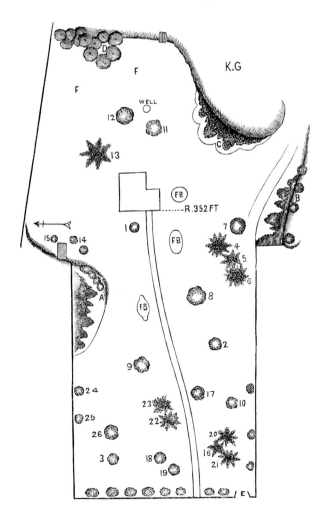

Grounds improved. *Vick's Monthly Magazine*, 1882.

favorites on the lawn with a flower bed or two of bedding plants could accomplish a modern rendition.

MOUNTAIN STATES AND THE WEST
Arizona, California, Colorado, Idaho, Montana, New Mexico, Nevada, Oregon, Utah, Washington, Wyoming

The Mountain States and the West are characterized by great diversity of climate and topography. The Rocky Mountains, Death Valley, and the mild, rainy coast of Oregon all fall within this region, as well as temperate valleys, high plains, and warm subtropical coastal areas. Because of this, it is difficult to identify an all-encompassing garden tradition, if indeed one ever existed. Historically, the region attracted groups seeking religious freedom, gold, and fertile farm and ranch lands. Settlement of the western portion of this country took place with immigration from all directions: eastern North America, Mexico, and different nationalities who chose the oceanic route to the West via the Pacific.

Water and the lack of it was a constant challenge for horticultural purposes in many parts of this region. In gardening styles a tension existed from the beginning between following the fashionable trends of the East—cultivating water-thirsty, exotic plants—and establishing a more regionally responsible form of gardening that relied on drought-tolerant and native plants. By the end of the nineteenth century, this tension was finally resolved in the gardens of the bungalows of California—in the often ecofriendly Craftsman or Arts-and-Crafts garden style.

It is easy to romanticize the early Spanish missions in California and envision luscious, tropical-looking pleasure gardens. The literature contradicts this vision. The missions' gardens were mainly for subsistence, as were other early gardens across the country. A few ornamentals might have been grown for altar decoration. California's ornamental garden history begins in earnest in the late 1800s, when changing land use, from huge rancheros to smaller fruit farms and urban properties, and the heightened availability of ornamental plants coincided for the advancement of the gardening art.

Both Streatfield (1992) and Padilla (1961) suggest the same list of ornamental plants grown in mission gardens prior to secularization in the 1830s. Included on their lists are calla and Madonna lilies, the Castilian rose (a damask rose), musk rose, jasmine, lavender, pennyroyal, giant reed, castor oil plant thought to have been introduced in California by Father Junipero Serra in 1769, wild cherry (*Prunus illicifolia*), pepper tree (*Schinus molle*), Matalija poppy (*Romneya coulteri*), date palm (*Phoenix dactylifera*), Canary Island palm (*Phoenix canariensis*), and the Mexican and native fan palms (*Washingtonia robusta* and *W. filifera*, respectively).

Victorian gardens in California resembled gardens of that era in the East, with emphasis on strategic placement of trees and curvilinear paths in the Downingesque mode, as well as implementation of the gaudy ribbon bedding style of brightly colored annuals. Some elaborate estates bore testimony to the diversity of plants available to the California gardener with their many individual specimens of trees in the lawn. Besides the wonderfully diverse native

Durand's residence. Pasadena, California, 1909.

flora, California gardens were graced by plants from all over the world. Australian plants, in particular, were in vogue, with scores of species offered by the more savvy nurseries.

Modest California homes typically had one or two palms planted along the front path. Often they were a species of *Washingtonia* or *Phoenix*, although twelve to twenty different palms were available (Wickson 1915). Palms were both drought-tolerant and easily trans-planted, making them a practical choice for the vernacular California land-scape. By the end of the nineteenth century, Cali-fornia gardens of varied economic status enjoyed a reputation of widespread verdure and ornamental plantings.

After the beginning of the twentieth century, Cali-fornians increasingly adopted a definitive regional style that set them apart from other areas of the country. Some credit Kate O. Sessions (1857–1940), a San Diego garden designer and horti-culturist, with sowing the seeds of the idea that Cali-fornia gardens were best served by the use of drought-tolerant and primarily native plants. In the early 1900s, a house architectural style called the Bungalow origi-nated and gained prominence in California. Bungalows were relatively modest dwellings that emphasized simplicity

Vernacular garden with poppies. Jamestown, California, 1902.

A California bungalow is swathed in verdant vines. 1907.

A residential street. Cheyenne, Wyoming, 1908.

and the use of natural building materials. The gardens that developed around these houses synthesized man-made elements with the natural world. They promoted the outdoors as additional living space with the use of terraces and patios, in the tradition of colonial Spanish courtyards and verandas.

Vines and lush plantings dominated these landscapes, and ground covers helped obscure the boundaries between the man-made and natural features. Emphasis on native plants punctuated the connection with the natural world, although gardeners still cultivated many exotic plants, including bougainvillea, banana, eucalyptus, palms, and roses. California became known for the diversity of species and colors in its plant palette. Its reputation claimed that any plant could be grown bigger and better in California. The *Ladies' Floral Cabinet* of 1876 described the lush scenery: "California climate is wonderfully exuberant in its development of flowers and trees, and it is a frequent sight to have Geraniums clambering up the garden fence and covering a space six feet high by ten feet long, and all one brilliant mass of scarlet blossoms" (California gardens and homes 1876).

Correspondents to nineteenth-century horticultural periodicals provide us with some modest vignettes of gardening by early settlers in the other areas of the West. Mrs. A. A. E. of Evanston, Wyoming Territory, wrote in the 1878 *Vick's Monthly Magazine* that planting conditions were so inhospitable that flowers could be grown only

indoors in her area. A photo postcard of a street in Cheyenne thirty years later illustrates the transformation of the Wyoming landscape to a more domesticated nature. The placement of street trees and yard plantings on this street could be from almost anywhere in the United States.

Neighboring Montana had a more extensive nineteenth-century garden tradition, including the cultivation of many fruit trees due to the greater availability of water in that state (Bailey 1906a). The Montana State Board of Horticulture reported in 1901 that ten nurseries were operating in the state, offering trees, fruit, shrubs, and flowers. The State Nursery in Helena grew "the hardiest of trees and plants, ornamental trees and shrubs; palms, bulbs and flowers . . . [and] over one acre in roses." The City Nursery of Great Falls grew thousands of shade trees, including elm, ash, and maple, for municipal use. In all areas of the West, including the Central states and Great Plains, shelterbelts built of trees to protect against the prairie winds were important. State Nursery advertised a bargain group of trees for this purpose in their 1941 catalog, including, for $7.95, 25 poplars, 100 white ash, 25 Russian willows, and 200 buckthorns.

Any rumor of inhospitable conditions in Montana was summarily dispelled by a correspondent to the Gurney Seed and Nursery Company of Yankton, South Dakota, who wrote that she had moved to Montana in 1913 and brought three peonies with her from her previous home in Wisconsin. Her new neighbors claimed her peonies would not grow in the unfriendly prairie climate, but she reported that six years later the peonies boasted over eighty-six blooms. Horticultural authorities recommended the following plants for cultivation in northeastern Montana: green ash, elm, hackberry, Russian olive, poplar, pine, caragana, lilac, iris, peonies, and tulips (South Dakota Horticultural Society 1921).

Early settlers, hoping to become wealthy from gold or land acquisitions, usually did not take the time to make a flower garden. Some exceptions certainly occurred, and

A RESIDENCE STREET, PORTLAND, OREGON

A residence street. Portland, Oregon, 1913.

correspondents from gold-mining regions in both Nevada and Oregon reported on the success of their horticultural ventures. "C. L." of Franktown, Nevada, notified the readers of *Vick's Monthly Magazine* in 1879 that he had grown a number of ornamentals in his Nevada valley since 1861, including *Hydrangea paniculata* 'Grandiflora', phlox, hollyhocks, weigela, deutzia, spiraea, roses, lilacs, and Virginia creeper. Another Nevada gardener from the 1870s added to this list sweet peas, cockscomb, and marvel of Peru or four-o'clocks (Greenleaf 1878).

Similarly, a correspondent from Althouse, Oregon, wrote, also to the 1879 *Vick's Monthly Magazine*, that he grew crown imperial, hyacinths, dahlias, gladiolus, stock, sweet pea, candytuft, China pink, zinnia, pansies, snapdragons, and petunias.

> We cannot get vegetables and flowers to grow easily here. To raise anything like decent vegetables we have to work up our garden soil very well and give it plenty of water. Our garden soil is sand with gravel bottom. To irrigate my garden I run water from the Mining ditch, and all the time I have to attend to it is in the evening, after my day's work is done. (L. E. L. 1879)

Many plants that gardeners cultivated in these remote places were grown from seeds or bulbs that were easily carried or transported across the country to the West.

Pioneers who followed the Oregon Trail all the way to the West Coast encountered a more congenial site for gardening than those people who stopped in the mountainous or prairie areas of the Far West. Many Oregon settlers brought roses with them, including *Rosa virginiana*, *Rosa* 'York and Lancaster', and *Rosa* 'Queen of the Prairie', and established ornamental gardens as they developed their new communities (Albro 1936). Following the same evolution of the cultivated landscape as elsewhere, a photo postcard of a street in Oregon in 1913 confirms the idea that landscapes in the East and the West became fairly homogenized after the beginning of the twentieth century.

The Mormons in Utah cultivated a rich horticultural history. U. P. Hedrick (1988) declared "horticulture began in Utah around 1850 [and] it is doubtful that in any other state in the Union the growing of fruits, vegetables, and flowers made so rapid progress in so short a time." Della Barnett, a sixth-generation Utah resident, reported that her grandmother, Helen Price Hyde, cultivated a lovely flower garden in the 1920s. Helen's mother and aunts brought plants, including sweet woodruff and lily-of-the-valley, with them from their native Sweden in the nineteenth century and transplanted them to the short-seasoned northern Utah landscape. Hedges surrounded the Hyde property and a weeping birch was the focal point of the front yard. Virginia creeper covered the two-story brick house. Helen cultivated flowers for their beauty in the garden and also to fill vases that she placed throughout the house, as well as for the cemetery. She proudly exhibited her flowers and vegetables at the county fair (Barnett 2003).

Sometimes early travelers in an area recorded their observations of the landscape. Zebulon Pike, traveling through New Mexico in 1806, commented on the adobe dwellings and said they had courtyards adorned with fountains, pools, trees, and shrubs. Hedrick (1988) believed that Pike exaggerated the beauty of the scene. His skepticism seems to have been substantiated by another traveler six decades later, who reported to *The Cultivator & Country*

Street scene, midwinter. Phoenix. Arizona Seed & Floral Company, 1921.

of natives more than others. Still, since joining the world of historic garden and plant research, I have often heard two generalizations concerning the use of native plants in nineteenth-century American gardens. First, all native plants had to be exported to Europe for "improvement" before being appreciated here. Second, native plants are always appropriate for period gardens because they obviously were widely available and it was an easy task to dig them up and transplant them to gardens.

Let us look at the horticultural literature for clues as to how natives could (or should) have been used in nineteenth-century gardens and landscapes. Early writers both recommended their use and lamented their neglect. Bernard M'Mahon's 1806 *American Gardener's Calendar* is usually cited as the beginning of the written American gardening tradition. M'Mahon observed, "Here, we cultivate many foreign trifles, and neglect the profusion of beauties so bountifully bestowed upon us by the hand of nature." Some gardeners apparently agreed (even if they had never heard of him), because Thomas Ashe in his *Travels in America in 1806* described the garden of an Ohio woman, Miss L. Livingston, residing at North Bend, who

Gentleman that the area was barren, although interesting cacti abounded. He also noted that peaches and grapes were raised "in abundance" but that no one knew how to preserve them (T. S. H. 1869).

Although the lack of water was an issue in many states of the western region, Arizona was the driest state of all. J. W. Tourney wrote in Bailey's *Cyclopedia* (1906), "All of this region has very limited possibilities from a horticultural standpoint, the flow of the few available streams being small and very uncertain." As in other areas of the country, residents sought to emulate the garden traditions of the eastern states where they had previously lived. A photo of a relatively lush ornamental planting along a Phoenix sidewalk, just nine years after the territory became a state, successfully evokes nostalgia for landscapes of eastern areas. A 1925 Phoenix floral catalog directed that, "The successful garden requires good irrigation and cultivation." Thus, the availability of water defined early Arizona gardens as it did elsewhere.

> collects seeds from such plants and flowers as are the most conspicuous in the prairies and cultivates them with care on the banks, and in the vicinity of the house . . . she is forming a shrubbery also, which will be entirely composed of magnolia, catalpa, papaw, rose, and tulip tree and all others distinguished for blossom and fragrance. (Ashe 1809)

"THE NEGLECTED AMERICAN PLANTS"— FACT OR FALLACY?

Whether or not to use native plants in period gardens is always a controversial question in the absence of any documentation. As noted above, some regions promoted the use

Writers cited *beauty* and *ornamentation* as compelling reasons to cultivate native plants. Edward Sayers, in his 1839 *The American Flower Garden Companion*, echoed M'Mahon's observations, "the native shrubs and plants are much neglected in culture here . . . it is their finely woven texture and rich coloring that should engage our admiration, and not the country that has given birth to a particular variety." Some horticulturists complained that savvy gardeners tended to avoid anything that was perceived as "common."

Joseph Breck resorted to *economic* reasoning in his 1851 tome. "Many beautiful plants may be selected from the woods and fields, by those who wish to ornament their grounds at the least expense." Economic benefits applied only if the gardener obtained the plant from the wild. J. C. Loudon observed in his 1838 *Encyclopedia of Gardening* that the retail prices of the American growers were as high as those of England and that many American trees and shrubs were as cheap in Britain as in the United States.

Another crusader for the use of natives in the American garden was Andrew Jackson Downing. He was particularly enamored of the broadleaf evergreens and recommended in 1851 that all readers of *The Horticulturist* should plant some laurels and holly. "A bed of these fine evergreens . . . will be a feature in the grounds, which will convince you far better than any words of ours, of the neglected beauty of our American plants" (Downing 1851a).

Economy and beauty are reasonable motivators by our standards. Add to that a compatibility with *design* precepts of the nineteenth century. Downing included native plants in his landscape designs. In 1855 *The Horticulturist* featured a design by William Saunders that used these native trees: hemlock, sweet gum, Virginia fringe tree, umbrella magnolia, yellowwood, silver bell, and nettle tree (or hackberry). Likewise, Robert Copeland in his 1867 *Country Life* wrote, "However liberally you introduce foreign trees, retain a large number of the native and common kinds, that they may connect the home-place with the general landscape." He published a list of foreign trees frequently cultivated, alongside possible substitutions, and graded both for quality. Interestingly, he ended his discussion with the observation, "We generally depend on the taste of the nursery-man, who prefers to sell the trees he can grow most easily, and thus a great deal of rubbish has been foisted upon the public."

Speaking of design, nature was a good source for inspiration in how to arrange trees and shrubs. "T" wrote in the 1847 *Cultivator* that one should look to nature for the good combinations. "The owner may be at a loss how to arrange his trees to the best advantage. Let him try to imitate as nearly as he can . . . the finest natural groupings he can find in the country."

Native plants provided easy ornamentation of a farmhouse as Jared Kirtland eloquently asserted:

The most homely log house with its portals covered with the everblooming Honeysuckle, and some of the climbing roses, its ends deeply enshrouded with the luxuriant grape vine and the running Ampelopsis, over-shadowed either with the native trees, or those that are fruit-bearing, presents more pleasing associations than the gaudily painted farmhouse. (Kirtland 1845)

Other writers cited additional reasons to grow indigenous plants. J. L. Comstock, writing to *The Horticulturist* in 1850, described the reasons why he grew native plants:

1. Native plants are easy to grow, being already acclimatized to the area. (At least one grower cautioned readers not to dig up plants themselves, as they were better if coming from the nursery.)

2. Comstock felt "a mixture of national pride in the consideration that our woods, swamps and barrens afford as beautiful specimens of the gifts of Flora, as can be brought from any other country."

3. Watching the development and adaptation of a wild plant to cultivation is a distinctive pleasure.

4. Comstock found amusement in stumping his friends over the identity of common plants. This last motive seems to have infected others as well. A member of the 1879 Iowa Horticultural Society (IHS) described how an eastern friend of his had a lovely garden of azaleas that he had obtained from an English firm. He was entertained by the friend's chagrin upon learning that his "rare" plants grew wild all over his section of the country. The IHS member, a Professor Arthur of Madison, Wisconsin, repeated M'Mahon's words of seventy years before, "the value of the indigenous plants of Iowa for ornamental purposes is not well appreciated by our own people." That refrain seems to have been constant throughout the first seventy-five years of the 1800s.

The hardiness of native plants in their home countryside was another benefit for the garden. George Gurney of Yankton, South Dakota, wrote in 1921, "Of the shrubs . . . some of our natives . . . are among the best, if not the very best, on account of their extreme hardiness, and hardiness means considerable." His was good advice for South Dakota gardeners.

Occasionally, an article would appear extolling the virtues of native plants in containers. Mrs. E. B. R. wrote enthusiastically to the *New England Farmer* in 1857 that she had particular success growing "the common plants of the woods: dandelion, Buttercup, and violet" in pots. The large-flowered yellow lady's slipper was featured in the 1883 *Vick's Monthly Magazine* as a particularly handsome subject for pot culture.

By the 1880s and 1890s American gardening tastes were moving from geometric, well-manicured but gaudy bedding schemes to looser-edged wild gardens and old-fashioned borders. This seems to have generated a greater interest in growing native plants. The wild garden, according to a writer for *Vick's* in 1882, was not to be placed in the center of the lawn or another conspicuous place, but in a hideaway place where it could become a refuge of sorts. Shady sites are practicable as long as they have been thoroughly amended to approximate the soil conditions where the plants normally thrive. He recommended growing ferns, trilliums, and other beauties of the woods (Arnold 1882).

Wild gardens were repositories not only for native plants. Wild gardens were a "look" creating a soothing atmosphere rather than merely a collection of indigenous plants—as Elias Long pointed out in 1893. The natural or wild garden was "a place where interesting wild and cultivated plants are brought together in the most natural manner, and allowed to live and struggle, much as they do when wild" (Long 1893).

A major event that added to the late nineteenth-century interest in native plants was the 1892 World's Fair in Chicago. The Olmsted firm designed an island landscape, which featured the type of scenery to be found along U.S. lakes and lagoons. Trainloads of native plants, including poplars, maples, cherries, elms, and lindens, were planted. For the understory, dogwoods, spiraeas, loniceras, along with some exotics like snowballs, lilacs, and barber-ries were included. The end result, according to a writer for the 1893 *American Gardening* magazine, "will doubtless have an effect of arousing an interest in our decorative native plants and flowers of which many are yearly exported for cultivation" (Seavey 1893).

About this time a number of nurseries began to specialize in natives. Edward Gillette of Southwick, Massachusetts, offered a catalog of primarily natives by 1880 and wrote, "The demand for this class of plants has fully doubled within the past two years." Thomas Meehan's nursery (established 1853) in Germantown, Pennsylvania, was also noted for its extensive selection of native plants.

So, all this suggests conflicting evidence for the presence of native plants in the gardens of nineteenth-century America. Prominent designers and growers certainly promoted their use. It is not unreasonable to think that some people were so awed by their beauty or motivated to obtain something useful for little effort and no cash that plants were taken from the fields and forests and cultivated in gardens. Still, the overriding lament heard throughout the century was that American plants were sadly neglected.

The twentieth century promised to be a better showcase for native plant treasures. The prominent horticulturist Liberty H. Bailey made the following observation in the 1893 *Annals of Horticulture*:

> The ornamental gardening of this country is very rapidly undergoing a change, particularly in its application to home or private grounds. The formal and purely conventional features of ornamentation are giving place to the freer use of hardy perennials and native plants. . . . The interest in native plants has never been so great as now . . . many of the so-called old-fashioned plants are coming into favor, at least in their improved forms. All this indicates an evolution in taste which must be abiding.

ENCYCLOPEDIA OF
HEIRLOOM ORNAMENTAL PLANTS

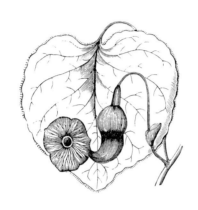

· 4 ·

HOW TO USE THE ENCYCLOPEDIA OF HEIRLOOM ORNAMENTAL PLANTS

THE ENCYCLOPEDIA of Heirloom Ornamental Plants is a compendium of more than 1000 heirloom ornamental plants. These plants are not merely known to have been cultivated sometime in America's past. They represent the most frequent offerings of the nursery trade—out of more than 25,000 taxa that were actually listed in more than 300 catalogs and newspaper advertisements. These trade citations originated from firms from across the contiguous forty-eight states, with each state except Nevada represented at least once. The earliest commercial listing dates from 1719 and the most recent is from 1939. See Appendix C for a list of these historic commercial sources.

Not all of these formerly popular ornamental plants are appropriate for contemporary landscapes by virtue of their inclusion in this encyclopedia. They are important plants in American garden history—but some have proved too invasive or disease-prone to be of practical use any longer. Please refer to the *Remarks* for each entry for cautionary advice about the use of a particular plant. Appendix D is a list of heirloom plants found on regional invasive species lists.

Phlox was the plant offered most frequently in the old catalogs. Other popular plants in the commercial trade were sweet William, snowball viburnum, and American arborvitae. However, other plants that were easy to propagate and share with other gardeners rarely made it to nurseries or seed houses. These are difficult to document quantitatively. A few of these plants are also included in the encyclopedia—plants like gardener's garters or the plume poppy, neither of which made a huge showing in catalogs, but which tradition tells us might have been planted frequently. Other considerations for listing were those plants that were introduced later in the period—like the regal lily—or that had significant regional, rather than national, presence such as the blue gum in California. The incidences of these plants in the catalogs might not have compared favorably with the overall total, but they were important enough to include in the encyclopedia. Under *Related species* I document additional plants that were particularly prevalent in the trade catalogs, but were not in the first ranking. The Encyclopedia of Heirloom Ornamental Plants is extensive, but inevitably it will exclude someone's favorite old-time plant. I apologize for this in advance.

The number of citations for plants should not be compared between categories. The number of references that were available varied between perennials and bulbs, for example. Perennials as a group are represented more often than any other plant category. This was enhanced by the fact that early in my research I concentrated solely on perennials before moving on to other plant classifications. Catalog lists of bulbs, on the other hand, were in the minority, so plants in that chapter do not have high numbers of historic commercial source citations. Bulbs typically were imported and the distributor in this country might not have known until he received his shipment exactly which varieties he could offer. In each chapter I have included those species that appeared most often within their own particular category.

Plants are arranged alphabetically by genus. In most cases, the main entry is a species, although a few genera, for example *Paeonia* and *Tulipa*, are exceptions. Common names are included with the botanical nomenclature. Common names are always ambiguous because they reflect the jargon of a particular region. Fortunately, most of the catalogs and garden literature of the nineteenth century included both scientific and common names, so accurate identification usually, but not always, was possible. Occasionally, a common name referred to more than one species; for example, Jupiter's beard could be *Centranthus ruber*, a red-flowering herbaceous perennial, or *Chionanthus virginicus*, the native shrub also known as fringe tree. The index provides a cross-reference of common names with botanical names.

Introduction dates include previously published dates for introduction of the plant into the western world. Most of these are European plant introductions. The years come from a variety of sources, mainly secondary, all of which are listed in the bibliography. In some cases, I found an American citation that predates a widely published general introduction date. In those plant entries, the previously published year appears in brackets following the earlier citation. Unfortunately, no record is complete—in some cases no introduction date was found.

Earliest American citation is the first year for which I found documented evidence that the plant was cultivated on American soil or was offered by an American nursery or seed house. Obviously, written records are scarce for the first three centuries of American garden history. Thus, the American cultivation of some plants inevitably predated the first written citation. These dates do not claim to be the *actual years of introduction* into American gardens. Much more research is needed on this topic and I hope garden historians will continue to add to our knowledge of actual dates of introduction of American heirloom ornamental plants.

In order to distinguish them from general text citations, the format for the earliest American citation takes four forms. Citations from a nursery catalog or trade advertisement show name, location of business, and year. These catalogs are listed in Appendix B. Citations from literature in the bibliography show last name, year. The third type of citation relies on secondary works to reference the plant cultivation activities of people in the early days of the country and includes the first and last name of the actual cultivator and the year. Finally, a few citations are unique enough to require the typical author-date citation used elsewhere in this book.

Many of the earliest American citations come from the work of scholars who have researched the plants and gardens of colonial plant collectors. Two early presidents, Washington (deForest 1982) and Jefferson (Betts 1981, 1986) were avid plantsmen and left detailed records concerning their gardening activities. Eighteenth-century plant collectors like John Bartram of Philadelphia (Berkeley 1992) and John Custis of Williamsburg (Swem 1957) not

only cultivated their own gardens, but also engaged in plant exchanges with British gardeners who introduced American plants into England. The assumption is made here that if Custis or Bartram sent a plant to England, they very likely cultivated the plant in their own gardens as well. In addition to the above references, please consult the bibliography for works by Faris, Leighton, Lockwood, and Sarudy, which further describe the role that these early plant enthusiasts, along with others like William Byrd, Jr., Lady Jean Skipwith of Virginia, and William Faris of Annapolis, played in the introduction of plants into American gardens. The Southern Garden History Society compilation of early southern plant lists (Chappell 2002) is an additional source with contributions by Flora Ann Bynum responsible for references to the Bethabara settlement in North Carolina.

The *Description* for each plant might have come from the pages of a trade catalog or the details of a garden writer, or it might be my own observations. The description was chosen to convey the essence of the plant—and the reason why early gardeners cultivated and cherished it. Please refer to contemporary horticultural references to expand upon those descriptions and to obtain more detailed cultural information for modern gardens.

The *Design notes* make suggestions for placement of the plant in the landscape or describe historic plant combinations. This attention to plant combinations plays to our own contemporary tendency to look at garden plants in artful combinations rather than see each as a individual specimen, cherished for singular attributes, as often was the case in the past. Although the art of garden design using plant combinations has evolved over the years, it was not unusual, particularly after the beginning of the twentieth century, for garden writers to suggest a complementary planting scheme or to describe the components of a natural scene that they found particularly attractive.

Remarks include miscellaneous information with regard to the plant, its history, or culture. Particular attention should be paid to this section for notes on potential invasiveness of some of the more aggressive heirloom plants. In some cases, it might be better to plant a substitute rather than a particularly vigorous plant, in spite of any historical significance.

Heirloom varieties include plants that had a presence in the past and are still available in the modern nursery trade. Cultivars are the most transient of all plants since they are propagated and offered only until something supposedly improved or different comes along. The preservation of old cultivars has become a passionate pursuit for

'Bella Donna' is an undocumented rose in gardens east of the Mississippi. Photograph by author.

many heirloom plant enthusiasts. Sources in Appendix C offer many of these rare treasures. For each selection, the date of international introduction, where known, is followed by the earliest American citation in my records. Descriptions in this section are from the earliest American citation unless indicated otherwise.

Historic commercial sources provide the number of times a plant was cited in the researched literature. This documentation is very incomplete. While extant publications like seed catalogs and periodical advertisements compose the foundation of what we have to work with, *they are not the complete record*. We are limited severely by which catalogs are still available and the time needed to study them.

If a plant is not listed in the encyclopedia that does not mean it was not available or past gardeners did not grow it.

The published record is scanty and has many holes. In my own garden I have a lovely, deep pink, fragrant damask rose, 'Bella Donna' (thanks to the Reverend Douglas Seidel for the identification), which grew in the yards of a number of mid-1800s houses in central Ohio. This rose was also commonly grown in Pennsylvania Dutch areas, but it did not show up even once in my commercial lists that included 3500 different taxa of *Rosa*. We can assume that many, many other plants are undocumented and have not made these pages. The written record is the easiest to research. The more challenging task will be for someone to construct an accurate picture of heirloom ornamental plant cultivation combining written documentation with the anecdotal and otherwise unpublished records. That challenge is yours.

· 5 ·

HEIRLOOM TREES

A tree, undoubtedly, is one of the most beautiful
objects in nature.
> —Andrew J. Downing, 1841

The culture of trees for shelter, shade and ornament, has been in practice from time immemorial
. . . civilization and arboriculture have always traveled together.
> —Walter Elder,
> *The Gardener's Monthly*, 1861

Sometime when you have nothing else to do, plant
a tree. It will be growing while you sleep.
> —George W. Gurney, Yankton,
> South Dakota, 1921

THE NINETEENTH CENTURY in America was the
Century of the Tree. Emblematic of the passing of the frontier, trees were initially cleared to provide room for settlements. Then, as communities became more established and
secure, trees were planted—fruit trees for sustenance and
shade trees for protection. When permanent dwellings rose
up, so also did the ornamental plantings around them,
anchored by the placement of beautiful or picturesque
trees. Some scholars have argued that the presence of a tree
nursery in an early American village signaled that the transition from frontier to permanent settlement was complete.
The symbolism inherent in the presence of trees in the
landscape was not lost on early gardeners. As F. R. Elliott
(1868) so aptly put it:

> We are yet a young people, and in many places the
> trees that adorn our homes and our streets have
> grown with our growth; and while we are to pass
> away, they are to remain life-enduring monuments
> of our labors and examples of instruction to our
> children's children for generations to come.

Trees, according to Andrew Jackson Downing in his
Treatise, can impart all that is beautiful about nature to the
landscape.

A few fine trees, scattered and grouped over any
surface of smooth lawn, will give a character of
simple beauty; lofty trees of great age, hills covered
with rich wood, an elevation commanding a wide
country, stamp a site with dignity; trees of full and
graceful habit or gently curving forms in the lawn,
walks, and all other objects, will convey a sense of
grace; as finely formed and somewhat tall trees of
rare species, or a great abundance of bright
climbers and gay flowering shrubs and plants, will
confer characters of elegance and gaiety.

The diversity among the many species of trees both excited and challenged the early garden designers. Frank Scott
extolled the virtues of trees in his 1870 *The Art of Beautifying
Suburban Home Grounds of Small Extent*. According to Scott,
trees have nearly infinite variety based on

> their multitude of features and forms, their oddi-
> ties of bark, limb, and twig, their infinitude
> of leaves and blossoms of all sizes, forms and
> shades of color, their towering sky outlines, and
> their ever varying lights and shadows. . . . Sunny
> cheerfulness, gayety, gloom, sprightliness, rude-
> ness, sweetness, gracefulness, awkwardness, ugli-
> ness, and eccentricities, are all attributes of trees as
> well as human beings.

Most obvious is the variety of forms that trees exhibit in the landscape. Trees with a rounded crown were the largest group employed in landscape gardening. Ash, oak, and beech are examples of round-headed trees. Downing described their forms as "elegant and beautiful" and noted that they usually attain a more picturesque character as they age. The round-headed trees "harmonized with almost all scenes" (Downing 1859).

The conical-shaped trees in this landscape echo the architectural lines of the house, ca. 1905.

Conical or spire-topped trees include most of the evergreen conifers as well as trees such as the larch. Use of these trees typically was tempered with restraint in acknowledgment of their sometimes rigid forms at maturity and the accompanying evergreen foliage that cast a somber perspective on the landscape.

Downing (1859) described another class of trees: "Oblong-headed trees show heads of foliage more lengthened out, more formal, and generally more tapering than round-headed ones" (Downing 1859). The typical example of oblong-headed was the Lombardy poplar, popular for lining avenues or providing relief in the outline of a group of round-headed trees.

Weeping trees or those with exaggerated forms complete the list of typical tree habits. Writers differed in their opinion of how "drooping" trees might best be used in the landscape. Downing thought them appropriate for the edge of groupings or used singly and with restraint in the lawn. Another proponent of weeping trees was Patrick Barry, who wrote in an article for the 1850 *The Horticulturist* that "the peculiar gracefulness of drooping trees, render them of great importance in the embellishment of landscapes . . . they are equally capable of producing charming effects" (Barry 1850). Contrary to these opinions, *Vick's Monthly Magazine* editorialized in 1878, "Drooping trees we do not admire. An occasional specimen as a curiosity, is well, but a lawn abounding in Weeping Trees would be a sorry place" (Lawns and lawn trees 1878).

The landscape design philosophy of the great Andrew Jackson Downing revolved around the characteristics of trees important to his landscape designs. Downing divided his theories into the Beautiful and the Picturesque. Trees exemplified very clearly the differences in these two perspectives:

> The Beautiful in Landscape Gardening is produced by outlines whose curves are flowing and gradual. . . . In the form of trees, by smooth stems, full, round, or symmetrical heads of foliage, and luxuriant branches often drooping to the ground— which is chiefly attained by planting and grouping, to allow free development of form; and by selecting trees of suitable character, as the elm, the ash, and the like.

> The Picturesque in Landscape Gardening aims at the production of outlines of certain spirited irregularity. . . . The trees should in many places be old and irregular, with rough stems and bark; and pines, larches, and other trees of striking, irregular growth, must appear in numbers sufficient to give character to the woody outlines . . . trees and shrubs are often planted closely together; and intricacy and variety—thickets—glades—and underwood—as in wild nature are indispensable.

Whether to use deciduous trees or conifers was a recurring problem for designers. Downing himself felt that evergreen trees were neglected and could be used more often. He suggested that they be planted to provide contrast in a group of deciduous trees or for the ever important function of screen or windbreak. Evergreens were also useful for hedges. One particularly effective planting combined evergreen trees in a group of trees that bore brightly colored fall fruit, such as the mountain ash and the strawberry tree (*Euonymus*), the dark foliage of the evergreens providing great contrast and effect (Elliott 1868). One of the disparagers of the evergreen tree was Frank Scott, who wrote in 1870 that evergreens "did not deserve to be valued" because when they matured they became rigid, somber, and monotonous in the landscape. He did concede that evergreens and snow do make a lovely combination, an observation that was repeated in many books into the twentieth century.

The positive edge, however, appears to have belonged to the evergreen enthusiasts, with Walter Elder summing it up in an 1863 *Gardener's Monthly* article: "The gorgeous grandeur of the rich and many evergreens, standing erect in their majestic beauties, with their ponderous branches far out-spread over the grassy sod, and in such density that only a mass of foliage is seen, excites our highest admiration."

America was home to many indigenous species of trees, and early gardeners apparently appreciated the native trees as much as they did the exotic species. If we look at the trees that were most often featured in nursery catalogs of the 1800s, we find that seven of the top ten were native species, the exceptions being Norway spruce, weeping willow, and European mountain ash. Most often featured in those catalogs was the American arborvitae, followed by the balsam fir and the white pine. Rounding out the list is Virginia red cedar, silver maple, tulip tree, and Canadian hemlock. If we expand our criteria to include the early years of the twentieth century, the American elm joins the list of popularly cultivated natives. Garden designers published landscape designs featuring native trees in the major horticultural periodicals and writers often entreated their readers not to take the common plants of their land for granted or avoid them in their plantings. Robert Copeland (1867) wrote, "However liberally you introduce foreign trees, retain a large number of the native and common kinds, that they may connect the home-place with the general landscape."

People placed trees in their landscapes for both practical and aesthetic reasons. Shade was perhaps the foremost consideration, although Grace Tabor wrote in 1916 that the shade of trees should never touch the house, but rather the ground surrounding the house. Nineteenth-century writers often cautioned against too much shade as being bad for the health and stifling to the atmosphere surrounding a house. Trees therefore were placed near, but not too close to the house. Trees were planted on the boundary line of the property to emphasize the extent of the landscape or to direct a view. They were arranged to imitate natural groupings and thickets and also placed singly in the lawn to draw particu-

lar attention to the majesty or grandeur of the tree itself. Trees were chosen for these placements on the basis of height, form, and seasonal interest, which could include spring and summer flowers, fall color, and winter berries.

Discussion in the garden literature of trees for the landscape declined after the beginning of the twentieth century. In the early 1900s, trees were never ignored, but their individual attributes and virtues for the landscape were not covered as often as in the books of the 1800s because attention had turned to herbaceous plants.

In many garden books of the early 1900s that featured descriptions of herbaceous borders and gardens, trees provided the background and framing for the flower garden. Neltje Blanchan (1913) provided her list of the functions of trees in the garden:

To break the sky line

To give diversity of outline and color at different seasons

To increase the interest of the home grounds

To unite the house and the garden with the surrounding landscape

To form windbreaks and boundary belts

To afford shelter and shade

To screen off unsightly places

To emphasize the height of a hill top

To draw the eye toward a lovely view

To improve the quality of the atmosphere around a dwelling

To furnish masses of bloom

To attract birds

To make a place comfortable and beautiful in winter as well as summer

To line a drive or walk

To beautify the lawn

A CATALOG OF HEIRLOOM ORNAMENTAL TREES

These heirloom ornamental trees are found most often in 300 nursery catalogs for the period 1771–1939.

Green's Nursery Co., Rochester, New York, 1894.

Abies balsamea

balsam fir, American silver fir, balsam, balm of Gilead
Synonyms: *Pinus balsamea*, *Picea balsamina*
Pinaceae
Native
Introduction: 1696
Earliest American citation: John Bartram, ca. 1760
Zone: 3–5
Description: Evergreen, 45–75 ft. "Among the beauties of this tree may be mentioned the bright green of its foliage and the clusters of erect and purplish cones borne upon the upper branches.... The Balsam fir is one of the most hardy of American trees . . . it is well adapted for planting as a protection to other plantations that would otherwise be exposed to winds" (Flagg 1856b).
Design notes: "There is something about it, while it is young that attracts the attention of the crowd, and has caused it to be very generally planted as an ornamental tree. As it increases in stature, it is found unworthy of its reputation, and inferior to all other species of this tribe" (Flagg 1856b).

"It is one of the most beautiful evergreens for planting in grounds near the house, and is perhaps more cultivated for that purpose than any other in the Union. . . . The deep green color of the verdure of the Balm of Gilead fir is retained unchanged in all its beauty through the severest winters, which causes it to contrast agreeably with the paler tints of the Spruces" (Downing 1859).
Remarks: "No sight is more common in our New England villages than a little cottage close to the street, with two or more tall Balsam Firs tyrannizing over it" (Copeland 1867).
Historic commercial sources: 71
Related species:
Abies alba (syn. *Abies pectinata*). European silver fir. Long cultivated. Prince, New York, 1790.
Abies concolor. White fir, Colorado fir, concolor fir. Intro: 1872. Waukegan Nursery, Illinois, 1878.
Abies nordmanniana. Nordmann's silver fir. Intro: 1848. Downing, 1859.

Acer negundo

ash-leaved maple, box elder, Manitoba maple
Synonyms: *Negundo fraxinifolium, N. acerifolium*
Aceraceae
Native
Introduction: 1688
Earliest American citation: John Bartram, ca. 1760
Zone: 3–9

Description: Deciduous, 30–50 ft. "Its foliage is of a peculiar lively, light green, which gives it a striking and marked appearance among other trees; while its long racemes of pale green seeds, which hang all summer on the tree, and the peculiar pea-green bark of the young wood, are all features of novelty and interest to the arboriculturist" (Downing 1847a).

Design notes: "It groups admirably with pines" (Elliott 1868). "Very hardy and long-lived, it is not a beautiful tree but is desirable in your windbreak or groves on the farm" (Gurney, South Dakota, 1927).

Remarks: "Much prized in the West, where it withstands cold and dryness. Largely used for shelter belts and for planting timber-claims" (Bailey 1906a).

Historic commercial sources: 52

Acer platanoides

Norway maple
Aceraceae
Exotic
Introduction: Long cultivated
Earliest American citation: Bartram, Philadelphia, 1792
Zone: 4–7

Description: Deciduous, 40–50 ft. "Large handsome tree, with round spreading head . . . the leaves turn pale yellow in autumn" (Bailey 1906a).

Design notes: Used as a specimen lawn tree and as a street tree. "The beautiful Norway Maple standing by the curbstone is a common sight in our city streets" (Keeler 1900).

Remarks: "The Norway Maple, fine in shape and quick growing . . . [is an] especially valuable variety" (Ely 1903).

Acer platanoides has proved to be invasive in some areas of the United States. Please refer to Appendix D for specific regional information concerning invasive species.

Heirloom variety:
'Schwedleri'. Purple-leaved Norway maple. Intro: 1870. Storrs & Harrison, Ohio; California Nursery, 1894. "Leaves bright red when young, changing to dark green" (Bailey 1906a).

Historic commercial sources: 53
Related species:

Acer campestre. European cork maple. Long cultivated. Prince, New York, 1826.

Acer palmatum (syn. *Acer polymorphum*). Japanese maple. Intro: about 1830. Hogg, New York, by 1870. Heirloom cultivars include: 'Atropurpureum', blood-leaved Japanese maple and 'Dissectum', cut-leaf Japanese maple, known in the United States by 1870; and 'Dissectum Purpureum', purple cut-leaf Japanese maple, offered by the California nursery of Mrs. Theodosia Shepherd in 1891.

Acer pseudoplatanus. European sycamore maple. Long cultivated. M'Mahon, 1806. "Of special notice as a street shade or park tree or as a shade tree for an area near to the house—appearance is intermediate between the sycamore and the sugar maple" (Elliott 1868).

Other *Acer* species of concern for invasiveness include *A. palmatum* and *A. pseudoplatanus*. Please refer to Appendix D for additional information.

Purple-leaved Japanese maple, *Acer palmatum* 'Atropurpureum'. Photograph by author.

Acer saccharinum

silver maple, soft maple
Synonyms: *Acer dasycarpum, A. argenteum*
Aceraceae
Native
Introduction: 1725
Earliest American citation: John Bartram, ca. 1760
Zone: 3–9
Description: Deciduous, 50–70 ft. "Fast growing . . . one of the most graceful as well as lofty of the species" (Elliott 1868).
Design notes: "The Silver Maple is now more extensively planted than any other maple, being of very rapid growth, and adapted to almost any soil or climate" (Barry 1872).
Remarks: Some cultivators felt that the silver maple ranked a poor second to the sugar maple: "I prefer the hard maple, but most people live only for today; they do not live for next

Acer saccharinum, silver maple, was a popular nineteenth-century choice for a fast-growing lawn tree. William C. Moore, Newark, New York, ca. 1910.

year or the next generation. The people want soft maple" (Dintlemann 1910). Similarly, Mr. Neeley, a fellow member with L. F. Dintlemann of the Horticultural Society of Southern Illinois, lamented in 1909, "I do not know of a single soft maple tree that ever made a respectable shade tree. They are always diseased and the storm will break them, while the hard maple stands the storm much better" (Dintlemann 1910).
Heirloom variety:
'Laciniatum Wieri'. Wier's cut-leaf maple. Intro: 1872 by D. B. Wier of Illinois.
Historic commercial sources: 81

Acer saccharum

sugar maple, rock maple
Synonym: Occasionally in the literature you will see an allusion to *Acer saccharinum* referring to sugar maple, rather than silver maple.
Aceraceae
Native
Introduction: by 1735 [1753]
Earliest American citation: John Bartram, ca. 1735
Zone: 3–8
Description: Deciduous, 60–70 ft. "The Sugar Maple is a beautiful tree at all seasons. In early spring, when the greenish yellow flowers suddenly burst forth with the first leaves, the tree has an appearance altogether distinct from that presented by any other. Standing in the sunshine, a tree in full flower seems enveloped with a luminous mist, and is an object of striking beauty. Later in the season, its light green and very abundant foliage give it what has been aptly termed a peculiarly sunny appearance, and it stands for the very type of cheerfulness among trees. In the autumn none of our trees blaze with brighter or more varied colors, and in the winter its light, ash-colored bark is a pleasant relief from the more somber hue of other Native trees" (Sargent 1891b).
Design notes: "One of our best trees for ornamental planting, and that few trees can excel it in situations where it will thrive. In some of the old places on the Hudson River long avenues were planted with it, three-quarters of a century ago, and some of them are now worth a journey to see" (Sargent 1891b).
Remarks: "Chieftain of its tribe; straight, spreading, symmetrical, of grand proportions, often 120 ft. in height . . . hardy here when planted among other trees" (Gurney, South Dakota, 1921).
Historic commercial sources: 64

Early gardeners were attracted by the fall color as well as the summer flowers of *Aesculus parviflora*, dwarf horse chestnut. Photograph by author.

Aesculus hippocastanum, the horse chestnut, (right) has distinct pinnately compound foliage. Photograph, early 1900s.

Related species:

Acer rubrum. Red maple, scarlet maple. Intro: 1656. John Bartram, ca. 1760. "During the spring, the Scarlet maple is certainly the most beautiful tree of our forests" (Downing 1859).

Aesculus hippocastanum

European horse chestnut, candle tree

Hippocastanaceae

Exotic

Introduction: 1576

Earliest American citation: John Custis, ca. 1734

Zone: 4–7

Description: Deciduous, 50–75 ft. "This tree, when planted in a rich soil, grows to a large size, and is beautiful in shape, foliage, and flower" (Breck 1858).

"Each leaf is composed of five or seven leaflets, which radiate from the petiole like parts of a fan. . . . Following immediately [the] splendid bursting into leaf, its blossoms glow in spikes like giant hyacinths set in the green young foliage, and lifted upon a tree stem to form a colossal bouquet (Scott 1870).

Design notes: The horse chestnut was useful for bordering streets, for public squares, for single lawn use, and for limited use in grouping with Scotch and Austrian pines (Elliott 1868).

"It makes a very dark shadow, and should not be planted closely in rows, nor very near to the windows of a residence" (Scott 1870).

"Much planted along roads and in parks and private grounds in this country. It is particularly adaptable for bowers and places where seats are desired, as the top stands heading-in and makes a very dense shade" (Bailey 1906a).

Remarks: "The Horse-chestnut has its own peculiar, stubby branches, its uniform shape, its dense shade; is in a word, a cabbage on a stick" (Copeland 1867).

Heirloom variety:

'Flore Pleno' (syn. 'Baumannii'). Double-flowered horse chestnut. Intro: 1820. Downing, 1859.

Historic commercial sources: 56
Related species:
Aesculus flava (syn. *Aesculus octandra*). Yellow buckeye. Intro: 1764. Bartram, Philadelphia, 1783.
Aesculus glabra. Ohio buckeye. Intro: 1809. Spring Garden, Cincinnati, 1843.
Aesculus parviflora (syn. *Aesculus macrostachya*, *Pavia macrostachya*). Bottlebrush buckeye, dwarf horse chestnut. Intro: 1785. George Washington, ca. 1786. The dwarf horse chestnut is a shrub bearing "long slender spikes of white flowers with very long projecting stamens tipped in red" (Manning 1884).
Aesculus pavia (syn. *Pavia rubra*). Scarlet-flowering horse chestnut, red buckeye. Intro: 1711. John Bartram, ca. 1760.

Ailanthus altissima

tree-of-heaven, paradise tree, celestial tree, Tillou tree
Synonym: *Ailanthus glandulosa*
Simaroubaceae
Exotic
Introduction: 1784
Earliest American citation: William Hamilton, Philadelphia, 1784
Zone: 4–8
Description: Deciduous, 40–60 ft. "Its strong shoots or arms of rusty brown young wood, taken with its long and singular foliage and profusion of whitish green flowers, create a tree of no mean attraction" (Elliott 1868).
Design notes: "The Ailanthus is a picturesque tree, well adapted to produce a good effect on the lawn, either singly or grouped; as its fine foliage catches the light well, and contrasts strikingly with that of round-leaved trees. . . . The sole objection to this tree is its unpleasant odor at flowering time" (Long 1893). The tree-of-heaven sometimes was used when young for subtropical bedding (Massey 1893).
Remarks: *Ailanthus altissima* has had both fans and detractors throughout its history in American gardens. For example, Robert Copeland described it in 1867 as "bad as possible." However, an 1851 correspondent to the *Western Horticultural Review*, who identified himself only as M. K., earlier had rallied to its defense.

> The Ailanthus, sir, is not only the best shade tree we possess, but it is immensely superior as a city shade tree to any other Native or foreign. Its rapid growth, its entire exemption from the attacks of insects, its power of enduring our dryest summers without apparent injury, the luxuriant verdure of its foliage, which never changes or decays during summer, and its splendid Palm-like form, so suitable in proximity to fine buildings, give it a superiority which no other tree possesses for such purposes. True, it has a few faults, one of which, and that most objected to, is the disagreeable smell of the blossoms of the male plant. . . . But this nuisance, if such it should be, lasts for only about two weeks in the year, and it may be greatly abated if the pavements and roofs are swept three or four times during the period of flowering.

Ailanthus altissima has proved to be invasive in some areas of the United States. Please refer to Appendix D for specific regional information concerning invasive species.
Historic commercial sources: 31

Betula pendula

white European birch
Synonym: *Betula alba*
Betulaceae
Exotic
Introduction: Long cultivated
Earliest American citation: M'Mahon, 1806
Zone: 2–6
Description: Deciduous, 50–60 ft. "Their graceful habit, the slender, often pendulous branches, and the picturesque trunks, make them conspicuous features of the landscape" (Bailey 1906a).
Design notes: The birches were considered very ornamental park trees.
Remarks: Bronze birch borer is a major pest of the European birch that prevents it from being used effectively in contemporary landscapes without chemical intervention.
For regional invasiveness concerns regarding *Betula pendula*, see Appendix D.
Heirloom variety:
'Laciniata' (syn. sometimes 'Dalecarlica'). Cut-leaf weeping birch. Brighton, Boston, 1841. "The cutleaf birch is, to our taste, one of the most elegant trees recently introduced" (Sargent 1854).
Historic commercial sources: 40
Related species:
Betula papyrifera. Paper birch, canoe birch. Intro: 1750. John Bartram, ca. 1760.
Betula populifolia. American white birch. Intro: 1750. John Bartram, ca. 1760. "Small, graceful, but short-lived tree" (Bailey 1906a).

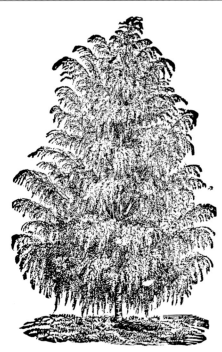

Betula pendula 'Laciniata', cut-leaf weeping beech. Call's Nursery, Perry, Ohio, 1901.

Castanea dentata

American chestnut
Synonym: *Castanea americana*
Fagaceae
Native
Introduction: ca. 1760 [1783]
Earliest American citation: John Bartram, ca. 1760
Zone: 4–8
Description: Deciduous, 70–100 ft. "Fine massy foliage and sweet nuts. . . . When old, its huge trunk, wide-spread branches, lofty head, and irregular outline, all contribute to render it a picturesque tree of the very first class" (Downing 1859). "It is most beautiful when in flower, its abundant long racemes appearing in great numbers at the end of every twig, and the effect of the whole is one of airiness and grace" (The chestnut as an ornamental tree 1869).
Design notes: "A very fine tree, partaking much of the character of the oak for a broad and picturesque outline. . . . Every planter of private grounds who has room should use the chestnut, as it is itself as a tree beautiful, whether singly or in groups, of easy cultivation, and produces fruit of value as profitable one year with another as an apple-tree" (Elliott 1868).
Remarks: The demise of the American chestnut is one of the tragedies of America's wars with imported pests. The blight *Cryphonectria parasitica* was introduced to the eastern states in 1904 and rapidly killed off the native stands of American chestnut. Its impact must not have been clearly understood at first, since as late as 1932 nurseries east of the Mississippi were still offering this majestic tree. Since 2002, some progress is being made in Virginia and Ohio to cultivate American chestnut trees that are resistant to the chestnut blight.
Historic commercial sources: 29
Related species:
Castanea sativa. Spanish chestnut. Long cultivated. M'Mahon, 1806. Rose Hill, Maryland, featured an avenue of Spanish chestnut ca. 1820 (Lockwood 1934).

Catalpa

Indian bean, catalpa, catawba tree
Bignoniaceae
Native
Introduction: 1726
Earliest American citation: Ratcliffe Manor, Maryland, 1750 (Lockwood 1934)
Zone: 4–9
Description: "Catalpa" referred to two different species of a deciduous tree, but rarely did early writers distinguish be-

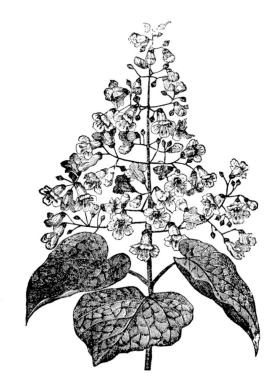

Flowers of the *Catalpa*. Peter Henderson, *Henderson's Handbook of Plants*, 1890.

Catalpa speciosa bears fragrant white flowers in early summer. Photograph by Steven Still.

Catalpa bungii, the umbrella catalpa, was used as a specimen tree in this ca. 1910 Lima, Ohio, front yard.

tween them. *Catalpa bignonioides* is slightly smaller and less hardy than *C. speciosa*. Both species average 40 ft. tall with *C. bignonioides* 30–40 ft. and *C. speciosa* 40–60 ft.

"The leaves of this tree are very large, often measuring six or seven inches broad; they are heart-shaped in form, smooth, and pale green. . . . The blossoms are extremely beautiful, hanging like those of the Horse-chestnut, in massy clusters . . . the color is a pure and delicate white . . . wide-spreading head" (Downing 1859).

Design notes: "Decidedly tropical appearance . . . good lawn tree" (Hooker, Wyman, & Co., New York, ca. 1905).

"May be mingled with other large round-leaved trees, as the basswood, etc. when it produces a very pleasing effect" (Downing 1859).

Remarks: The particular species of catalpa that was recommended for landscape use seemed to depend on the location. *Catalpa speciosa* typically was the northern or

western catalpa and *C. bignonioides* was the eastern or southern catalpa.

Catalpa bignonioides (syn. *Catalpa syringafolia*). Intro: 1726. Bartram, Philadelphia, 1783.

Catalpa speciosa. Intro: 1754. George Washington, ca. 1786.

Historic commercial sources: 80

Related species:

Catalpa bungei: Umbrella catalpa. Intro: by 1860 [1877]. Ellwanger & Barry, New York, 1860.

Cedrus deodora

deodar cedar, Himalayan cedar, Indian cedar

Pinaceae

Exotic

Introduction: 1831

Earliest American citation: W. E. Johnson, South Carolina, 1835 (Lockwood 1934)

Zone: 7–9

Description: Evergreen, 40–70 ft. "Those who have seen it in its native localities on the mountains of northern Hindostan, describe it as a tree of colossal dimensions, uniting gracefulness and grandeur beyond all other evergreens" (Scott 1870).

Design notes: "As lawn trees, the light airy, graceful characters of the Japan and Deodar cedars render them specially beautiful . . . wherever the climate is such that they can be grown safely, their planting should not be omitted" (Elliott 1868).

Branch of *Cedrus libani*, cedar of Lebanon. Andrew J. Downing, Rural Essays, 1853.

Remarks: "Surely, because a few plants are occasionally lost, people will not give up growing this exquisite Evergreen?" (Saul 1857).
Historic commercial sources: 27. More commonly found in trade lists of the Deep South and Far West than elsewhere.
Related species:
Cedrus libani. Cedar of Lebanon. Intro: 1638. John Custis, ca. 1735. "The noblest evergreen of the old world" (Saul 1857).

Cercis canadensis
redbud, Judas tree
Fabaceae
Native
Introduction: 1641
Earliest American citation: John Custis, ca. 1735
Zone: 4–9
Description: Deciduous, 20–30 ft. "Valuable as an ornamental tree . . . exceedingly neat foliage, which is exactly heart-shaped and of a pleasing green tint . . . pretty pink blossoms" (Downing 1859).
Design notes: Downing (1859) recommended that these trees be placed near the house "where their pleasing vernal influences may be observed."
Remarks: The blossoms could be eaten in salads and were pickled by French Canadian families.
Historic commercial sources: 55

Chamaecyparis pisifera
Sawara cypress, retinospora, Japan cypress
Synonym: *Retinospora pisifera*

Chamaecyparis pisifera 'Filifera Aurea', golden thread-leaf Japan cypress, was available from a California nursery by 1891. Photograph by author.

Cupressaceae
Exotic
Introduction: 1861
Earliest American citation: A. C., *The Gardener's Monthly*, 1868
Zone: 4–8
Description: Evergreen, 50–70 ft. "Beautiful feathery foliage" (Blanchan 1913).
Design notes: Initially, the main concern about the newly introduced trees in the *Chamaecyparis* genus among nineteenth-century gardeners (or to them, the Retinosporas) was whether or not they would be hardy. The 1870 *Gardener's Monthly* recommended "a place in the cool conservatory, as a companion of the noble Norfolk Island pine," but acknowledged that "in mild moist climates it may be planted out with safety" (New and rare plants. Retinospora Plumosa 1870). By the 1890s, the Japan cypress had proved

Cornus florida in pink and white lines the Adams's driveway. Photograph by author.

itself hardy to New York. Henderson (1890) suggested, "The Japanese Retinosporas are among the most beautiful of small evergreen trees. They are fine subjects for the lawn . . . and make very pretty hedges."

Neltje Blanchan (1913) recommended that only the young Japan cypress be used in the garden, either in ornamental groupings or as a lawn specimen. She observed that the golden 'Plumosa Aurea' was much used in bedding.

Remarks: "This new botanical family in general appearance resemble [sic] the junipers, and the arbor-vitaes, as much as the cypress. . . . Its Japanese name signifies 'tree of the sun'" (Scott 1870).

Heirloom varieties:

'Filifera'. Thread-branched Japan cypress. Intro: 1861. Berger, San Francisco, 1892.

'Filifera Aurea'. Golden thread-leaf Japan cypress. Intro: by 1889. Shepherd, California, 1891.

'Plumosa'. Plumed Sawara cypress. Intro: 1861. Moon, Pennsylvania, 1870.

'Plumosa Aurea'. Golden Sawara cypress. Intro: 1861. Moon, Pennsylvania, 1870.

'Squarrosa'. Veitch's silver cypress. Intro: 1843. Moon, Pennsylvania, 1870.

Historic commercial sources: 26

Related species:

Chamaecyparis lawsoniana (syn. *Cupressus lawsoniana*). Lawson's cypress. Intro: 1858. Downing, 1859. "One of the greatest acquisitions that has been made for many years to our list of hardy evergreens" (Elliott 1868).

Cornus florida

flowering dogwood

Cornaceae

Native

Introduction: 1731

Earliest American citation: John Custis, 1735

Zone: 5–9

Description: Deciduous, 20–30 ft. "This species . . . is a conspicuous object, in some of our woods, the last of May. The tree is then loaded with a profusion of large, showy, white flowers, which are produced at the ends of the branches." In the autumn "the leaves early begin to change to purple, and turn to a rich scarlet, or crimson above, with a light russet beneath. . . . These, surrounding the scarlet bunches of berries, makes the tree as beautiful an object, at the close of autumn, as it was in the opening summer" (Breck 1858).

Design notes: "Quite a picturesque small tree and owes its interest chiefly to the beauty of its numerous blossoms and fruit . . . one of the gayest ornaments of our Native woods. . . . Taking into consideration all these ornamental qualities, and also the fact that it is every day becoming scarcer in our

Native wilds, we think the Dogwood tree should fairly come under the protection of the picturesque planter, and well deserves a place in the pleasure-ground and shrubbery" (Downing 1859).

An article in the 1872 *The Horticulturist* suggested a good combination to feature fall color, which included in the back row a red maple, scarlet oak, and sour gum and in the front flowering dogwood, two common sumachs, with a few vines of smilax and Virginia creeper (Hoopes 1872b).

Remarks: "Its profusion of white flowers in early spring have [sic] drawn attention of ornamental planters to it, until it is now sought for and planted by every landscapist of every taste" (Elliott 1868).

Heirloom varieties:

'Pendula'. Weeping dogwood. Meehan, Philadelphia, 1880.

f. *rubra* (syn. 'Rubra'). Red-flowering dogwood. John Custis, ca. 1738. Mrs. Frances King (1925) was impressed with a combination of two to three dark-leaved Japanese maples planted with a pink-flowering dogwood in Richmond, Virginia.

Historic commercial sources: 43

Crataegus laevigata

European hawthorn, Maythorn
Synonym: *Crataegus oxycantha*
Rosaceae
Exotic
Introduction: Long cultivated
Earliest American citation: George Washington, ca. 1786
Zone: 4–7

Description: Small deciduous tree or shrub, 15–20 ft. "The growth of the tree is more rambling than that of our best Native thorns, and its outer branches, intercurving, and well covered either with flowers or leaves, often convey the impression of trees composed of garlands, blossoms, and leaves" (Scott 1870).

Design notes: Andrew J. Downing (1859) recommended that hawthorns "be planted singly, or two or three together, along the walks leading through the different parts of the pleasure-ground or shrubbery."

"There can be no prettier deciduous gateway arch than may be made by planting a white-flowering hawthorn on one side, and some of the pink or scarlet varieties on the other, for the purpose of weaving their branches together overhead, and then clipping to perfect the arch, but not so closely on the outside as to mar the graceful freedom of the outline that is one of the most pleasing features of the hawthorn" (Scott 1870). Scott also echoed the rec-

Crataegus laevigata 'Plena', double-flowering thorn. *Vick's Monthly Magazine*, 1881.

ommendation of the English landscape gardener, Uvedale Price, that the hawthorn was a good tree for filling in the spaces in a large planting of trees. All of the hawthorns were suitable plants for hedging.

Remarks: "The berries, or haws, as they are called, have a very rich and coral-like look when the tree, standing alone, is completely covered with them in October" (Downing 1859).

Heirloom varieties:

'Paul's Scarlet' (syn. 'Coccinea Plena'). Paul's Scarlet thorn, double red thorn. Intro: by 1832 [1858]. Kenrick, Boston, 1832. 'Coccinea Plena' was the earlier name for the double red thorn and 'Paul's Scarlet' was used after 1858.

'Plena'. Double white thorn. Kenrick, Boston, 1832.

Historic commercial sources: 44

Related species:

Crataegus crus-galli. Cockspur thorn, red haw. Intro: 1656. John Bartram, ca. 1734. This hawthorn provided good hedge material, being heavily "armed."

Pyracantha coccinea (syn. *Crataegus pyracantha*). Evergreen thorn. Intro: 1629. George Washington, ca. 1786. "A greater variety of beautiful small trees and ornamental shrubs can be formed of several species of Thorn, than of any kind of tree whatever" (Breck 1858).

Eucalyptus globulus

blue gum, Tasmanian blue gum, fever tree
Myrtaceae
Exotic
Introduction: 1804
Earliest American citation: ca. 1860. James Vick speculated that a huge tree in Oakland, California, had been planted about that time.
Zone: 9

Description: The blue gum can grow to 300 ft. high. It has
smooth, grayish bark and aromatic, thick, lanceolate leaves.

Design notes: Eucalyptus trees were commonly used in early
California landscapes as ornamentals, street trees, and
windbreaks. Bailey (1906a) described the use of blue gum in
the eastern states as a bedding plant, for lawn groupings, or
for subtropical effect. He recommended that the seed be
planted indoors the autumn preceding when it is to be
placed outdoors for summer effect.

Remarks: "On the 28th of January, this year, there was cut
down in the city of Oakland, Cal., a Eucalyptus Globulous
[sic], or Blue Gum, as it is commonly called in that state,
which was planted early in the 'fifties' by Rear Admiral Mc-
Dugall. This tree was probably the oldest tree of the species
in the United States, and had attained a height of nearly a
hundred feet, and was four feet eight inches in diameter at
the butt" (California gleanings 1886).

"No other single Exotic has so altered the California countryside as this one tree" (Padilla 1961).

Historic commercial sources: 13

Related species:

Eucalyptus camaldulensis (syn. *Eucalyptus rostrata*). Red gum.
Santa Rosa Nursery, California, 1880.

Eucalyptus citriodora. Lemon-scented gum. Berger, California, 1892. This was a favorite pot plant in eastern conservatories.

Fagus sylvatica

European beech

Fagaceae

Exotic

Introduction: Long cultivated

Earliest American citation: M'Mahon, 1806

Zone: 4–7

Description: Deciduous, 50–60 ft. The beeches are "tall, deciduous, hardy trees of noble symmetrical habit, with
smooth light gray bark and clean dark green foliage, which
is rarely attacked by insects or fungi . . . [especially] attractive in spring, with the young foliage of a tender, delicate
green, and the graceful, drooping heads of the staminate
flowers" (Bailey 1906a).

Design notes: Designers designated the European beech as
appropriate for the pleasure ground or parks, but considered it too large for the shrubbery. It was also sometimes
used for tall hedges.

Remarks: The purple-foliaged European beech was the most
common beech cultivated in nineteenth-century American
gardens.

Victorian gardeners used weeping or drooping trees as specimen lawn
trees. *Fagus sylvatica* 'Pendula', weeping beech. Photograph by author.

Heirloom varieties:

var. *heterophylla* 'Aspleniifolia'. Cut-leaf beech. Intro: by 1804.
Barrett, Boston, 1841. 'Comptoniifolia' (fern-leaf beech) is
a form of the European beech similar to 'Asplenifolia'.

'Atropurpurea' (syn. Atropurpurea Group, var. *purpurea*, 'At-
ropunicea'). Purple European beech, copper beech. Intro:
before 1680. Thomas Jefferson, ca. 1807. "Common in gardens" (Downing 1859).

'Pendula' (syn. var. *pendula*). Intro: 1836. Barrett, Boston,
1841.

Historic commercial sources: 36

Related species:

Fagus grandifolia. American beech. Intro: 1783. Bartram,
Philadelphia, 1783.

Fraxinus americana

American ash, white ash
Synonyms: *Fraxinus acuminata, F. alba*
Oleaceae
Native
Introduction: 1724
Earliest American citation: John Bartram, ca. 1760
Zone: 4–9
Description: Large deciduous tree, 50–80 ft. "Straight trunk
. . . with light-colored or gray bark, latticed into ridges and
deep furrows. . . . In leaf it is occasionally a superb tree, sym-
metrically globular or ovate, with abundant foliage, of a dull
or bluish-green color. . . . In autumn the leaves change to a
deep brownish-purple" (Scott 1870).
Design notes: "The White Ash . . . [is] one of the most beau-
tiful of our Native trees . . . one of the best of Native trees for
ornamental planting" (Sargent 1894d).
"Used in large plantations, for parks, squares or streets"
(Breck 1858).
Remarks: "[The ash] is most valuable of all for North and
South Dakota . . . absolutely the best for high and dry places.
. . . It will grow with less rainfall than any other forest tree.
. . . Your home, whether it is in the city or on the farm, will
be just as beautiful as the tree-covered portions of south-
eastern South Dakota. This is a great tree for Montana and
Colorado. . . . The ash tree is one of the easiest to transplant,
it seldom fails to grow, but requires care after planting just
as your cornfield does" (Gurney, South Dakota, 1921).
Historic commercial sources: 56
Related species:
Fraxinus excelsior. European ash. Long cultivated. M'Mahon,
1806. Elliott (1868) stated that the European ash was the
Fraxinus species most often sold in American nurseries.
Several nineteenth-century nurseries carried the gold-
barked ash (*F. excelsior* 'Aurea'), the earliest being Prince
Nursery in their 1826 catalog. The weeping European ash
(*F. excelsior* 'Pendula') was also available from Prince and
over a dozen other nurseries, both east of the Mississippi
and in California.
Fraxinus nigra (syn. *Fraxinus sambucifolia*). Black ash. Intro:
by 1760 [1800]. John Bartram, ca. 1760. Downing noted in
his *Treatise* (1859) that this tree was of "less stature" than the
American ash, while Copeland (1867) labeled it "good" for
the landscape.
Fraxinus ornus. Flowering ash, manna ash. Intro: 1700.
M'Mahon, 1806. "Chief beauty lies in the beautiful clusters
of pale or greenish-white flowers borne in terminal
branches in May and June . . . in blossom it resembles the
Carolina fringe tree" (Downing 1859).
Fraxinus pennsylvanica (syn. *Fraxinus viridis*). Red ash, green
ash. Intro: by 1810 [1824]. Booth, Baltimore, 1810. Although
the American ash was overwhelmingly the most popular ash
among American growers, green ash occasionally turned up
on the pages of their catalogs. Both Downing (1859) and
Copeland (1867) gave this species their approval for landscape use. Scholars have noted that in some early literature
the name *Fraxinus pennsylvanica* was used for the tree we
now refer to as *F. americana*.

Gleditsia triacanthos

honey locust, three-thorn acacia, Kentucky locust
Fabaceae
Native
Introduction: ca. 1700
Earliest American citation: John Bartram, ca. 1760
Zone: 4–9
Description: Deciduous, 30–70 ft. "A large and curious tree of
our forests, armed at all points with enormous compound
thorns which grow even through old bark of the trunk as
well as on the branches, and arm all parts of the tree in the
most formidable manner" (Scott 1870).
Downing (1859) considered this a much finer tree in appearance than the common locust, "although the flowers are
greenish and inconspicuous, instead of possessing the
beauty and fragrance of the [locust] . . . [it has] a particular
elegance about its light green and beautiful foliage."
Design notes: "It is a tree very desirable in the composition of
groups, and also for roadsides or streets where only a partial, not deep shade is desirable" (Elliott 1868). The honey
locust also was favored as a hedge plant throughout the
nineteenth century. Scott (1870) recommended that the
armed honey locust not be cultivated in areas frequented
by children.
Remarks: *Vick's Monthly Magazine* of 1881 declared the three
best hedge plants to be honey locust, Osage orange, and
Japan quince (Vick 1881a).
Heirloom variety:
var. *inermis*. Thornless acacia. Intro: 1700. M'Mahon,
Philadelphia, 1804.
Historic commercial sources: 47

Ilex opaca

American holly
Aquifoliaceae
Native
Introduction: 1744

Earliest American citation: Bartram, Philadelphia, 1783

Zone: 5–9

Description: Evergreen tree or shrub to 40–50 ft. Conical in shape. "The leaves are waved or irregular in surface and outline . . . and their color is a lighter shade of green. They are armed on the edges with thorny prickles and the surface is brilliant and polished" (Downing 1859). Bright red berries in the autumn.

Design notes: "There is no plant that would make a more quaintly beautiful and striking hedge than this our native Ilex. In the open ground it is of remarkably thick growth, and its stiff and well-armed leaves would render it impenetrable even to fowls and smaller animals" (Richardson 1854).

"In foundation plantings it is best used where the large evergreens are needed, unless it is trimmed occasionally, when it may be kept low and compact" (Johnson 1927).

Remarks: "We regret that the American sort, which may be easily brought into cultivation, is so very rarely seen in our gardens or our grounds" (Downing 1859).

"The American Holly (*Ilex opaca*), with its dull green leaves is much inferior to the English Holly (*I. Aquifolium*), which has lustrous foliage, but it has the merit of being fairly hardy in northern Massachusetts, whereas its European relative is not" (Wilson 1932).

Historic commercial sources: 24

Related species:

Ilex aquifolium. English holly. Long cultivated. George Washington, ca. 1786.

Ilex verticillata (syn. *Prinos verticillata*). Deciduous holly. Intro: 1736. George Washington, ca. 1786.

Juglans nigra

black walnut

Juglandaceae

Native

Introduction: 1686

Earliest American citation: Bartram, Philadelphia, 1783

Zone: 4–9

Description: Deciduous tree, 50–75 ft., with a "massive straight trunk, and a light and airy broad top . . . one of the noblest trees of the American forest" (Bailey 1906a).

"In open ground it becomes not only a tree of majestic size but of marked beauty, from the light color and softly blended masses of its long pinnate leaves, each leaf having from thirteen to seventeen leaflets" (Scott 1870).

Design notes: A valuable park tree.

Remarks: Even in the mid-nineteenth century, garden writers were aware that "there is something in the emanations from its leaves and roots injurious to trees near it, and grass under" (Scott 1870).

Historic commercial sources: 28

Juniperus communis 'Hibernica'

Irish juniper

Synonym: *Juniperus communis* 'Stricta'

Cupressaceae (Pinaceae)

Exotic

Introduction: 1560 (species)

Earliest American citation: The Irish juniper was brought to the United States from Ireland about 1836.

Zone: 2–6

Description: A small evergreen tree, 10–15 ft. "This is, we believe, the most slender and fastigiate of all evergreens" (Scott 1870).

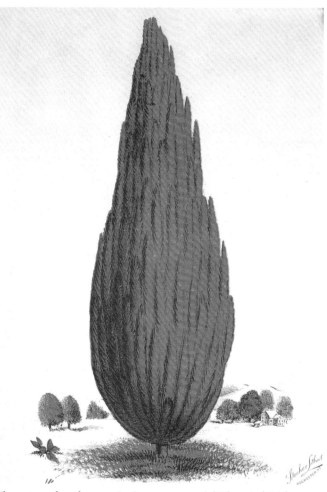

The extremely columnar *Juniperus communis* 'Hibernica', Irish juniper, served as an accent plant in early gardens. Leo Weltz, Wilmington, Ohio, ca. 1905.

Juniperus sabina. Savin juniper. Intro: before 1580. Bartram, 1792. This 4–6 ft. shrubby juniper was used in shade plantings. Staunton Nurseries in Virginia offered the variety 'Tamariscifolia', gray carpet juniper, in 1858. *Juniperus prostrata*, the dwarf savin or carpet juniper, was available in Ohio by 1845 and may be the same plant as *Juniperus sabina* 'Tamariscifolia'.

Juniperus virginiana
Virginia red cedar, Rocky Mountain juniper
Cupressaceae (Pinaceae)
Native
Introduction: before 1664
Earliest American citation: John Bartram, Philadelphia, ca. 1735
Zone: 3–9
Description: Evergreen, 40–50 ft. "The red cedar just falls short of being one of the most beautiful evergreens.... While young ... the length of its side branches, which take a horizontal direction near the ground, give it the appearance of a free-growing evergreen shrub, of a less formal character than any other evergreen we have.... The foliage in spring and summer varies greatly in color on different trees, from a bluish to a yellowish green" (Scott 1870).

"The Red Cedar has less to recommend it to the eye than most of the evergreens which we have already described, the color of the foliage is dull and dingy at many seasons ... when old we have seen it ... become an interesting, and indeed a picturesque tree" (Downing 1859).

Design notes: "Landscape architects have learned to appreciate its value ... [cedars] have a perfect columnar growth and take the place of the handsome pyramidal evergreens of rare varieties used in formal gardens" (Ely 1917).

Remarks: Elliott (1868) said the red cedar was only occasionally planted because of its "rather stiff habit and dull dingy brown color of foliage in winter and spring." It would be interesting to look into the past to see if his observations were indeed the reality or if the high number of nursery catalogs that featured the red cedar reflected the actual usage of the tree.

Juniperus virginiana, Virginia red cedar, stands as a sentinel in this photograph of a home of the early 1900s.

Design notes: "Peculiarly useful on small places, where, while occupying a minimum of space, it is conspicuous by its height; and by its vertical growth breaks with pleasant contrasts, when not too frequently repeated, the level lines of lawns and terraces" (Scott 1870).

"This we consider one of the best of all Junipers for planting on small cemetery lots" (Trees for rural cemeteries 1854).

Remarks: Although modern gardeners have found the Irish juniper to be hardy, nineteenth-century writers like Frank Scott (1870) referred to this plant as being tender and a candidate for winter mulch to protect it from freezing.

Heirloom variety:
Juniperus communis 'Suecica'. Swedish juniper. Intro: 1768. M'Mahon, 1806. "Hardy and handsome" (Gray 1854).

Historic commercial sources: 51

Related species:
Juniperus chinensis. Chinese juniper. Intro: before 1764. M'Mahon, 1806. A number of varieties of Chinese juniper appeared in early-twentieth-century catalogs, including a golden and a silver-variegated variety.

Juniperus ×*pfitzeriana* (syn. *Juniperus chinensis* 'Pfitzeriana'). Ernst, Ohio, 1926. This old standby of modern gardens originated in Germany around the beginning of the twentieth century.

For regional invasiveness concerns regarding *Juniperus virginiana*, see Appendix D.

Heirloom varieties:

'Canaertii'. Intro: 1868. Storrs & Harrison, Ohio, 1925. A compact form usually with bountiful blue fruit.

'Glauca'. Blue Virginia cedar. Intro: 1850. Langdon, Alabama, 1881.

'Pendula'. Weeping red cedar. Intro: ca. 1850. Ellwanger & Barry, New York, 1860.

Historic commercial sources: 70

Koelreuteria paniculata

golden rain tree, varnish tree, pride of India, Japan bladder tree

Synonym: *Paulina aurea*

Sapindaceae

Exotic

Introduction: 1763

Earliest American citation: Thomas Jefferson, ca. 1809

Zone: 5–8

Description: Deciduous, 30–40 ft. Chinese dwarf tree, with distinct divided foliage, covered during July and August with panicles of beautiful golden flowers (Buist, Philadelphia, 1859).

Design notes: "We know of no tree which, without being variegated, has such decidedly yellowish-green foliage; and this quality, together with the airy delicacy of its leafy outline, its brilliant flowers, and autumn color, combine to make it one of the most desirable trees for even a small collection; and especially beautiful where its low golden top can be seen projecting from a mass of dark-foliaged trees" (Scott 1870).

Remarks: Recommended for the short stocky growth of its blunt shoots, double pinnate foliage, bright yellow flowers, abundance of interesting seed vessels, and all-season interest.

Historic commercial sources: 34

Lagerstroemia indica

crape myrtle, crepe myrtle, Chinese myrtle, pride of India

Synonym: *Lagerstraemia vulgaris*

Clethraceae

Exotic

Introduction: 1747

Earliest American citation: George Washington, ca. 1786

Zone: 7

Description: Deciduous shrub or small tree, to 25 ft. Summer-blooming flowers are the main feature. Pink is the species color. White and light purple flower were introduced by 1825, crimson by the 1870s. The exfoliating bark gives it a winter character as well.

Design notes: "The Crape [sic] Myrtle, *Lagerstroemia Indica*, is to the South what the lilac and snowball are to the North—an inhabitant of nearly every home yard" (Bailey 1906a).

"It is found in all gardens, forming the background of groups of Bridal-Myrtles (*Myrtus communis*) and dense specimens of banana shrub (*Michelia figo*).... Its huge trusses of brilliant rose-colored flowers contrast charmingly with the dark foliage of the evergreens" (Nehrling, ca. 1925, in Read 2001).

Remarks: Pride of India was a common name for several plants, including *Lagerstroemia indica*, *Koelreuteria paniculata*, and *Melia azedarach*.

Historic commercial sources: 44

Larix decidua

European larch, Scotch larch

Synonyms: *Larix europaea*, *Pinus larix*

Pinaceae

Exotic

Introduction: Long cultivated

Earliest American citation: John Custis, ca. 1736

Zone: 3–6

Description: Deciduous coniferous tree of pyramidal habit, 70–75 ft. "In the spring when it is covered with its new growth of feathery, light green foliage, it is a very striking and beautiful object" (Bailey 1906a).

Design notes: "For picturesque beauty, the Larch is almost unrivalled. Unlike most other trees which must grow old, uncouth, and misshapen before they can attain that expression, this is singularly so, as soon almost as it begins to assume the stature of a tree. It can never be called a beautiful tree.... But it has what is perhaps more valuable ... the expression of boldness and picturesqueness peculiar to itself, and which it seems to have caught from the wild and rugged chasms, rocks, and precipices of its Native mountains.... It should be introduced sparingly, and always for a special purpose ... to give spirit to a group of trees, to strengthen the already picturesque character of a scene, or to give life and variety to one naturally tame and uninteresting" (Downing 1859).

Bailey (1906a) noted that the European larch was used as a park tree and was "one of the best lawn trees."

Remarks: "Almost indispensable in ornamental planting of grounds" (Elliott 1868).

Historic commercial sources: 48

Related species:

Larix laricina. American larch, tamerack, hackmatack, larch

Larix deciduas, European larch. F. R. Elliott, *Popular Deciduous and Evergreen Trees and Shrubs*, 1868.

pine. Intro: 1737. Bartram, Philadelphia, 1783. "The American larches are well worthy a place where sufficient moisture can be commanded, as their peculiar forms are striking, though not so finely picturesque as that of the European species" (Breck 1851).

Larix kaempferi. Japanese larch, money pine of Japan. Intro: 1861. Berger, San Francisco, 1892.

Liquidambar styraciflua

sweet gum, alligator wood
Hamamelidaceae
Native
Introduction: 1681
Earliest American citation: John Bartram, ca. 1760
Zone: 5–9
Description: Large deciduous tree, 30–50 ft., featuring brilliant fall color—a deep red that persists for quite a while. "The fine proportions of its somewhat pyramidal head—the dark green of its glossy foliage in summer and the brilliant hues of its autumn tints—the refreshing aroma exhaled from the opening leaves in spring, as well as the beautifully starry form of their mature growth—all combine to give it a distinctive character, and to render it a conspicuous ornament of the pleasure ground, every lawn, or rural plantation" (Hovey 1856).
Design notes: A. J. Downing (1859) recommended planting the sweet gum among maples and ashes for a "magical" autumn color effect.
Remarks: Thomas Meehan, writing for *The Horticulturist* in January 1854, praised the virtues of the sweet gum: its beautiful fall foliage, starlike leaf shape, corky bark, insect resistance, and "It is American!"
Historic commercial sources: 28

Liriodendron tulipifera

tulip tree, white wood, yellow poplar, white poplar
Magnoliaceae
Native
Introduction: 1668
Earliest American citation: John Custis, 1737
Zone: 4–9
Description: Deciduous tree, 70–90 ft. "No tree is handsomer than the Native tulip, which grows to a great height, has large, glossy leaves, and bears lovely yellow-orange tulip-shaped flowers at the end of May" (Ely 1903).
Design notes: "In the stately appearance of its magnificent trunk; in the richness and profusion of its singular-shaped and pleasing green foliage; in the brilliancy and abundance of its large, tulip-shaped blossoms, and in its freedom from the depredations of insects, it is preeminently fitted to adorn our public avenues, our parks, and ornamental grounds" (Hovey 1856).
"The most stately tree in North America. . . . This tree should stand alone or near a mass of trees on the lawn or in a park [may also be used for an avenue]" (Downing 1859).
Remarks: A writer in *The Horticulturist* of March 1854 reported that the people of England were in wonderment over the report of a tree covered with tulips. "The excitement was great and the *Liriodendron tulipifera* was all the fashion" (An Observer 1854).
Heirloom variety:
Long (1893) reported that the "Gold-margined-leaved Tulip Tree is a recent Introduction, with most beautifully margined leaves."
Historic commercial sources: 64

Maclura pomifera

Osage orange, yellow wood, Bodac (bois d'arc—bow-wood)
Synonyms: *Maclura aurantiaca*, *Toxylon pomiferum*
Moraceae
Native
Introduction: Expedition of Lewis and Clark, ca. 1805
Earliest American citation: Thomas Jefferson, 1807
Zone: 4–9

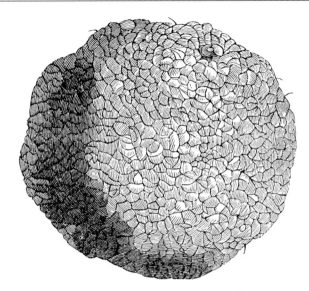

The fruit of the Osage orange. A. J. Downing, *Rural Essays*, 1853.

Description: Deciduous, 20–40 ft. "When grown singly it makes a tree of medium size, with a regular round head, covered with clean glossy foliage and rich golden fruit, in appearance resembling oranges of commerce" (Elliott 1868).

Design notes: Valued mainly as a hedge plant.

Remarks: *The Horticulturist* reported in 1857 that "One of the most extraordinary things in these grounds [Edmondson residence near Baltimore] and one of the most beautiful we ever saw, was an Osage Orange-tree, about twenty- four years old. Its leading shoot had been destroyed and it had become recumbent to a surprising degree. By pacing the circumference over which it spread itself, we found it covered the space of one *hundred* and sixty-five feet! The limbs laid [sic] about with a profusion that was positively beautiful and wonderful. We recommend experiments with this tree where a large space (say a circular drive) is to be filled" (Visits to country places—no. 9 around Baltimore 1857).

For regional invasiveness concerns regarding *Maclura pomifera*, see Appendix D.

Historic commercial sources: 32

Magnolia acuminata

cucumber tree, blue flowering magnolia
Magnoliaceae
Native
Introduction: 1736
Earliest American citation: John Bartram, ca. 1736
Zone: 3–8
Description: Deciduous tree, 80 ft. "Growth is perfectly straight and symmetrical, flowers are 6–8 in. in diameter and are bluish or white, with a tinge of yellow. Coarse fruit is 3 in. long and 8–10 in. in diameter, resembling a cucumber. A magnificent tree and very ornamental; umbrella-shaped head; virtues: deep green foliage, white flowers, unusual fruit, rose-colored seeds" (Hovey 1856).

Design notes: Harmonizes with the architecture of the house.

Remarks: Hovey (1856) observed that magnolias, both foreign and domestic, were among the best of ornamental trees.

Heirloom variety:

var. *subcordata*. Heart-leafed magnolia, yellow flowering magnolia, yellow cucumber tree. Intro: ca. 1800. Bloodgood, New York, 1819.

Historic commercial sources: 50

Related species:

Magnolia macrophylla. Large-leaved magnolia, splendid magnolia, large-leaved cucumber-tree. Intro: 1800. Bloodgood, New York, 1819.

Magnolia tripetala. Umbrella magnolia. Intro: 1752. Thomas Jefferson, 1767. "From its fine tufted foliage and rapid growth this is one of the most desirable species for our pleasure-grounds" (Downing 1859).

Magnolia grandiflora

southern magnolia, laurel-leaved magnolia, evergreen laurel, big bull bay, big laurel, Carolina laurel
Magnoliaceae
Native
Introduction: 1734
Earliest American citation: John Bartram, ca. 1760
Zone: 7–9

Magnolia grandiflora, the native southern magnolia, was cherished particularly in landscapes of the region. Photograph by author.

Description: Evergreen, 60–80 ft. "The large deep green, glossy foliage glistening like a thousand mirrors in the bright sunshine, the large pure milky-white, deliciously fragrant flowers, and the dense and noble growth combine to create a most noble effect. And even the seeds are very ornamental. As soon as the cones open their seed receptacles, the brilliant red, oily, highly aromatic seeds are displayed" (Henry Nehrling, ca. 1924, in Read 2001).

Design notes: In the more northern latitudes gardeners cultivated the southern magnolia in tubs or boxes and sheltered it during the winter. The magnolia was used to line avenues in many parts of the South.

Remarks: "No garden is complete without it" (California Nursery, 1894).

"Of the broad-leaved evergreens, this is unquestionably the finest" (Saul 1857).

"A friend of mine, who traveled in many countries, compared the fragrance of Magnolia grandiflora with the mockingbird's song, being typical and purely American" (Nehrling, ca. 1924, in Read 2001).

Heirloom varieties:

'Exmouth' (syn. 'Oxoniensis'). Exmouth magnolia. Intro: 1734. Prince, New York, 1826. Throughout the nineteenth century various nurseries offered this double-flowered variety and also another called 'Double Nantais'.

'Gloriosa'. Intro: before 1856. Berckmans, Georgia, 1861. Because of its huge flowers and extra broad foliage, Dirr (1998) reported that this cultivar is considered one of the finest in cultivation.

Historic commercial sources: 56

Magnolia ×soulangeana

saucer magnolia, pink magnolia
Magnoliaceae
Exotic
Introduction: 1820
Earliest American citation: Winter, New York, 1844
Zone: 4–9

Description: Deciduous tree about 30 ft. high. The flowers "are borne singly, are irregularly cup-shaped, from four to six inches in diameter, white, tinged with purple, and somewhat fragrant." The foliage is glossy green (Scott 1870).

Design notes: "These succeed well in sheltered situations in our pleasure grounds, and add greatly to their beauty early in the season" (Downing 1859).

Remarks: *Magnolia ×soulangeana = Magnolia denudata × M. liliiflora*

Heirloom varieties:

Magnolia denudata, Chinese white magnolia. F. R. Elliott, *Popular Deciduous and Evergreen Trees and Shrubs*, 1868.

'Lennei'. Lenne's magnolia. Intro: 1854. Elliott, 1868. Dark purplish blooms appear a little later than the species.

'Norbertii' (syn. 'Nobertiana'). Norbert's magnolia. Intro: before 1835. Ellwanger & Barry, New York, 1860. Flowers are more deeply tinted and much later than *M. ×soulangeana*; has the habit and growth of *M. denudata*, but flowers are dark purple and very fragrant (Elliott 1868).

Historic commercial sources: 27

Related species:

Magnolia denudata (syn. *Magnolia conspicua, M. Yulan*). Chinese white magnolia, Yulan magnolia, Gulan, lily-tree. Intro: 1789. Kenrick, Boston, 1832. An additional common name in the old literature—Chinese white chandelier—said it all.

Magnolia liliiflora (syn. *Magnolia gracilis, M. purpurea*). Chinese purple magnolia, lily magnolia. Intro: 1790. Kenrick, Boston, 1832. "Remarkable for fragrance" (A select list 1857).

Malus ioensis 'Plena'

Bechtel's double-flowering crab, prairie crabapple
Synonyms: *Pyrus angustifolia flore pleno, P. iowensis, Malus ioensis* var. *plena*
Rosaceae
Native
Introduction: by 1840
Earliest American citation: Cleveland Nursery, Ohio, 1845
Zone: 4–7

Description: Deciduous tree with double pink, fragrant flowers, 30 ft., rounded habit. "All the crab-apples are noted for their beauty and the exquisite fragrance of their blossoms, which exceed in size those of the common apple tree" (Scott 1870).

Design notes: "The apple tree need never be discarded from the decorated grounds of anyone who will keep his lawn closely shaven, and clean of falling fruit" (Scott 1870).

Remarks: *Malus angustifolia* differs from other native crabapples in its narrow pointed leaves. It is apparent that M'Mahon (1806) was speaking of this species. Prior to 1850, a crabapple in the garden probably would have been either *M. angustifolia* or *M. coronarius*.

Bailey, in 1935, said that the double-flowered form has been listed as *Pyrus (Malus) angustifolia*, but should be *P. ioensis*. Entries for *Malus angustifolia* and *M. ioensis* are combined in this book because of the obvious overlap. The bottom line is that this is an heirloom, late-flowering, double-blooming crabapple.

Heirloom varieties:

The popular flowering crabapple as we know it is a twentieth-century phenomenon. Breeders seriously began to select for fruiting and flowering characteristics, as well as disease resistance, in crabapples in the 1900s.

Historic commercial sources: 31

Related species:

Malus ×adstringens 'Hopa'. Hopa crabapple. Intro: 1920. Fairbury, Nebraska, 1933. The single, rose-colored 'Hopa' is one of the earliest hybrids still in cultivation.

Malus spectabilis (syn. *Pyrus spectabilis*). Chinese flowering crabapple. Intro: by 1780. Kenrick (1841) wrote, "The tree is handsome and upright, does not grow large; the flowers are large, very double, and in clusters, and are beautiful, resembling small roses, of a delicate rose color. It is not uncommon with us."

Melia azedarach

pride of India, bead tree, chinaberry tree, Persian lilac, pride of China

Meliaceae

Exotic

Introduction: Sixteenth century

Earliest American citation: Thomas Jefferson, 1778

Zone: 7–10

Description: Deciduous tree, from 30–40 ft. "The leaves are pinnate . . . with many leaflets of a beautiful deep green hue; in spring the pretty lilac or pink flowers appear in racemes, having a delicate odour, and these are succeeded by round green berries, which in autumn turn of a bright yellow, and the skin becomes shriveled. It grows rapidly, but does not attain a great altitude" (Gosse 1859).

Design notes: Basil Hall, a nineteenth-century traveler, recorded that the streets of Savannah were lined with

"Pride-of-India" trees ca. 1825. Alice Lockwood (1934) translated this to mean *Melia azedarach*, while J. C. Loudon (1834) wrote that Hall had observed *Lagerstroemia indica*, the crepe myrtle. The sketch that accompanied Loudon's observations is on page 42.

Bailey (1906a) called *Melia azedarach* a valuable shade tree, but observed that it had already naturalized throughout the South.

Remarks: The pride of China has been known as "the most ornamental tree of the South" (Lockwood 1934). However, it did have detractors, such as Thomas Affleck, who wrote in the Natchez, Mississippi, *Daily Courier* of 23 October 1854, "The perpetually recurring Pride of China tree, beautiful though it be, to the exclusion of the scores of magnificent trees, native and introduced, is to say the least of it, in very bad taste. It is a filthy tree, too, about the yard, when compared with many others" (Stritikus and Johns 1996).

Melia azedarach has proved to be invasive in some areas of the United States. Please refer to Appendix D for specific regional information concerning invasive species.

Heirloom variety:

'Umbraculiformis'. Umbrella China tree. Intro: before 1860 US. Langdon, Alabama, 1881. "There is a variety called the Umbrella China Tree, which, as a low, lawn tree, is surpassingly lovely, and is well named from its symmetrical top and thick foliage of deep green. This variety is thought to have been introduced around 1870 in the South, but no one knows by whom or where" (Sargent 1894c). "It grows exactly in the shape of an umbrella" (Massey 1893).

Historic commercial sources: 32

Palmae

palms

No encyclopedia of heirloom plants would be complete without featuring species of palms, so important to the landscapes of the South and Far West. Palms generally are easy to propagate and cultivate. "Their tall, straight, unbranched trunks surmounted by a spreading canopy of huge pinnate or digitate foliage distinguish them from nearly all other forms of vegetation" (Bailey 1906a). In the nineteenth century, palms bordered southern avenues in stately alignment and often provided singular ornamentation of a vernacular landscape. "They group well with other trees and shrubs and very beautiful foliage contrasts and harmonies may be secured" (Hume 1929). In the North, greenhouses and conservatories featured different species of palms. They were also used in the bedding known as subtropical bedding (see chapter 9.) The species below were those most often

Washingtonia filifera, native fan palm, graces an early California landscape.

deep green leaves curved outward from the center" (Perfection, Alabama, 1927). "One of the best known and handsomest of the order, and as it is quite hardy, it is well adapted for the subtropical garden" (American Exotic, Florida, 1894).

Latania lontaroides (syn. *Latania borbonica*). Fan palm. Intro: 1816. Santa Rosa Nursery, California, 1880. "A beautiful Palm, with large, deeply divided, fan-shaped leaves" (Storrs & Harrison, Ohio, 1908).

Phoenix canariensis. Canary Island date palm. Intro: 1597. California missions by 1800. "It [and other varieties of *Phoenix*] comprise the grandest ornaments of our gardens, parks, and lawns, contributing a graceful and charming tropical appearance to any landscape. . . . Fully as hardy as the native fan palm and differing so widely from that variety in its habit of growth, color, and style of foliage, a finer contrast cannot readily be imagined when the two are planted either opposite, or alternately in rows (California Nursery, 1894). "Suitable for large lawns" (Ashby, California, 1908).

encountered in the early nursery catalogs. In addition to these, species of *Areca*, *Kentia*, *Brahea*, *Howea*, *Serenoa*, and *Livistona* also were included in commercial publications.

Chamaerops humilis. Fan palm. Intro: before 1600. M'Mahon 1806. A hardy dwarf palm that was suitable for the small garden.

Cycas revoluta. Sago palm, Japanese fan palm. Intro: 1737. R. Morris, ca. 1760. Not a true palm. "Palm-like cycad reaching a height of 3 to 4 ft., with a handsome crown of

Cycas revoluta, Japanese fan palm. Peter Henderson, *Henderson's Handbook of Plants*, 1890.

Phoenix dactylifera. Date palm. Long cultivated. California missions by 1800. "Not so ornamental as others of the genus, [but] was extensively planted in early days" (Bailey 1906a).

Ptychosperma elegans (syn. *Seaforthia elegans*). Alexander palm, solitaire palm. Intro: 1822. Henderson, 1890. Very tender palm, suitable for cultivation only in southernmost tip of Florida or as a conservatory plant. For regional invasiveness concerns regarding *Ptychosperma elegans*, see Appendix D.

Sabal palmetto. Cabbage palmetto, blue palmetto. Intro: 1788. George Washington, ca. 1800.

Trachycarpus fortunei (syn. *Chamaerops excelsus*). Japanese fan palm, windmill palm. Intro: 1849. One early planting took place in Butte County, California, ca. 1870 (Shinn 1894). In the southeast, this palm is hardy in areas bordering on the Gulf of Mexico.

Washingtonia filifera. Fan palm. Intro: by 1840. Early cultivation of the native *Washingtonia* took place at the Ramirez residence in the Los Angeles area in 1840 (Parish 1890). Ernest Braunton, writing in Bailey (1906a), observed, "Washingtonias, natives of San Bernardino and San Diego counties, have been most extensively planted, and may be found everywhere." *W. robusta* is a less hardy species and was used more commonly in the extreme south.

Paulownia imperialis

empress tree, blue trumpet tree, cotton tree
Scrophulariaceae
Exotic
Introduction: 1834
Earliest American citation: McIntosh, Ohio, 1845
Zone: 6–9
Description: 30–40 ft. "Ornamental deciduous trees, in habit and foliage similar to Catalpa, with ample, long-petioled, opposite leaves, and pale violet large flowers, resembling those of foxglove in shape, in terminal panicles opening before the leaves" (Bailey 1906a).
Design notes: "They would be ornamental in the shrubbery, even without bloom, on account of their showy foliage" (Breck 1858). Bailey (1906a) observed that the empress tree occasionally was used as an "avenue tree" in temperate climates and that it had escaped from cultivation in the South.
Remarks: "Remarkable for the size of its foliage, and the great rapidity of its growth . . . leaves resemble those of the common Sunflower" (Downing 1859).
For regional invasiveness concerns regarding *Paulownia imperialis*, see Appendix D.
Historic commercial sources: 25

Picea abies

Norway spruce, Norway spruce fir
Synonyms: *Abies excelsea, Picea excelsa, Pinus picea*
Pinaceae
Exotic
Introduction: Long cultivated
Earliest American citation: Prince, New York, 1771
Zone: 3–8
Description: Evergreen, 40–60 ft. "It is a beautiful spiry-topped tree; the branches sweep downward with a graceful curve and the branchlets, after the tree reaches the height of thirty feet or more, become pendulous" (Keeler 1900).
Design notes: Garden writers from Downing (1853) to Keeler (1900) recommended the Norway spruce for hedges and also as an ornamental tree, particularly useful for parks.

Remarks: "Now the [Norway spruce] is the popular evergreen tree for all planting. Unfortunately, it is used without regard to appropriateness of position or space" (Elliott 1868).
For regional invasiveness concerns regarding *Picea abies*, see Appendix D.
Heirloom varieties:
f. *pendula* (syn. 'Pendula', 'Inversa', 'Inverta'). Weeping Norway spruce. Intro: by 1836. Downing (1849a) noted a seedling Norway spruce with a pendulous habit. It does not appear with frequency in nursery lists until after 1900.
'Pumila'. Dwarf Norway spruce. New England Nurseries, Massachusetts, 1910. This petite Norway spruce is usually 3–4 ft. high.
Historic commercial sources: 88
Related species:
Picea polita (syn. *Abies polita*). Tigertail spruce. Intro: 1861. Parsons, 1882. "One of the finest and most valuable of the Japanese conifers" (Parsons 1882).

Picea glauca

white spruce, silver spruce, white spruce fir
Synonyms: *Pinus alba, Abies alba, Picea canadensis, P. alba*
Pinaceae
Native
Introduction: 1700
Earliest American citation: M'Mahon, 1806
Zone: 2–6
Description: "A slender, conical, evergreen tree, usually sixty to seventy feet high. . . . Resinous; foliage ill-smelling" (Keeler 1900).
Design notes: "For planting in small grounds, for the outskirts of groups and masses, for points on roadways, and for cemeteries, the American White and Red Spruces are deserving of far more general use than they have received . . . the White Spruce is far more suited to position on small lawns or outside masses, or borders of half-acre lots, than the Norway, which is much more commonly planted" (Elliott 1868).
Remarks: Hovey, in *The Magazine of Horticulture* for 1856, said the white spruce was common in the swamps—it was a smaller tree with light green foliage that gave a "lively appearance."
For regional invasiveness concerns regarding *Picea glauca*, see Appendix D.
Heirloom variety:
'Densata'. Black Hills spruce. Shenandoah, Iowa, 1899. This is the state tree of South Dakota.
Historic commercial sources: 38

Picea pungens

Colorado spruce
Pinaceae
Native
Introduction: 1862
Earliest American citation: Reading Nursery, Massachusetts, 1881
Zone: 3–7

Description: Evergreen, 30–60 ft. "Stiff, pungent foliage and clusters of cones. No evergreen tree can excel it, as it has the advantage of growing vigorously where many evergreens fail" (New England Nurseries, Massachusetts, 1910).

Design notes: Mrs. Frances King (1925) wrote about the appropriateness of using the blue form of *Picea pungens* in the cultivated landscape, "Never use a Colorado blue spruce under any circumstances whatever, unless you live in Denver or the region of the Rockies. Those trees are not fitted for Eastern gardens, and look out of place from the very beginning." Obviously, in modern times no one has taken her opinion to heart.

Remarks: Although the Colorado spruce, along with its blue form, frequented the pages of nursery catalogs in the last two decades of the nineteenth century, garden writers rarely discussed it in the period garden literature.

Heirloom varieties:

Glauca Group (syn. f. *glauca*). Colorado blue spruce. Intro: 1877. Reading Nursery, Massachusetts, 1881. The Colorado blue spruce was a common variety in nurseries, as it remains to this day, although some nurseries such as Good & Reese found it to be in short supply: "There is nothing in the Evergreen line that is as fine as the Colorado Blue Spruce. It is entirely hardy, growing into a shapely tree without any pruning, while the color of the foliage is a beautiful blue. It is scarce and always will be" (Good & Reese, Ohio, 1906).

'Koster'. Koster's blue spruce. Intro: before 1885. Wagner Park, Ohio, 1905. Consistent steel blue color.

Historic commercial sources: 32

Related species:

Picea engelmannii. Engelmann's spruce. Intro: 1862. Biltmore, North Carolina, 1907.

Picea mariana (syn. *Picea nigra*, *Abies nigra*). Black spruce. Intro: 1700. Prince, New York, 1771. "Scarce as an ornamental tree. Norway spruce is generally preferred; black spruce has very dense foliage, medium size tree, pendulous cones, egg-shaped, 1-inch in length, purple hue" (Flagg 1856b).

Pinus nigra

Austrian pine, black spruce pine, black spruce fir
Synonym: *Pinus austriaca*
Pinaceae
Exotic
Introduction: 1759
Earliest American citation: M'Mahon, 1806
Zone: 4–7

Description: Evergreen, 50–60 ft. "There is a liveliness, purity, and depth in its green not surpassed by any tree we know of; forming a marked contrast in this respect to the rather grayish-green of the Scotch pine, and the lighter green of the white pine. It is, however, a stiffer, coarser, and more robust tree in its growth than either of them. . . . When young the tree has the usual conical or pyramidal character of the pines, but after it reaches middle size the top begins to round out somewhat, and at maturity it becomes rather a round-headed tree, sometimes even flat-topped when old" (Scott 1870).

Design notes: "It is of rapid growth, with rich deep blue-green foliage, that for backgrounds or masses is admirably suited. As a single tree, also, upon a lawn, it is always beautiful; and when the scenery will admit, groups of this pine with the tulip tree, mountain ash, dogwood, etc. are exceedingly effective" (Elliott 1868).

Pinus nigra, Austrian pine. F. R. Elliott, *Popular Deciduous and Evergreen Trees and Shrubs*, 1868.

Remarks: "The Austrian pine is extensively planted throughout the north in parks and lawns" (Keeler 1900).

For regional invasiveness concerns regarding *Pinus nigra*, see Appendix D.

Historic commercial sources: 51

Pinus strobus

white pine, Weymouth pine, sapling pine, apple pine

Pinaceae

Native

Introduction: 1705

Earliest American citation: John Bartram, ca. 1760

Zone: 3–7

Description: The white pine typically grows 50–80 ft. "Its wide-spread and nearly horizontal branching and dense foliage . . . does not totally block out sunlight." Like many evergreens it has a symmetrical outline but it is softer in form with "tasseled foliage of lively green" and "long silky tufts at the end of branches that are gracefully pendulous" (Flagg 1856c).

Design notes: Wilson Flagg wrote that the white pine was serviceable for all purposes of shade or shelter. "In the white pine, this symmetry, being united with grace and majesty, increases the grandeur of its appearance, like architectural proportions in certain noble edifices." He observed that all evergreens were too somber to be planted near the house and that deciduous trees should be used for that purpose. A good site for the white pine was a little distance away from the house to provide protection from the wind (Flagg 1856c).

"The most beautiful American tree of the genus . . . desirable for planting in the proximity of buildings . . . growth is rapid" (Downing 1859).

Remarks: White pine formed an avenue at Rose Hill in Cecil County, Maryland, in 1823 (Lockwood 1934). This was considered an unusual use of the tree and was copied at other estates in the area.

Historic commercial sources: 62

Related species:

Pinus ponderosa. Ponderosa pine, Bentham's pine, bull pine, western yellow pine, heavy wooded pine. Intro: 1827. Gray, 1854. Henry Sargent in Downing (1859) said the Ponderosa pine was the hardiest of all of the pines with the exception of the white pine.

Pinus rigida. Pitch pine, resin pine. Intro: 1759. Prince, New York, 1771. Wilson Flagg (1856c) wrote that the pitch pine with its shaggy appearance was not as beautiful as the white pine. Usually it was seen massed in the forest and single

specimens were comparable to the white pine. The pitch pine's branches ran up at an angle, but it had little symmetry so could be pruned without losing its character. Flagg considered the salt-tolerant pitch pine to be a valuable tree for a seaside planting or for erosion control.

Pinus sylvestris

Scotch pine, Scots pine, pinaster, mountain pine

Pinaceae

Exotic

Introduction: Long cultivated

Earliest American citation: John Bartram, ca. 1760

Zone: 2

Description: Evergreen, 30–60 ft. "Its form is generally rounded rather than pyramidal; the branches radiate more irregularly, and are not so straight and formal in their disposition as those of the white and Austrian pines, and the foliage therefore breaks into less stratified and more oaklike masses. . . . The dull color of the foliage is the one thing that prevents the Scotch pine from being the most popular of evergreens" (Scott 1870).

Design notes: "It may be sparingly introduced in the formation of groups or masses; and for picturesque distant views, and for belts or masses for breaking the force of storms and wind, it is very desirable; but as a single tree, or for groups in small grounds, we prefer to leave it out" (Elliott 1868).

Henry Sargent wrote in the 1859 edition of Downing's *Treatise* that *Pinus mugo* was perfectly hardy but not very attractive. Photograph by author.

Remarks: Scott (1870) described five varieties of the Scotch pine, including a dwarf less than 3 ft. in height, a variegated-foliage form with both straw-colored and green needles, and "the silvery Scotch pine" with foliage and cones having a silvery aspect.

For regional invasiveness concerns regarding Pinus sylvestris, see Appendix D.

Historic commercial sources: 55

Related species:

Pinus cembra. Swiss stone pine, Siberian stone pine. Long cultivated. M'Mahon, 1806. "A very compact, upright growing tree. Should have a place in every collection" (Gray 1854).

Pinus mugo. Dwarf mugho pine, mountain pine. Intro: 1779. M'Mahon, 1806.

Pinus wallichiana (syn. *Pinus excelsa*). Lofty pine, Bhotan pine. Intro: 1827. Gray, 1854. "I consider [Bhotan pine] the best of the hardy pines" (Saul 1857). "A splendid tree, with long silvery foliage" (Gray 1854).

Platanus occidentalis

American sycamore, buttonwood, button tree of Virginia
Platanaceae
Native
Introduction: 1640
Earliest American citation: Bartram, Philadelphia, 1783
Zone: 4–9
Description: Deciduous tree, 75–100 ft. The sycamore and the tulip tree are our tallest native trees. Professor Lindley, a prominent nineteenth-century plant scientist, said that owing to its deficiency in the expansive power of the fiber common to the bark of other trees, "a striking and peculiar characteristic of the plane, is its property of throwing off or shedding continually the other coating of bark here and there in patches" (Downing 1859).
Design notes: The sycamore was a favorite shade tree particularly in the South because of the density of foliage (Gosse 1859).
Remarks: "The great merit of the plane, or buttonwood, is its extreme vigor and luxuriance of growth" (Downing 1859). Writers of the nineteenth century lamented the presence of a disease (assumed to be anthracnose) in the American sycamore, which limited its use in the landscape. Breck (1858) said, "the mysterious disease, which has prevailed throughout the country for a number of past years, has so disfigured them that they are not desirable at the present time. No cause or remedy for the disease has yet been discovered, but it is said to be passing away."
Historic commercial sources: 32

Related species:

Platanus ×hispanica (syn. *×acerifolia*). London plane tree. Intro: 1663. Thomas Jefferson, ca. 1812.

Platanus orientalis. Oriental plane tree. Long cultivated. Bartram, Philadelphia, 1792.

Platycladus orientalis

Chinese arborvitae
Synonyms: *Biota orientalis*, *Thuja orientalis*
Cupressaceae
Exotic
Introduction: by 1737
Earliest American citation: Bartram, Philadelphia, 1792
Zone: 6–11
Description: Small tree or large shrub of 18–25 ft. "This is a little beauty when young, and marked by a warmer-toned green, and a finer quality of foliage, than the common American" (Scott 1870).
Design notes: "All the above [*Thuja* species] as well as the Chinese and the variegated foliaged varieties, are adapted for planting as single trees; and as they bear the knife perfectly, may be kept clipped and pruned into any shape or form desired to harmonize with their position" (Elliott 1868).
Remarks: The Chinese arborvitae proved to be too tender for use in northern gardens.
Heirloom variety:
'Aurea'. Golden Chinese arborvitae. Pomaria, South Carolina, 1856. "Its rare shade of green is truly golden, and its compact growth, pretty ovate form, and dwarf habit, combine to make it one of the most indispensable of shrubs" (Scott 1870).
Historic commercial sources: 52

Populus alba

silver leaf poplar, silvery leaf abele, white poplar, silver aspen
Salicaceae
Exotic
Introduction: 1784
Earliest American citation: M'Mahon, 1806
Zone: 3–8
Description: Deciduous tree, 40–70 ft. "The silver poplar—abele—is a tree remarkable for its silvery white underside of foliage, that every rustle of the wind gives it, when seen from a distance, very much the appearance of a tree covered with white blossoms" (Elliott 1868).
Design notes: "It was once pretty generally planted in lawns and groups, but the disposition to sucker makes it extremely

objectionable for such positions . . . as a tree to make conspicuous some particular high point, or where possible, to form the foreground of a group of dark firs, it is very desirable and always effective" (Elliott 1868).

Mrs. James Madison reported that silver poplar was used to conceal outbuildings at Montpelier (Lockwood 1934).

Remarks: Robert Copeland (1867) obviously did not care for this plant when he wrote, "bad, leaves out late, and loses its foliage." One attribute of the poplars was that they were considered to be smoke and smog tolerant, making them good urban trees.

For regional invasiveness concerns regarding Populus alba, see Appendix D.

Heirloom variety:

'Pyramidalis' (syn. 'Bolleana'). White-leaved pyramidal poplar, Bolle's silver poplar. California Nursery, 1894.

Historic commercial sources: 41

Populus deltoides

cottonwood, Carolina poplar, Virginia poplar, necklace poplar

Synonyms: *Populus carolinensis, P. monolifera*

Salicaceae

Native

Introduction: 1750

Earliest American citation: John Bartram, ca. 1760

Zone: 3–9

Description: Deciduous tree, 75–100 ft. "In its early growth the cottonwood is simply rank, upright, and uninteresting; but after it has reached fifty or sixty feet in height, its branches begin to bend gracefully, the foliage breaks into fine rounded masses, and it spreads into a park tree of noble proportions" (Scott 1870).

Design notes: Scott (1870) recommended that the cottonwood never be planted near dwellings or as a street tree.

Remarks: "They [cottonwoods] make rather excellent firewood, mighty good thick shelter, and are always pleasing to the eye" (Gurney, South Dakota, 1921).

Historic commercial sources: 52

Related species:

Populus ×canadensis. The Carolina poplar is a hybrid between *Populus deltoides* and *P. nigra*, which was introduced about 1750 in France. The literature often referred to Carolina poplar, but the descriptions lacked details, so a confirmed identification is lacking. *Populus deltoides* subsp. *monilifera* also was called the Carolina poplar. The commercial sources listed for *P. deltoides* probably include some of *Populus ×canadensis.*

Populus nigra 'Italica'

Lombardy poplar, sudden saw log

Synonyms: *Populus dilatata, P. pyramidalis, P. fastigiata*

Salicaceae

Exotic

Introduction: Prior to 1750

Earliest American citation: W. Hamilton, Philadelphia, 1784

Zone: 3–9

Description: Deciduous tree, 70–90 ft. A "tall, narrow, and rigid tree . . . [with] architectonic qualities" (van Rensselaer 1900). "When the wind blows, unlike other trees that wave in parts, it waves in one simple sweep from top to bottom" (Keeler 1900).

Design notes: "It is the most formal of deciduous trees, and therefore, the most effective when properly used and the worst when abused. . . . A single poplar, if a thrifty and vigorous tree, is never out of place. It supplies as no other tree can the want of perpendicular forms in the level or rounded lines of our landscapes. . . . When backed or supported by other trees, and especially if water in front be added . . . three poplar trees, of different heights, produce a magically picturesque effect" (Lenox 1849).

Allen (1856) observed that the Lombardy poplar had gone out of fashion and he decried the former use of the trees "like a line of grenadiers with shouldered arms, guarding an outpost" or "naked, stalk-like" lining an avenue. Allen asserted that the beauty of the tree was realized when mixed in with other trees "like the tall spires of a church . . . giving variety, point, and character to a finished picture."

J. J. Smith, editor of *The Horticulturist*, made this comment following an 1856 article on the Lombardy poplar by L. F. Allen: "It is a rule in the composition of a landscape, that all horizontal lines should be balanced and supported by perpendicular ones; hence the Lombardy Poplar becomes of great importance in scenery when contrasted with round-headed trees."

"No tree is more useful in the right place or more ugly in the wrong place than the Lombardy poplar" (van Rensselaer 1900).

Remarks: The Lombardy poplar was easy to propagate, required low maintenance and no pruning to maintain its distinctive shape, provided a conspicuous landmark, was a vigorous grower, matched the Italian architecture of houses, and even made a good fuel. The 1856 *Horticulturist* reported that earlier reports of a poisonous "poplar worm" were unfounded (Allen 1856).

"A great deal of senseless ridicule has been cast upon this tree; though it is indeed the only tree that ought to be planted in

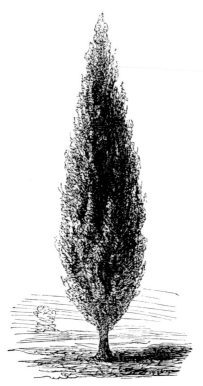

Populus nigra 'Italica', Lombardy poplar. F. R. Elliott, *Popular Deciduous and Evergreen Trees and Shrubs*, 1868.

the narrow streets and enclosures of some of our villages. . . . The Lombardy poplar is . . . a favorite resort for our familiar singing birds . . . robin, vires, the summer yellow bird, indigo bird are constantly found among their branches, which, on account of their dense and peculiar growth, afford them unusual facilities for building and concealing their nests" (Flagg 1857).
Historic commercial sources: 65

Prunus persica 'Plena'
double-flowering peach
Synonym: *Amygdalus persica plena*
Rosaceae
Exotic
Introduction: before 1636
Earliest American citation: John Custis, ca. 1734
Zone: 5–9
Description: Deciduous, 15–25 ft. "The tree is cultivated for the beauty of its flowers, which are often semi-double and very large. Fruits good and pretty numerous" (Kenrick, Boston, 1841). As the century progressed, forms with distinctive double flowers became available in a variety of colors.

DOUBLE FLOWERING PEACHES. ALBA PLENA, WHITE. ROSEA PLENA, PINK.

Prunus persica 'Plena', double flowering peach. Leo Weltz, Wilmington, Ohio, ca. 1905.

Design notes: Henry Sargent, writing for Downing's *Treatise* in 1859, suggested that both the white-flowering peach and the pink-flowered variety be planted side by side for the best effect.
The "double flowering peach is very beautiful in shrubberies. It blossoms early, and sometimes bears fruit, but it is cultivated entirely for its beautiful blossoms" (Bridgeman 1857).
Remarks: "Its finely cut vivid green foliage and symmetrical form make it a beautiful small tree" (Scott 1870).
Heirloom varieties:
Bailey (1906a) listed different varieties of the ornamental peach including white-flowered, dark-flowered, purple-flowered, and variegated-leaved.
Historic commercial sources: 34

Related species:

Prunus cerasifera 'Pissardii'. Purple-leaf plum. Intro: 1880. Thomas Meehan, 1885. The purple-leaf plum appears to have become exceedingly popular after the beginning of the twentieth century. "Covered with single white flowers in spring, when they first appear the leaves are a lustrous crimson, changing to a rich purple" (Dreer, Philadelphia, 1925).

Pseudotsuga menziesii

Douglas fir, Douglas spruce
Synonyms: *Pinus douglasii*, *P. taxifolia*, *Abies douglasii*, *Pseudotsuga taxifolia*
Pinaceae
Native
Introduction: 1827
Earliest American citation: Gray, 1854
Zone: 4–6
Description: Evergreen, 40–70 ft. "It [Douglas fir] resembles most the Norway Spruce as one occasionally sees the finest form of that tree, having that graceful, downward sweep of the branches, and feathering out quite down to the turf; but it is altogether more airy in form, and of a richer and darker green color. At this size [the specimen he was looking at was 62 ft. high] it is the symbol of stately elegance" (A. J. Downing, in Scott 1870).
Design notes: "It is desirable to have groups of Douglas Spruce, because the foliage is so soft that single specimens are sometimes injured by high winds" (C. S. Harrison, in Bailey 1906a). "Among the most congenial conifers for park planting" (Bailey 1906a).
Remarks: "The Douglas Spruce is a tree for the million. It would be difficult to overrate its beauty" (C. S. Harrison, in Bailey 1906a).
Early attempts to cultivate the Douglas fir in the eastern states were inhibited by the seed provenance—seed from the Pacific Northwest was not hardy. Finally, seed originating on the eastern slope of the Rocky Mountains proved to be both hardy and drought tolerant enough for widespread cultivation. A separate species called *Abies menziesii*, with stiff, pointed needles, could have been confused with *Pseudotsuga menziesii* in the early literature.
Heirloom variety:
Bailey (1906a) mentioned that a var. *glauca* was the best form of Douglas fir for cultivation in the eastern states.
Historic commercial sources: 25

Quercus

oaks

Although many catalogs listed oaks, only a few species stand out as being commonly commercially available and even these were not as prevalent as one would imagine. With the exception of *Quercus robur*, the English oak, oaks were free for the taking from the woods. Although no clear evidence shows that this happened, I would have to speculate, based on the many 100-year-old-plus oak trees that are in cultivated landscapes today, that they indeed were transplanted from woods to home. Downing (1859) described the nineteenth-century fondness for the oak: "As an ornamental object, we consider the oak the most varied in expression, the most beautiful, grand, majestic, and picturesque of all deciduous trees." Elliott (1868), however, commented that the difficulty in transplanting oaks made them a scarcer commodity in the catalogs than other tree species. These were the favorite oaks of the nursery trade:

Quercus alba

white oak
Fagaceae
Native
Introduction: 1724
Earliest American citation: John Bartram, ca. 1760
Zone: 3–9
Description: Deciduous tree, 50–80 ft. Early garden designers felt the white oak displayed its best characteristics when it had attained maturity. "Then its deeply furrowed trunk is covered with mosses; its huge branches, each a tree, spreading horizontally from the trunk with great boldness, its trunk of huge dimension" (Scott 1870). Writers differed on the autumn color effect of the white oak leaves, alternatively complaining that they persisted on the tree too long and remained a dull purplish brown or else exclaiming that the fall color was a wonderful deep wine red.
Design notes: The white oak needs a large landscape to expand to its full size and glory. It was a good choice for parks or large estates.
Remarks: "The white oak is the grandest, the most common, and the most useful of our northern oaks" (Scott 1870).
Historic commercial sources: 17
Related species:
Quercus macrocarpa. Bur oak, mossycup oak. Intro: 1804. M'Mahon, Philadelphia, 1804.
Quercus robur. English oak. Long cultivated. M'Mahon, 1806. For regional invasiveness concerns regarding *Quercus robur*, see Appendix D.

Quercus palustris

pin oak, swamp red oak, marsh oak
Fagaceae
Native
Introduction: by 1770
Earliest American citation: Prince, New York, 1790
Zone: 4–8
Description: Deciduous tree, 60–70 ft. Scott (1870) referred to the pin oak as the "graceful savage." "When grown in open ground the lower branches droop to the ground, and the light-green of its fine foliage, the sharpness of its stratified lights and shadows, and the general downward sweep of its branches, altogether make it a pleasing tree." The foliage is bright red in the autumn.
Design notes: Often used for avenues at the beginning of the twentieth century according to Bailey (1906a).
Remarks: The pin oak has a shallow fibrous root system that eases the process of transplanting. It is intolerant of calcareous soils.
Historic commercial sources: 25

Quercus rubra

red oak
Fagaceae
Native
Introduction: 1783
Earliest American citation: Bartram, Philadelphia, 1783
Zone: 3–7
Description: Deciduous, 60–75 ft. "Beautiful Oak, of rapid growth, growing into a large majestic tree, with usually broad, round head, the foliage turning dark red in fall" (Bailey 1906a).
Design notes: The red oak, like the other oaks, must be planted where there is ample space. It was not considered appropriate for small home grounds.
Remarks: "However much grand old oaks may be admired, their use for ornamenting lawns, or for producing cool shades on roadsides or grandeur in parks, as yet has been very limited, and they cannot claim to be classed as popular in comparison with the elm and the maple" (Elliott 1868).
Historic commercial sources: 26
Related species:
Quercus coccinea. Scarlet oak. Intro: 1691. John Bartram, ca. 1760.
Quercus virginiana (syn. *Quercus virens*). Live oak. Intro: 1739. Middleton Place, South Carolina, 1742. Although not common in the nursery trade, the live oak was prevalent in the landscape of the South, as it has remained to the present time. Avenues of live oak, festooned with tendrils of Spanish moss, were symbolic of the lush southeastern landscape. New settlers clearing land in the South would often preserve the best specimens of live oak to stand near their dwellings. Isabella Oakley, describing the landscape of San Francisco in 1886, wrote, "Live-oaks and various Firs and Cypresses, cluster around the home-sites and shade the public squares."

Robinia pseudoacacia

black locust, yellow locust
Fabaceae
Native
Introduction: 1635
Earliest American citation: John Bartram, ca. 1760
Zone: 4–8
Description: Deciduous tree, 30–50 ft. "The locust is another tree of rapid growth which attains great height. From the end of May, for about two weeks, they are covered with white blossoms of delicious odor, which attract the bees for miles around" (Ely 1903).
Design notes: The locust was commonly used as a shade tree in Tennessee and Virginia—considered to have fine foliage and flowers, but lacking autumn color (Flagg 1856a). Downing, however, did not think this tree was appropriate for ornamental use with "its meagerness and lightness of foliage, producing but little shade ... brittle branches, which are liable to be broken and disfigured by every gale of wind; and lastly the abundance of suckers" (Downing 1859).
Remarks: Ely (1903) reported that many old homesteads on Long Island had the locust in their yards.
For regional invasiveness concerns regarding *Robinia pseudoacacia*, see Appendix D.
Historic commercial sources: 49
Related species:
Albizia julibrissin. Silk-tree, mimosa, acacia of Constantinople. Intro: 1745. Thomas Jefferson, 1805. The mimosa is an almost ubiquitous legume in the southern states, originating in Iraq and China. E. Plank, writing about Texas plants for the 1894 *Garden and Forest*, called the *Albizia* "handsomest of our native or naturalized trees of the Pea family." *Albizia julibrissin* has proved to be invasive in some areas of the United States. Please refer to Appendix D for specific regional information concerning invasive species.
Gymnocladus dioica. Kentucky coffee tree, Bonduc. Intro: 1748. George Washington, ca. 1786. "A very beautiful tree. ... In summer, its charming foliage and agreeable flowers

render it a highly beautiful lawn tree; and in winter, it is certainly one of the most novel trees in appearance, in our whole native sylva" (Downing 1859).

Salix babylonica

weeping willow, Napoleon's weeping willow
Salicaceae
Exotic
Introduction: 1730
Earliest American citation: Cocke, Virginia, 1775 (see Remarks)
Zone: 5–8
Description: Deciduous tree, 30–40 ft. "In their first year of growth the branches aim bravely upward, but the slender subsidiary branches soon give up all struggle with the laws of gravity, and resign themselves to their fall with a graceful *abandon* that is bewitching. The trunk and great branches become ruggedly massive as the tree reaches maturity, and their deeply furrowed bark contrasts finely with the delicacy of the spray" (Scott 1870).
Design notes: Andrew J. Downing (1859) said that all willows should be used to "embellish low grounds, streams of water, or margins of lakes." He claimed they did not combine well with other species and should not be placed near a house because the shape of the willow would not complement the architecture of the building.
Remarks: Ann Leighton reported that General Cocke of Virginia received from Madeira a willow basket that took root in his yard. Thomas Jefferson observed that particular tree, reputedly the first *Salix babylonica* grown in America, in 1775 (Leighton 1986b).
For regional invasiveness concerns regarding Salix babylonica, see Appendix D.
Heirloom variety:
'Crispa' (syn. *'Annularis'*). Ring-leaved willow. Intro: 1827. Brighton, Boston, 1833.
Historic commercial sources: 60

Salix babylonica, weeping willow. F. R. Elliott, *Popular Deciduous and Evergreen Trees and Shrubs*, 1868.

Sorbus aucuparia, European mountain ash, was valued in the landscape for its bright red berries. Leo Weltz, Wilmington, Ohio, ca. 1905.

Related species:
Salix alba subsp. *vitellina*. Golden willow, golden osier. Long cultivated. George Washington, ca. 1786. For regional invasiveness concerns regarding *Salix alba* var. *vitellina*, see Appendix D.
Salix caprea 'Kilmarnock' (syn. 'Pendula'). Kilmarnock willow. Intro: 1853. Buist, Philadelphia, 1859. "The handsomest weeping tree in cultivation" (Kilmarnock 1861).
Salix pentandra. Laurel-leaved willow, bay-leaf willow, Huntington willow. Long cultivated. Bartram, Philadelphia, 1807.

Sorbus aucuparia

European mountain ash, Rowan tree of Scotland
Rosaceae
Exotic
Synonym: *Pyrus aucuparia*

Introduction: Long cultivated

Earliest American citation: Bartram, Philadelphia, 1792

Zone: 3–7

Description: Small deciduous tree, 20–40 ft. "The foliage is composed of pinnate leaves, forming a delicate spray, but of dull color. . . . The tree is compactly ovate when young, but becomes round-headed with age. The European variety has the brighter-colored fruit, and is rather more desirable" (Scott 1870).

Design notes: It "is a charming tree . . . but it must be backed by tall evergreens to be seen to advantage" (Lenox 1849).

Remarks: "Planted principally for the beauty in autumn of their large drooping clusters of bright red fruit, which remain a long time on the tree, and produce a brilliant effect" (Scott 1870).

For regional invasiveness concerns regarding *Sorbus aucuparia*, see Appendix D.

Heirloom variety:

'Pendula'. Weeping European mountain ash. Intro: prior to 1853. Bloomington Nursery, Illinois, 1859.

Historic commercial sources: 66. *Sorbus aucuparia* was the default species for listings that merely said "mountain ash."

Related species:

Sorbus americana (syn. *Pyrus americana*). American mountain ash. Intro: 1783. Bartram, Philadelphia, 1783. Copeland (1867) commented that the American mountain ash was "very good . . . rarely plant it singly but rather in masses." Most writers of the nineteenth century expressed a preference for the European mountain ash.

Thuja occidentalis

American arborvitae, flat cedar, white cedar

Synonym: *Thuya oderifera*

Cupressaceae

Native

Introduction: 1536

Earliest American citation: John Bartram, ca. 1760

Zone: 3–7

Description: Evergreen tree, 40–60 ft. "Very formal and regular in outline; distinguished from other evergreens by its flat foliage" (Downing 1859).

Design notes: Used as a screen or hedge plant. "One of our most valuable evergreens . . . it can rarely be used in grouping; but as a single point tree, or for screen belts and hedges, it is one of the most desirable" (Elliott 1868).

Remarks: The American arborvitae was a good landscape plant because it was low maintenance, did not have to be

Thuja occidentalis, American arborvitae, was the number one tree found in nineteenth-century American nursery catalogs. Leo Weltz, Wilmington, Ohio, ca. 1905.

pruned into shape, was disease-free, and had good summer foliage color—no browning (Saul 1846).

Heirloom varieties (descriptions from the 1910 New England Nurseries catalog):

'Aurea'. George Peabody's arborvitae, golden arborvitae. Intro: before 1860. Berckmans, Georgia, 1858.

'Lutea'. George Peabody's arborvitae, golden arborvitae. Downing, 1859. Bright yellow on terminal branches. Frank Scott (1870) suggested a decorative grouping of shrubs— with andromeda (*Pieris*) in front and a golden arborvitae and two Irish yews in the back. Michael Dirr (1998) distinguishes between the two golden arborvitaes by describing 'Aurea' as broad and conical in habit and 'Lutea' as pyramidal.

'Ellwangeriana'. Storrs & Harrison, Ohio, 1908. Low, broad pyramid, with slender branches clothed with two kinds of foliage. The name suggests that this cultivar originated at Mount Hope Nurseries, owned by Ellwanger & Barry in Rochester, New York, in the nineteenth century.

Tilia americana, American linden. F. R. Elliott, *Popular Deciduous and Evergreen Trees and Shrubs*, 1868.

'Fastigiata' (syn. 'Pyramidalis'). Intro: by 1853 [ca. 1865]. Rennie, Virginia, 1853. This citation could refer to *Platycladus orientalis* 'Pyramidalis'. The fastigiated arborvitae is very much like the Irish juniper. The foliage is light green and compact.

'Globosa'. Moon, Pennsylvania, 1870. Low, thick, globe form with attractive foliage.

Historic commercial sources: 93

Related species:

Thuja plicata. Plicate-leaved arborvitae, western arborvitae, giant arborvitae. Intro: 1853. Rennie, Virginia, 1853.

See also *Platycladus*.

Tilia americana

American linden, basswood, American lime tree

Synonym: *Tilia heterophylla*

Tiliaceae

Native

Introduction: 1752

Earliest American citation: John Bartram, ca. 1760

Zone: 3–8

Description: Deciduous tree, 60–80 ft. "More formal, and less varying and graceful in outline, than some others" (T. 1847). "Forms an oval, symmetrical head, and the branches, which are smooth and regular, droop with a fine

curve from the lower part of the trunk, and, rising again at their extremities, form a graceful sweep most pleasing for an open lawn tree. . . . The flowers appear in June and July, and hang in loose, pale yellow clusters, and are fragrant" (Scott 1870).

Design notes: "When planted singly on the lawn, and allowed to develop itself fully on every side, the linden is one of the most beautiful trees. Its head then forms a fine pyramid of verdure, while its lower branches sweep the ground and curve upwards in the most pleasing form" (Downing 1859). Downing was describing both the American and European species of *Tilia*.

Remarks: The American linden was extensively used in the middle states as a shade tree, while the European lime was more common in the northern states (Flagg 1856c).

Historic commercial sources: 54

Tilia platyphyllos

European linden, lime

Synonym: *Tilia europaea* (syn. *Tilia ×europaea*, a hybrid species in its own right that may be the actual plant of some of the listings)

Tiliaceae

Exotic

Introduction: Long cultivated

Earliest American citation: Cambridge, Massachusetts, ca. 1646 (Browne 1846)

Zone: 4–6

Description: Deciduous, 60–80 ft. "The European lime is distinguished from the American sorts, by its smaller and more regularly cordate and rounded leaves . . . the foliage is rather deeper in hue than the native sorts, and the branches of the head more regular in form and disposition" (Downing 1859).

Design notes: "A favorite tree in the ancient style of gardening, as it bore the shears well and was readily clipt [sic] into all manner of curious and fantastic shapes" (Downing 1859). Downing also noted that streets in Philadelphia were lined with the European linden or lime.

Remarks: Not everyone was enamored of the linden trees. Robert Copeland (1867) wrote in disgust, "very inferior; loses its leaves early, much attacked by worms, etc."

Heirloom varieties:

'Laciniata.' Fern-leaved linden. Intro: before 1835. Brighton, Boston, 1841.

'Rubra' (syn. *Tilia rubra*). European red-twigged linden. Intro: 1755. Bloodgood, New York, 1819.

Historic commercial sources: 43

Tsuga canadensis, hemlock. F. R. Elliott, *Popular Deciduous and Evergreen Trees and Shrubs*, 1868.

Tsuga canadensis

hemlock spruce fir, Canadian hemlock
Synonyms: *Abies canadensis, Pinus canadensis*
Pinaceae
Native
Introduction: 1736
Earliest American citation: Prince, New York, 1771
Zone: 4
Description: Evergreen tree, 40–70 ft. "The foliage, when the tree has grown to some height, hangs from the branches in loose pendulous tufts, which gives it a peculiarly graceful appearance . . . when the tree attains more age, it often assumes very irregular and picturesque forms" (Downing 1859).
Design notes: Use in a group with other evergreens for a windscreen and also for winter interest. "At that season, when, during three or four months the landscape is bleak and covered with snow, these noble trees (all evergreens) properly intermingled with the groups in view of the house, give an appearance of verdure and life to the scene that cheats winter of half its dreariness" (Downing 1859).
Remarks: "The most beautiful of the coniferous trees." Wilson Flagg also stated in the 1856 *Magazine of Horticulture* that the hemlock was difficult to transplant from the woods

and had superior gracefulness, and the leaves moved in the wind like a "network of spangles," the undersides showing as "silvery glitter." The full beauty of the hemlock was apparent when it grew singly and could expand. It was less formal than other conifers. "The branches of its summit being slender and flexible, do not stand upright like the lightning rod of a spire; they bend slightly over, and wave gracefully in the breeze" (Flagg 1856b).
Heirloom varieties:
'Pendula'. Weeping hemlock. One North Carolina firm, the Biltmore Nursery, carried this variety and also 'Compacta' in 1907.
Historic commercial sources: 58

Ulmus americana

American elm, drooping elm, white elm, weeping elm
Ulmaceae
Native
Introduction: 1670 [1752]
Earliest American citation: Daniel Henchman, Boston, ca. 1670 (Browne 1846)
Zone: 3–9
Description: Deciduous, 60–80 ft. The American elm was "a tree greatly admired for its combination of the graceful and magnificent. Its enormous rounded head of foliage in soft rolling masses, and the luxuriance of its pendant branches present a most striking appearance" (T. 1847).
Design notes: "From the abundance of elms, everywhere native, over our country, and the almost perfect certainty of their living and growing freely when transplanted with ordinary care, it has become one of our most popular street and park trees" (Elliott 1868).
"[The American elm is] graceful and elegant . . . particularly adapted for planting, in scenes where the expression of elegant or classical beauty is desired" (Downing 1859).
Charles Latrobe wrote in 1835, "The weeping elm is the glory of New England, and trees of great beauty and size not unfrequently line both sides of the streets, and cluster about the older mansions."
Remarks: Most people know the sad story of the American elm. Valued as an ornamental, shade, and street tree in the 1800s and early 1900s, thousands of elms were planted. Many have since succumbed to Dutch elm disease as well as a variety of other problems. That is not to say that the American elm is extinct. Some cities are attempting to preserve their plantings with maintenance programs and sometimes, traveling through the countryside, you can spot a thriving tree, isolated by distance from its diseased rela-

Camperdown Weeping Elm.
THE GRANDEST OF WEEPERS.

REPRODUCED FROM NATURE.

THIS IS TRULY NATURE'S UMBRELLA,

A BEAUTIFUL ADDITION TO THE LAWN.

A DELIGHTFUL RETREAT IN SUMMER.

A FINE spreading tree of rapid growth and large, luxuriant, deep-green glossy leaves, covering the tree with a luxuriant mass of foliage, forming one of the most picturesque drooping trees. Of rank growth, the shoots often making a zigzag growth outward and downward of several feet in a season.

The Camperdown elm provided an interesting silhouette in the Victorian landscape. Rice Brothers, Geneva, New York, ca. 1905.

tives. Few trees compare with the beauty and grandeur of the American elm, and finding a substitute for it in the historic landscape is a difficult challenge. Some have used the vase-shaped *Zelkova serrata*, but it is a poor substitute. This is probably one of the few cases where a modern cultivar of a species is an appropriate substitute. Michael Dirr (1998) recommends the following clones of *Ulmus americana* as respectably disease resistant: 'Valley Forge', 'New Harmony', and 'Princeton'.

Historic commercial sources: 72

Related species:

Ulmus carpinifolia (syn. *Ulmus campestris*). English elm, cork bark elm, Dutch elm, European elm, smooth-leaf elm. Long cultivated. Paddock & Ballard, Boston, 1762 (Browne 1846). Some confusion exists in the literature between this species and *Ulmus ×hollandica* (also Dutch elm), which is a hybrid of *U. carpinifolia* and *U. glabra*. That name did not appear in American nineteenth-century catalogs, but was known in Europe by the eighteenth century.

Ulmus glabra. Scotch elm, Wyck elm, witch elm. Long cultivated. M'Mahon, 1806.

Ulmus glabra 'Camperdownii'. Scotch weeping elm, Camperdown elm. Intro: by 1850. Lindley, North Carolina, 1854.

Ulmus procera. English elm, Dutch elm, cork bark elm. Long cultivated. M'Mahon, 1806.

· 6 ·

HEIRLOOM ORNAMENTAL SHRUBS

Every yard ought to have its quota of shrubs. They give to it a charm which nothing else in the plant-line can supply, because they have a greater dignity than the perennial and the annual plant, on account of size, and the fact that they are good for many years, with very little care.

—Eben Rexford, *Amateur Gardencraft*, 1912

EARLY GARDENERS PRIZED SHRUBS for their architectural forms or for their functional capabilities as screens or hedges. Shrubs obviously were the basis for shrubberies, were used to construct screens and hedges, defined the boundary of a landscape, and punctuated architectural features of the house, such as entries, porches, and corners. Occasionally, wealthy garden owners imitated European traditions in pruning shrubs into artistic forms of topiary or in making mazes and labyrinths, but these were not common features in most early American gardens. Bernard M'Mahon reminded gardeners in 1806 that such garden effects were reminders of the ancient style and not of the current fashion. Shrubs were also combined with perennials and annuals in artistic combinations called mixed borders. Following World War I, another use for shrubs became fashionable—ornamenting the base of a house with deciduous and evergreen shrubs in foundation plantings. Additionally, shrubs were placed throughout the landscape as specimen plants to highlight a beautiful spring flowering habit, decorative fruit, or distinctive variegated foliage or fall color.

HEDGES

Dr. John A. Warder of Cincinnati, Ohio, discussed the history of hedges in his 1858 book and reminded his readers that the use of shrubs for hedging dated at least to the time of ancient Greece. The need for enclosure—either to keep something within a boundary or to prevent entry from without—has always been a priority in land cultivation, and hedges were important as economical and ornamental solutions to the problem. Certain "armed" species like cockspur hawthorn, buckthorn, or a well-pruned honey locust also provided a protective element to the enclosure if needed. In the South and Far West, the warmer climate enabled the use of other thorny species for hedging, including the Cherokee rose, Spanish bayonet, and certain species of cactus.

Most writers agreed that the premier hedging plant for agricultural uses in America was the Osage orange or hedge apple, a native to Arkansas, Oklahoma, and Texas. Among its agreeable characteristics were ornamental glossy foliage and unusual fruit, rapid and dense growth, durability and longevity, lack of insect predators, and thorns. Remnants of those early live fences can be found today in both urban and rural areas across the United States.

Hedges to shelter a garden were important to many early gardeners. Among good performers for this function were the two natives, red cedar and American arborvitae. Both species bear pruning well and grow fast and dense enough to provide protective shelter from the wind. Other evergreens that were valued for hedging included the Chinese arborvitae, Norway spruce, hemlock, and American holly. Like the red cedar and the arborvitae, their tolerance for extensive pruning and their dense growth were defining qualifications. *The Gardener's Monthly* of 1870 declared the hemlock to be the most popular hedge plant in the Philadelphia area (Hemlock hedges 1870). In New England, common privet got the nod from the *New England Farmer* as "the prettiest thing for an ornamental hedge that has come to my notice" (French 1857). Southern garden hedges for wind protection or pure ornamentation might have been constructed of wild orange, yaupon holly, or laurustinus.

The use of flowering deciduous shrubs to screen undesirable views was a common practice. Mock orange, lilac, and roses were both beautiful and practical for this purpose. In order to give an upright, bushy appearance, roses were sometimes trained on a wire fence. In the mid-nineteenth century, William Reid of Elizabethtown, New York, grew a 400-ft.-long hedge of Japanese quince, which gave a unique flowering effect with its brilliant scarlet blooms. Such a hedge interspersed with a multiflora or prairie rose was considered the "most ornamental of screens" (Warder 1858). Other decorative hedges might have included lilac alternated with sweetbriar rose; a cockspur hawthorn hedge with elder, roses, clematis, and honeysuckle providing floral relief; or a hedge completely formed of Vanhoutte spirea or rugosa rose.

One of the requirements for constructing a hedge was to have plants that were the same age and height all growing together in a uniform manner. Acknowledging that this was a difficult ideal, Thomas Fessenden (1857) recommended that anyone serious about having a successful hedge should keep a nursery with the same plants of the same age as those used

An evergreen hedge defines the perimeter of this property, ca. 1890.

972 — FLORAL HEDGE, PASADENA, CAL.

Floral hedge featuring roses in Pasadena, California, 1907.

in the hedge. In that way there would always be a ready supply of substitutions should there be any casualties along the way.

Like so many other features of garden history, conflicting testimonials obscure the record of the actual use of shrubs for hedges in the United States. While many recommendations and observations confirmed this practice, a small dissenting group of writers bemoaned the fact that hedge making was not as important in the United States as it was in England. Hedgerows were not common features in the American landscape. American properties were extensive and fences were cheaper and lower maintenance than hedges. Ornamental hedges surrounded formal grounds and gardens, but wooden fences more typically defined the boundary of a large country property.

THE SHRUBBERY

Shrubs were combined in groupings referred to as "shrubberies," or they were placed individually in the lawn. Most garden writers recommended grouping shrubs, as the editor of *The Gardener's Monthly* observed in July 1863: "No one who has seen the beautiful effects of light and shade in summer, playing through a mass of shrubbery, where the soil is kept raked and clean around the plants, would ever think about keeping them in the lawn in the usual way"

(Treatment of shrubbery 1863). The use of the word *usual* suggests that planting shrubs indiscriminately in the lawn, while not the most fashionable arrangement, was nonetheless the norm.

Andrew Jackson Downing (1859) reported that a collection of flowering shrubs was "to be found in almost every residence of the most moderate size." He recommended that shrubs could be placed in the same manner as herbaceous flowering plants, in formal, intricately designed beds and along walkways, arranged according to height. He also advocated that, for a different effect, shrubs could be placed in irregular groups throughout the lawn.

Grace Tabor in *Making the Grounds Attractive with Shrubbery* (1912) described the different uses for a shrubbery: to mark boundaries; to provide a screen; as a transition between different elements of the garden, such as between lawn and woods; and for its own intrinsic beauty. Shrubberies were used to outline walkways or driveways and could have been curvilinear or straight in outline depending on the circumstances of the landscape. After the beginning of the twentieth century, such groupings of shrubs more typically were planted along the sides and in the back of a small lot rather than in the front of the house.

Early American gardeners chose the plants for their shrubberies on the basis of many characteristics, foremost of which were foliage color, flowers, and autumn fruit. Fragrance was important if the shrub was to be placed near the house. Early writers exhorted their readers to learn about the cultural requirements of shrubs and their requisite soil and light needs and to keep the mature height in mind. F. R. Elliott wrote in 1868, "A shrubbery should be planted for general effect. . . . Boldness of design should be attempted; but although boldness is what the planter should aspire to, all harshness or too great abruptness must be avoided by a judicious mixture of plants whose colors will blend easily with one another."

In 1909, Wilhelm Miller wrote an article for *The Gar-*

Many different shrubs are distributed throughout this Texas front yard, ca. 1900.

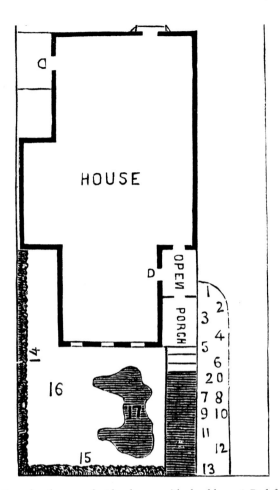

A planting plan for a modest landscape with shrubbery. 1-Red-fruited Berberry. 2-Euonymous or Strawberry. 3-Weigela Rosea. 4-Variegated Weigela. 5-Weigela Amabilis. 6-Gordon's Syringa. 7-Spirea Lanceolata fl. plena. 8-Spirea Revesii Robusta. 9-Deutzia Crenata, floraplena. 10-Magnolia Rubra. 11-Deutzia Gracilis. 12-Hydrangea Paniculata Grandiflora. 13-Variegated-leaved Dogwood. 14-Hedge of Norway Spruce. 15-(Assorted Rocks and Boulders covered with Vines). 16-Purple-leaved Maple. 17-Bed for flowering plants. F. R. Elliott, *Handbook of Practical Landscape Gardening*, 1881.

den Magazine entitled "What America Can Teach England About Shrubs." Obviously impressed with the predominance of ornamental shrubs in the landscape, he remarked, "I believe the instinct of the American people in making shrubbery a national institution is thoroughly sound." His recommendations included the following points:

Never mix deciduous shrubs with broad-leaved evergreens.

Large shrubs and small trees can be used to hide ugly details in the landscape.

The outline of a shrubbery should be bold and irregular.

Select twelve different kinds of shrubs—one for each month—and arrange for best effect.

Place the rapid growers in the back of the border and the slower growers in front.

Place broadleaf evergreens against the house.

Place evergreens behind the deciduous shrubs to provide a green background for colorful flowers and fruits.

Place smaller, arching-branched shrubs on the edges of the shrubbery "to ease the transition from lawn to shrubbery."

Interlace the large masses of shrubs by including several specimens of each preceding group with the next mass.

Often tall and stately herbaceous plants filled in the "holes" in the shrubbery and provided additional color and ornamentation. Gardeners employed lilies, delphiniums, and hollyhocks, among other flowering plants, for this purpose. This variation of the shrubbery that provided a more deliberate blending of shrubs with other plant material, such as roses, perennials, and bulbs, was called the mixed border.

As early as 1806, Bernard M'Mahon described a landscape setting that coincides with our present-day idea of a mixed border. He recommended constructing shrubberies so that shrubs, trees, and herbaceous perennials were planted together according to height, with a diversity of foliage and flowering types and times. The herbaceous perennials could be grouped together to add variation to the scene. One hundred years later, American garden writers developed the idea of the mixed border into a form of garden art.

Many of these writers admittedly were influenced by the writings of Gertrude Jekyll, the *grand dame* of English flower border design and horticultural color theory. In 1918 Louise B. Wilder wrote *Colour in My Garden* in which she described some of her favorite shrub-perennial combinations:

Purple barberry . . . used behind Irises of the pinky-mauve tones, Fraxinella, hybrid Pyrethrums.

Golden Privet . . . attractive used in a section of the border where dim blue flowers, Campanulas, Veronicas, and Aconites prevail; or employed to accentuate the sunshiny effect of groups of yellow and white flowers.

Strong purple Dutch crocuses thickly planted about the scarlet Japanese Quince.

A blue and gold carpet that spreads beneath the Lilac bushes . . . woven of the Grape Hyacinth called Heavenly Blue and the little wild yellow Tulip, *Tulipa sylvestris*, so full of grace and gracious sweetness.

FOUNDATION PLANTINGS

Probably no other landscape feature with roots in the past has been more assiduously adhered to in contemporary landscapes than those belts of shrubs and small trees called "foundation plantings." One of the earliest recommendations for these appeared in the 1891 *Garden and Forest*. Charles Eliot wrote:

Most American suburban houses stand in naked enclosures. The ugly fact has been pointed out and the obvious remedy. . . . It has been shown that even in the smallest house-yards one helpful thing can be easily accomplished—the building may be connected with the ground and the appearance of

nakedness removed by massing shrubs along the bases of the walls or piazzas.

In his short article, Eliot included four designs, each showing a planting arrangement of at least forty different shrubs and herbaceous plants that could be used for a formal effect at the base of a suburban house. Other writers also promoted this type of planting. In 1906, Liberty H. Bailey wrote that shrubbery masses should be used to mark

the lines between properties, the foundations of buildings, the borders along walks and drives. Judicious planting may relieve the angularity of foundations. . . . It is not to be understood, however, that boundaries are always to be planted or that foundations are always to be covered. (Bailey 1906a)

The circa-1905 catalog of the Wagner Park Conservatories of Sidney, Ohio, referred to "the banking of the foliage against the porches and foundation of the house" as a fashionable idea in landscape gardening.

Landscape historians disagree on the exact timing for the *popular* adherence to the practice of covering the foundation of a house with plantings. Evidence seems to indicate that foundation planting did not become widespread in the United States until well after World War I—and perhaps the adjective *popular* should not be applied until at least the 1930s. Photographs from the early years of the twentieth century typically fail to show foundation plantings around houses. Additionally, the writings of garden designers from the period do not describe the practice except to comment that it is not commonly seen. In his 1925 *Design in the Little Garden*, Fletcher Steele described a house with the implied *novel* " 'planting around the foundation,' which they [prospective buyers of the house] had seen recommended in nursery catalogs."

In 1927, Leonard H. Johnson wrote the book *Foundation Planting*, which the editors stated was a "field

No foundation plantings are in sight on this Midwestern street, ca. 1917.

unusually rich and broad and comparatively unexplored." Johnson analyzed an array of foundation plantings for different architectural styles ranging from Colonial Revival frame houses to Tudor Revival half-timbered designs. His basic tenant was that the foundation planting should tie the architecture of the house to its vegetative surroundings and occupy the natural transition space between the lawn and the structure.

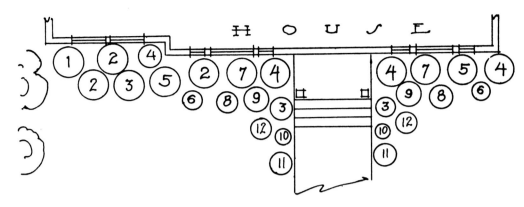

A typical suburban foundation planting of evergreens. 1. Goldenplume Retinospora, 2. Plume Retinospora, 3. Moss Retinospora, 4. Oriental Arborvitae, 5. Compact Oriental Arborvitae, 6. Sulphur Retinospora, 7. Obtuse-leaved Retinospora, 8. Swiss Stone Pine, 9. Upright Japanese Yew, 10. Berckmans Golden Arborvitae, 11. White-leaved Retinospora, 12. Dwarf Hinoki Cypress. Leonard H. Johnson, *Foundation Planting*, 1927.

Early foundation plantings were not monocultures of yew or juniper. Johnson recommended different combinations of plants, including evergreen-only plantings, flowering shrub plantings, and mixed evergreen and deciduous plantings. In a typical design, Johnson suggested a foundation planting that depended on evergreen foliage. He cautioned that the plants would look good when newly planted, but would need attention over the years to keep their sizes balanced and in check.

Another design from Leonard concentrated on low-growing, flowering, or variegated-leaved shrubs for effect. Vanhoutte spirea was repeated along the foundation line, combined with weigela and other species of spirea. On the right side of the front of the house, Japanese barberry was flanked by jetbead. Leonard's only note of caution was to prune the Japanese flowering quince to keep it in scale with the other plantings.

Shrubs were, and are, important components of historic landscapes and ornamental gardens. As "An Old Gardener" wrote in 1822:

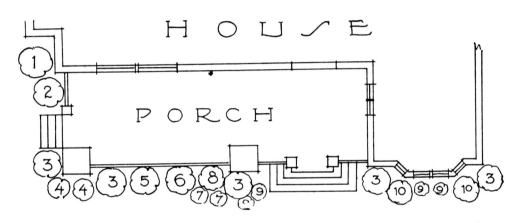

"For low foundations and small plantings, this selection is about ideal." 1. Aralia, 2. Variegated leaf Weigela, 3. Vanhoutte Spirea, 4. Thunberg Spirea, 5. Single globe flower, 6. Japanese Flowering Quince, 7. Anthony Waterer Spirea, 8. Lemoine Deutzia, 9. Japanese barberry, 10. Jetbead. Leonard H. Johnson, *Foundation Planting*, 1927.

The diversity created by shrubs, in combination with flowers, will, if judiciously arranged, always delight. It is certain, that the improver of grounds, without this class of plants, would be deprived of one of the most easily disposed, and most beautiful materials.

A CATALOG OF HEIRLOOM ORNAMENTAL SHRUBS

These plants showed up most frequently among over 2500 shrub species and varieties offered in American nursery catalogs that were distributed between 1770 and 1940.

Peter Henderson Co., New York, 1903.

Amorpha fruticosa

indigo shrub, bastard indigo, wild indigo, false indigo
Synonym: *Amorpha fragrans*
Fabaceae (Leguminosae)
Native
Introduction: 1724
Earliest American citation: Bartram, Philadelphia, 1783
Zone: 4–9

Amorpha fruticosa, indigo shrub. Photograph by Steven Still.

Description: Deciduous, 5–20 ft. "Fine feathery foliage; remarkable for the unusual color of its dark violet-purplish flowers [in June]" (Bailey 1906a).
Design notes: "The pleasing, pinnate foliage . . . contrasts well with that of most other shrubs" (Long 1893).
"Very ornamental for the lawn" (Henderson 1890).
Remarks: Both Thomas Jefferson and George Washington cultivated this native beauty. Keeler (1912) noted that it was "frequently cultivated." Considered by several writers as "rather weedy."
Amorpha fruticosa has proved to be invasive in some areas of the United States. Please refer to Appendix D for specific regional information concerning invasive species.
Historic commercial sources: 32

Berberis thunbergii

Japanese barberry, Japan berberry
Synonym: *Berberis japonica* (not the *B. japonica* in Downing [1859], which was *Mahonia bealei*)
Berberidaceae
Exotic
Introduction: ca. 1864
Earliest American citation: Langdon, Alabama, 1881
Zone: 3–9

Berberis thunbergii, Japanese barberry. Lovett & Co., Little Silver, New Jersey, 1898.

Description: Deciduous, 3–4 ft. "Especially remarkable for its low, dense, horizontal growth, its large, brilliant red fruits, remaining fresh till the following spring, and for its bright scarlet fall coloring" (Bailey 1906a).

Design notes: Effective when used for a low hedge or for a foundation planting.

Combine Japanese barberry with Japanese quince, goldenbell, Thunberg's spirea, and wayfaring-tree in the shrub border (Tabor 1906).

Remarks: "Even if it bore no berries, this shrub would be worth growing for the winter effect of its branches, its innumerable, slender arching branches being full of feathery grace" (Dunbar 1906).

Berberis thunbergii has proved to be invasive in some areas of the United States. Please refer to Appendix D for specific regional information concerning invasive species.

Heirloom variety:

f. *atropurpurea*. Purple-leaved Japanese barberry. Intro: 1913. Breck, Boston, 1917.

Historic commercial sources: 43

Berberis vulgaris 'Atropurpurea'

purple barberry, red-leaved berberry
Synonym: *Berberis vulgaris* var. *purpurea*
Berberidaceae
Exotic
Introduction: Long cultivated
Earliest American citation: Saco, Maine, 1853
Zone: 3–9
Description: Deciduous, 4–8 ft. Purple-leaved variety of the common barberry; red berries in clusters.

Design notes: *Berberis vulgaris* is an alternate host for the wheat rust and is outlawed in several states—and is inadvisable to use in the others due to potential for invasiveness. See Appendix D for additional information. An alternative purple-leaved shrub for the heirloom garden might be pur-

ple filbert (*Corylus avellana* 'Fuscorubra', formerly var. *atropurpurea*) or the larger *Corylus maxima* 'Purpurea'. The common name of purple filbert is found in nursery catalogs as early as 1859, but it is difficult to distinguish which species was meant, since the identification depends on the relative size of the husk to the nut in the fruit, a distinction undisclosed by early writers.

Remarks: Dunbar (1906) reported that this barberry was seen "everywhere."

Heirloom varieties: Bailey (1906a) described a variegated-foliaged barberry and varieties with purplish-black, white, or yellow fruit.

Historic commercial sources: 38

Buxus sempervirens

common boxwood, tree boxwood, box tree
Buxaceae
Exotic
Introduction: Cultivated since ancient times
Earliest American citation: Cornelia Horsford, New York, 1652 (Earle 1901)
Zone: 5(6)–8
Description: "It becomes a tree from twelve to twenty feet in height, growing very slowly and attaining great age . . . grown . . . in partial shade, and in the cool, deep soils the color is a deep glossy green" (Scott 1870).

Design notes: "The tree box . . . forms a pretty dwarf ornamental tree for decorating small lawns or grass-plots, or for rounded points of pathways, etc" (Elliott 1868). Could be pruned to any desirable shape so was used for the infrequent practice of topiary as well as for hedges.

"Allow [boxwood] to grow naturally, rather than prune, in order to blend in with other broad-leaved evergreens in a foundation planting" (Johnson 1927).

Remarks: "Fast becoming extinct in the northern sections of the Middle and Eastern States, where a quarter of a century ago it was largely used for a low hedge or border or as specimen plants" (Maynard 1903).

Heirloom varieties: In the South, a distinction is often made between English and American box. Both refer to *Buxus sempervirens*, but American box is the cultivar 'Arborescens', a larger-leaved form.

Historic commercial sources: 39

Buxus sempervirens 'Suffruticosa'

dwarf English boxwood, edging box, Dutch edging box
Buxaceae
Exotic

Introduction: Cultivated since ancient times

Earliest American citation: John Custis, 1737

Zone: 5–8

Description: "Usually seen from six to eighteen inches in height. . . . No other evergreen shrubs form so naturally into smoothly rounded surfaces, or present such a velvety tone of foliage, as old dwarf box-woods" (Scott 1870).

Design notes: Primarily used for edging of formal flower beds. "Forms a pretty bush when planted alone" (Long 1893).

"The very best dwarf edging plant for flower-beds and borders that is known" (Elliott 1868).

Remarks: Thomas Jefferson did not mention box, which leads some historians to question exactly how extensive was the use of boxwood in the early years of this country.

Historic commercial sources: 31

Calycanthus floridus

sweet shrub, spice bush, allspice, Carolina allspice, bubby flower, sweet Betsy, strawberry bush

Synonym: *Butneria floridus*

Calycanthaceae

Native

Introduction: 1726

Earliest American citation: Thomas Jefferson, 1778

Zone: 4–9

Description: "A low shrub with broad, dark brownish green foliage and dark brown wood, producing a dull, dusky, chocolate-colored flower highly perfumed, as is also the foliage, but less strong. . . . Its growth is usually three to four feet high and as broad" (Elliott 1868).

Design notes: One recommended shrub grouping with long season appeal consisted of "three sweet shrubs (June to August) plus three syringa [*Philadelphus*] (May to June) plus three lilac, common purple (May to June) combined with three Japan quince (April to May)" (Neosho, Missouri, 1917).

Remarks: "Recommended, remarkable for [pineapple] fragrance" (Beecher 1859).

Historic commercial sources: 86

Camellia japonica

camellia, China rose, japonica, Japan-tree-rose

Synonym: *Thea japonica*

Theaceae

Exotic

Introduced: by 1740

Earliest American citation: John Stevens, New Jersey, 1798 (Hume 1951)

Zone: 7–9

Description: Glossy evergreen foliage on shrub or small tree, 10–15 ft. Flowers may be semidouble to double in many colors, including pink, white, red, variegated, scarlet, white with carmine stripe, pink with carmine stripe. Bourne noted in 1833 that there were at least fifty varieties available in the trade at that time.

Design notes: A "striking group" for a southern garden included tea olive, banana shrub, and abelia, with *Camellia japonica* (Nehrling 1894).

Remarks: Eastern nurseries sold *Camellia* for greenhouse cultivation and western and southern nurseries supplied *Camellia* varieties for the shrubbery. Noel Becar was an amateur col-

The flower of *Calycanthus floridus*, sweet shrub, was cherished for its fruity fragrance. Photograph by author.

Camellia japonica 'C. M. Hovey'. Photograph by Bobby Green, Green Nurseries.

Camellia japonica 'Fimbriata'. Photograph by Bobby Green, Green Nurseries.

Chaenomeles speciosa, Japan flowering quince. Storrs & Harrison, Painesville, Ohio, 1896.

lector from Brooklyn who in 1848 had a 100-ft.-long camellia house. Berckmans 1861 catalog pointed out that this plant was hardy in Augusta, Georgia and suggested "a coat of pure sand should be put around the body and upon the roots, to prevent the frost from splitting the bark." In the West, A. P. Smith of Sacramento, California, was renowned for his offerings of *Camellia* in 1858. Smith had over 2000 plants of 200 varieties, with rare selections selling for $100 apiece (Lockwood 1934).

Heirloom varieties:

'Alba Plena'. Double white camellia. Intro: 1597. Floy, New York, 1800 (Hume 1951). One of the oldest camellias that remains in cultivation.

'C. M. Hovey'. Intro: ca. 1850. An imbricated double flower in carmine, splashed with white. Named for Charles Hovey, editor of *The Magazine of Horticulture*.

'Debutante'. Intro: Early twentieth century. Kiyono, Alabama, 1939. Peony form, light pink.

'Fimbriata'. Intro: by 1816. Berckmans, Georgia, 1861. "Clear white, with the petals finely imbricated" (Storrs & Harrison, Ohio, 1874).

'Gigantea' (syn. 'Magnolia King'). Magnolia, South Carolina, 1840s. Peony form, large, flowers are red, marked with white.

'Kumasaka'. Intro: 1895. Kiyono, Alabama, 1939. Peony form, deep pink, late season.

'Otome' (syn. 'Pink Perfection'). Intro: 1875. Kiyono, Alabama, 1939. Small, double light pink.

'Professor Charles S. Sargent'. Intro: 1925. Magnolia, South Carolina, 1925. Peony form, crimson.

Historic commercial sources: 34

Chaenomeles spp.

Japanese scarlet quince, flowering quince, burning bush, fire bush, japonica

Synonyms: *Pyrus japonica*, *Cydonia japonica*, *C. maulei*, *Cidonia Japonica*

Rosaceae

Exotic

Introduction: *Chaenomeles japonica*, 1784; *Chaenomeles speciosa*, 1815

Earliest American citation: Kenrick, Boston, 1832

Zone: 4–8

Description: Deciduous shrub, 5–6 ft. "Its clean, smooth foliage makes it always attractive, but when in bloom in early spring, it is a showy and admirable plant, bright scarlet flowers are best known . . . the fruits are 1.5–2 inches in diameter, yellow shaded with purple and have the odor of violets" (Vick 1882b).

Design notes: The Japanese flowering quince was popular for single plantings in the lawn or as an addition to the shrubbery. Also used as hedge material and for foundation plantings.

"Use if possible near it . . . bushes of *Rosa rubrifolia* with its 'plum-red' foliage . . . or else near the reddish kinds of Japanese maple" (King 1923).

"Underplant with forget-me-not (*Myosotis*)" (King 1925).

For a colorful foundation planting, group Anthony Waterer

spirea (magenta-pink) and Japanese quince (orange-red) with a planting of several white Thunberg spirea in between (Johnson 1927).

Remarks: "The Japanese quince is an adorable subject for the small place" (King 1923).

"Valuable, if not indispensable . . . hardy and requiring only common soil . . . two sorts, white and scarlet" (A select list 1857).

The two species of *Chaenomeles* are hopelessly confused in the old gardening literature. Japanese quince referred to either plant. Alice Coats (1992) believed *C. speciosa* was cultivated more frequently.

Historic commercial sources: 76

Chionanthus virginicus

fringe tree, snowdrop, weeping ash, Daddy Greybeard, grandfather's beard, Virginia snow flower

Oleaceae

Native

Introduction: 1736

Earliest American citation: John Bartram, ca. 1760

Zone: 4–9

Description: Deciduous, small tree or shrub, 12–20 ft. "Long drooping panicles of delicate flowers with elongated, narrow, nearly thread-like, pure white petals . . . a charming object when in flower" (Sargent 1894a).

On female plants, the "large clusters of grape-like fruit have singular beauty" (Meehan 1857).

Design notes: Used as a specimen plant in the open lawn (Scott 1870).

Remarks: "One of the most beautiful of our flowering shrubs. . . . Its blossoms last but a short time, but the heavy green foliage is ornamental all summer" (Maynard 1903). A close relative to our native fringe tree, *Chionanthus retusus*, Chinese fringe tree, was known to late-nineteenth-century American gardeners.

Historic commercial sources: 50

Clethra alnifolia

alder-leaved clethra, sweet pepperbush, summer sweet, white alder

Clethraceae

Native

Introduction: 1731

Earliest American citation: John Bartram, ca. 1751

Zone: 4–9

Description: Deciduous shrub, 3–10 ft. Ornamental features include late-flowering, exquisitely fragrant spikes of white

Clethra alnifolia, sweet pepperbush. F. R. Elliott, *Popular Deciduous and Evergreen Trees and Shrubs*, 1868.

flowers and bright yellow fall foliage (Manning 1884b).

Design notes: "Although a native shrub . . . the clethra is nevertheless deserving, on account of its beautiful and numerous spikes of white flowers, a place in every collection" (Elliott 1868).

"Should be seen much more frequently in the choice shrubbery" (Ellwanger 1889).

Remarks: "Recommended, fragrant . . . will grow in wet places; will grow in shade" (A select list 1857).

"This shrub, though indigenous in our woods, has been brought into notice in the New York Central Park, more than ever before" (Scott 1870).

Hume (1929) claimed that for years large quantities of clethra were grown in foreign countries and imported to the United States, with gardeners unsuspecting that they were growing a native species.

Historic commercial sources: 35

Colutea arborescens

bladder senna

Fabaceae

Exotic

Introduction: 1570

Earliest American citation: Prince, New York, 1790

Zone: 5–7

Description: Deciduous shrub, 5–7 ft. "Chiefly desirable for its pretty orange-colored, pea-shaped blossoms, which are produced throughout the summer. These are succeeded by very curious, bladdery fruit, which, if they might not be

Colutea arborescens, bladder senna, bears attractive seedpods for late-season interest. Photograph by Steven Still.

called handsome, are, at least, highly interesting" (Meehan 1857). "Delicate acacia-like leaves" (Scott 1870).

Design notes: Position *Colutea* in the interior of a mass of shrubbery (Scott 1870).

"The Colutea, or bladder-senna, attractive for its reddish seed-pods, [should not] be overlooked in the collection of shrubs" (Ellwanger 1889).

Remarks: "The plant will do well in any soil or situation, but is seen in perfection only in dry, rich soils, and well exposed to the sun" (Meehan 1857).

Historic commercial sources: 31

Cornus stolonifera

redosier dogwood, red-twig dogwood, bloody dogwood, American red-rod

Synonyms: *Cornus sericea, C. sanguinea* (also a separate species)

Cornaceae

Native

Introduction: 1656

Earliest American citation: Bartram, Philadelphia, 1783

Zone: 2–7

Description: Deciduous shrub, 7–9 ft. Grown for bright crimson stems, particularly effective in the winter. Flowers are inconspicuous. Berries are white, slightly tinged bluish.

Design notes: "Best red-barked shrub for winter effects" (Blanchan 1913).

Remarks: "Accustomed from childhood to see this dogwood in the copses of wet alluvial soils, and to associate its brilliant-colored sprouts principally with the whips used in school chastisements, it has surprised me to see how beautiful a shrub it makes in open ground" (Scott 1870).

For regional invasiveness concerns regarding *Cornus stolonifera*, see Appendix D.

Heirloom variety:

'Flaviramea'. Golden-barked dogwood. Intro: ca. 1900. Biltmore, North Carolina, 1907.

Historic commercial sources: 29

Related species:

Cornus sanguinea. Bloody dogwood, European redosier. Long cultivated. M'Mahon, 1806.

Cotinus coggygria

purple fringe, purple mist tree, smoke tree, Jupiter's beard, Venetian sumach, smoke bush, green fringe, mist tree, blue fringe tree, wig-tree

Synonym: *Rhus cotinus*

Anacardiaceae

Exotic

Introduction: 1656

Earliest American citation: George Washington, ca. 1786

Zone: 5–8

Description: "Planted for the filmy effect of the plumose fruiting panicles and the yellow and purple autumn tints of the leaves" (Rehder 1940).

Design notes: Cultivated as a specimen in the lawn or in the garden (Maynard 1903).

Remarks: "It is beautiful, curious, and desirable" (Scott 1870).

Heirloom varieties: Although the species itself displays a purple tinge to the flowers and seed plumes, the var. *purpureus* with deeper coloration has been in cultivation since 1870.

Historic commercial sources: 61

Small hairs on the stalks of the flowers and fruit form the "smoke" of *Cotinus coggygria*. Photograph by the author.

Daphne mezereon

mezereon, February daphne
Thymelacaceae
Exotic
Introduction: 1561
Earliest American citation: Bartram, Philadelphia, 1792
Zone: 4–7
Description: Semievergreen to deciduous shrub, 3–5 ft. Fragrant, rose-purple flowers appear in spring before the leaves. "Its charming little pink blossoms thickly scattered along the branches, render it highly interesting in every garden" (An Amateur 1848). "The fruit is of a bright red color when ripe and it matures by midsummer when the plants are again conspicuous for a while" (Jack 1894).
Design notes: "Recommended, fragrant, will grow in shade" (A select list 1857).
Remarks: "Almost the first flowering shrub that blossoms in the spring, (coming out even before the crocus)" (An Amateur 1848).
"For centuries it has been a favorite garden plant in Europe, but in this country is too rarely seen" (Keeler 1903).
Heirloom varieties: Prince Nurseries offered a white-flowered daphne by 1826.
Historic commercial sources: 25
Related species:
Daphne cneorum. Garland flower, widow wail. Intro: 1752. M'Mahon, 1806.

Deutzia gracilis

slender-branched deutzia, dwarf deutzia
Hydrangeaceae
Exotic
Introduction: 1840
Earliest American citation: Sargent, *The Horticulturist*, 1854
Zone: 4–8
Description: Deciduous shrub. 2–4 ft. "Of low compact growth, with pure white flowers; may be sheared to a perfect globe" (Long 1893).
Design notes: Useful for border or shrubbery. Deutzia was considered one of the best flowering shrubs for planting around the foundation of the house (Johnson 1927).
Remarks: "The Deutzias are universally esteemed for their hardiness, good forms, and free-flowering habits, producing a great profusion of delicately-formed, white, or tinted flowers in June" (Long 1893).
Heirloom varieties: Nurseries offered at least five different varieties of *Deutzia*, including those with gold-margined foliage or rose-colored blossoms.

Flower of *Deutzia*. The Good & Reese Co., Springfield, Ohio, 1889.

Historic commercial sources: 52
Related species:
Deutzia ×*lemonei*. Lemoine deutzia. Intro: 1891. Wagner Park, Ohio, 1905. A 5–7 ft., double white deutzia.
Deutzia scabra. Rough-leaved deutzia, pink mezereum, fuzzy deutzia. Intro: 1822. Brighton, Boston, 1841. "Its numerous white flowers are not unlike those of the orange, though the general habit of the plant is that of the syringo, to which it is related. . . . Unquestionably one of the best of all the new shrubs" (An Amateur 1848). 'Pride of Rochester', the double-flowered fuzzy deutzia, was quite popular in the early 1900s.

Eriobotrya japonic

loquat, Japanese medlar, Japan plum
Synonym: *Mespilus japonica*
Rosaceae
Exotic
Introduction: 1784
Earliest American citation: Simpson, Virginia, 1793
Zone: 7–10
Description: Small ornamental tree or spreading shrub, 10–20 ft. Has large evergreen leaves and produces yellow, plum-sized fruits that, when fully ripe, have a rich, sweet flavor.
Design notes: "Loquat is an extremely decorative plant, either as an evergreen lawn tree south of Charleston, or as a pot-plant in the North" (Bailey 1906a). Nehrling wrote in 1894 that *Eriobotrya* should be in every garden, no matter how small. "It looks best as an isolated specimen. Crowded with other shrubs and trees, it soon loses its characteristic beauty" (Read 2001).

Remarks: Loquat was a common plant in nineteenth-century gardens of the South and West.

Historic commercial sources: 17

Euonymus americanus

strawberry tree, American spindle tree, burning bush, hearts-a-burstin'

Synonym: *Evonimus Semper Virens*

Celastraceae

Native

Introduction: 1697

Earliest American citation: Bartram, Philadelphia, 1783

Zone: 5–9

Description: Deciduous, 4–6 ft. Inconspicuous flowers in late spring are followed by brilliant scarlet fruits. "A pretty little umbrella-shaped tree, with pretty green striped bark" (Scott 1870).

Design notes: "Use in combination with low-growing evergreens, that assist in bringing more prominently forward their bright-colored, crimson, or white fruit, which generally hangs all winter" (Elliott 1868).

Remarks: This species is particularly susceptible to *Euonymus* scale.

Historic commercial sources: 33

Related species:

Euonymus atropurpureus. Wahoo, burning bush. Intro: 1756. Bartram, Philadelphia, 1783.

Euonymus europaeus. European spindle tree, strawberry tree. Long cultivated. M'Mahon, 1806.

Euonymus fortunei var. *radicans.* Winter creeper. Intro: 1865. Scott, 1870. A silver-edged, variegated foliage form appears in my U.S. catalogs after 1894.

Euonymus japonicus. Japan spindle tree. Intro: 1804. McIntosh, Ohio, 1845.

For regional invasiveness concerns regarding *Euonymus* spp., see Appendix D.

Forsythia viridissima

golden bell, sunshine bush, greenstem forsythia

Oleaceae

Exotic

Introduction: 1844

Earliest American citation: Saco, Maine, 1853

Zone: 5–8

Description: Deciduous, shrub, 6–10 ft. high. "The flowers are the brightest yellow and produced all over the young branches" (Maynard 1903).

Design notes: Mrs. Francis King (1925) suggested an ornamental combination that included forsythia, blooming pears, pale yellow tulips, and blue myosotis. Another suggestion was to mass forsythia in front of evergreens to highlight the golden blooms against dark green.

Golden bell was used to provide bright yellow, contrasting color to a foundation planting (Johnson 1927).

Remarks: Frank Scott (1870) was skeptical about the continued popularity of *Forsythia* when he noted, "Its luxuriance, the earliness of its bright small yellow flowers, and the fact that it is a comparatively new thing, has given this shrub a reputation that it may not sustain."

Historic commercial sources: 53

Related species:

Forsythia ×*intermedia.* Intro: ca. 1880. Bailey, 1906a. The offspring of *F. viridissima* × *F. suspensa.*

Forsythia suspensa. Weeping forsythia, drooping golden bell. Intro: 1850. Buist, Philadelphia, 1859. Bailey (1906a) wrote that *F. suspensa* was less common in gardens than *F. viridissima*, but that it was the better plant, with better growth and vigor and more versatility in the landscape. The Hunnewell estate in Wellesley, Massachusetts, used *F. suspensa* as a pillar plant in 1891. Weeping forsythia also provided quick coverage of porches and trellises (The forsythia as a pillar plant 1891).

Gardenia augusta

cape jasmine, jessamine

Synonyms: *Gardenia florida, G. jasminoides, G. radicans*

Rubiaceae

Exotic

Introduction: 1754

Earliest American citation: Alexander Garden, Charleston, 1762 (Berkeley 1969)

Zone: 7b–10

Description: Shrub, 4–6 ft. with fragrant waxlike blossoms and evergreen, leathery foliage. The double-flowered form was the most prevalent.

Design notes: Used as a greenhouse plant in the North and in the shrub border in the South.

"It blooms from June to September in the South, where it is often used for hedges" (Bailey 1906a).

Remarks: "With the Camellia and the Rose, the Gardenia belonged to a trio of the most fashionable flowers during antebellum days. Its glorious fragrance was particularly valued and the pure white color of the waxy double flower was another point in its favor" (Henry Nehrling ca. 1925, in Read 2001).

Heirloom varieties:

'Fortuniana'. Berckmans, Georgia, 1906. Larger-flowered variety of cape jasmine.

Historic commercial sources: 34

Hibiscus syriacus

rose of Sharon, althea, shrubby althaea

Synonym: *Althaea Frutex*

Malvaceae

Exotic

Introduction: Before 1600

Earliest American citation: John Custis, 1736

Zone: 5–8

Description: Deciduous shrub with flowers that are most commonly double white and double purple, but also available in double rose, double red, double blue, white blush, and striped with red (among other colors and forms).

"It rises to the height of 12–15 feet, with a full spreading body; profusely covered with pink flowers, much resembling those of the hollyhock of our gardens, but rather smaller . . . an unfailing resort of the Humming-birds" (Gosse 1859).

Design notes: "The Altheas are fine, free growing and free blooming shrubs, of the easiest cultivation. Very desirable on account of blooming in the autumn months, when scarcely any other tree or shrub is in blossom" (Ellwanger & Barry, New York, 1860).

May be used in the center of a group of smaller shrubs so that its top with showy flowers will show over and behind the lower shrubs in front or it may be planted singly in the lawn as a specimen plant. Can also be massed in the lawn for spectacular effect (Scott 1870; Vick 1882c).

Remarks: Of the flowering shrubs used in early gardens, *Hibiscus syriacus* turned up most often on the pages of early U.S. garden literature and nursery catalogs.

Hibiscus syriacus, rose of Sharon, was the most popular shrub in the nineteenth-century nursery trade. Photograph by author.

Heirloom varieties: Descriptions are from earliest American citation unless otherwise noted.

'Albus Plenus'. Jean Skipwith, ca. 1800. Double white.

'Ardens'. Ellwanger & Barry, New York, 1860. Double, bluish-purple.

'The Banner'. Storrs & Harrison, Ohio, 1896. "Striped variety, nicely marked white and deep rose." Current references describe this shrub as single white with a reddish eye.

'Foliis Variegatus' (syn. 'Meehanii'). Bloodgood, New York, 1819. Double, purple blooms, creamy edged foliage. "One of the very best variegated-leaved shrubs" (Long 1893).

'Jeanne d' Arc'. Biltmore, North Carolina, 1907. Double, white.

'Paeoniflorus' (syn. 'Amplissimus'). Ellwanger & Barry, New York, 1860. "Peony-flowered double, pink."

'Totus Albus'. California Nursery, 1894. Single, white.

Historic commercial sources: 100

Related species:

Hibiscus rosa-sinensis. Chinese hibiscus. George Washington, ca. 1800. "No shrubs are more common or more showy in southern Florida" (Hume 1929).

Hydrangea macrophylla

changeable hydrangea, bigleaf hydrangea

Synonym: *Hydrangea hortensis*

Hydrangeaceae

Exotic

Introduction: 1790

Earliest American citation: M'Mahon 1806

Zone: 6–9

Description: Deciduous, 3–6 ft. "The old favorite; well-known and favorite plants, producing large heads of flowers, in great profusion; the color of Hortensis varieties can be changed to a beautiful blue by mixing iron scales or

Hibiscus syriacus 'Albus Plenus', double white rose of Sharon. *Vick's Monthly Magazine*, 1882.

Nineteenth-century gardeners enjoyed using shrubs with variegated foliage in their borders. *Hydrangea macrophylla* 'Maculata'. Photograph by author.

sparks from a blacksmith's shop among the soil . . . large pink flowers" (Dreer, Philadelphia, 1876). Two separate classes of the garden hydrangea were distinguished in the literature: the hortensias had round heads of mainly sterile flowers, and the lacecaps bore relatively flat flower heads with a center of small fertile flowers and an outer ring of large sterile flowers. Flower colors were white, pink, or blue.

Design notes: Hydrangeas were used as lawn decorations, often grown in large pots that could be moved indoors in areas where it was not hardy. They were also a common greenhouse plant in the North. "The common bushy plant grown in boxes and seen in or near almost every New England village porch" (Scott 1870).

Although their hardiness was questionable in many parts of the country, Johnson (1927) recommended *Hydrangea macrophylla* 'Otaksa' for use as a base planting around a foundation, combined with other plants.

Remarks: "Give plenty of water, and as often as once a week give liberal dosages of cow manure water . . . watering with rusty iron water, adding iron borings to the soil, and watering with alum water, is said to change the color of any of the varieties to a blue shade" (Hydrangeas for lawn decoration 1894).

Heirloom varieties:

'Goliath'. Michell, Philadelphia, 1931. Flowers of pale purple to soft pink. Hortensia type.

'Maculata' (syn. 'Variegata'). Ellwanger & Barry, New York, 1860. 'Variegata' was described as silver-striped or gold-striped in the old literature. Current descriptions refer to the variegation as creamy white margins. Lacecap.

'Nikko Blue'. Fremont Nursery, Ohio, 1932. Mophead type, deep blue globular flowers. Hortensia type.

'Otaksa'. Denson, North Carolina, 1871. Large heads, pale pink flowers. Hortensia type.

'Thomas Hogg'. Thompson, Kentucky, 1888. One of the first hortensias to be introduced from Japan and popular in the early 1900s. Blooms profusely with pure white sterile flowers.

Historic commercial sources: 38

Hydrangea paniculata 'Grandiflora'

large double hydrangea, peegee hydrangea, Japanese hydrangea

Synonyms: *Hydrangea paniculata* var. *grandiflora*, *H. deutziafolia*

Hydrangeaceae

Exotic

Introduction: 1862

Earliest American citation: Moon, Pennsylvania, 1870

Zone: 3–8

Description: Deciduous shrub, 10–15 ft. Dark green glossy foliage with nearly all sterile flowers. "A splendid late-flowering shrub, with its immense panicles and changeable shades, and it should enliven every garden in September" (Ellwanger 1889).

"It is too well known to need description" (Rexford 1912).

Design notes: Used in the shrubbery or in the border. Also made a good lawn specimen. Blanchan (1913) recommended the use of this shrub as a late-season flowering hedge, but also observed that everyone who had at least a 20-ft. lot, planted one of these. The fact that they were easy to propagate and cultivate made them ubiquitous in the landscape. *Garden and Forest* described a design solution for using the Japanese hydrangea:

> Shoots about a foot long, of the Hydrangea, were planted out at intervals near the grass border and backed by dwarf Cannas and annual Euphorbias. Some low-growing Snapdragons or similar flowering plants occupied the spaces toward the front and gave splashes of color during the season. In late summer the drooping heads of the Hydrangea flowered low, and were relieved by the background and the surrounding masses of foliage. The whole effect, with glints of color from Cannas and other flowers, was cheerful, but quiet withal and in excellent taste for a moderate sized lawn. (The hardy hydrangea 1891)

HYDRANGEA PANICULATA GRANDIFLORA.
(LARGE FLOWERED HYDRANGEA.)
Perfectly hardy ; grows rapidly, eventually attaining a height of 6 to 8 feet ; commences
to flower in August, when very few shrubs are in bloom, and lasts
until cut off by severe frosts.

Hydrangea paniculata 'Grandiflora', Japanese hydrangea. Leo Weltz, Wilmington, Ohio, ca. 1905.

Remarks: "Continues to be one of the best and ornamental shrubs grown" (Jackson, Georgia 1904).

Historic commercial sources: 58

Related species:

Hydrangea arborescens. Snowball hydrangea. Intro: 1736. George Washington, 1786. Heirloom varieties of this native snowball include subsp. *radiata* (M'Mahon, Philadelphia, 1804) and 'Hills of Snow' (Biltmore, North Carolina, 1907).

Hydrangea quercifolia. Oakleaf hydrangea. Intro: by 1786 [1803]. George Washington, 1786.

Kalmia latifolia

calico bush, mountain laurel, Virginia laurel, forest laurel, green ivy
Ericaceae
Native

Bailey (1906a) reported that *Kalmia latifolia* was once considered for the honor of being the national floral emblem of the United States. Photograph by the author.

Introduction: 1734

Earliest American citation: John Custis, 1734

Zone: 4–9

Description: Evergreen shrub, 7–15 ft. Bears clustered, showy flowers in late spring with pink, white, or purplish blooms.

Design notes: Kalmia was massed in groups or placed as a specimen plant in the lawn. Gardeners also cultivated it in containers.

Effective when used in combination with azaleas and andromeda (*Pieris*) for a foundation planting (Johnson 1927).

Remarks: "One of the finest shrubs to adorn a farmer's grounds . . . if the common Kalmia was an imported shrub and was imported and sold at $5 or $10 a plant, it would be seen and found in most of the amateur's grounds in this country. But as it can be had for the asking or nothing as a wild shrub no cultivator takes any notice of it" (Durand 1857).

"Kalmia latifolia . . . would be one of the most desirable medium-sized shrubs if it could be grown as it grows itself" (Ellwanger 1889).

Historic commercial sources: 36

Related species:

Kalmia angustifolia. Intro: 1736. Bartram, Philadelphia, 1783. The bright red flowers of the sheep laurel were favored by early gardeners.

Kerria japonica 'Pleniflora'

corchorus, globeflower, double yellow Japan globe flower, Japanese rose

Synonyms: *Kerria japonica* var. *pleniflora, Corchorus*

Besides bright yellow flowers, *Kerria japonica* 'Pleniflora', double corchorus, has conspicuous green stems. Photograph by Steven Still.

Rosaceae
Exotic
Introduction: ca. 1800 [1805]
Earliest American citation: George Washington, ca. 1800
Zone: 4–9
Description: Deciduous shrub, 3–6 ft., with green branches and bright yellow, double flowers.
Design notes: Use "in simple masses or in front of a shrubbery group or border" (Bailey 1906a). The bright green stems are conspicuous in the winter.
"Pink-flowering Peach, Lilac, Redbud and Kerria japonica make a charming early spring grouping" (Scruggs 1931).
Remarks: "Although Kerria is among our most valuable shrubs we can no longer recommend it because of a blight that is almost sure to kill it wherever it is planted" (Fremont Nursery, Ohio, 1932).
Heirloom varieties:
'Foliis Variegata' (syn. 'Picta'). Variegated corchorus. Columbus Nursery, Ohio, 1877.
Historic commercial sources: 43

Laburnum anagyroides

English laburnum, golden chain, bean tree
Synonyms: *Cytisus laburnum*, *Laburnum vulgare*
Fabaceae
Exotic
Introduction: 1560
Earliest American citation: John Custis, 1735
Zone: 5–7
Description: Deciduous small tree or shrub to 20 ft. Golden yellow, pea-shaped flowers develop in pendulous racemes.

Design notes: Planted in the shrubbery and particularly effective in front of evergreens that displayed the bright yellow flowers. "Where this half-hardy shrub or small tree succeeds, it is one of the most beautiful yellow-flowering trees in existence.... It must be grown slowly in the lawn" (Maynard 1903).
Remarks: Scott (1870) observed that the golden chain was grown more commonly and successfully in England and Scotland than in the United States.
Historic commercial sources: 43

Lantana camara

shrub verbena, yellow sage
Synonym: *Lantana aculeata*
Verbenaceae
Exotic
Introduction: 1692
Earliest American citation: Jean Skipwith, ca. 1800
Zone: 9
Description: Deciduous shrub, 1–4 ft. Flowers open yellow or pink and may change to shades of scarlet or orange.
Design notes: Grown in northern greenhouses and used as a bedding plant. Cultivated as a specimen plant in southern gardens. "They are very desirable for any situation where sun-loving bedding plants are used, in groups or borders, window-boxes, baskets and vases" (Rawson, in Bailey 1906a). "Among the few shrubs that grow well on the poor-

Lantana camara, shrub verbena. Peter Henderson, *Henderson's Handbook of Plants*, 1890.

est sand are the lantanas. From early spring to late autumn in the colder sections, and all through the year in the lower end of the Florida peninsula, these shrubs with their bright yellow, orange, white, scarlet or lavender blossoms make gay any spot planted with them" (Hume 1929).

Remarks: *Viburnum lantana*, is occasionally confused with *Lantana camara* in the literature.

"This is one of those plants that will remain in popularity for a long time, both on account of the beauty and abundance of its flowers at all seasons of the year" (Vick 1878c).

Lantana camara has proved to be invasive in some areas of the United States. Please refer to Appendix D for specific regional information concerning invasive species.

Heirloom variety: Gardeners also cultivated a weeping form of lantana.

Historic commercial sources: 44

Ligustrum ovalifolium

California privet, oval-leaved privet
Synonyms: *Ligustrum californicum, L. ovifolium*
Oleaceae
Exotic
Introduction: 1847
Earliest American citation: Pomaria, South Carolina, 1856
Zone: 5–7
Description: Deciduous or half-evergreen shrub, 10–15 ft. Fragrant white flowers are followed by blackish berries.
Design notes: Privet is the classic hedge plant. A shrub grouping with long-season ornamental interest could include:

12 California privet—June to July

Lilac, common purple—May to June

2 althea—August to September

Hedge of *Ligustrum ovalifolium*, California privet. The Templin Co., Calla, Ohio, 1904.

9 Japanese barberry—May to December (Neosho, Missouri, 1917)

Remarks: The salt-tolerant California privet was a good plant for seaside plantings.

Historic commercial sources: 26

Ligustrum vulgare

common privet, English privet, prim
Oleaceae
Exotic
Introduction: Cultivated since ancient times
Earliest American citation: George Washington, ca. 1800
Zone: 4–7
Description: Deciduous to part-evergreen shrub, 12–15 ft. Common privet has dark green foliage with white, odoriferous flowers in early summer and dark purple or black autumn fruit.
Design notes: "Greatly valued for deciduous hedges . . . no shrub bears clipping better" (Scott 1870). Privet was suitable for massing and screens or for use in a foundation planting.
Remarks: This plant had naturalized in the northeast by the beginning of the twentieth century, according to Bailey (1906a). Please refer to Appendix D for regional information concerning the invasive status of *Ligustrum vulgare*.
Heirloom varieties:
Gardeners grew several different varieties of *Ligustrum* in early American gardens, based on diverse leaf shapes or fruit color, including the varieties *buxifolium, xanthocarpum, myrtifolium, leucocarpum, laurifolium,* and *variegatum.*
Historic commercial sources: 36
Related species:
Ligustrum amurense. Amur River privet. This privet was imported to the South in 1860, according to *Georgia Garden History* (1933), and was particularly popular in the South. By the 1920s it had naturalized in some areas.

Lonicera tatarica

bush honeysuckle, upright honeysuckle, Tatarian honeysuckle, tree honeysuckle
Synonym: *Xylosteum tartaricum*
Caprifoliaceae
Exotic
Introduction: 1752
Earliest American citation: Prince, New York, 1826
Zone: 3–8
Description: Deciduous, multistemmed shrub, 10–12 ft.,

Lonicera tatarica, Tatarian honeysuckle. F. R. Elliott, *Popular Deciduous and Evergreen Trees and Shrubs*, 1868.

Just as its name suggests, the magnolialike blossom of *Michelia figo*, banana shrub, emits a bananalike fragrance. Photograph by the author.

with delicate, blue-green foliage that appears early in the season. Different varieties had diverse flower colors including red, yellow, pink, and white.

Design notes: Used in the shrubbery, border, or as a lawn specimen as well as in foundation plantings.

Remarks: "Were we to have but one shrub . . . we would probably choose the honeysuckle" (Scott 1870).

Shrubby honeysuckles, including *L. tatarica* and *L. fragrantissima* have proved to be invasive in some areas of the United States. Refer to Appendix D for specific regional information concerning invasive species.

Heirloom variety:

Long (1893) described a variegated form of the Tatarian honeysuckle, but it appears to be lost from cultivation.

Historic commercial sources: 61

Related species:

Lonicera fragrantissima. Sweet breath of spring, winter honeysuckle. Intro: 1846. Langdon, Alabama, 1875. Louise B. Wilder (1935) could not imagine a garden without the "the rich fragrance emitted by the creamy, paired blossoms before the leaves appear that informs all the air for yards around them, in March."

Magnolia virginiana

sweet bay magnolia, swamp laurel, beaver tree
Synonym: *Magnolia glauca*
Magnoliaceae
Native
Introduction: 1688
Earliest American citation: John Bartram, ca. 1736
Zone: 5–9

Description: Semievergreen to evergreen shrub, 10–20 ft., with same spread. "The fragrance of its flowers, together with the rich, glossy, pale-green foliage and young shoots, form for it a shrub tree that were it to be newly introduced, would cause an excitement rarely known in the arboricultural world" (Elliott 1868).

Design notes: Does best in partial shade and deep moist soil (Scott 1870).

"This tree is not sufficiently appreciated as an ornamental one in landscape gardening" (Bailey 1906a).

Remarks: "Of which so many fragrant and beautiful bouquets are gathered in the season of its inflorescence, brought to New York and Philadelphia, and exposed for sale in the markets" (Downing 1859).

Dr. Jared Kirtland of Cleveland, Ohio, experimented with the sweet bay magnolia ca. 1870, grafting it onto rootstock of *Magnolia acuminata* in order to have a more adaptable tree.

Historic commercial sources: 29

Related species:

Magnolia stellata (syn. *Magnolia halleana*). Star magnolia, Hall's Japan magnolia. Intro: 1862. Henderson, 1890. "It's form is low and shrub-like, flowers pure white and delicately fragrant."

Michelia figo. Banana shrub. Intro: by 1789. On list of plants grown in Georgia, 1820–1840 (Lockwood 1934). "One of the most popular garden shrubs in the southern states . . . very desirable conservatory shrub in northern sections" (P. J. Berckmans, in Bailey 1906a). "A jewel among evergreen Exotic shrubs" (Nehrling, ca. 1924, in Read 2001).

Mahonia aquifolium

mahonia, Oregon grape holly, Oregon Hollygrape, holly-leaved berberry, ashberry, evergreen barberry

Synonym: *Berberis aquifolium*

Berberidaceae

Native

Introduction: 1823

Earliest American citation: Saco, Maine, 1853

Zone: 5–8

Description: Deciduous shrub, 4–5 ft. "The young leaves are very green and glossy, the yellow flowers very fragrant, and the racemes of purple berries (ripe in September) peculiarly pretty" (Meehan 1857).

Design notes: Used in the front of the shrub border or in a foundation planting.

Johnson (1927) described a low, informal foundation planting to include Oregon Hollygrape with California privet, *Chamaecyparis pisifera*, azaleas, *Hosta plantaginea*, and taller pyramidal arborvitaes to anchor the planting.

Remarks: "The finest low evergreen shrubs that we have" (Scott 1870).

Historic commercial sources: 34

Nerium oleander

oleander

Apocynaceae

Exotic

Introduction: 1596

Earliest American citation: Christopher Witt, Pennsylvania, ca. 1760

Zone: 9

Description: Evergreen shrub, 10–12 ft. "Their large and handsome flowers, either double or single, pink or white ... having made them general favorites" (Henderson 1890).

Design notes: "In the North, the Oleander is a common house plant, being grown in tubs for summer decoration, and ranking in popularity after the sweet bay and hydrangea" (Bailey 1906a).

Remarks: The oleander was popular as a garden plant throughout the South as the following testimonials confirm:

"[Galveston] is emphatically the Oleander City. . . . It is planted on the outer edge of the sidewalk and just inside the fence of many residences, the two rows of trees forming a perfect arch of flowers, as they are thick with bloom the whole summer long. The red is the common variety, and seems to be hardier and grow larger than the white, though the white is far from being a rare sight. . . . They are common, but it seems as though I could never tire of looking at

Nerium oleander, single-flowered pink oleander. Photograph by Steven Still.

them. The perfume of the flowers seems more like Vanilla than anything else" (R. B. S. 1880).

"Found in almost every dooryard of Florida, thriving vigorously without any care" (Nehrling 1894).

"Oleanders are much grown in S. Calif. . . . we have five colors here . . . white, light pink, dark pink, scarlet and buff . . . in single and double forms. . . . One Los Angeles man planted the red variety thirteen years ago for sidewalk trees" (Ernest Braunton, in Bailey 1906a).

"It must be noted that the wood, bark, and leaves of this plant are poisonous. Death has resulted from eating meat in which skewers of oleander have been used; the powdered bark is used as a rat poison, and an infusion of leaves is a powerful insecticide" (Floramant 1882).

Heirloom varieties:

At least fifty named garden forms are found in old-time catalogs. These are still in commercial production:

'Sister Agnes'. Boardman, California, 1889. "Very large trees, pure, the very best single white."

'Mrs. F. Roeding'. Fancher Creek, California, 1895. Double, pink or salmon flowers.

'Variegata'. Berckmans, Georgia, 1873. Variegated foliage.

Historic commercial sources: 41

Osmanthus fragrans

tea olive, sweet olive, fragrant olive

Synonym: *Olea fragrans*

Oleaceae

Exotic

Introduction: 1856

Earliest American citation: Pomaria, South Carolina, 1856

Zone: 7–10

The fragrance of *Osmanthus fragrans*, sweet olive, permeates the garden in which it is cultivated. Photograph by the author.

Description: Evergreen shrub, 20–30 ft. "The small creamy white flowers among the dense foliage appear from early spring until late in the fall, and shed a delicious fragrance" (Nehrling 1894).

Design notes: "One of the most beautiful and valuable evergreen shrubs for the extreme south Atlantic and Gulf states. . . . Planted with Michelia fuscata, Gardenia florida, Abelia rupestris, etc., striking groups are formed" (Nehrling 1894). Tea olive was occasionally grown as a conservatory plant in the North.

Remarks: Nehrling suggested that for the best growth the sweet olive should be grafted on a good species of privet (Read 2001).

Historic commercial sources: 18

Old-timers referred to *Philadelphus coronarius*, mock orange, as "syringa." Photograph by the author.

Philadelphus coronarius

mock orange, syringa, garland syringa, jasmine
Hydrangaceae
Exotic
Introduction: 1560
Earliest American citation: Prince, New York, 1771
Zone: 4–8

Description: Deciduous shrub, 10–12 ft. Fragrant, white, four-petaled flowers are reminiscent of orange blossoms.

Design notes: May be used for massing or screens. Useful for foundation plantings around tall buildings or those with particularly high foundations (Johnson 1927).

Contrast the golden-foliaged *Philadelphus* with purple filbert for a beautiful effect (Maynard 1903).

Remarks: The leaves of *Philadelphus* are said to taste like cucumber (Henderson 1890).

Three shrubs: *Spiraea*, golden spirea; *Viburnum plicatum*, Japan snowball; *Philadelphus coronarius* 'Aureus', golden syringa. Hooker, Wyman, & Co., Rochester, New York, ca. 1903.

For regional invasiveness concerns regarding *Philadelphus coronarius*, see Appendix D.

Heirloom varieties:

'Aureus'. Golden-leaved syringa. Intro: 1878. California Nursery, 1894. James Vick wrote in 1884, "its strikingly distinct feature is its foliage, which . . . is golden-yellow tinted, contrasting strongly with ordinary green foliage, and giving the plant an individuality that is attractive during the whole season of leafage."

'Flore Pleno'. Double-flowered mock orange. Elder, 1850.

'Variegatus'. Variegated-leaved syringa. Intro: 1770. Prince, New York, 1826.

Historic commercial sources: 94

Related species:

Philadelphus ×*lemonei*. Hybrid syringa. Intro: 1884. Wagner Park, Ohio, 1905. The Lemoine hybrids offered a number of named varieties, including 'Mont Blanc' (Berckmans, Georgia, 1906), a single-flowered, hardy selection.

Pittosporum tobira

tobira, Japanese pittosporum

Pittosporaceae

Exotic

Introduction: 1804

Earliest American citation: Paulsen, 1846

Zone: 8–10

Description: Evergreen shrub, 10–12 ft., with small, fragrant, white flowers.

Design notes: Used for hedges in late-nineteenth-century southern California. Pittosporum was a favorite specimen small tree in Houston, Mobile, and New Orleans, according to Henry Nehrling (Read 2001).

Remarks: Bailey (1906a) reported that this was grown in the open in the West and South and in greenhouses in the North.

Heirloom variety:

'Variegata'. Pomaria, South Carolina, 1856. Leaves variegated with white.

Historic commercial sources: 20

Related species:

Pittosporum eugenioides. Tarata, lemonwood. Santa Rosa Nursery, California, 1880. Bailey (1906a) said that this was the most commonly cultivated species in California.

Prunus glandulosa

dwarf double-flowering almond

Synonyms: *Prunus pumila, Amygdalus nana, A. pumila, A. flora plena*

Rosaceae

Exotic

Introduction: 1683

Earliest American citation: Prince, New York, 1790

Zone: 4–8

Description: "A small shrub of the nut-bearing almond family, bearing in March or April an abundance of small double rose-like flowers, closely set upon the twigs, before the appearance of the leaf. The latter is similar to the leaf of the peach tree. Height from two to six feet" (Scott 1870).

Design notes: Earle (1901) noted that dwarf flowering almonds were commonly planted under windows because they did not grow tall enough to shade the windows.

"A most elegant flowering shrub, ornamental in vases, for courtyard, etc." (John Bartram, per Leighton 1986a).

"Found in all gardens and yards" (Beecher 1859).

Remarks: "It is one of the most common of early flowering spring shrubs, but rarely makes a handsome bush when out of bloom" (Scott 1870).

"Much-loved shrub of spring" (King 1925).

Heirloom varieties:

'Sinensis' (syn. 'Rosea Plena'). Intro: 1683. McIntosh, Ohio, 1845. Double, pink flowers; considered to be earlier in cultivation than 'Albo Pleno', the double white form.

Historic commercial sources: 68

Related species:

Prunus dulcis. Almond. Cultivated since ancient times. The almond tree occasionally appeared in ornamental plant catalogs as the double-flowering almond, but without descriptions was difficult to distinguish from dwarf double-flowering almond citations. It is a 30-ft. tree, hardy to zone 8 and also has pink and white double-flowering varieties.

Prunus laurocerasus. Cherry laurel. Intro: 1576. Custis, 1736. "Bright shining green foliage and large panicles of creamy white fragrant flowers succeeded by large purple berries" (California Nursery, 1894).

Prunus triloba (syn. *Amygdalopsis lindleyi*). Double rose-flowering plum, flowering almond. Intro: 1856. Elliott, 1868. "The flowers are of a soft rose color, semi-double, from an inch to an inch and a quarter in diameter, appearing like little roses growing closely along the branches . . . numerous fruits [are] similar to small almonds" (Vick 1882b).

Rhododendron calendulaceum

flame azalea, sky paint flower
Synonyms: *Azalea calendulacea, A. lutea*
Ericaceae
Native
Introduced: 1800
Earliest American citation: Kenrick, Boston, 1832
Zone: 5–7
Description: Deciduous shrub, 5–12 ft. high and wide. This showiest of the American azaleas bears flowers in shades of yellow, orange, and red.
Design notes: The best shrubberies always had a selection of azaleas in the late 1800s.
"With the azalea should be associated the native tall-growing lilies, Canadense, Canadense rubrum, and superbum" (Ellwanger 1889).
Remarks: "Extensively cultivated in England . . . it is, without exception, the handsomest shrub in North America" (Buckley 1847).
Historic commercial sources: 11
Related species:
Rhododendron ×gandavense. Ghent hybrid azaleas. Intro: 1840. Southern Nurseries, Mississippi, 1851. Series of hybrids between the American native *R. ponticum* and the oriental *R. molle.* The Ghent azaleas were produced primarily in Europe and then exported to the United States.
Heirloom varieties:
'Bouquet de Flora'. Intro: before 1869. Pilkington, Oregon, 1912. Early descriptions of "soft rose" differ from later "orangish-red with yellow centers."
'Daviesii'. Intro: ca. 1840. Biltmore, North Carolina, 1907. Fragrant, pure white flowers.
'Nancy Waterer'. Intro: by 1876. Pilkington, Oregon, 1912. Pure yellow blooms.
'Narcissiflora'. Intro: by 1871. Biltmore, North Carolina, 1907. Double, light yellow flowers.
'Pallas'. Intro: before 1875. Pilkington, Oregon, 1912. Orange-red blossoms.
Rhododendron periclymenoides (syn. *Rhododendron nudiflorum, Azalea nudiflora*). Pinxter flower, pink azalea, wild honeysuckle. Intro: 1730. Thomas Jefferson, 1767.
Rhododendron viscosum (syn. *Azalea viscosa*). White swamp azalea, honeysuckle. Intro: 1731. Bartram, Philadelphia, 1783. Native azalea with very fragrant, white flowers.

Rhododendron catawbiense. The Gardener's Monthly, June 1870.

Rhododendron catawbiense

Catawba rhododendron
Ericaceae
Native
Introduction: 1809
First American citation: Brighton, Boston, 1841
Zone: 4–8
Description: Evergreen shrub, 6–15 ft. Lilac-purple flowers are borne in 5–6 in.-diameter trusses. "The Catawba Rhododendron grows dwarfer than the R. maximum, and has far more change of color" (Meehan 1870).
Design notes: Catawba rhododendrons and hybrids were effective both as single specimen plants and massed. Bailey recommended that rhododendrons be grouped in front of conifers, both to provide a dark green background to the bright flowers and also for shelter. "One of the most beautiful of native shrubs" (Bailey 1906a).

Remarks: The successful cultivation of rhododendrons was challenging to the early gardeners. Proper culture required appropriate soil, moisture, and light conditions, including the addition to the soil of 25 percent—no more—of well-rotted leaf humus.

"The Rhododendron takes its name from two Greek words, which signifies [sic] 'Rose tree'; and next to the Rose itself, there are few flowers more worthy of bearing its name than this. Our own *Rhododendron catawbiense*, which we figure, has particular right to the name, for amongst its flowers are produced almost every shade of color, rivaling the Rose in abundance and beauty" (Meehan 1870).

Heirloom varieties:

Between 1800 and 1820, hybrids between *Rhododendron* species were recorded, but Bailey (1906a) reported the 1826 cross, *R. catawbiense* × *R. ponticum* × *R. arboreum*, as the beginning of "official" *Rhododendron* breeding in the nineteenth and early twentieth centuries. Some early hybrids that still are available include:

'Catawbiense Album'. Intro: ca. 1865. Rhododendron expert David Leach (1961) explained that this cultivar is different from *R. catawbiense* var. *album*, which usually is said to be its synonym. According to Leach, 'Catawbiense Album' has hybrid origins and var. *album* is "quite distinct . . . an extraordinary fine and beautiful garden Rhododendron."

'Album Elegans'. Intro: by 1861 [before 1876]. Miellez, 1861. Blush changing to white.

'Boule de Neige'. Intro: ca. 1878. California Nursery, 1894. Michael Dirr (1998) considers this lovely white, hardy form one of the best of all-time *Rhododendron* hybrids.

Historic commercial sources: 19; *Rhododendron* spp. 54

Related species:

Rhododendron maximum. Great bay, rose bay, mountain laurel. Intro: 1736. Bartram, Philadelphia, 1792.

A Mr. Russell reported that the flower that generated the most interest at the 1837 Massachusetts Horticultural Society exhibition was *R. maximum* from Thomas Lee of Brookline, a "known fancier of native plants." He wrote, "a number of the visitors were completely taken up with its unique and beautiful appearance, and were not a little astonished when they were informed that the plant that produced such charming flowers was a *native* of North America and could be obtained at a trifling expense" (Russell 1837).

Rhododendron indicum

Chinese azalea, Indian azalea
Synonym: *Azalea indica*
Ericaceae
Exotic
Introduction: 1680
Earliest American citation: Middleton Place, South Carolina, 1815 (Lockwood 1934)
Zone: 6–9
Description: Evergreen shrub, 2–5 ft. Flowers are brightly colored in shades of red, pink, magenta, or white and may be single, double, hose-in-hose, frilled, or otherwise variable.
Design notes: Often grown as greenhouse plants in the North and planted out into the garden or in containers for summer color. Azaleas were very showy, particularly with a dark green background of conifers or broad-leaved evergreens. They were used in the shrubbery, for hedges, and later in foundation plantings. In an 1859 article, Thomas Affleck observed that he did not often see many azaleas being cultivated in the South except for an occasional planting in a pot (Stritikus 1992).
Remarks: Hume (1929) observed that by the late 1920s, *Rhododendron indicum* was rarely available. Most commercial azaleas were hybrids. E. H. Wilson introduced the Kurume azaleas in 1917. According to Hume, "A Kurume azalea plant in bloom is a solid mass of color, and it may be so full of flowers as completely to hide the foliage . . . [colors] white, salmon, red, pink, and lavender."
Historic commercial sources: 21
Related species:
Rhododendron molle (syn. *Azalea sinensis*, *A. mollis*). Intro: 1823. California Nursery, 1894. Species has striking yellow flowers.

Robinia hispida

rose acacia, flowering acacia, moss locust, bristly locust
Fabaceae
Native
Introduction: 1758
Earliest American citation: Bartram, Philadelphia, 1783
Zone: 5–8
Description: Deciduous shrub, 2–8 ft. with blue-green foliage and bright purplish rose-colored flowers in pendulous racemes. "Dwarf acacia with red flowers" (Prince, New York, 1790).
Design notes: "Have a single stem tied to a strong cedar post six or eight feet high . . . with a wire parasol-like frame fixed

to the top to support the branches and allow them to fall on all sides from it. Thus trained there is no more exquisite shrub" (Scott 1870).

Remarks: "There are few more superb bloomers among shrubs than the rose acacia, but its habit of growth is so straggling and tortuous that it needs much care to keep it in a form suitable in polished grounds" (Scott 1870).

"It is in both foliage and fruit, one of our most delightful of hardy shrubs, and has but one fault: It suckers most abominably, and will soon take possession of the tract where it is planted" (The rose acacia 1887).

For regional invasiveness concerns regarding *Robinia hispida*, see Appendix D.

Historic commercial sources: 40

Spiraea japonica '**Anthony Waterer**'
dwarf red spirea, Anthony Waterer spirea
Synonym: *Spiraea* ×*bumalda* 'Anthony Waterer'
Rosaceae
Exotic
Introduction: ca. 1895

Neltje Blanchan (1913) called this spirea "Anthony Waterer's magenta nerve shocker." Photograph by author.

Earliest American citation: Call, Ohio; Dunning, Maine, 1901
Zone: 3–8
Description: Deciduous shrub, 2–3 ft. "With the most beautiful large clusters of pink flowers, and continues to bloom throughout the summer" (Maynard 1903).
Design notes: Used for edging along a walkway or for a border. Also was effective to add color to a foundation planting or for the foreground of the shrubbery.
Remarks: The genus *Spiraea* is important for heirloom plants, encompassing species both native and exotic, woody and herbaceous. The old-time herbaceous spiraeas have been moved to *Filipendula*, *Aruncus*, and *Astilbe*. For regional invasiveness concerns regarding *Spiraea japonica*, see Appendix D.

Historic commercial sources: 41

Early artists sometimes glorified the attributes of their plant subjects. Compare this *Spiraea* 'Anthony Waterer' with the facing photograph. Leo Weltz, Wilmington, Ohio, ca. 1905.

It is not hard to understand why the beautifully floriferous *Spiraea prunifolia*, bridal wreath spirea, was so popular with early gardeners. Photograph by Marge Garfield.

Vanhoutte spirea, 1932.

Related species:

Spiraea japonica 'Bumalda' (syn. *Spiraea ×bumalda*). Intro: 1824. Parsons, New York, 1857 (Visits 1857). This was very visible in early commercial offerings. The dark green foliage combined with pink to red flowers or the white-flowered var. *albiflora* provided a stunning accent for shrubberies or lawn.

Spiraea prunifolia

Rosaceae
Exotic
plum-leaved spirea, double white spirea, bridal wreath spirea
Synonym: *Spiraea prunifolia* var. *plena*
Introduction: 1843
Earliest American citation: Wilson, 1849
Zone: 4–8
Description: Deciduous shrub, 4–9 ft. "It produces long, slender branches that in the spring are covered with beautiful white double flowers" (Maynard 1903). The autumn foliage has been compared to that of a sugar maple, gradually changing from glossy green to a reddish hue and mellowing into gold or amber.
Design notes: Used in shrubberies or as a single specimen on the lawn. Rexford (1912) noted that a particularly ornamental combination was a group of pink and white spireas together.
Remarks: "One of the most common and most beautiful, but apt to be undervalued" (Scott 1870).
"One of the oldest and most hardy of the spiraeas" (Maynard 1903).
Historic commercial sources: 58

Spiraea ×vanhouttei

Vanhoutte spirea, St. Peter's wreath
Rosaceae
Exotic
Introduction: ca. 1866
Earliest American citation: Scott, 1870
Zone: 3–9
Description: Deciduous shrub, 6–8 ft. "It is dwarf in habit, with graceful pendulous branches that, when in bloom, are weighted down with pure white blossoms" (Maynard 1903).
Design notes: *Spiraea ×vanhouttei* was a favorite shrub to include in foundation planting designs in the 1920s catalogs. Use for a hedge or in formal gardens "as it does not run riot" (Blanchan 1913).
Remarks: *Spiraea trilobata* × *S. cantoniensis* = *S. ×vanhouttei*
Historic commercial sources: 56
Related species:
Physocarpus opulifolius (syn. *Spiraea opulifolia*). Common ninebark. Intro: 1687. Bartram, Philadelphia, 1783. For regional invasiveness concerns regarding *Physocarpus opulifolius*, see Appendix D.
Spiraea ×billardii. Billard's spirea. Intro: before 1854. A select list, 1857. A hybrid that originated in France with two American species, *Spiraea salicifolia* × *Spiraea douglasii*.
Spiraea cantoniensis (syn. *Spiraea reevesii*). Reeve's spirea. Intro: 1824. Saco, Maine; Rennie, Virginia, 1853.
Spiraea douglasii. Douglas spirea. Downing, 1847b. A native spirea with rosy lilac flowers.
Spiraea salicifolia. Willow-leaved spirea, bridewort. M'Mahon, Philadelphia, 1804.
Spiraea thunbergii. Snow garland. Intro: 1863. Moon, Pennsylvania, 1870.

Symphoricarpos albus, snowberry. *Garden Magazine*, 1919.

Symphoricarpos albus

snowberry, St. Peter's wort, waxberry

Synonyms: *Symphoricarpos racemosus, Symphoria racemosa*

Caprifoliaceae

Native

Introduction: 1807 [1817]

Earliest American citation: Bartram, Philadelphia, 1807

Zone: 3–7

Description: Deciduous shrub, 3–6 ft. "Small pink flowers followed by large white berries . . . very showy and desirable" (Iowa Seed, Des Moines, 1914).

"Clusters of snowy balls" (Keeler 1903).

Design notes: "One of the favorites of old-time gardens, and is holding its own fairly well in the new. . . . A good combination in the fall is snowberry and *Rosa rugosa*, "the white berries of the one contrasting with the red hips of the other" (Keeler 1903; Leonard, 1927).

Both species of *Symphoricarpos* can be used "for covering the ground under trees, for massing in lower parts of beds or borders, or for detached groups where something low is desired" (Bailey 1906a).

Remarks: "Considered troublesome, when planted by itself or near borders, on account of its numerous suckers" (El-

liott 1868). Bailey (1906a) considered this a virtue for covering the ground "rapidly and effectively."

"Few garden owners now plant the Snowberry . . . once seen in every front yard and even used for hedges . . . the clusters of berries were as pure as pearls" (Earle 1901). "Will grow in poor, dry soil" (Meehan 1857).

"The berries are much used for winter bouquets" (Scott 1870).

Heirloom variety:

'Variegatus'. Brighton, Boston, 1841.

Historic commercial sources: 57

Symphoricarpos orbiculatus

Indian currant, red snowberry, coralberry, St. Peter's wort

Synonyms: *Symphoricarpos vulgaris, S. rubra, Symphoria glomerata, Lonicera symphoricarpos*

Caprifoliaceae

Native

Introduction: 1727

Earliest American citation: Bartram, Philadelphia, 1783

Zone: 2–8

Description: Deciduous shrub, 3–4 ft. with "drooping wands of crimson berries adorned with leaves" (Keeler 1903).

Design notes: "The shrub forms the most perfect of miniature trees when growing quite alone" (Scott 1870).

"Branches are somewhat recurved and pendulous, making it a useful plant for facing shrub groups and borders" (Leonard 1927).

Remarks: "The abundance of fruit on the Indian Currant is little short of marvelous . . . the birds leave them alone" (Keeler 1903).

For regional invasiveness concerns regarding *Symphoricarpos orbiculatus*, see Appendix D.

Historic commercial sources: 50

Syringa ×persica

Persian lilac, Siberian lilac

Oleaceae

Exotic

Introduction: 1614

Earliest American citation: John Custis, 1738

Zone: 3–7

Description: Deciduous shrub "of medium size, with small bright green leaves and large compound panicles of rather brighter flowers than the common species" (Maynard 1903). "Though the growth of this species is every way more delicate than the common lilac, it forms at maturity a broader bush" (Scott 1870).

Syringa ×persica 'Alba', white Persian lilac. Photograph by Marge Garfield.

Design notes: The Persian lilac was popular among savvy plant collectors. George Washington, Thomas Jefferson, and Lady Skipwith all grew this shrub at the beginning of the nineteenth century.

Remarks: *Syringa ×persica* probably is a backcross between *Syringa ×laciniata × Syringa vulgaris*.

Heirloom variety:

'Alba'. Persian white lilac. Prince, New York, 1826. "Flowers a delicate lavender-white in May" (Scott 1870).

Historic commercial sources: 59

Related species:

Syringa ×laciniata. Cut-leaf lilac. Intro: before 1614. Prince, New York, 1826. In the early literature this was considered to be a variety of the Persian lilac (*S. persica* var. *laciniata*); now we believe it to be a parent of the Persian lilac.

Syringa vulgaris

common lilac, laylock, pipe tree
Synonym: *Syringa purpurea*
Oleaceae
Exotic
Introduction: 1563
Earliest American citation: ca. 1652. Father Fiala (1988) reported that lilacs growing in northern Michigan were large enough to verify that they were planted in the 1650s.
Zone: 3–7
Description: Deciduous shrub, 8–15 ft. Fragrant lilac, pink, or white flowers in panicles. "Too well known to need description" (Scott 1870).
Design notes: "Group with the snowball, red-bud, and other small-sized trees or large shrubs, it makes always an attractive appearance, and should not be thrown to one side because it is common" (Elliott 1868).
Lilacs are beautiful when massed, but it is important to limit the number of different varieties in the group, so as not to spoil the effect (Bailey 1906a).
Used for hedges, both pruned and unpruned (Earle 1901).
Many writers recommended that lilacs be placed near the door or window of the house so the delicious fragrance would waft inside.
Remarks: "The universal flower in the old time garden was the Lilac . . . gave a name to Spring—Lilac tide . . . it is the emblem of the presence of spring . . . in many colonial dooryards it is the only shrub" (Earle 1901). For regional invasiveness regarding *Syringa vulgaris*, see Appendix D.
Heirloom varieties:
The old catalogs listed over 120 varieties of lilac. Among those more frequently included were:
var. *alba*. White lilac.

The lilac was planted by homesteaders across the country.

Prince, New York, 1771. "If there is a more beautiful shrub than the white Lilac I do not know what it is" (Rexford 1912).

'Belle de Nancy'. Intro: 1891. Berckmans, Georgia, 1906. Satiny rose with dark center.

'Charles X'. Intro: ca. 1830. Brighton, Boston, 1841. Reddish purple.

'Congo'. Intro: 1896. Ellwanger & Barry, New York, 1917. Single flower, deep reddish purple.

'Madame Casimir Perier'. Intro: 1894. Berckmans, Georgia, 1906. Double, white.

'Madame Lemoine'. Intro: 1890. Berckmans, Georgia, 1906. Vigorous white blossoms.

'Marie LeGraye'. Intro: 1840. Wagner Park, Ohio, 1905. Single flowers, pure white.

'President Grevy'. Intro: 1886. Reid, Ohio, 1893. Huge blue panicles.

Historic commercial sources: 94

Related species:

Syringa ×*chinensis* (syn. *Syringa rothomagenesis*, *S. dubia*). Chinese lilac. Intro: 1777. Prince, New York, 1826.

Syringa josikaea. Rough-leaved lilac. Intro: 1830. Saco, Maine, 1853. Valued for its late blooming season.

Syringa reticulata (syn. *Syringa amurensis* var. *japonica*). Japanese tree lilac. Intro: 1876. Berger, California, 1892.

Viburnum opulus 'Roseum'

snowball, Guelder's rose

Synonym: *Viburnum opulus* 'Sterile'

Caprifoliaceae

Exotic

Introduction: Long cultivated

Earliest American citation: Prince, New York, 1771

Zone: 3–8

Description: Deciduous shrub, 10–12 ft. Large globose heads of white sterile flowers. The viburnums as a group were cherished for their ornamental foliage, lovely flowers, and good fruiting effect. "When well grown few shrubs can surpass it in beauty" (Rexford 1912).

Design notes: Placed in the shrub border or along a walkway or roadway. Also used as a single specimen in the lawn.

Remarks: Bailey (1906a) was convinced that the old-fashioned snowball was doomed due to infestations of aphids.

For regional invasiveness concerns regarding *Viburnum* spp., see Appendix D.

Heirloom variety: Prior to 1860, nurseries offered a variegated-leaved form of the common snowball that seems to have disappeared from gardens.

Viburnum opulus 'Roseum', snowball, was one of the most popular shrubs offered by American growers in the 1800s. Photograph by author.

Historic commercial sources: 100

Related species:

Viburnum dentatum. Arrow-wood viburnum. Intro: 1736. Bartram, Philadelphia, 1783. Scott (1870) noted that this native shrub was nicely cultivated in New York's Central Park.

Viburnum lantana. Way-faring tree. Long cultivated. Booth, Baltimore, 1810.

Viburnum opulus. European highbush cranberry. Long cultivated. Thomas Jefferson, 1798. This species has particularly ornamental fruit and good fall color.

Viburnum plicatum. Japanese snowball. Intro: 1844. Buist, Philadelphia, 1859. Ellwanger (1889) felt that this *Viburnum* was the finest of all, "surpassing the common variety in habit, foliage, and flowers."

The variegated weigela in the author's garden is not quite as flamboyant as the one in the illustration to the left. Photograph by the author.

A nursery's advertising chromolithograph for *Weigela florida* 'Variegata'. Leo Weltz, Wilmington, Ohio, ca. 1905.

Viburnum plicatum var. *tomentosum*. Doublefile viburnum. Intro: 1865. Berger, San Francisco, 1892.

Viburnum tinus. Laurustinus. Intro: Sixteenth century. Bartram, Philadelphia, 1807. This evergreen viburnum is hardy only to zone 7b; however, savvy gardeners frequently cultivated laurustinus in pots in the northern states. Bailey (1906a) described a purple-leaved and also a variegated-leaved variety.

Viburnum trilobum (syn. *Viburnum oxycoccus*). Highbush cranberry. Bartram, Philadelphia, 1783.

Weigela florida

Chinese weigela
Synonyms: *Spiraea weigelia*, *Weigela rosea*, *Diervilla florida*
Caprifoliaceae
Exotic
Introduction: 1843
Earliest American citation: Breck, 1851
Zone: 5–9

Description: Deciduous shrub, 6–9 ft. "The flowers which are trumpet-shaped, are borne in spikes in which bloom and foliage are so delightfully mixed that the result is a spray of great beauty" (Rexford 1912). "Its robust habit, profuse bloom, and easy culture have combined to rank it in popular estimation with those dear old shrubs the lilacs and the honeysuckles" (Scott 1870).

Design notes: This old-fashioned favorite "is found in most foundation plantings" (Johnson 1927).

Remarks: "I should condemn the Weigela as a garden shrub were it limited to its common form. The white varieties, on the contrary, are desirable, and so are some of the dark reds, which are not frequently seen" (Ellwanger 1889).

Heirloom varieties:

'Eva Rathke'. Wagner Park, Ohio, 1905. Erect habit, carmine red blossoms.

'Variegata'. Denmark Nursery, Iowa, 1868. Distinctive gold-variegated leaves and rose-colored funnelform flowers.

Historic commercial sources: 77

· 7 ·

HEIRLOOM VINES AND CLIMBING SHRUBS

Nothing will more quickly destroy the appearance of "newness" about a home than an appropriate planting of vines.

—Ernest H. Wilson,
The Garden Magazine 1915

IF WE COULD DESIGNATE any specific plant type as symbolic of historic American garden style, it would have to be the vine or climbing shrub. From honeysuckle strung loosely on the front of a rustic log cabin, to Boston ivy completely covering the front of a Queen Anne–style house, vines have been prominent in American landscape adornment since the earliest years of settlement.

Vines have various morphological structures to aid them in their climbing habits. Many vines climb by twining stems, twining either clockwise (Chinese wisteria) or counterclockwise (Dutchman's pipe), depending on the species. Some vines use tendrils to adhere to a support, for example, the grapevine and *Smilax*. Modified tendrils can be found on Boston ivy where each tendril ends in several adhesivelike tips that have the ability to stick to almost any surface. The most tenacious of the vines produce rootlike holdfasts along the stem, causing the vine to fasten to everything in its path, as exemplified by climbing hydrangea. Each vine's climbing apparatus dictated the type of architectural structure for which it was best suited.

Vines and climbing roses adorn the sides of this early-twentieth-century dwelling.

Annual vines, including *Ipomoea purpurea*, morning glory, cover the front of this simple cottage, ca. 1880.

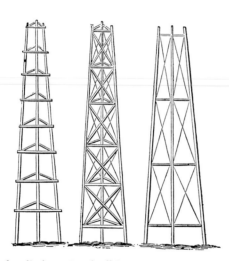

Structures for climbers. *Rural Affairs*, 1858.

Commercial nurseries and seed houses promoted vines from their earliest years. In *The Boston Evening-Post*, 31 March 1760, John Townley advertised "sweet scented pease." John Bartram listed native vines such as trumpet creeper, Carolina jasmine, and scarlet trumpet honeysuckle in his 1783 broadside. In 1810, William Booth of Baltimore offered exotic favorites like English ivy and periwinkle. The term *vines* in the early literature usually meant grapevines, as in the publications of M'Mahon (1806) and An Old Gardener (1822). However, among the

shrubs recommended by early writers are "climbing shrubs." M'Mahon includes almost forty varieties and An Old Gardener, twenty-six. As the nineteenth century developed, vines and climbing shrubs received continuing and accelerated attention in the garden literature and remained popular with nurseries.

Between 1850 and 1875, Andrew Jackson Downing, Robert Morris Copeland, and other nineteenth-century horticulturists recommended the use of climbing plants to camouflage and obscure the disagreeable and to highlight and emphasize decorative features of architecture and landscape. Downing was particularly enamored of vines, citing their versatility, gracefulness, and variety. He recommended covering trees, both alive and dead, with vines. The evergreen English or European ivy was his special favorite.

Patterns and designs for the use of versatile climbing plants varied. On simple folk dwellings throughout the 1800s and early 1900s, vines such as morning glory and cardinal climber crept up strings that hung limply from roofs and overhangs. Wooden trellises supported wisteria or roses, sometimes against a house or on freestanding lattice fences, perhaps to screen a drying yard or chicken house. A dead tree or stump covered with the brilliant orange blossoms of the trumpet creeper or the bright reddish orange fruit of bittersweet was transformed into a living garden sculpture. The *Gardener's Monthly* for June 1868 suggested the following combination of plants to cover a 5-ft.-high cherry tree stump: various loniceras including the golden-netted honeysuckle, creeping Jenny, and evergreen ivy, "all to trail over the sides" (W. H. C. 1868). To aid in the coverage or decorative effect of vines, several writers suggested the use of climbing plants to outline and highlight each window (Copeland 1867; Long, 1893). Vines were also useful in window boxes for their trailing effect or to train on a wall.

Robert Morris Copeland (1867) described an elaborate plan for ornamenting a "modest" house with an extensive variety of vines:

On each side of the eastern side of the house are vines: 2 Woodbines at each corner; next, 2 monthly Honeysuckles; next, 2 Roses (Queen of the Prairie and Rosa-ruga); in the middle, a Virgin's Bower or Clematis Virginiana and Clematis Azurea, Grandiflora, and Flammula (white and fragrant). On the front of the house, on either corner, a Monthly Honeysuckle; on each side of the door, Woodbine; between door and either corner, Boursault Rose and Mrs. Hovey (Prairie). On west side 8 vines; at north-west corner, Monthly Honeysuckle; at south-west, Wisteria; next to each of these a variety of Clematis; next, Trumpet-creeper and Woodbine; in the middle, Sweetbrier, and annual vines. In each hole may be planted some tubers of the Apios, the wild Ground-nut, and of the Madeira vine; and in the proper places where it will show to advantage, the Ipomea Learii and others. . . . On the west and north L of the house, Grape-vines are put, and if the varieties are well selected, and carefully pruned and trained, you will be able to ripen the Grapes on the north exposure, though the east and south are better of course.

In the early twentieth century, the use of vines was integral to the Craftsman style of garden design, which emphasized the connection of the architectural elements of the structure with the natural materials of the landscape. Vines obscured the lines between house and garden and provided a sense of a continuous canvas. Bungalow owners in southern California took advantage of their favorable subtropical climate and grew lush and vigorous climbing flowering plants, including bougainvillea and climbing roses. In the eastern regions of the country, displays were less exuberant, but colorful and lovely nonetheless.

The eminent horticulturist Ernest Wilson proposed including pergolas in fashionable gardens in the early twentieth century. He noted that such structures covered with climbing plants would offer a shady retreat, particularly in gardens of the South and Southwest.

Garden designer Grace Tabor (1916) recommended that vines be planted first, immediately after the builders had left the house, and that their placement should be independent of plans for the garden. "The vital thing is that every building must have vines upon it to impart that sense of oneness with the earth which is the first essential." Vines furnish the "greatest possible results in the least possible space." Tabor suggested that care be taken with the trelliswork that supported

Bougainvillea vine on a California residence, ca. 1910.

vines on porches and that strings and chicken wire should be avoided in such conspicuous places. She and other writers also urged that vines not be allowed to cover windows.

Often writers and designers would recommend using several vines in combination. Tabor asserted that, "Lovely and striking hedges may be made of a tangle of two or three climbers like honeysuckle and Wisteria, supported by and mingling with the common wild rose of the fields and roadside, *Rosa lucida* (*Rosa virginiana*)." Another combination was wisteria and trumpet creeper grown together to take advantage of the similarity of their pinnate foliage and the successive bloom of their flowers.

CATALOG OF HEIRLOOM VINES AND CLIMBING SHRUBS

During the nineteenth century, nursery catalogs featured more than 500 taxa of vines and climbing shrubs.
By the first half of the twentieth century, that number had increased to almost 900. The vines in this encyclopedia appeared
most frequently in the gardening literature from the eighteenth through the early twentieth centuries.

Probably no other type of landscape plants will produce as striking effects as vines.
—C. L. Burkholder, *Better Homes and Gardens*, 1926

James Vick, Rochester, New York, 1881.

Akebia quinata

Japan akebia, fiveleaf akebia

Lardizabalaceae

Exotic

Introduction: 1845

Earliest American citation: Akebia quinata, *Gardener's Monthly*, 1868

Zone: 4–8

Description: Deciduous or semievergreen twining vine, bearing a "mass of rich plum colored fragrant bells" (Akebia quinata 1868). "Its five-fingered leaves are of a type not common with us" (Keeler 1910). The fruit is a berrylike pod, of a drab purplish color, with a slight bloom.

Design notes: Akebia was a good climbing plant for sun or shade on large arbors or trellises and porch pillars. "The delightful odor of its blossoms makes it very desirable near the house" (The Akebia in fruit 1869).

Plant this with sweet autumn clematis to "clothe its bare lower branches" (Tabor 1916).

Remarks: Akebia's delicate appearance belies its vigorous growth; one nineteenth-century observer recorded 15-ft. growth in a single season (Hardy vines and creepers 1884).

Nineteenth-century taxonomists placed this genus in the barberry family.

For regional invasiveness concerns regarding *Akebia quinata*, see Appendix D.

Historic commercial sources: 28

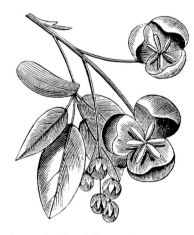

Akebia quinata, Japan akebia. *Vick's Monthly Magazine*, August 1881.

Anredera cordifolia

Madeira vine, mignonette vine

Synonym: *Boussingaultia baselloides, Basella tuberosa* (also a separate species)

Basellaceae

Exotic

Introduction: by 1846

Earliest American citation: Lake Erie Nursery, Cleveland, 1846

Zone: 9

Description: Madeira vine is a tropical, tuberous-rooted climber. It covers a space rapidly with attractive, thick, shiny green foliage and fragrant white flowers.

Design notes: "A common vine, prized for porches and arbors . . . sometimes grown in the conservatory and window garden" (Bailey 1906a).

Remarks: The tuberous roots traditionally were overwintered in cellars and planted out after the danger of frost was past.

Historic commercial sources: 28

Apios americana

potato bean, tuberous-rooted wisteria, wild bean, groundnut

Synonyms: *Glycine apios, Apios tuberosa*

Fabaceae (Leguminosae)

Native

Introduction: 1640

Earliest American citation: Bartram, Philadelphia, 1783

Zone: 3

Description: Climber, 4–8 ft. Groundnut features roots that develop strings of edible tubers. The flowers are fragrant and chocolate brown.

Design notes: *Apios americana* would provide a rapid covering for porch or trellis. Bailey (1906a) recommended groundnut for the wild border, but cautioned that this plant could become weedy in a rockery.

"Makes a pleasing addition to the various ornaments of the border" (Breck 1851).

"Rarely found in cultivated gardens . . . but if used will cover a fence or trellis in a short time" (Keeler 1910).

Remarks: The name *Apios* means "pear," referring to the shape of the tubers.

Historic commercial sources: 25

Aristolochia macrophylla

Dutchman's pipe, birthwort

Synonyms: *Aristolochia sipho, A. durior*

Aristolochiaceae

Native

Introduction: 1783

Earliest American citation: Bartram, Philadelphia, 1783

Zone: 6

Description: Dutchman's pipe is a twining climber. "Its gigantic circular leaves, of a rich green, form masses such as delight a painter's eye,—so broad and effective are they; and as for flowers which are about an inch and a half long,—why they are so like a veritable meerschaum—the pipe of a true Dutchman from 'Faderland'—that you cannot laugh but outright at the first sight of them" (Downing 1849b).

Design notes: The large leaves quickly afforded a dense shade when used on an arbor or a porch. Because of its twining habit, it was not suitable for walls.

"One of our best hardy climbing vines for screen or shade as its great leaves overlap each other and quickly form a leafy wall" (Keeler 1910).

Apios americana, potato bean. Peter Henderson, *Henderson's Handbook of Plants*, 1890.

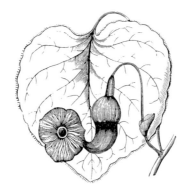

Aristolochia macrophylla, Dutchman's pipe. *Vick's Monthly Magazine*, August 1881.

Remarks: This native vine was sometimes observed in the wild growing to lengths of 80 ft. or more and with leaves over 1 ft. long. Andrew J. Downing considered the Dutchman's pipe to be one of the most picturesque climbing plants in cultivation (Downing 1849b).

Historic commercial sources: 52

Campsis grandiflora

Chinese trumpet creeper
Synonyms: *Bignonia grandiflora*, *Tecoma grandiflora*
Bignoniaceae
Exotic
Introduction: 1800
Earliest American citation: Prince, New York, 1826
Zone: 7
Description: Deciduous climbing shrub. "Large, more open, and equally brilliant flowers, [however] not as vigorous as trumpet creeper" (Bridgeman 1840).
Design notes: Considered a good climber for fences or brickwork.
Remarks: This is the Chinese version of our native trumpet creeper. Henry Nehrling wrote in Bailey's *Cyclopedia* (1906) that this plant covered a 16-ft. pine stump in his Florida garden, "the brilliant, fiery orange-scarlet flowers which can be seen at a distance of half a mile."
Historic commercial sources: 35

Campsis radicans

trumpet creeper, scarlet jasmine, creeping Ginny, trumpet flower, trumpet vine, trumpet honeysuckle
Synonyms: *Bignonia radicans*, *Tecoma radicans*
Bignoniaceae
Native
Introduction: 1640
Earliest American citation: Brickell, 1737
Zone: 4
Description: Trumpet creeper is deciduous with long, pinnate foliage and large trumpet-shaped, orange-scarlet flowers.
Design notes: Many garden writers described the native trumpet creeper as the perfect climber to rise on the trunk of trees, particularly on evergreens where its bright reddish orange blooms would contrast with the green foliage. In the 1870 *Gardener's Monthly*, H. T. Williams described an impressive planting of trumpet creeper growing on the sides and tops of Osage orange hedges "eliciting expressions of admiration from the passers by." He recommended that this vine be planted to intertwine with *Wisteria* (Williams 1870).

Early garden writers suggested planting *Campsis radicans*, trumpet creeper, at the base of a tree so its bright orange blossoms would contrast with the green foliage. *Vick's Monthly Magazine*, 1884.

"A general utility vine—it will adorn a fence, cover a porch, climb a post, and supply foliage and flowers to the dead trunk of a tree. Climbs by means of aerial rootlets . . . the blossoms are full of nectar and the hummingbirds come for it in numbers. . . . Can be made into a hedge—space plants 3 ft. apart and tie each plant to a stake, allowing only one branch to grow, cutting this back at 3 ft. high to form the head which should be made to branch freely. By the time the stake has rotted the plant will have a trunk as large as a wrist and be perfectly self-supporting . . . can also be grown on the lawn, trained to a stake and grown the same as a Kilmarnock Willow" (Bennett 1903).

"This is an excellent plant for covering the bare trunks of palmettos" (H. Nehrling, speaking of his Florida garden, in Bailey 1906a).

Remarks: "A very picturesque climbing plant . . . very beautiful effects are sometimes produced by planting it at the foot of a tall-stemmed tree, which it will completely surround with a pillar of verdure, and render very ornamental by its little shoots, studded with noble blossoms" (Downing 1859).

Heirloom variety:

Campsis radicans var. *flava*. Yellow-flowered trumpet creeper. Intro: by 1842. Scott, 1870.

Historic commercial sources: 61

Cardiospermum helicacabum

balloon vine, love-in-a-puff, heart pea, heartseed
Sapindaceae
Exotic
Introduction: by 1827
Earliest American citation: Thorburn, New York, 1827
Zone: 9
Description: Balloon vine is a short-lived vine, "remarkable for its inflated membraneous capsule . . . flowers are green and white, without any claim to beauty" (Breck 1851). "The leaves, which are thin in texture, are handsomely cut. The flowers are in axillary clusters, very small. . . . The fruit is a large bladdery capsule, with a single seed in each of its three cells. Each seed is marked by a heart-shaped spot (aril) which suggested the generic name of *Cardiospermum*, or Heartseed." (The balloon-vine or heartseed 1872).
Design notes: A tropical vine for summer ornamentation on porches and trellises, the balloon vine also was useful in the conservatory.

Cardiospermum helicacabum, love-in-a-puff. James Vick, Rochester, New York, 1881.

"The plant is a low climber . . . and in cultivation it should have some support about four feet high" (The balloon-vine or heartseed 1872).

Remarks: Balloon vine was a favorite with children.

Cardiospermum helicacabum has proved to be invasive in some areas of the United States. Please refer to Appendix D for specific regional information concerning invasive species.

Historic commercial sources: 33

Celastrus scandens

bittersweet, staff tree, wax work
Celastraceae
Native
Introduction: 1736
Earliest American citation: Bartram, Philadelphia, 1783
Zone: 3–8
Description: Bittersweet is a deciduous, twining, dioecious vine with glossy, pointed leaves and showy red berries, which are held above the leaves.
Design notes: Bittersweet has neither tendrils nor discs so must have something to twine around.
"It twines so tightly around the stems of young trees as frequently to kill them" (Scott 1870).
"Best seen as a tangle on a rock" (Wilson 1915a).
Remarks: In the article "Hardy Vines and Creepers," the January 1884 *The Ladies' Floral Cabinet* observed that American bittersweet was only occasionally cultivated in gardens at that time. The catalog list bears this out with most of the commercial activity documented for either before 1850 or after 1900.
Historic commercial sources: 44
Related species:
Celastrus orbiculatus. Oriental bittersweet. Intro: 1860. Biltmore, North Carolina, 1907. Vigorous and invasive and a serious weed in some states (see Appendix D). Michael Dirr (1998) has observed that hybridization between the two plants blurs the species delineation.

Celastrus scandens, bittersweet. James Vick, Rochester, New York, 1881.

Clematis flammula

sweet-scented virgin's bower, European sweet-scented clematis

Ranunculaceae

Exotic

Introduction: 1590

Earliest American citation: Thorburn, New York, 1827

Zone: 6

Description: Vigorous climber, 10–15 ft. "Has compound leaves, with very narrow leaflets. The flowers are quite small, white, borne from July to October, and exceedingly fragrant" (Scott 1870).

Design notes: Despite the fact that this clematis dies to the ground in many regions of the country, cultivators valued it for its rapid growth, furnishing shade late in the season.

Remarks: "Very beautiful" (Bailey 1906a).

Historic commercial sources: 28

Related species:

Clematis vitalba. Traveler's joy. Long cultivated. M'Mahon, 1806.

Clematis viticella. Virgin's bower. Intro: 1597. Prince, New York, 1826. *Clematis viticella* is one of the parents of the popular *C.* 'Jackmanii'.

Clematis 'Jackmanii'

Jackman's clematis, virgin's bower

Ranunculaceae

Exotic

Introduction: 1858

Earliest American citation: Dreer, Philadelphia, 1876

Zone: 4–8

Description: Woody climber with large velvety purple-violet flowers.

Design notes: The large-flowered clematis was useful to cover old tree stumps and sod heaps or to train over a rustic arch. *Vick's Monthly Magazine* (1883b) promoted the combination of Jackman's clematis with Hall's honeysuckle, "the contrasting white and purple for a fine effect." *Vick's* also recommended clematis to train on a pillar. To achieve the best effect, the magazine gave these directions: "Taking three poles and setting them into the soil so as to make them secure, bring their tops together and fasten them. A plant of a different variety can occupy each pole, and they will form a most beautiful garden ornament." Jackman's clematis was also used in bedding schemes by pegging down the sprawling stems and shoots to cover the designated area.

Remarks: *Clematis lanuginosa* × *C. viticella* = *Clematis* 'Jackmanii'

CLEMATIS, OR VIRGIN'S BOWER.

Group of clematis—white 'Henryi', red 'Kermisina', and purple 'Jackmanii'. Hooker, Wyman, & Co., Rochester, New York, ca. 1905.

The horticulturally outspoken Mrs. Frances King (1925) observed that Jackman's clematis was "usually seen in the country (I regret to add) against a house wall of orangish-red brick."

Prior to 1890, Bailey (1906a) reminded his readers that the majority of large-flowered *Clematis* were imported into the United States from Holland.

Heirloom varieties:

'Duchess of Edinburgh'. Intro: 1887. Good & Reese, Ohio, 1889. Double, white-flowered variety.

'Henryi'. Intro: by 1872. *Vick's Monthly Magazine*, 1883. A white form. The purple and white clematis were sometimes planted together, "the stems of both plants intermingling" (Clematis Jackmanii 1883).

'Hybrida Sieboldii' (syn. 'Ramona'). Intro: 1874. Storrs & Harrison, Ohio, 1896. Deep blue.

'Kermisina'. California Nursery, 1894. Wine red.

'Lady Caroline Neville'. Intro: 1866. Reid, Ohio, 1893. White

Clematis terniflora, star clematis, a vigorous vine, covers this archway at Gwinn, near Cleveland. Photograph by author.

Design notes: "Invaluable for covering porches, arbors, etc. . . . covers a large space the first season" (Sedgwick 1907).

Remarks: "Popular because of its adaptability as a porch plant . . . introduced into the US from Japan in the early seventies and immediately achieved great popularity as a porch climber for several reasons . . . the root will bear a sunny exposure, the growth is vigorous, the bloom is abundant . . . this bloom appears in September" (Keeler 1910).

For regional invasiveness concerns regarding *Clematis terniflora*, see Appendix D.

Historic commercial sources: 45

Clematis virginiana

virgin's bower, woodbine, American white clematis, leather flower, devil's darning needles
Ranunculaceae
Native
Introduction: 1720
Earliest American citation: Bartram, Philadelphia, 1783
Zone: 4
Description: Climbing vine, 12–15 ft. Small white flowers bloom in late summer. Compared with *C. vitalba*, the flowers are "more profuse and conspicuous . . . less showy seed plumes" (Scott 1870).
Design notes: "The species is worthy of cultivation as a fence cover or to give wildwood effects; it is not as good a porch plant as C. paniculata, and its flowers are not as fragrant as C. flammula" (Keeler 1910).
Remarks: Downing (1859) reported that this vine was frequently seen in the woods, covering trees with its pale white blossoms.
Historic commercial sources: 27

Clematis 'Madame Edouard André'. Leo Weltz, Wilmington, Ohio, ca. 1905.

with mauve-colored stripe down the center of each petal.
'Madame Edouard André'. Intro: 1892. Lovett, New Jersey, 1898. Crimson.
'Ville de Lyon'. Intro: 1900. Henderson, New York, 1910. Bright red.
Historic commercial sources: 54

Clematis terniflora

sweet autumn clematis, star clematis, Japan virgin's bower
Synonym: *Clematis paniculata*
Ranunculaceae
Exotic
Introduction: ca. 1864
Earliest American citation: Storrs & Harrison, Ohio, 1896
Zone: 5
Description: Japan virgin's bower is a deciduous woody climber bearing a profuse autumn display of fragrant, star-like white flowers.

Cobaea scandens

Mexican morning glory, cathedral bells, cup and saucer vine
Polemoniaceae
Exotic
Introduction: 1792
Earliest American citation: Thorburn, New York, 1827
Zone: 9
Description: The Mexican morning glory is a tender, climbing, tendriled shrub used as an annual, with large, bell-shaped, purple flowers.
Design notes: Besides being used outdoors on trellises and arbors, the Mexican morning glory was popular for parlor window decorations and in conservatories.
Remarks: This old favorite was considered one of the best climbing annuals because of its rapid growth and interesting purple flowers.
Historic commercial sources: 48

Dioscorea batatas

Chinese yam, cinnamon vine
Synonym: *Dioscorea divaricata*
Dioscoreaceae
Exotic
Introduction: 1827
Earliest American citation: Prince, New York, 1857
Zone: 5
Description: Climbing vine to 30 ft. The leaf axils bear small clusters of cinnamon-scented, white flowers. The shiny, opposite leaves were deemed attractive.
Design notes: "Cinnamon vine likes the sun and is not at all capricious as to soil" (McCurdy 1927).

Dioscorea batatas, cinnamon vine. The Templin Co., Calla, Ohio, 1904.

Remarks: This hardy climber was introduced for the food potential of its tuber, but accelerated in popularity for its ornamental qualities. A letter from Melford, Nebraska, to Gurney Seed in 1921 stated, "I want to let you know I received the cinnamon vine all o.k. Thank you very much for it."
Historic commercial sources: 23

Gelsemium sempervirens

yellow jessamine, Carolina jasmine, false jasmine
Synonym: *Gelsemium nutidum*
Loganiaceae
Native
Introduction: 1640
Earliest American citation: Bartram, Philadelphia, 1783
Zone: 7
Description: Evergreen twining shrub that produces a profusion of bright yellow, fragrant flowers in springtime.
Design notes: This vigorous native vine was used successfully to cover flat trellises, porches, and banks. In the North, Carolina jasmine could be found in conservatories.
Remarks: "During the war between the North and South, when medicines in popular use were cut off by the blockade, this plant was commonly employed as a narcotic" (Meehan 1878).
Heirloom variety: Several nurseries offered a double-flowered form.
Historic commercial sources: 20

Gourds, ornamental

Cucurbitaceae
Exotic
Coccinia grandis—ivy gourd, scarlet-fruited gourd
Cucurbita pepo var. *ovifera*—egg-shaped gourd, pear-shaped gourd, globular gourd
Curcubita argyrosperma—silver seed gourd, cushaw
Lagenaria siceraria—Hercules' club, sugar trough, dipper gourd, bottle gourd, snake gourd, calabash
Trichosanthes cucumerina var. *anguina*—serpent gourd, snake gourd, snake cucumber
Introduction: by 1597 (*Lagenaria*)
Earliest American citation: John Custis, ca. 1741 (*Lagenaria*)
Description: Mainly annual or tender perennial vines. The ornamental gourds came in many sizes, from several inches to 4 ft. long as in Hercules' club. The shapes ranged from long and slender to bottle-shaped and apple-shaped.
Design notes: Gardeners used ornamental gourds for rapid coverage of fences, trellises, and old tree stumps. Some of

the tender perennials like *Abobra viridiflora* also grew in greenhouses providing winter ornamentation.

Remarks: The term *gourd* historically referred to hard-shelled fruits of the Curcurbitaceae family that were used ornamentally or for making household utensils. The author Nathaniel Hawthorne, quoted in *Vick's Monthly Magazine* for 1878, rhapsodized, "A hundred gourds in my garden were worthy, in my eyes at least, of being rendered indestructible in marble" (Vick 1879a).

"Very useful ... an ornamental feature of the summer garden and afford an economic and unique addition to the winter's supply of plant receptacles, hanging baskets, low bowls for Tulips, Crocus, and other bulbs ... highly ornamental and graceful climbers ... delicate foliage and showy fruit ... good for covering rear fences or unsightly outbuildings ... some have large white flowers that are finer than a Clematis" (Bennett 1903).

Historic commercial sources: 34

Hedera helix

English ivy, European ivy, Irish ivy
Synonym: *Hedera vulgaris*
Araliaceae
Exotic
Introduction: Cultivated since ancient times
Earliest American citation: Peter Kalm, 1748 (Leighton 1986a)
Zone: 5
Description: English ivy climbs by means of tiny rootlike structures along the stems that affix the plant tenaciously to any structure. It has evergreen, dark green, palmate foliage. Yellow flowers are produced on the adult form, most often by allowing the plant to gain some height in full sun. 30–40 ft.
Design notes: "A desirable evergreen for covering naked walls or any other unsightly object" (Bridgeman 1840).

> A whole ugly village might be changed in its appearance by a plentiful planting of evergreen ivy. ... Trained to a pole, or an irregular cedar tree, and allowed to branch out at its summit, it forms a very striking object in small gardens—giving in winter a green aspect and cheerful tone. ... Trained against espaliers, lattice work, iron hurdles, or wire frames, it forms in a very short time, most beautiful evergreen walls, or hedges, for the separation or shelter of flower gardens. ... By placing pots of ivy in the balconies of the different windows of a per-

fectly new house, the whole front, in one day, may be covered with rich evergreen leaves. (Notes on the evergreen ivy 1849)

Downing (1859) suggested growing ivy at the base of a dead tree—"by planting Ivy at their roots, we have converted them into more beautiful objects than they were when arrayed in their own natural foliage. ... Bare walls or fences [also] may thus be clothed with verdure and beauty equal to the living hedge, in a very short time by planting young ivy roots at the base."

"Every few feet around the pool, just back of the wall, English Ivy is planted, which as it grows is fastened down with hairpins, those most valuable implements of femininity, and will, it is hoped, in time surround the edge of the pool so that the water will be framed in green. ... English Ivy is [also] an excellent substitute for Box-edging as a border for paths or beds" (Ely 1903).

"The English ivy is more formal in growth ... and is therefore especially suited to buildings of a very formal nature or style" (Tabor 1916).

Remarks: Because of the tenacious nature of ivy's hold, it was not recommended for use on wooden houses, as it could cause rot. "But [it] holds stone and mortar together in stone buildings" (Downing 1859).

For regional invasiveness concerns regarding *Hedera helix*, see Appendix D.

Heirloom varieties: Several variegated-leaved forms of *Hedera helix* were available, but they were less hardy, although more decorative.

Historic commercial sources: 54

Ipomoea purpurea

morning glory
Synonyms: *Convolvulus major, C. carolinus, C. purpurea*
Convolvulaceae
Exotic
Introduction: 1621
Earliest American citation: Bartram, Philadelphia, 1783
Description: Annual vine. Flower colors include white, rose, dark red, violet.
Design notes: The morning glory was much loved in the nineteenth century. Several pioneers in the West described the comfort of having a blue morning glory on the front of their log cabin. Fancy trelliswork was eschewed in favor of simple strings and wires to guide the morning glory to the roof. By the twentieth century, it seemed that the morning glory was out of favor. Harriet Keeler wrote in 1910:

The flowers of *Ipomoea lobata* were described as appearing as sky-rockets. Photograph by author.

Ipomoea quamoclit, cypress vine. Photograph by author.

> Somewhat of a rascal when given too free a hand in the garden . . . it must be kept within bounds or kept not at all. . . . A flower that is seen at its best only at sunrise . . . it will never be a favorite with the American people, and the morning-glory vine, despite all its virtues, will probably remain . . . a utility plant loved by a few, outlawed by others, tolerated by the many. (Keeler 1910)

Remarks: Nurseries typically sold morning glory seeds rather than the plant. *Ipomoea purpurea* is a prohibited noxious weed in Arizona (USDA 2002). Other species have also proved invasive. Please refer to Appendix D for regional information on invasive species. Members of the garden race of morning glories are hybrids developed chiefly from *I. purpurea* and *I. hederacea*.

Historic commercial sources: 35

Related species:

Ipomoea alba. Moonflower. M'Mahon, 1806.

Ipomoea lobata (syn. *Mina lobata*). Spanish flag, skyrocket vine. Intro: 1841. Manda, 1887.

Ipomoea tricolor 'Heavenly Blue'. Blue moon flower. Storrs & Harrison, Ohio, 1896.

Ipomoea quamoclit

cypress vine, star glory, Indian pink
Convolvulaceae
Exotic
Introduction: 1629
Earliest American citation: Thomas Jefferson, 1791
Zone: 8
Description: Annual climber with small, white, rose, or red trumpet-shaped flowers. The foliage is delicate and ferny.

Design notes: This vine needs wires or strings to guide its ascent. Jefferson's daughter planted cypress vine in window boxes.

Remarks: "No annual climbing plant that exceeds the Cypress Vine, in elegance of foliage, gracefulness of habit, or loveliness of flowers" (Breck 1851). This is a prohibited noxious weed in Arizona (USDA 2002).

Historic commercial sources: 41

Jasminum officinale

common jasmine, hardy jasmine, jessamine
Synonym: *Jasminum grandiflorum* is *J. officinale* f. *grandiflorum*
Oleaceae
Exotic
Introduction: Cultivated since ancient times
Earliest American citation: Jean Skipwith, ca. 1800
Zone: 7
Description: Perennial vine. "It grows quite rapidly and will clamber all about the window in one season. It has fine foliage, and bears star-shaped, pure white flowers in great profusion. These are delightfully sweet" (Rexford 1890).
Design notes: Thomas Bridgeman (1840) wrote eloquently about jasmine:

> This delicious climbing shrub has from time immemorial been common in Europe for covering arbours. Its delicate white fragrant flowers render it very desirable; but it is rather tender for our Northern winter, unless well protected. In the Southern States, this plant, and also the yellow Jasmine, revolutum, grow luxuriantly and bloom profusely.

Remarks: Louisa Johnson recorded her observations in England (1856), but she wrote for American women in hopes of instilling in them a similar gardening aesthetic:

> I have seen very fanciful and beautiful devices invented to display the beauty of jasmine. Their shoots grow so rapidly and luxuriantly, that if the plant is allowed to luxuriate, it will soon cover any frame-work with its drooping beauty. The jasmine loves to hang downwards; and I have admired inventive little arbors, where the plant has been trained up behind them, and the branches allowed to fall over their front in the richest profusion, curtained back like the entrance of a tent. The effect, during their time of flowering, was remarkably elegant.

Historic commercial sources: 26

Lablab purpureus

hyacinth bean, Jack bean, purple hyacinth bean
Synonym: *Dolichos purpurea*
Fabaceae (Leguminosae)
Exotic
Introduction: 1790
Earliest American citation: M'Mahon, 1806
Description: Annual twining climber with purple flowers. "[The] clusters of seed pods are a lasting ornament, as they turn a rich dark purple and keep the color until killed by the frost" (Keeler 1910).
Design notes: "The Flowering Bean is a pretty vine for training up verandas, but it does not grow to a sufficient height to make it of much value elsewhere. It is fine for covering low trellises or a fence" (Rexford 1912).

Lablab purpureus, purple hyacinth bean, provides coloration in both flower and pod. Photograph by author.

Remarks: Cultivated in this country as an ornamental bean, but in the tropics the seeds are eaten (Bailey 1906a).
Heirloom variety:
'Alba' or 'Daylight'. White-flowered hyacinth bean. M'Mahon, 1806.
Historic commercial sources: 35

Lathyrus latifolius

everlasting sweet pea
Fabaceae (Leguminosae)
Exotic
Introduction: Before 1635
Earliest American citation: Townley, Boston, 1760, "sweet scented pease"
Zone: 5
Description: The sweet pea vine bears branching tendrils and a "full raceme of beautiful rose and white blossoms . . . the pod is 4–5 inches long" (Keeler 1910).
Design notes: "Excellent for covering rocks, stumps, banks, etc. Good for cutting" (Sedgwick 1907).
Plant the everlasting pea (The Pearl) among delphiniums to continue their bloom by clouds of white flowers (King 1915).
Remarks: The everlasting sweet pea was the most commonly found vine species on the nursery and seed lists of the nineteenth and twentieth centuries. Naturalized plantings escaped from early gardens may be found in culvert and waste areas today.

Lathyrus latifolius, perennial sweet pea. Storrs & Harrison, Painesville, Ohio, 1908.

Lathyrus odoratus 'America' (1896). Photograph by Pat Sherman, Fragrant Garden Nursery.

Lathyrus odoratus 'Black Knight' (1898). Photograph by Pat Sherman, Fragrant Garden Nursery.

For regional invasiveness concerns regarding *Lathyrus latifolius*, see Appendix D.

Historic commercial sources: 100

Lathyrus odoratus

annual sweet pea

Fabaceae (Leguminosae)

Exotic

Introduction: 1699

Earliest American citation: George Washington, ca. 1800

Description: "Every curve in its peculiar form is graceful and its colors are bright, or soft, and contrasting.... The lower pair (of petals) is called the keel, while the petals enclosing them are the wings, and the uppermost petal is called the banner" (Old-fashioned flowers 1882).

Design notes: The annual sweet peas were valued for cut flowers and to provide a quick-growing screen in summer. "There is not a more lively garden ornament or a better nosegay flower than the Sweet Pea, which is also very fragrant" (O'Keefe, New York, 1870).

Remarks: More than 400 varieties of annual sweet pea were available from U.S. nurseries and seed houses during the nineteenth and early twentieth centuries. Important breeders introduced new varieties from California as well as from Europe. Selections were made on the basis of color, form, and bloom time. The first dwarf sweet pea was discovered in California in 1893. "In this form the plant makes a mat of low foliage, the blossoms are the usual size" (Keeler 1910). Another significant type was the Spencer sweet pea, introduced in England in 1902. Spencers are vigorous and upright with waved standards and open keels. They immediately became important for cut flowers.

Lathyrus odoratus 'Butterfly' (1878). Arrangement by Alexia Newman. Photograph by Pat Sherman, Fragrant Garden Nursery.

Heirloom varieties:

American introductions are indicated by "US" after the year. Descriptions are from earliest American citation unless otherwise indicated.

'America'. Intro: 1896 US. Griswold, Nebraska, 1908. "Brightest blood red, striped white."

'Black Knight'. Intro: 1898. Cox, California, 1907. "Deep maroon, veined black."

'Blanche Ferry'. Intro: 1889 US. Storrs & Harrison, Ohio, 1896. "Standard bright carmine rose, wings white tinged with pink" (Morse 1917). This was the first of the early-flowering sweet peas.

'Butterfly'. Intro: 1878. Good & Reese, Ohio, 1889. "White laced with lavender blue."

'Captain of the Blues'. Intro: 1891. Imlay, Ohio, 1899. "Standard bright blue and purple, wings pale blue."

'Dorothy Eckford'. Intro: 1903. Storrs & Harrison, Ohio, 1908. "One of the best pure white varieties. Is semi-hooded of the best form with large wings and very large standard which averages two inches across" (Morse 1917).

'Flora Norton'. Intro: 1904 US. Storrs & Harrison, Ohio, 1908. "Bright clear blue, self colored with just a hint of purple which is only perceptible at times" (Morse 1917).

'Janet Scott'. Intro: 1903 US. Storrs & Harrison, Ohio, 1908. "Clear deep but bright pink, showing buff at the top of the standard, with the upper or top blossom and the bud lighter pink and more buff" (Morse 1917).

'King Edward VII'. Intro: 1903. Storrs & Harrison, Ohio, 1908. "Bright red or crimson scarlet. Almost self colored, but the standard is a little brighter than the wings. Very large size, open form" (Morse 1917).

Lathyrus odoratus 'Senator' (1891). Photograph by Pat Sherman, Fragrant Garden Nursery.

'Lady Grisel Hamilton'. Intro: 1899. Griswold, Nebraska, 1908. "Standard light mauve, wings lavender" (Morse 1917).

'Lord Nelson'. Intro: 1907. Henderson, New York, 1910. Navy blue.

'Painted Lady'. Intro: 1731. Booth, Baltimore, 1810. This is the oldest sweet pea with rose and white coloration.

'Prince Edward of York'. Intro: 1897. Cox, San Francisco, 1907. "Standard is cerise with crimson wings."

'Queen Alexandra'. Intro: 1906. Henderson, New York, 1910. "Almost a true scarlet."

'Senator'. Intro: 1891. Storrs & Harrison, Ohio, 1908. "Maroon and violet striped on white."

Historic commercial sources: 58

Lonicera flava

yellow trumpet honeysuckle
Synonym: *Lonicera fraseri*
Caprifoliaceae
Native
Introduction: 1810
Earliest American citation: Prince, New York, 1826
Zone: 5
Description: Vigorous grower with yellow flowers.
Design notes: "For particular situations we wish nothing better than the old Red and Yellow Coral; they are unique in flower, bright in color, and bloom freely" (Hoopes 1874).
Remarks: C. S. Sargent in "Two American Honeysuckles" (1890) stated that this plant was first discovered in 1802 and sent to England in 1810; but he does not confirm when it was actually *cultivated* in American gardens.
Historic commercial sources: 32
Related species:
Lonicera ×*heckrottii*. Intro: before 1895. Berckmans, Georgia, 1906. A hybrid of unknown origin, "the flowers which are borne in clusters are deep rose color without and pale yellow within and though not fragrant are very beautiful" (Wilson 1915a).

Lonicera japonica 'Aureareticulata'

gold-netted honeysuckle, golden-leaved honeysuckle
Synonym: *Lonicera aurea reticulata*
Caprifoliaceae
Exotic
Introduction: ca. 1860
Earliest American citation: Denmark Nursery, Iowa, 1868
Zone: 4–9
Description: Leaves "netted" and laced with yellow; flowers are also yellow. Nice crimson fall color.
Design notes: A rapid climber that may be pegged down to function as an edger for a pathway or flower bed (Vick 1878g).
Remarks: Bailey (1906a) noted that the climbing honeysuckles as a group are usually deficient in ornamental foliage characteristics. This variety of the Japanese honeysuckle is an exception.
Historic commercial sources: 21

Lonicera japonica 'Halliana'

Hall's Japan evergreen honeysuckle
Caprifoliaceae
Exotic
Introduction: 1862

Group of honeysuckles—*Lonicera periclymenum* 'Belgica', *Lonicera japonica* 'Halliana' and 'Aureareticulata', and *Lonicera sempervirens*. *Vick's Monthly Magazine*, September 1878.

Earliest American citation: Moon, Pennsylvania, 1870
Zone: 4–9
Description: Twining, semi-evergreen vine. Fragrant flowers open white and develop to creamy yellow.
Design notes: Hall's Japan honeysuckle is a rapid grower, useful for trellises. Rexford (1912) suggested that Hall's honeysuckle and the red trumpet honeysuckle be planted together for "pleasing effect. . . . In whatever manner you train them they lend grace and beauty to a porch without shutting off the outlook wholly."
Remarks: Blanchan (1913) said that Hall's honeysuckle was "one of the most popular climbers in cultivation. . . . It needs wire netting or a lattice, but will climb any support it finds."
Please refer to Appendix D for specific regional information concerning invasiveness of *Lonicera japonica*.
Historic commercial sources: 52

This woman stands before *Lonicera japonica*, Japanese honeysuckle, the apparent source of this background verdant screen. Photograph ca. 1906.

Lonicera periclymenum Belgica

Belgian honeysuckle, European sweet honeysuckle, striped monthly honeysuckle, monthly fragrant honeysuckle, Dutch sweet-scented honeysuckle

Synonyms: *Caprifolium periclymenum* var. *belgicum, Lonicera belgicum*

Caprifoliaceae

Exotic

Introduction: Long cultivated

Earliest American citation: Prince, New York, 1790

Zone: 4–8

Description: The Belgian honeysuckle is a twining, somewhat shrubby, fragrant vine that blooms all summer. Buds are purplish red with the flower itself having shades of white, cream, and orange, giving it a variegated appearance (Vick's 1878g).

Design notes: Useful for porches and trellises or for growing up trees or over shrubs.

Remarks: "With many this is the favorite of the whole family" (Vick 1878g). Rehder (1940) remarked that the Belgian monthly was one of the most commonly cultivated varieties of the European woodbine.

Historic commercial sources: 42

Lonicera sempervirens

scarlet trumpet honeysuckle

Synonyms: *Caprifolium sempervirens, Lonicera coccinea*

Caprifoliaceae

Native

Introduction: 1686

Earliest American citation: Bartram, Philadelphia, 1783

Zone: 3

Description: Scarlet trumpet honeysuckle is an evergreen vine in the South, but deciduous in the North. It bears clusters of long tubular flowers that are scarlet with deep orange shading. Rapid growth. Not fragrant.

Design notes: Suitable for verandas and porches. "Extremely beautiful, flowering the whole of the Summer, with its thousands of scarlet bunches" (Bridgeman 1840).

Remarks: Old-time gardeners valued the light red fruit clusters on this native vine as much as they cherished the flowers.

Historic commercial sources: 64

Momordica balsamina

balsam apple

Cucurbitaceae

Exotic

Introduction: 1568

Earliest American citation: William Faris, 1793

Description: Balsam apple is an annual vine with distinctive, deep rich orange fruit, about 12 in. in length. A beautiful climber with ornamental foliage . . . fruit is smaller than balsam pear (Henderson 1890).

Design notes: An Old Gardener (1822) said that balsam apple required a trellis at least 12 ft. tall and that strings would be

Momordica balsamea, balsam apple. Vick's Monthly Magazine, 1879.

Momordica charantia, balsam pear, has longer fruit than the balsam apple. Photograph by author.

required to train it. "When it begins to produce fruit, the appearance is beautiful; they are sometimes from twelve to fifteen inches in length, and as they begin to ripen, are of a high rich orange colour." Charles Parnell, writing for the 1880 *Vick's Monthly Magazine* described the use of balsam apple saying that it was "often allowed to ramble over rockwork, stumps of trees & c." and was valued for its rapid healthy growth and the fact that it was free of insects.

Remarks: The balsam apple was considered edible and was also used medicinally in other cultures. "This fruit in Syria is famous for curing wounds. They cut it open when unripe, and infuse it with sweet oil, exposed to the sun for some days until the oil becomes red. It may then be applied to a fresh wound, dropped on cotton" (Henderson 1890).

Although a separate species, the balsam pear (*Momordica charantia*) was frequently lumped with balsam apple, but was described as a shorter vine with longer fruit.

Historic commercial sources: 28

Parthenocissus quinquefolia

American ivy, Virginia creeper, American woodbine, woodbine

Synonyms: *Ampelopsis quinquefolia*, *A. hederacea*, *A. Engelmannii*, *Hedera quinquefolia*,

Vitaceae

Native

Introduction: 1622

Earliest American citation: M'Mahon, Philadelphia, 1804

Zone: 3–9

Description: A woody vine that climbs by tendrils that end in sticky, flattened disks, Virginia creeper has ornamental five-fingered (*quinquefolia*), dark, glossy green foliage with wonderful scarlet fall color.

Design notes: Readily available, Virginia creeper was used on porches, pillars, vases, summer houses, outbuildings, walls, stone fences, and old tree stumps as well as trained to ascend evergreen trees and shrubs. It climbed the walls of houses, both wood and brick, and festooned balconies and windows.

Remarks: The Virginia creeper was esteemed for its tenacity, vigor, lustrous green foliage, and brilliant fall cover. "It grows more rapidly than Ivy, clings in the same way to wood or stone, and makes rich and beautiful festoons of verdure in summer, dying off in autumn, before the leaves fall, in the finest crimson. Its greatest beauty . . . when running up in the centre of a dark cedar or other evergreen" (Downing 1849b).

"Extensively cultivated—a favorite wall-covering vine in the north . . . this one is more three-dimensional [than] Boston ivy" (Keeler 1910).

Historic commercial sources: 69

Parthenocissus quinquefolia, Virginia creeper, was the most commonly available native vine from nurseries in nineteenth-century America. Photograph by author.

Parthenocissus tricuspidata

Vitaceae
Exotic
Boston ivy, Japan ivy
Synonyms: *Ampelopsis veitchii, A. japonica*
Introduction: 1862
Earliest American citation: Denmark Nursery, Iowa, 1871
Zone: 4–8
Description: Woody climber. Uses holdfasts (small sticky disks on the ends of tendrils) for very tenacious hold. Lustrous dark green foliage is three-lobed. Brilliant fall color in shades of crimson and maroon. Flowers are inconspicuous.
Design notes: Recommended for smoky cities. Will cover a

A Queen Anne–style house is clothed in ivy, probably *Parthenocissus tricuspidata*. Albany, New York, 1890.

wall uniformly without much manipulation. Boston ivy literally "sheaths a wall in leafy armor" (Keeler 1910).
Remarks: First coming to the United States ca. 1860 as a conservatory plant, "it surpasses all other vines for covering brick and stone walls. Thrives in all locations" (Keeler 1910).
For regional invasiveness concerns regarding *Parthenocissus tricuspidata*, see Appendix D.
Historic commercial sources: 55

Passiflora caerulea

Passifloraceae
Exotic
passion vine, blue passion flower, fleur-de-la-passion, mercuria
Introduction: 1699
Earliest American citation: M'Mahon, 1806
Zone: 7
Description: Vine with tendrils. Passion vine bears unusual purplish flowers. One catalog advertised blue, white, and pink varieties.
Design notes: Gardeners cultivated passion vine in greenhouses and conservatories, but they also used it on trellises in the South and Far West.
Remarks: Passion flower received its name because early missionaries, discovering it in South America, thought the plant represented the history of the Passion of Christ: ten petals = ten apostles; small purple threads = crown of thorns, and so on.
Heirloom variety:
'Constance Elliot' (syn. var. *alba*). Thompson, Kentucky, 1888. Pure white.
Historic commercial sources: 27
Related species:
Passiflora incarnata. Maypop. Intro: 1699. Bartram, Philadelphia, 1807. *Passiflora incarnata*, with white waxy flowers, was also available throughout the country. It is hardier than blue passion flower and apparently was used more often for arbors and verandas. Maypop was a troublesome weed in cotton fields of the South (Keeler 1910).

Periploca graeca

Virginia silk vine, Grecian silk
Asclepiadaceae
Exotic
Introduction: 1597
Earliest American citation: Bartram, Philadelphia, 1792
Zone: 6

Description: "A prolific climber. . . . Established plants will grow thirty or forty feet in one season, and yield flowers in clusters, of a brownish yellow colour, from May to July" (Bridgeman 1840).

The fruits are similar to those of other species in the milkweed family.

Design notes: "Well suited for covering arbors, trellis work and trunks of trees" (Bailey 1906a).

Remarks: Despite a common name of Virginia silk vine, *Periploca* was native to southern Europe and parts of Asia and Africa.

Historic commercial sources: 24

Pueraria montana var. *lobata*

kudzu vine, Jack and the beanstalk
Synonym: *Pueraria thunbergiana*
Fabaceae (Leguminosae)
Exotic
Introduction: 1885
Earliest American citation: Columbian Exposition, Chicago, 1893
Zone: 5
Description: "Woody climber with large, dark-green three-foliate leaves, and bearing short, compact racemes of violet colored pea-shaped flowers, followed by brown, hairy pods" (Keeler 1910).

Design notes: "When a dense screen is needed on a kitchen porch or one for a lattice around a drying ground, the Kudzu is invaluable" (Blanchan 1913). Adaptable to porches, arbors, fences, rockeries, old trees, etc. "If you wish a vine that will grow anywhere in the best or poorest soil, then plant the Chinese Kudzu" (Comal Springs Nursery, Texas, 1917).

Remarks: "One of the most rampant growers ever introduced into our gardens, and it well to think twice before planting it" (Keeler 1910). "The famous Chinese Kudzu grows more in three months than most vines do in five years." Although gardeners of the past did use kudzu in the landscape, do *not* use this noxious weed in the interest of historic accuracy. Substitutions can be made with other vines in this section, particularly those featured multiple times by southern nurseries.

Historic commercial sources: 28

Thunbergia alata

black-eyed Susan vine
Acanthaceae
Exotic

Thunbergia alata, black-eyed Susan vine. James Vick, Rochester, New York, 1881.

Introduction: 1823
Earliest American citation: Brighton, Boston, 1833
Description: Twining perennial vine that was cultivated as an annual. Flowers are white, buff, or orange with a deep, purplish brown throat.
Design notes: Used both in the garden and in the greenhouse and conservatory. The black-eyed Susan vine is "valuable for covering low trellises, the foundations of porches, window-boxes, urns, or rock-work" (Bennett 1903).
Remarks: "Thunbergias . . . are great favorites in central and southern Florida, being used on verandas, arbors, small trees, old stumps, trellises, and buildings" (Nehrling, in Bailey 1906a).
Historic commercial sources: 35 (*Thunbergia* spp.)

Tropaeolum peregrinium

canary bird vine, canary creeper
Synonyms: *Tropaeolum canariensis*
Tropaeolaceae
Exotic
Introduction: 1810
Earliest American citation: Buist, 1839
Zone: 9
Description: Annual, trailing vine. "Its canary colored flowers, like little birds on the wing, give it its name" (Wright 1924).
Design notes: Useful for any structure that needs a quick cover, but must be fastened to strings or trellises since it has no natural means of fastening.
Remarks: "It needs a light soil to produce many flowers" (Hale 1868).
Historic commercial sources: 36

The flowers of *Tropaeolum peregrinium*, canary vine, reminded early gardeners of a fluttering yellow bird. Photograph by author.

Vinca major
larger periwinkle, running myrtle
Apocynaceae
Exotic
Introduction: 1789
Earliest American citation: M'Mahon, 1806
Zone: 7
Description: Evergreen, vining plant. "The Vinca is a fine drooping plant, having rich, smooth foliage of a bright, shining green. . . . All varieties have a pretty, light blue flower" (Rexford 1890).
Design notes: Gardeners used this plant outside in the South and indoors in the conservatory or as a parlor plant in areas where it was tender. It was recommended as a covering for the ground beneath shrubbery.
Remarks: The white variegated-leaved form was particularly valued for baskets, vases, and window boxes.
For regional invasiveness concerns regarding *Vinca major*, see Appendix D.
Historic commercial sources: 24

Vinca minor
creeping periwinkle, hardy myrtle, grave myrtle
Apocynaceae
Exotic
Introduction: Cultivated since ancient times
Earliest American citation: Bartram, Philadelphia, 1807
Zone: 4

Description: "A hardy trailing plant with shining evergreen foliage and blue salver-shaped, 5-lobed flowers about 1 inch across, appearing in spring or early summer" (Bailey 1906a).
Design notes: "One of the commonest and best plants for covering the ground in deep shade, especially under trees and in cemeteries . . . a capital plant for clothing steep banks, covering rocks and carpeting groves . . . will live in city yards under trees where grass will not thrive" (Bailey 1906a).
Remarks: Bourne (1833) claimed this was a common plant in early gardens.
For regional invasiveness concerns regarding *Vinca minor*, see Appendix D.
Heirloom varieties:
'Alba'. Prince, New York, 1857. White flowers.
'Flore Pleno'. Prince, New York, 1826. Double-flowered variety.
'Variegata'. There were several variegated forms ('Argenteo-variegata', 'Aureovariegata') with white or golden variegation and with blue or white flowers.
Historic commercial sources: 31

Wisteria frutescens
American glycine, American wistaria
Synonym: *Glycine frutescens*
Fabaceae (Leguminosae)
Native
Introduction: 1724
Earliest American citation: Prince, New York, 1790
Zone: 5
Description: Woody, twining vine. The flowers typically are light purple, although a white form was known also. "Climbing plant, several stems as big as a man's thumb twisting around each other like a cable, so tight a knife could scarce be thrust between. It bears a long and thick spike of flowers, of a pink or lilac colour of pleasant odour" (Gosse 1859).
Design notes: Downing (1859) suggested that the American glycine be planted so that it will drape gracefully over tree limbs. Philip Gosse wrote eloquently from Alabama in 1838 about the use of *Wisteria frutescens* on modest dwellings in the area to ornament and camouflage the logs.
Remarks: "The American Wistaria should be planted in every garden with other creepers, or to run up the trees in the shrubbery" (Bridgeman 1840).
Historic commercial sources: 31

Wisteria sinensis

Chinese wisteria, wistaria

Fabaceae (Leguminosae)

Exotic

Introduction: 1816

Earliest American citation: Kenrick, Boston, 1832

Zone: 5

Description: "20–30 ft. May, large, pendant clusters of [lavender] pea-shaped flowers" (Sedgwick 1907).

Design notes: *The Horticulturist* reported in 1848 that this climber was still relatively unknown in small gardens. Recommendations included planting Chinese wisteria with English ivy to maintain an evergreen appearance or with laburnum or golden chain—"their similar racemes of blue and yellow blossoms would create a peculiar and pleasing effect." Wisteria also could be used against a wall, to decorate an arbor of wood or iron at the entrance to a flower garden, or to cover a rustic, open-roofed pavilion (Valk 1848).

Andrew J. Downing (1859) suggested that wisteria "be allowed to grow up and hang from the branches of similar light airy foliaged trees like *Gleditisia* and *Robinia*."

Wisteria could be trained as a standard—for example, on Long Island in 1884, the wisteria resembled "fine shade trees" (Hardy climbers: the Wisteria 1884).

"Commonly trained around piazza and pergola pillars (which it sometimes weakens), over arches and fences and along walls . . . best when grown to trail its way at will among trees" (Blanchan 1913).

Remarks: Other early writers commented on the vigorous nature of *Wisteria*, one calling it the "boa constrictor" of vines (Miller 1909a). Another observed wisteria reaching the top of the lightning rod of a five-story building within four years after planting (Hardy climbers: the *Wistaria* 1884).

"The wisteria alone holds a whole summer of fragrance in its June cascade of bloom" (Ellwanger 1889).

Wisteria sinensis has proved to be invasive in some areas of the United States. Please refer to Appendix D for specific regional information concerning invasive species.

Heirloom varieties:

'Alba'. White Chinese wisteria. Intro: 1844. Breck, 1851.

'Plena' (syn. 'Flora Plena'). Double-flowered Chinese wisteria. Intro: 1869. Parkman, 1871b.

Historic commercial sources: 92

The white Chinese wisteria was nearly as popular as the violet-blue variety during the second half of the nineteenth-century. Photograph by author.

· 8 ·

HEIRLOOM HARDY HERBACEOUS PLANTS

OFTEN NINETEENTH-CENTURY garden writers discussed "flowers," without distinguishing between perennials, biennials, and annuals. Gardeners did recognize that hardy herbaceous plants had their own intrinsic virtues though, as noted in the catalog of Woolson Nursery & Co. of Passaic, New Jersey, in 1879:

Herbaceous and other Hardy Plants . . . have been favorites from early gardening times, and still hold a place in popular favor—eminently the people's, or everybody's plants.

Why Hardy Herbaceous Plants
Should be Cultivated

The first reason is for their beauty. They afford not only a great variety in habit of the plant, but much diversity and beauty of foliage, while the flowers present an interminable variety in form and color. In time of blooming, they range from the earliest spring to latest autumn, and by a proper selection a continuous bloom can be kept up the entire season.

Another reason is their permanence. When the foliage fades, or the frost ends their career, that is not the last of them, but we know that they will appear the following spring in new strength and beauty.

Another reason is that they pay good dividends. One can give away the increase, and still be as rich as he was before; at the same time he can do good to his neighbors and friends by adding to their enjoyments. [That] they are but little trouble is a reason that will commend itself to many. When once planted, they may usually be left for three or

four years, and in some cases much longer. They are generally abundant bloomers, and many are excellent for cut flowers.

As the nineteenth century progressed, gardeners considered several alternatives for garden design. English garden writers like J. C. Loudon, Humphry Repton, and William Robinson influenced gardeners from across the Atlantic. The popular sentiment was to break ties with English traditions and develop a uniquely American style of gardening. Edward Sayers (1839) described the dilemma faced by garden designers of the age:

It is difficult to give a correct method for laying out flower gardens owing to the diversified opinions of different persons, which are much at variance with one another. Some say that nature should be copied, as much as possible, others that formal lines and geometrical figures, such as circles, ovals, & c. are best.

HISTORIC DESIGN CONSIDERATIONS FOR THE FLOWER GARDEN

Beginning with Bernard M'Mahon and his 1806 *The American Gardener's Calendar*, it is possible to trace the development of perennial garden design in the United States. M'Mahon recommended that the pleasure ground, in the so-called "natural style" of gardening, be enclosed by a fence, wall, or hedge, and that it should range in size from one-quarter acre to thirty to forty acres, depending on the size of the house.

M'Mahon suggested that both annual and perennial flowers be combined with trees and shrubs in curvilinear beds placed in the front of the residence. In deference to the well-established ancient-style garden design, M'Mahon advised that, for contrast, some straight walks and geometric flower borders could be incorporated into the landscape. Box, thrift, pinks, and sisyrinchiums provided edging material. M'Mahon also recommended parterre-style flower gardens, noting that they appeared "more gay and sprightly."

Although the 1806 edition of M'Mahon's *Calendar* included a list of hundreds of perennials, later editions contained none. It is difficult to determine if this omission reflected an actual decreased enthusiasm for these plants in fashionable gardens or the diminished availability of these plants from M'Mahon's own business following his death in 1818.

In the 1830s and 1840s several discourses on gardens included directions for laying out flower gardens. Herman Bourne in *Flores Poetici* (1833) combined botanical observations with horticultural recommendations. Although his focus was florists' flowers, he included perennials in his list of four ranks of ornamental plants, classified according to their respective heights. Most hardy herbaceous perennials, including pinks and other small flowering plants, belonged to the first rank. Their landscape function was to occupy the borders and edges of walks and avenues. Bourne described a border with the shrubs mixed with tall-growing, showy, herbaceous, flowering plants. Among perennials that he recommended for placement in this shrubbery setting were lily-of-the-valley, wood anemone, hollyhock, goatsbeard spirea, foxglove, monkshood, larkspur, columbine, willow herb, double feverfew, tall asters, goldenrods, sunflowers, tiger lily, sweet woodruff, and yucca. Bourne also suggested that traditional perennial borders be 3–6 ft. wide with a collection of perennials arranged according to height.

Robert Buist in *The American Flower Garden Directory* (1839) recommended that a large area be enclosed with serpentine walks "as would allow an agreeable view of the flowers when walking for exercise." Buist theorized that "the arrangement of a flower garden is rather a matter for the exercise of fancy, than one calling for the application of refined taste . . . a design should be kept in view that will tend to expand, improve, and beautify the situation." For his choice of plants, Buist called for a good selection of perennials: "They are lasting ornaments; and when judiciously selected, will give yearly gratification. In making a choice, a view should be to have those that flower abundantly, are of free growth, beauty, and continuation of bloom."

In *The Flower Garden* (1851), Joseph Breck acknowledged that plant selection was a key feature of successful garden making and admonished his readers to become knowledgeable about the habit, culture, and appearance of annuals, perennials, biennials, and shrubs. He recommended the use of native plants as a cost-cutting measure. "Many beautiful plants may be selected from the woods and fields by those who wish to ornament their grounds at the least expense." He also enjoined gardeners not to neglect the old-fashioned flowers, "among the many follies which the gardening world commits, none is more striking to the looker-on, than the eagerness with which old favorites are deserted for new ones."

Andrew Jackson Downing distinguished between several forms of the flower garden. It might be "a place exclusively devoted to the cultivation of flowers or . . . it may be an architectural flower-garden." An artistic mélange of plants, sculpture, urns, and vases, the architectural flower garden complemented the formality and symmetry of the accompanying building.

Downing described the irregular flower garden, the old French flower garden, and the modern or English flower garden. For each of these styles, the flower beds were either cut out of the turf or each bed was surrounded by a low hedging material such as box or by a hard material, for example, tiles or cut stone, with the pathways filled with gravel.

The irregular flower garden incorporated a variety of irregular shapes that stood singly or were grouped in a somewhat haphazard arrangement. The flower garden itself was surrounded by trees and ornamental shrubs arranged informally. This style of garden was to be located out in the grounds rather than immediately adjacent to the house.

The French flower garden was "most fanciful" with intricate planting beds or parterres. This took its inspiration from seventeenth-century European gardens. French flower gardens were filled with "low growing herbaceous plants or border flowers, perennials and annuals . . . such as will not exceed on an average, one or two feet in height."

"In the English flower-garden, the beds are either in symmetrical forms or figures, or they are characterized by irregular curved outlines." Each bed is planted with a single variety or possibly a combination of two species. "Only the most striking and showy varieties are generally chosen, and the effect, when the selection is judicious, is highly brilliant." The English flower garden resembled carpet bedding, although it did offer opportunity for using a greater variety of plants. Bulbs started the display in the early spring, followed by annuals and greenhouse plants, which Downing noted must be renewed every season. In the absence of a greenhouse, he recommended that a combination of perennials and biennials with the "finer species of annuals" be used in the English flower garden. G. M. Kern, the Cincinnati designer, following Downing's lead, singled out the English flower garden as most appropriate for perennials. For a smaller landscape, Kern espoused placing flower beds beneath windows where they could be admired (Kern 1855).

> The desideratum, however, with most persons is, to have a continuous display in the flower-garden from the opening of the crocus and snowdrop in the spring, until the autumnal frosts cut off the last pale asters, or blacken the stems of the luxuriant dahlias in November. This may be done with a small catalogue of plants if they are properly selected: such as flower at different seasons, continue long time in bloom, and present fine masses of flowers. (Downing 1859)

Most writers agreed that the flower garden should be near the main house so it might be viewed from a favorite room or else located within one-quarter mile of the dwelling so it was easily accessible. Only one voice dissented from this simple rule of proximity. Henry Winthrop Sargent, writing a supplement to Downing's sixth edition of the *Treatise*, asserted that flowering plants should never be used near a house except for an occasional fragrant rose or honeysuckle beneath some windows. Even in the case of the architectural flower garden, he argued that it should not be visible from the front of the house. Flowers, according to Sargent, detracted from the sweeping views.

Even the question of correct exposure was controversial. Usually, an eastern or southeastern exposure for the flower garden was deemed most beneficial. A southern exposure would cause a glaring sun to "wither the flowers" and a northern exposure should also be avoided (Johnson 1856). On the other hand, Joseph Breck (1851) recommended that a well-drained plot with a southern exposure be used. He said the garden should be "trenched two spades deep" and compost and rotten manure be added. Today, we call this procedure "double-digging." Several recipes were published for compost that was particularly beneficial to flowers; for example—four parts good loam, four parts well-rotted cow manure, four parts road-wash or clean sand, two parts good surface loam, one part poudrette (Watson 1859). Robert Copeland (1867) exhorted his readers to prepare for the next season by making into "convenient heaps old leaves, straw manure, wood

mould, muck and clay, or sand. These mixed with lime and ashes will make excellent compost, ready for use when you want it."

Arranging plants by height was a recommendation for improvement of the flower garden:

> The larger flowers, such as hollyhocks, sunflowers, & c. look to the best advantage as a background, either planted in clumps, or arranged singly. Scarlet lychnis, campanula, or any second-sized flowers, may range themselves below, and so in graduated order, till the eye reposes upon a foreground of pansies, auriculas, polyanthuses, and innumerable humbler beauties. Thus all are seen in their order, and present a mass of superb color to the observer, none interfering with the other. . . . Each flower is in this mode of planting distinctly seen, and each contributes its beauty and its scent, by receiving the beams of the sun in equal proportions. (Johnson 1856)

An informal look was achieved by the use of tall plants for vertical emphasis spaced throughout the planting. If less precision were desirable, plants like plume poppy, Madonna lily, and gladiolus could be scattered throughout the bed (Neill 1851).

Flower and foliage color were sometimes highlighted, but were not the main consideration as "the management of color is more difficult" (Neill 1851). This advice on color probably was written specifically for carpet bedding schemes, but was also appropriate for the arrangement of perennials in flower beds:

> Color Arrangements—A few simple rules in the arrangement of flower beds will materially enhance the effect produced. Among these are:
> 1. Avoid placing rose-colored next to scarlet, orange or violet.
> 2. Do not place orange next to yellow, or blue next to violet.
> 3. White relieves any color, but do not place it next to yellow.
> 4. Orange goes well with blue, and yellow with violet.
> 5. Rose color and purple always go well together.
> (Color arrangements 1875)

Frank Scott wrote the first book aimed at "suburbia," *The Art of Beautifying Suburban Home Grounds of Small Extent* (1870). For Scott, flowers were the finishing accessory to the landscape rather than a focal point. He urged restraint in the quantity of selection of flower species. According to Scott, perennials, with annuals and bedding plants, could be placed in three different modes:

> First, in narrow beds bordering a straight walk to a main entrance, or skirting the main walk of a kitchen-garden. Second, in a variety of beds of more or less symmetrical patterns, grouped to form a flower garden or parterre, to be an object of interest independent of its surroundings. Third, as adjuncts and embellishments of a lawn, of groups of shrubs, of walks and window views, to be planted with reference to their effect in connection with other things.

COTTAGE AND VERNACULAR GARDENS

The oft-romanticized English cottage garden occasionally had a modest counterpart in America: "There is a pleasure and beauty in all styles, by which the man of money and leisure may amuse himself; but there is far more pleasure in the neatly laid out, the well stocked and well kept cottage garden, where everything is under the immediate care and observation of its owner" (Elder 1850).

Describing a farm garden in 1837, Edward Sayers wrote that in addition to the requisite beds of fruits and vegetables:

> The southwest part of the garden was appropriated to a small flower garden neatly laid out which occupied the leisure hours of the female part of the family in an exercise that was at once pleasing to the mind and healthy to its constitution. The garden was well stocked with the best kinds of hardy shrubs and herbaceous plants.

A writer for the 1886 *Gardener's Monthly* reminisced about an old-fashioned cottage garden:

> The dear old-fashioned flower garden, which consisted of little more than a two or three feet border through or around a vegetable garden, is still one of the best places to pass a pleasant hour among outdoor flowers. Here are the Paeonias—"pineys" our mothers called them—Phloxes, Sweet Williams, Hollyhocks, old hundred-leaved Roses, and everything that is the sweetest and the best are gathered together. (Seasonable hints 1886)

In *The Rescue of An Old Place* (1892), Mary Robbins wrote about an old garden that she inherited. Flowers that persisted among the weeds in a shady nook and along the fence were hardy English violets, tulips, and star of Bethlehem. Crocus endured along with "clumps of Tiger Lilies, and old fashioned small bluebells, and Sweet Williams.... Under the Box-arbor I found Spiderwort growing in great clusters."

Occasionally, a prominent garden designer would offer advice for the vernacular garden. Included in a plan for a small homestead, F. L. Olmsted counseled that the "pleasure ground" should be near the bedrooms of the house for practicality. All bed lines should be undulating. Shrubs should be grown next to the fences, and low-growing shrubbery and herbaceous plants were to be placed in front of taller material in a tiered effect. Olmsted suggested goatsbeard spirea as a companion for the shrubs. Goldenrods and asters were to be located in wilder areas of the landscape (Olmsted 1888).

FASHIONABLE PERENNIAL BORDERS AT THE CLOSE OF THE NINETEENTH CENTURY

By the last quarter of the nineteenth century, savvy garden designers began to emphasize hardy herbaceous plants. In recognition of their lower maintenance in contrast to the bedding plants, and as a result of a nostalgia for the old-fashioned garden, writers promoted perennials to a more prominent position in the landscape. In England, garden stylists William Robinson and Gertrude Jekyll advocated the use of hardy herbaceous plants in a natural setting as an alternative to garish bedding schemes.

Liberty H. Bailey (1891) hailed the change in landscape sensibilities:

> The ornamental gardening of the country is very rapidly undergoing a change, particularly in its application to home or private grounds. The formal and purely conventional features of ornamentation are giving place to the freer use of hardy perennials and native plants. . . . Carpet bedding seems to have passed its zenith. . . .
>
> The interest in native plants has never been so great as now. . . . Many of the so-called old-fashioned plants are coming again into favor, at least in their improved forms. All this indicates an evolution in taste which must be abiding.

In *Ornamental Gardening for Americans* (1893), Elias Long noted "the increasing attention this class of plants [hardy herbaceous plants] is now attracting in ornamental gardening in this country and Europe." Long advised that borders be placed at the foundations of a house to "hide the natural limits of the place, thus giving an idea of increased largeness of the garden area." He made the point that since a wavy line is actually longer than a straight line, such beds were more spacious than they at first appeared. He advocated careful placement of hardy perennial or annual plants with woody plants "to render them attractive in flowers and foliage from early spring until freezing weather in the fall."

Flowers should be massed for the best appearance: "much finer than the same plants scattered in driblets too small to make an impression."

THE OLD-FASHIONED GARDEN

The "old-fashioned" or grandmother's garden was actually a new style incorporated into gardens in the late nineteenth century, perhaps as an attempt to romanticize the American cottage-type garden described above. A horticultural exhibit at the 1892 Columbian Exposition reinforced the popularity of this style.

> There is a fresh call for the perennials and annuals which enlivened the borders of long ago, and those who are fortunate enough to possess one of these old-time gardens show with pride the long-treasured plants which have bloomed for so many years. . . . The charm of those old gardens was in their wealth and tangle of bloom. . . . The spirit of those gardens came from the hands that tended them and culled their fragrant produce. . . . The fairest of these gardens were unsymmetrical ones, with winding paths that led by unexpected turns to some half-hidden bower wreathed in roses.

> An old-fashioned garden appeals to the mind as well as the eye, and whether formal or informal has about it something individual suggested by the mind of the owner. Its very tangles have a meaning and its stiffness a significance. . . . The plants of an old-fashioned garden were beloved, and are still justly beloved, for beauty or fragrance or for picturesque habit. (Sargent 1895)

These informal gardens were places of quiet dignity and "quaint simplicity." Samuel Parsons (1891) was inspired by his own grandmother's garden to design them for others, but acknowledged that the resultant new garden did not absolutely copy the old:

> I have introduced a plan of a place near Orange, N. J., where just this arrangement for a grand-

mother's garden was undertaken. It is not, of course, exactly what we remember our grandmother's garden to have been—other times, other manners—but it is built on the same plan, amplified and perfected in accordance with the richness of our modern list of perennial garden plants. It is less quaint, I acknowledge, less old-timey, but it has as much quaintness as the old rooms with grandmother's furniture seen in modern houses, and is quite as much in keeping.

Parsons' grandmother's garden was lined with clipped California privet. The four corners contained the striped giant reed. The border contained over 100 hardy perennial plants against the dark background of the hedge. "As in the grandmother's garden, there is plenty of color scattered about in somewhat promiscuous fashion, and ready to the hand for plucking or not, as the passing mood may determine."

The overall effect of the plants, rather than the individual plants themselves, determined the success of this style. The selling points of the grandmother's garden included a tidiness and neatness of design; economical use of perennials as opposed to annuals that would have to be replaced each year; profusion and variety of bloom; and "individuality of beauty."

The plants of the grandmother's garden were those that had been cherished for years and years. C. S. Sargent, editor of *Garden and Forest*, recommended peonies, lilies, and roses, as well as bee balm, sweet William, scarlet lychnis, clove and maiden pinks, Canterbury bells, phloxes, marvel-of-Peru, pansies, and buttercups (Sargent 1895).

An old-fashioned garden for $10.00. *The Garden Magazine*, 1910.

ROCK GARDENS

Rockeries and rock gardens are another canvas on which to paint a floral portrait. "A rockery properly located and tastefully arranged is capable of affording much of interest and pleasure to those who can appreciate the beauties of nature" (*Report of the Commissioner 1869*). The first published American reference to a rock garden was in M'Mahon's 1806 *Calendar*: "Likewise in some parts are exhibited artificial rock-work, contiguous to some grotto, fountain, rural piece of water & c. and planted with a variety of saxatile plants, or such as grow naturally on rocks and mountains."

Throughout the nineteenth-century, writers like Buist, Bridgeman, and Elder exclaimed the virtues of rock gardening to attract the sophisticated gardener. In their catalogs, the growers advertised suitable plants for those special ecosystems: "plants, which would be swallowed up or would not thrive in the border—delicate Alpines, little creeping vines, cool mosses, rare orchids, and much of the minute and charming flora of the woods and mountains" (Ellwanger 1889).

Rock gardens were distinguished from rockeries:

I speak of the rock-garden as distinguished from the "rockery"—that embellishment to be found in company with the geranium-bed, surrounded by whitewashed stones; and iron stags or greyhounds standing guard over the growth of a hopvine up a mutilated Norway spruce. With the "rockery" we are all familiar—that nightmare of bowlders [sic], that earthquake of stones dumped out on to the hottest portion of the lawn, with a few spadefuls of soil scattered among them. Into this scant pasturage, where even a burdock would cry out for mercy, dainty plants are turned to graze. Fancy the rude shock to a glacier-pink or a Swiss harebell! (Ellwanger 1889)

"The best possible rockery is nature's and she is the best teacher as to how to form an artificial one," stated Robert Manning in his 1889 catalog. Also, "rock work should not be placed on level ground, but on the side of a slope, bank, or side of a ravine—just at those places where in nature, beds of rocks are to protrude" (Thomas 1855b). Directions for the construction of rock gardens emphasized particularly the imitation of the natural stands of alpine plants and strict adherence to their cultural requirements:

To grow Alpine plants successfully, it is necessary to understand the object of the rock-garden—its special adaptation to a very large class of beautiful plants, which find in it the root-moisture and natural surroundings they require. Many of these are too minute, many too fastidious, to be grown in any other way. The novelty, the delightful variety and charm which the rock-garden lends to the cultivation of flowers can scarcely be over estimated. From the very requirements of most Alpine plants, which love to run deeply into the soil in search of moisture, it is self-evident that there should be no unfilled spaces left between the base and the surface. The rocks should be firmly embedded in the soil, with sufficient space left between them for root-development of the plants. While the hideous chaos of stones of the average "rockery" can not be too severely condemned, half-buried bowlders [sic], showing here and there their weather-beaten sides, have a picturesque look, especially when the flowering season is over. (Ellwanger 1889)

J. E. Teschemacher, writing for the *Horticultural Register* (1835) on the construction of rock gardens, cautioned "see that it does not resemble a pile of loose stones" and observed that "few of these artificial structures exist."

Plants recommended for the rock garden

Anemonella thalictroides (rue anemone)

Campanula (bellflower)

Cerastium tomentosum (snow-in-summer)

Dianthus montanus (mountain pink)

Duchesnea indica (mock strawberry)

Gaultheria procumbens (wintergreen)

Geranium sanguineum (bloody geranium)

Geranium wallichianum (hardy geranium)

Hepatica nobilis

Houstonia caerulea (bluets)

Lobelia

Lysimachia nummularia (moneywort)

Mitchella repens (partridge berry)

Sedum (stonecrop)

Sempervivum (hens-and-chicks)

Tiarella cordifolia (foamflower)

Verbena

Viola pedata (bird's foot violet)

Waldsteinia fragrarioides (barren strawberry)

WATER GARDENS

Water features provided another way to enhance the landscape, and perennials were a natural accompaniment to these features.

> There is nothing that I am acquainted with, that gives more ease, and has so fine an effect in the ornamental and flower garden department, as ornamental water, in any form it can be introduced; it gives a relief to the eye, from too much sameness of the living part of the created world; and calls to mind, the utility that is derived from its presence as a medium conductor of food, to an organized kingdom. Independent of this, the cooling aspect it assumes, forms a fine feature in rural scenery. (Sayers 1839)

Scott (1870) cautioned, "of water, we can only require that it be pure and clear, and in motion." The water feature might have been a small pond or a stream, either natural or contrived. Enthusiasm for water plants reached a pinnacle when the first blossoming in the United States of *Victoria regia*, "The Great Water Lily of America," was recorded in 1851 (Cope 1851).

In his *Treatise*, Downing devoted an entire chapter to water. He observed that the smaller scale of landscapes in America, as compared with England, did not call for the expense and labor of major aquatic features. Nature provided the main water features in the landscape. Downing was not complimentary on the state of the art of water gardening:

> There is no department of Landscape Gardening which appears to have been less understood in this country than the management of water . . . the occasional efforts that have been put forth in various parts of the country, in the shape of square, circular, and oblong pools of water, indicate a state of knowledge extremely meagre, in the art of Landscape Gardening. The highest scale to which these pieces of water rise in our estimation is that of respectable horse-ponds; beautiful objects they certainly are not. They are generally round or square, with perfectly smooth, flat banks on every side, and resemble a huge basin set down in the middle of a green lawn.

Downing gave directions for the construction of lakes and ponds for the grounds of country residences. He recommended taking inspiration from the forms of natural lakes.

As for the plantings, trees and shrubs of different heights and shapes were to be placed on the banks maintaining a connection and a blending of the different forms. Herbaceous plants, including ferns and moneywort, formed the lower layer. Although native plants were appropriate, Downing observed that the introduction of foreign species to this situation would provide novelty in the landscape.

Only in the flower garden "where a different and highly artificial arrangement prevails" may accessories such as fountains "be employed with good taste." Otherwise, Downing suggested that "with water especially . . . all appearance of constraint and formality should be avoided."

Horticultural treatises and nursery catalogs featured aquatic and bog plants as composing "an interesting class of plants and quite easy to grow." For instance, Long (1893) provided this list:

Plants recommend for the water garden

Acorus calamus (sweet flag)

Arisaema dracontium (green dragon)

Brasenia peltata (water shield)

Calla palustris (marsh calla)

Calopogon tuberosum (calopogon)

Caltha palustris (marsh marigold)

Calypso borealis (northern calypso)

Cypripedium spp. (lady's slipper)

Darlingtonia californica (pitcher plant)

Drosera spp. (sundew)

Habenaria spp. (orchis)

Lobelia cardinalis (cardinal flower)

Nuphar advena (yellow water lily)

Nymphaea odorata (water lily)

Orontium aquaticum (golden club)

Parnassia asarifolia (grass of Parnassia)

Pogonia (hardy orchid)

Pontederia cordata (pickerel weed)

Sabatia (centaury)

Sagittaria variabilis (arrow head)

Sarracenia spp. (side-saddle flower)

Trollius spp. (globe flower)

Typha (cattail)

PERENNIALS IN BEDDING SCHEMES

Bedding scheme designs of the second half of the nineteenth century usually emphasized annuals and tropical plants chosen for their vivid colors and compactness or a strong vertical habit for accent. Interestingly, some herbaceous perennials were also considered appropriate for this style.

In one intricate design, the planting starts at the center circle with a focal point, such as a vase or a sundial, and works outward. The scale is 16 ft. to 1 in. The next four irregular beds contain perennials such as aconites, bleeding heart, phlox, and delphinium. Japanese lilies are the feature of the subsequent eight beds. Each small circle near the perimeter holds a rose and the outer scalloped edge contains annuals or dwarf phlox or pinks (Design for a flower garden 1855).

Scale 16 feet to the inch.

Design for a carpet-bed flower garden using perennials. *The Magazine of Horticulture*, 1855.

Perennials used for their color, interesting habit, or foliage effect in Victorian bedding schemes

Achillea tomentosa (woolly yarrow)

Aegopodium podagraria 'Variegatum' (goutweed)

Alcea rosea (hollyhock)

Anemone vitifolia (anemone)

Aubrieta deltoidea (false rock cress)

Bellis perennis (English daisy)

Cerastium tomentosum (snow in summer)

Convallaria majalis (lily-of-the-valley)

Delphinium grandiflorum (delphinium)

Dianthus barbatus (sweet William)

Dicentra spectabilis (bleeding heart)

Hosta spp. (variegated yellow and green hosta)

Iris species and cultivars

Lilium speciosum (Japan lily)

Lobelia cardinalis (cardinal flower)

Lychnis ×*haageana* (orange lychnis)

Melissa officinalis 'Variegata' (variegated lemon balm)

Miscanthus sinensis 'Variegatus' (variegated Japanese silver grass)

Penstemon hybrids (beardtongue)

Phalaris arundinacea var. *picta* (gardener's garters)

Phlox spp. and varieties

Primula spp. (primrose)

Saccharum ravennae (ravenna grass)

Salvia leucantha (sage)

Sedum acre (stonecrop)

Sedum carneum 'Variegatum' (variegated stonecrop)

Stachys byzantina (lamb's ears)

Tanacetum parthenium 'Flore Pleno' and 'Aureum' (double and golden feverfew)

Thymus serpyllum 'Aurea' (golden thyme)

Trillium grandiflorum (wake robin)

Viola odorata (sweet violet)

PERENNIALS FOR LAWNS

Perennials had many functions in the residential landscape, some more fashionable than others. Old photographs often illustrate a specimen perennial in the lawn. Suitable perennials for this practice were large and symmetrical in form with showy, colorful flowers. Appropriate perennials for the lawn included gasplant, peony, oriental poppy, baptisia, *Clematis recta*, goatsbeard, and perennial phlox.

> The more central and open parts [of lawns] may be interspersed with shrubbery and with the larger growing and more showy flowering perennial plants. If the latter are selected among the hardier and stronger sorts, they will maintain their appearance and thriftiness with a small amount of cultivation—no more than shrubs commonly require for their successful growth. (Thomas 1855a)

Perennials for lawns. *Illustrated Annual Register of Rural Affairs for 1855–56–57.*

THE WILD GARDEN

Although M'Mahon and others had been recommending American native plants from the earliest years of the century, the wild garden as a separately designed landscape entity became fashionable under the influence of England's William Robinson, who wrote *The Wild Garden* in 1870. "A wild garden . . . is a delightful feature of a place." This style of garden was in retaliation to the garish bedding schemes that had enjoyed popularity in both countries. The wild garden was a natural repository for hardy herbaceous plants, both native and exotic. They were placed in a setting where they were allowed to thrive without further care. A rockery or a water feature might also have been an element of a wild garden.

Elias Long (1893) promoted the natural or wild garden as

> a place where interesting wild and cultivated plants are brought together in the most natural manner, and allowed to live and struggle, much as they do when wild. . . . Where space will admit, hardy flowers, grasses, ferns, and

creepers should be scattered about, and thickets be formed of shrubs, including brambles. . . . Here is a place where the Fennel-leaved Paeony will be enjoyed more than would an improved variety with large globular flowers.

Another example of the informal wild garden is found in Ella Rodman Church's *The Home Garden* (1884):

> Says a writer on flowers: "I would have, in a large flower garden, a corner or a belt, where nature and apparent neglect should reign throughout the season. I say *apparent* neglect, for, of course, noxious weeds must be exterminated everywhere. Yet in this unmolested ground should grow aquilegia, lychnis, hollyhock, aconite, delphinium, dicentra, foxglove, lathyrus, cardinal-flower, peonies, phlox, campanula, yucca filamentosa, sweet-briers also, and many other low bushes, if there were room enough. I would have creepers, there too, such as vines, moneyworts, partridge-berry, ground-pine, and all hardy trailers, native or foreign, that will endure our climate. The lower plants of my lazy bed should be hellebore, trilliums, hepaticas, star of Bethlehem, hardiest of the asphodels, *Clematis erecta* should be there, also mullein-pink, daisies, gentian, alkanet, violets, and sedum, while mother-

A peony in the middle of an Illinois lawn, 1908.

of-thyme, hyssop, and other hardy herbs should sun themselves on the borders of my natural garden."

As the nineteenth century closed, the future for flower gardens looked promising, as Mary Robbins observed in 1892:

> Fashionable freaks and follies pass away, and flowers would have their brief day like any other craze, if the regard for them was artificial or fictitious. The flower-dealers of the country need have no apprehension as to the future of their industry. It is based on the elementary wants of our nature. Flowers will be loved until the constitution of the human mind is radically changed.

COLOR IN THE MODERN FLOWER GARDEN

The beginning of the twentieth century was marked in gardening literature by a preponderance of garden books in which the gardener, usually female and wealthy, described her adventures making and maintaining her perennial borders. Many of these gardens were Americanized versions of the colorly borders of Gertrude Jekyll. Ida Bennett, Neltje Blanchan, Mrs. Francis King (Louisa Yeoman King), Alice Morse Earle, Louise Beebe Wilder, and Helena Rutherfurd Ely were included in this august group. Their energetic and vivid recollections inspired a generation of gardeners to plant hardy herbaceous plants in their gardens. The best of the old-fashioned flowers as well as the most fashionable new plants were interwoven into intricate and simple designs.

The hallmark of the modern, twentieth-century flower garden was the judicious and artful use of color in addition to considerations of bloom sequence and arrangement of plant forms and structures. Perhaps Louise B. Wilder (1918) said it best, "The enjoyment of colour is, in the garden as elsewhere, entirely a matter of individual feeling and, whatever the result, it is mete that every garden should be a personal manifestation." Gardeners were exhorted to create beautiful pictures and vignettes in their gardens and writers offered many suggestions of effective, colorful plant combinations.

Planting composition became a sophisticated activity involving color combinations, color harmony, color balance, color accent, the play of light on color, color sequences, and color schemes. Monochromatic garden schemes, which evolved around the use of a single color, were sometimes implemented. The lack of any uniformity or standards in published flower color descriptions occasioned some discussion.

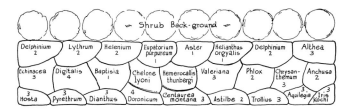

Perennial border design. Victor Ries, *The Home Flower Garden*, 1936.

Mabel Sedgwick's 1907 *The Garden Month by Month* provided an early color chart to help alleviate this concern.

Garden designers looked to nature for ideas for plant combinations. As Stuart Ortloff observed in 1931, "Nature is a good colorist. Follow her and you cannot go far wrong." No matter what the inspiration, the best plans for perennial borders were simple and concentrated on single harmonious pictures placed throughout the garden. Ortloff suggested that the gardener apply general landscape design principles to flower garden making. To achieve balance, he recommended that equal masses of color with proportionate weight be used. For unity, it was important to use one color predominantly throughout the composition. Coherence depended on progressive color changes. In order to break any monotony, contrasting or accenting colors could be used sparingly.

A simple plan for a border of herbaceous perennials (above) is appropriate for a small yard and measures 5 ft. by 20 ft. The numbers in the design indicate the number of each particular species. This plan could easily be reproduced in a modern landscape.

HERB GARDENS

Herb gardens are often erroneously attributed to historic ornamental landscapes. They simply did not exist in the manner in which we appreciate them today. Herbs in the earliest American gardens were grown alongside vegetables and fruits in a kitchen garden. An early doctor or pharmacist might have had a medicinal herb garden, but even these were rare after the mid-nineteenth century. However, some individual herbs were valued for their ornamental qualities. Early catalogs included plants like lavender, rosemary, lemon verbena, various thymes, and some wormwoods in their ornamental sections. Many plants that we use today primarily for their decorative qualities have old-time herbal origins, either medicinal or fragrant—plants like foxgloves, pinks, and roses.

In her book *Old-Time Gardens* (1901), Alice Morse Earle documented one of the first gardens completely for herbs in the United States. This Chicago garden was the forerunner of the formal herb gardens that became popular in the Colonial Revival period. Earle described how one could replicate her friend's herb garden:

> Let two garden walks be laid out, one at the lower edge, perhaps of the bank, the other parallel, ten, fifteen, twenty feet away. Let narrow paths be left at regular intervals running parallel from walk to walk, as do the rounds of a ladder from the two side bars. In the narrow oblong beds formed by these paths plant solid rows of herbs, each variety by itself, with no attempt at diversity of design. You can thus walk among them, and into them, and smell them in their concentrated strength, and you can gather them at ease.

The herb gardens of the early 1900s typically followed the ancient style of garden design with geometric and symmetrical beds of traditional herbs often enclosed with a boxwood hedge or a picket fence. Leonard Meager's seventeenth-century garden designs on page 26 illustrate several popular forms. Sometimes knot gardens were constructed with herb foliage textures and colors forming a design that resembled verdant needlework.

By the 1930s, not only were herb gardens more prominent in American landscapes, but herbs themselves had become recommended features of fashionable gardens:

> I believe that some place in the home grounds may be found for any herb to grow; so no one need despair for lack of opportunity or space for an herb garden. But at the same time all herbs respond gratefully to their individual needs of shade, sunlight, soil and moisture.

> A rough bank around an old house . . . makes an ideal green bank for thymes. Rosemary leans against the underpinning of the house for it likes the warmth of the supporting walls. (Webster 1939)

Helen Webster recommended herbs as ground covers to replace lawn grass: chamomile, ajuga, Corsican mint, and thyme. "A good combination planting is that of the crimson and woolly thymes." As edging plants, she advised hyssop, rue, santolina, and sage. Tender herbs like the scented geraniums and lemon verbena were thought appropriate for porch boxes or incorporated into the flower or herb garden as annuals (Webster 1939).

The attraction of cultivating herbs was practical, aesthetic, and nostalgic. Henry Beston (1935) perhaps expressed the sentiments of herb growers across the country when he wrote

> A garden of herbs is a garden of things loved for themselves in their wholeness and integrity. It is not a garden of flowers, but a garden of plants which are sometimes very lovely flowers and are always more than flowers. It is a garden of colour seen as a part of garden life and not as its climax and close, of the pleasures and refreshments of fragrance, of the fantasy and beauty of leaves, of the joy of symmetry and design in nature, of that neglected delight to be found in garden contrasts and harmonies of green.

A CATALOG OF HEIRLOOM HARDY HERBACEOUS PLANTS

These perennials and biennials are those most often featured in the seed and nursery catalogs associated with the early American gardening aesthetic to the year 1940.

James Vick, Rochester, New York, 1881.

Achillea ptarmica

sneezewort, yarrow, white tansy

Asteraceae

Exotic

Introduction: 1597

Earliest American citation: M'Mahon, 1806 (double-flowered)

Zone: 3–9

Description: Most of the early documents refer to a perennial with double, as opposed to single, small white flowers on 2 ft. stems.

Design notes: Breck (1851) considered the double-flowered sneezewort to be a desirable border plant because of its long season of bloom. "A hardy, popular perennial herb, much used for cut flowers, appearing in gardens principally in its double variety" (Keeler 1910).

"Unsurpassed for cemetery planting" (Old Colony, New York, 1857).

Remarks: This plant can be floppy and vigorous in the garden.

Heirloom varieties:

'Boule de Neige' (syn. 'Ball of Snow'). Ellwanger & Barry (1917) called this a dwarf form of 'The Pearl', although some sources consider 'The Pearl' and 'Boule de Neige' to be synonymous.

'Perry's White'. Intro: 1912. Michell, Philadelphia, 1931. A 24-in. double white variety.

'The Pearl'. The double form of sneezewort was mentioned in 1806, but the name 'Pearl' appears to be newer: " 'The Pearl' . . . new variety" (Jackson, Georgia, 1904). "The Pearl is one of the most popular of all hardy herbaceous plants" (Bailey 1906a).

Historic commercial sources: 73

Achillea 'Boule de Neige'. Photograph by Steven Still.

Related species:

Achillea filipendulina. Golden yarrow. Intro: 1739. Hovey, Boston, 1859.

'Parker's Variety'. Park, South Carolina, 1938.

Achillea millefolium. White yarrow. Long cultivated. Lawson, 1718. Breck (1851) reported growing the rose-colored form 'Roseum'. 'Cerise Queen' was a variety available in the United States by 1931.

Aconitum napellus

monkshood, wolfsbane, helmet flower, bear's foot, turk's cap

Ranunculaceae

Exotic

Introduction: by 1551

Earliest American citation: John Winthrop, Jr., 1631

Zone: 4–8

Description: The helmet-shaped, dark blue-violet flowers are held on 3–4 ft. plants for middle to late summer bloom.

Design notes: Old-time gardeners planted monkshood in a shady corner of the border or allowed it to blend with natives in a wild garden.

Remarks: "Formerly used much in borders . . . but not much favored in new ones; for its acrid juices are exceedingly poisonous and consequently it has been banished" (Keeler 1910).

Heirloom varieties:

var. *versicolor*. Intro: 1820. Downing, 1842.

subsp. *neomontana*. Autumn aconite. Jean Skipwith, ca. 1800. The deep blue autumn aconite made a pleasing combination with white Japanese anemone

Historic commercial sources: 65

Related species:

Aconitum carmichaelii (syn. *Aconitum fischeri*). Azure monkshood. Ellwanger & Barry, New York, 1862. A shorter-growing monkshood at 2–3 ft.

Aconitum lycoctonum subsp. *lycoctonum* (syn. *Aconitum septentrionale*). Intro: 1800. Prince, New York, 1844. An early bloomer with small white flowers.

Alcea rosea

hollyhock, holy-hock

Synonym: *Althaea rosea*

Malvaceae

Exotic

Introduction: by the 15th century

Earliest American citation: John Winthrop, Jr., 1631

Zone: 5

Alcea rosea, hollyhock. B. K. Bliss and Sons, New York, 1869.

Description: "Old-time plant of vigorous growth, noble aspect, and ornamental character. . . . The double forms are popular, but the singles hold their own because of their individuality and real beauty" (Keeler 1910). Height typically was 5–6 ft.; although hollyhocks occasionally grew to 10–13 ft. Colors ranged from shades of red and rose to purples, yellow, and white.

Design notes: Here is a chronologically arranged list of the uses of hollyhocks in the garden:

"This is a fine showy plant for a shrubbery. There are single and double, and none but the double should be cultivated" (Cobbett 1821).

The Gardener's Monthly for 1863 recommended the hollyhock for use as a bedding plant or as a complement to a shrubbery. "To give summer grace to the evergreen, nothing surpasses the Hollyhock" (The hollyhock 1863).

"For a prominent bed on the lawn, or for a hedge, or to conceal a fence, I know of nothing better than the beautiful double Hollyhock" (Rexford 1886).

Use to hide an untidy corner, or "for the purpose of forming a back-ground for smaller growing plants; and in small lots the hollyhock is invaluable for the breaking up of the formal lines of the boundary wall or the fence" (The hollyhock—cover illustration 1894).

"No one can have too many hollyhocks. Plant them at the back of borders among the shrubbery, along fences, and in good clumps in any odd corner, or around buildings; they are never amiss, and always beautiful" (Ely 1903).

"Set directly against an old weather-worn building, they screen the evidence of decay with a thrilling suggestion of comfort and loving care" (Allen, Ohio, 1930).

Remarks: Diseases on hollyhocks did not appear to squelch any enthusiasm for this plant. An 1871 correspondent to *The Gardener's Monthly* inquired, "What is the matter with [my] Hollyhocks? The leaves get spotted in summer and appear as if burnt, and the spikes of flowers are poor and weak in consequence." Editor Thomas Meehan assumed that the problem was symptomatic of the attack of a "minute fungus." He recommended occasionally starting fresh plants from seed (Disease of hollyhock 1871). The 1894 *American Gardening* recommended burning all diseased hollyhocks and treating healthy-appearing ones with Bordeaux mixture (The hollyhock—cover illustration 1894).

For regional invasiveness concerns regarding *Alcea rosea*, see Appendix D.

Heirloom varieties:

James Vick wrote in 1878 about how the single hollyhock, so popular in the first half of the 1800s, had been replaced by a flower that

> was as double as a Rose, the plant has lost half its height and gained much more than this in beauty. The slender shaft has become a gorgeous mass of flowers, possessing more grace and beauty than art ever produced. . . . A good, double, clear white Hollyhock is a very good substitute for a Camellia or a white Rose, at the center of a bouquet.

Anemone 'Honorine Jobert' (1851). Photograph by Robert Herman.

The 1857 Prince Nursery catalog listed thirty named varieties, but currently available selections are not so extensive:

'Chater's Double'. Breck, Boston, 1917. Double flowers were available in yellow, red, pink, purple, white, and maroon.

'Nigra'. Owens & Leckie, Virginia, 1831. Deep maroon flowers, almost black.

Historic commercial sources: 129

Anemone ×*hybrida*
Anemone hupehensis
Anemone hupehensis var. *japonica*

Japanese anemone, fall-blooming anemone

Synonym: *Anemone japonica*

Ranunculaceae

Exotic

Introduction: 1844

Earliest American citation: Breck, Boston, 1851

Zone: 4–8

Description: Of the perennial Japanese anemone, Keeler (1910) wrote, "the color of type is rose-red, but the white variety seems to be the present favorite although the silvery-pink is much in evidence."

Anemone 'September Charm' became available in the United States in the 1930s. Photograph by author.

Design notes: Use in a container or as a single specimen in the mixed border. May also be planted in large masses (Parnell 1882b).

Mrs. Francis King (1915) delighted in the combination of a coral pink gladiolus towering above an established grouping of the double white *Anemone* 'Whirlwind'.

The double white *Anemone* 'Whirlwind' originated in a plot of 'Honorine Jobert' in the 1890s. Photograph by Robert Herman.

Antirrhinum majus, snapdragon. Peter Henderson, *Henderson's Handbook of Plants*, 1890.

Remarks:

"The autumnal equinox comes and goes, but the Anemones bloom on, careless of threatening skies or pinching cold" (Keeler 1910).

Heirloom varieties:

Anemone ×hybrida:

'Honorine Jobert' (syn. *Anemone japonica* var. *alba*). Intro: 1851. *The Gardener's Monthly* of 1863 reported "a beautiful, new, hardy, herbaceous plant, being a pure white-flowered variety of *Anemone japonica*."

'Königin Charlotte' (syn. 'Queen Charlotte'). Biltmore, North Carolina, 1907. The flowers are semidouble and early growers described the color of 'Queen Charlotte' as "La France pink," referring to the color of the La France rose.

'September Charm'. Lamb, Washington, 1939. "Beautiful new early bloomer, lovely silvery-pink shaded rose and mauve."

'Whirlwind'. Intro: 1894. This double white anemone originated in a plot of 'Honorine Jobert' in Rochester, New York.

Anemone hupehensis var. *japonica* 'Prinz Heinrich' (syn. 'Prince Henry'). Biltmore, North Carolina, 1907. Double pink.

Historic commercial sources: 37

Related species:

Anemonella thalictroides (syn. *Anemone thalictroides*, *Thalictrum anemonoides*). Rue anemone. M'Mahon, Philadelphia, 1804. "A charming little plant . . . bearing the leaves of the meadow rue and a cluster of three to five long stemmed Anemone blossoms" (Keeler 1910).

Pulsatilla vulgaris (syn. *Anemone pulsatilla*). European pasque flower. Long cultivated. Thomas Jefferson, 1782.

Antirrhinum majus

snapdragon

Scrophulariaceae

Exotic

Introduction: Long cultivated

Earliest American citation: Thomas Jefferson, 1767

Zone: 7

Description: "The flower bears a perfect resemblance to the snout or nose of some animal; by applying the thumb and the finger to the side of the corolla, it opens and shuts, as with a spring. . . . The flowers grow at the top of the stalkes [sic], of a purple color, fashioned like a frog's mouth, or rather a dragon's mouth, from whence the women have taken the name Snap-Dragon" (Breck 1858). The flowers came in many colors: purple, rosy crimson, yellow, red and yellow, red and white, striped, mottled, and tipped snapdragons. Bailey (1906a) described both tall and dwarf varieties and also referred to a double-flowered *Antirrhinum*.

Design notes: "All the varieties of *A. majus* are esteemed in the flower borders; the pure white, bright red, and variegated are very showy" (Buist 1839).

Grow tall yellow snapdragons in front of white perennial phlox or tall pink snapdragons before hybrid delphiniums (Wright 1924).

Useful for the cutting garden or as a filler in the perennial border.

Remarks: By the beginning of the twentieth century, some writers felt that the snapdragon had been so overdeveloped as to lose any charm it once had had.

Heirloom varieties: Over 115 named varieties were offered in the catalogs.

'Black Prince'. Gregory, Massachusetts, 1915. Dark crimson, 18–20 in.

'Tom Thumb'. Wendel, Massachusetts, 1867.

Historic commercial sources: 102

Aquilegia canadensis

American columbine, scarlet columbine, turk's cap, meeting houses, wild honeysuckle

Ranunculaceae

Native

Introduction: by 1640

Earliest American citation: Jean Skipwith, ca. 1800

Zone: 3–9

Description: "Our beautiful native species, *A. canadensis*, whose pendant scarlet and yellow flowers enliven many a

Aquilegia canadensis, American columbine. Martin Doyle, *The Flower Garden*, 1835.

hill-side in June, has ever been scarce in cultivated grounds" (A few words for herbaceous plants 1856).

Design notes: "The debonair little red-and-yellow native sort [of columbine] . . . is fit to bring into the garden to shine among the best. . . . The persistent fine foliage of Aquilegias makes them particularly valuable in the borders" (Wilder 1918).

Remarks: "A wild creature, it submits to cultivation if it must, but loses something of its rare grace thereby" (Keeler 1910).

Historic commercial sources: 57

Related species:

Aquilegia caerulea. Rocky Mountain columbine. Prince, New York, 1829.

Aquilegia chrysantha. Intro: 1873. Breck, Boston, 1875. Longest bloom time of all of the columbines.

Aquilegia vulgaris

European columbine, granny's bonnets

Ranunculaceae

Exotic

Introduction: by 1310

Earliest American citation: John Winthrop, Jr., 1631

Zone: 3–9

Description: "It is variable in character under cultivation, and many beautiful and some extremely curious varieties have sprung from it. . . . There are white, pink, lilac, blue, purple, dark-crimson, red, yellow and variegated colors in double forms" (Hardy herbaceous plants 1884).

Design notes: Useful when massed or planted in beds or for the cutting garden. "The White English Columbine should be planted together [with *A. canadensis*] for the contrast of color. When thus situated, beautiful hybrids can easily be

'Nora Barlow' is a new name attached to an old type of short-spurred, double columbine. Photograph by author.

obtained from the seeds of the English Columbine, partaking of the character of both species, and distinct from either" (Bement 1860).

Remarks: In the nineteenth century growers introduced many new hybrids of columbine, short-spurred, long-spurred, single and double, the offspring of crosses between *A. canadensis*, *A. caerulea*, and *A. vulgaris*.

Heirloom varieties:

'Adelaide Addison'. Modern name for an old blue and white double form.

'Crimson Star'. Lamb, Washington, 1939. "An immense flower of deep crimson, having a snowy white corolla."

'Helenae'. Pilkington, Oregon, 1912. Blue and white.

Mrs. Scott Elliot hybrids. Wing, Ohio, 1918. An English seed strain consisting of long-spurred columbines in many shades and combinations of red, yellow, purple, and blue.

'Nivea' (syn. 'Alba'). White columbine. New England Nurseries, Massachusetts, 1910.

var. *stellata* 'Nora Barlow'. In the early 1980s, the English grower Alan Bloom gave this name to a columbine that, according to experts, was known in the sixteenth century. Double, fringed petals in rose and greenish-white.

Historic commercial sources: 49

Armeria maritima

cushion pink, sea thrift, statice
Synonyms: *Statice armeria*, *Armeria vulgaris*, *A. lauchiana*
Plumbaginaceae
Exotic
Introduction: by 1600
Earliest American citation: M'Mahon, 1806
Zone: 4–8
Description: "Its pink flowers are produced in June or July, on stems six inches high, in little heads or clusters" (Breck 1858). Thrift was also available with white flowers.
Design notes: After boxwood, gardeners considered thrift to be the best plant for a low edging for the flower border. "An

George Ellwanger (1889) called *Asclepias tuberosa* "the most brilliant flower of summer." Photograph by author.

edging of double white or single white fringed Pinks, Nepeta Mussini [sic] and gay pink Thrift is the very prettiest thing I know" (Wilder 1918).

"The common variety, Statice Armeria or A. vulgaris or A. maritima, serves successfully in the spring garden if given a place in pockets of the shrubbery, along edgings, in the rock garden, or dry wall" (Wright 1924).

Remarks: "The tiny sea-pinks (*Armeria maritima*) will cover bare slopes with a mass of deep pink in May and June and will grow on the steepest incline" (Hill 1923).

Heirloom variety:

'Splendens'. Dreer, Philadelphia, 1872. Deep red flowers.

Historic commercial sources: 51

Asclepias tuberosa

butterfly weed, pleurisy root, orange milkweed
Asclepiadaceae
Native
Introduction: 1690
Earliest American citation: Bartram, Philadelphia, 1783
Zone: 4–9
Description: "Flowers numerous, erect, and of a beautiful bright orange color . . . blooms in August" (Breck 1858).
Design notes: "All or any of these (Asclepias tuberosa, Trilliums, Dodecatheons, etc.) added to the more popular and familiar kinds [of herbaceous plants] render the garden doubly attractive" (A few words for herbaceous plants 1856).

Grace Tabor (1916) included butterfly weed in her list of suggested plants for a sunny rock garden. The 1931 F. M. Horsford catalog of Charlotte, Vermont, suggested combining *Asclepias* with the blue of *Platycodon* for a pleasing grouping in the border.

Remarks: George Ellwanger (1889) spoke of the butterfly weed as the most brilliant flower of summer, but did not admit to digging any up for his own garden or nursery.

Historic commercial sources: 64

Related species:

Asclepias incarnata. Swamp milkweed, water-silk weed. Intro: 1710. M'Mahon, Philadelphia, 1804. Norman Taylor (1915) of the Brooklyn Botanic Garden confirmed that swamp milkweed was equally at home in garden soil as in a swamp.

Aster novae-angliae

New England aster, Michaelmas daisy

Asteraceae

Native

Introduction: 1710

Earliest American citation: John Bartram, ca. 1737

Zone: 4–8

Description: "The faint grayish tones, the hundred tints and shades of lavender, mallow pink, mauve, and heliotrope, and even deep-toned violet and purple sorts lend themselves happily to almost any association" (Wilder 1918).

Design notes: In the 1800s, the perennial blue aster graced the gardens of native plant collectors, but in general was not fashionable. Hardy asters enjoyed more widespread appreciation after the beginning of the twentieth century when they were used for late-season color in the back of the hardy border or for naturalizing in the wild garden.

Eben Rexford (1912) enjoyed the effect of asters in his garden. "These plants have captured the charm of the Indian Summer and brought it into the garden, where they keep it prisoner during the last days of the season. By all means give them a place in your collection. And it will add to the effect if you plant alongside them a few clumps of their sturdy, faithful companion of the roadside and pasture, the Golden Rod."

Mrs. Francis King (1915) recommended planting lavender-blue Michaelmas daisies in the border with *Salvia patens* and a lavender pink gladiolus to produce "one of the loveliest imaginable companion crops of flowers."

Louise B. Wilder (1918) planted the reddish asters "that approach magenta in color . . . among the fleecy Boltonias, the tall stiff stems reaching well up among the crowding white blossoms."

Remarks: Landscape architect O. C. Simonds visited the garden of English garden author William Robinson in 1892 and reported,

> As we approached the house, I noticed, some distance ahead, quite large areas of delicate color, mostly light blue. On coming nearer, these areas were found to be large beds of American asters. "Oh, you have some of our flowers!" I exclaimed. "Yes," said Mr. Robinson, "you Americans do not appreciate your wild flowers. We have to bring them over to England and cultivate them a while before you will notice them." (Simonds 1909)

"The hardy Asters of the New York and New England roadsides have been hybridized into glorious, hardy border flowers dependable for bloom when other flowers are scarce" (Wright 1924).

Heirloom varieties:

'Mrs. J. F. Raynor'. Intro: before 1900. Horsford, Vermont, 1931. "Good sized, almost double; ageratum blue flowers" (Fremont, Ohio, 1932).

'William Bowman'. Intro: ca. 1898. Pilkington, Oregon, 1912. Dark violet. Late.

Historic commercial sources: 46

Related species:

Aster ×frikartii 'Wunder von Stäfa'. Intro: ca. 1924. Lamb, Washington, 1939. "One of the most constant blooming plants in existence producing freely branching sprays of clear lavender-blue flowers in lavish profusion." 'Mönch' was introduced in Germany about 1918.

Aster novi-belgii. New York aster, starwort. Intro: 1687. M'Mahon, Philadelphia, 1804. In the early 1900s, a flurry of hybridization in Europe produced many named varieties.

'Beauty of Colwell'. Intro: by 1907. Breck, Boston, 1917. Double lavender.

'Climax'. Intro: ca. 1906. Farr, Pennsylvania, 1920. Large, light lavender-blue flowers.

'Queen of Colwell'. Intro: 1922. Howard, Los Angeles, 1937. "Semi-double mauve pink flowers with rays beautifully curved."

'Saint Egwyn'. Intro: before 1907. Farr, Pennsylvania, 1920. Delicate pink.

'White Climax'. Farr, Pennsylvania, 1920. White form of 'Climax'.

Aurinia saxatilis
madwort, golden alyssum, basket of gold, golden-tuft
Synonym: *Alyssum saxatile*
Brassicaceae
Exotic
Introduction: 1710
Earliest American citation: Goldthwaite & Moore, Philadelphia, 1796
Zone: 3–7
Description: Perennial, 12 in. high. The flowers are golden yellow and produced in "little compact clusters . . . makes a spreading mat" (Bailey 1906a).
Design notes: For a spring garden, grow golden alyssum with red *Phlox stolonifera* and pink or white *Phlox subulata* (Breck 1851).
An excellent edging for the flower border included the compact form of golden alyssum with aubrietia and perennial candytuft (Wright 1924).
Remarks: Golden alyssum was popular in the 1800s for rockwork.
Heirloom varieties:
'Citrinum'. Wright, 1924. Flowers are lemon yellow.
'Compactum' (syn. var. *compactum*). Hovey, Boston, 1862. 6–8 in.
'Variegata'. Bailey (1906a) notes a "pretty variegated variety."
Historic commercial sources: 58

Baptisia australis
false indigo
Synonyms: *Podalyria australis, P. caerulea, Sophora australis*
Fabaceae
Native
Introduction: 1758
Earliest American citation: Bartram, Philadelphia, 1783
Zone: 3–9
Description: "A native plant with the appearance of the Lupin, growing two to three feet high and bearing spikes of pale blue flowers in June and July" (Wright 1924).
Design notes: Baptisia was well situated in the wild garden. Often it was used as a single lawn specimen.
In *The Horticulturist* for 1846, John J. Thomas suggested the combination of blue *Baptisia* with red and white *Dictamnus* and *Aquilegia canadensis.*
Remarks: Thomas Lea wrote in Cincinnati's *Western Farmer* in 1844: "This handsome plant is rare here . . . it succeeds well in the garden."
Historic commercial sources: 65

Related species:
Baptisia tinctoria. Yellow podalyria. Intro: 1750. Bartram, Philadelphia, 1783.

Bellis perennis
English daisy, double daisy, Belgian daisy, mountain daisy, Herb Margaret
Asteraceae
Exotic
Introduction: Long cultivated
Earliest American citation: Bethabara, North Carolina, 1761
Zone: 4–10
Description: "The daisy, as it grows wild in England, has a yellow center, surrounded by numerous rays in a single row, but the favorite cultivated forms are double, the rays rising in tier upon tier, and frequently crowding out every trace of a yellow center . . . essentially a pink or pinkish flower in its general effect" (Bailey 1906a).
Design notes: The English daisy was particularly popular for bedding designs.
"For the small space it occupies, no flower is more satisfactory . . . particularly well adapted for edgings and for ground covers under Darwin Tulips. . . . Pink and white daisies massed together also make an effective carpet" (Wright 1924).
Remarks: *Bellis perennis* traditionally appeared in U.S. markets with pansies in early spring.
Heirloom variety:
'Monstrosa'. Henderson, New York, 1910. The largest of all; flowers were from 1–1.5 in. in diameter and of deep, rose-pink color.
Historic commercial sources: 91

Campanula carpatica
Carpathian bellflower
Campanulaceae
Exotic
Introduction: 1774
Earliest American citation: M'Mahon, 1806
Zone: 3–8
Description: The large, delicate-looking bells, 6–12 in., appear in shades of blue or white.
Design notes: Authors at the beginning of the twentieth century recommended the Carpathian bellflower for the rock garden or for the front of the border.
Remarks: "Unfortunately Campanula culture is at an low ebb in America today, partly because the plants are less hardy

Campanula persicifolia 'Alba Plena', double white peach-leaf bell-flower, was known in early-nineteenth-century U.S. gardens. Photograph by Marge Garfield.

Seed packets—"Canterbury Bells, Cup and Saucer Mixed" and "Wallflower, Finest Mixed." Inland Seed Co., Spokane, Washington, ca. 1928.

Campanula rotundifolia. Harebell, blue bells. Long cultivated. M'Mahon, Philadelphia, 1804.

Campanula trachelium. Nettle-leaved bellflower, Our Lady's glove. Intro: 1578. Spurrier, 1793. Alice Coats (1956) noted that in the old English literature, this plant was called Canterbury bells, as was the *Campanula medium.*

Campanula medium

Canterbury bells, cups and saucers, hose-in-hose
Campanulaceae
Exotic
Introduction: 1597
Earliest American citation: Townley, Boston, 1760
Description: Two to three-foot biennial with single or double flowers in blue, white, purple, rose, and lilac. The earliest forms were single and blue or white. The double-flowered varieties were either "cup-and-saucer" or "hose-in-hose."
Design notes: Ann Leighton (1986a) reported that Thomas Jefferson grew Canterbury bells in combination with white poppies and African marigolds.
An artistic combination that an article in *The Garden Magazine* described in 1905 included blue, white, and purple larkspurs, Canterbury bells in lavender and white, with *Lilium elegans*, "just a touch to spice up the whole" (Artistic color combinations 1905).
Mrs. Frances King (1915) suggested combining pink *Campanula medium* with lamb's ears and a delicate rosy pink annual poppy with "the white mist of gypsophila."
Remarks: "Flowers have friendships and antipathies ... how Canterbury bells and Foxgloves love to grow side by side" (Earle 1901).

here, and also because rock-gardens and amateur's collections are less frequent than in England" (Wilhelm Miller, in Bailey 1906a).
Heirloom varieties:
f. *alba* (syn. 'Alba'). White Carpathian bellflower. Ellwanger & Barry, New York, 1860.
var. *turbinata* 'Isabel'. Michell, Philadelphia, 1931. Rose.
'White Star'. Michell, Philadelphia, 1931.
Historic commercial sources: 59
Related species:
Campanula persicifolia. Peach-leaf bellflower, peach bells. Intro: 1596. M'Mahon, 1806. Available in double and single forms, white, blue, and later a shade of lavender.
Heirloom varieties available today:
'Alba Plena'. Intro: 1596. Buist, 1839.
'Caerulea'. Bloomington Nursery, Illinois, 1859.
'Moerheimii'. New England Nurseries, Massachusetts, 1910.
'Telham Beauty'. Horsford, Vermont, 1931.

Heirloom variety:

'Calycanthema'. Intro: by 1889. Bailey, 1906. "The Cup-and-Saucer Canterbury Bell is another lauded development far inferior to the normal type" (Wilder 1918).

Historic commercial sources: 101

Campanula pyramidalis

chimney bellflower

Campanulaceae

Exotic

Introduction: 1596

Earliest American citation: M'Mahon, 1806

Zone: 7

Description: Biennial. "This is a great ornament, when cultivated in perfection, forming a pyramid four to six feet high, producing innumerable flowers [blue or white] for two or three months, if shaded from the sun" (Breck 1858).

Design notes: Mrs. Francis King (1915) wrote of interplanting chimney bellflowers among her Oriental poppies to fill in with late summer blue and white blooms after the poppies are gone.

Remarks: In spite of its tall size, gardeners often cultivated the chimney bellflower in pots. Joseph Breck considered this an old-fashioned flower, even in 1858.

Historic commercial sources: 59

Centranthus ruber

garden heliotrope, red valerian, Jupiter's beard

Synonym: *Valeriana rubra*

Valerianaceae

Exotic

Introduction: Long cultivated

Earliest American citation: M'Mahon, 1806

Zone: 5–8

Description: Red valerian "forms numerous flower stalks densely covered with smooth green leaves and clusters of airy flowers almost continually. One of the easiest perennials to grow and will run wild in the garden if neglected. We have white and rose-red varieties" (Howard, Los Angeles, 1937).

Design notes: "Good for cutting. Attractive border plant found frequently in old gardens" (Sedgwick 1907).

Remarks: "The name Jupiter's Beard serves to emphasize a peculiar development of the calyx of all the Valerians. Before the corolla falls the calyx is represented by a mere thickened margin to the ovary, but as the fruit matures this unrolls and shows itself to be a whorl of feathery ap-

The old-fashioned *Valeriana officinalis* has an overpowering, intensely sweet fragrance that people love to hate. Photograph by author.

pendages. Apparently this is a very large name for a very small thing" (Keeler 1910).

Historic commercial sources: 56

Related species:

Valeriana officinalis. Common valerian. Long cultivated. Spurrier, 1793. In the old literature, the name "valerian" could refer to *Centranthus ruber* or to this old-fashioned herb said to have a "most delicious odour like vanilla" (Ely 1903). One artistic combination for valerian was to plant it with a purple perennial *Campanula* and *Cerastium tomentosum* (King 1925).

For regional invasiveness concerns regarding common valerian, see Appendix D.

Chrysanthemum

Chinese chrysanthemum, winter pink, goldblume, October pink, garden chrysanthemum

Synonyms: *Chrysanthemum hortorum, Dendranthema ×grandiflorum*

Asteraceae

Exotic

Introduction: 1688

Earliest American citation: John Bartram, ca. 1735 (possibly a reference to pyrethrum or feverfew)

Zone: 4

Description: The chrysanthemums of the nineteenth century are thought to have been the offspring of *C. morifolium* × *C. indicum*. They came in many shapes and colors. One 1846 list described blooms in shades of purple, blush, buff, various tints of rose and pink, red, and yellow. The following classification of *Chrysanthemum* is from Laurie and Kiplinger, 1947:

This semi-double purple mum is known to predate the 1940s.

Convallaria majalis 'Albostriata' was a collector's plant even in the nineteenth century. Photograph by author.

(Current classifications include thirteen forms.)

Incurved—"The flowers are of globular form and regular outline. The (ray) florets are broad, smooth, rounded at tips and regularly arranged."

Japanese—"Florets may be flat, fluted, quilled, or tubular of varying length." This type has great variation.

Japanese Incurved—"Distinguished by incurving florets, broad and grooved."

Hairy—"Flowers covered with short, globular hairs on the reverse side of the florets."

Reflexed—"Flowers . . . circular in outline, full at center, globular, with broad overlapping florets."

Large Anemone—Flowers are large with neat centers and uniformly arranged flat ray florets. The disc florets are quilled. This and the large pompons were developed in the United States by Elmer Smith around the beginning of the twentieth century. The other forms allegedly were developed in the Orient.

Japanese Anemone—"Ray florets vary in length, breadth and arrangement. They may be narrow and twisted, broad and curled, or drooping to form a fringe."

Pompons—Both foliage and flowers are diminutive and flowers are either flat or globular. Pompons may be classified as large, intermediate, or button forms.

Singles—"Should not have more than a row of ray florets arranged sufficiently close together to form a dense fringe."

Spidery, Plumed, and Feathery—"Flowers of eccentric shape but of a light and graceful character."

Design notes: Used in pots, beds, and borders. Until the middle of the nineteenth century, chrysanthemums were cultivated for the garden. After that time many chrysanthemums were grown in the greenhouse, primarily for autumn display, and others were used as annuals, referred to as "summer chrysanthemums."

"Chrysanthemums look best scattered, for at their time of glory they have the field almost alone" (Warner 1872).

Remarks: "Few plants afford more gratification than a good collection of chrysanthemums" (Hovey 1846).

"The chrysanthemum, next to the rose, is at present the most fashionable flower . . . border or pot plant" (Good & Reese, Ohio, 1889).

Heirloom varieties: Apparently none of the old-timers are still available by name, although some old forms remain, passed down in families and between friends.

Historic commercial sources: 90

Convallaria majalis
lily-of-the-valley, May-flowers, May-lily, valley lilies
Synonym: *Funkia*
Convallariaceae (Liliaceae)
Exotic
Introduction: by 1568
Earliest American citation: John Custis, ca. 1738
Zone: 2–7
Description: This 6–10-in. perennial has dark green, lancelike leaves with fragrant, nodding, white, bell-like flowers in May. Flowers in white, double white, and red (pink) were known by 1829.
Design notes: Lily-of-the-valley was a good choice for shady sites. It was also considered appropriate for the old-fash-

ioned garden. "It succeeds well in the shade in any soil, and soon spreads itself, by its slender creeping roots, beyond the desire of the cultivator" (Breck 1858).

"There are plenty of places where Lily-of-the-Valley would not be suitable but in any position at the entrance to the wild garden, as a transition between the cultivated area and the wild area, it will look well" (Wister 1930).

Remarks: Lily-of-the-valley was a favorite for forcing into winter bloom in nineteenth-century households.

For regional invasiveness concerns regarding *Convallaria majalis*, see Appendix D.

Heirloom varieties:

'Flore Pleno'. Double-flowered lily-of-the-valley. Prince, New York, 1829.

var. *rosea*. Red (pink) lily-of-the-valley. Prince, New York, 1829.

'Variegata' (syn. var. *foliis variegatus*) and 'Albostriata' (syn. *foliis striata*). Gold or white-striped lily-of-the-valley. Prince, New York, 1841.

Historic commercial sources: 98

Coreopsis lanceolata

lance-leaf coreopsis
Asteraceae
Native
Introduction: 1724
Earliest American citation: M'Mahon, Philadelphia, 1804
Zone: 4–9

Description: "A fine species, with lanceolate leaves, producing a profusion of large, rich, yellow flowers, upon long peduncles (flower-stems), which begin to open on June, and give a continual succession until autumn" (Breck 1858). "A showy yellow composite" (Ellwanger 1889).

Design notes: Richardson Wright (1924) recommended planting *Coreopsis lanceolata* with belladonna delphiniums. Coreopsis was also a good flower for the cutting garden and the wild garden.

"Coreopsis lanceolata is a very charming plant for front rows, especially if it can have a place where it is given the benefit of contrast with a white flower, like the Daisy" (Rexford 1912).

Remarks: Some contemporary authorities lump *C. lanceolata* and *C. grandiflora* together. Old-time writers always distinguished between the two.

Historic commercial sources: 57

Related species:

Coreopsis verticillata (syn. *Coreopsis tenuifolia*). Fine leaf coreopsis. Intro: 1759. M'Mahon, Philadelphia 1804. "C. verti-

cillata is a small and pretty species, with delicate foliage and numerous small yellow flowers" (Ellwanger 1889).

Gaillardia ×*grandiflora*. Blanket flower. Trumbull, California, 1873. *G. aristata* × *G. pulchella*.

Cortaderia selloana

pampas grass
Synonym: *Gynereum argentea*
Poaceae
Exotic
Introduction: 1848
Earliest American citation: Hovey, Boston, 1862
Zone: 8

Description: "Foliage long, narrow, drooping; 8 to 10 feet. Not hardy in extreme North. . . . Beautiful white silken plumes in the fall, but in some varieties varying to carmine, violet and purple" (Blanchan 1913).

Design notes: [In San Francisco] "A faint suggestion of semi-tropical flora is preserved by the bunches of Pampas Grass, a yucca, a Palm, a shining East India Rubber Tree, a Tree fern, or less frequently a giant Century Plant" (Oakley 1886).

Pampas grass was ornamental next to a pond or other water feature.

"Pampas grass may be used in informal hedges and screens or in groups with bamboos and other grasses" (Hume 1929).

Remarks: "The Pampas Grass . . . has long been considered the finest of all tall, plumy grasses, as also the most important commercially, of all ornamental grasses. Plumes of Pampas Grass are shipped in large quantities from California to Europe, and are dyed various colors" (Bailey 1906a).

Historic commercial sources: 46

Related species:

Arundo donax var. *versicolor* (syn. 'Variegata'). Striped reed. Prince, New York, 1822. Used for screens in the South.

Miscanthus sinensis 'Gracillimus' (syn. *Eulalia gracillima univittata*). Maiden grass, Japanese rush. Reid, Ohio, 1893. "Effective for small gardens" (Blanchan 1913).

Miscanthus sinensis 'Zebrinus'. Zebra grass. Intro: by 1873. The 1876 *American Agriculturist* declared, "One of the most beautiful of ornamental grasses, is the variegated Eulalia Japonica."

Phalaris arundinacea var. *picta*. Ribbon grass, gardener's garters. William Faris, ca. 1792.

Saccharum ravennae (syn. *Erianthus ravennae*). Ravenna grass, hardy pampas grass. Hovey, Boston, 1862. Ida Bennett (1903) recommended this design for a 9-ft. bed of ornamental grasses to be placed in the lawn: "Large clumps of Arundo Donax in center; First row, three feet out, three

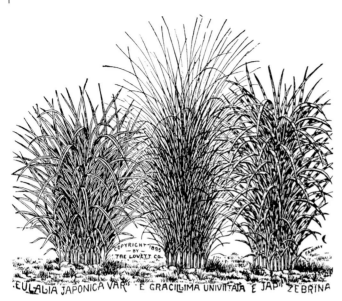

(l–r) *Miscanthus sinensis* 'Variegatus', 'Gracillimus', 'Zebrinus'. Lovett & Co., Little Silver, New Jersey, 1898.

Erianthus Ravennae, six feet apart; second row, twelve Eulalia gracillima univittata, two feet apart. . . . I cannot too highly recommend the planting of ornamental grasses on the lawn."

Several grass species including plants in *Miscanthus*, *Saccharum*, and *Phalaris* are potentially invasive in some areas of the United States. Please refer to Appendix D for specific regional information concerning invasive species.

Delphinium elatum

bee larkspur
Synonyms: *Delphinium alpinum*, *D. intermedium*
Ranunculaceae
Exotic
Introduction: by 1578
Earliest American citation: M'Mahon, 1806
Zone: 2–7
Description: "Numerous flowers marked with violet, in long wands. Finely divided foliage. Two to six feet" (Sedgwick 1907).
Design notes: The bee larkspur was a good plant for the border. "I have never seen Delphiniums poorly placed, they seem to grace every situation as to make inharmony impossible" (Wilder 1918).
Remarks: What is the "bee?" The bee of the delphinium is the visible part of the true petals in the throat of the flower. The ornamental petal-like structures that give the delphinium its appearance are actually sepals.

Bailey (1906a) commented that it was his belief that nearly all the plants sold as *D. elatum* in the United States at the beginning of the twentieth century were actually the native species, *Delphinium exaltatum*.
Historic commercial sources: 58
Related species:
Delphinium formosum. Perennial larkspur. Prince, New York, 1857. This was the old-fashioned deep blue delphinium.

Delphinium grandiflorum

great-flowered larkspur, Chinese delphinium
Synonyms: *Delphinium sinensis*, *D. chinense*
Ranunculaceae
Exotic
Introduction: by 1800
Earliest American citation: M'Mahon, 1806
Zone: 3
Description: Flowers on long spikes in shades of deep indigo blue to white; attractive cut-leaf foliage. "Best of blue flowers for border use" (Blanchan 1913).
Design notes: Delphiniums should be planted near *Lilium candidum*, as the two bloom at the same time (Ely 1903).
"There is no period of the year when the garden is so exuberantly beautiful as that when there are climbing, tumbling, reaching Roses in all directions and spires and spires of Delphiniums gleaming against them or shooting upward like jets of blue flame to touch the fragrant sprays above" (Wilder 1918).
Blue delphiniums were frequently placed near yellow flowers in gardens of the early 1900s. Writers recommended as companions yellow foxglove, yellow meadow rue, evening primrose, or dyer's chamomile. Often pink flowers were added for additional contrast, such as pink hollyhocks, pink lupins, or pale pink roses.
"Plant them at the rear of the borders, and place at the sides and in front some bushy plant of medium height in order to hide their temporary untidiness when cut back after their first period of bloom. . . . *Cleome pungens* or the four o'clock among annuals, are good for the purpose" (Egan 1911).
Remarks: In the early 1900s, gardeners lamented that delphiniums were short-lived because of a blight. *Delphinium grandiflorum* is a parent to the modern hybrid groups with *D. elatum* and *D. belladonna*. In 1926, a *Delphinium* hybridizer in Oregon, Charles E. Barber, produced the first *fragrant* delphiniums.
Heirloom varieties:
'Album'. White Chinese delphinium. Henderson, New York, 1910.

'Blue Butterfly'. Intro: by 1900. Field, Iowa, 1927. Bright blue, short-lived perennial, 1–2 ft. tall.

Blackmore & Langdon hybrids. Intro: 1907. Michell, Philadelphia, 1931.

Wrexham hybrids (syn. Hollyhock Strain). Michell, Philadelphia, 1931. These hybrids were developed ca. 1920 in Wrexham, Wales. The spikes had "unsurpassed stature and substance" and the strain was widely acclaimed, particularly in America (Phillips 1933).

Historic commercial sources: 77

Related species:

Delphinium Belladonna Group (syn. ×*belladonna*). Intro: by 1890. *The Garden Magazine*, 1911.

Mrs. Francis King (1925) recommended combining "Delphinium belladonna with white petunia and sweet alyssum in front, next to sweet alyssum is ageratum, hardy pinks, blue lyme-grass, pink larkspur, and a magenta phlox that looks lovely because of the Delphinium belladonna."

'Cliveden Beauty'. Michell, Philadelphia, 1931. An early, taller belladonna variety of Cambridge blue that is still available.

Delphinium ×*bellamosum*. Storrs & Harrison, Ohio, 1925. Dark blue hybrid between *D. belladonna* and *D. formosum*.

Dianthus barbatus

sweet William, poetic pink, pickery carnation pink, bunch pink, sweet John

Caryophyllaceae

Exotic

Introduction: 1533

Earliest American citation: Townley, Boston, 1760

Zone: 4

Description: *Dianthus barbatus* is a biennial or short-lived perennial with "flowers in dense, flat head, fragrant, various colors, chiefly red or reddish and white and pink" (Blanchan 1913).

Design notes: "They . . . make a beautiful edging for a border, or give great effect when planted in masses" (Ely 1903).

Mrs. Francis King (1915) alternated groups of a dark velvety-red sweet William with *Stokesia laevis* in her garden. "As soon as the fine heads of sweet-william begin to crisp and dry, the beautiful lavender-blue flowers of the Stokesia take up the wondrous tale, and a veil of delicate blue is drawn over the spots which a few days since ran red with a riot of dark loveliness."

Remarks: The William Prince catalog of 1857 offered two pages of named varieties of sweet William, with the observation, "there is no class of flowers which presents a more

Dianthus barbatus, sweet William. *Vick's Floral Guide*, 1899.

brilliant display of varied colors and tints than this. Our collection has commended universal attention."

Rand (1876) summarized the popular attitude toward *Dianthus barbatus*: "As a popular garden flower, the Sweet William takes first rank; it is preeminently a flower for everybody, and none is of easier culture."

Heirloom varieties: The old catalogs listed over seventy-five different varieties of *Dianthus barbatus*. These three are currently available:

'Holborn Glory'. Duckham, New Jersey, 1924.

'Newport Pink' (syn. 'Pink Beauty'). Porter-Walton, Utah, 1926.

'Nigricans'. (Nigrescens Group). O'Keefe, New York, 1870. Brilliant dark red with white anthers.

Historic commercial sources: 135

Dianthus plumarius

pheasant's eye, grass pink, feathered pink, hardy garden pink, clove pink

Synonym: *Dianthus hortensis*

Caryophyllaceae

Exotic

Introduction: 1629

Earliest American citation: Townley, Boston, 1760

Zone: 3–9

Description: "Fragrant fringed flower, originally pink or purplish, the petals fringed for about one-fourth their length" (Blanchan 1913).

Design notes: "Much used in old gardens as edging for beds; double form common" (Keeler 1910).

Dianthus 'Rose de Mai' is a nineteenth-century variety that is rarely found by name in American listings prior to the 1900s. Photograph by author.

Remarks: Many antique *Dianthus plumarius* varieties in the trade today are undocumented in early American horticultural literature. These heirlooms include 'Inchmery', 'Rose de Mai', 'Margaret Curtis', 'Lady Granville', and 'Bat's Double Red', among others. Although it is possible that they were cultivated chiefly in Europe during the nineteenth century, it is more likely that they were distributed among U.S. growers and their customers on the basis of color or fragrance, rather than with a variety name. Barrett's of Boston listed twenty-five different pinks in their 1841 catalog—by description only.

Heirloom varieties:

'Essex Witch'. Storrs & Harrison, Ohio, 1908. Delicate pink, finely fringed.

'Her Majesty'. Ellis, New Hampshire, 1894. Double flowers are a lovely clear white and arranged on long stiff stems. Exquisite clove-scented fragrance.

'Mrs. Sinkins' (syn. 'Mrs. Sinkit'). Intro: 1880. *The Ladies' Floral Cabinet*, 1884. Dwarf plant with a mass of pure white flowers. "A model of perfection."

'Spring Beauty'. Harris, New York, 1934. Double flowers, showy colors.

Historic commercial sources: 77

Related species:

Dianthus deltoides. Maiden pink. Goldthwaite & Moore, Philadelphia, 1796. The selection 'Brilliant' was known in the United States by 1931.

Dianthus superbus. Superb pink. Intro: 1596. Goldthwaite & Moore, Philadelphia, 1796.

Dicentra spectabilis

bleeding heart

Synonyms: *Dielytra spectabilis*, *Fumaria spectabilis*

Fumariaceae

Exotic

Introduction: 1846

Earliest American citation: *The Horticulturist*, July 1854

Zone: 2–9

Description: "Very curious and beautiful, immensely hardy, long in bloom, foliage neat, flowers pendant from arcs or sprays, fine crimson with white, gem-like stamen or border protruding, admirable for forcing, two feet, May, June" (Bloomington Nursery, Illinois, 1868).

"Pink . . . heart-shaped flowers on long, gracefully arching sprays . . . fragile looking, but quite hardy" (Blanchan 1913).

Design notes: Plant bleeding heart in front of a lilac or group of lilacs along with irregular clumps of "pearly" lavender, *Iris germanica*, and groups of the tulip 'Clara Butt'. "The slightly bluish cast of Clara Butt's pink binds the dicentra and the lavender, lilac, and iris to each other and the effect can be deepened by adding a strong lavender tulip" (King 1915).

Remarks: The 1854 *Horticulturist* reported that finest specimen in the United States was at the home of Abijah Reed of Hulberton, New York, who considered this one of the finest hardy herbaceous border plants he had ever seen. "It is a plant for the million. It is adapted for house or garden culture and as easy to grow as the peony, easy to multiply as the dahlia." One English journal had reported a plant that was 5 ft. tall and 30 ft. in circumference (Barry 1854).

The Chinese name for *Dicentra spectabilis* was "Hong pak Moutan Wha," or the "red and white moutan flower" (Parnell 1882a).

Heirloom variety:

'Alba'. "The white-flowered variety has a weak growth and sickly appearance" (Bailey 1906a).

Historic commercial sources: 84

Related species:

Dicentra eximia. Fringed bleeding heart. Intro: 1793 [1812]. William Faris, 1793.

Dicentra formosa (syn. *Corydalis formosa*). California bleeding heart, red-flowered corydalis, wild bleeding-heart. Kenrick, Boston, 1835.

Dictamnus albus var. *purpureus*, gasplant. William Prince in his 1831 catalog exclaimed, "this plant exhales inflammable gas!" Photograph by Marge Garfield.

Dictamnus albus

gas plant, fraxinella, white dittany, burning bush
Rutaceae
Exotic
Introduction: by 1600
Earliest American citation: John Custis, ca. 1741
Zone: 3–9
Description: The foliage of *Dictamnus* resembles that of the ash (*Fraxinus*), thus the name "fraxinella." Flowers are purplish red or white on a 2-ft. plant. George Ellwanger (1889) described the fragrance of *Dictamnus* as suggestive of "anise, sweet-clover, and lavender." To others, it smells lemon-y.
Design notes: Gasplant is "one of the most permanent and beautiful features of the hardy herbaceous border. Instances are known where it has outlived father, son, and grandson

in the same spot" (Bailey 1906a).
Remarks: "Will flash at dusk, on still summer eve, if a lighted match is brought near" (Blanchan 1913).
Heirloom variety:
var. *purpureus* (syn. 'Purpureus', 'Flore Rubra'). Pink gasplant. Goldthwaite & Moore, Philadelphia, 1796.
Historic commercial sources: 75

Digitalis purpurea

foxglove
Scrophulariaceae
Exotic
Introduction: by 1600
Earliest American citation: John Custis, 1737 (white)
Zone: 4–9
Description: Foxglove is a biennial that may self-sow in the border. "Purplish pink, [or] white . . . large, thimble-shaped flowers two inches long, in long spikes on long stems" (Blanchan 1913).
Design notes: Earle (1901) recommended growing sweet Williams with foxgloves. She commented that foxglove was "a plant of dignity and beauty, admirably adapted for shrubberies and woodland walks."
"Foxgloves . . . are the pride of the garden. Plant them back of Sweet Williams, in clumps of six or eight, or else with Peonies" (Ely 1903).
Waugh (1905) said the common foxglove had two uses—the purple-flowered variety was for wild gardens or for borders that had a loose appearance and could deal with the self-sowing nature of the plant. In a refined border, the gloxinia-flowered type was preferred.
Remarks: "We have heard complaints of the foxglove dying out: and there seems to be popular ignorance of the nature of biennial plants. . . . A biennial is only a longer-lived annual; the plant takes more than one season to produce its

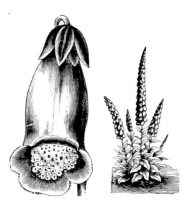

Digitalis purpurea, foxglove. *Vick's Monthly Magazine*, 1882.

Digitalis lutea was sometimes called straw foxglove. Photograph by author.

flower; that done, it ripens seed, and dies" (Rand 1876).
Heirloom varieties:
f. *albiflora* (syn. 'Alba'). White foxglove. John Custis, 1737.
'Gloxiniiflora' (syn. Gloxinioides Group, 'Gloxiniaeflora', 'Gloxinoides'). Hovey, Boston, 1862. A foxglove with a stiffer and more formal habit.
Historic commercial sources: 103
Related species:
Digitalis ferruginea. Rusty foxglove. Intro: 1597. M'Mahon, 1806.
Digitalis grandiflora. (syn. *Digitalis ambigua, D. orientalis, D. aurea*). Great-flowered foxglove. Intro: 1566. Thorburn, New York, 1827. "Ranks next to the common foxglove" (Blanchan 1913).
Digitalis lutea. Yellow foxglove, straw foxglove. Intro: 1620. M'Mahon, 1806.

Dodecatheon meadia

shooting star, American cowslip, pride of Ohio, Indian-chief, bear's ear of Virginia
Synonym: Meadia
Primulaceae
Native
Introduction: 1704
Earliest American citation: Bartram, Philadelphia, 1783
Zone: 4–8
Description: "The root is like the root of the Cowslip, the flower like the Cyclamen. It sends up a flower stem the same as the Cyclamen, but on this stem, instead of one bloom, it sends out six or eight, pure white, with ears thrown back, and bright yellow nose or center.... The first impression on looking at them is that they are laughing at you" (E. S. S. 1878).

Design notes: "The rockery with a northern or eastern aspect suits them to a dot" (Bailey 1906a).
Remarks: Thomas Lea wrote in Cincinnati's *Western Farmer* in 1844, "This beautiful plant is now very rare and will soon be extinct, in a wild state, in this vicinity, being much sought after for gardens." Perhaps the absence of *Dodecatheon* in Ohio and Great Lakes nursery catalogs is explained by this observation—apparently everyone knew to dig it up in the woods.
Heirloom varieties:
The Prince Nursery in 1857 offered the shooting star in white plus four different shades of purple. Bailey (1906a) reported that the 1897 French *Revue Horticole* described twenty-six horticultural varieties of *Dodecatheon*.
Historic commercial sources: 53

Echinacea purpurea

purple coneflower, red sunflower
Synonyms: *Rudbeckia purpurea, Brauneria purpurea*
Asteraceae
Native
Introduction: 1699
Earliest American citation: Bartram, Philadelphia, 1783
Zone: 3–8
Description: "The disk of the flower is very rich, appearing, in the sun, of a golden crimson; the rays are purple, and, in some of the varieties, quite long" (Breck 1851).
Design notes: Useful for the wild garden or for a cutting garden. "*Echinacea purpurea* and *Echinacea angustifolia* are well adapted for grouping in open bays in shrubby borders, as their flowers are extremely durable and seem in harmony with such surroundings" (W. C. Egan, in Bailey 1906a).
Remarks: While the long bloom time was an asset for *Echinacea*, the stiff habit caused some garden designers to shy away from it, at least in the early 1900s.
Historic commercial sources: 66

Erysimum cheiri

wallflower
Synonym: *Cheiranthus cheiri*
Brassicaceae
Exotic
Introduction: by fourteenth century
Earliest American citation: John Winthrop, Jr., 1631
Zone: 3–7
Description: The wallflower is a biennial with yellow, red, orange, or brownish fragrant flowers in spikes 6–12 in. long. "This ornamental plant has been greatly improved in the

Erysimum cheiri, wallflower, has been known in America since the seventeenth century. Photograph by author.

multiplication of its varieties, in its varied colors, and enlargement of its flowers,—single, semi-double, and double; varying from light yellow to orange, and reddish brown to violet" (Breck 1851).

Design notes: Used as edging for spring borders and for bedding schemes. Recommended for the "old-fashioned" garden by writers of the early 1900s.

Remarks: Wallflowers prefer cooler weather and were frequently treated as annuals.

Heirloom variety:

'Bloody Warrior'. Intro: by 1596. French, Virginia, 1799. Double, dark crimson variety

Historic commercial sources: 73

Filipendula vulgaris

dropwort, meadowsweet

Synonyms: *Spiraea filipendula*, *Filipendula hexapetala*

Rosaceae

Exotic

Introduction: Long cultivated

Earliest American citation: M'Mahon, 1806

Zone: 3–8

Description: "A very elegant species, with tuberous roots like the Peony. Flowers white; the buds shaded with pink; in corymbs; two feet high; from June to August. The foliage is beautiful" (Breck 1851).

Design notes: "Of the herbaceous Spiraeas the Filipendula is very desirable for the border or for edging shrubbery. . . . It is [also] very fine for cut flowers, and for forcing in winter" (Bennett 1903).

Remarks: Blanchan (1913) reported that dropwort had naturalized throughout the northeast by the early twentieth century.

Heirloom variety:

'Multiplex' (syn. 'Flore Pleno', 'Plena'). Hovey, Boston, 1834. The double-flowered dropwort is shorter than the species.

Historic commercial sources: 47

Related species:

Filipendula rubra (syn. *Spiraea palmata*, *S. lobata*). Queen-of-the-prairie. Intro: 1765. M'Mahon, Philadelphia, 1804. "Vivid crimson, June to August, 3 ft." (New England Nursery, Massachusetts, 1910).

Filipendula ulmaria (syn. *Ulmaria pentapetala*, *Spiraea ulmaria*). Meadowsweet. Long cultivated. M'Mahon, 1806. "Excellent for wild effects" (Blanchan 1913).

For regional invasiveness concerns regarding *Filipendula ulmaria*, see Appendix D.

Gypsophila paniculata

baby's breath, chalk plant

Caryophyllaceae

Exotic

Introduction: 1759

Earliest American citation: Hovey, Boston, 1862

Zone: 3–9

Description: "Has gray-green delicate foliage that begins to take shape when the Peonies are passing. The plant rounds itself out and, in a few days, a white cloud rests comfortably on the border" (Wright 1924).

Design notes: They "make an excellent effect as filling amongst shrubbery; also good for covering unkempt places with a mass of delicate bloom" (Bailey 1906a).

Outstanding for the middle of the border with a sweet pea as a companion that can cover the baby's breath after its period of bloom is over. Also useful for the cutting garden and "for giving mist-like effects in borders" (Blanchan 1913).

Mrs. Francis King (1915) recommended several companions for *Gypsophila* including the Shasta daisy 'Alaska' and the white *Lilium longiflorum*.

Remarks: The double-flowered baby's breath was valued for its better appearance, but the single varieties flowered for a longer period of time.

Gypsophila paniculata has proved to be invasive in western regions of the United States. Please refer to Appendix D for specific regional information concerning invasive species.

Heirloom varieties:

'Bristol Fairy'. Wagner Park, Ohio, 1905. Strong growing, 3–4 ft., with large panicles of small, white double flowers.

'Apricot' daylily (1893) was the first of many hybrids for the genus *Hemerocallis*. Photograph by John Pike.

Hemerocallis 'Mikado' (1929). Photograph by John Pike.

'Hyperion' daylily has remained a garden favorite for over seventy-five years. Photograph by John Pike.

Hemerocallis 'Mrs. W. H. Wyman' (1929). Photograph by John Pike.

Hemerocallis 'Iris Perry' (1925). Photograph by John Pike.

Hemerocallis fulva 'Rosea' (1924) was the first red daylily used for breeding programs. Photograph by John Pike.

'Snowflake' (syn. 'Schneerflocke'). Park, South Carolina, 1938. Robust plant with small white flowers.

Historic commercial sources: 57

Related species:

Gypsophila repens. Creeping baby's breath. Intro: 1774. Prince, New York, 1829. For the rockery.

Hemerocallis lilioasphodelus

lemon lily, yellow lily, asphodel lily, custard lily, daylily

Synonyms: *Hemerocallis flava, H. formosissima*

Liliaceae

Exotic

Introduction: 1570

Earliest American citation: Spurrier, 1793

Zone: 3–9

Description: The yellow daylily has narrow, grass-like foliage and yellow, fragrant, funnel-shaped flowers.

Design notes: The lemon lily is a "most satisfactory garden plant on account of its early bloom, its beauty, and its ability to live without coddling" (Keeler 1910).

"These Day Lilies (H. flava and H. fulva) are particularly effective used as a base planting for spring-flowering shrubs. Their blossoming does not begin until that of the shrubs is past" (Wilder 1918).

"To make a border of Day Lilies alone is a dream I hope eventually to attain, for here is a flower that, in the individual specimen, has a lovely shape and affords variation of color, and in the mass is very striking" (Wright 1924).

Early gardeners used *Hemerocallis* in the hardy border and along the edges of ponds or in semishady situations. "Surely no more modern flower for our modern-day busy life can be found than the Day Lily" (Lamb, Washington, 1939).

Remarks: In early catalogs, members of the *Funkia* or *Hosta* genus were also called "day lilies."

Heirloom varieties:

Since the breeding of *Hemerocallis* is a dynamic process with new varieties introduced annually, it is not surprising that many of the old varieties are no longer available. By 1940, daylilies were available in shades of yellow, orange, bronze, copper, and maroon. The following heirlooms are currently available:

'Apricot'. Intro: 1893. Farr, Pennsylvania, 1920. The first hybrid daylily, a cross between *H. lilioasphodelus* × *H. middendorffii.*

'Hyperion'. Intro: 1925 US. Lamb, Washington, 1939. Fragrant, yellow favorite. "Generally conceded to be the finest yet introduced."

'Iris Perry'. Intro: 1925. Lamb, Washington, 1939. "Gorgeous

Kniphofia uvaria 'Pfitzeri'. Storrs & Harrison, Painesville, Ohio,

bronzy orange blooms with golden center in late June on 4 ft. branching stalks."

'Mikado'. Intro: 1929 US. Lamb, Washington, 1939. "Rich bright orange with large ruddy purple blotch on each petal."

'Mrs. W. H. Wyman'. Intro: 1929. Lamb, Washington, 1939. "Perfectly rounded flowers of clear gold."

'Ophir'. Intro: 1924 US. Lamb, Washington, 1939. "Delightful golden yellow. Late."

'Orangeman'. Intro: 1906. New England Nurseries, Massachusetts, 1910. Orange-yellow.

'Sovereign'. Intro: 1906. Ellwanger & Barry, New York, 1917. Chrome yellow with brown shading.

Historic commercial sources: 67

Related species:

Hemerocallis dumortieri. Prince, New York, 1857. This orange-gold daylily is the earliest to bloom.

Hemerocallis fulva. Homestead lily, ditch lily, tawny daylily. Intro: 1576. Jean Skipwith, ca.1800. Dr. Arlow Stout named this daylily 'Europa' in 1929. A white-variegated foliage form of the tawny daylily was available by 1826.

Hemerocallis fulva 'Flore Pleno' (syn. 'Kwanso'). Double orange lily, crown daylily, double corn lily. Brighton, Boston, 1841. The name 'Kwanso' appeared in A. Blanc's catalog ca. 1895.

Hemerocallis fulva 'Rosea'. Intro: 1924. A parent of *Hemerocallis* hybrids in shades of red and pink.

Hemerocallis minor (syn. *Hemerocallis graminea*). Prince, New York, 1822. "A splendid dwarf sort with large rich orange blossoms on 8-inch stems. A glorious rock garden subject" (Lamb, Washington, 1939).

Kniphofia uvaria (syn. *Tritoma uvaria*). Torch lily, red hot poker. Intro. 1707. Prince, New York, 1860. 'Pfitzeri' (Wagner Park, Ohio, 1905) featured large, orange-scarlet flowers that bloomed from August till frost.

Hesperis matronalis

rocket, dame's violet, damask violet, sweet rocket
Synonym: *Hesperis fragrans*
Brassicaceae
Exotic
Introduction: by 1562
Earliest American citation: Spurrier, 1793
Zone: 3–8
Description: "A vigorous, hardy herbaceous perennial plant forming clumps 2–3 ft. high, branched from the base, and covered with showy terminal pyramidal spikes of 4-petaled flowers, resembling stocks. The colors range from white through lilac and pink to purple" (Bailey 1906a). Many horticulturists classify *Hesperis matronalis* as a biennial.
Design notes: An old favorite that was appropriate for the hardy border or, in the early 1900s, for the old-fashioned garden. Said to be particularly fragrant at night.
Remarks: Throughout the nineteenth century the common rocket was popular in gardens; however, garden writers recommended the double-flowered rocket, which had been known since the sixteenth century in England, to be superior to the single.

Hesperis matronalis has proved to be invasive in some areas of the United States. Please refer to Appendix D for specific regional information concerning invasive species.
Heirloom varieties:
var. *albiflora*. Single white rocket. Intro: 1759. Hovey, Boston, 1834.
'Alba Plena'. Double white rocket. Intro: 1597. M'Mahon, 1806.
'Lilacena Flore Plena' (syn. 'Purpureo Plena'). Double purple rocket. Intro: 1597. M'Mahon, 1806.
Historic commercial sources: 72
Related species:
Lunaria annua (syn. *Lunaria biennis*). Honesty, moonseed, moonwort. Intro: 1595. Josselyn, 1672. Despite its name, this plant is considered to be a biennial. "It is a most interesting thing to grow because of its beautiful oval seedvalves, made apparently of mother-of-pearl, set like an eye-glass in a delicate but firm rim" (Mrs. Hattie Knight, in Bailey 1903). For regional invasiveness concerns regarding *Lunaria annua*, see Appendix D.

Hibiscus moscheutos

mallow, musk-smelling hibiscus, marsh mallow, swamp rose mallow, wild cotton
Malvaceae
Native
Introduction: by 1783
Earliest American citation: Bartram, Philadelphia, 1783
Zone: 4–9
Description: "Rose or white . . . 3 to 7 feet. For swamps and brackish marshes. Large, expanded flower, four inches across, sometimes with crimson eye" (Blanchan 1913).
Design notes: Good for wet places, and for the wild garden or hardy border. "When a handsome plant of large dimensions is needed an occasional hibiscus is very striking when the bed is broad enough to permit its use. In colony plantings it makes a gorgeous display" (Cloud 1927).
Remarks: Liberty H. Bailey (1906a) mentioned that sometimes these plants are set in large pots in the spring. "They then make excellent specimens."
Heirloom varieties:
subsp. *palustris* (syn. *Hibiscus palustris*). Marsh hibiscus, sea hollyhock. Intro: 1759. M'Mahon, Philadelphia, 1804. Three-lobed foliage, pink flower. "Well-adapted for planting in the shrubbery" (Breck 1858).

Hesperis matronalis, dame's rocket. James Vick, Rochester, New York, 1873.

'Crimson Eye'. William Bassett & Son introduced 'Crimson Eye' from a New Jersey swamp in 1894. The flowers are clear white with a crimson center.

'Mallow Marvels'. Storrs & Harrison, Ohio, 1925. "A giant race derived from the common native Hibiscus, which has elevated this type almost to the dignity of shrubs. Massed in great groups or generously interspersed among shrubs, these 'Marvels' grow very rapidly, sometimes getting up to 8 to 10 ft. in height—various shades red, pink, crimson, and white."

Historic commercial sources: 44

Related species:

Hibiscus militaris. Halbert-leaved hibiscus. Intro: by 1783 [1804]. Bartram, Philadelphia, 1783. Large white flowers with a red center.

Hibiscus trionum. Flower-of-the-hour, bladder ketmia. Intro: by 1597. M'Mahon, 1806. Bladder ketmia has proved to be invasive in some areas of the United States. Please refer to Appendix D for specific regional information concerning invasive species.

Hosta plantaginea

fragrant plantain lily, hosta, white day lily, Japan lily, funkia

Synonyms: *Funkia japonica, F. alba, F. grandiflora, F. subcordata, Hemerocallis japonica*

Liliaceae

Exotic

Introduction: by 1784

Earliest American citation: Landreth, Philadelphia, 1828

Zone: 3–8

Description: The white day lily has "large, pure white, fragrant flowers, which open daily in the month of August, on stems one and a half to two feet high; leaves broad ovate, nerved" (Breck 1858).

Design notes: "The old-fashioned Plantain or Day Lily is one of the finest hardy plants for isolated groups on the lawn" (Henderson 1901).

"Funkias are hardy and of the easiest culture. Their dense stools or clumps of foliage are in place along walks or drives and in the angles against buildings. A continuous row along a walk gives a strong and pleasant character" (Bailey 1906a).

Remarks: "The common daylily of old yards" (Keeler 1910).

An 1883 West Virginia correspondent to *Vick's Monthly Magazine* preferred these "white day lilies" to all other lilies as they are "so pure and daintily sweet" (Darling 1883).

Historic commercial sources: 62

Hosta ventricosa

blue day lily, blue hemerocallis

Synonyms: *Funkia caerulea, F. ovata, Hemerocallis caerulea*

Liliaceae

Exotic

Introduced: 1790

Earliest American citation: Landreth, Philadelphia, 1811

Zone: 3–8

Description: "Blue day lily, is a plant with broad ovate leaves; flowers blue, in June and July; two feet high" (Breck 1858).

Design notes: "Too often associated with the foundation borders of suburban homes, the Funkia is apt to be neglected by gardeners in the country; yet it has its varieties that are both beautiful and useful—useful in that they thrive in shade, beautiful for the greenery or variegation of the foliage and the tall spikes of white and purple bell flowers" (Wright 1924).

Remarks: "From their neat habit and showy flowers these plants should be generally cultivated. . . . If the spikes are cut when the lowest flower is just opening, and placed in the parlor in water, every flower will expand day after day; they are thus desirable for cut flowers" (Rand 1876).

Historic commercial sources: 59

Related species:

Hosta lancifolia. Lance-leaved hosta. Intro: 1829. Cleveland Nursery, Ohio, 1845.

Hosta sieboldiana. Siebold's funkia. Intro: 1829. Downing, 1844. The cultivar 'Frances Williams' originated in Bristol, Connecticut, in 1936.

H. undulata var. *albomarginata* (syn. 'Thomas Hogg'). Intro: ca. 1880. Thomas Hogg of New York introduced this hosta directly into American gardens, bypassing the usual European route.

Iberis sempervirens

evergreen candytuft, edging candytuft

Brassicaceae

Exotic

Introduction: 1739

Earliest American citation: Townley, Boston, 1760, "candy tuff" (possibly the annual)

Zone: 3–9

Description: "The perennial Candytufts . . . form low spreading plants with dense and dark green foliage, and are covered the last of May and first of June with compact bunches of flowers [white or pink] an inch or more in diameter" (Manning 1886).

Design notes: Designers recommended the perennial candytuft for use in Victorian bedding schemes because of its short, uniform habit and bright flowers.

Candytuft is "adapted to the front of shrubberies, where they connect taller plants with the surrounding lawn ... may mingle with other genera in the herbaceous border ... and hang well over walls and ledges" (A. Wyman, in Bailey 1906a).

"The ideal home for it is in the rock garden where its rambling habit will receive no check; when used as a border plant or for edging, constant pruning is necessary to keep it within bounds" (Cloud 1927).

Remarks: Besides its landscape uses, candytuft was easily forced into winter bloom and it was grown indoors in containers.

Heirloom varieties: Bailey (1906a) noted that a double form of *Iberis sempervirens* was cultivated at the beginning of the twentieth century, but considered it less desirable than the single-flowered species.

Historic commercial sources: 52

Iris ensata

Japanese iris, sword-leaved iris

Synonym: *Iris kaempferi*

Iridaceae

Exotic

Introduction: 1857

Earliest American citation: Moon, Pennsylvania, 1870

Zone: 4–9

Description: "The great floppy petals of the singles are in accord with the languor of the season, and the broad doubles, on slim stalks in ranked file, are superb offerings carried aloft in the procession celebrating summer." The flower colors range from "the blues and violets of fine porcelain ... lilac-pinks that image treasured remnants from the cupboards of our grandmothers . . . cool, clear whites and whites of softest ivory marked with gold ... pale clarets and deep wines. . . . There are sometimes delicately lined and misted flowers of great beauty and some of lively vivacity" (McKinney 1927).

Design notes: The Japanese iris was primarily a collector's plant, useful in the border and, at the end of the nineteenth century, in fashionable Japanese-style gardens.

Remarks: Early gardeners recognized that Japanese iris required extensive watering for the best bloom. "I hear that in Japan they actually flush water over the entire iris field just before flowering time, treating them almost as they do rice, but of course we can't emulate this" (Rion 1912).

A young woman admires her irises, ca. 1930.

The vibrant colors of *Iris ensata*, Japanese iris, have excited American gardeners for decades. John Lewis Childs, Floral Park, New York, 1894.

Heirloom varieties:

'Eleanor Parry'. Fremont, Ohio, 1932. Double, claret red, flamed with white and blue.

'Gold Bound'. Intro: ca. 1895. Storrs & Harrison, Ohio, 1896. Large, pure white with gold-rayed center.

'Manadzuru'. New England Nurseries, Massachusetts, 1910. White, veined with blue.

'Mount Hood'. Storrs & Harrison, Ohio, 1896. Deep purplish violet, yellow center.

'Queen of the Blues'. Fremont, Ohio, 1932. Double, delft blue, veined white.

'Waria Hotei'. Intro: by 1900. Fremont, Ohio, 1932. "Flowers are extra large, six-petaled, lavender blue with primrose blotches, surrounded by a light blue halo and radiating into dark blue veins. Stigmas dark blue. Late flowering."

'Yezo-nishiki'. New England Nurseries, Massachusetts, 1910. Velvety dark red; center purple.

Historic commercial sources: 37

Iris germanica
fleur de lis, bearded iris, rainbow flower, flag
Synonym: *Iris violacea*
Iridaceae
Exotic
Introduction: 1000 B.C.E.
Earliest American citation: Josselyn, 1672
Zone: 3–10

Description: "The flowers of all the varieties are large and handsome, often stately, exhibiting beautiful variegation and shades of color. They are borne on stout, erect, branched stalks much exceeding the clumps of spreading leaves. All are hardy, and form excellent border plants, flowering in May and June" (Bailey 1906a).

Design notes: Bearded iris selections made perfect companions for the plants included in the fashionable, color-conscious borders of the early twentieth century. Mrs. Frances King (1915) raved about the following combination: "masses of . . . wonderful pinkish-mauve Iris pallida var. dalmatica Queen of May, tall lupines of rich blue, with Iris Madame Chereau back of this, while before the group . . . the luscious silken salmon-pink flowers of two Oriental poppies . . . [and] below these, coral bells of Heuchera."

"The true garden lover succumbs to Iris by these gradual steps—first a few in the perennial border, then an Iris-lined bank or wall, then an Iris garden. If he is wise, he will not permit the Iris in a border to exceed one-fifth of the total area" (Wright 1924).

Iris germanica 'Florentina', orris root, has been known in America since colonial days. Photograph by the author.

Ella McKinney devoted an entire book to cultivating iris in the "Little Garden" series (1927) and noted these successful combinations:

Iris 'Florentina' beneath a Bechtel's flowering crab with [rose-pink] tulip 'Pride of Haarlem'.

Iris 'Quaker Lady' [lavender and gold] with dark red pyrethrums.

A pale rose or light violet bearded iris with pale yellow lupines.

Remarks: *Iris* was sometimes known as the "poor man's orchid."

Several species of *Iris* have proved to be invasive in western areas of the United States. Refer to Appendix D for specific regional information concerning invasive species.

Heirloom varieties:

'Amas'. Intro: 1885. Biltmore, North Carolina, 1907. Inner segments sky blue, the outer segments deep violet.

The fragrant *Iris* 'Missouri' was a Dykes Award winner in 1937. Robert Wayman, Bayside, New York, 1938.

Iris 'Honorabile' is a charming relic of the past. Photograph by author.

'Caterina'. Intro: 1909. State Nursery, Montana, 1923. Standards: clear blue; falls: soft lilac.

'Flavescens'. Intro: 1813. Kenrick, Boston, 1835. Light primrose yellow.

'Florentina' (syn. var. *florentina*). Orris root. Long cultivated. Brickell, 1737. Outer segments tinged with lavender, inner are white.

'Honorabile'. Intro: 1840. Wagner Park, Ohio, 1905. Standards: bright Indian-yellow; falls: chestnut-red.

'Lent A. Williamson'. Intro: 1918. Storrs & Harrison, Ohio, 1925. Standards: blue-violet; falls: royal purple with yellow beard.

'Madame Chereau'. Intro: 1844. Buist, Philadelphia, 1866. Standards and falls: white-edged and feathered with violet and pale blue. "Among the best of the so-called German irises" (Blanchan 1913).

'Mildred Presby'. Intro: 1923 US. Lovely duet of purple and pure white.

'Missouri'. Intro: 1933. Very fragrant. A large flower of true deep blue coloring and perfect form, with flaring velvety falls and good substance. Dykes Award winner, 1937.

'Quaker Lady'. Intro: 1909 US. Standards: smoky lavender; falls: blue and bronzy gold.

'Seminole'. Intro: 1920. Standards: dark violet-rose; falls: rich velvety crimson.

'Sweet Lavender'. Intro: 1919. Horsford, Vermont, 1931. Standards: pale lavender; falls: pinkish lavender.

Historic commercial sources: 81

Related species:

Iris cristata. Crested iris. Intro: 1756. M'Mahon, 1806. "Exquisite for edging" (Blanchan 1913).

Iris pallida. Dalmatian iris, pale Turkey iris. Intro: by 1600. Bloodgood, New York, 1819. One of the parents of the modern hybrid irises.

Iris pseudacorus. Yellow flag, fleur-de-lis. Long cultivated. Thomas Jefferson, 1767.

Iris pumila. Dwarf iris. Intro: 1596. M'Mahon, 1806.

Iris sibirica. Siberian iris. Intro: 1596. M'Mahon, 1806. "Veritable fountains of grace" (Wilder 1918).

'Caesar'. Intro: 1930. Lamb, Washington, 1939. "Fine delicate violet with deeper markings."

'Caesar's Brother'. Intro: ca. 1930. Lamb, Washington, 1939. "A rich glossy black-purple of perfect form."

'Perry's Blue'. Intro: 1916. Horsford, Vermont, 1931. Clear turquoise blue and white.

'Snow Queen'. Intro: ca. 1900. New England Nurseries, Massachusetts, 1910. Pure white. "Masses of pure white Siberian Irises with their delicate poised blossoms are particularly beautiful following the shore of lake or stream with a background of good green shrubbery" (Wilder 1918).

Leucanthemum ×superbum

Shasta daisy, moonpenny daisy

Synonyms: *Chrysanthemum maximum*, *Leucanthemum maximum*

Asteraceae

Exotic

Introduction: Luther Burbank, Santa Rosa, California, 1890

Zone: 5–9

Description: "Very closely resembling the ox-eye daisy, its parent, but larger and more floriferous. Flowers all season, but does not succeed anywhere in the East" (Blanchan 1913).

Design notes: "These fill in after the Peonies and Irises have gone, and before the late Phlox appears" (Wright 1924). For the middle of the border, Shasta daisy 'Alaska' combines well with double baby's breath (King 1915). Also recommended for massing in the garden.

Remarks: *Leucanthemum maximum* × *L. lacustre* = Shasta daisy

Heirloom varieties:

'Alaska'. Santa Rosa Nursery, California, 1904. Large, white, single flowers with golden center.

'King Edward'. New England Nurseries, Massachusetts, 1910. White flowers.

Historic commercial sources: 43

Liatris spicata

gayfeather, long-spiked liatris, blazing star, devil's bit

Synonyms: *Liatris macrostachya*, *L. pilosa*, *Laciniaria*

Asteraceae

Native

Introduction: 1732

Earliest American citation: M'Mahon, Philadelphia, 1804

Zone: 3–9

Description: "Strange flowers these, a club covered with tiny blossoms" (Wright 1924). The flowers of *Liatris* came in purple or white.

Design notes: "Best adapted to the wild-flower border." *Liatris* should be massed in the garden (Bailey 1906a).

"[Gayfeathers] grown in groups behind Lyme Grass or Rue and mingled with clumps of white Moon Daisies are very effective" (Wilder 1918).

Remarks: Although a surprisingly large number of early catalogs offered *Liatris*, the garden literature did not support interest in cultivating this American native. Few writers discussed or described this plant.

Historic commercial sources: 46

Related species:

Liatris pycnostachya. Button snakeroot. Intro: 1732. Prince, New York, 1844.

Liatris scariosa. Blue blazing star, button snakeroot. Intro: 1739. Bartram, Philadelphia, 1807.

Linum perenne

perennial flax, Austrian flax

Synonym: *Linum sibiricum*

Linaceae

Exotic

Introduction: Sixteenth century

Earliest American citation: Goldthwaite & Moore, Philadelphia, 1796

Zone: 5–8

Description: Flowers are sky blue, 1-in. across, atop delicate-looking medium green foliage.

Design notes: Appropriate for the front to middle of the hardy border or for the wild garden.

Linum perenne, perennial flax. James Vick, Rochester, New York, 1873.

The bright red of the native cardinal flower provides a pleasing contrast with the golden *Solidago*. Photograph by author.

Remarks: Thomas Meehan (1878) said this was a native plant and cited a Colorado flora as proof. He most likely was referring to the western indigenous *Linum perenne* subsp. *lewisii*, (prairie flax). He also observed that "Dr. Gray thinks the American Perennial Flax . . . may . . . be a distinct species."

Heirloom variety:

'Album'. White perennial flax. O'Keefe, New York, 1870.

Historic commercial sources: 65

Related species:

Linum narbonense. Narbonne flax. Intro: 1759. O'Keefe, New York, 1870.

Lobelia cardinalis

cardinal flower, Indian pink

Campanulaceae

Native

Introduction: 1629

Earliest American citation: Bartram, Philadelphia, 1783

Zone: 3–9

Description: "A splendid native plant. . . . It has an erect stem, two to three feet high, with broad lanceolate, serrate leaves; [scarlet] flowers in terminal spikes pointing one way" (Breck 1858).

Design notes: Breck asserted that the cardinal flower would grow quite nicely in dry sites as well as in conditions resembling its native marshes.

Remarks: Liberty H. Bailey wrote in his *Cyclopedia* (1906), "One of the most showy of all native flowers, and worthy of cultivation in any moist border. It has been long in cultivation."

Heirloom varieties:

The 1831 Prince catalog featured both the red- and white-flowering varieties with the white selling for the exorbitant price of $3.00.

Lobelia New Hybrids. This 1937 seed strain from Paul Howard of Los Angeles embraced various vivid shades of crimson, cerise, carmine, purple, deep lilac, and mauve.

Historic commercial sources: 92

Related species:

Lobelia fulgens 'Queen Victoria' (syn. Lobelia ×*speciosa* 'Queen Victoria'). O'Keefe, Son & Co. of Rochester, New York, announced 'Queen Victoria' as a "new" hybrid in 1870. Originally thought to be the offspring of *L. cardinalis* × *L. siphilitica* × *L. fulgens*, current nomenclature assigns 'Queen Victoria' to *Lobelia fulgens* alone. Gardeners prized this variety for it large scarlet flowers and dark reddish foliage.

Lobelia siphilitica (syn. *Lobelia caerulea*). Blue cardinal flower, great lobelia. Intro: 1665. Bartram, Philadelphia, 1783. This stately, blue-flowered native plant was frequently offered at New England and Middle Atlantic nurseries, particularly between 1825 and 1875.

Lupinus polyphyllus

hardy lupin, lupine

Fabaceae

Native

Introduction: 1826

Earliest American citation: Hovey, Boston, 1834

Zone: 3–6

Description: "The flowers are disposed in long terminal clusters, of a beautiful azure blue, with a reddish border, forming a kind of whorls, very near each other around the stem. The leaves are composed of from twelve to fifteen green, lanceolate leaflets, hairy on the underside. The flowers resemble those of the Blue Sophora but far more elegant" (Breck 1858).

By 1934 lupine hybrids embraced vivid shades of crimson, cerise, carmine, purple, deep lilac, and mauve.

Design notes: At home in the wild garden, lupines also made good companion plants for German iris selections in the border.

Remarks: "This flower has become quite 'smart' of late" (Wright 1924).

Heirloom variety:

'Alba'. White perennial lupin. McIntosh, Ohio, 1845.

Historic commercial sources: 48

Related species:

Lupinus perennis. Lupine, sun-dial. Intro: 1658. M'Mahon, 1804.

Lychnis chalcedonica, scarlet Maltese cross, "glows in the border." Photograph by author.

Lychnis coronaria 'Alba', white rose campion. Photograph by author.

Lychnis chalcedonica

Maltese cross, ragged robin, London pride, burning star, Jerusalem cross, scarlet lightning

Caryophyllaceae

Exotic

Introduction: by 1578

Earliest American citation: Goldthwaite & Moore, Philadelphia, 1796

Zone: 3–9

Description: "The flowers are usually brick-red to scarlet. . . . The arrangement of the petal-limbs suggests the Maltese cross, hence one of the common names" (Bailey 1906a).

Design notes: "One of the most splendid decorations of the border is the Double Scarlet Lychnis" (Breck 1851). Early-twentieth-century gardeners recommended *Lychnis* for the border or cutting garden.

"I am extremely fond of the very dark red Sweet William with blackish stems, and it is a splendid balance for high-pitched scarlet Geums and for Lychnis chalcedonica" (Wilder 1918).

Lychnis chalcedonica, Maltese cross. *Vick's Monthly Magazine*, February, 1882.

Remarks: "A lover of the sun, it glows in the border on a hot summer day with an air of contentment and satisfaction, and often rises head and shoulders above its neighbors. The typical color is scarlet or brick-red, but there are varieties with rose-colored, flesh-colored, and white blossoms, also with double flowers" (Keeler 1910).

Heirloom varieties:

var. *albiflora* ('Alba'). White lychnis. Sayers, 1839. A double white variety was also available.

'Flore Pleno'. Double scarlet lychnis. Bloodgood, New York, 1819.

Historic commercial sources: 123

Related species:

Lychnis ×haageana. Ellwanger & Barry, New York, 1848. *L. fulgens × L. coronata* produces "large clusters of orange-red, scarlet, or crimson flowers . . . very desirable" (Bailey 1906a).

Lychnis coronaria

rose campion, mullein pink, dusty miller

Synonyms: *Agrostemma coronaria*, *Campion rosea alba*

Caryophyllaceae

Exotic

Introduction: 1596

Earliest American citation: Thomas Jefferson, 1767

Zone: 4–8

Description: Perennial with "hoary foliage, forked style of growth, and splendid solitary flowers" in pink or white (Keeler 1910). "The mullein pink in bloom is an effect in grey and crimson. . . . There are three forms of this plant in cultivation: the single red, the single white, and the double red" (Keeler 1910).

Design notes: "Mullein Pink (Lychnis Coronaria) is splendid with the gray leafage and lilac flower spikes of Nepeta Mussini, or shining through a haze of Gypsophila with a background of creamy Mulleins" (Wilder 1918).

"Rose campion was beloved of our grandmothers and, despite its magenta, should find a corner in the garden today" (Wright 1924).

Neltje Blanchan (1913) found rose campion to be a good perennial for bedding.

Remarks: "The glowing flowers and white foliage make it a conspicuous plant" (Bailey 1906a).

Heirloom variety:

'Alba'. White campion. Prince, New York, 1845. Louise Beebe Wilder (1918) described the white campion to be "fine but far less beautiful" than the magenta variety.

Historic commercial sources: 64

Lychnis flos-cuculi

ragged robin, meadow lychnis, London pride
Synonym: *Agrostemma flos-cuculi*
Caryophyllaceae
Exotic
Introduction: by Elizabethan period
Earliest American citation: M'Mahon, 1806
Zone: 4–8
Description: "Double red or rosy flowers, the petals cut in four stripes. Perennial. Blooming all summer; 1 to 2 feet" (Blanchan 1913).
Design notes: "An old inhabitant of the flower garden" (Breck 1858).
Remarks: "Common in old gardens and also naturalized in parts of the eastern country. The double form (red or white) is prized for its close-packed, fimbriate flowers. An old-time and deserving favorite blooming profusely and for most of the season" (Bailey 1906a).
For regional invasiveness concerns regarding *Lychnis flos-cuculi*, see Appendix D.
Heirloom variety:
'Plena'. M'Mahon, 1806. The double ragged robin was available in both red and white forms.
Historic commercial sources: 45

Monarda didyma

Oswego tea, red balm, bergamot, scarlet sage, sweet Mary
Lamiaceae
Native
Introduction: 1744
Earliest American citation: Bartram, Philadelphia, 1783

Zone: 4–9
Description: "The leaves possess a strong mint-like odor, and the dark red of its flowers is striking" (Ellwanger 1889).
Design notes: A good plant for the wild border or shrubbery. "When it is used in the border, dispose it carefully, for it increases at great speed, and is apt to choke out less avaricious things" (Wright 1924).
Remarks: Many Middle Atlantic firms like Thorburn, Landreth, Prince, Albany Nursery, and Buist promoted this showy native perennial.
Heirloom variety:
'Cambridge Scarlet'. Ellwanger & Barry, New York, 1917. Brilliant crimson scarlet.
Historic commercial sources: 58
Related species:
Monarda fistulosa. Purple bee balm. Intro: 1656. M'Mahon, Philadelphia, 1804. This plant did not show up on any early commercial lists west of the Mississippi.

Myosotis palustris
Myosotis scorpioides
Myosotis sylvatica

forget-me-not
Boraginaceae
Exotic
Introduction: by 1817
Earliest American citation: Breck, 1851
Zone: 3–8
Description: "The flowers are blue, with yellow eye, and in most places are produced all summer, and ripen abundance of seed" (Forget-me-nots 1867).
Design notes: "The best all-purpose hardy plant of its color for feathery and foreground effects" (Blanchan 1913).

"Forget-me-nots are invaluable in a dozen different situations—mixed with Arabis for an edging, mixed with Alyssum saxatile and Iberis, as a ground cover for flowering bulbs, on top of a wall, in cracks of the rock pavement, and

Myosotis spp., James Vick, Rochester, New York, 1881.

to take the curse of bareness off the soil of the Rose garden" (Wright 1924).

Remarks: Forget-me-nots had escaped gardens and naturalized in the eastern states by the beginning of the twentieth century. Bailey (1906a) remarked that *Myosotis sylvatica* was "common in cultivation"; however, it appeared in only one of the more than 275 catalogs. It seems that several *Myosotis* species were in early cultivation in the United States and that the names were interchanged, including *M. palustris*, *M. scorpioides*, *M. sylvatica*, *M. dissitiflora*, and *M. alpestris*. According to *Hortus Third*, these last two names were frequently used for *Myosotis sylvatica* and other writers have noted that *Myosotis palustris* was often used for *M. scorpioides*.

For regional invasiveness concerns regarding *Myosotis scorpioides*, see Appendix D.

Historic commercial sources: 86

Oenothera macrocarpa

Ozark sundrops
Synonym: *Oenothera missouriensis*
Onagraceae
Native
Introduction: 1811
Earliest American citation: Buist, 1839
Zone: 3–7
Description: "This showy species . . . producing in succession through the summer, numerous large yellow flowers, four or five inches in diameter" (Breck 1858).
Design notes: Sundrops provided a "glowing display of yellow" in the hardy border or the wild garden (Bailey 1906a).
Remarks: "Though an American plant, it is very seldom to be found in our collections, while the inferior species are seen in every garden" (An Amateur [Hogg] 1847a). The genus *Oenothera* is divided into the evening flowering plants (evening primroses) and the day bloomers (sundrops).
Historic commercial sources: 44
Related species:
Oenothera biennis var. *grandiflora* (syn. *Oenothera lamarckiana*). Large flowering evening primrose. Hovey, Boston, 1862. "One of the most showy flowers, large, yellow, half shrubby habit, beautiful" (Wendel, Boston, 1867). "It is the fairest thing at night-fall, and in the moonlight, and until the sun gets hot next day" (Warner 1872).
Oenothera fruticosa subsp. *glauca* (syn. *Oenothera youngii*, *O. frazerii*, *O. fraserii*, *O. glauca fraserii*). Sundrops. Intro: 1811. Prince, New York, 1818. According to Bailey (1906a) this *Oenothera* was commonly cultivated at the beginning of the twentieth century.

Oenothera speciosa. White evening primrose, gumbo lily, cowboy lily. Intro: 1821. Prince, New York, 1826.

Paeonia

pioneiss, peony, piney, pioney
Paeoniaceae
Exotic
Introduction: by the fifteenth century
Earliest American citation: Brickell, 1737
Zone: 3–8
Description:

> Starting with single blooms, like huge anemones, through semi-double flowers, resembling water-lilies, and various forms of doubling up to the solid mass of petals, as in Avalanche, the peony holds one spell-bound in admiration. . . . The leaves of certain sorts of peonies are much divided and fern-like; of others, broad and strong with leathery quality. Usually varnished and lustrous, they run in colour range through many shades of green—often tinged with copper or with red. Some kinds are dwarf and bushy, and others tall with a bold outline. All, however, have an air of sturdy character and self-reliance. (Harding 1917)

Design notes: The peony was often situated in the middle of the lawn so it could be admired from all angles.
Bailey (1906a) noted that peonies provided such a diversity of color and form that they offered great opportunity for creativity in the design of herbaceous borders. Their foliage also provided ornamental appeal. "They grow from 1–3 ft. high, and are therefore suitable for planting in front of shrubbery, along driveways, and are especially pleasing when entering into a distant vista. When planted in a border with fall-blooming perennials, such as phlox, funkia, etc. their rich glossy foliage is very effective."
"In the Maryland garden where I grew up I remember that there were many clumps of these [May-flowering peonies in crimson, pink, and white] massed against the evergreens that formed a windbreak for my mother's Rose garden" (Wilder 1918).
Mrs. Francis King (1921) suggested combining peonies with iris, lupine, foxglove, and columbine.
Remarks: "No flowering plants capable of enduring our northern winters are more satisfactory than the Paeonies. Massive without being coarse, fragrant without being pungent, grand without being gaudy, various in form and color, beyond the possibility of being successfully superseded,

Paeonia 'Baroness Schroeder' (1889). Photograph by Roy Klehm, Klehm's Song Sparrow Farm Nursery.

'Karl Rosenfeld' peony is a 1908 American introduction that is still commercially available. Photograph by Roy Klehm, Klehm's Song Sparrow Farm Nursery.

Paeonia 'Monsieur Jules Elie' (1888). Photograph by Roy Klehm, Klehm's Song Sparrow Farm Nursery.

Paeonia 'Sarah Bernhardt' (1906) honored the French actress. Photograph by Roy Klehm, Klehm's Song Sparrow Farm Nursery.

Lemoine of France introduced the tree peony 'Alice Harding' in 1935. Photograph by Roy Klehm, Klehm's Song Sparrow Farm Nursery.

Paeonia ×*lemoinei* 'Souvenir de Maxime Cornu' (1907). Photograph by Roy Klehm, Klehm's Song Sparrow Farm Nursery.

they stand in the first rank of hardy flowers" (Paeonies 1879).

The first peony reputedly cultivated in New England and the Middle Atlantic states was the double red peony (*P. officinalis* 'Rubra Plena'), which is still a favorite. For many years the main peony in American gardens was this red peony, but breeding started in earnest in the nineteenth century and by 1900 growers had introduced hundreds of varieties.

Heirloom varieties:

Peonies are not referred to as "century plants" for nothing. Many old varieties have persisted in private gardens and in the nursery trade. When my husband and I moved into our 1845 Ohio house years ago, one of the first things we did was bring in loads of top soil to make a garden on top of a neglected dump area at the rear of the house. Ten years later, a peony peeked out of the soil, having been buried for a decade but reappearing to take on the next hundred years. From its position in the yard, as it aligned with other peonies that had been left undisturbed, it was obvious that once a row of peonies of the Festiva Maxima-type had bordered the path from the back door to the outhouse.

Here is just a sample of commercially available antique peonies. All are selections or hybrids of *Paeonia lactiflora*

'Albert Crousse.' Intro: 1893. Ellwanger & Barry, New York, 1917. "Soft shell pink with faint salmon tints. . . . Immense size, rose type" (Fremont, Ohio, 1932).

'Amabilis'. Buist, Philadelphia, 1859. "Outer petals rose, inner straw."

'Baroness Schroeder'. Intro: 1889. Ellwanger & Barry, New York, 1917. "Very large, globular flowers, flesh-white passing to milk-white. A strong tall grower, very free flowering and very fragrant" (Fremont, Ohio, 1932).

'Duchess de Nemours'. Intro: 1856. Breck, 1851. Although experts give the introduction date for 'Duchess de Nemours' as 1856, Breck discussed this peony as a new introduction in his 1851 *The Flower-Garden*: "Broad exterior petals a blush white, while the centre is filled up with numerous fine petals of a sulphur color, quite a novelty."

'Edulis Superba'. Intro: 1824. Prince, New York, 1844. Dark rose; very fragrant. Said to have edible roots (Harding 1917).

'Felix Crousse'. Intro: 1881. Ellwanger & Barry, New York, 1917. Large, brilliant red, bomb-shaped blossoms.

'Festiva Maxima'. Intro: 1851. Hovey, Boston, 1852. Early type with pure white flowers with splashes of crimson stripes in center. "The finest white peony in existence" (Pilkington, Oregon, 1912).

'Francois Ortegat'. Intro: 1850. Prince, New York, 1860. Dark purple-crimson.

'Humei'. Intro: 1810. Booth, Baltimore, 1810. Double rose peony.

'Karl Rosenfeld'. Intro: 1908 US. Farr, Pennsylvania, 1920. "Pure rich intense crimson. Of half-rose type." (Ernst, Ohio, 1926).

'Louis Van Houtte'. Intro: 1867. Prince, New York, 1860. Bright violet-red. As with 'Duchess de Nemours', a discrepancy exists between the "official" introduction date and a listing in an American catalog.

'Marie Lemoine'. Intro: 1869. Wagner Park, Ohio, 1905. Color descriptions ranged between ivory white and flesh white.

'Monsieur Jules Elie'. Intro: 1888. Ellwanger & Barry, New York, 1917. Peerless deep pink with a silvery sheen.

'Sarah Bernhardt'. Intro: 1906. Brand, Minnesota, 1919. "Semi-rose type. Full and double, blooming in clusters. Apple blossom pink with each petal silver tipped, giving it the appearance of pure white. Very fragrant" (Fremont, Ohio, 1932).

'Whitleyi'. Intro: 1808. Brighton, Boston, 1833. Single, white with yellow center, in clusters. Authorities believe this peony to be the closest peony in appearance to the original species *Paeonia lactiflora*, from which most modern cultivars descended.

Historic commercial sources: 106

Related species:

Paeonia officinalis. Common peony. Intro: 1548. Thomas Jefferson, 1782.

'Alba Plena'. Manning, Massachusetts, 1875. Double, white.

'Rubra Plena'. Prince, New York, 1822. Double, red.

Paeonia suffruticosa (syn. *Paeonia moutan*, *P. arborea*). Tree peony, moutan peony. Intro: 1787. Prince, New York, 1822. The tree peony typically stood 3–4 ft. bearing huge flowers, often measuring 7–10 in. across. The tree peony was a collector's plant in the past as it is now. The American peony expert Alice Harding (1917) remarked, "The tree peony deserves a much wider appreciation and cultivation in this country than it now receives." The following heirloom varieties are still commercially available:

×*lemoinei* 'Alice Harding'. Intro: 1935. Fragrant, semidouble, yellow with red highlights

'Osirus'. Wilder, 1871. Double, purple.

'Reine Elizabeth'. Intro: before 1846. Ellwanger & Barry, New York, 1867. "Finest of all the tree peonies. The flowers are massive—salmon pink with brilliant copper tints" (Harding 1917).

×*lemoinei* 'Souvenir de Maxime Cornu' (syn. 'Kinkaku'). Intro: 1907. Farr, Pennsylvania, 1920. Double yellow and red.

'Zenobia' (syn. 'Alexandre de Humbolt'). Ellwanger & Barry, New York, 1860. "Imperial purple, semi-double" (Wilder 1871).

Paeonia tenuifolia. Fern leaf peony. Intro: 1765. M'Mahon, 1806. Available in both single and double flowering ('Flore Pleno') forms.

Papaver orientale

oriental poppy, Armenian poppy
Synonym: *Papaver pulcherrima*
Papaveraceae
Exotic
Introduction: 1714
Earliest American citation: John Bartram, ca. 1741
Zone: 3–7

Description: "This is a most magnificent perennial, worth all the rest of the Poppy tribe. Its large, gorgeous, orange scarlet flowers display themselves in the month of June. The bottoms of the petals are black; the stigma is surrounded by a multitude of rich purple stamens" (Breck 1858). After the 1880s, varieties had white, orange, pink, or salmon-colored flowers.

Design notes: "Planted in groups with Lyme Grass and Nepeta, Stachys lanata and Valerian they are among the loveliest of early June's pictures.... There is some magic appeal to this great Poppy, too, and one wants to splash it about the garden regardless of consequences" (Wilder 1918).

Remarks: How to deal with the bare space left in the garden after the poppies have bloomed and died back has challenged gardeners for years. One suggestion in *The Garden Magazine* (1909) was to plant ageratum blue 'Mrs. F. W. Raynor' hardy asters among the poppies for late-season bloom (Duffy 1909). Other writers recommended filling the spaces between poppy plants with hostas, baby's breath, or sea lavender.

Heirloom varieties:

'Beauty of Livermere'. Breck, New York, 1917. Crimson with black blotch.

'Mrs. Perry'. Farr, Pennsylvania, 1920. Orange-apricot.

'Perry's White'. Farr, Pennsylvania, 1920. Satiny white with a crimson-maroon blotch at the base of each petal.

'Princess Victoria Louise' (syn. 'Princess Louise', 'Prinzessin Viktoria Luise'). Dreer, Philadelphia, 1908. "Princess Victoria Luise [sic], the huge bloom of a delicious rosy-salmon

Papaver orientale 'Queen Alexandra'. Photograph by Marge Garfield.

hue, was a sensation" (King 1915).

'Queen Alexandra'. Intro: 1906. Breck, New York, 1917. Rosy-salmon, crimson spots.

var. *bracteatum* (syn. *Papaver bracteatum*). Intro: 1821. Prince, New York, 1829. This variety has blood-red flowers.

Historic commercial sources: 100

Related species:

Papaver nudicaule. Iceland poppy. Intro: 1759. Buist, 1839. Most trade references occur after 1850 for this colorful member of the poppy family.

Macleaya cordata (syn. *Bocconia cordata*). Plume poppy. Intro: 1795. Prince, New York, 1829. "A flower much admired in gardens during the early years of the nineteenth century" (Earle 1901). The 6–10-ft. plume poppy is often identified with the Victorian penchant for the dramatic.

Penstemon barbatus

beardtongue, scarlet penstemon
Synonyms: *Penstemon coccineum*, *Chelone barbata*
Scrophulariaceae
Native
Introduction: 1794
Earliest American citation: Landreth, Philadelphia, 1811
Zone: 3–8

Description: "They bear long-tubular often two-lipped flowers in terminal usually interrupted or leafy clusters" (Bailey 1906a).

Design notes: "For the hardy border, Pentstemons [sic] are the most satisfactory plants, and the great number of showy species allows much latitude in the choice of color and habit" (Bailey 1906a).

Combine with cream-white zinnias and allow a salmon-pink sweet pea to rise up the back of the Penstemon (King 1915).

Penstemon barbatus, beardtongue. James Vick, Rochester, New York, 1881.

Richardson Wright (1924) suggested a warm perennial grouping composed of "Bee Balm, Monarda didyma, and red Penstemons."

Remarks: The early growers offered many species of *Penstemon*, both hardy and tender, but they referred to the scarlet *P. barbatus* most frequently. "There are many choice varieties cultivated; many of them are not hardy" (Kern 1855). Another species, *Penstemon digitalis*, also appeared frequently in the catalogs. Although writers continued to recommend it, beardtongue disappeared from the trade catalogs after the beginning of the twentieth century.

Historic commercial sources: 52

Phlox

perennial phlox, bastard lichnis, lychnidea, hardy phlox
Synonym: *Lychnidea*
Polemoniaceae
Native
Introduction: 1732
Earliest American citation: Bartram, ca. 1737
Zone: 4–8

Description: Phlox are 2–4 ft., hardy perennials bearing panicles of flowers in various shades of rose, lilac, red, white, mauve, and pink. Many have beautifully contrasting eyes.

Design notes: Phlox was at home in the border as well as a single lawn specimen. "The phlox may be termed a necessary garden-flower" (Ellwanger 1889). The many colors of *Phlox* were not only advantageous, but also challenging to the garden designer. Eben Rexford, writing for the 1900 publication *How to Grow Flowers*, cautioned, "Be careful not to use the lilac or magenta sorts in combination with the reds. They never harmonize. But these colors can be used with the white very effectively."

Perennial Phlox. Rice Brothers, Geneva, New York, ca. 1905.

Recommended combinations from garden writers of the early 1900s:

Harriet Keeler (1910): Phlox with baby's breath, sea holly, globe thistle, and blue salvia.

Mrs. Francis King (1915): "A tall white Phlox makes a beautiful background for the lavender plumes of Buddleia."

Richardson Wright (1924): White speedwell, Culver's root, red phlox, and yarrow with blanket flower in front.

Mrs. Francis King (1925): Rose-colored *Gladiolus* 'Indian Maid' positioned below salmon pink *Phlox* 'Rheinlander', with rose-pink zinnias nearby.

Remarks:

Breck (1846a) observed that, although most of the early interest in *Phlox* had been in England, breeders in Massachusetts, including himself, Hovey, and Warren, were introducing new selections that rivaled the European varieties. Breck recommended *Phlox* as the best of all hardy perennials for the ornamental border because of its ease of culture, propagation, and the long season of bloom attained by using different species and varieties.

Powdery mildew, the scourge of many twentieth-century varieties, was seldom referred to in the historical literature. Breck mentioned a blight that had attacked some of his prize seedlings, but without a description it is difficult to say exactly what had infected his plants.

Heirloom varieties: The first garden variety of *Phlox paniculata* was 'Wheelerii', with pink flowers and red eye, developed in England in the 1820s. Literally hundreds of selections were to follow, with a continuous debate as to their true parentage. Some writers believed all to be offspring of *Phlox paniculata* and others determined that interspecific hybridization was responsible for the diversity, with *P. paniculata* and *P. maculata* as the probable parents of many. My research into a sampling of American catalogs yielded over 800 named selections of *Phlox*. At least one nineteenth-century horticulturist was overwhelmed by the many varieties:

> The number of new varieties announced each year is altogether too great for any one except the professional florist to think of purchasing. It is to be feared that in the race for new varieties, the real marked distinction between them is often overlooked . . . the endless variety of colors which may be obtained from seeds constitutes one of its greatest charms. (Fuller, 1868)

These heirloom varieties were commercially available in 2002:

'Graf Zeppelin'. Fremont, Ohio, 1932. White with deep red eye.

'Hindenberg'. Horsford, Vermont, 1931. Brilliant deep crimson red, darker eye.

'Le Mahdi'. New England Nurseries, Massachusetts, 1910. "Darkest purple phlox in existence."

'Rheinlander'. Henderson, New York, 1915. A rare shade of salmon-pink, intensified by a distinct claret-red eye.

'Rijnstroom'. Henderson, New York, 1915. Immense trusses of flowers, superb salmon-rose.

'Septemberglut'. Storrs & Harrison, Ohio, 1925. Tall growth and vivid color effect; dark salmon-carmine.

'Widar'. Henderson, New York, 1915. Light reddish violet with large white center.

'William Ramsey'. Horsford, Vermont, 1931. Dark purple.

Historic commercial sources: 148

Related species:

Phlox carolina 'Miss Lingard' (syn. *Phlox suffruticosa* 'Miss

Phlox 'Widar' is nearly 100 years old. Photograph by Marge Garfield.

Lingard'). Manning, Massachusetts, 1889. Early waxy, snow-white flowers with lavender eye (some said pink) and sweetly fragrant.

"The best modern white variety for general use" (Blanchan 1913).

Phlox subulata

moss pink, ground-pink, mountain-pink, moss phlox

Synonyms: *Phlox setacea*, *P. perfoliata*, *P. nivea*

Polemoniaceae

Native

Introduction: by 1745 [1786]

Earliest American citation: John Bartram, ca. 1745

Zone: 3–9

Description: Gardeners were familiar with pink, white, and red varieties of *Phlox subulata* by 1850, as well as a lilac flower with a dark eye and a pink selection with a red eye (Breck 1846).

Design notes: "Especially desirable for carpeting under shrubs and dwarf evergreens" (Manning 1886). The moss pink also was a desirable plant for the front of the border.

'Miss Lingard' phlox is a nineteenth-century garden phlox still available today. Photograph by author.

Remarks: "In the Spring of 1831, an eminent British collector [Mr. Drummond] exclaimed, on seeing a patch of Phlox subulata in one of the pine barrens of New Jersey, 'The beauty of that alone is worth coming to America to see, it is so splendid'" (Buist 1839).

Heirloom variety:

'Snowflake'. Prince, New York, 1857. "Fine white."

Historic commercial sources: 53

Related species:

Phlox stolonifera (syn. *Phlox reptans*). Creeping phlox. Intro: 1800. M'Mahon, 1806.

Physostegia virginiana

obedient plant, false dragon head, Virginia dragon's head

Synonyms: *Dracocephalum physostegia, D. virginica, D. denticulatum, D. variegatum*

Lamiaceae

Native

Introduction: 1683

Earliest American citation: M'Mahon, Philadelphia, 1804

Zone: 3–9

Description: Hardy herbaceous perennial, with spikes of gaping flowers in shades of purple, rose, or white.

Design notes: Mrs. Frances King (1915) included in her list of good "companion crops" for August: perennial phlox in shades of pink and white, zinnias in light flesh tones, the lavender pink *Physostegia*, sea-holly, stocks, and a salmon-colored *Dianthus*.

"In planning the rear of a broad border this is almost indispensable for it has height, a clean foliage and pleasant spikes of pink or white flowers from July to frost. It makes a fine background for Phlox and an excellent companion for tall Veronica" (Wright 1924).

Remarks: The corolla of *Physostegia virginiana* will stay indefinitely in whatever position it is turned, thus the common name "obedient plant."

Heirloom varieties:

'Alba'. White false dragon's head. Storrs & Harrison, Ohio, 1908.

'Vivid'. False dragon's head. Manning, Massachusetts, 1931. Bright rosy pink.

Historic commercial sources: 59

Platycodon grandiflorus

balloon flower, Japanese or Chinese bellflower

Synonyms: *Campanula grandiflora, Wahlenbergia grandiflora*

Campanulaceae

Exotic

Introduction: 1782

Earliest American citation: M'Mahon, 1806

Zone: 3–8

Description: Handsome hardy herbaceous perennial with blue or white bell-shaped flowers. The bud has an inflated appearance giving it the name of balloon flower.

Design notes: "They resemble Canterbury bells, and . . . are valuable in continuing the period of blue flowers, with the advantage of being perennials" (Ely 1903).

Balloon flower is 2–3 ft. tall and thus suitable for the middle of the border.

For a blue garden vignette in July, surround a group of *Platycodon* with ageratum (Hill 1923).

Remarks: "A charming plant with great bell-shaped flowers, which is less well-known than it deserves" (Hill 1923).

Platycodon grandiflorus, balloon flower. Peter Henderson, *Henderson's Handbook of Plants*, 1890.

Primula veris has naturalized on this Vermont roadside. Photograph by Susan E. Schnare, Mountain Brook Primroses.

Heirloom varieties:

'Albus'. White balloon flower. Storrs & Harrison, Ohio, 1896. Combine white *Platycodon* with double rose-pink poppies.

'Mariesii' (syn. var. *mariesii*). *Gardener's Monthly*, 1885. Deep violet, dwarf, 1-ft. tall, also known as var. *nana compacta*.

Historic commercial sources: 77

Polemonium caeruleum

Jacob's ladder, Greek valerian

Polemoniaceae

Native

Introduction: by 1600

Earliest American citation: Hepburn & Gardiner, 1804

Zone: 3–7

Description: Hardy herbaceous perennial with "beautiful pinnately-cleft leaves" and nodding bright blue flowers, on the ends of the stems (Breck 1858).

Design notes: Useful for the front of the border or in the wild garden. Breck (1858) called it a standard for the flower border.

Remarks: "The solid mass of pale lavender with which the valerian bed will be covered in the spring must delight the heart of anyone who loves color or profusion" (Hill 1923).

Heirloom variety:

'Alba'. White Jacob's ladder. M'Mahon, 1806.

Historic commercial sources: 54

Related species:

Polemonium reptans. Creeping Greek valerian, blue-eyed Susan. Intro: by 1757. M'Mahon, Philadelphia, 1804.

Primula veris

English cowslip, primrose, polyanthus

Synonym: *Primula officinalis*

Primulaceae

Exotic

Introduction: Long cultivated

Earliest American citation: Katherine Risteau, Maryland, 1747 (Lockwood 1934)

Zone: 3–8

Description: A dwarf hardy herbaceous perennial. "The flowers are produced in trusses . . . but look pretty in the garden. The flowers generally are of a pale-yellow, but there is a variety with red flowers" (Breck 1858).

Design notes: Primulas grow well in cool, moist, shady sites. Garden writers of the early 1900s recommended them as premier rock garden plants. Mrs. Frances King (1915) recommended using a brilliant scarlet tulip as a companion for the subtle yellow primrose.

Remarks: *Primula veris* means "the first in spring."

Historic commercial sources: 50

Related species:

Primula auricula. Primrose. Long cultivated. Thomas Jefferson, 1767. "A hardy plant for the border, much esteemed in Europe . . . rich colored flowers are freely produced in spring" (Columbus Nursery, Ohio, 1877).

Primula elatior. Primrose, oxlip. Intro: 1764. M'Mahon, 1806.

Primula ×*polyantha* . Intro: by 1693. Thomas Jefferson, 1812. "Most generally used as spring bedding plants" and the *Primula* species most often cultivated in American gardens (Bailey 1906a).

This *Primula* is called 'Daisy Eastman' to honor the photographer's great-grandmother, who grew it decades ago. Photograph by Susan E. Schnare, Mountain Brook Primroses.

Primula sinensis. Chinese primrose. Bridgeman, 1840. Cultivated in the greenhouse during the nineteenth century.
Primula vulgaris. Primrose, sweet keys. Long cultivated. Thomas Jefferson included this species on his 1771 garden plan.

Rudbeckia laciniata

coneflower, golden glow, thimble flower
Synonym: *Rudbeckia digitata*
Asteraceae
Native
Introduction: 1640
Earliest American citation: M'Mahon, Philadelphia, 1804
Zone: 4–10
Description: "*Rudbeckia laciniata* is one of the tall vigorous composites which brighten the tangle and adorn the roadsides in August. It often stands seven feet high, bearing a loose collection of long peduncled heads, with disks somewhat elongated. The bright-yellow rays droop a little, but

Rudbeckia 'Golden Glow' (syn. 'Hortensia') was all the rage in gardens at the beginning of the twentieth century. Rice Brothers, Geneva, New York, ca. 1905.

the general effect of the flower-head is that of a sunflower" (Keeler 1910).
Design notes: Prefers moist locations in the hardy border or wild garden.
Remarks: As a recipient of numerous species of yellow composites, Collinson wrote to Custis in the mid-eighteenth century, "I often reflect what a numerous train of yellow flowers your continent abounds."
Heirloom varieties:
'Hortensia' (syn. 'Golden Glow', 'Flore Pleno'). *The Mayflower* of December 1895 reported that *Rudbeckia laciniata flore pleno*, also called "Golden Glow," was to be introduced by Childs for the next growing season (Rudbeckia "Childs' Golden Glow" 1895). One correspondent exclaimed that he had never seen a double-flowered *Rudbeckia* before: "I unhesitatingly regard it

as the most desirable introduction among hardy perennials since we got *Clematis paniculata* . . . five to seven feet high." While most garden writers praised golden glow's presence in gardens, Richardson Wright disagreed in 1924: "The pariah of all good gardens is Golden Glow. Not that it lacks beauty, but because it is greedy, wormy, and, after blooming, is not good to look upon."

Historic commercial sources: 62

Related species:

Helenium autumnale. Autumn sneezeweed, false sunflower. Intro: 1729. Bartram, Philadelphia, 1783. 'Riverton Beauty'. Ellwanger & Barry, New York, 1917. Lemon yellow ray flower and a purplish black cone. 'Riverton Gem'. Gregory, Massachusetts, 1914. "Old gold suffused with terra cotta."

Helianthus ×multiflorus. Perennial sunflower. Intro: before 1596. M'Mahon, Philadelphia, 1804. The perennial double-flowered sunflower was known only in cultivation.

Rudbeckia fulgida. Black-eyed Susan. Intro: 1760. M'Mahon, 1806.

Rudbeckia hirta. Black-eyed Susan, yellow daisy. Intro: 1714. Bartram, Philadelphia, 1783. Biennial or annual.

Senna marilandica

Maryland cassia, American senna
Synonyms: *Cassia marilandica*, *Ditremexa marilandica*
Caesalpiniaceae (Fabaceae)
Native
Introduction: by 1800 [1823]
Earliest American citation: Jean Skipwith, ca. 1800, "cassia"
Zone: 4–7
Description: "A hardy indigenous perennial, four feet high, with yellow flowers, from August to September" (Breck 1851).

Design notes: "Cassia Marylandica—a wild native beauty—will thrive and flower without stint, if transplanted to your garden; needing plenty of room and giving in return plenty of handsome yellow flowers" (Warner 1872).

Remarks: Although *Senna marilandica* appeared frequently in the catalogs of the nineteenth and early twentieth centuries, the gardening literature rarely mentioned it.

Historic commercial sources: 52

Related species:

Hedysarum coronarium. French honeysuckle. Intro: 1596. Spurrier, 1793. White or scarlet flowers.

Tanacetum parthenium

feverfew
Synonyms: *Pyrethrum parthenium*, *Chrysanthemum parthenium*
Asteraceae
Exotic
Introduction: Long cultivated
Earliest American citation: Josselyn, 1672
Zone: 5-8
Description: The single feverfew looks like a small ox-eye daisy. The double has white buttons, a little less than an inch across.

Design notes: Originally valued for medicinal uses, feverfew gained popularity for the front of borders, as edging, and for bedding schemes in the 1800s. The double and golden-foliaged varieties were also grown in greenhouses.

Remarks: "Old favorite that grew in Pilgrim gardens and still finds a place in the hardy border" (Keeler 1910). The double feverfew was the favorite variety throughout the 1800s and

Senna marilandica, Maryland cassia. Photograph by author.

Tanacetum parthenium 'Flore Pleno', double white feverfew, was a popular bedding plant in Victorian times. Photograph by author.

1900s. Breck (1851) claimed that the species was no better than a weed for "there is no beauty in the single flowers."

Heirloom varieties:

'Flore Pleno'. Double white feverfew. Intro: before 1614. Hepburn & Gardiner, 1804. Extremely popular throughout the nineteenth century.

'Aureum'. Golden feather, golden feverfew. Wells, Boston, 1871. Used in bedding schemes.

'Golden Ball'. Double golden feverfew. Ferris, Iowa, 1927.

Historic commercial sources: 87

Related species:

Tanacetum coccineum (syn. *Pyrethrum roseum*). Insect powder plant, painted daisy, Persian daisy. Intro: by 1826. Hovey, Boston, 1859. Was available in many colors in single- and double-flowered forms.

Tradescantia virginiana

Virginia spiderwort, starflower, star of Bethlehem, widow's tears

Commelinaceae

Native

Introduction: 1629

Earliest American citation: Jean Skipwith, ca. 1800

Zone: 3–9

Description: "The Spiderwort is rather an unusual type of flower. The blossoms are at the summit of what looks like an iris stem; usually two or three are open, but more drooping buds are clustered between long, blade-like bracts. The rich blue petals, the brilliant orange anthers set upon a cluster of blue bearded filaments, and the dark-green sepals and leaves, form a pleasing combination of color" (Keeler 1910).

Thomas Meehan (1878) described many beautiful colors of the spiderwort: reddish violet, pale rose, deep rose, vermilion, carmine, light purple, white. Some doubles were also available.

Design notes: Meehan said spiderwort was esteemed as a border plant in the second half of the nineteenth century. Neltje Blanchan (1913) placed it in the wild garden and also recommended spiderwort to be cultivated in the foreground of the shrubbery.

Remarks: *Tradescantia virginiana* was thought to provide a remedy for spider bites.

Heirloom varieties:

'Alba'. White spiderwort. Hovey, Boston, 1834.

'Rubra'. Red spiderwort. Prince, New York, 1857.

Historic commercial sources: 49

Viola odorata

single blue violet, hardy violet, sweet violet

Violaceae

Exotic

Introduction: Long cultivated

Earliest American citation: Lawson, 1718

Zone: 5–8

Description: The sweet violet was a fragrant, diminutive perennial, blooming in early spring. The species had single, deep blue-purple flowers. There were also doubles and additional colors including white and reddish tones.

Design notes: Violets were appropriate for the front of the border and for rockwork. "Viola odorata,—or the Sweet-scented Violet,—should not be wanting in any collection of plants, on account of its fragrance and early appearance" (Breck 1858).

Viola odorata, sweet violet. Columbus Nursery, Columbus, Ohio, 1877.

Tradescantia virginiana, spiderwort. The Lovett Co., Little Silver, New Jersey, 1898.

Remarks: Breck noted that a single violet could scent an entire room with its sweet fragrance.

Heirloom varieties:

'Alba Plena'. Double white sweet violet. Sayers, 1839.

'The Czar'. Sunnyside, Iowa, 1871. Rich bluish purple, large and fragrant.

'Queen Charlotte'. Park, South Carolina, 1938. Large dark blue.

Historic commercial sources: 66

Related species:

Viola pedata. Bird's-foot violet. Intro: by 1804 [1826]. M'Mahon, Philadelphia, 1804. Native violet.

Yucca filamentosa

yucca, Adam's needle, bear grass, thready yucca

Agavaceae

Native

Introduction: 1675

Earliest American citation: George Washington, ca. 1800

Zone: 5–10

Description: "The leaves are sharp-pointed, stiff, and rigid. . . . Yucca filamentosa . . . is called Thready Yucca, from the long threads that hang from the leaves. The flower stem grows to the height of five or six feet, and nearly the whole of it is covered with large, bell-shaped, white flowers . . . in July and August" (Breck 1858).

Design notes: *Yucca* was native to the American Southeast and adapted well to the climate of the Northeast and Midwest. Besides winter hardiness, its bold habit and vertical interest were alluring virtues both for the garden and for bedding schemes, as Thomas Meehan (1871) explained:

> Since Mr. Robinson's works and the writings of other leaders in horticulture have called attention to the great beauty of the more tropical styles of northern gardening, there is much demand for this class of plants. One Landscape gardener tells us he makes great use of the Yuccas for this purpose; as its sword like evergreen leaves have a pretty effect in winter as well as summer. The Yucca filamentosa is the one employed chiefly. There are other species still rare, which will no doubt become very useful for this purpose, also when they become cheap and common, of these are Y. recurva, Y. gloriosa, and Y. angustifolia.

William Falconer, writing for the 1876 *The Gardener's Monthly*, recommended a pleasing combination with yucca as the featured plant:

> Yucca filamentosa, a common but noble plant, with tall tree-like flower, stem laden with yellowish white blooms. I lately saw a pretty effect produced on a sunny slope by having these Yuccas planted some three to four feet apart, and interplanted with low-growing red-flowered Cannas, banded with white variegated grass.

Helena R. Ely (1903) reported that yuccas "are most effective when grown in clumps, but look very well along a fence with Hollyhocks at the back."

Remarks: Keeler (1910) observed that yucca was particularly effective when seen in the moonlight.

Historic commercial sources: 80

Related species:

Yucca aloifolia. Intro: 1696. M'Mahon, Philadelphia, 1804. Phillip Gosse recorded in 1838 that the *Yucca aloifolia* was a common inhabitant of Alabama gardens.

Yucca gloriosa. Spanish dagger. Intro: 1596. M'Mahon, Philadelphia, 1804.

· 9 ·

HEIRLOOM ANNUALS AND
TROPICAL PLANTS

The cultivation of Annual Flowers is a delightful employment, and well adapted to the amusement of a Lady, who, with the assistance of a labourer to prepare the ground, may turn a barren waste into a beauteous flower garden with her own hands.

—Thomas Bridgeman, *The Florist's Guide*, 1840

DEFINITIONS OF THE TERM *ANNUAL* tend to be quite straightforward. The English agriculturist William Cobbett, visiting in America in 1821, wrote: "[Annuals] . . . first blow and die the year they are sown; [biennials] . . . blow the second year and then die; [perennials] . . . sometimes blow the first year and sometimes not, and die down to the ground annually, but spring up again every spring." However, the plants that were actually used as annuals in gardens exceeded the conventional definition to include all those plants that flowered the first year from seed and also plants that were perennials in warmer climates, but which were not hardy to the area in question and had to be either overwintered in a warm place or replaced each year.

Annuals occupy a distinctive position in the earliest annals of American horticultural history. The obvious reason is that their seeds were easily produced and transported. Annual flowers efficiently and practically fulfilled the demand for ornamentation in early landscapes. When growers and seed houses west of the Mississippi began to publish catalogs in the second half of the nineteenth century, they emphasized annual plants for the same reasons.

Early writers, particularly those using the calendar format for their books, described the process of successfully sowing and growing annual flowers. "Under favorable conditions, annual flower plants, in general, will produce their flower buds within two months from the period of sowing the seed. Some species, soon after exhibiting their brilliant blossoms, disappear, while others embellish the borders by their successional bloom for two or three months" (Bridgeman 1840). The key to seedling vigor was a well-cultivated, fertile soil.

Horticulturists typically categorized annuals into three classes that were defined by the timing and conditions of their cultivation:

1. Hardy Annuals are sown directly into the open ground where they are to grow. They are vitally strong, developing without artificial heat, and may be sown from February to May, according to the season and latitude—for example, sweet peas, poppies, eschscholzias, bartonia, lupine, malope, and the dwarf convolvulus.

2. Half-hardy annuals are usually sown in February or March in a window or a warm frame. The season is usually not long enough to enable them to reach full development in the open. In the early stages of development they need protection and warmth. Pansies are half-hardy annuals.

3. Tender annuals require still more warmth and are started from January to May in the greenhouse or other suitable place. (Ernest Walker, in Bailey 1906a)

Annuals provided the primary focus of a flower garden and could also perform an ancillary function. For example, annuals filled in bulb gardens, the annuals' season of bloom being consecutive to the season of flowering for the bulbs. Annuals also served as fillers in the herbaceous border, particularly as that garden style became more important with the progression of the 1800s into the 1900s. As Louise Shelton wrote in 1931:

Unless the flowering season is to be of short duration, I have yet to see a satisfactory plan for a perennial garden without any annuals to complete its bloom. When long and continuous bloom is required, a plentiful supply of certain annuals is recommended. . . . Annuals from good seed never fail to develop quickly; therefore, the perennial bed should be more or less dependent upon a certain number and variety of annuals.

The relatively temporary nature of annuals caused some gardeners to be unappreciative of their garden use. Grace Tabor wrote in 1916, "Annuals, lovely though they may be, can hardly be seriously considered in a composition that must, primarily, be permanent in order to enjoy that charm which is one of a garden's chiefest—that exquisite mellowing, like fine wine, under the lapse of time."

BEDDING SCHEMES

When we think of annuals in a historic sense, we often envision the bedding schemes so popular in Victorian United States and Europe. Bedding consisted of arranging plants—annuals, biennials, and perennials, but usually annuals and tender exotics—in parterres or other designs cut out of the lawn and often viewed from a window or other perspective in the dwelling or associated building. "Some cultivators prefer the promiscuous arrangement; others like the Ribbon Style, and some set the dwarfs and those of stately growths upon separate beds, so that all will display their peculiar beauties to the best advantage" (Elder 1870).

Carpet bedding might have involved simple geometric figures such as circles and ovals or it could have entailed an intricate cutout design for a tapestry effect. The ribbon style consisted of long, narrow strips and coils. Bedding required "besides good taste in arranging colors harmoniously, judgment to select those kinds that will continue in bloom the whole season, withstanding the summer drouth [sic], and

Group of annuals—1. Agrostemma. 2. Lobelia. 3. Mirabilis. 4. Lantana. 5. Salpiglossis. 6. Vinca. 7. Myosotis. 8. Mimulus tigrinus. 9. Honeysuckle. 10. Sweet William. *Vick's Monthly Magazine*, 1884.

Eight designs for carpet bedding. Design 1: Three different foliage colors of Achyranthes. Design 2: White and red geraniums. Design 4: A-Dusty Miller, B-Coleus, 3-Abutilon. Design 8: Canna in the center with two different colors of *Pelargonium*. Design 9: Caladium in center, surrounded by two colors of *Pelargonium*. Design 10: White *Phlox drummondii* alternates with purple phlox, surrounded by bronze geranium. Design 11: Outer circle: white and scarlet verbena, center is blue heliotrope. Design 12: A. Blue lobelia, B. Scarlet Verbena, C. Striped Petunia. *Vick's Monthly Magazine*, 1881.

that will harmonize in habit and growth with one another" (Hints for May 1863). Bright and sustained color was the most important achievement.

Andrew Jackson Downing visited Montgomery Place on the Hudson River in 1847 and remarked on the beauty of the garden of annuals:

> Here all is gay and smiling. Bright parterres of brilliant flowers bask in the full daylight, and rich masses of color seem to revel in the sunshine. . . . The beds are surrounded by low edging of turf or box, and the whole looks like some rich oriental pattern or carpet of embroidery. . . . The whole garden is surrounded and shut out from the lawn, by a belt of shrubbery, and above and behind this . . . the background of trees.

Bedding schemes emphasized contrasting color, either of flowers or, more importantly, of foliage. The plants had to be uniform in habit and maintain their ornamental features throughout the season. Bedding required strict attention to maintenance and garden writers cautioned that it was an expensive style of gardening. A circular bed 10 ft. in diameter might cost $15.00 (Vick 1878e). Owners of small properties were encouraged to adopt the style on a simple scale by cutting only a few designs in their lawns and filling them with colorful annuals. The more complex patterns were reserved

for public institutions, such as the Dayton, Ohio, Soldiers' Home.

Eben Rexford wrote in 1912, "Carpet-Bedding is not the most artistic phase of gardening, by any means, but it has a great attraction for many persons who admire masses of harmonious and contrasting colors more than the individual beauty of a flower." The best foliage plants for carpet-bedding included coleus, *Alternanthera* (red was best), golden feather feverfew, dusty miller, and variegated-leaved geraniums.

Subtropical gardening was a distinctive category of the bedding designs. In these beds, the form of the foliage was more important to the gardener than color or flowers. Savvy gardeners in America expressed interest in this style in the late 1800s and early 1900s. Charles Henderson wrote in the 1901 *Henderson's Picturesque Gardens*:

> There is a growing taste for additional bold picturesque effects—something suggestive of the stately grandeur of luxuriant tropical vegetation. . . .
>
> This taste has led to the introduction into gardens of large-leaved so-called "subtropical" foliage plants, the characteristics of which, nobility of form and habit, luxuriant growth, and exuberant and graceful leafage, render them of high decorative value, either grown as specimens or boldly grouped.

Henderson and others recommended certain plants for this style of gardening, including plants that had to be overwintered like palms, *Agave*, *Musa*, *Dracaena*, and *Cycas*; bul-

Man admiring his simple bedding garden featuring a canna in the center of the bed, ca. 1910.

Intricate bedding designs at the Dayton, Ohio, Soldiers' Home, ca. 1880.

bous plants like *Canna*, *Colocasia*, *Crinum*, and *Caladium*; annuals such as coleus, ornamental-leaved beet, castor bean, and amaranthus; perennials, particularly plume poppy, tritoma, yucca, and verbascum; and the ornamental grasses, for example, the giant reed, pampas grass, and bamboo. Woody plants with luxuriant, tropical-looking foliage like *Paulownia* and *Ailanthus* were used with the plant cut back to the ground each year to stimulate new seasonal growth of the foliage.

Ida Bennett (1903) suggested a simple plan for a subtropical bed that could be adapted to contemporary gardens. She recommended that a 12-ft.-diameter bed of castor bean be cut in the lawn in a remote space, but visible from a window. The castor bean should be surrounded with scarlet sage and edged with white sweet alyssum. Another bed, 8 ft. in diameter, could be filled with large-flowered cannas and edged with coleus. Another suggestion was to feature ornamental grasses: giant reed, ravenna grass or hardy pampas grass, and maiden grass. "Such beds are rich in tropical effects and give more distinction to a lawn than any other class of plants."

Bed of subtropical plants. Vick's *Monthly Magazine*, 1880.

Not everyone enjoyed the flamboyant bedding style of gardening. "I have heard it sarcastically called by some of the old-school gardeners the 'scarlet fever and yellow jaundice style' in allusion to so many red Geraniums and yellow Calceolarias being used," observed a correspondent to *Vick's Monthly Magazine* in 1881 (J. B. 1881). Neltje Blanchan (1913) also lamented that in the bedding system, "there can be no possibility of adding a favorite plant throughout the season or allowing a single one to grow in a natural way." She was vehement in her criticism of geometric beds in the lawn that were filled with coleus or cannas or purple China asters. "Such excrescences on a fair green lawn can be likened only to pimples on the face of nature." The popularity of bedding schemes began its decline when the writings of the English horticulturists and garden designers William Robinson and Gertrude Jekyll became fashionable. Still, even in the twenty-first century, the bedding system is widely implemented in the grounds of public institutions.

CONTAINER GARDENING

Annuals were particularly appropriate for another style of gardening, that of filling containers like urns, pots, vases, and window boxes and placing them around the garden or even on the roof. William Faris of Annapolis recorded in his 1804 diary that he filled wooden half-barrels with ice plant, Jerusalem cherry, eggplant, tulips, wallflowers, India pinks, and tuberose and set them around his property (Sarudy 1998).

A particularly interesting reference to a roof garden composed of flowers in containers appeared in the 1878 *Vick's Monthly Magazine*. The gardener, Isaac Blauvelt of Paterson, New Jersey, wrote, "My garden is on the roof of my black-smith shop, two stories high . . . still I have had some success. My balsams were superb, and every plant that bloomed was a beauty." In addition to the balsams, Blauvelt grew anemones, zinnias, verbenas, petunias, portulacas, pansies, ten-week stocks, and China asters, as well as a few perennials.

> If any lovers of flowers, without a garden, have a house with a flat roof, they can grow enough flowers to satisfy any reasonable demand. The way I managed it was to place boxes around the edges of the roof, put in the bottom three or four inches of fresh horse manure, no litter, then fill the boxes with good soil mixed with well rotted manure, and transplant from my hot-bed after the boxes have

stood three or four days. I also grew all the Lettuce and Radishes our family used, in a box on the same roof. Of course, much water is needed.

Outdoor window-box gardening appeared to gain some popularity by the last quarter of the nineteenth century. Indoors, window gardening was a hallmark of the proper Victorian housewife. Window boxes were particularly useful for city dwellers who lacked outdoor space for gardening, but they also were used to embellish country homes. According to an enthusiastic window gardener writing to *The Ladies' Floral Cabinet* of 1883:

Doubtless the idea originated in the city where there was not ground for flower-beds, but there is not reason why it should be confined there, for it furnishes a rare opportunity to embellish the country home. It is a great saving of labor, as the boxes can be watered from within, which is far less work than to water garden vases and flower-beds. (J. E. J. 1883)

Window boxes were of two types: indoor for parlor windows; or outdoor, affixed under windows or on the porch or veranda, or even the roof, as we have seen above. If the box was a distance up from the street, care was needed in the choice of plants so that bright colors could be seen from below. At any level, trailing and creeping plants were effective to drape and cover the container. Ida Bennett (1903) cautioned that "the outside window-box is a thing of beauty if well cared for, a disfigurement if neglected." Eben Rexford wrote in Vick's 1890 *Home Floriculture* that he was "glad to note the increasing popularity of the window-box." His suggestions for planting the boxes might be followed today:

Morning glories are excellent for planting at the ends of a window-box to train up and over the windows. Madeira vines can be used instead, if preferred. Nasturtiums and Petunias can be made to droop over the sides in such luxuriance that the box will be hidden by their flowers and foliage. The Heliotrope is an excellent plant for the center. Pansies will grow well in a partially shaded window, and in north windows Ferns and Lycopodiums can be used with charming results. A Tea Rose or a Geranium will make an effective plant for the center of a box, and an edging of Mme. Salleroi Geraniums, with their pretty green and white leaves will give a pleasing effect. If you want one that will be ablaze of brilliant color all

summer long, fill it with crimson and yellow Coleus, Alternantheras and Achyranthes. In an eastern window where the sun is not so intense, the fancy Caladiums can be used with charming effect.

A correspondent to *The Gardener's Monthly* of October 1885 described the effect of container gardening in Delaware County, Pennsylvania:

This place . . . is one of the prettiest, cleanest, neatest and best laid out in town. . . . Every cottage has a flower and vegetable garden attached. The flowers in front of the cottages were a mass of bloom and in great variety, including the inevitable sunflower. . . . Some people cultivate their plants in pots, boxes, tubs, etc., which decorate the window sills of the houses. (Wooding 1885)

Sometimes the memories of annuals in the flower garden were as evocative as an actual garden. Anna Bartlett Warner (1872) delighted in the old-fashioned annual garden and wrote:

Fair, rich confusion is all the aim of an old-fashioned flower garden, and the greater the confusion the richer. You want to come upon mignonette in unexpected places, and to find sprays of heliotrope in close consultation with your roses. . . . Sweet peas bow to phloxes here, and the gladiolus straightens itself with harmless pride among its more pliant companions, and the little white sweet alyssum goes visiting all day. There is the most exquisite propriety and good fellowship, with utter absence of "deportment"; and the perennials that pass out of flower are kindly hid and merged by their blooming neighbors. No stiffness, no ceremony—flowers, and not a garden—this is the beauty of the old style.

A CATALOG OF HEIRLOOM ANNUALS AND TROPICAL PLANTS

From annual seeds in the pocket of a pioneer moving west—to annuals in brilliant and luxuriant bedding schemes— to annuals used to complement perennial borders—to annuals flowing from barrels and window boxes, these plants have enjoyed a rich history of use in American gardens. These annuals are most often listed in the pages of nursery and seed catalogs and nursery advertisements, 1719 to 1939.

James Vick, Rochester, New York, 1881.

Ageratum houstonianum

Asteraceae

Exotic

floss flower, Mexican ageratum

Synonym: *Ageratum mexicanum*

Introduction: 1822

Earliest American citation: Barrett, Boston, 1836

Description: Annual, 4–12 in. Small, tuftlike, compact flowers that may be azure blue, white, or less frequently, rose. "Very pretty, but not remarkable for its beauty" (Breck 1858).

Design notes: Because the ageratum was a compact, dependable long-bloomer, it was valuable for ribbon bedding and massing. Nineteenth-century gardeners cultivated it in conservatories and as a container plant.

"Ageratum is lovely for edging beds of pink Geraniums, its soft lavender tones being in perfect harmony with their color. It is equally satisfactory when used with pale rose Phlox drummondi, or the soft yellow shades of that flower.... One of the prettiest beds I saw last summer was filled with Sweet Alyssum, and edged with Ageratum . . . it was suggestive of old blue-and-white Delft" (Rexford 1912).

Use light blue ageratum "to bring together the harsh, discordant colors of a mixed planting of *Zinnia*" (King 1915).

"In many respects this Half Hardy Annual is one of the most desirable summer flowering plants we have. It may be used alone for beds and borders, or planted in connection with geraniums, coleus, cannas, etc" (Breck, Boston, 1917).

Remarks: In his 1906 *Cyclopedia*, Bailey stated that the ageratum of old gardens was *Ageratum conyzoides*—a name that does not appear in other garden literature of the nineteenth century and a plant that is considered a weed in the tropics. In the 1935 edition, Bailey cited *Ageratum houstonianum* as the ageratum most frequently cultivated at that time.

Historic commercial sources: 62

Amaranthus caudatus

love-lies-bleeding, velvet flower, tassel flower, nun's whipping rope, *discipline des religieuses*

Synonyms: *Amaranthus melancholicus*, *Amarantus*

Amaranthaceae

Exotic

Introduction: 1665

Earliest American citation: Townley, Boston, 1760

Amaranthus caudatus, love-lies-bleeding. James Vick, Rochester, New York, 1881.

Description: "Well-known hardy annual, from three to four feet high, with blood-red flowers, which hang like pendant spikes, and, at a little distance, look like streams of blood" (Breck 1858).

Design notes: Place in the center of flower beds, in the mixed border, or in the shrubbery. Eben Rexford (1912) recommended planting something of a contrasting color like nasturtium or double yellow French marigold at the base of amaranthus for "fine effect."

Remarks: Peter Henderson (1890) raved about the grace and ornamental character of the brightly colored members of the *Amaranthus* genus. Bailey (1906a) termed love-lies-bleeding "an old favorite."

Historic commercial sources: 31

Amaranthus tricolor

Joseph's coat, floramor, amaranth

Synonyms: *Amaranthus Gangeticus, A. bicolor, A. melancholicus*

Amaranthaceae

Exotic

Amaranthus tricolor, Joseph's coat, provided a flashy effect when massed in the garden. Photograph by author.

Introduction: by 1596

Earliest American citation: Thomas Jefferson, 1786

Description: "Annual, and is admired for its beautiful foliage, red, green, and yellow—tender" (Green 1828). Heights from 18 in. to 5 ft.

Design notes: Cultivated in the flower garden or in the conservatory. The brightly colored foliage of *Amaranthus tricolor* made this a useful plant for a tropical effect (Long 1893).

Remarks: *Gomphrena* and *Celosia* were often called amaranth in the old gardening literature. Joseph's coat sometimes referred to *Alternanthera*.

"One of the most beautiful of ornamental-leaved plants" (Henderson 1890).

Heirloom variety:

Amaranthus tricolor var. *salicifolius*. Berckmans, Georgia, 1873.

Historic commercial sources: 35

Related species:

Alternanthera bettzickiana. Intro: by 1826. Truett, Nashville, 1868. This brightly colored foliage plant often occupied a place of prominence in Victorian bedding designs.

Amaranthus hypochondriacus. Prince's feather. Intro: 1684. Lawson, 1714. Erect red spikes on 3–5-ft. plants. Also called *Amaranthus cruentus* and *A. atropurpureus*. Breck (1858) considered this to be most appropriate for the shrubbery. Prince's feather also referred to *Polygonum orientale*.

Calendula officinalis

pot marigold

Asteraceae

Exotic

Introduction: by 1573

Earliest American citation: John Winthrop, Jr., 1631

Description: An annual, 12-in. high, with flower colors ranging from whitish-yellow to deep orange.

Design notes: "Avoid the orange shade, unless it is to be used in a yellow bed" (Shelton 1931).

Remarks: Although we know *Calendula* was grown in this country from the seventeenth century, it does not show up with any regularity in the ornamentals listings until the twentieth century because of its earlier usefulness in the garden for herbal purposes. Pot marigold, as its common name suggests, occupied the vegetable garden in early American homesteads rather than decorating ornamental beds and borders.

"One of the most universal garden flowers" (Bailey 1906a).

Historic commercial sources: 42

Callistephus chinensis

China aster, German aster

Synonyms: *Aster hortensis, A. chinensis, A. sinensis, Callistemma hortensis, Callistephus hortensis*

Asteraceae

Exotic

Introduction: 1728

Earliest American citation: John Custis, 1735

Description: China asters are half-hardy annuals that range in height from 6 to 30 in. tall. In the nineteenth century they were available in both single and double forms with ray florets, sometimes quilled, in colors of white, purple, red, blush, lilac, red-striped, and purple-striped, accompanied by yellow disks. Shelton (1931) observed that the peony-flowered and the late-branching varieties were the most popular China asters in the 1930s.

Design notes: "White Asters may be combined with Marigolds, and will produce a charming—if rather prim—effect" (Moberly 1899). The tall asters were used in the middle of a border and the shorter-growing dwarf varieties were favorites for carpet bedding. The semidwarfs were prized for container culture.

Remarks: The first asters were single-flowered and red or white. Other colors and forms followed: violet in 1736; double red, 1752; and double white, 1753. M'Mahon observed in 1806 that the China aster was "one of the desirable garden annuals." Bourne (1833) reported that the China aster, rather than the native aster, was most often found in American gardens. During the nineteenth century dozens of varieties of the China aster were introduced. By 1910 garden races included plants with ray flowers of diverse structural forms, including curved inward, curved outward, and quilled (Keeler 1910).

"This annual disputes popularity with the Sweet Pea. Very many persons would prefer it to any other because of its sturdy habit, ease of culture, profusion of bloom, and great variety of color. It is one of the indispensables" (Rexford 1912).

Heirloom varieties:

'California Giant'. Henderson, New York, 1899. "Ostrich feather" type of aster, with extreme spikes on very long stems, in pink, lavender, and white.

'Giant Crego'. Union, Idaho, 1916. Flowers 4–5 in., white, shell pink, rose pink, crimson, lavender, dark blue, and purple.

Historic commercial sources: 56

Celosia argentea var. *cristata*

crested cockscomb, red fox, amaranth

Synonym: *Celosia cristata*

Amaranthaceae

Exotic

Introduction: 1570

Earliest American citation: John Custis, ca. 1738

Description: Crested cockscomb is a 9–12-in. annual with crested flower heads in colors of yellow, rose, and red. "The color of the scarlet varieties is highly brilliant. None of the other colors are so rich" (Breck 1858).

Design notes: Bailey (1906a) observed that the crested cockscomb was a popular subject for pots, with the goal being to have the largest crested flower on the smallest possible plant.

A flamboyant red combination for a window box included dwarf red cockscomb, coleus, and dark crimson sweet William (Hill 1923).

Remarks: "To produce fine combs the soil cannot be made too rich" (Breck 1858).

"A plant with the most peculiar flowers. What we *call* the flower is really a collection of hundreds of tiny individual blossoms set so close together that they seem to complete one large blossom" (Rexford 1912).

Heirloom varieties:

Plumosa Group. Feathered or plumed cockscomb. Dreer, Philadelphia, 1876. Shelton (1931) recommended that groups of three to four plumed cockscombs be placed to rise above a planting of vincas or dwarf zinnias.

Celosia argentea Childsii Group. Chinese woolflower. Arizona Seed, Phoenix, 1925. Plants grow 2–3 ft. high, "the bloom starting early with a central head, round and globular, which often reaches the immense size of two ft. in circumference" (Porter-Walton, Utah, 1926).

Historic commercial sources: 38

A gardener admires his China asters.

Centaurea cyanus

Asteraceae

Exotic

bachelor's button, great blue bottle, ragged sailor, bluet, corn-
flower, bluebottle, French pink, bleuette

Introduction: before 1600

Earliest American citation: Townley, Boston, 1760, "cyanus"

Description: Annual to biennial, 18 in. Bachelor's buttons
may have single and double flowers in blue, white, pink, and
rose shades.

Design notes:

> Of course we can never reflect the sky too often in
> our gardens, so all blue flowers are to be grown
> profusely. Of these the king is the cornflower. . . . It
> is at its best in masses where it does not need, nor
> make you desire, any other flower to perfect the
> beauty. Then sprinkled throughout the garden,
> preferably near the white and golden flowers, it is
> also a harmonizer. (Rion 1912)

"A mass of these plants close-set makes an effective group,
especially when surrounded with two close lines of Silene
armeria." Since their blooms are of short duration in the
early summer, plan to fill in the spaces with a later-bloom-
ing cockscomb (Shelton 1931).

Remarks: "*Centaurea cyanus*—is a common weed throughout
Europe, and also a popular border annual" (Breck 1858).

For regional invasiveness concerns regarding *Centaurea
cyanus*, see Appendix D.

Heirloom variety: Templin & Sons, a Calla, Ohio, firm,
termed the double bachelor's button as "new" in 1904.

Historic commercial sources: 52

Clarkia unguiculata

farewell to spring, godetia, rose-colored clarkia

Synonyms: *Godetia, Clarkia elegans*

Onagraceae

Native

Introduction: 1832

Earliest American citation: Barrett, Boston, 1833

Description: Annual, 1–3 ft. Clarkia has reddish stems with
double or single flowers of purple, rose, or white.

Design notes: Useful for low masses or for edgings; also for
vases and baskets. "They have been much improved by do-
mestication" (Bailey 1906a).

Use in a large garden to add variety (Shelton 1931).

Remarks: "Discovered by Captain Clark, in his expedition,
with Captain Lewis, to the Columbia River" (Breck 1858).

Clarkia. B. K. Bliss & Sons, New York, 1869.

"One of the commonest annual flowers" (Bailey 1906a).

Historic commercial sources: 46

Related species:

Clarkia amoena var. *lindleyi.* Evening primrose. Bartram,
Philadelphia, 1807.

Clarkia pulchella. Beautiful clarkia. Intro: 1826. Bridgeman,
1840.

Consolida ajacis

larkspur, rocket larkspur, branching larkspur

Synonyms: *Delphinium ajacis, D. consolida, Consolida ambigua*

Ranunculaceae

Exotic

Introduction: before 1572

Earliest American citation: Townley, Boston, 1760

Description: Bailey (1906a) described *Delphinium consolida*
and *D. ajacis* as separate species with *D. ajacis,* "the common annual larkspur," being the more floriferous rocket
form and *D. consolida* described as being the candelabrum
or branching form. Larkspurs are 18–36-in. erect annuals
with single or double flowers of blue, violet, pink, and
white.

Design notes: The annual larkspur was used to fill in gaps in
the herbaceous border and as a bedding plant. Used also as
a cut flower.

ANNUAL LARKSPUR.

Consolida ajacis, larkspur. *Vick's Monthly Magazine*, 1883.

Remarks: Typically sold as seed. The common name larkspur traditionally could refer to both annual and perennial types of *Delphinium*.

Historic commercial sources: 53

Coreopsis tinctoria
bright eyes, brown-eyed Susan
Synonyms: *Calliopsis tinctoria, C. elegans*
Asteraceae
Native
Introduction: 1823
Earliest American citation: Bourne, 1833
Description: Annual, 2–3 ft. "The flowers are large and rich,

having a dark crimson-brown center with yellow rays" (Breck 1858).

Design notes: "It has been said that no combination of flowers is complete without yellow; if this is so, Nature is under great obligations to the composite family, in which this color predominates.... It is to *Calliopsis* that we must look for the fine annual species that are so showy in the garden" (Rand 1876).

Remarks: "A common garden annual, showy and good" (Bailey 1906a).

Heirloom variety:

Breck (1858) described a dark-flowered variety of *Calliopsis*: "The center is yellow, surrounded by a circle of dark purple, beyond which to the extremity of the petals, is of a fine scarlet color."

Historic commercial sources: 33

Related species:

Gaillardia pulchella. Indian blanket. Intro: 1833. Breck, 1851. The var. *picta* was frequently offered.

Double-flowered 'Lorenziana' was available in the United States by 1889.

Cosmos bipinnatus
cosmos, Mexican aster
Synonym: *Cosmos hybridus*
Asteraceae
Exotic
Introduction: 1799
Earliest American citation: Allen, Vermont, 1889
Description: Annual; 2–4 ft. *Cosmos* was the subject of early-twentieth-century breeding efforts of Mrs. Theodosia Shepherd in Ventura, California. Her description of this lovely annual would have convinced gardeners everywhere to cultivate it:

> There are white and pink flowers with full, round petals, slightly incurved, very large, resembling camellias, pink and white frilled ones, with very large, broad petals with edges fringed . . . flowers in pink, white and mauve, with plain round petals and large flat eye, having a waxen appearance and yet much resembling Anemone Japonica . . . flowers with a maroon ring around the eye; large pink and white star-like flowers; charming crimson flowers of infinite variety of shape; measuring four and five inches across; white flowers with a delicate mauve ring around the eye. Indeed, there are so many beautiful combinations of shapes, shades

and colors that I cannot find language to properly describe them. (Wickson 1915)

Design notes: Shelton (1931) urged her readers to forego the more intense purplish shades of cosmos because they approached the despised color of magenta. She suggested using only white or pink cosmos in the border. "A tall grower, branching freely, therefore well adapted to back rows or massing" (Rexford 1912).

Remarks: *Cosmos bipinnatus* and *Cosmos sulphureus* are considered weeds in some areas of the Southeast (USDA, NRCS 2002). Deadhead to keep down the seed production in these areas.

Heirloom variety:

'Sensation'. All-American Award of Merit 1936. Four-ft. plants bear white and pink flowers.

Historic commercial sources: 44

Related species:

Cosmos sulphureus. Intro: 1896. Ashby, California, 1908. The golden-yellow variety, 'Klondyke', was available from Breck in 1917.

Dianthus caryophyllus

carnation, clove pink, sops-in-wine, gillyflower

Caryophyllaceae

Exotic

Introduction: Ancient

Earliest American citation: Josselyn, 1672

Zone: 8

Description: Early florists categorized carnations into three classes. *Flakes* had two colors only, with large stripes. *Bizarres* had at least three colors and were variegated in irregular stripes and spots. *Picotees* had a white ground that was spotted with scarlet, red, or purple and had either an even or a serrated edge. The stems typically were 2–3 ft. tall.

Design notes: Gardeners esteemed the carnation for bedding, but it is not clear how often they used it in the traditional border. "A well-grown superior variety, cannot be surpassed, in elegance, beauty, or odor, by any other flower; yet we scarcely ever see it to perfection" (Breck 1858).

Remarks: Grown as a hardy border flower in earlier times, now cultivated as an annual and greenhouse flower. Although carnations were typically categorized as perennials in the early catalogs, prominent horticulturists such as Liberty H. Bailey and Harriett Keeler reported that more Americans grew the greenhouse or tender varieties of carnations, while in England the border carnation was more popular. In 1894 at the American Carnation Society meeting in Indianapolis, Bailey

Dianthus caryophyllus, carnation. Columbus Nursery, Columbus, Ohio, 1877.

urged the growers to encourage more cultivation of the border carnation (Bailey 1906b).

Heirloom varieties:

The Prince Nursery, New York, listed nearly 200 named selections of the carnation in their 1831 catalog. Overall, at least 400 varieties appeared in catalogs throughout the nineteenth and early twentieth centuries. Of these, 'Grenadin' (Allen, Vermont, 1889), a double carnation that bloomed the first season in bright rose, white, vivid scarlet, or soft yellow, is available today.

Historic commercial sources: 121

Dianthus chinensis

China pink, Indian pink

Synonym: *Dianthus sinensis*

Caryophyllaceae

Exotic

Introduction: 1716

Earliest American citation: Townley, Boston, 1760

Description: Biennial or short-lived perennial; 12–15 in. "This species is a biennial of great beauty, but without fragrance; of dwarf habit. The foliage is of a yellowish green. . . . The colors are exceedingly rich; crimson, and dark shades of that color approaching to black, are often combined in the same flower, with edgings of white, pink, or other colors" (Breck 1858).

Design notes: "The single varieties are particularly effective when used behind sweet alyssum or try placing a same color *Portulaca* sparingly around a group of China pinks" (Shelton 1931).

Remarks: *Dianthus chinensis* performed as a perennial for early gardeners, but since then has been bred for use as an annual. Traditionally, its value lay in its long bloom time. China pink has no fragrance; the color range was "anything as long as it is red" (Keeler 1910).

Heirloom variety:

'Heddewigii'. Japan pink. Wendel, Boston, 1867. Growers of the second half of the nineteenth century frequently listed what they called *Dianthus heddewigii*, which, in this century, has been considered a variety of *D. chinensis*. Currently, *Dianthus* ×*heddewigii* is in use to designate hybrid offsprings of *D. barbatus* × *D. chinensis*.

Historic commercial sources: 64

Eschscholzia californica

California poppy, copa-de-oro, cups of gold

Synonym: *Chriseis californica*

Papaveraceae

Native

Introduction: 1792

Earliest American citation: Barrett, Boston, 1836

Zone: 7

Description: Eschscholzia is a showy, short-lived perennial, 12–15 in., used as an annual, originally portrayed as having flowers of yellow, orange, and white. Later writers also described rose, carmine, and scarlet varieties.

Design notes: "A bed of it will be a sheet of richest golden yellow for many weeks" (Rexford 1912).

Remarks: Keeler (1910) said that one of the early names for California was Land of Fire because of the brilliant colors of poppies blooming on the hillsides.

Heirloom varieties:

'Alba'. Plant, St. Louis, 1875. White California poppy.

'Carmine King'. Ferguson, Oklahoma, 1920. Beautiful carmine rose.

'Golden West'. Cox, San Francisco, 1907. "Intense shining yellow fading to orange."

'Mandarin'. Cox, San Francisco, 1907. "Large scarlet, inside orange."

Historic commercial sources: 45

Eschscholzias, or California poppies, came in different shades of orange and gold. *Vick's Monthly Magazine*, 1884.

Gomphrena globosa

globe amaranth, bachelor's buttons, everlasting, English clover

Synonym: *Amaranthus*

Amaranthaceae

Exotic

Introduction: 1714

Earliest American citation: Townley, Boston, 1760

Description: Annual, 1–3 ft. Everlasting flowers resemble clover heads with blooms in shades of white, red, and orange, as well as white-striped, flesh-colored, and purplish-crimson.

Design notes: "Plant a patch 3 by 2 feet of the garnet red *nana compacta*, 8 inches apart, margined with a band of the pink variety" (Shelton 1931).

Gomphrena was considered to be a "grandmother's garden" flower.

Gomphrena globosa, globe amaranth. James Vick, Rochester, New York, 1881.

Remarks: Usually offered as seeds; Joseph Breck's (1858) advice for successful germination was to soak them in milk for twelve hours before planting.

Historic commercial sources: 37

Gypsophila elegans
annual baby's breath
Caryophyllaceae
Exotic
Introduction: 1828
Earliest American citation: Bridgeman, 1840
Description: Annual, 12–30 in. "A plant of great daintiness, both in foliage and flowers. . . . White and pink" (Rexford 1912).
Design notes: "Useful for mist-like effects in mixed borders and containers" (Bailey 1906a).
Baby's breath was also a valuable plant for the cutting garden or for rockwork.
Remarks: "Much cultivated and handsome" (Bailey 1906a).
Heirloom varieties:
'Carminea'. Michell, Philadelphia, 1931. Bright carmine-rose flowers.
'Covent Garden'. Grand Junction Seed, Colorado, 1936. Single, white flowers.
Historic commercial sources: 31

Helichrysum bracteatum
strawflower, everlasting, immortelle
Synonym: *Helichrysum monstrosum*
Asteraceae
Exotic
Introduction: 1799
Earliest American citation: Buist, 1839
Description: The strawflower is a hardy annual, 1–3 ft., prized for its showy papery bracts. The main colors were orange and yellow, but red, pink, and white also were represented.
Design notes: "I should never consider a garden of pleasant

Helichrysum bracteatum, strawflower. James Vick, Rochester, New York, 1881.

annual flowers to be complete that did not contain some of the 'everlastings,' or immortelles. . . . The colours are bright, the blooms hold longer on the plant, and most of the kinds are very easy to grow. My favorite groups are the different kinds of xeranthemums and helichrysums" (Bailey 1903).
Remarks: "A family of plants much admired on account of the beauty of their flowers, when dried; which, if gathered when they first open, and carefully dried, retain their color and shape for many years" (Breck 1858).
"This blossom, which is of the everlasting type, should be sown where it is to grow, and does better if not transplanted" (Hill 1923).
Heirloom varieties:
Monstrosum Series (syn. *Helichrysum monstrosum*). Wendel, Boston, 1867. The extra-large flowers of what we refer to now as the Monstrosum Series were available in singles and doubles and in many colors including purple, white, rose, crimson, bright-scarlet, red, and yellow. Bailey used this name to designate double flowers only.
Historic commercial sources: 41
Related species:
Acroclinium roseum (syn. *Helipterum roseum*). Pink and white everlasting. Wendel, Boston, 1867.
Rhodanthe manglesii. Swan River everlasting. Intro: 1832. Breck, 1851. Like *Acroclinium*, *Rhodanthe* spent some time in the genus *Helipterum* before being reclassified to *Rhodanthe*. Bailey cited this everlasting as one of the most long lasting after it was dried.

Heliotropium arborescens
heliotrope, cherry pie
Synonym: *Heliotropium peruviana*
Boraginaceae
Exotic
Introduction: 1757
Earliest American citation: Thomas Jefferson, 1786
Description: "They are hardy greenhouse shrubs, with rough

foliage and corymbs of fragrant purplish flowers" (Rand 1876). Heliotrope was available in colors ranging from white to shades of lavender, purple, and blue.

Design notes: Bedding, border, or greenhouse and house-plant. Heliotropes were also popular in Victorian times for window gardens and as a florists' cut flower.

"There is no more desirable bedding plant than the Heliotrope. . . . It is admirable for replacing Pansies. . . . Combines with purple Ageratum for excellent effect" (Bennett 1903).

"A mass of low-growing Heliotrope with a border of Sweet Alyssum or white Petunia is also desirable" (Shelton 1931).

Remarks: Victorian writers and growers referred to heliotrope for both *Heliotropium peruviana* (now *H. arborescens*) and *H. corymbosum*, described by some as having a scent more like a narcissus. It is likely that some heliotropes were also hybrids between these two species.

"Heliotropes are universally esteemed for their delightful fragrance, and should be in every garden" (Columbus Nursery, Ohio, 1862). Unfortunately, heliotropes in the twenty-first century rarely have the signature vanilla scent. The white or lighter colored heliotropes have the most consistently sweet fragrance. Modern selections based on good old-fashioned fragrance include 'Old-fashioned Purple' and 'Iowa'.

Historic commercial sources: 56

Impatiens balsamina

touch-me-not, lady's slipper, balsam, somer-sots
Synonym: *Balsamina hortensis*
Balsaminaceae
Exotic

Impatiens balsamina, balsam. Storrs & Harrison, Painesville, Ohio, 1896.

Introduction: 1596

Earliest American citation: Townley, Boston, 1760

Description: Tender annual, 12–24 in. The flowers of the type were single and rose-red, but under cultivation very double blossoms developed. Full-double flowers were called "camellia-flowered." Nineteenth-century seed producers offered balsams in rose, variegated, "fire-colored," purple, white, and crimson.

Design notes: "Balsams are grown chiefly for their value as flower-garden plants; but some years ago the fls. were largely used as 'groundwork' in florists' designs, particularly the double white varieties. The flowers were wired to toothpicks, and were then thrust into the moss which formed the body of the design" (Bailey 1906a).

Remarks: "What can be compared to the Camellia Balsam, as double as a rose; no wax work nor any other imitation of man, can compare with it in rich appearance and dazzling beauty. The white and scarlet spotted is unequalled among flowers" (Elder 1863).

"Widely cultivated" (Bailey 1906a, Keeler 1910).

Heirloom variety:

'Camellia-flowered'. Elder, 1863. "An old favorite, producing large masses of beautiful brilliant-colored flowers in the greatest profusion . . . camellia-flowered" (Ullathorne, Memphis, 1895).

Historic commercial sources: 56

Related species:

Impatiens walleriana (syn. *Impatiens sultana*). Sultan's balsam. "Recent introduction. . . . It is without question, destined to become very popular" (Vick 1884).

Lobelia erinus

edging lobelia
Campanulaceae
Exotic
Introduction: 1752

Earliest American citation: Wendel, Boston, 1867

Description: Trailing annual or perennial, 6–12 in. *Lobelia erinus* has "small blue flowers in great profusion" (Rand 1876). Edging lobelia was quite variable in form and color. Some had very dwarf habits that were well suited to bedding. Foliage colors could be green and there were also golden-foliaged and bronzy types. Flowers, in addition to the standard dark violet blue, were available in light blue, white, crimson, and rose by 1900, some of these with the additional variation of a white eye.

Design notes: "One of the commonest of all edging plants particularly for early season effects" (Bailey 1906a).

"It is beautiful as an edging plant or for a mass effect" (Wickson 1915).

Lobelia was an important bedding plant and was considered useful for baskets.

Remarks: "Lobelia erinus is also a good pot-plant for the winter conservatory" (Bailey 1906a).

Heirloom variety:

'Crystal Palace'. Wendel, Boston, 1867. This dark blue lobelia was a good variety for bedding at a compact 6 in. in height.

Historic commercial sources: 49

Lobularia maritima

sweet alyssum

Synonyms: *Alyssum odoratum, A. calycinum, A. balsamifolium, Koeniga maritima*

Brassicaceae

Exotic

Introduction: Long cultivated

Earliest American citation: M'Mahon, 1806

Description: Hardy annual, 6–9 in. Sweet alyssum bears small, honey-scented, usually white flowers in terminal racemes in combination with light green foliage. There was a variegated-leaf form by 1874 and in the early 1900s rose and lilac varieties were for sale.

Design notes: Sweet alyssum is a dwarf, spreading annual that was popular as an edging plant and for flower borders. It could also be found in bedding schemes and in rockwork and was used as a pot plant and window garden plant. One late-nineteenth-century recommendation was to use sweet alyssum to carpet under *Gladiolus* beds, "the baby faces . . . received nearly as much admiration as the gay spikes above them" (Beers 1895).

Remarks: Most firms offered this as seed.

Isabella G. Oakley (1886), speaking of gardens in San Francisco, observed that sweet alyssum was "much used for borders."

Heirloom variety: 'Carpet of Snow'. I'm not sure how the old 'Carpet of Snow' compares with the currently available 'New Carpet of Snow'. Plants with this type of name have been popular at least since 1904.

Historic commercial sources: 57

Matthiola incana 'Annua'

dwarf ten-week stock, stock gillyflower, Julyflower, cut-and-come-again

Synonyms: *Matthiola annua, Cheiranthus annuus*

Brassicaceae

Exotic

Matthiola incana 'Annua', ten-week stock. Storrs & Harrison, Painesville, Ohio, 1896.

Introduction: 1596

Earliest American citation: John Winthrop, Jr., 1631

Description: Biennial or perennial, usually treated as an annual, 12–30 in.

"Elegant leaf, elegant plant, beautiful, showy, and most fragrant flower" (Breck 1858).

"Most of the garden forms are double. . . . The colors are most various, running from white through rose, crimson, purple and parti-colored" (Bailey 1906a).

Design notes: "Stocks are among the most common of all garden flowers" (Bailey 1906a).

Remarks: *Matthiola* was the subject of intensive breeding in the nineteenth century. In 1836 only the white and purple selections were offered, but by the 1860s one Massachusetts nursery offered twenty-four varieties of the dwarf ten-week stock as well as seven other categories of stock. Early books distinguished between the autumn-flowering Brompton stock, *Matthiola incana*, and the summer-blooming variety, *M. annua*, now designated as *M. incana* 'Annua'.

Historic commercial sources: 52

Mesembryanthemum crystallinum

ice plant, diamond ficoidas, frozen plant, diamond-fig-marygold

Synonym: *Mesembryanthemum glaciale*

Aizoaceae

Exotic

Mesembryanthemum crystallinum, ice plant. Peter Henderson, *Henderson's Handbook of Plants*, 1890.

Introduction: 1773

Earliest American citation: William Faris, 1793

Description: A tender, succulent annual, 6–10 in., with thick, fleshy leaves that have the appearance of being covered with crystals of ice. Flowers were white to light rose.

Design notes: A common houseplant that was also used in hanging baskets and vases. According to Liberty H. Bailey (1906a), many species in *Mesembryanthemum* were good for bedding and edging. They were also suitable for rock gardens. Ice plant was grown primarily for its interesting foliage.

Remarks: "The plants are highly ornamental and contrast well with other annuals" (Breck 1858). Although many sources insist that this was primarily cultivated as a houseplant, in catalogs it was commonly found on the same page with annuals for the out-of-doors.

Historic commercial sources: 36

Mirabilis jalapa

four-o'clock, marvel of Peru, noon-sleep, dwarf morning-glory

Nyctaginaceae

Exotic

Introduction: 1596

Earliest American citation: Thomas Jefferson, 1767

Description: Treated as a tender annual, 2–3 ft. "A great favorite, combining beauty of foliage, profuseness of bloom, of rich and varied colors, and delicious fragrance" (Michel, St. Louis, 1876). The four-o'clock has tubular flowers and in the nineteenth century it was available in many colors, including crim-son, red-striped with white, lilac-striped with white, chamois, yellow, yellow and red, violet, and white.

Design notes: Useful as a bedding plant or as a filler for the border. Bailey (1906a) suggested that *Mirabilis jalapa* made a good hedge at the rear of a flower garden, with plants spaced 1 ft. apart.

Remarks: Often the seed was available rather than plants. The common name four o'clock came from the fact of its blooming every day in late afternoon.

"Hawkmoths love this plant" (Gosse 1838).

Historic commercial sources: 48

Related species:

Mirabilis longiflora. Long-flowered four-o'clock. Intro: 1759. M'Mahon, 1806.

Papaver somniferum

poppy, annual poppy, opium poppy

Papaveraceae

Exotic

Introduction: Long cultivated

Earliest American citation: Townley, Boston, 1760

Description: Annual, 2–3 ft. "The Poppy displays to perfection all color-tones, beginning with white and ranging through pink, blush, salmon, scarlet, and 'red to blackness.' Indeed such diversity does this flower show in form, color, and habit of growth, that a collection of Poppies is a complete flower garden in itself" (Moberly 1899).

Design notes:

Sow Poppy seed freely wherever there is a corner to spare, especially if there is a corner that would otherwise be neglected and grow up in weeds. It is surprising how many places can be found to sow them. A barren angle of a fence, a vacant strip behind or at the side of some outbuilding, an

Papaver somniferum, annual poppies. Photograph by author.

exposed spot among trees where nothing else will grow, a foot of ground here and there, in the perennial border and among late flowering plants, where the Poppies will have danced through their brief season of bloom and passed on before the former have discovered that they need the room ... also plant a long narrow bed of poppies. Where there is sufficient shade, Myosotis and Anchusa are lovely among the poppies. (Bennett 1903)

Mrs. Francis King (1915) suggested planting double rose-pink poppies with pearly white platycodon.

Remarks: Often the catalogs and books discussed "annual poppies" without specifying which species. Most of the listings were probably for *P. somniferum*, but also included *P. rhoeas*, and possibly even a few *Eschscholzia*.

"*Papaver somniferum* is the best known and the most variable ... [the] chief objection is the shortness of the flowering season and the death of the plant immediately after; thus leaving its place in the garden bare in midsummer" (Keeler 1910). *Papaver somniferum* may not be grown legally in many areas of the United States. Please refer to Appendix D for regional invasiveness information and your state department of agriculture for laws impacting poppy's cultivation.

Heirloom varieties:

'Carnation-flowered'. Double-flowered opium poppy. Townley, Boston, 1760.

'Paeony-flowered'. Wendel, Boston, 1867.

Historic commercial sources: 53

Related species:

Papaver rhoeas. Shirley seed strain. Shirley poppy. Intro: 1880. Ullathorne, Memphis, 1895. The four characteristics of a Shirley poppy: always single, white base, stamens yellow or white, and never any black. "The Shirley Poppies are almost like fairy flowers, they are so delicate and beautiful" (Ely 1903).

Pelargonium ×hortorum

bedding geranium, crane's bill
Geraniaceae
Exotic
Introduction: 1732
Earliest American citation: Spurrier, 1793
Description: Tender subshrub, used as an annual, with single or double flowers in shades of red, rose, salmon, and white. The foliage may be green or variegated with white or yellow.

'Crystal Palace Gem' geranium is a nineteenth-century variety that is still available. Photograph by author.

Design notes: "Among the most showy and popular bedding plants, after verbenas" (Columbus Nursery, Ohio, 1863).

"For bedding, hedges, and border plants" (Ashby, California, 1908). The geranium was also popular for window gardens and container culture.

Remarks: *Pelargonium ×hortorum* = *P. zonale* × *P. inquinas*. At the beginning of the twentieth century, Liberty H. Bailey remarked, "If a window or a garden can have but one plant, that plant is likely to be a geranium" (Wilson 1946).

Heirloom varieties: Approximately 875 varieties were listed in the old catalogs. The following are among those still available commercially:

'Crystal Palace Gem'. Intro: by 1876. Good & Reese, Ohio, 1889. "Broad, golden-yellow margin, with a central disc of green." Other geraniums with similar names and descriptions are: 'Crystal Palace', "leaf disk bright green, broadly margined golden yellow" (Allen, Vermont, 1889) and 'Crystal Gem', "crimson, tall" (Michel, St. Louis, 1876).

Historic commercial sources: 66

Related species:

Pelargonium ×domesticum. Regal pelargonium. Martha (Lady) Washington geranium. Intro: before 1830. Brookfield, Missouri, 1869.

Pelargonium graveolens. Rose geranium. Intro: before 1787. Jean Skipwith, ca. 1800. Harriet Keeler (1910) observed that the rose geranium was primarily used in borders.

Pelargonium inquinans. Stained geranium. Intro: before 1753. M'Mahon, 1806. The parent of many of the later hybrids.

Pelargonium odoratissimum. Apple-scented geranium. Intro: before 1753. M'Mahon, 1806.

Pelargonium quercifolium. Oak-leafed geranium. Intro: before 1787. M'Mahon, 1806.

Pelargonium tomentosum. Peppermint geranium. Intro: 1790. M'Mahon, 1806.

Pelargonium zonale. Zonal geranium. Intro: before 1753. George Washington, ca. 1800.

Petunia ×hybrida

hybrid petunia
Synonym: *Nierembergia Atkinsiana*
Solanaceae
Exotic
Introduction: 1837
Earliest American citation: *The Horticulturist,* 1847
Description: *Vick's Monthly Magazine* described the following sorts of *Petunia* as being in cultivation in the 1870s:

1. Grandiflora varieties—"Strong succulent growth." Stems and leaves are sticky to the touch. Few flowers, but very large—3–4 in. across. The fringed petunia is a type of grandiflora.

2. Double petunias.

3. Small-flowered varieties—"Slender, wiry growth . . . bear an immense number of flowers." Colors are bright and variable.

The striped petunias appear to be a subgroup of the small-flowered types—singles, stripes are variable—in one illustration, the stripes form a star shape and in the other they outline the petals. (Vick 1878d; 1879b).

Design notes: "The single petunia is too coarse for the front yard, still for its beauty of colors and fragrance it deserves a place and I would suggest an oval bed beside the carriage drive . . . distance lends enchantment" (Kulp 1879).

The old-fashioned 'Balcony' petunia attracts the dew in the early morning. Photograph by author.

"Particularly useful for massing against shrubbery, for they make a florid undergrowth with almost no care" (Bailey 1906a).

Remarks: Liberty H. Bailey chronicled the history of the petunia in his book of essays dealing with evolutionary topics, *The Survival of the Unlike.* In 1823, the first *Petunia* was introduced into cultivation from South America. *Petunia nyctaginiflora* had an upright habit, sticky leaves and stems, and long-tubed white flowers that were fragrant at night. *Petunia violacea* from Argentina bloomed for the first time in the Glasgow Botanic Garden in 1831. It was originally known as *Salpiglossis integrifolia* and had narrower leaves than the white petunia and small violet-purple flowers.

The first hybrids between these two were observed in 1837. These hybrids were taxonomically placed in their own species, *Nierembergia Atkinsiana.* The early hybrids were described as pale pink with dark center, sulphur with dark center, white with dark center, and others streaked and veined with darker color. Bailey observed that the double-fringed petunia was the culmination of *Petunia* breeding and that interest had died down by the beginning of the twentieth century.

Contemporary hybrids are a complex group and are descendents of the originally cultivated species, now called *Petunia axillaris* (*P. nyctaginiflora*) × *P. integrifolia* (*P. violacea*).

Heirloom varieties: Of over 200 varieties listed in pre-1940 catalogs, these two are still available commercially:

'Balcony'. Porter-Walton, Utah, 1926. Large, single forms in colors of blue, rose, white, royal purple, and violet blotched with white. "The Balcony type, of trailing habit, are excellent for porch and window boxes."

'Howard's Star'. "About the center is a star, merged into the ground color at the margin, mixed colors" (Storrs-Harrison, Ohio, 1908).

Historic commercial sources: 52

Phlox drummondii

annual phlox, Drummond's phlox
Polemoniaceae
Native
Introduction: 1835
Earliest American citation: Buist, 1839
Description: Annual, 6–15 in. "The Phlox Drummondii was only discovered about 40 years ago, in Texas, by Mr. Drummond. . . . No annual excels the Phlox for a brilliant and constant display. . . . The colors range from the purest white to the deepest crimson, including purple, and striped, the

Drummond's Phlox. Peter Henderson, *Henderson's Handbook of Plants*, 1890.

clear eye of the Phlox being peculiarly marked. There is a yellow variety, but the color is not very clear" (Vick 1878i).

Design notes: *Phlox drummondii* was popular for planting in beds, combining the different colors available in the species for contrasting effects as Eben Rexford suggested in 1912: "Charming effects are easily secured by planting the pale rose, pure white, and soft yellow varieties together, either in rows or circles. The contrast will be fine and the harmony perfect." The white varieties can be used freely as they "heighten the effect of the strong colors."

Remarks: "This is essential for the smallest collection" (Gold 1850).

"If we could have but one flower for our garden it would be Phlox" (Iowa Seed, Des Moines, 1914).

Heirloom varieties: In the old catalogs there were over sixty named varieties, all of which appear to be lost to cultivation.

Historic commercial sources: 54

Portulaca grandiflora

flowering moss, moss rose, great-flowered purslane, sun plant, eleven o'clock

Portulacaceae

Exotic

Introduction: 1827

Earliest American citation: Buist, 1839

Description: Annual, 4–8 in. "Portulaca is a lovable little creature, living in the sand and the sun . . . has varied into many garden forms. The present color range varies from pure-white to yellow, orange, rose, scarlet, crimson, and deep-red. Double forms are common, but not desirable. A bed will often perpetuate itself, and in some places the plant persists about old gardens" (Keeler 1910).

Design notes: Portulaca was a good plant to use to cover a bulb bed. The single varieties also could be used for ribbon gardening.

"Portulaca is a consistent bloomer affording a constant mass of color over the summer months. . . . . A package of mixed seed will stock any garden for years at a cost of five cents" (Rand 1876).

Remarks:

"This plant might well be called a vegetable salamander, as it flourishes in dry, hot locations, where other plants would utterly fail" (Rexford 1912).

One gardener from Oregon wrote to *Vick's Monthly Magazine* in 1878 to report, "For gorgeous, brilliant show of color, nothing, I think, can surpass the Portulaca. I have a large bed of them . . . and it is of the most metallic brilliancy imaginable" (Olney 1878).

Historic commercial sources: 50

Reseda odorata

sweet scented mignonette, Frenchman's darling

Synonym: *Reseda alba* (also a species in its own right)

Resedaceae

Exotic

Introduction: 1752

Earliest American citation: William Faris, 1792

Description: Annual, 12–24 in. The old variety of mignonette had small spikes of inconspicuous flowers with delightful fragrance, "perfuming the whole region about the premises" (Breck 1851). After breeders began working with it, several cultivars were described as having red or white in them. However, the editor of *The Ladies' Floral Cabinet* observed in 1883 that there really was not a true scarlet or white mignonette and that the description had to be taken in a relative sense—perhaps a reddish tinge to flowers that had appeared white at first glance (Answers to correspondents 1883).

Design notes: Bridgeman (1840) recommended that mignonette be planted with *Clarkia pulchella*, which thrived in the same poor soil.

"This is one of the plants that is greatly desired in every garden, not because of the beauty of its flowers, but because of

Castor bean attracts the eye in this simple flower bed, ca. 1910.

Heirloom varieties:

'Grandiflora'. Wendel, Boston, 1867. "An universal favorite on account of its delicate fragrance" (Ullathorne, Memphis, 1895).

'Machet'. Allen, Vermont, 1889. "Dwarf and vigorous growth with massive spikes of deliciously scented red flowers" (Lippincott, Minnesota, 1898).

Historic commercial sources: 55

Ricinus communis

castor bean, palma-Christi

Euphorbiaceae

Exotic

Introduction: Long cultivated

Earliest American citation: Brickell, 1737

Description: Shrub treated as an annual, 6–8 ft. "Valued for its striking green or reddish foliage topped by brilliant red blossoms" (Hume 1929). "Almost everyone has admired a fine specimen of the Castor-oil plant. There is a luxuriance of growth, a breadth of foliage of an attractive form, and an altogether unusual air . . . about the plant that arrest the attention of the most indifferent observer" (A bit of the subtropical 1872).

Design notes: The castor bean was deemed useful as a large, dramatic accent. "The best effect is secured by growing four or five plants in a group. None of the tropical plants that have come into prominence in gardening, during the past ten or twelve years, are nearly as effective as this easily grown annual, whose seed sell at five cents a package" (Rexford 1912).

Although its fragrance can sometimes be elusive, *Reseda odorata*, sweet mignonette, is a charming addition to any heirloom garden. Photograph by author.

the beauty of the plant, its fragrance, and poetical association" (Allen 1894).

Remarks: The catalogs all praised the heady fragrance of mignonette, but that attribute seems to have been lost in modern seed strains. I conducted an experiment in the summer of 2002 when I planted seeds from four different companies, trying to find the ever elusive fragrant mignonette. The resulting plants were attractive, but scentless. Isabella Oakley in *Vick s Monthly Magazine* (1886) wrote, "The reason that some Mignonette has scarcely any scent, is, because the soil in which it is cultivated is too rich." Harriet Keeler also discussed the subject of fragrance in her 1910 book. She wrote that mignonette is a "well-known garden favorite . . . the reddish anthers give the color . . . [the] ideal plant has large spikes, but enlarging the spikes has not improved fragrance—in some cases the fragrance has turned disagreeable . . . the old garden form, with its light, sweet, pleasant fragrance, holds its own among the fifty improved varieties offered by the trade" (Keeler 1910).

"Castor-bean is a perennial far South, assuming tree-like proportions, with trunks six or eight inches in diameter and ten to fifteen feet high, often planted to secure quick shade" (Hume 1929).

Remarks: *Ricinus communis* is the source of the old-time medicinal tonic, castor oil. All parts of the plant are poisonous.

For regional invasiveness concerns regarding *Ricinus communis*, see Appendix D.

Heirloom varieties:

'Borboniensis'. Wendel, Boston, 1867. Huge foliage.

'Cambodgensis'. Allen, Vermont, 1889. Maroon foliage, black stems.

'Gibsonii'. Allen, Vermont, 1889. Dwarf, purplish leaves and stems, with metallic tinge.

'Sanguineus'. Wendel, Boston, 1867. Blood red stalks and foliage.

'Zanzibarensis'. O'Keefe, New York, 1870. Immense leaves, green, brown, or purplish; contemporary descriptions say that it is veined with white.

Historic commercial sources: 33

Salpiglossis sinuata

large flowering salpiglossis, painted tongue, velvet trumpet, tube tongue

Synonym: *Salpiglossis variabilis*

Solanaceae

Exotic

Introduction: 1824

Earliest American citation: Bridgeman, 1840

Description: Annual, 18–24 in. "Resembles a petunia, but taller (2 ft.) and different colors—purple, blue, red, yellow, orange, and cream in bewildering combinations, and then each flower veined and penciled with darker lines than the basic color" (Keeler 1910).

Design notes: Plant in masses to avoid the appearance of a single bare stem (Keeler 1910).

"This is an indispensable annual to give color to the garden or border" (Allen, Sterling & Lothrop, Maine, 1937).

Remarks: "Really freakish in its peculiar markings" (Rexford 1912). Some of the older references place this genus in Scrophulariaceae (snapdragon) family.

Historic commercial sources: 46

Salpiglossis resembles a petunia, but is variously colored in shades of purple, orange, and red. *Vick's Monthly Magazine*, 1883.

Salvia splendens

scarlet sage

Lamiaceae

Exotic

Introduction: 1822

Earliest American citation: Brighton, Boston, 1833

Description: Annual, 12–24 in. "One of the most brilliant red-flowered plants in cultivation. The mass of color of a well-grown bed defies description; it is magnificent, and it is barbaric" (Keeler 1910).

Design notes: Scarlet sage was popular in bedding. "Another excellent flower for producing strong effects when used in masses. . . . I have seen it planted among clumps of white perennial Phlox with very satisfactory results" (Rexford 1886).

Salvia splendens. W. A. Manda, South Orange, New Jersey, 1897.

Mrs. Helen Boyd cradles a bouquet of annual flowers including *Salvia splendens*, ca. 1885.

"An exceedingly brilliant combination can be made by the use of scarlet Salvia, as the center of a bed six or eight feet across, with the Calliopsis surrounding it. The scarlet and yellow of these two flowers will make the place fairly blaze with color and they will continue to bloom until frost comes" (Rexford 1912).

Remarks: Ornamental sages "are beautiful plants for masses, or beds, when properly managed" (Breck 1858).

Heirloom varieties:

'Alba'. Berckmans, Georgia, 1873. White form of the scarlet bedding salvia.

'Bonfire'. Henderson, New York, 1910.

Historic commercial sources: 59

Related species:

Salvia argentea. Silver sage. Intro: 1759. Wendel, Boston, 1867. A biennial that features dramatic, woolly, silver, basal foliage.

Salvia azurea. Meadow sage. Intro: 1806. Saco, Maine, 1853. This is a native perennial sage. The subspecies *pitcheri* was also used in nineteenth-century gardens.

Salvia farinacea. Mealy cup sage. Lippincott, Minnesota, 1898. "Entirely distinct from all other Salvias, producing pretty, long spikes of delicate silvery sky-blue flowers" (Templin, Ohio, 1904).

Scabiosa atropurpurea

mourning bride, sweet scabiosa, scabious, pincushion flower, mourning widow

Dipsacaceae

Exotic

Introduction: 1621

Earliest American citation: Townley, Boston, 1760

Description: Annual, 1–3 ft. The flowers are in long-peduncled heads and may be either single or double. Colors vary from deep purples to shades of red, blue, white, and salmon rose.

Design notes: "A hardy ornamental plant, suitable for the border; it may be sown any time in May, and will produce its flowers from July to October" (Breck 1858).

"An annual plant producing beautiful flowers; but they soon
fade, continuing only an hour or two" (Green 1828).

Remarks: "A garden favorite because of easy culture, extended
period of bloom, and richness of color range" (Keeler 1910).

Historic commercial sources: 47

Schizanthus pinnatus

butterfly flower, poor man's orchid, fringe flower
Solanaceae
Exotic
Introduction: 1822
Earliest American citation: Barrett, Boston, 1836
Description: Annual, 18–24 inches. Butterfly flower usually
has a darker lower lip in shades of violet or purple, a paler
upper section of the flower, and a yellow and purple mid-
section. There were white forms and marbled forms (Bai-
ley1906a).
Design notes: Used for bedding or in pots.
Remarks: Several species of *Schizanthus* were known to early
gardeners.
Historic commercial sources: 34

Solenostemon scutellarioides

coleus, painted nettle
Synonyms: *Coleus ×hybrida, C. blumei*
Lamiaceae
Exotic
Introduction: 1851
Earliest American citation: Truett, Nashville, 1868
Description: Annual, 10–16 in. Coleus is a colorful foliage
plant with leaves deeply serrated to crenately edged, in colors
ranging from green to diverse variegations involving red,
purple, orange, gold, brown, maroon, pink, or white.
Design notes: Gardeners considered coleus to be "indispensable for ornamental bedding" (Bennett 1903). It also was
valued as a container plant.
Remarks: "Would that the Coleus might vanish from the
land! But, after all, it is not the plants, poor things, but the
people who grow them who are to blame" (Ely 1903).
Heirloom varieties:
Over 150 varieties of coleus were described in early catalogs
of which these names are still in the nursery trade. It is always important to cross-check descriptions when trying to
locate heirloom flowers to be sure that a modern grower
has not used an old name on a new plant.
'Beckwith's Gem'. Storrs & Harrison, Ohio, 1908. "Large
leaves of heavy texture and finely scalloped edges. The cen-

A Dozen Good Coleus. *Vick's Monthly Magazine*, 1880.

'Beckwith's Gem' coleus was available in the United States by 1908.
Photograph by author.

ter of the leaf is dark velvety maroon, bordered with fiery
red; the edge is green, changing to creamy yellow at the
point of the leaf."

'Brilliancy' coleus (by 1908). Photograph by author.

The 'Striped Dwarf' marigold has been known in this country since the early 1800s. Photograph by author.

'Brightness'. Storrs & Harrison, Ohio, 1896. "Bright red center, bounded with maroon, edged light green."

'Brilliancy'. Storrs & Harrison, Ohio, 1908. "Rich, lustrous carmine merging into maroon; the margins capriciously outlined in yellow and green."

'Buttercup'. Louisville Rose, Kentucky, 1881. "Marbled, bright green, mottled and marked with pure yellow spots."

'Chameleon'. Dreer, Philadelphia, 1876. "Variegated violet, rich scarlet and chocolate, with white edge."

'Firebrand'. Thompson, Kentucky, 1888. "Maroon, flamed and shaded with brilliant fiery red" (Storrs & Harrison, Ohio, 1896).

'Joseph's Coat'. Good & Reese, Ohio, 1889. "Mottled violet, white, purple and green."

'Kentish Fire'. Good & Reese, Ohio, 1889. "Bright crimson edged with carmine."

'Midnight'. Storrs & Harrison, Ohio, 1896. "Dark maroon, flamed with crimson."

'Sunbeam'. Dreer, Philadelphia, 1876. "Dark bronzy crimson, golden edge."

Historic commercial sources: 51

Tagetes erecta
African marigold, Indian pink
Asteraceae
Exotic
Introduction: by 1535
Earliest American citation: Townley, Boston, 1760, "Africans"
Description: Hardy annual, about 24 in. high with an open, branching habit. Bailey (1906a) observed that the African marigold has flowers that are three to four times the size of those of *T. patula* and that they are typically a single color,

lemony yellow being the favorite. One of the forms had quilled petals.

Design notes: The African marigold was considered more suitable for the shrubbery or mixed border than for bedding.

Remarks: The African marigold was the "common marigold of old gardens" (Bailey 1906a).

Heirloom variety:
'El Dorado'. Storrs & Harrison, Ohio, 1896. Extra large double flowers in shades of primrose, gold, and yellow.

Historic commercial sources: 50

Tagetes patula
French marigold
Asteraceae
Exotic
Introduction: 1572
Earliest American citation: Spurrier, 1793
Description: Annual about 12 in. tall with dark green, pinnately divided foliage. Single and double flowers were available in shades of red, orange, yellow, or gold.

Design notes: Used for bedding or edging.

Remarks: "A well-known tender annual; one of the old-fashioned flowers; deservedly popular, from the brilliancy and variegation of its flowers" (Breck 1858).

"The French [marigolds] are variously hued and striped and are very handsome, both in flower and foliage, but one never gets very affectionate with any of the marigolds because of their somewhat medicinal odors" (Wickson 1915).

Heirloom variety:
'Striped Dwarf'. Jean Skipwith, ca. 1800.

Historic commercial sources: 45

Related species:

Tagetes tenuifolia 'Pumila' (syn. *Tagetes signata*). Intro: 1797. Wendel, Boston, 1867. "A beautiful delicate plant of dwarf habit; covered with hundreds of bright yellow blossoms, marked with a brown stripe through the center of each petal."

Tropaeolum majus

tall nasturtium, Indian cress

Tropaeolaceae

Exotic

Introduction: 1684

Earliest American citation: Bethabara, North Carolina, 1759

Description: Climbing annual 1–5 ft., with irregularly shaped flowers in shades, primarily, of yellow, orange, and red, although one 1889 catalog offered purple. The leaves are peltate (rounded) in shape. Double-flowered forms were available after 1885. Bourne (1833) observed that the nasturtium was "phosphorescent, or emits light in the dark." Unfortunately, this characteristic is not apparent in contemporary forms.

Design notes: "The two chief groups among nasturtiums are those in which the plants are of small compact, bushy growth and those which throw out long running branches. . . . The dwarf type of nasturtium is most desirable for edging flower beds and garden walks. . . . The tall or running varieties . . . [are useful] for pot culture, hanging baskets, vases, window boxes . . . or for planting along the fences, walls . . . or for a long border" (Darlington 1909).

Eben Rexford (1912) described a pleasing combination as a bed of vibrant nasturtium flowers edged with the dull red annual candytuft.

"The prettiest blue border I ever saw was one wherein a few nasturtium seeds had been accidentally dropped, and between the elegantly aspiring stalks of Larkspur and Anchusa one got little sparkles of flame and saffron and buff that endowed the blue flowers with a shimmering spirit" (Wilder 1918).

Remarks: Besides their obvious ornamental effect, nasturtiums have been used for centuries for their edible qualities. The leaves were used to provide a peppery flavor to salads, thus the name Indian cress. The seeds and pods were sometimes pickled. Early offerings of *Tropaeolum* might have been in the ornamental or in the vegetable and herb section of a catalog.

Verbena. James Vick, Rochester, New York, 1881.

Listings typically offered "climbing nasturtiums," "tall nasturtiums," or "dwarf nasturtiums." All of these common names could indicate *T. majus* or they also might be used for *T. peltophorum* (climbing) or *T. minus* (dwarf).

Heirloom varieties:

'Empress of India'. Allen, Vermont, 1889. Brilliant crimson; dark tinted foliage.

'Golden Gleam'. Intro: by 1931. Clear yellow, fragrant, and double. AAS winner for 1933.

'King Theodore'. Dreer, Philadelphia, 1876. "Bluish-green foliage; flowers almost black."

'Moonlight'. Henderson, New York, 1910. Enormous, creamy white flowers.

'Variegatum'. Storrs & Harrison, Ohio, 1908. Foliage variegated with creamy white.

Historic commercial sources: 47

Related species:

Tropaeolum minus. Dwarf nasturtium. Intro: 1596. Bethabara, North Carolina, 1759.

Tropaeolum peltophorum. Lobb's nasturtium, climbing nasturtium. Intro: 1843. Wendel, Boston, 1867.

Verbena ×hybrida

verbena

Verbenaceae

Exotic

Introduction: ca. 1840

Earliest American citation: Lelievre, 1838

Description: Colorful, often fragrant, and tender subshrubs used as annuals, 12 in. Verbenas featured clusters of flowers throughout the summer season in shades of white, lilac-purple, dark blue-purple, red, rose, and pale yellow.

Design notes: "The Verbena is the most valuable of bedding plants. It is perfectly adapted to our climate, delighting in the hot sunshine, and withstanding severe drouth" (Columbus Nursery, Ohio, 1862). Verbena was also used for containers. Bailey (1906a) cited 1850 to 1870 as the period of the greatest popularity of verbenas in the United States.

Viola 'Engelmann's Giants' (by 1930s). Photograph by Susan E. Schnare, Mountain Brook Primroses.

'Homestead Purple'. This selection was discovered at the site of an old homestead in Georgia and is believed to be an early variety. Historic commercial sources: 80

Related species:

Verbena bonariensis. Purple top. Intro: 1726. Buist, 1839. Although this currently popular verbena was listed in two prominent flower books of the first half of the nineteenth century, it does not appear in old-time commercial sources.

Verbena canadensis. Rose-colored vervain. An Old Gardener, 1822.

Viola tricolor

pansy, ladies' delight, jump-up-and-kiss me, little flame, garden violet, three-faces-under-a-hood, tres-colores

Synonym: *Viola grandiflora*

Violaceae

Exotic

Introduction: 1587

Earliest American citation: Lawson, 1718

After that time, the increasing prominence of bedding geraniums, annual phlox, and tuberous begonias contributed to decreased interest in *Verbena* ×*hybrida* as a bedding plant.

"The verbena has been judged on merits alone . . . better bedding plants than Verbenas are now to be had (Keeler 1910). By the 1930s one California nursery was calling verbena, "One of the most popular plants grown. For beds, borders and window boxes it is particularly fine" (Howard, Los Angeles, 1937).

Remarks: *Verbena* ×*hybrida* was the result of extensive hybridization beginning ca. 1840 between four species of *Verbena*: *V. chamaedryfolia*, *V. phlogiflora*, *V. incisa*, and *V. teucrioides*.

Heirloom varieties (almost 400 in catalogs):

'Royal Purple'. Southern Nurseries, Mississippi, 1851.

Description: A perennial grown as an annual, 4–8 in. The 2–3 in. flower was often described as having a "face," with single colors or various combinations of white, purple-black, yellow, blue, violet, and red-purple. Orange was not mentioned until the twentieth century.

Design notes: "Carpet your rose beds with Pansies" (Ely 1903).

"Our garden treatment of the Pansy leaves much to be desired. We set out beds of blooming plants in April and for a short time they are dreams of beauty; the plants are then either taken up or allowed to deteriorate and slowly to perish. . . . But with the proper selection of location (shade and moisture) a pansy bed will be a pleasure all summer long. . . . The Pansy is the flower for all. Cheap, hardy, beautiful, bright, cheerful, etc." (Keeler 1910).

Viola 'Bowle's Black' (1901). Photograph by Susan E. Schnare, Mountain Brook Primroses.

Zinnias. James Vick, Rochester, New York, 1881.

"Combine apricot violas with primrose, Aubretia and Anchusa myosotidiflora" (King 1921).

Remarks: "Not an annual, but generally treated as such. An universal favorite that almost everybody grows" (Rexford 1912).

The bedding pansies were developed from *Viola tricolor* over the course of the nineteenth century. Most of the races that existed in the early twentieth century came from three French developers, Bugnot, Cassier, and Trimardeau. Today the hybrid *Viola ×wittrockiana* includes some of the old cultivars.

Mrs. J. D. H. of Ladonia, Texas, wrote to *Vick's* magazine in 1878, "Those superb Pansies, that are the admiration of the country! People who are strangers to me come here to see "them flowers that have faces," they say. One poor fellow, who perhaps had never admired a flower before, the other day exclaimed, "I'd give five dollars if that 'ere was in my yard."

Heirloom varieties:

'Bowle's Black'. Intro: 1901. Horsford, Vermont, 1931.

'Engelmann's Giants'. Park, South Carolina, 1938. "Scottish show type of pansy, long stems, deep bronze, golden, purple and reddish shades, blues, yellows, and creams, blotched and marked to perfection."

Historic commercial sources: 116

Related species:

Viola cornuta. Tufted pansy. Intro: 1776. Hovey, Boston, 1873.

Zinnia elegans

zinnia, youth-and-old-age

Asteraceae

Exotic

Introduction: Single zinnia, by 1793 [1796]; double zinnia, 1858

Earliest American citation: Spurrier, 1793, "zennia"

Description: Fifteen zinnia flower colors were noted in old catalogs and references, including white, sulfur yellow, golden yellow, orange, scarlet-orange, scarlet, light tan, lilac, rose, magenta, crimson, violet, purple, and dark purple. There were also variegated forms, but the solid double flowers were the most popular. This hardy annual ranged in size from the dwarfs at 3–12 inches to the tall zinnias that were 20–30 inches (Bailey 1906a).

Design notes: Zinnias did not appear to their best advantage in masses—but looked well in mixed borders. They were also effectively grown as single plants in the lawn.

Rexford (1912) recommended using zinnias to make a low hedge due to their dense branching habit and height of 3 ft.

"Plant rose-colored giant zinnias (of the new type) with dwarf white cosmos" (King 1915).

Remarks: "[This] grand old flower of our grandmothers, such vivid colors, yellow, red, bronze and mixed, fit for little fairies to play hide-and-go-seek around, it was the brightest spot in the garden to me and cost for such beauty only 25 cents" (R. S. B. 1894).

"Few would recognize the zinnia of today as the Youth-and-age of their grandmother's garden, yet they are identical" (Mattiers 1880).

Zinnia 'Cactus' is still a favorite after almost 100 years in American gardens. Photograph by author.

Heirloom varieties:

'Cactus'. Bolgiano, Washington, D.C., 1928. Resembles the cactus-flowering type of *Dahlia*.

'California Giants'. Bolgiano, Washington, D.C., 1928. A cactus-flowered variety.

'Lilliput'. Henderson, Philadelphia, 1910. Button-flowered on 2-ft. stems.

Historic commercial sources: 51

Related species:

Zinnia haageana. Dreer, Philadelphia, 1876. "A double variety of *Zinnia mexicana*; flowers deep orange, margined in bright yellow." This species was bred with *Z. elegans* to produce a number of the garden hybrids.

Zinnia peruviana (syn. Zinnia *pauciflora, Z. multiflora*). Intro: 1770. M'Mahon, 1806. In 1838, Philip Gosse described fields in Alabama that he said were filled with masses of the red *Zinnia multiflora*, having "a showy effect, something like that of a bank covered with the common scarlet poppy in England." Since zinnias have not been known in the wild in Alabama or anywhere else in the United States, considerable curiosity exists among garden historians concerning which plant Gosse actually had observed.

· 10 ·

HEIRLOOM BULBS
AND TUBEROUS PLANTS

In proportion to cost and subsequent care, bulbs offer a maximum of attraction both to the novice in garden affairs and to the enthusiast of many seasons.

—Elizabeth Strang, landscape architect, 1915

SOME OF THE EARLIEST OBSERVATIONS of ornamental gardening in this country cite the cultivation of bulbous plants. Adrian van der Donck, visiting New Netherland in 1642, reported several bulbs in the landscape including white lilies, the "lily frutilaria," anemones, native red and yellow lilies, and red, white, and yellow maritoffles (van der Donck 1655). Garden historians have translated maritoffles as lady's slippers.

Farther north, William Bradford in 1654 had described in verse the state of gardening in Massachusetts ending with

Here grow fine flowers many, and, 'mongst those,
The fair white lily and th' sweet, fragrant rose.
(Bradford 1654)

It is not too difficult to figure out why lilies or anemones should be planted in New World gardens. Bulbs are naturally and efficiently constructed to carry their own individual food source with them. Minimal special packaging considerations had to be made for them to make the trip across the Atlantic in good shape for immediate cultivation.

Bulbs definitely made the trans-Atlantic voyage in good condition. In a 1740 letter to his plant-swapping buddy John Bartram, Peter Collinson remarked:

Inclosed is the Mate's receipt for a box of bulbs, directed for thee. Make much of them; for they are such a collection as is rarely to be met with, all at once: for, all the sorts of bulbous roots being taken up this year, there is some of every sort. There is above twenty sorts of Crocus—as many of Narcissus—all our sorts of Martagons and Lilies–with Gladiolus, Ornithogalums, Moleys, and Irises, with many others I don't now remember, which time will show thee. (Darlington 1849)

Around 1800 Lady Jean Skipwith of southern Virginia recorded the plants that she grew in her garden. She cultivated a wide assortment of bulbous and tuberous-rooted plants, including meadow saffron; double hyacinths; lily-of-the-valley; *Lilium canadense*; great white lily; large and common snowdrop; grape and feathered hyacinths; double, single, and polyanthus *Narcissus*; bulbous iris; Florentine white and blue iris; star-flower; tulip; and crown imperial (Lockwood 1934).

In his 1806 *American Gardener's Calendar*, Bernard M'Mahon encouraged the inclusion of bulbs in a flower garden. He described an area of ground in a geometric shape with a boundary of flowering shrubs and the interior divided into many narrow beds, similar to a parterre, but simpler. The beds that were to contain bulbs were raised and edged with boards.

In this division you may plant the finest hyacinths, tulips, polyanthus-narcissus, double jonquils, anemones, ranunculus's, bulbous-irises's, tuberoses, scarlet and yellow amaryllis's, colchicums, fritillaries, crown-imperials, snowdrops, crocus's, lilies of various sorts, and all other sorts of bulbous and tuberous-rooted flowers.

In other beds you may exhibit a variety of sorts, both bulbous, tuberous, and fibrous rooted kinds, to keep up a succession of bloom in the same beds during the whole season.

Andrew Jackson Downing did not neglect the versatile bulb. In a plan from his 1844 *Cottage Residences*, he included two circular beds of 10–16 ft.-diameter, cut into the lawn near the house and destined to be filled with double dahlias for bright late summer color.

The Victorians did with bulbs what they did with any brightly colored flowers—they used them in brilliant, flamboyant bedding schemes and carpet patterns. Tulips and hyacinths were particularly valued for this purpose, chosen for their bright clear colors, uniform height, and concurrent periods of bloom. Geometric beds were filled with one or the other, with admonitions from the arbiters of taste not to mix the two in a single bed. A bedding plan advertised by the Peter Henderson Company (below) featured hyacinths in concentric rows filling a 5-ft.-diameter bed. The outside row was crimson, then white, purple, and white, with repeated crimson in the center.

After the beginning of the twentieth century, many directives for the use of bulbs appeared in popular gardening books. Three choices predominated: bulbs could be used for naturalizing; they could be planted in beds to be followed by annuals to complete the flowering season; or bulbs could be part of a hardy herbaceous garden design or a formal garden layout. Bulbous plants, particularly the smaller ones like *Chionodoxa* and *Scilla* were appropriate for the rock garden. Gardeners also used bulbs as fillers in the shrubbery throughout the nineteenth century and as Mrs. Frances King described in 1921:

While shrubs are growing in these informal borders, the ground between them, as has been

A bed of hyacinths. Peter Henderson Co., New York, 1910.

noticed, affords a capital planting-place for spring bulbs. Here snow-drops, crocuses, daffodils, make themselves at home, and seed of the best myosotis or forget-me-not gives a sweet blue harvest, if left undisturbed for a year or two. Tulips are delightful among the budding spireas, honeysuckles, or lilacs.

Naturalizing bulbs involved planting large quantities for a massed, wild effect in the grass or in a meadowlike area. Writers cautioned that to make this type of planting effective hundreds or even thousands of bulbs must be used—it was not a method for limited finances. Long irregular drifts of daffodils or scattered large plantings of diminutive crocus exemplified this practice.

Gardeners like Wilhelm Miller, writing for *The Garden Magazine* (1909b), urged Americans to look at English bulb gardens for inspiration on how to plant bulbs in this country. In regard to naturalizing daffodils, Miller wrote

The grand effects in English woods come in April with the daffodils, ending with the poet's narcissus in May. The most artistic result is secured, not by merely scattering the bulbs as we commonly do, but by arranging a dense mass, with small outlying colonies in the direction of the prevailing wind, so that the latter seem to owe their origin to seeds borne on the breeze from the large group. We often make the mistake of planting bulbs in solid blocks, like a nursery, or in immense areas of equal density. Also, and it pains me to write these words, we often set them in straight rows or patterns.

Designers frequently cited the poet's narcissus as the perfect naturalizing daffodil. Miller also advised on using bulbs in the hardy border. He suggested that low-growing, carpeting perennials should be planted among daffodils and Darwin tulips. Plants useful for this purpose included the pinks, sedums, thrift, rock cress, and any other "mossy little plants."

Peter Henderson, writing for Bailey's *Cyclopedia* (1906), described the mixed border as "a favorite place for most hardy bulbs." Gardeners positioned bulbs in small colonies among hardy herbaceous plants and shrubs. Louise Beebe Wilder (1918) proposed many beautiful combinations of bulbs with herbaceous plants and flowering shrubs. Springtime in Wilder's garden must have been a gloriously colorful season, with little yellow *Crocus* planted at the feet of lilac-pink *Daphne mezereum*, grape hyacinths carpeting the ground beneath a star magnolia, and sky-blue *Chionodoxa* and yel-

low and white *Crocus* beneath the forsythia. Daffodils were particular favorites of Wilder and she praised their effect.

> There they go streaming the length of one bor-der—pale starlike hosts with a ribbon of purple Aubrietia wound among them; there they stand, long golden trumpets, in a flutter above a cloud of silver-lilac Phlox, and again how they pick their way among the fallen Cherry blossoms. Why plan color harmonies for those to whom inharmony is impossible?

Bulbs, of course, were of two types: the hardy autumn-planted, spring-flowering varieties such as tulips and daffodils and the tender spring-planted, summer-flowering species like dahlias and cannas. The tender sorts were planted out in situations suited to each type. Dahlias were perfect for bedding, particularly the double-flowered varieties available in a multitude of rich vibrant colors. The imposing cannas and elephant ears often grew in the middle of the bedding designs providing a dramatic vertical focal point or they appeared in groupings by themselves in beds scattered in the lawn.

Old-time gardeners also planted bulbs in pots for winter flowering in the parlor or conservatory. Certain alliums, lily-of-the-valley, single hyacinths, gladiolus, lilies, narcissus, and both single and double tulips were in demand for this pur-pose. Most important to the success of bulb forcing in pots was the normal de-velopment of the roots. To this end, writers recom-mended that bulbs be planted as soon as possible in the fall in pots filled with rich and well-draining gar-den loam. The pots were then sunk in the ground or covered and placed in a cool cellar. Most potted bulbs should remain in this location for about eight weeks and then brought to a cool porch or unheated room for the growth of stems and leaves to take place. The final step was to put the container in a sunny, warm window for

Bulbs in assorted containers. *Vick's Monthly Magazine*, 1881.

the flowers to develop. The Victorian housewife typically took great pride in her window or parlor garden.

Another method of forcing bulbs out of season was to place hyacinth bulbs in glasses of water or special vases made for the purpose. The water filled the container just to the bot-tom of the bulbs and the glass was stored in a dark place for six weeks. As in the procedure above, the glass was first put in a cooler location for the growth of stems and leaves and then on a sunny, warm window for the conclusion of the process—a brightly colored, fragrant hyacinth. Besides hyacinths, old-time gardeners grew Jacobean lily, tulips, Roman hyacinths, crocus, and various daffodils in this manner.

Elephant ears dominate this small garden, ca. 1910.

Growers imported most of the bulbs they offered in their catalogs. Often an advertisement for bulbs was very general; for example, it might state that bulbous roots would be available in the autumn, with the final selection of the varieties left to the Dutch or English bulb producer. This makes it difficult to determine which *Tulipa* or *Narcissus* selections were most often cultivated in early gardens.

In 1878, James Vick reported that up to that time tuberose bulbs had been grown in Italy for American gardens, but in the 1870s "American grown Tuberoses are advertised by many of the Florists of Europe" (Vick 1878h). C. L. Allen, writing for Bailey's *Cyclopedia of Horticulture* (1906), observed that there had been limited success at growing tulip bulbs in nineteenth-century America. Many people felt that Holland was uniquely endowed with the appropriate soil and conditions for successful bulb growth and, indeed, growers imported most bulbs sold in this country. Allen cited the efforts of men like Isaac Buchanan of Astoria, Long Island, and David Thomas of Cayuga County, New York, as examples of successful tulip production on a limited basis. Allen referred to tulip production in the western states that he felt showed some promise, but provided no details. He reported that one hundred thousand saleable bulbs could be grown in three years' time on a single acre and suggested that Americans should pay more attention to the prospect of raising bulbs on their home ground.

The U.S. federal government enacted a quarantine that assisted in bringing some bulb production to the homeland. Plant Quarantine 37 went into effect in 1919 with the stated intention of eliminating nematodes and insects from the American bulb supply. Initially, the quarantine affected only small-bulb importation and tulips, daffodils, crocus, hyacinths, lilies, and lily-of-the-valley were exempt. Then, in 1926, *Narcissus* was added to the genera prohibited from entry. Nurseries in Washington state, which already had an established bulb industry, as well as in Texas, Virginia, and other states, expanded bulb production for American consumers. John Wister reported on the progress of bulb production in the United States by 1930. Large quantities of regal lilies were grown from seed in various places in the country. Daffodils and a small selection of tulips were available from American producers and tender bulbs like calla lilies, dahlias, and gladiolus were grown in nurseries in the southern states and along the Pacific Coast. Wister observed that foreign sources would always predominate in bulb production, but that American growers had made good progress during the 1920s.

CATALOG OF HEIRLOOM BULBS AND TUBEROUS PLANTS

These bulbs topped the lists offered by growers in America from the earliest years of settlement to the pre–World War II years.

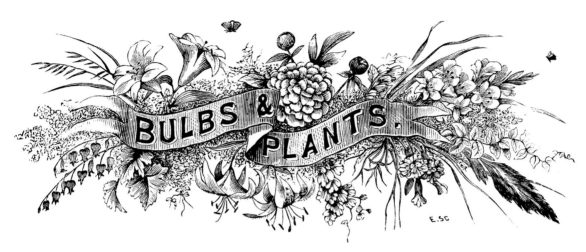

James Vick, Rochester, New York, 1881.

Agapanthus africanus
African blue lily, love flower, blue lily-of-the-Nile
Synonym: *Agapanthus umbellatus*
Lilaceae (Alliaceae)
Exotic
Introduction: 1629
Earliest American citation: M'Mahon, 1806
Zone: 8
Description: "The stems are about three feet high and produce umbels of [blue] trumpet-shaped flowers in mid-summer" (Wister 1930). The foliage is dark and evergreen.
Design notes: The African blue lily thrives well in a large tub. Writers cautioned that this plant's strong roots were apt to break clay pots. Northern gardeners cultivated these half-hardy plants in the conservatory or in a window garden. They were also bedded out and then overwintered indoors.
"These are noble ornaments on lawns in pots or tubs on terraces or piazzas, or for the decoration of the greenhouse" (Henderson, New York, 1915).
"Our Southern readers would find it [*Agapanthus*] an excellent plant to introduce upon the borders of ponds and streams" (The African lily 1887).
Remarks: "A. umbellatus, with bright blue flowers, is very celebrated, and well known in the collections of this country.

There is a variegated variety of it highly desirable, the foliage being white striped" (Buist 1839).
Heirloom variety:
'Albus'. White lily-of-the-Nile. Dreer, Pennsylvania, 1876.
Historic commercial sources: 22

Anemone coronaria
wind flower, poppy anemone, garland anemone
Ranunculaceae
Exotic
Introduction: 1596
Earliest American citation: van der Donck, 1655
Zone: 6–9
Description: "The flowers are large, brilliant, and varied. The foliage is attractively cut." Wind flower was available in both single and double flowers. Colors ranged from cerise to rosy carmine to blue to salmon to white (Wright 1911).
Design notes: Suitable for the hardy border. "A few we can try in the rock garden, but except in favored climates we cannot grow them in great masses. . . . Some gardeners like to plant them between violets in cold frames" (Wister 1930).
Remarks: "The early tuberous anemones bloom with the tulips and daffodils and require essentially the same treatment" (Keeler 1910).

239

Anemone coronaria, wind anemone. Peter Henderson, *Henderson's Handbook of Plants*, 1890.

Heirloom varieties:

'St. Brigid'. Bailey, 1906a. "The flowers are large as breakfast cups" (Wright 1911).

'De Caen'. Bailey, 1906a. Single flowers in shades of violet-blue, red, and white.

Historic commercial sources: 24

Related species:

Anemone nemorosa. Wood anemone. Long cultivated. Bourne, 1833.

Begonia

tuberous begonia, flowering begonia

Begoniaceae

Exotic

Introduction: 1777

Earliest American citation: Buist, 1839

Zone: 10

Description: "Begonias are often at their best in October.... The colors are not more brilliant than those of Zonal Geraniums, but the flowers are finer, and the foliage is more handsome. Some of the shades are exquisite, notably the soft pinks, yellows, and blushes. The whites are as pure as snow" (Wright 1911).

Design notes: Useful for bedding; cultivated in the greenhouse and conservatory; considered an elegant border plant.

Remarks: In southern California, begonias did wonderfully bedded out in sheltered localities, according to the Theodosia Shepherd catalog of 1891. Early horticulturists rec-

Tuberous begonias. *Vick's Monthly Magazine*, July 1878.

ognized three or sometimes four categories of begonias, including fibrous-rooted or winter-flowering, tuberous or summer-flowering, and rex or ornamental-leaved. The tuberous begonias were the most popular for outdoor culture in borders and bedding, as well as in pots. Modern wax begonias, *Begonia* Semperflorens-Cultorum Hybrids are more recent introductions.

Heirloom varieties:

'Countess Louise Erdody'. Vick, 1884. "The leaf has a metallic luster, shading into coppery rose towards the margin, the spiral twist of the leaf giving it a very curious appearance" (Jackson, Georgia, 1904).

'Margaritae'. Intro: 1884. Good & Reese, Ohio, 1889. "Leaves bronze green, with purplish cast.... Large trusses of delicate cream and rose-colored flowers" (Storrs & Harrison, Ohio, 1896).

'Thurstonii'. Flowering begonia. Storrs & Harrison, Ohio, 1896. "The undersides of the leaves are a rich purplish-red,

Canna indica

Fancy-leaved caladiums and rex begonias. John Lewis Childs, Floral Park, New York, 1907.

Canna 'America' (1893). Photograph by Scott Kunst, Old House Gardens.

the veinings very prominent . . . the upper side is a bronzy-green, shaded crimson and olive, with a peculiar glossy metallica lustre over all" (Jackson, Georgia, 1904).

Historic commercial sources: 48

Related species:

Begonia albopicta. Intro: 1885. Good & Reese, Ohio, 1889. "Long pointed slender leaves, thickly spotted with silvery-white foliage, small and elegant" (Jackson, Georgia, 1904). A rose-flowered variety ('Rosea') of this fibrous-rooted begonia was available by 1908.

Begonia ×argenteoguttata. Angel wing begonia. Good & Reese, Ohio, 1889. "Rich green leaves spotted with silver . . . white flowers" (Jackson, Georgia, 1904).

Begonia metallica. This fibrous-root begonia had "pale pink flowers . . . covered with bright coral-red hairs, bronzy green leaves" (Parnell 1883).

Begonia rex. Painted-leaved begonia. Intro: 1858. Storrs & Harrison, Ohio, 1874. "Very desirable for house and garden decorations, in shady positions" (Dreer, Philadelphia, 1876). "In no other class of plants are the rich metallic shades of various colors found so satisfactorily blended" (Bailey 1906a).

Begonia sanguinea. Flowering begonia. Intro: 1829. Storrs & Harrison, Ohio, 1874. Fibrous rooted. "A showy variety, with large leaves; upper side rich olive, underside crimson, and of a peculiarly leathery substance; flowers light rose and white" (Jackson, Georgia, 1904).

Canna indica

Indian shot plant, Indian frill, arrow root
Cannaceae
Exotic
Introduction: 1596
Earliest American citation: John Custis, 1735
Zone: 9

Canna 'Florence Vaughan' (1892) has brightened American landscapes for over 100 years. Photograph by author.

Canna 'Mme. Paul Casaneuve' (1902). Photograph by author.

Description: "In habit they are either standard or dwarf; the foliage is either bronze or green; the flowers are self-colored, spotted, blotched, or edged, all brilliant and all beautiful" (Keeler 1910).

Design notes: "Cannas are the most useful of all subtropical plants for general effect, whether as backgrounds in the border or for large clumps, or masses on the lawn. A large bed filled with the different varieties [of Canna], with an outer border of Coleus verschafeldti, on the lawn, is one of the most beautiful features of ornamental gardening. A still better effect is produced by planting a row of Salvia splendens between the Cannas and Coleus" (Cannas 1884).

"They do well in all parts of the country. . . . For best effect plant in large masses of one color, setting out the plants 18 inches apart" (Gurney, South Dakota, 1921).

Remarks: "Cannas were formerly foliage plants, now they are among the most brilliant flowering plants of the garden" (Rand 1870).

"Cannas are favorites largely because they give such generous return for the care expended upon them. Can make a 'leafy hedge' with the taller ones, the lower will give a brilliant bed of color. . . . At the present time the Crozy cannas are the most popular . . . first fashion was for tall, late-flowering types c. 1850. Dwarf cannas began in the mid-1860s" (Keeler 1910). Dwarf is a relative term. Nineteenth century growers described a canna as dwarf if it was less than 5 ft. tall.

Heirloom varieties:

'America'. Intro: 1893. Henderson, New York, 1899. The first red-leaved canna in the giant-flowered class. "Ht. 4–5 ft. Foliage, fine glossy bronze, almost as if varnished. Flowers . . . deep orange flamed and striped with deeper shade; entirely distinct from any other Canna, both in foliage and flower."

Canna ×ehemanii. Photograph by Scott Kunst, Old House Gardens.

'City of Portland'. Intro: 1916. Porter-Walton, Utah, 1926. Bright rosy pink flower, green foliage. Modern growers describe this pink canna as closer to salmon in color.

'David Harum'. Intro: 1900. Wagner Park, Ohio, 1905. "Dark bronze foliage . . . color is bright vermilion-scarlet with crimson spots." "The best of all dark bronze Cannas. Strong, robust grower, and one of the freest blooming varieties" (Vick, New York, 1906).

'Florence Vaughan'. Intro: 1892. Storrs & Harrison, Ohio, 1896. "The finest yellow spotted canna . . . color brilliant yellow, spotted with bright red."

'Königin Charlotte' (syn. 'Queen Charlotte'). Intro: 1892. Storrs & Harrison, Ohio, 1896. "A bright orange scarlet, deeply edged with bright canary yellow . . . dwarf habit."

'Mme. Paul Casaneuve'. Intro: 1902. With bronze foliage setting off its soft peach blossoms, this antique canna is one of my favorites in the garden. Unfortunately I have never been able to find an early American citation for 'Mme. Paul Casaneuve', although as a Crozy hybrid, it may have been sold here as part of a color mixture that the breeder offered in the early 1900s.

'Richard Wallace'. Intro: 1902. Dreer, Philadelphia, 1908.

Canna musifolia, banana-leaved canna. John Lewis Childs, Floral Park, New York, 1914.

A tall growing canna, with wide canary yellow flowers in heavy trusses.

'Roi Humbert'. Intro: 1902. Wagner Park, Ohio, 1905. The flower is a bright orange-scarlet, streaked with crimson. The foliage is bronze with brownish-green stripes, large, thick, and leathery.

'Semaphore'. Intro: 1895. Vick, New York, 1907. "A decidedly new and novel color in Cannas. The flowers are of a pure orange color, and are produced in large trusses. Foliage in light shade of bronze. Very showy." Modern growers describe this canna as being more a golden orange.

'Shenandoah'. Intro: 1894. Wagner Park, Ohio, 1905. "Beautiful pink flowers standing out in striking contrast with its rich red foliage… very dwarf [under 5 ft.] and compact habit."

'Souvenir de President Carnot'. Intro: by 1889. Storrs & Harrison, Ohio, 1896. "Orange scarlet, slightly shaded pink." The foliage is marked in rifts of sea green and purple.

'Wyoming'. Intro: 1906. Iowa Seed, Des Moines, 1914. "A beautiful new variety with purplish bronze foliage. Flowers are bright orange, slightly rimmed and flaked rose" (Ernst, Ohio, 1926).

'Yellow Humbert'. Ferguson, Oklahoma, 1920. Ernst Nursery (1926) described this canna as having "graceful heart-shaped leaves, but rich all-green instead of bronze . . . flower a brilliant yellow instead of red and produced more abundantly."

Historic commercial sources: 69

The purplish stems of *Colocasia* 'Fontanesii' are a truly startling feature. Photograph by Scott Kunst, Old House Gardens.

Caladium 'Lord Derby' would be a perfect accompaniment to pink-flowered tuberous begonias. Photograph by Scott Kunst, Old House Gardens.

Related species:

Canna ×*ehemanii*. Intro: 1863. *The Ladies' Floral Cabinet*, 1884. "The most distinct of all cannas on account of its large, oval, soft, green leaves and carmine flowers" (Good & Reese, Ohio, 1889).

Canna musifolia. Intro: 1858. Rand, 1876. "Large green leaves, and red flowers." Some contemporary references lump this species with the *Canna indica*.

Colocasia esculenta

elephant ears, colocasia, caladium

Synonyms: *Caladium esculentum, Arum esculentum, A. colocasia*

Araceae

Exotic

Introduction: by 1739

Earliest American citation: M'Mahon, 1806

Zone: 8–11

Description: Leaves bright green, often 3 ft. long or more, nearly as wide. The varieties have different variegation. "One of the most beautiful and ornamental of the ornamental foliage plants" (Allen, Vermont, 1889).

Design notes: "This species makes a beautiful plant for lawn decoration, either planted singly, in clumps, or for borders of sub-tropical groups" (Allen 1902).

"Much grown for tropical bedding" (Bailey 1906a).

Remarks: *Colocasia* differs from *Caladium* mainly in the structure of the flower. Both were grown for foliage effects.

Colocasia esculenta has proved to be invasive in some areas of the United States. Please refer to Appendix D for specific information concerning invasive species.

Heirloom varieties:

'Fontanesii'. Intro: by 1865. Bailey, 1906a. Leaf petiole is violet, blade is green with violet edges.

'Illustris'. Intro: by 1902. Royal Palm, Florida, 1904. "Petioles violet; blade . . . with black-green spots between the primary veins" (Bailey 1906a).

Historic commercial sources: 47

Related species:

Caladium bicolor. Fancy-leaved caladium. Intro: 1773. M'Mahon, 1806. In the 1920s, Henry Nehrling cultivated over 1500 named varieties of fancy-leaved caladiums. Nehrling wrote that he saw the caladium for the first time at the 1893 Chicago World's Fair. "When I admired the richness, brilliancy, delicacy of these often translucent colors, I was reminded of art, not nature. In this, as many other cases, nature simply surpasses art" (Nehrling, in Read 2001).

'Candidum'. Henderson, New York, 1899. "White ground with strongly marked green ribs."

'Lord Derby'. Reuter, New Orleans, 1928. "Pink with green ribs."

Crinum bulbispermum

crinum, milk and wine lily, peppermint lily, deep sea lily, southern lily

Synonyms: *Amaryllis longifolium, Crinum capensis, C. longifolium*

Amaryllidaceae

Exotic

Introduction: early 1800s

Earliest American citation: Prince, New York, 1820

Zone: 6–10

Description: Crinums have lush, wide, straplike foliage topped with fragrant, white, trumpet-shaped blossoms, striped with bands of pink or rose.

Design notes: "For placing in conspicuous positions on terraces or lawns, or in corners where flowers are wanted to combine with architecture or statuary for summer effect, they are of the greatest value" (W. Watson, in Bailey 1906a).

"Fine for planting along fences and center of beds" (Perfection, Alabama, 1927).

Remarks: "When we first offered these bulbs three years ago, we had no idea how immensely popular they would become" (American Exotic, Florida, 1894).

Henry Nehrling (ca. 1925) reported that true lilies did not grow well in Florida gardens and that crinums took their place; "though not generally as regal and distinguished, they form wonderful substitutes" (Read 2001).

Crinums are a group of plants that apparently sidestepped the commercial nurseries in their distribution throughout the Deep South. Milk and wine lilies or peppermint lilies are known in old gardens in the region. Crinums are as tra-

Crinium, peppermint lily. A. Blanc, Philadelphia, Pennsylvania, 1895.

ditional in the South as peonies are in Midwestern gardens. In early years, crinum bulbs were delivered from foreign suppliers via cargo ships to southern gardeners, who in turn passed them along to fellow cultivators.

Heirloom variety:

'Ellen Bosanquet'. Royal Palms, Florida, 1930. Beautiful rich burgundy, spicily fragrant flowers.

Historic commercial sources: 15

Crocus

crocus, herald of spring

Iridaceae

Exotic

Introduction: Long cultivated

Earliest American citation: William Byrd, Virginia, 1684

Zone: 3–8

Description: "The most prominent sorts [of Spring Crocus] are the great yellow, deep blue, light blue, white with blue stripes, blue with white stripes, white with a purple base, pure white, cloth of gold, etc. It flowers in April" (Breck 1858).

Design notes: Mrs. Frances King (1915) suggested a bulb composition of a white crocus ('Reine Blanche') with alternating groups, some dense and others more open, of blue *Scilla sibirica*, accented by the yellow water-lily tulip, *Tulipa kaufmanniana*.

"Crocus can be naturalized in the lawn. . . . In planting these, fling handfuls across the grass and dibble the bulbs in where

Crocus 'Mammoth Yellow' is a recent cultivar name for the old giant yellow crocus. Photograph by Scott Kunst, Old House Gardens.

Early gardeners were able to enjoy an additional season of bulb color by planting *Colchicum autumnale*, autumn crocus. Photograph by author.

they fall. Crocuses can also be used for pockets in the rockery" (Wright 1924).

Remarks: "No bulb gardener has tasted all the joy in his hobby until he has planted crocuses liberally in his lawn and among his other flowers" (Sherlock 1922).

Heirloom varieties:

Crocus angustifolius (syn. *Crocus susianus*). Cloth of gold. Intro: 1587. M'Mahon, 1806. "Golden yellow, striped with brown on outside" (New England Nurseries, Massachusetts, 1910).

Crocus vernus 'Purpureus Grandiflorus'. Intro: 1870. New England Nurseries, Massachusetts, 1910. "Among the florists' varieties of crocus, the one with true magnificence of form and color" (King 1915).

'King of the Blues'. New England Nurseries, Massachusetts, 1910. Large, purplish blue.

Crocus ×*luteus* 'Mammoth Yellow' (syn. 'Golden Yellow'). Intro: 1665. Storrs & Harrison, Ohio, 1908. The large yellow crocus was available under other names in the nineteenth century, for example, 'Giant Yellow'.

Historic commercial sources: 46

Related species:

Colchicum autumnale. Autumn crocus. Intro: before 1600. M'Mahon, 1806. Wister (1930) recommended planting this bulb among the spring bloomers like *Arabis*, *Iberis*, and *Phlox subulata* where it would not be disturbed and would give an additional season of bloom to the spot.

Dahlia

dahlia

Synonym: *Georgina*

Asteraceae

Exotic

Introduction: 1789

Earliest American citation: Bloodgood, New York, 1819

Zone: 8–10

Description: Dahlias came in so many shapes, sizes, and colors that it is difficult to arrive at an all-compassing description. Breck wrote in his 1858 *The Flower-Garden*: "The flowers are large, gorgeous in color, sporting in every tint except blue. The shape too is perfect, although a little too set and prim, as though it was made for the occasion. The habits of the plant are coarse and vulgar, and the smell thereof rather repulsive; but with all its failings, it is a popular flower,—one which will find favor with the multitude."

Design notes: "The best disposition or arrangement in planting the Dahlia, I think, is in groups; each group should be composed of a different section of colour: this affords a close comparison, and gives a greater diversity of landscape, than combining the colours; the tallest growing sorts should be carefully planted in the center or at the back of the group . . . they [also may be] planted in rows along walks or avenues" (Buist 1839).

"The Dahlia will be found one of our very best plants for use in the border where something is needed for a filler. It is very effective as a hedge, and can be used to great advantage to hide a fence. Single specimens are fine for prominent locations on the grounds about the house. In fact it is a plant that can be useful anywhere" (Rexford 1912).

Remarks: The diverse forms of *Dahlia* have prompted their classification into distinct categories. In the twenty-first century in America, *Dahlia* is divided into ten categories.

Early growers referred to *Dahlia* 'Jersey's Beauty' as a "decorative" dahlia. Photograph by Scott Kunst, Old House Gardens.

The carmine-tipped, quilled petals of *Dahlia* 'Kaiser Wilhelm' made this dahlia a favorite among early-twentieth-century gardeners. Photograph by Scott Kunst, Old House Gardens.

However, the *Vick's Floral Guide* of 1881 split the genus into three categories according to the form and size of the flower:

1. Ordinary or Show Dahlia
2. Dwarf or Bedding Dahlia—compact bush with flowers full size
3. Pompon or Bouquet Dahlia—small flowers on a normal size plant

The first cactus dahlia appeared in England in 1879. It resembled in flower the *Cereus speciosissimus* and was originally called *Dahlia Juarezii*. The cactus dahlia was offered by American nurseries by the late 1880s.

Heirloom varieties: From over 1200 named varieties in the old catalogs, these are still in the commercial trade:

'Bonnie Blue'. Ernst, Ohio, 1926. "The nearest approach to a *blue* yet approached. Not washy, but a full, strong, dark, solid, color . . . perfect in form, full, round, short, quilled, and profuse bloomer."

'Jane Cowl'. Intro: 1928. Park, South Carolina, 1938. "Large flowers of old gold and buff, shading to salmon" (Will, North Dakota, 1939). Decorative.

'Jersey's Beauty'. Intro: 1923. Bolgiano, Washington, D.C., 1928. Clear pink.

'Kaiser Wilhelm'. Intro: 1892. Storrs & Harrison, Ohio, 1908. "Very large, with quilled petals, yellow, lightly tipped carmine."

'Thomas Edison'. Intro: 1929. Barteldes, Kansas, 1939. "Deep royal purple—a gorgeous *Dahlia*!"

'Tommy Keith'. Intro: 1892. Manning, 1931. Deep burgundy red, splotched with white. Pompon type.

'Union Jack'. Intro: 1911. Manning, 1931. This sprightly dahlia features single flowers that are red with a white stripe down the middle.

'Yellow Gem'. Intro: 1914. Manning, 1931. Small, cheerful, clear yellow pompon.

Historic commercial sources: 93

Fritillaria imperialis
crown imperial, fritillary
Liliaceae
Exotic
Introduction: Long cultivated
Earliest American citation: van der Donck, 1655
Zone: 5–8
Description: "In every old-fashioned garden one used to see the fritillary or crown imperial erect its tall stem, bearing near the top a graceful umbel of red, yellow, or orange bell-

Fritillaria imperialis 'Aurora' is a red crown imperial. Photograph by Brent Heath, Brent & Becky's Bulbs.

Fritillaria meleagris, checkered lily, is a good candidate for the wild garden. Photograph by author.

Fritillaria imperialis 'Aureomarginata' is a flamboyant selection for the spring border. Photograph by Scott Kunst, Old House Gardens.

shaped flowers with a tuft of foliage above them" (Blanchan 1913).

Design notes: The crown imperial was considered to be a good plant for the hardy border. "They are very effective, and if left undisturbed for years they form gigantic and picturesque groups, bearing gorgeously colored flowers" (Henderson, New York, 1915).

Remarks: "This species is less esteemed than its beauty merits, on account of its strong, and to some, disagreeable scent" (Breck 1858).

Heirloom varieties:

'Aurora'. Briggs, New York, 1873. Red flowers.

'Argenteovariegata' (syn. 'Folius Argenteus'). White-striped crown imperial. Thomas Jefferson, 1812.

'Aureomarginata' (syn. 'Folius Aureus'). Gold-striped crown imperial. Prince, New York, 1820.

Historic commercial sources: 37

Related species:

Fritillaria meleagris. Guinea hen flower, checkered lily. Long cultivated. M'Mahon, 1806. "Exceedingly pretty when grown in large groups in the garden border or wild garden" (Henderson, New York, 1915).

Galanthus nivalis

Amaryllidaceae

Exotic

snowdrop, snowflake, milk-flower, snow-piercer, fair maid of February

Introduction: by 1500

Earliest American citation: Brickell, 1737

Zone: 3–7

Galanthus nivalis, snowdrops, are welcome harbingers of spring. Photograph by Scott Kunst, Old House Gardens.

Description: The snowdrop has nodding flowers of three concave white petals surrounding a tube made of three parts, each white and marked with green (Keeler 1910). Often *Galanthus* (snowdrop) and *Leucojum* (snowflake) are confused. *Galanthus* has sepals that are longer than the petals; in *Leucojum*, they are the same size. Only the petals in the snowdrop are tipped green, while both petals and sepals in the snowflake are tipped (Snowdrops and snowflakes 1885). The snowdrop is a winter bloomer— "snow organized in flower form" (Keeler 1910).

Design notes: Snowdrops looked best planted in clumps or beds rather than singly or in straight lines. Some gardeners preferred to scatter them throughout the lawn grass: "Irregular clumps or masses on lawns near the borders of walks appear to great advantage (Snowdrops and snowflakes 1885). "Snowdrops can be planted thickly in the borders, and also,

like Crocuses, in the grass. The foliage of both will die before it is time to mow the grass" (Ely 1903).

Remarks: "With what triumph the first one is found (after a long winter) and brought to the house, and what a thrill of joy it gives to know that spring will soon be here" (Ely 1903).

"The fragile little white snowdrop with 'heart-shaped seal of green,' nodding from its slender stem in the meadow, is not impressive, it is true; but because it is the very earliest flower cultivated . . . it is dear to the hearts of the people" (Blanchan 1913).

Heirloom variety:

'Flore Pleno'. Double snowdrop. John Bartram, 1735.

Historic commercial sources: 21

Related species:

Galanthus elwesii. Intro: 1875. *Garden and Forest*, 1890. "A better gardener's flower, flowers are slightly larger" (Keeler 1910).

Eranthis hyemalis (syn. *Helleborus hyemalis*). Winter aconite. Long cultivated. M'Mahon, 1806. Although early writers like M'Mahon and "An Old Gardener" of 1822 included *Eranthis* in their lists of recommended bulbs, this plant was not offered frequently in the catalogs. Wister (1930) noted that winter aconite succeeded better in the United States than in England, "where a mild December may start them into premature growth and bloom only to be hurt by later cold."

Gladiolus

sword lily, corn lily

Iridaceae

Exotic

Introduction: 1629

Earliest American citation: John Bartram, 1735

Zone: 9

Description: "Gladiolus communis is a hardy, showy borderflower, of which there are several varieties in cultivation, viz. white, purple, and red. . . . They have a flag-like foliage, and produce their flowers on long, one-sided spikes or racemes, about two feet high, in June and July. . . . [G. psittacinus] the flowers are scarlet, on a greenish-yellow ground . . . sometimes four feet high. . . . G. gandavensis, producing long spikes of the most vivid scarlet flowers . . . four and five feet high" (Breck 1858). As the nineteenth- and early-twentieth-century hybridizers took over, the gladiolus flowers became larger and arranged more evenly on the stem and the color selection was more varied and vibrant.

The old catalogs featured *Gladiolus* more often than any other bulb except *Dahlia. Vick's Monthly Magazine*, 1878.

Gladiolus communis subsp. *byzantinus*, Byzantine glad, has been cultivated for nearly 200 years in America. Photograph by Scott Kunst, Old House Gardens.

Design notes:

"The cultivation of the gladiolus is so exceedingly simple; the results so wonderfully rewarding; the color effects so certain of accomplishment with flowers which come as true to type and color as these; there is everything to praise in this flower.... Gardens of enchantment might easily be created by the use of two annuals such as dark heliotrope, ageratum Stella Gurney, and the lavender, cool pink, and palest-yellow gladiolus" (King 1915).

Gladiolus were good companions with ornamental grasses—a yellow glad among yellow-green grasses, a deep violet or salmon-pink among the bluish-green types. "Stems of gladiolus must ever be concealed. This would do it gracefully and well" (King 1915). In her 1925 book, Mrs. Frances King suggested planting white gladiolus with buddleia or planting glads in the peony border for an aftercrop of fine flowers—the peony foliage would hold up the gladiolus stems.

Remarks: Nineteenth-century efforts at hybridization of *Gladiolus* took place in Belgium and England and resulted in the successful hybrid *Gladiolus* ×*gandavensis* in 1841, which was then crossed with species and other hybrids to develop the modern strains. Through hybridization, the form of the gladiolus was changed, colors separated, markings changed, delicate stripes became bold, some flowers had conspicuous blotches, and round symmetrical petals emerged instead of sharp-pointed ones. Flowers were arranged compactly on long spikes, with many more flowers on a spike, time of bloom manipulated, and the endurance of the flowers increased (Childs 1893).

"The gladiolus [parrot] in my earliest recollection, which was found in gardens about the middle of the nineteenth century, was dull red mingled with greenish yellow, appearing red at a distance. The flowers were small and pinched-look-

"Carolina Primrose" is the working name for this example of the lovely, old-fashioned *Gladiolus dalenii*. Photograph by Scott Kunst, Old House Gardens.

ing, with pointed petals, and were scattered at regular intervals along one side of the leaning stem" (Crawford 1911).

The gladiolus became popular from about 1870 on because it was easily grown, bloomed up to four months, was available in many colors, and was excellent for cut flowers.

Heirloom varieties: Over 500 selections appeared in the early catalogs. Today's gardeners should be aware that some of the old names have been recycled to new plants. If you find a glad with one of these names and the description does not match, it probably is not an heirloom gladiolus. This warning holds, of course, for cultivars in other genera as well.

'Halley'. Trumbull, 1916. "Soft toned, large salmon-pink petals with creamy blotch."

'Obelisk'. Allen, 1902. "Flowers large, violet, lower petals blotched brown, spotted with sulphur."

'Princeps'. Amaryllis-flowered gladiolus, thousand dollar gladiolus. In 1903 Dr. Walter Van Fleet introduced this first scarlet hybrid glad, which he distributed through Vaughan's Seed Store of Chicago.

'The Bride'. Allen, Vermont, 1889. Pure white, this is a selection of *Gladiolus ×colvillei*.

Historic commercial sources: 78

Related species:

Gladiolus communis subsp. *byzantinus* (syn. *Gladiolus byzantinus*). Intro: 1629. Prince, New York, 1820.

Gladiolus dalenii (syn. *Gladiolus primulinus*). "New, 3–4 feet tall and very vigorous. The flowers are of a good size and are a clear primrose-yellow. Blooms late in July" (Thorburn, New York, 1908). Thorburn also listed 'Primulinus Hybrids'—"Grow 3–5 feet high, with long spikes of richly colored blooms, varying in color from clear yellow to crimson, the latter with large soft orange or golden throats; exceedingly desirable."

Crocosmia ×crocosmiiflora. Montbretia, golden sheaf. Henderson, New York, 1890. "A fine, free-flowering garden plant producing orange-scarlet flowers from July to frost" (Wister 1930).

'Etoile de Feu'. Wagner Park, Ohio, 1905. A bright vermilion-scarlet selection.

Hippeastrum ×johnsonii

St. Joseph lily, Bermuda spice lily

Synonym: *Amaryllis johnsonii*

Amaryllidaceae

Exotic

Introduction: 1799

Earliest American citation: Buist, 1839

Zone: 7–10

Description: "The flowers are a deep scarlet, with a white streak in the center of each petal, four blooms on a stem of about two feet, each flower about six inches in diameter" (Buist 1839).

Design notes: The St. Joseph's lilies were grown as pot plants and subjects for greenhouse culture in the North. Buist expressed the hope that "in a few years many of them [the Amaryllis] will be so acclimated, as to keep as garden bulbs, planting about the end of April, and lifting them in October."

In the warmer regions, St. Joseph lily provided a brilliant companion to spring-blooming iris in the flower garden.

Hippeastrum ×johnsonii, St. Joseph lily, is an example of an early hybrid amaryllis. Photograph by Greg Grant.

Remarks: "One of the earliest hybrids, a cross between *Hippeastrum reginae* and *H. vittatum*, and still is a popular variety; it is one of the most robust and showy, and a wonderful bloomer" (Allen 1902).

Historic commercial sources: 21

Related species:

Nerine sarniensis (syn. *Amaryllis sarnienesis*). Guernsey lily. John Custis, 1736. *Amaryllis belladonna* sometimes was called Guernsey lily.

Zephyranthes atamasca (syn. *Amaryllis atamasco*). Atamasco lily, stagger-grass. Jean Skipwith, ca. 1800.

Hyacinthus orientalis
common hyacinth, oriental hyacinth
Liliaceae (Hyacinthaceae)
Exotic

Double hyacinths. Leo Weltz, Wilmington, Ohio, ca. 1905.

Introduction: 1543

Earliest American citation: Watson, South Carolina, 1765

Zone: 3–7

Description: "Hyacinths are double and single; of various colors, embracing every shade of red, from a deep crimson pink down to white; of blue, from white to almost black, and some few yellow and salmon color. . . . Some of the white and other light varieties have red, blue, purple or yellow eyes, which add much to the beauty of the flower" (Breck 1858).

Design notes: Hyacinths were traditional candidates for bedding, with the brightest colors chosen for splashy colorful designs. They were also distributed in the flower border.

"In a previous generation, given to bedding, Hyacinths enjoyed a wide popularity; but I cannot say that I like them for the average garden. Their stiffness calls for a formal planting, even though this may be mitigated by using a ground cover" (Wright 1924).

A bouquet of hyacinths—(from lower left) mauve 'Lord Balfour' (1883), pale blue 'Queen of the Blues' (1870), double white 'Madame Sophie' (1929), mid-blue 'Bismarck' (1875), pink 'Lady Derby' (1875), double blue 'General Köhler' (1878), orange 'Gipsy Queen' (1927), yellow 'Prins Hendrik' (1910), and, in the center, dark blue 'Marie' (1860). Photograph by Scott Kunst, Old House Gardens.

Hyacinthus 'Chestnut Flower' (1880). Photograph by Scott Kunst, Old House Gardens.

Remarks: Joseph Breck reported in 1858 that over 1000 varieties of hyacinth were cultivated in Holland, from where they were exported to other countries, including America.

Heirloom varieties:

var. *albulus* (syn. *Hyacinthus romanus*). Roman hyacinth. Intro: 1613. M'Mahon, 1806.

'Chestnut Flower'. Intro: 1880. State Nursery, Montana, 1923. "Rose color, extra large and considered the best of its color."

'City of Haarlem'. Intro: 1898. State Nursery, Montana, 1923. Single, golden yellow.

'General Köhler'. Intro: 1878. New England Nurseries, Massachusetts, 1910. Although New England Nurseries described this hyacinth as deep yellow, contemporary sources agree this cultivar is pale purple or blue.

'King of the Blues'. Intro: 1863. New England Nurseries, Massachusetts, 1910. "Deep purplish blue; fine close spike, one of the best for forcing."

'Lady Derby'. Intro: 1875. State Nursery, Montana, 1923. Bright rose-pink.

'L' Innocence'. Intro: 1863. New England Nurseries, Massachusetts, 1910. Large and pure white.

'Lord Balfour'. Intro: 1883. Storrs & Harrison, Ohio, 1925. Lilac shaded violet.

'Marie'. Intro: 1860. New England Nurseries, Massachusetts, 1910. "Dark purplish blue; fine spike."

'Queen of the Blues'. Intro: 1870. New England Nurseries, Massachusetts, 1910. "Beautiful azure blue; large bells; handsome truss."

Historic commercial sources: 71

Related species:

Galtonia candicans (syn. *Hyacinthus candicans*). Summer hyacinth. Intro: by 1880. Manning, Massachusetts, 1887. "A batch of Galtonia interplanted with Chrysanthemums enlivens with its spikes of white drooping flowers what would otherwise be a dead corner of a border" (Wright 1924).

Muscari botryoides (syn. *Hyacinthus muscari*). Grape hyacinth. Intro: 1596. Spurrier, 1793. This wonderful small blue hyacinth was seldom offered in the nursery catalogs—merely eight times compared with sixty-eight for the oriental hyacinth. Wister (1930) mentioned that the grape hyacinth was frequently found in old gardens and often naturalized in areas as an escapee from gardens.

Iris xiphium

Spanish iris

Synonym: *Iris hispanica*

Iridaceae

Exotic

Introduction: by 1600

Earliest American citation: M'Mahon, 1806

Zone: 6–9

Description: "A very pretty border flower, of many varieties, all rich and elegant; embracing the most delicate shades of light and dark blue, brown, purple, yellow, and white" (Breck 1858).

Design notes: "As for the Irises that can be grown in the sunny, well-drained borders in most localities, and in sunny rockeries with even greater security, their name is legion. We all know the Poor Man's Orchid, or the Spanish Iris, one of the cheapest of all floral charmers.... This Iris is finest when left out for three years, yet it is not absolutely certain to survive winters, so it is often lifted and stored each autumn" (Hampden 1922).

Remarks: "This is one of the most common species known to the trade, the bulbs being annually sent out with the Dutch bulbs in autumn" (Allen 1902).

Historic commercial sources: 33

Related species:

Iris latifolia (syn. *Iris xiphioides*). English iris. Intro: by 1571. Bartram, Philadelphia, 1807. "The flowers are exceedingly showy ... of various colors, blue, white, lavender, crimson and yellow" (Allen 1902).

Lilium

lilies

The common name lily refers to many plants in American gardening history: May lily or lily-of-the-valley (*Convallaria*); white or blue day lily, plantain lily (*Hosta*); yellow or orange daylily (*Hemerocallis*); lily leek (*Allium*); water lily (*Nymphaea*); wood lily (*Trillium*); milk and wine lily (*Crinum*); Persian lily, checkered lily (*Fritillaria*); Guernsey lily (*Nerine*); St. Bruno's lily, St. Bernard's lily (*Anthericum*); blackberry lily (*Belamcanda*); toad lily (*Tricyrtis*); triplet lily (*Triteleia*); Belladonna lily (*Amaryllis*); St. Joseph lily (*Hippeastrum*); August lily, surprise lily, magic lily (*Lycoris*); rain lily (*Zephyranthes*); calla lily (*Zantedeschia*); Chinese sacred lily (*Narcissus*); spider lily (*Hymenocallis*); and angular-stalked lily-of-the-valley (*Polygonatum*). This section will deal with the "true" lilies, members of the genus *Lilium*.

Lilium 'Fire King' is a 1933 example of an Asiatic hybrid lily. Photograph by Scott Kunst, Old House Gardens.

Nineteenth- and twentieth-century garden writers always referred to lilies in superlative terms, citing the distinctive form, flowers, and fragrance, all of which made the lily indispensable for cultivation in the garden. Indeed, the Madonna lily was one of the first ornamental plants to be cultivated with documentation going back to 3000 B.C.E. It was also one of the earliest ornamental plants cultivated in the New World, as recorded by Governor William Bradford of Plymouth, Massachusetts, in 1654.

Others in the early days of America enjoyed the cultivation of lilies, including John Bartram, who in 1740 received a packet of bulbs from his English correspondent, Peter Collinson, including "all our sorts of Martagons and Lilies." Bartram reciprocated to Collinson with American natives, *Lilium canadense* and *L. superbum*. Thomas Jefferson grew several types of lilies at Monticello, including the "fiery" lily, white lily, and the "yellow [lily] from the Columbia." Lady Jean Skipwith at the end of the eighteenth-century cultivated the "Large White Lily" and the "spotted Canada Martagon lily" in her southern Virginia garden. America's love affair with the lily has lasted for three centuries.

By mid-nineteenth century, plant explorers had introduced many new species of *Lilium* from the western United States and the Orient, and the American nursery trade was quick to supply the latest finds to gardeners. In the 1800s, U.S. nursery and seed catalogs offered over sixty-eight species and selections of lilies including ten native species. Lilies were used in borders and in the foreground of shrubberies. Occasionally, lilies were used to provide vertical effect in the center of a bedding scheme. The genus *Lilium* was so diversified and had so many beautiful members that several garden writers proposed that a garden of nothing but lilies be cultivated. The nineteenth century has been called the "Century of the Lily," and George Ellwanger, the prominent Rochester grower of that period, called the lily "one of the greatest treasures of the hardy flower garden" (1889).

The popularity of lilies waned somewhat in the early years of the twentieth century with only the appearance of Ernest H. Wilson's *Lilium regale* in 1910 adding any new excitement to the genus. In addition to the regal lily, tiger lilies and *L. speciosum* varieties were popular garden plants in the early 1900s.

The 1920s and '30s saw renewed interest in the genus *Lilium* with breeders, particularly in the United States and Holland, crossing different species, such as *L. bulbiferum*, *L. lancifolium*, *L. pumilum*, and others, in order to produce new and even more splendid varieties. Jan deGraaff of Oregon Bulb Farm was one such breeder who worked in Holland and Oregon to produce many of the Asiatic hybrids. Early examples of these include 'Enchantment' (1944, de-Graaff), orange-red, flared upright flowers, 3–4 ft., and 'Fire King' (1933, Stooke), orange-red, outward-facing, recurved tips, 3 ft. In France, the Aurelian hybrids, crossing *L. henryi* with *L. sargentiae*, were produced in 1938. Earlier, in 1924 an American breeder, Griffith, had introduced a cross of American species called the Bellingham hybrids, now known as the Bellingham Group. In the '20s, the Backhouse hybrids, *L. martagon* × *L. hansonii*, originated.

Lilium auratum

Japan lily, gold-banded lily, glorious Queen of the Lilies, golden-rayed lily

Liliaceae

Exotic

Introduction: 1861

Earliest American citation: Parsons, New York, 1861

Zone: 6

Description: Large white petals are thickly spotted with rich chocolate crimson and have a bright golden yellow band through the center of each (Iowa Seed, Des Moines, 1914).

Design notes: "Alternate clumps of a dozen each of Lilium auratum and Lilium album planted in a border just behind Foxgloves and Canterbury Bells will come into bloom when these two biennials have finished, the Auratum first, then the Album; these four flowers will keep the border gay from early in June until the middle of September" (Ely 1903).

"Lilies should be planted among Ferns, or dwarf shrubs such, for example, as Lavender, wild Roses, Deutzias, Indigoferas, Lespedezas, Comptonia, Vacciniums, Ericas, Calluna, native Azaleas, [and] Rhododendrons" (Wilson 1932).

Lilium auratum, gold-band lily. B. K. Bliss & Sons, New York, 1869.

Remarks: For successful cultivation, gold-banded lilies need good drainage, a light porous, fertile soil, deep planting (8–12 in.), and a mulch of light litter, in order "to maintain an even, cool soil temperature" (The gold-banded lily 1882).

Allen (1902) observed, "In a small room its fragrance is overpowering and sickening."

Heirloom variety:

var. *platyphyllum*. Intro: by 1880. The largest of the *L. auratum*, with broader petals and spotted yellow. "This is the best one for the garden. . . . The flowers are more massive, sometimes 12 inches across. They are creamy, with fewer pinky brown spots and have a pale gold stripe" (Fox 1928).

Historic commercial sources: 72

Related species:

Lilium brownii. Intro: 1835. Prince, New York, 1854. "Trumpet-shaped; delicate yellow throat, with purple outside, one of the most beautiful lilies" (Berger, California, 1892).

Lilium regale. Regal lily. Intro: 1905. Wilson, Boston, 1910. "The most satisfactory . . . and the finest of all lilies for our northern climate. No flower is finer, no stalk more graceful, no fragrance sweeter."

Lilium canadense

Canada martagon lily, nodding meadow lily, orange field-lily

Liliaceae

Native

Introduction: 1620

Earliest American citation: Thomas Jefferson, 1786

Zone: 5

Description: "Has been known to grow five feet high, with a pyramid of at least twenty of its pendulous flowers; color from yellow to deep orange scarlet. The flowers are profusely spotted, on the inside, and are but little reflexed" (Breck 1858).

Design notes: Wilder (1918) suggested planting *Lilium canadense* with perennial baby's breath.

Remarks: Although it was already quite beautiful, some writers suggested this lily could be improved under cultivation.

Historic commercial sources: 33

Related species:

Lilium philadelphicum. Philadelphia lily, wood lily, wild orange lily, common red lily. Intro: 1730. John Bartram, ca. 1730. "The color of the wood lily is rich and brilliant, dark vermilion color, spotted with black, and the corolla is bell-shaped" (Breck 1846).

Lilium candidum

Madonna lily, Annunciation lily, white lily, St. Joseph's lily, old white lily, Ascension lily

Liliaceae

Exotic

Introduction: Cultivated since ancient times

Earliest American citation: William Bradford, 1654

Zone: 6

Description: "It is a beautiful and stately plant, often growing four feet high, and bearing from one to a dozen flowers [white]" (Rand 1876).

Design notes: "A mass of White Lilies is always upheld with admiration and they perfume the air with their delicious fragrance. The White Lily is, therefore, indispensable, and should be found in every garden" (Breck 1858).

"It [Madonna lily] is especially effective when grown in bold masses or in rows bordering back garden walks, drives, etc.

Lilium candidum, the Madonna lily, is one of the oldest cultivated flowers in the world. Photograph by Brent Heath, Brent & Becky's Bulbs.

where the brilliancy of the snow-white flowers makes its influence felt against the greenery of surrounding trees and shrubs" (Henderson 1901).

"Although the combination of Madonna Lilies and Delphinium is almost as hackneyed as Chopin's Minute Waltz, repetition has not lessened the beauty of either" (Fox 1928).

Gardeners in the early years of the twentieth century recommended using the Madonna lily in combination with monkshood and phlox in the hardy border or planted by itself in a bold clump in the lawn.

Remarks: "A mass of white lilies is always beheld with admiration, and they perfume the air with their delicious fragrance" (Breck 1846).

"The Madonna lily is fixed in our affections. . . . But many gardeners have found, to their sorrow, that this is a fickle and uncertain lily" (King 1921).

Heirloom varieties:

Nurseries offered double-flowered and golden-striped-leaved Madonna lilies in the first half of the nineteenth century. Of the double white, Joseph Breck (1858) remarked, "curious, but not beautiful."

Historic commercial sources: 67

Related species:

Lilium longiflorum. Japan lily, long-flowered lily, Easter lily, Bermuda lily. Intro: 1820. Buist, 1939. The flowers were twice the size of the common white lily. Usually cultivated in commercial greenhouses as a florist's flower.

Lilium lancifolium, tiger lily, is often associated with grandmothers' gardens. Photograph by author.

Lilium lancifolium

Japan lily, tiger lily, Chinese lily
Synonym: *Lilium tigrinum*
Liliaceae
Exotic
Introduction: 1804
Earliest American citation: Albany Nursery, New York, 1827
Zone: 4
Description: "Fine, reflexed, orange flowers, with black spots" (Breck 1851).
Design notes: Tiger lily was a suitable plant for the border or shrubbery, according to nineteenth century garden writers like Joseph Breck (1858).
"The tiger lily is, next to the Phlox, the most important plant in the early August garden" (Wilder 1918).
"Excellent with blue and white Monkshood, yellow and brown Helenium and white Boltonia" (Wright 1924).
Remarks: "This old fashioned flower is becoming very popular the last several years and is now planted extensively in all gardens. On account of its extreme hardiness it is one of the most valuable of all lilies" (Gurney, South Dakota, 1921).
Heirloom varieties:
'Flore Pleno'. Double tiger lily. Briggs, New York, 1873. "Double flowers are not generally thought more beautiful than single ones, but the double tiger lily is really beautiful" (Some plants little grown 1888).
var. *splendens*. Briggs, New York, 1873. "Sometimes twenty-five flowers to a stem; tall grower" (California Nursery, 1894). "Large pyramids of orange-red flowers spotted with black" (Iowa Seed, Des Moines, 1914).
Historic commercial sources: 55

Lilium martagon

scarlet martagon lily, turk's cap lily
Liliaceae
Exotic
Introduction: 1596
Earliest American citation: In 1739 Collinson sent a red martagon lily to John Custis—either *Lilium martagon* or *L. chalcedonicum*.
Zone: 4
Description: "Many varieties . . . pure white, others with purple, spotted or variegated flowers . . . petals are very much reflexed, giving the appearance of caps" (Breck 1851).
Design notes: "Lilies of many sorts are highly agreeable when scattered—not massed—somewhat freely through shrubbery borders, or with large hardy perennials" (Bailey 1906a).
Remarks: "Much cultivated in Europe, less in America. . . . The plant is vigorous, upright and thrifty, with good foliage, but the flowers are small, dull-colored and not showy, as compared with our more popular kinds" (Bailey 1906a).
Historic commercial sources: 30
Related species:
Lilium chalcedonicum. Thomas Jefferson, 1782. *The Ladies' Floral Cabinet* asserted that *Lilium chalcedonicum* was the lily most often referred to as the martagon lily. "A general favorite . . . with its number of scarlet, pendulous flowers contrasting admirably with the *Candidum* and *Excelsum*" (Lilium martagon 1884).

Lilium pumilum

Japan lily, coral lily
Synonym: *Lilium tenuifolium*
Liliaceae
Exotic
Introduction: 1816

The Iowa Seed Company catalog declared *Lilium speciosum* var. *rubrum* the most popular lily grown in 1914. Photograph by author.

Lilium speciosum
Japan lily
Synonym: *Lilium lancifolium*
Liliaceae
Exotic
Introduction: 1830
Earliest American citation: Kenrick, Boston, 1835
Zone: 6
Description: "Flower, ground color, clear rose, shading to white, covered with numerous small projections of bright crimson, and which gives it the appearance, as Dr. Lindley remarks, of being 'all rugged, with rubies and garnets and crystal points'; a plant of two to three feet in height" (Wilder 1847).

"Flowers are white with a deep rosy or crimson band on each petal, with deeper colored spots between, 5–6 in. in diameter" (Iowa Seed, Des Moines, 1914).

Design notes: One successful combination described by Elizabeth Strang in the 1915 *Garden Magazine* used the "pink speciosum lilies with pink phlox Elizabeth Campbell [another salmon pink phlox could be substituted], cloudy sea lavender and tall steely blue eryngium."

Remarks: When this lily first drew the attention of American gardeners, they thought it was winter-tender for the northern states. James Vick conducted a hardiness experiment, planting some in the greenhouse and some outdoors. He explained his results:

> In the spring, on removing the covering of coarse manure, which we had used as a slight protection,

Lilium pumilum, coral lily, is a member of the lily family appropriate for the front of the border. Photograph by Scott Kunst, Old House Gardens.

Earliest American citation: Breck, 1846
Zone: 5
Description: "A diminutive, jewel-like Lily, from 14 to 18 inches high, with narrow grass-like leaves, mainly about the center of the stem, and nodding revolute flowers of shiny deep coral red" (Fox 1928).
Design notes: "Plant them among white and blue Campanula persicifolia" (Wright 1924).
"It is a gem in the rock garden and in the border" (Vobeyda 1938).
Remarks: "One of the smallest as well as one of the prettiest of the lily family" (Parkman 1871c).
Historic commercial sources: 25

The late-blooming *Lilium henryi* was an excellent lily to plant in the shrubbery. Photograph by Scott Kunst, Old House Gardens.

our surprise and pleasure was great on finding the strong, noble shoots had made several inches of growth above the surface of the ground. During the summer, these out-door plants far exceeded in strength and beauty those raised in the houses. Lancifolium lily. Rubrum. 1879

Heirloom varieties:
var. *album*. Intro: ca. 1830. Breck, 1846. This was considered to be the finest of the pure white lilies.
var. *roseum*. Intro: ca. 1830. Kenrick, Boston, 1835.
var. *rubrum*. Red Japanese lily, rubrum lily. Intro: ca. 1830. Hovey, Boston, 1852.
Historic commercial sources: 79
Related species:
Lilium henryi. Orange speciosum lily. Intro: 1888. Henderson, New York, 1910. "It is very hardy and attractive, espe-

cially as it comes after most of the lilies are over" (Fox 1928). "An excellent variety for planting among Rhododendrons or other shrubs" (Marshall 1928).
Lilium maculatum (syn. *Lilium elegans*). Japan lily. Prince, New York, 1854. Cup-shaped flowers of yellow, orange, or red, usually with black spots.

Lilium superbum
superb Lily, turk's cap lily, swamp lily, wild tiger lily
Liliaceae
Native
Introduction: 1665
Earliest American citation: John Bartram, ca. 1738
Zone: 3
Description: "Stem erect, straight, from three to six feet high, bearing a large pyramid of orange coloured flowers, amounting not infrequently to thirty or forty in number . . . corollas reflexed. There appears to be a variety in the colours from a yellow to an orange scarlet" (Breck 1846).
Design notes: Recommended by Miller in 1909 for massing in a moist meadow setting similar to its natural environment: "a glorious sight."
"They form striking plants and look their best naturalized in the bay of a shrubbery rising from grass with near-by trees casting a little shade on them" (Fox 1928).
"Excellent in large masses in border, in the peat soil of a Rhododendron planting, or near water" (Wright 1924).
Remarks: "One of the most magnificent of our native plants" (Manning 1884a).
Historic commercial sources: 43

Lilium ×testaceum
Japan lily, Nankeen lily
Synonyms: *Lilium excelsum*, *L. isabellinum*
Liliaceae
Exotic
Introduction: ca. 1840
Earliest American citation: Ellwanger & Barry, New York, 1860
Zone: 6
Description: "The flowers are pendulous, in whorls of from three to nine each, nearly flat, of a beautiful salmon buff, with bright scarlet anthers, thus making a very fine contrast" (Hovey 1871).
"An exquisite willowy Lily, smelling faintly like the candidum" (Fox 1928).
Design notes: "This is one of the choicest all Lilies and should be included in every collection. . . . The coloring is effec-

Narcissus 'Conspicuus' (1869). Photograph by Scott Kunst, Old House Gardens.

Narcissus 'Golden Spur' (1885). Photograph by Scott Kunst, Old House Gardens.

tively produced in planting against a green background of shrubbery or tall Delphiniums" (Marshall 1928).

Remarks: Generally supposed to be *L. candidum* × *L. chalcedonicum*. Hovey insisted that it flowered first in England in 1842, although Fox (1928) asserted that it was discovered in a garden in 1836, the progeny of *L. candidum* × *L. monadelphum*. Allen (1902) said there was little evidence to support either theory and *Lilium* ×*testaceum* was found in a bed of seedlings in Erfurt in 1846.

Historic commercial sources: 22

Related species:

Lilium ×*hollandicum* (syn. *Lilium umbellatum*). Japan lily, umbel-flowered orange lily. McIntosh, Ohio, 1845. "In contrast with the white lily, it makes an imposing appearance" (Breck, 1846).

Narcissus

daffodil, narcissus, jonquil, daffy-down-dilly

Amaryllidaceae

Exotic

Introduction: Long cultivated

Earliest American citation: Brickell, 1737

Zone: 4–8

Description: "Of the common Daffodil, there are many varieties, with a white flower and yellow cup; a yellow flower and deep golden cup; a double flower, with several cups one within another; the Great Yellow Incomparable, double and single" (Breck 1851).

Design notes: "Daffodils are most happily placed when growing in clumps in the foreground of a border of mixed shrubs and herbaceous plants. . . . Daffodils may also be bedded

Besides being a good garden daffodil, Narcissus 'Princeps' was an excellent forcer. Photograph by Scott Kunst, Old House Gardens.

Narcissus 'Seagull' (1903). Photograph by Scott Kunst, Old House Gardens.

out like hyacinths and tulips, and very effectively too" (Kirby 1909).

The smaller daffodils are suitable for the rock garden (Wright 1911).

"Naturalized, scattered colonies of these incomparable flowers beside little lakes, in meadows, along woodland borders, old stone walls and entrance drives would seem to be the ideal way of planting them. . . . Some gardeners sow sweet alyssum, mignonette or some other low-growing annual over them to carpet their area with flowers during the summer and autumn" (Blanchan 1913).

"My general scheme [for using Narcissus] is to use the higher priced kinds for definite corners and protected spots in the borders, and the cheaper varieties for naturalizing" (Wright 1924).

Remarks: As the number of cultivated *Narcissus* increased, so did attempts to classify their forms. Mr. J. G. Baker, in

1869, explained an arrangement of the genus, which was described by Kirby (1909). In Baker's system there were three main subdivisions: magni-coronati, medio-coronati, and parvi-coronati, "wittily interpreted into 'long-nosed,' 'short-nosed,' and 'snub-nosed,' now spoken of as trumpet, cup and saucer."

Heirloom varieties:

'Albus Plenus Odoratus'. Double poet's narcissus. Intro: by 1629. Sayers, 1839. "Double, pure white, very sweet scented" (New England Nurseries, Massachusetts, 1910).

'Bath's Flame'. Intro: 1913. Michell, Philadelphia, 1931. "Deep yellow perianth; deeply edged orange red trumpet."

'Beersheba'. Intro: 1923. Stumpp & Walter, New York, 1938. "A magnificent pure white flower. Large, perfectly flat perianth; trumpet long and beautifully flanged at the mouth. A flower of great size, measuring nearly 5 inches across."

'Conspicuus' (syn. 'Barrii Conspicuus'). Intro: 1869. New

In his 1930 catalog, John Scheepers noted that *Narcissus* 'Van Sion' (1620) was "showy when naturalized in woodland." Photograph by Scott Kunst, Old House Gardens.

Narcissus 'W. P. Milner' (1880). Photograph by Scott Kunst, Old House Gardens.

England Nurseries, Massachusetts, 1910. "Perianth soft yellow; broad cup illumined with scarlet."

'Emperor'. Intro: 1870. New England Nurseries, Massachusetts, 1910. "Immense flower; clear golden yellow trumpet, deep primrose perianth."

'Golden Spur'. Intro: 1885. New England Nurseries, Massachusetts, 1910. "Immense golden trumpet; early fine flower." Florists often used this variety for forcing in the early 1900s.

'Grand Monarque'. Intro: 1780. Prince, New York, 1820. "Splendid trusses of white flowers, with lemon-yellow cups" (Kirby 1909).

'Grand Primo'. Intro: 1780. Prince, New York, 1860. "Citron color; perianth pure white" (New England Nurseries, Massachusetts, 1910).

'King Alfred'. Intro: 1899. Vaughan, Chicago, 1914. "Deep golden yellow; a new variety of great richness, size and strength of flower."

'Laurens Koster'. Intro: 1906. Wister, 1930. A white Poetaz (*N. poeticus × N. tazetta*) type of *Narcissus*.

'Mrs. R. O. Backhouse'. Intro: 1921. Stumpp & Walter, New York, 1938. "The famous original 'Pink Daffodil.' Beautifully proportioned perianth of ivory-white; long graceful trumpet of apricot-pink, changing to shell-pink at the deeply fringed edge."

'Orange Phoenix'. Intro: 1731. Prince, New York, 1820. This narcissus also has been called 'Double Incomparabilis' (syn. *Narcissus incomparabilis albus aurantius plenus*): "Considered the handsomest of all the species. It has large and small petals; the large lemon color, filled with small orange-colored ones" (Breck 1851).

'Princeps'. Intro: 1830. Griswold, Nebraska, 1908. "Large yel-

Narcissus: Double Roman, Paper White and Poeticus. *Vick's Monthly Magazine*, 1884.

low trumpet with sulphur perianth; excellent forcing" (New England Nurseries, Massachusetts, 1910).

'Seagull'. Intro: 1903. Duffy, 1916. "Very large flower; perianth white, expanded cup canary yellow, edged apricot" (Storrs & Harrison, Ohio, 1925).

'Sir Watkin'. Intro: 1884. Henderson, New York, 1890. "Perianth sulphur yellow, deep golden cup" (Storrs & Harrison, Ohio, 1925). "Planted in America by the million; and a thoroughly useful, dependable and satisfactory plant in every way" (Wister 1930).

'Thalia'. Intro: 1915. Wister, 1930. Pure white, Leedsii Group. "If I had to pick favourites among my Daffodils, it would probably result in my placing the Leedsi group first of all. They are pure white, come early, [and] last well" (Wister 1930).

'Van Sion' (syn. 'Telemonius Plenus'). Intro: 1620. Prince, New York, 1860. Golden yellow. "Very double form of *N. pseudonarcissus*" (Rand 1876; Bailey 1906a).

'White Lady'. Intro: 1898. Storrs & Harrison, Ohio, 1925. "An exquisite flower with broad white perianth, and daintily crinkled cup of canary yellow."

'W. P. Milner'. Intro: 1880. Vaughan, Chicago, 1914. "An exceedingly charming little Daffodil for rock gardens or naturalizing" (Wister 1930).

Historic commercial sources: 54

Related species:

Narcissus bulbocodium. Hoop petticoat daffodil. Intro: by 1629. M'Mahon, 1806.

Narcissus jonquilla. Jonquil. Intro: 1612. Thomas Jefferson, 1766. "Very slender and graceful. . . . One of the old-fashioned flowers" (Bailey 1906a).

Narcissus poeticus. Poet's narcissus, pheasant's eye. Long cultivated. M'Mahon, 1806. Flowers snow-white with cups suffused with bright orange-red. Helena R. Ely (1903) described the poet's narcissus in her garden:

> Everything is in rows. . . . Along the edge is Narcissus Poeticus; back of Narcissus Poeticus a row of Sweet Williams, pink, white and very dark red; back of the Sweet Williams, Foxgloves; back of the Foxgloves, Peonies and Hydrangea grandiflora planted alternately. About two feet behind this border, a row of Rudbeckia (Golden Glow) grows like a tall hedge.

Narcissus pseudonarcissus. Lent lily, trumpet daffodil, wild daffodil. Long cultivated. M'Mahon 1806. *N. pseudonarcissus* is the old daffodil, with several variants, that has naturalized throughout the South from Virginia to Alabama. Bailey (1906a) described it as "one of the hardiest and commonest of Narcissi." The var. *moschatus* has white segments and a primrose corolla.

For regional invasiveness concerns regarding *Narcissus* species, see Appendix D.

Ornithogalum umbellatum

star-of-Bethlehem, star-flower
Liliaceae (Hyacinthaceae)
Exotic
Introduction: Long cultivated
Earliest American citation: M'Mahon, 1806
Zone: 5
Description: "It is a dwarf, hardy, bulbous plant, which bears umbels of green and white flowers in May. . . . In the Star-of-Bethlehem the green and white of the leaf is curiously re-

peated in the white and green of the flower, which is a pretty six-pointed star, opening in sunshine" (Keeler 1910).

Design notes: "Gardeners seldom admit this flower now to their gardens, it so quickly crowds out everything else; it has become on Long Island nothing but a weed" (Earle 1901).

Remarks: "Although one of our prettiest early summer flowers, its dissemination should be avoided, as it is sure to assume the mastery over every other form of vegetation when it once gets started. If this species could be confined within reasonable limits, its presence in the garden would be most desirable" (Allen 1902).

For regional invasiveness concerns regarding *Ornithogalum umbellatum*, see Appendix D.

Heirloom varieties: Early growers described a blue star-of-Bethlehem and also a striped variety.

Historic commercial sources: 17

Polianthes tuberosa

tuberose, tube rose, polyanthus
Synonym: *Polyanthus tuberosa*
Agavaceae
Exotic
Introduction: 1530
Earliest American citation: John Custis, 1735
Zone: 9

Description: "The Tuberose is a tender tuberous-rooted plant, with linear leaves of whitish green, and stems four or five feet high, terminating in a sparse spike of white flowers, of very powerful fragrance, which display themselves in August" (Breck 1858).

Design notes: "The American or Pearl varieties will also succeed if the bulbs are potted in April, plunged in their pots in cinder beds, in the warmest parts of the garden, yard, rooftop, or balcony, and removed to the moderately warm greenhouse to blossom in October" (Hampden 1922).

Remarks: A letter to the editor of the 1878 *Vick's Monthly Magazine* reported sensational success with the tuberose by a southern gardener: "Mr. Vick: I had a tuberose last fall that had eighty-four buds and twenty-three flowers at one time, a double one you sent me, and it was six feet high. Mrs. M. H. Lowry, Washington, Arkansas" (Vick 1878h).

Harriet Keeler 1910) reported that the tuberose had fallen from favor because of its heavy fragrance and an untoward association with funerals.

Heirloom varieties:

'Flore Pleno'. Double tuberose. Prince, New York, 1790.

'Foliis Variegata'. Dreer, Philadelphia, 1876. Leaves striped with yellow or creamy white.

Polianthes tuberosa, tuberose, was valued for its pure white flowers and sweet fragrance. Photograph by Scott Kunst, Old House Gardens.

'Pearl' (syn. 'Excelsior'). Intro: 1870 US. Berckmans, Georgia, 1873. Dwarf habit and larger flowers than the species.

Historic commercial sources: 66

Sprekelia formosissima

Jacobean lily, Aztec lily, Jacobson lily
Synonym: *Amaryllis formosissima*
Amaryllidaceae
Exotic
Introduction: 1658
Earliest American citation: William Faris, Annapolis, 1802
Zone: 9

Description: "The flowers are large and of a very deep red. The under petals hang down, the upper curl up, and the whole flower stands nodding on one side of the stalk, making a fine appearance" (Breck 1858).

Design notes: "We have not the smallest doubt that in a few years . . . this superb South American bulb will adorn our flower gardens" (Buist 1839).

Tulipa 'Couleur Cardinal' (1845). Photograph by author.

The Jacobean lily was set out in borders after danger of frost was passed and overwintered indoors.

Remarks: "Old garden favorite, whose brilliant crimson flowers are seemingly, in the sun, dusted with gold, making them attractive objects" (Allen 1902).

Historic commercial sources: 27

Tulipa

tulip

Liliaceae

Exotic

Introduction: by 1554

Earliest American citation: Thomas Ash, 1682

Zone: 5–8

Description: "There is no question that the Tulip is the most popular spring flower that grows.... From the first Duc Von Thol scarce peeping above the ground, to the last Gesneriana Tulip, holding its flaming cup high aloft, there is a constant succession of Tulip Beauties—single, double, dwarf, tall, early, medium, and late, with blossoms, cup-shaped, star-formed, bowl-like, Paeony-flowered, imbricated like a Rose, twisted, waved and horned, like the plumage of some fantastic bird. No garden can be complete without plenty of Tulips" (Childs, New York, 1910).

Design notes:

"Plant double tulips with some parrot types among shrubs and other plants ... or planted out in separate beds" (Breck 1851).

Henderson (1901) illustrated a bed of tulips planted in the form of a multicolored butterfly. He used almost 5000 bulbs in the design, including yellow, crimson, and pink.

"Large May tulips are better for hardy borders than the small early ones, not only because they are more effective, but be-

This lovely rose tone is just one color found in the 'Duc van Thol' double tulips. Photograph by Scott Kunst, Old House Gardens.

cause they may be left undisturbed in the ground for four or five years without deteriorating" (Blanchan 1913).

Mrs. King (1921) encouraged the use of tulips in the perennial border: "little groupings of these bulbs among the perennial plants may easily be managed.... Tulips ... may be set between plants of delphinium or peony. Two objects are then achieved. The tulips bloom in encircling clusters of fresh foliage, and this foliage, as it rises and grows strong, covers the tulip leaves as they brown to ripeness in the border or bed."

"Tulips should be planted in clumps or masses to have the best effect and they need a background. Evergreens are ideal for this but flowering shrubs can also be used.... They are particularly attractive when lilac or mauve varieties ... are planted with Lilacs" (Wister 1930).

Remarks: "A bed for two hundred and fifty Tulips, should be thirty six feet long by four wide. The bulbs to be planted in rows, seven inches apart, and seven inches distant from each other" (Breck 1858).

Tulipa 'Generaal de Wet' (1904). Photograph by Brent Heath, Brent & Becky's Bulbs.

'Keizerskroon' (1750) is an extant eighteenth-century tulip. Photograph by author.

A butterfly-shaped bed for tulips. Charles Henderson, *Henderson's Picturesque Gardens*, 1901.

"So far as I can find, no one ever blamed Holland for the Tulip craze. You can't imagine a nation going mad over Golden Glow or Wild Cucumber. The Tulip has qualities that make for madness. It comes at a time when the eye hungers for color" (Wright 1924).

Heirloom varieties:

'Clara Butt'. Intro: 1889. King, 1915. "Darwin tulip. Soft salmon-pink, shaded rose; one of the finest of this class" (Storrs & Harrison, Ohio, 1925).

'Couleur Cardinal'. Intro: 1845. Briggs, New York, 1873. Early single. Crimson scarlet (New England Nurseries, Massachusetts, 1910). Combine this tulip with *Phlox divaricata* (King 1915).

'Duc van Thol'. Intro: 1700. Prince, New York, 1820. Early double. "Some of the most esteemed early types [of tulips]

'Zomerschoon' (1620) is an example of the early "broken" style of tulip. Photograph by Scott Kunst, Old House Gardens.

noted for the depth and purity of their colors and they bloom two weeks ahead of the others" (Childs, New York, 1910). Colors included crimson, orange, red and yellow, rose, white, yellow.

'Electra'. Intro: 1905. Storrs & Harrison, Ohio, 1925. Early double. Violet with light shading.

'Generaal de Wet'. Intro: 1904. Fiske, Boston, 1927. Early single. "Enormous yellow flowers, flushed with orange." Very fragrant.

'Keizerskroon'. Kaiser Crown. Intro: 1750. Bloomington Nursery, Illinois, 1859. Early single. Scarlet, tipped yellow. "Keizerkroon [sic], in my opinion, should never be planted with any other tulips. Its gaudiness is too harsh unless seen by itself" (King 1915).

'Lac van Rijn'. Intro: 1620. Barrett, Boston, 1836. Early single. Various colors with white margin.

'Peach Blossom'. Intro: 1890. Storrs & Harrison, Ohio, 1925. Early double. Brilliant rosy pink.

'Prince of Austria'. Intro: 1860. Bloomington Nursery, Illinois, 1859. Early single. Straw and crimson.

'Van der Neer'. Intro: 1860. Briggs, New York, 1873. Early single. Fine mauve.

'Zomerschoon'. Intro: 1620. King, 1915. "Flamed and feathered with a true cream-white, with a slightly bluish sheen on the centres of the outer petals, the flower is of indescribable beauty. There is not one to equal it for charm, for luscious combination of salmon and cream. It is never likely to become plentiful."

Historic commercial sources: 64

Zantedeschia aethiopica

Ethiopian lily, lily of the Nile, calla lily
Synonyms: *Calla aethiopica, Richardia africana*
Araceae
Exotic
Introduction: 1731
Earliest American citation: An Old Gardener, 1822
Zone: 8–9

Description: The flower consists of a spathe, 3–10 in. long, white, creamy inside at the base, flaring outward and narrowing to a cuspidate tip. Fragrant (Bailey 1906a).

Design notes: Some early gardeners planted callas in the spring after the last frost and dug them up like dahlias in the fall. They were also cultivated in the greenhouse and conservatory, particularly in the northern states. At least one early-twentieth-century writer recommended sinking pots of callas in the garden for the summer and then lifting and bringing them indoors for the cold weather. Bailey

Zantedeschia albomaculata, spotted calla. Columbus Nursery, Columbus, Ohio, 1877.

(1906a) suggested using them for bog plants and also on the margins of ponds for a tropical effect. In California, the calla lily was planted along fences or even used as a hedge between properties. It was also frequently grown in a long narrow bed along the side of a house. "For effective planting it is much in demand for grouping around hydrants and unsightly objects in damp places" (Ernest Braunton in Bailey 1906a).

Remarks: "For the window garden there is no more satisfactory plant than the Calla; it will endure more heat than most others, and there is no danger from overwatering" (Allen 1902).

Historic commercial sources: 42

Related species:

Zantedeschia albomaculata. Spotted calla. Michel, St. Louis, 1876.

· 11 ·

HEIRLOOM ROSES

The rose has been an esteemed shrub among all civilized nations. The flowers are double, semi-double, and single; the colours are pink, red, purple, white, yellow, and striped, with almost every shade and mixture; the odour universally grateful. This plant is cultivated in every garden, from the humblest cottager to the loftiest prince, and by commercial gardeners in Europe extensively, for distilling rose water, and making the essential oil of roses.

—Robert Buist, *The Rose Manual*, 1854

[The rose] is a flower beloved by every one, not only in the present age, but has been in all ages past, and will no doubt continue to be the most prominent and desirable flower as long as the world stands. It may, with propriety, be styled the Queen of Flowers.

—Joseph Breck, *The Flower-Garden or Breck's Book of Flowers*, 1851

THE ROSE WAS PRESENT—and appreciated—in American gardens and landscapes from the first years of settlement. Early travelers and naturalists noted the presence of native roses growing "spontaneously" in the meadows and woods. Daniel Denton, writing in 1670, observed in the future New York, "Yea, in May you shall see the Woods and Field so curiously bedecked with Roses, and an innumerable multitude of delightful Flowers, not only pleasing the eye, but smell, that you may behold Nature contending with Art, and striving to equal, if not excel many gardens in England." Also in the seventeenth century, John Josselyn (1672) described in New England, "Wild Damask Rose, single, but very large and sweet." American

gardeners cultivated native roses, although they never were as popular as the highly bred varieties that came from Europe and, to a more limited extent, from America's own rose breeders like Samuel and John Feast of Baltimore who introduced 'Baltimore Belle' in 1843 or Walter Van Fleet of Glenn Dale, Maryland.

In his 1867 book *Country Life*, Robert Copeland discussed the virtues of the native roses:

They are single, mostly rather low growing, and with small leaves. But they are perfectly hardy, accommodating themselves to all soils, and growing freely among other bushes, or in the Grass; are very fragrant, and their blossoms are succeeded by red hips, or seed vessels, which contribute much toward the enlivenment of the shrubbery during the winter. A bank of these Roses has often seemed to me more beautiful than any garden collection. . . . To fill a bend in a path or road, to skirt a plantation or fringe a pond, they are as beautiful as anything.

Copeland's favorites included *Rosa carolina*, *R. blanda*, and *R. nitida*. He also exclaimed over *Rosa setigera*, the prairie rose, which was used extensively in the West as a climber.

Besides valuing the native roses in the wild, early gardeners grew roses in ornamental settings. The rose's fragrant properties also made it a candidate for inclusion in kitchen gardens with other herbs and scented flowers. John Lawson reported in his 1718 *The History of Carolina* that Carolina gardeners cultivated two sorts of roses. Some years later in faraway California, where settlement was occurring somewhat independently of the activity in the east, the Castile rose was a noted inhabitant of the early mission gardens. Bernard M'Mahon in Philadelphia included fifty-seven species and

Rosa 'Champneys' Pink Cluster' is an original American hybrid. Photograph courtesy of the Thomas Jefferson Foundation.

Rosa wichurana and *Rosa rugosa*. Hooker, Wyman, & Co., Rochester, New York, ca. 1905.

varieties of rose, including the multiflora rose, six varieties of sweetbriar, and five different damasks in his 1806 book.

The first American-bred hybrid rose came from Charleston, South Carolina. John Champneys crossed *Rosa moschata* with *R. chinensis* to produce 'Champneys' Pink Cluster' in 1810. Charleston florist Philippe Noisette then selected a blush variety of 'Champneys' Pink Cluster', which he sent to France as 'Blush Noisette'. The class has been known since as the Noisettes on both sides of the Atlantic.

Nineteenth-century gardeners like Parkman, Ellwanger, Scott, and others classified rose blossoms on the basis of bloom time and frequency of flowering and grouped roses within those categories. Joseph Breck's classification in 1851 borrowed from Samuel Parsons and exemplified this style of organization, offered below with additional descriptions from Henry Havens' 1885 article, "The Classes of Roses."

I. Those that make distinct and separate periods of bloom throughout the season, as the Remontant Roses. . . . Includes only the present Damask and Hybrid Perpetuals. . . . Perpetual does not express their true character. "A most valuable class, and in England, standing at the head of all roses" (Havens).

II. Those that bloom continually, without any temporary cessation. [Actually most repeat roses do go temporarily dormant when summer temperatures exceed their heat tolerance.] These roses are divided into five classes [plus two newer categories].

1. The Bourbon, which are easily known by their luxuriant growth, and thick, leathery leaves. These are, moreover, perfectly hardy. [Bourbon roses actually are hardy to zone 5 and might require winter protection farther north.]

2. The China, which includes the present China, Tea, and Noisette Roses, which are now much confused, as there are many among the Teas which are not tea-scented, and among the Noisettes which do not bloom in clusters. "The China roses are of moderate, branching growth, flowers of medium size . . . they give a greater quantity of flowers during the season than any other class. . . . [The Noisette is] naturally of vigorous growth and produces large clusters of flowers. Through hybridization with the Tea section the varieties have partially lost the clustering tendency, but the flowers have more substance, and are far more beautiful" (Havens).

3. Musk, known by its rather rougher foliage.

4. Macartney, known by its very rich, glossy foliage, almost evergreen.

5. Microphylla, easily distinguished by its peculiar foliage and straggling habit.

6. Polyantha, introduced after Breck made this list and which Havens described: "As a class they are ever-blooming, of slender growth, producing a great quantity of exquisitely beautiful flowers."

7. Hybrid Tea, a new category in 1885, represented by 'La France' [which was introduced to commerce in 1867].

III. Those that bloom only once in the season, as the French and others.

1. *Garden Roses.* This includes all the present French, Provence, Hybrid Provence, Hybrid China, Hybrid Bourbon, White, and Damask Roses.

2. *Moss Roses.* "They are distinguished from other roses, by the moss-like substance which sur-rounds the flower buds and by the marked Provence scent" (Havens).

3. *Brier Roses,* which will include the Sweet Brier, Hybrid Sweet Brier, and Austrian Brier. [Breck spelled this rose "brier," whereas other writers used "briar," which is used later in this text.]

4. *The Scotch Rose.* [Distinguished by their small leaves, prickly stems, abundant bloom, delicate habits, early bloom.]

5. *Climbing Rose* [Climbing Teas, Hybrid Climbers, Prairie Roses]. "Three of our finest climbing roses [are] Climbing Devoniensis, Gloire de Dijon, and Reine Marie Henriette; all of vigorous growth when well established" (Havens).

How to place or arrange roses in the landscape was a much-discussed topic. In the vernacular landscape, placement was usually very simple, as per Joseph Breck who reminisced about the rose of his childhood, "Who can forget the old white Rose, as it was trained up the side of the house?" (Breck 1851). Porches or verandas were also traditional settings for a climb-

Caroline Testout Roses, Portland, Oregon.

A hedge of 'Caroline Testout' roses. Portland, Oregon, 1910.

A moveable rose trellis. Andrew J. Downing, *Rural Essays*, 1853.

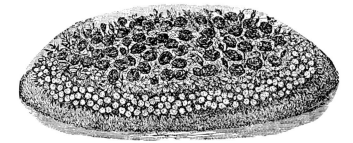

A bed of roses. C. E. Allen, Brattleboro, Vermont, 1889.

ing rose, which might have been the only plant ornamentation. A custom in many parts of the country was to put a favored rose on the grave of a loved one. Today many of those old roses persist in cemeteries, usually with no identification. "Rose Rustlers" and other interested persons are rescuing these roses, often in advance of a dedicated weedeater. Good & Reese Co., Florists and Seedsmen, of Springfield, Ohio (1907), advertised a "Superb Cemetery Collection of Pure White, Hardy Roses" including 'Lady Emily Peel', 'Coquette des Alps', 'Ball of Snow', 'Madame Alfred Carrière', and 'Madame Alfred de Rougemont'. One newer class of roses that was particularly valued for this purpose was the Wichurana class, also called the Memorial Roses. The species Memorial Rose was single and pure white. Its habit, if so allowed, was to creep along the ground as an effective ground cover on a grave.

Roses were used to construct hedges, particularly in the southern states and in the West. When Frederick Olmsted visited St. Francisville, Mississippi, just prior to the Civil War, the landscape impressed him with its rose hedges. He observed,

> The roadside fences are generally hedges of roses—Cherokee and sweet brier. These are planted first by the side of a common rail fence, which when they are young, supports them in the manner of a trellis; as they grow older they fall each way, and must mat together, finally forming a confused, sprawling, slovenly thicket, often ten feet in

breadth and four to six feet high. Trumpet creepers, grape-vines, green-briers, and in very rich soil, cane, grow up through the mat of roses, and add to its strength. It is not as pretty as a trimmer hedge, yet very agreeable. (Olmsted 1860)

Climbing roses offered special features for the landscape. A climbing rose might be trained along the side of a house or allowed to clamber over shrubs and small trees. Another attractive way to grow the climbers was on a pillar. Charles Henderson (1901) observed a "row of pillar roses bordering a lawn driveway, dotting with novel effect the level greensward and background of shrubbery with spires of red, white, yellow, and blush." Climbing roses covered porches and verandas as noted above, as well as rustic houses, arbors, pergolas, and trellises of various shapes and forms. Again, Henderson remarked, "Garden walks are rendered most charming by spanning them with arches to form arcades over which climbing Roses scramble in picturesque freedom; the Roses so trained are not only seen to best advantage, but the effect of arches and pillars of Roses or other flowers relieves gardens of monotonous flatness."

Nineteenth-century gardeners recognized that the special cultivation needs of roses dictated that they be grown in beds by themselves. The bright colors and the long season of bloom of the ever-blooming sorts made those varieties good candidates for bedding in gardens of the 1800s. Roses were massed one color per bed with each bed cut out of the lawn. A method to insure complete coverage of the bed was to peg down a tall-growing or climbing type of rose so that a ground cover effect might be obtained. H. B. Ellwanger wrote in *The Rose* (1910), "The requisites for a good bedding rose are, freedom of bloom, healthy habit of growth, and pure, steadfast color. Symmetry of form, fragrance, and fullness of flower should also be taken into consideration." Some popular bedding roses included: 'Bougere' (Tea), 'Catherine Mermet' (Tea), 'Clotilde Soupert' (Polyantha), 'Coquette des Alps' (Bourbon), and 'Gruss an Teplitz' (Bourbon).

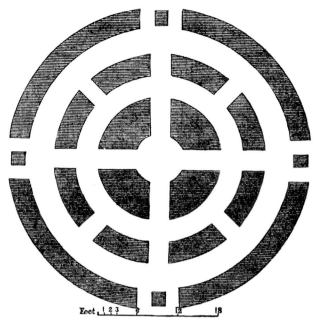

An English-style rose garden. Robert M. Copeland, *Country Life*, 1867.

Another place for roses was the shrubbery. Robert Buist in 1854 recommended that roses were "designed for open or close shrubberies, clumps, or thickets." Other writers agreed, including H. B. Ellwanger who suggested scattering roses throughout the border or shrubbery, keeping the more delicate ones in the front. Liberty H. Bailey in *How to Make a Flower Garden* (1903) disagreed with this design style, arguing that most roses were inappropriate for the shrubbery since they need extra care. He suggested that roses be planted by themselves in gardens or masses and definitely *not* scattered all over the lawn. Helena R. Ely (1903) agreed and went so far as to suggest that roses be planted in rows so that a cultivator could be run between them. Ely allowed, however, that a few noncompetitive plants could be grown with roses, including pansies and gladioli.

Many writers suggested planning an entire garden around a collection of roses as in this recommendation from Robert Buist (1854):

> The most interesting disposition, and one that offers the greatest variety, is to plant the whites, blushes, pinks, roses, reds, crimsons, and purples, each into separate clumps, figures, or patches; and to carry out a grand arrangement, let each division of the rose have its appropriate locality. . . . This Rosary can be formed on any piece of ground, from a quarter of an acre to any required extent, either on the lawn or any other spot for the purpose.

A design for a rose garden had the purpose of the "exhibition of the single plants with their peculiarities, and of the full beauty of their blossoms," rather than an effect of form or color (Copeland 1867). Many writers like Copeland felt that for the best presentation roses should be in formal beds. The design facing is from his book *Country Life* and measured 48 ft. across. The center of the design was raised about 4 ft. above the surrounding ground with a "temple" or structure upon which to grow climbing roses of various kinds. Each outlying bed contained eight rose bushes, one type of rose—that is, Bourbons, Albas, and so on—per bed. A hedge of Scotch roses surrounded the entire garden. The number of roses in the total design did not exceed 300, which as Copeland noted, could be obtained from European suppliers at $20.00 per hundred.

By the twentieth century, the design of the rose garden had changed very little. Hanna Rion (1912) recommended that a formal garden for roses be enclosed by a hedge. If the hedge was to be made of rugosa roses, then so much the better, and she suggested a mixture of the white 'Sir Thomas Lipton', red *Rosa rugosa*, and pink 'New Century'. A typical design, according to Rion, might be overall circular with a central circle-bed to hold spring-flowering bulbs, followed by annuals, and paths leading from the circle at right and left angles to form beds like the slices of a pie. Those beds would hold the roses, arranged individually by color.

Robert Huey, writing for Bailey's 1906 *Cyclopedia*, asserted that roses could be grown anywhere there is a love of the plant and plenty of sunshine. For city dwellers, he recommended digging the rose beds deeply and amending with topsoil brought in from the country and plenty of horse manure. The bed should be dug out to 3 ft. and the bottom foot filled with crushed stone, bricks, or cinders to allow better drainage to the bed. Hybrid Perpetuals would do fine in a heavy clay soil, he counseled, while the delicate Teas preferred a lighter soil. Care should be taken not to crowd the rose plants; planting them a distance of at least 30 in. apart was recommended.

The same writers of the early 1900s who revolutionized the approach to using color in American perennial gardens included roses in their ideal color combinations. Louise B. Wilder (1918) suggested massing delphiniums against groups of pink roses. She then suggested appropriate backgrounds for various roses, explaining, "New red brick is utterly unsuitable as a background for pink or Red roses." White buildings were deemed the best for growing a variety of roses. "What is prettier than a white house smothered beneath pink and scarlet Roses of all shades, with the starlike flowering in May of Clematis montana, with ropes of purple Wisteria and

some space left for the scarlet autumn hangings of Virginia Creeper." Stone furnished a good neutral background for roses as did stucco. Wilder suggested that arbors and pergolas be painted white, although she described an arbor that was painted light apple green. "Upon it grew white and pale lemon coloured Roses with now and then a splash of purple Clematis, and in the narrow beds at the base of the posts were crowding purple and lavender Violas, delicate Ferns, and white Stocks. It was most unusually fresh and pretty."

The horticultural periodicals of the nineteenth and twentieth centuries contained many articles of advice concerning rose care. Writers particularly addressed remedies for the ravages of pests and diseases. In their 1882 catalog, rose producer Dingee & Conard Company of Chester County, Pennsylvania, discussed both rose pests and their remedies.

Insect Enemies of the Rose

Aphis or green fly—
  The best remedy is tobacco smoke.
The Rose Slug—
  The body of this slug is green and soft, almost transparent like jelly. . . . They must be attacked instantly. Dust the plants thickly with powdered or air-slaked lime, plaster of Paris, ashes, or even road dust, and repeat the same vigorously as often as may be necessary.
The Rose Bug . . .
  of a grayish color and almost one-half an inch in length. . . . The only cure is hand picking.
Mildew—
  When plants suddenly become covered with a whitish looking mould or dust, the disease is known as Mildew. Unless a very severe attack it will not probably kill them, but only retard their growth. . . . For out-door plants, a thorough stirring of the soil, with a view to encourage strong growth, is probably the best thing that can be done.
Red Spider
  is a very minute insect, first appearing on the underside of the leaves. . . . It flourishes best in a hot, dry atmosphere, either indoors or out; moisture is its greatest enemy. Sprinkle or wash your plants frequently.
White Worms at the Root—
  Take up and wash the roots clean in warm water and repot.

Hanna Rion (1912) summed it up with two sentences: "You will realize, of course, that raising roses is not eating ice cream and cake. Believe me, the rose grower cannot be either a fool man or a lazy woman."

Roses are well documented in the annals of garden history. Fortunately, many of the old cultivars are available and can provide the basis for an authentic period garden. Early nursery catalogs offered over 3500 varieties of roses. The diversity and selection were truly overwhelming. The following 100 roses are those most commonly available in eighty trade notices that included roses, beginning with a 1786 advertisement for Peter Crowells & Company in the *South Carolina Gazette* through nursery catalogs of the 1930s. Interestingly, some of the varieties that made this list were not the best for planting out-of-doors and some were even panned by garden writers as not being very attractive. Commercial availability was based on many factors. Ease of propagation, low versus high cost of production, and availability from European sources all contributed to the inventory of the American grower.

The dates of introduction are from three sources: Dickerson's *The Old Rose Advisor* (1992), *The Combined Rose List 2002*, and Ellwanger's *The Rose* (1910). The rapidity with which roses introduced in Europe reached American gardens is amazing. Sometimes descriptions varied between nursery catalogs. Different descriptions do not mean that growers were not selling the correct rose. Color instability based on climate and soil conditions, particularly among the tea roses, often contributed to differing descriptions for the same rose. An additional "Earliest American citation" is given for U.S. introductions, since there was often a lag time between introduction and nursery production to meet commercial demand.

ONE HUNDRED HEIRLOOM ROSES FOR AMERICAN GARDENS

George Thompson & Sons, Louisville, Kentucky, 1888.

'Adam'

Tea
Synonym: 'President'
Introduction: Adam, 1838
Earliest American citation: Valk, 1847
Description: "Light pink, large flower" (Berckmans, Georgia, 1859).
"Salmon rose, fragrant" (Ellwanger 1910).
Remarks: "One of the finest tea-scented roses" (Parsons 1869). Esteemed for forcing (Ellwanger 1910).
Historic commercial sources: 17

'Aglaia'

Hybrid Multiflora
Synonym: 'Yellow Rambler'
Introduction: Schmitt/P. Lambert, 1896
Earliest American citation: Mission Valley, Texas, 1898
Description: "Clear golden yellow; one of the best of the ramblers" (Ashby, California, 1908).
Remarks: Ernest Wilson wrote in *The Garden Magazine* in 1915, "We want a Rambler Rose with pure white flowers as large and freely produced as in the Crimson Rambler. Also we want yellow Ramblers" (Wilson 1915b) Apparently, 'Aglaia' did not fulfill the need as Wilson perceived it.
Historic commercial sources: 25

'Alfred Colomb'

Hybrid Perpetual
Introduction: Lacharme, 1865
Earliest American citation: Moon, Pennsylvania, 1870
Description: "Bright carmine crimson, very large, globular form" (Storrs & Harrison, Ohio, 1896).
Remarks: "A good rose for massing, although not continuously in bloom. Highly scented. The most useful in its class for general cultivation" (Ellwanger 1910).
Historic commercial sources: 24

'American Beauty'

Hybrid Perpetual
Synonym: 'Crimson American Beauty'
Introduction: A. Cook/Field Bros., 1886
Earliest American citation: Thompson, Kentucky, 1888
Description: "Good strong grower and free bloomer; full, double and extra sweet; color rich, rosy, crimson, exquisitely shaded; very handsome" (Jackson, Georgia, 1904).
"Delicious odor" (Ellwanger 1910).
Remarks: "The great Rose of the eastern United States, American Beauty, is almost a complete failure here [in Southern California]" (Bailey 1906a). By the beginning of the twentieth century the American Beauty rose was the most popular florist's rose in America.
Historic commercial sources: 42

YELLOW RAMBLER.

'Aglaia' was a popular yellow rambler rose in California gardens. Leo Weltz, Wilmington, Ohio, ca. 1905.

Climbing American Beauty rose. *Archias Seed Annual*, Sedalia, Missouri, 1917.

'American Beauty, Climbing'

Climber

Introduction: James A. Farell/Hoopes Bro. & Thomas Co., Westchester, Pennsylvania, 1909

Earliest American citation (other): Iowa Seed, Des Moines, 1914

Description: "Has all the characteristics of its relative, including form and fragrance" (Ernst, Ohio, 1926).

"Immense blooms measuring 3 to 4 inches in diameter; and each one is invariably produced on a separate stem. The color is glowing crimson red, the real American Beauty color" (Dingee & Conard, Pennsylvania, 1924).

Remarks: "For single specimens, for pergolas, for climbing over verandas, or any place that an ordinary vine will grow, Climbing American Beauty will thrive. It does not require any petting or coaxing." (Dingee & Conard, Pennsylvania, 1925)

Historic commercial sources: 17

'Anna de Diesbach'

Hybrid Perpetual

Synonym: 'Gloire de Paris'

Introduction: Lacharme, 1858

Earliest American citation: Berckmans, Georgia, 1861

Description: "Clear rose, beautifully cupped" (Atlanta Nurseries, Georgia, 1870).

"The most lovely shade of carmine, very large, double flowers, fragrant" (Ellwanger 1910).

Remarks: A good rose for massing, although not continuously in bloom, also one of the hardiest roses (Ellwanger 1910).

Historic commercial sources: 36

'Apolline'

Bourbon

Introduction: V. Verdier, 1848

Earliest American citation: Pomaria, South Carolina, 1856

Description: "Rosy-pink, large cupped flowers" (Ellwanger 1910).

Remarks: This rose is "half-hardy, will endure the winter with little protection by covering with straw, leaves, or any other coarse litter" (Good & Reese, Ohio, 1889).

Historic commercial sources: 21

'Archiduc Charles'

China

Synonym: 'Archduke Charles'

Introduction: Laffay, by 1837

Earliest American citation: Winter, New York, 1844

Description: "Rosy crimson" (Bloomington Nursery, Illinois, 1859).

"Rose, changing to crimson" (Columbus Nursery, Ohio, 1860).

"Having frequently a beautiful carnation-like appearance" (Parsons 1869).

Remarks: "A noble variety, opening a bright rose color and changing to crimson; the points of the petals are frequently tipped with bright red" (Buist 1854).

Historic commercial sources: 21

'Auguste Mie'

Hybrid Perpetual

Synonyms: 'Blanche de Beaulieu', 'Madame Rival'

Introduction: Laffay, 1851

Earliest American citation: Pomaria, South Carolina, 1856

Description: "Bright rosy scarlet" (Columbus Nursery, Ohio, 1860).

"Clear rosy pink, very large and finely cupped" (Atlanta Nurseries, Georgia, 1870).

Remarks: "A seedling of the well-known La Reine" (Parsons 1869). "One of the most tender of this type" (Ellwanger 1910). This rose does not appear in current availability listings.

Historic commercial sources: 18

'Baltimore Belle'

Hybrid Setigera, Prairie Rose, Michigan Rose

Introduction: Feast, Baltimore, Maryland, 1843

Earliest American citation (other): McIntosh, Ohio, 1845

Description: "Double, pale blush, clusters" (Bloomington Nursery, Illinois, 1859).

Rosa 'Baltimore Belle'. Photograph by Peggy Cornett, Thomas Jefferson Foundation.

"Pale blush, variegated carmine rose and white, very double, flowers in beautiful clusters, the whole plant appearing a perfect mass of bloom" (Good & Reese, Ohio, 1889).

Remarks: Gardeners often used the Baltimore Belle rose as a porch rose, for trellises and arbors, or as a screen for unsightly objects, including outbuildings and fences.

"One of the finest climbing roses known" (Parsons 1869).

Historic commercial sources: 53

'Baron de Bonstetten'

Hybrid Perpetual

Introduction: Liabaud, 1871

Earliest American citation: Louisville Rose, Kentucky, 1881

Description: "Very double, rich, dark red" (Storrs & Harrison, Ohio, 1896).

"Velvety maroon, shaded with deep crimson . . . shy in autumn, but a grand rose" (Ellwanger 1910).

Remarks: One of the hardiest roses (Ellwanger 1910).

Historic commercial sources: 17

'Baroness Rothschild'

Hybrid Perpetual

Synonyms: 'Baronne Adolphe de Rothschild', 'Madame de Rothschild', 'Baronne A. de Rothschild'

Introduction: Pernet, 1868

Earliest American citation: Moon, Pennsylvania, 1870

Description: "Light rose color, large and full" (Langdon, Alabama, 1881).

"A very large and very charming pink rose of cupped shape, full, standing upright, keeping its handsome shape to the end, sits in a frill of foliage on a rather short stem. . . . Everything so pleasing except one thing, a complete absence of fragrance—a beautiful bird without a song—lovable, nonetheless" (Keays 1935).

Remarks: A good rose for massing, although not continuously in bloom (Ellwanger 1910).

Another 'Baron de Rothschild' was amaranth red, according to Ellwanger (1910). That rose most likely was the introduction with the same name by Guillot in 1862.

Historic commercial sources: 17

'Baronne Prevost'

Hybrid Perpetual

Introduction: Desprez/Cochet, 1842

Earliest American citation: Southern Nurseries, Mississippi, 1851

Description: "One of the finest of this class" (Columbus Nursery, Ohio, 1860). "Blooming freely in autumn, and producing flowers of a bright rose color" (Parsons 1869). "Pure rose color, very large, very full, flat form, a free bloomer, fragrant, very hardy" (Ellwanger 1910).

Remarks: A good rose for massing, although not continuously in bloom. Highly scented (Ellwanger 1910).

Historic commercial sources: 26

'Bon Silène'

Tea

Introduction: Hardy, by 1837

Earliest American citation: McIntosh, Ohio, 1845

Description: "Carmine and salmon, good fall bloomer" (Berckmans, Georgia, 1859). "Deep salmon rose, illumined with carmine, medium size, semi-double, highly scented, very free flowering" (Ellwanger 1910).

Remarks: "Grown by every florist for its highly colored buds, dark crimson rose, often changing to crimson" (Good & Reese, Ohio, 1889). "Bon Silène, 1835, similar in form to Safrano, but a trifle fuller, is the sweetest of the sweet Tea roses" (Keays 1935).

Historic commercial sources: 30

'Bougere'

Tea

Synonym: 'Clotilde'

Introduction: Bougere, 1832

Earliest American citation: Winter, New York, 1844

Description: "Deep blush, large" (Bloomington Nursery, Illinois, 1859).

"Bronze rose or violet crimson, delicately shaded with lilac" (California Nursery, 1894).

Remarks: Recommended as an excellent bedding rose and it is one of the hardiest of the Monthly Roses (Ellwanger 1910).

Historic commercial sources: 31

'Caroline'

Tea

Introduction: Guerin, 1829

Earliest American citation: McIntosh, Ohio; Cleveland Nursery, Ohio, 1845

Description: "Blush-pink, centre delicate rose, large and full" (Parkman 1871a). "Fleshy rose, deeper toward center; prettily formed buds" (Ellwanger 1910).

Remarks: Parkman (1871a) recommended that the Tea roses be planted in a bed with good drainage, "in an open sunny situation, and sheltered, as far as may be, from strong winds."

Historic commercial sources: 16

'Caroline de Sansal'

Hybrid Perpetual

Introduction: Desprez, 1849

Earliest American citation: *The Horticulturist*, 1854

Description: "Clear delicate flesh color, becoming blush; large size and fine form" (Columbus Nursery, Ohio, 1860).

Remarks: One of the hardiest roses (Ellwanger 1910).

Historic commercial sources 17

'Catherine Mermet'

Tea

Introduction: J. B. Guillot fils, 1869

Earliest American citation: Langdon, Alabama; Louisville Rose, Kentucky, 1881

Description: "Flesh color, decidedly one of the finest teas" (Louisville Rose, Kentucky, 1881). "Clear, shiny pink" (Boardman, California, 1889).

Remarks: Recommended as an excellent bedding rose. "When the flowers expand they exhale a delightful perfume" (Ellwanger 1910).

Historic commercial sources: 24

'Chromatella'

Noisette

Synonym: 'Cloth of Gold'

Introduction: Coquereau, 1843

Earliest American citation: Cleveland Nursery, Ohio; McIntosh, Ohio, 1845

Description: "Deep yellow, very sweet, large and beautiful" (Columbus Nursery, Ohio, 1860).

"Deep yellow center with sulphur edges . . . difficult to grow well" (Ellwanger 1910).

Remarks: "Well adapted for training against trellis work or as a standard in the border or lawn." S. D. Morton of Petersburg, Virginia, claimed that his 'Cloth of Gold' had forty to fifty flowers on it at one time (Brackenbridge 1847). The editor of *The Horticulturist* (responding to Brackenbridge) wrote, "From all parts of the south, where it appears to grow with the greatest luxuriance, we have accounts of the great beauty of this Rose."

Historic commercial sources: 37

Rosa 'Cramoisi Supérieur'. Photograph by G. Mike Shoup, The Antique Rose Emporium.

'Clotilde Soupert'

Polyantha

Introduction: Soupert & Notting, 1890

Earliest American citation: California Nursery, 1894

Description: "Medium size, very double and beautifully imbricated, produced in clusters, liable to vary, producing often red and white flowers on same plant" (California Nursery, 1894).

"Medium size; full round flowers, beautiful pinkish amber or cream, delicately flushed with silver-rose" (Jackson, Georgia, 1904).

Remarks: "Continually in bloom. . . . The best bedding or pot culture Rose known. . . . It is entirely exempt from the disease usually affecting Roses in the house" (Good & Reese, Ohio, 1907).

Historic commercial sources: 18

'Comtesse de Murinais'

Moss

Synonym: 'White Moss'

Introduction: Vibert, 1843

Earliest American citation: Ramsdell, Connecticut, 1853

Description: "Pure white, large and double" (Columbus Nursery, Ohio, 1860).

"Blush white" (Dreer, Pennsylvania, 1876).

"White, tinged with flesh, not inclined to mildew" (Ellwanger 1910).

Remarks: "Perfectly hardy, flowers in June and occasionally through the summer" (Vick, New York, 1881).

Historic commercial sources: 22

'Coquette des Alpes'

Bourbon

Introduction: Lacharme, 1867

Earliest American citation: Dreer, Pennsylvania, 1876

Description: "Pure white, flowers in clusters" (Dreer, Pennsylvania, 1876).

"White, tinged with blush . . . semi-cupped form. A very desirable white rose" (Ellwanger 1910).

Remarks: Recommended as an excellent bedding rose (Ellwanger 1910).

"One of the finest White Hybrid Perpetuals" (Dingee & Conard, Pennsylvania, 1882).

Historic commercial sources: 20

'Cramoisi Supérieur'

China, Monthly Rose

Synonyms: 'Agrippina', 'Purple Superior', 'Crimson Hermosa', 'Cramoisie Superieure', 'Lady Brisbane'

Introduction: Coquereau/Vibert, 1832/1835

Earliest American citation: Prince, New York, 1841

Description: "Scarlet, with white center" (Prince, New York, 1841).

"Fine velvety crimson" (Bloomington Nursery, Illinois, 1859).

"Specially valued for its fine buds" (Ellwanger 1910).

"It is cupped, beautifully formed, and of a rich, brilliant crimson, with a delicate white stripe in the centre of each petal" (Parsons 1869).

Remarks: "Should be in every collection" (Buist 1854). Recommended as an excellent bedding rose (Ellwanger 1910).

CRESTED MOSS.

Rosa 'Crested Moss'. Leo Weltz, Wilmington, Ohio, ca. 1905.

Rosa centifolia cristata, *Rosa* 'Crested Moss'. Louisville Rose Co., Louisville, Kentucky, 1881.

"Cramoisie Supérieure . . . is excellent as a front planting in a rose-border, where its flashes of crimson are as arresting as the cardinal bird darting across our path in the woods" (Keays 1935).

Historic commercial sources: 36

'Crested Moss'

Moss

Synonyms: *Rosa centifolia cristata*, 'Cristata', 'Chapeau de Napoleon'

Introduction: Kitzer/Vibert, 1827

Earliest American citation: Winter, New York, 1844

Description: "Deep, pink-colored buds, surrounded by a mossy fringe and crest. Highly scented" (Ellwanger 1910).

Remarks: Mrs. Frederick Love Keays wrote, "probably not truly a Moss. Little whisk-brooms of bristly, resinous green edge the sepals so that the bud seems to wear a three-cor-

nered hat which breaks open and is lost to sight behind the cabbage bloom of rose-pink with Centifolia fragrance" (Keays 1935).

Historic commercial sources: 27

'Devoniensis'

Tea

Synonym: Magnolia Rose

Introduction: Foster, 1838

Earliest American citation: Winter, New York, 1844

Description: "Beautiful creamy white with rosy center; large, very full and double, delightfully Tea scent; one of the finest Roses" (Dingee & Conard, Pennsylvania, 1882).

Remarks: Lockwood (1934) cites the inclusion of this plant in a garden ca. 1845 laid out by William Battersby in Savannah.

"Most delightfully scented" (Ellwanger 1910).

Historic commercial sources: 34

'Dorothy Perkins'

Hybrid Wichurana

Introduction: Jackson & Perkins, Medford, Oregon, 1901

Earliest American citation (other): Dunning, Maine, 1901

Description: "Clear shell pink, very sweetly scented" (New England Nurseries, Massachusetts, 1910).

Remarks: "In my own garden a Dorothy Perkins Rose climbs the wall beside my group of Purple Plum-trees and throws its great trusses of pink blossoms across the purple branches with fine effect. . . . Dorothy Perkins . . . is lovely with the

Rosa 'Dorothy Perkins'. Hooker, Wyman, & Co., Rochester, New York, ca. 1903.

warm purple blossoms of Clematis Jackmanii unfolding among the fluffy pink draperies" (Wilder 1918).
Historic commercial sources: 39

'Duchesse de Brabant'

Tea
Synonyms: 'Comtesse de Labarthe', 'Comtesse Ouwaroff', 'Countess Bertha'
Introduction: Bernede, 1857
Earliest American citation: Sunnyside, Iowa, 1871
Description: "Soft, rosy pink petals, edged with silver; extra good bloomer" (Jackson, Georgia, 1904).
Remarks: "This Rose combines exquisite perfume, beautiful coloring, and a matchless profusion of flowers and foliage" (Good & Reese, Ohio, 1889).
Historic commercial sources: 24

Rosa 'Étoile de Lyon'. Photograph by Marlea Graham.

'Étoile de Lyon'

Tea
Introduction: Guillot, 1881
Earliest American citation: Correspondent from Kentucky to *The Gardener's Monthly*, 1882
Description: "Beautiful chrome-yellow, deepening at center to pure golden yellow" (Jackson, Georgia, 1904).
Remarks: A correspondent who called himself W. A. R. sent this rose to the editor of *The Gardener's Monthly* in May 1882, saying, "You can judge somewhat of its size, and that it has a fine form, but it has not its usual color, which is much deeper [yellow]."
Historic commercial sources: 22

'Excelsa'

Hybrid Wichurana
Synonym: 'Red Dorothy Perkins', 'Seven Sisters'
Introduction: Walsh, 1909

Rosa 'Excelsa', also known in the Midwest as the Seven Sisters rose. Photograph by the author.

Some growers claimed that 'Frau Karl Druschki' was the only pure white rose ever introduced. Leo Weltz, Wilmington, Ohio, ca. 1905.

Rosa 'Frau Karl Druschki'. Peter Henderson Co., New York, 1910

Earliest American citation: Breck, Boston; Ellwanger & Barry, New York, 1917

Description: "A remarkable grower, free from insects and producing a great quantity of blooms of crimson-maroon with tips of the petals scarlet. Flowers full and double and thirty or forty produced on a stem" (Dingee & Conard, Pennsylvania, 1925).

Remarks: "The undesirable features of the Crimson Rambler, the unsightly foliage, is eliminated in this Rose by the infusion of Wichuriana [sic] blood" (Dingee & Conard, Pennsylvania, 1925).

Historic commercial sources: 19

'Frau Karl Druschki'

Hybrid Perpetual

Synonyms: 'White American Beauty', 'Snow Queen', 'Reine des Neiges'

Introduction: Lambert, 1901

Earliest American citation: Weltz, Ohio, ca. 1905

Description: "Pure paper-white" (New England Nurseries, Massachusetts, 1910).

Remarks: Some said that this was the only absolutely pure white rose ever introduced.

Mrs. Frederick Love Keays was apparently not completely captivated by this rose because she observed in her 1935 book, "Frau Karl Druschki, as widely spread throughout gardens as the plebian cabbage, as beautiful and scentless as a Greek statue."

Others extolled its virtues: "You must have the Druschki rose, the finest white rose in existence, despite the fact that it has no fragrance. It blooms freely and is almost everblooming. There is nothing finer than a half-open Druschki rose" (Wilcox 1938).

Historic commercial sources: 35

'Géant des Batailles'

Hybrid Perpetual
Synonym: 'Giant of Battles'
Introduction: Nerard/Guillot père, 1846
Earliest American citation: Southern Nurseries, Mississippi, 1851
Description: "Brilliant fiery crimson" (Atlanta Nurseries, Georgia, 1870). Not fragrant. "Well known for its dazzling color, and in this respect unequaled" (Parsons 1869).
Remarks: "Very liable to mildew . . . of delicate constitution" (Ellwanger 1910).
'Géant des Batailles' is "the red prickled rose," with short-jointed, erect, stiff shoots covered with numerous red thorns" (Keays 1935).
Historic commercial sources: 32

'Général Jacqueminot'

Hybrid Perpetual
Introduction: Roussel/Rousselet, 1853
Earliest American citation: Berckmans, Georgia; Hopewell, Virginia, 1859
Description: "Brilliant crimson scarlet, free bloomer, vigorous" (Atlanta Nurseries, Georgia, 1870).
Remarks: "A strong grower, and when in bud, one of the most beautiful of roses" (Parsons 1869). A good rose for massing, although not continuously in bloom. Highly scented and one of the hardiest roses (Ellwanger 1910).
Historic commercial sources: 67

'General Washington'

Hybrid Perpetual
Introduction: Granger, 1861
Earliest American citation: Truett, Tennessee, 1868
Description: "Brilliant red" (Atlanta Nurseries, Georgia, 1870).
Remarks: "It is a good grower, very full bloomer, and a general favorite" (Parsons 1869). "The flowers are often malformed, greatly lessening its value" (Ellwanger 1910).
Historic commercial sources: 24

'Gloire de Dijon'

Climber, Noisette
Introduction: Jacotot, 1853
Earliest American citation: Pomaria, South Carolina, 1856
Description: "Salmon buff, rose centre; very vigorous, one of the very best" (Atlanta Nurseries, Georgia, 1870).
"Blending of amber, carmine, and cream" (Good & Reese, Ohio, 1889).

Rosa 'Général Jacqueminot' was available in more nineteenth-century nursery catalogs than any other rose. Leo Weltz, Wilmington, Ohio, ca. 1905.

Remarks: "One of the hardiest of the Monthly Roses . . . has long been a favorite as a pillar rose, both for conservatories and in favorable conditions out of doors" (Ellwanger 1910).
Historic commercial sources: 22

'Gloire des Mousseux'

Moss
Synonyms: Gloire des Mosseuses, Glory of Mosses
Introduction: Laffay, 1852
Earliest American citation: Bloomington Nursery, Illinois, 1859
Description: "Pale rose, very large, full and beautiful" (Columbus Nursery, Ohio, 1860).
Remarks: "Not attractive in the bud" (Ellwanger 1910).
Historic commercial sources: 18

'Gruss an Teplitz'

Bourbon, China

Synonym: 'Virginia R. Coxe'

Introduction: Geschwind/Lambert, 1897

Earliest American citation: Templin, Ohio; Jackson, Georgia, 1904

Description: "A bedding rose . . . color scarlet" (Jackson, Georgia, 1904). Very fragrant.

"Best red garden rose . . . field grown" (Pilkington, Oregon, 1912).

Remarks: "As a bedding Rose this is one of the finest and most useful varieties ever sent out. . . . It is a perfect sheet of richest crimson scarlet all summer" (Good & Reese, Ohio, 1907).

Historic commercial sources: 39

'Hermosa'

Bourbon, China, Monthly Rose

Synonyms: 'Armosa', 'Melanie Lemaire', 'Madame Neumann'

Introduction: Marcheseau/Rousseau, 1834

Earliest American citation: Winter, New York, 1844, as 'Armosa'

Description: "Blush, popular" (Bloomington Nursery, Illinois, 1859).

"Large pale rose, very perfect; double and blooms profusely" (Atlanta Nurseries, Georgia, 1870).

Remarks: Recommended as an excellent bedding rose and one of the hardiest of the Monthly Roses (Ellwanger 1910).

Historic commercial sources: 44

'Homère'

Tea

Synonym: 'Homer'

Introduction: Robert & Moreau, 1858

Earliest American citation: Truett, Tennessee, 1868

Description: "Rose, salmon centre" (Dreer, Pennsylvania, 1876)

"Extra good; large, very full and double; Tea-scented; color light flesh, changing to silvery rose; very fine" (Dingee & Conard, Pennsylvania, 1882).

Remarks: Recommended as an excellent bedding rose and one of the hardiest of the Monthly Roses (Ellwanger 1910).

Historic commercial sources: 17

'Isabella Sprunt'

Tea

Introduction: Rev. James Sprunt, Kenansville, North Carolina/Buchanan, 1855

Rosa 'Hermosa'. Photograph by G. Mike Shoup, The Antique Rose Emporium.

Earliest American citation (other): Parsons, 1869

Description: "Sulphur-yellow, very beautiful in the bud" (Ellwanger 1910).

Remarks: 'Isabella Sprunt' was known to occasionally sport double buds. "Its remarkably free blooming qualities make it a valuable acquisition for forcing and for cut flowers" (Parsons 1869).

Historic commercial sources: 25

'John Hopper'

Hybrid Perpetual

Introduction: Ward, 1862

Earliest American citation: Truett, Tennessee, 1868

Description: "Brilliant rose, crimson center, large and double" (Atlanta Nurseries, Georgia, 1870).

Remarks: A good rose for massing, although not continuously in bloom (Ellwanger 1910).

Historic commercial sources: 29

Rosa 'Killarney'. Peter Henderson Co., New York, 1910.

'Jules Margottin'
Hybrid Perpetual
Introduction: Margottin, 1853
Earliest American citation: Persimmon Grove, Illinois, 1858
Description: "Bright cherry red, large, full, superb" (Atlanta Nurseries, Georgia, 1870).
"Carmine purple; very large full and beautiful" (Columbus Nursery, Ohio, 1860).
Remarks: "One of the finest Remontant Roses. . . . It is particularly fine when in bud" (Parsons 1869). One of the hardiest roses (Ellwanger 1910).
Historic commercial sources: 21

'Kaiserin Auguste Viktoria'
Hybrid Tea
Synonym: 'K. A. Victoria'
Introduction: Lambert & Reiter, 1891
Earliest American citation: Storrs & Harrison, Ohio, 1896
Description: "Creamy white with shining center of yellow" (Jackson, Georgia, 1904).
Remarks: "The greatest hardy, white Hybrid Tea Rose in existence. A strong, sturdy grower; free flowering; it has become the most popular of all white Roses for general planting" (Dingee & Conard, Pennsylvania, 1925).
Historic commercial sources: 33

'Killarney'
Hybrid Tea, Irish Rose
Introduction: A. Dickson & Sons, 1898
Earliest American citation: Cox, San Francisco; Yates, Texas, 1907

Rosa 'La France'. *Vick's Monthly Magazine*, 1883.

Description: "Brilliant imperial pink; the blooms are large" (New England Nurseries, Massachusetts, 1910).
"Even each fallen petal is a poem—a deep, pink shallop with prow of gold" (Rion 1912).
Remarks: Dingee & Conard (1925) listed a pink, a white, and a yellow Killarney rose. They praised 'Killarney', "This queen of the Irish Roses excels any other of its class and color yet introduced, and by many recognized as the most beautiful, hardy, everblooming Hybrid Tea now under cultivation."
Historic commercial sources: 20

'La France'
Hybrid Tea
Introduction: Guillot fils, 1867
Earliest American citation: Dreer, Philadelphia, 1876

Description: "Delicate silvery rose, shaded with cerise pink, often silvery pink with peach shading" (Storrs & Harrison, Ohio, 1896).

Remarks: " 'La France' was the first of the Hybrid Teas. It was recommended as an excellent, highly scented bedding rose" (Ellwanger 1910).

Historic commercial sources: 40

'Lamarque'
Noisette
Synonym: 'Maréchal's Tea'
Introduction: Maréchal, 1830
Earliest American citation: Prince, New York, 1841
Description: "Large pale yellow" (Bloomington Nursery, Illinois, 1859).

"Yellowish white, large and full" (Atlanta Nurseries, Georgia, 1870).

"Pale canary yellow, almost white; beautiful buds; large full flowers; very double and sweet" (Dingee & Conard, Pennsylvania, 1882).

Remarks: "It makes a splendid pillar rose, frequently growing ten feet in one season" (Buist 1854).

"A superb climbing rose, quite too much neglected" (Ellwanger 1910).

Historic commercial sources: 46

'La Reine'
Hybrid Perpetual
Synonym: 'Rose de la Reine'
Introduction: Laffay, 1842
Earliest American citation: McIntosh, Ohio, 1845
Description: "Large, rose, sweet" (Bloomington Nursery, Illinois, 1859).

"It is finely cupped, almost globular, very double, and very fragrant. Its color is a bright rose, slightly tinged with lilac" (Parsons 1869).

"Deep rosy lilac; very large and full, double sweet, superb" (Atlanta Nurseries, Georgia, 1870).

Remarks: A good rose for massing, although not continuously in bloom; one of the hardiest roses (Ellwanger 1910).

Historic commercial sources: 37

'Le Pactole'
Tea
Synonym: 'Pactole'
Introduction: Miellez, by 1841
Earliest American citation: Cleveland Nursery, Ohio; McIntosh, Ohio, 1845

Rosa 'Lamarque' has adorned porches throughout the South for over a century. Photograph by G. Mike Shoup, The Antique Rose Emporium.

Description: "Pale sulphur yellow: large, full and double; beautiful buds, very sweet, Tea-scented" (Dingee & Conard, Pennsylvania, 1882).

Remarks: "Tea Roses are celebrated the world over for their delicious fragrance and the exquisite forms and rich, charming tints of their flowers, and may well be taken as a synonym for all that is delicately beautiful" (Long 1888).

Historic commercial sources: 26

'Louis Philippe'
China
Introduction: Guerin, 1834
Earliest American citation: Winter, New York, 1844
Description: "Rich, dark velvety crimson; free and beautiful. One of the best for bedding" (Good & Reese, Ohio, 1889).

Rosa 'Louis Philippe'. Photograph by G. Mike Shoup, The Antique Rose Emporium.

Remarks: "Has not an equal for growth, in good soils frequently making a shoot six feet long in one season; the flowers are large, perfectly double, of a globular form; the circumference of the bloom is of a dark crimson color; the center a pale blush, making it altogether perfectly distinct from any other rose in cultivation; it will give entire satisfaction" (Buist 1854).
"An inferior Agrippina" (Ellwanger 1910).
Historic commercial sources: 31

'Luxembourg'
Moss
Synonym: 'Ferrugineax du Luxembourg'. This appears to have been the original name.
Introduction: by 1840
Earliest American citation: Winter, New York, 1844
Description: "Superb crimson" (Bloomington Nursery, Illinois, 1859).
"Crimson purple, shaded" (Atlanta Nurseries, Georgia, 1870).
Remarks: Ellwanger (1910) said "Hardy. Crimson. Not attractive."
Prince (1846) wrote, "Robust . . . almost too much so, making here shoots six feet in length in growing seasons."
Historic commercial sources: 25

'Madame Bravy'
Synonyms: 'Madame Brevay', 'Adele Pradel', 'Danzille', 'Isidore Malton', 'Madame Denis', 'Madame de Sertot', 'Madame Maurin', 'Alba Rosea', 'Josephine Malton'
Introduction: Guillot père, 1846

Earliest American citation: Bloomington Nursery, Illinois; Berckmans, Georgia; Hopewell, Virginia, 1859
Description: "Creamy white" (Bloomington Nursery, Illinois, 1859).
"White, center rose" (Atlanta Nurseries, Georgia, 1870).
"Creamy white, blush centre, large perfect form" (Langdon, Alabama, 1881).
"Waxy white, center fawn and flesh, flowers large, full and cupped" (Good & Reese, Ohio, 1889).
Remarks: Highly scented (Ellwanger 1910).
Historic commercial sources: 22

'Madame Caroline Testout'
Hybrid Tea
Synonyms: 'City of Portland', 'Caroline Testout'
Introduction: Pernet-Ducher, 1890
Earliest American citation: Storrs & Harrison, Ohio, 1897
Description: "Satiny-pink with rose center" (Jackson, Georgia, 1904).
Flowers very double (Ellwanger 1910).
Remarks: Fine for bedding. "This is the Rose which grows so luxuriantly in the Far West that it has been adopted by the State of Oregon as its State Flower. The gardens of the cities along the Pacific Coast are the wonder of the world by the profusion of the bloom of this remarkable Rose" (Dingee & Conard, Pennsylvania, 1925).
Historic commercial sources: 29

'Madame Charles Wood'
Hybrid Perpetual
Introduction: Verdier, 1861
Earliest American citation: Moon, Pennsylvania, 1870
Description: "Dazzling crimson" (Storrs & Harrison, Ohio, 1896).
"One of the freest flowering kinds, but not of first quality" (Ellwanger 1910).
Remarks: A good rose for massing, although not continuously in bloom (Ellwanger 1910).
Historic commercial sources: 19

'Madame Gabriel Luizet'
Hybrid Perpetual
Synonyms: 'Madame Gabrielle Luizet', 'Madame G. Luiset'
Introduction: Liabaud, 1877
Earliest American citation: Good & Reese, Ohio; Allen, Vermont, 1889
Description: "Light, silvery pink" (New England Nurseries, Massachusetts, 1910).

Rosa 'Madame Norbert Levavasseur'. Photograph by author.

Rosa 'Madame Plantier'. Photograph by author.

"Pink, somewhat fragrant, long foliage, a promising kind, worthy of attention" (Ellwanger 1910).

Remarks: Although Ellwanger seemed to disagree, most nursery catalogs described this rose as "sweetly fragrant."

Historic commercial sources: 16

'Madame Laffay'

Hybrid Perpetual

Introduction: Laffay, 1839

Earliest American citation: Cleveland Nursery, Ohio; McIntosh, Ohio, 1845

Description: "Rosy crimson; large and full; one of the oldest and best" (Columbus Nursery, Ohio, 1860).

"Beautiful clear flesh color, changing to transparent rose; very full, large, double and sweet" (Dingee & Conard, Pennsylvania, 1882). Their rose appears to have been misnamed.

Remarks: "If delicacy describes the Teas, grandeur is the appellation peculiarly appropriate to the beauty of the Hybrid Perpetuals" (Long 1888).

Historic commercial sources: 19

'Madame Norbert Levavasseur'

Polyantha, Baby Rambler

Synonyms: 'Crimson Baby Rambler', 'Dwarf Crimson Rambler', 'Madame N. Levavasseur', 'Red Baby Rambler'

Introduction: Levavasseur, 1903

Earliest American citation: Berckmans, Georgia, 1906

Description: Crimson rambler.

Remarks: "Most popular bedding rose in existence . . . blooming the whole summer" (Archias, Missouri, 1917).

Historic commercial sources: 33

'Madame Plantier'

Hybrid Alba, Hybrid Noisette, Hybrid China

Introduction: Plantier, 1835

Earliest American citation: Winter, New York, 1844

Description: "White" (Bloomington Nursery, Illinois, 1859).

"Large and double in clusters" (Langdon, Alabama, 1881).

Remarks: "It is one of the most hardy Roses we have . . . a most desirable Rose for cemetery or garden" (Columbus Nursery, Ohio, 1877).

"The Madame Plantier . . . has never wavered in popularity nor waned in goodness since the first June when it opened its eyes on American soil . . . the Madame Plantier ever lavishes on us, whether in a formal garden or cottage border . . . a profusion of snowy blooms, as close gathered as the stars in the Milky Way" (Earle 1902).

Historic commercial sources: 42

Rosa 'Magna Charta'. Photograph by Marlea Graham.

'Magna Charta'
Hybrid Perpetual
Introduction: William Paul and Son, Ltd. of London, 1876
Earliest American citation: Louisville Rose, Kentucky, 1881
Description: "Bright clear pink, flushed with violet crimson" (Storrs & Harrison, Ohio, 1896).
Remarks: "A fragrant, excellent variety" (Ellwanger 1910).
Historic commercial sources: 35

'Maman Cochet'
Tea
Introduction: S. Cochet, 1893
Earliest American citation: Storrs & Harrison, Ohio, 1896
Description: "Deep rose" (Jackson, Georgia, 1904).
"Rich, rosy-pink, shaded silvery-rose on outer petals, exquisite in color and graceful in form" (Archias, Missouri, 1917).
Remarks: "Unquestionably the queen of pink tea roses and a leading cut flower variety" (Archias, Missouri, 1917).
Historic commercial sources: 25

'Maréchal Niel'
Noisette
Introduction: Pradel, 1864
Earliest American citation: Truett, Tennessee, 1868
Description: "Flowers beautiful deep yellow, large, full and of globe form; very sweet" (Atlanta Nurseries, Georgia, 1870).
Remarks: "It is of delicate constitution, and requires very careful treatment to produce satisfactory results" (Ellwanger 1910). Gardeners often cultivated 'Maréchal Niel' under glass. "To succeed with the Maréchal Niel I prefer plants budded on the Banksia or Solfaterre, as they tend to check too rampant growth for the first two or three years, and induce more freedom to bloom by producing wood that ripens well" (Capstick 1882).
"Of unexcelled loveliness and fragrance in the South, as well as in that paradoxical rose heaven, the Portland and Puget Sound region of the Pacific Northwest' (McFarland 1923).
Historic commercial sources: 42

'Marie Guillot'
Tea
Synonym: 'Mlle. Marie Guillot'
Introduction: Guillot fils, 1874
Earliest American citation: Vick, New York; Louisville Rose, Kentucky, 1881
Description: "Pure white" (Jackson, Georgia, 1904).
"White, tinged with a delicate shade of lemon" (Storrs & Harrison, Ohio, 1896).
Remarks: Recommended as an excellent bedding rose or for the conservatory. "One of the most beautiful Teas; would that it were fragrant!" (Ellwanger 1910).
Historic commercial sources: 19

'Marie van Houtte'
Tea
Synonyms: 'The Gem', 'Mlle. Marie Van Houtte'
Introduction: Ducher, 1871
Earliest American citation: Dreer, Pennsylvania, 1876
Description: "A lovely Rose; large, very double and full; delicious Tea scent; color, white tinged with yellow, delicately shaded with pale rose" (Dingee & Conard, Pennsylvania, 1882).
"Creamy white with the outer petals washed and outlined with a bright rose" (Storrs & Harrison, Ohio, 1896).
Remarks: Recommended as an excellent bedding rose. Highly scented. "The finest of all Teas for out-door culture" (Ellwanger 1910).
"The distinctive feature of this rose is in the carmine which edges the creamy yellow petals and drifts down the backs of the petals, making a fascinating shading in a large, very double, rather high-centered bloom which becomes pinker with the summer heat" (Keays 1935).
Historic commercial sources: 23

'Marshall P. Wilder'
Hybrid Perpetual
Introduction: Ellwanger & Barry, New York, 1884
Earliest American citation (other): Allen, Vermont; Good & Reese, Ohio, 1889

Rosa 'Marie Guillot'. Louisville Rose Co., Louisville, Kentucky, 1881.

Rosa 'Meteor'. Storrs & Harrison Co., Painesville, Ohio, 1896.

Description: "Perfectly double, bright cherry red shading to crimson" (Storrs & Harrison, Ohio, 1896).

Remarks: "It continues to bloom profusely long after the other Remontants are out of flower. In brief it may be described as an improved *Alfred Colomb*" (Ellwanger 1910).

Historic commercial sources: 23

'Meteor'

Noisette

Introduction: Geschwind, 1887

Earliest American citation: Thompson, Kentucky, 1888

Description: "Rich, velvety crimson" (Jackson, Georgia, 1904).

Remarks: "Very few dark Roses compare with this in richness and depth in color" (Dingee & Conard, Pennsylvania, 1925).

Historic commercial sources: 19

'Mistress Bosanquet'

Bourbon, Daily Rose, China,

Synonyms: 'Mrs. Bosanquet', 'Pauline Bonaparte'

Introduction: Laffay, 1832

Earliest American citation: Winter, New York, 1844

Description: "Flesh color, large, free color" (Bloomington Nursery, Illinois, 1859).

"Resembles wax" (Valk 1847).

Remarks: "A fine old variety, much esteemed" (Good & Reese, Ohio, 1889).

"Mrs. Bosanquet, found frequently in our neighborhood, is a very luxuriant variety, blooming abundantly . . . a rose of considerable complexity, is called a China in some lists, a Bourbon in others" (Keays 1935).

Historic commercial sources: 22

'Mrs. Aaron Ward'

Hybrid Tea

Introduction: Pernet-Ducher, 1907

Earliest American citation: Henderson, New York, 1910

Description: "Deep rich Indian-yellow, often tinted salmon" (Pilkington, Oregon, 1912).

Remarks: "There was a time when 'Mrs. Aaron Ward' was the only dependable yellow rose . . . it is yet one of the most desirable bedding roses" (McFarland 1938).

Historic commercial sources: 16

'Mrs. John Laing'

Hybrid Perpetual

Synonyms: 'Mrs. J. H. Laing', 'Mistress John Laing'

Introduction: Bennett, 1887

Earliest American citation: Allen, Vermont; Good & Reese, Ohio, 1889

Description: "Soft delicate pink with a satin tinge, very fragrant" (Storrs & Harrison, Ohio, 1896). "Exceedingly fragrant . . . flowers continuously in open ground" (Ellwanger 1910).

Remarks: Hybrid Perpetuals are "the best adapted for outdoor planting for perpetual effect" (Good & Reese, Ohio, 1889).

Historic commercial sources: 33

'Niphetos'

Tea

Introduction: Bougere, 1843

Earliest American citation: McIntosh, Ohio, 1845

Description: "Fine pure white" (Berckmans, Georgia, 1859).

"White sometimes tinged with pale yellow, long large buds, the petals thick and durable . . . entirely unsuited for growing in open air" (Ellwanger 1910).

Remarks: "It is highly valued for its lovely buds, which are remarkably large and fine, and particularly valuable for personal adornment, bouquet work, & c." (Dingee & Conard, Pennsylvania, 1882).

Historic commercial sources: 18

'Ophirie'

Noisette

Synonym: 'Ophire'

Introduction: Goubault, 1841

Earliest American citation: McIntosh, Ohio, 1845

Description: "Buff, with a tinge of red" (Columbus Nursery, Ohio, 1860).

"Deep salmon" (Berckmans, Georgia, 1859).

"Reddish copper, cupped, distinct and fragrant" (Truett, Tennessee, 1868).

"Clear sulphur yellow, very rich and beautiful; large full flowers, very fragrant and free" (Dingee & Conard, Pennsylvania, 1882).

Remarks: "It blooms in clusters, and its luxuriant habit would make it a good pillar rose" (Parsons 1888).

Historic commercial sources: 17

'Papa Gontier'

Tea

Introduction: Nabonnand, 1883

Earliest American citation: Thompson, Kentucky, 1888

Description: "One of the most fashionable roses, similar to old Bon Silène in its delightful fragrance, but larger, more double and far richer in color" (Jackson, Georgia, 1904).

"Rose, shaded yellow, reverse of petals crimson; large, semi-double, fragrant" (Ellwanger 1910).

Remarks: Papa Gontier rose sold for ten cents each in the 1889 Good & Reese catalog of Springfield, Ohio.

Historic commercial sources: 26

Beautiful pink 'Paul Neyron' was considered a good rose for massing. Leo Weltz, Wilmington, Ohio, ca. 1905.

'Paul Neyron'

Hybrid Perpetual

Introduction: Levet, 1869

Earliest American citation: Dreer, Philadelphia, 1876

Description: "Color deep pink, very full and double, finely scented" (Jackson, Georgia, 1904).

Remarks: A good rose for massing, although not continuously in bloom. Somewhat fragrant (Ellwanger 1910).

"Probably the largest Rose grown and one of the finest" (Dingee & Conard, Pennsylvania, 1882).

Historic commercial sources: 57

'Perle des Jardins'

Tea

Introduction: Levet, 1874

Earliest American citation: Louisville Rose, Kentucky, 1881

Description: "This magnificent Rose is undoubtedly the finest variety of its color ever introduced; it constantly grows in favor as it becomes better known; color beautiful clear golden yellow; extra large globular flowers, very full and highly perfumed" (Dingee & Conard, Pennsylvania, 1882).

Remarks: Recommended as an excellent bedding rose (Ellwanger 1910).

Historic commercial sources: 29

'Pie IX'

Hybrid Perpetual

Synonyms: 'Pius IX', 'Pius the Ninth', 'Pope Pius IX'

Introduction: Vibert, 1848

Earliest American citation: Pomaria, South Carolina, 1856

Description: "Bright crimson, fully imbricated; a very abundant bloomer; quite fragrant" (Buist 1854).

"Bright purplish red" (Columbus Nursery, Ohio, 1860).

"Clear bright rose, changing to rosy pink, delicately shaded; very large, fragrant and desirable" (Dingee & Conard, Pennsylvania, 1882).

Remarks: "Robust and a profuse bloomer; one of the best" (Columbus Nursery, Ohio, 1860).

Historic commercial sources: 18

'Prince Albert'

Hybrid Perpetual

Introduction: M. Laffay/Rivers, 1837

Earliest American citation: McIntosh, Ohio, 1845

Description: "Rich crimson, perfect cup form, inclining to globular; very fragrant" (Buist 1854).

"Deep rose changing to violet" (Columbus Nursery, Ohio, 1860).

Remarks: "Rather under medium size, which is made up in its profuse clusters of brilliant flowers" (Buist 1854).

Historic commercial sources: 18

'Prince Camille De Rohan'

Hybrid Perpetual

Synonym: 'La Rosiere'

Introduction: E. Verdier, 1861

Earliest American citation: Truett, Tennessee, 1868

Description: "Very dark, rich velvety crimson, passing to intense maroon, shaded black" (Storrs & Harrison, Ohio, 1896).

Remarks: "A good rose, of splendid color" (Ellwanger 1910).

"Prince Camille de Rohan, 1861, is the darkest, most velvety rose of the Général Jacqueminot derivation, thought to have come from crossing the General with old Giant of Battles. From whatever mystery of breeding, Camille de Rohan

Rosa 'Perle des Jardins'. George Thompson & Sons, Louisville, Kentucky, 1888.

is a little different. The bushes... spread more than the General. They have less numerous prickles, foliage of a darker shade. The bloom is a very deep velvety crimson to maroon ... with a quite nice fragrance" (Keays 1935).

Historic commercial sources: 38

'Princesse Adélaïde'

Moss

Introduction: Laffay, 1845

Earliest American citation: *Magazine of Horticulture*, 1845

Description: "Very stout grower, flower light blush" (Bloomington Nursery, Illinois, 1859).

"Rosy lilac" (Dreer, Philadlephia, 1876).

"Dark foliage, which is often variegated" (Ellwanger 1910).

Remarks: Parsons (1869) reported that 'Princesse Adélaïde' should not be closely pruned and that it was desirable as a pillar rose.

Historic commercial sources: 20

'Quatre Saisons Blanc Mousseux'

Moss

Synonyms: 'Perpetual White Moss', 'Quartre Saisons Blanche', 'Rosier de Thionville'

Introduction: Laffay, by 1837

Earliest American citation: Winter, New York, 1844

Description: "Large clusters of white flowers, often with pink stripe" (Bloomington Nursery, Illinois, 1859).

Remarks: This old-time variety continued in popularity into the twentieth century.

Historic commercial sources: 22

'Queen of the Prairies'

Hybrid Setigera, Prairie Rose

Synonyms: 'Prairie Belle', 'Prairie Queen', 'Beauty of the Prairies'

Introduction: Feast, Baltimore, Maryland, 1843

Earliest American citation (other): Cleveland Nursery, Ohio; McIntosh, Ohio, 1845

Description: "Large, double, rose" (Bloomington Nursery, Illinois, 1859).

"Bright pink, often with a white stripe" (Atlanta Nurseries, Georgia, 1870).

Remarks: The flowers "are produced in clusters, in which they appear cup-shaped, and stand for several days without being affected by our scorching sun" (Buist 1854).

Historic commercial sources: 58

'Reine Marie-Henriette'

Hybrid Tea

Introduction: Levet, 1878

Earliest American citation: Louisville Rose, Kentucky, 1881

Description: "Clear cherry red" (Jackson, Georgia, 1904).

"Cherry red, a pure shade, large, double; a beautiful, but rather unproductive sort" (Ellwanger 1910).

Remarks: One of the hardiest of the Monthly Roses (Ellwanger 1910).

Historic commercial sources: 21

'Safrano'

Tea

Synonym: 'Aimee Plantier'

Introduction: Beauregard, 1839

Earliest American citation: Southern Nurseries, Mississippi, 1851

Description: "Dark buff" (Berckmans, Georgia, 1859).

"Curious, coppery fawn" (Bloomington Nursery, Illinois, 1859).

Rosa 'Queen of the Prairies'. Louisville Rose Co., Louisville, Kentucky, 1881.

"Fawn, shaded with rose; beautiful dark foliage" (Atlanta Nurseries, Georgia, 1870).

"Saffron yellow" (Dreer, Pennsylvania, 1876).

"Bright apricot yellow, changing to orange and fawn, sometimes tinted with rose; valued highly for its beautiful buds: very fragrant, and one of the best" (Dingee & Conard, Pennsylvania, 1882).

"Bright apricot yellow tinted with rose" (Jackson, Georgia, 1904).

Remarks: In California, Safrano roses bloomed all winter. Isabella Oakley described their use and appearance for *Vick's Magazine* in 1886, "We gather Safranos and Pink Noisettes; poor winter-roses we call them, because they fall short of the luxuriance of spring, but they are 'not wholly mean.'"

Historic commercial sources: 38

'Salet'

Moss

Introduction: Lacharme, 1854

Earliest American citation: Berckmans, Georgia; Bloomington Nursery, Illinois, 1859

Description: "Perpetual moss, rosy red" (Bloomington Nursery, Illinois, 1859).

"Bright pink, rapid grower" (Atlanta Nurseries, Georgia, 1870).

"Light rose; flowers flattened, very freely produced. Both flowers and buds are covered with moss" (Biltmore, North Carolina, 1907).

"Crimson, shaded with purple" (Ellwanger 1910).

Rosa 'Safrano'. Louisville Rose Co., Louisville, Kentucky, 1881.

Remarks: "A good autumnal bloomer" (Parsons 1869). "The Moss Rose is a hardy, out-of-door plant; once set out will take care of itself if the ground is kept free of grass and weeds" (Good & Reese, Ohio, 1889).

Historic commercial sources: 22

'Sanguinea'

China rose
Synonym: 'Rose de Bengale'
Introduction: by 1824
Earliest American citation: Brighton, Boston, 1833
Description: "Anemone flowered. Deep crimson" (Prince, New York, 1841).
"Deep crimson; a most profuse and constant bloomer" (Columbus Nursery, Ohio, 1860).
Remarks: For bedding or pot culture. "Not capable of sustaining as severe cold as most other varieties" (Prince 1846).
Historic commercial sources: 16

'Seven Sisters'

Hybrid Multiflora Rose
Synonyms: 'Greville', 'Eugene Greville', *Rosa multiflora cathayensis*, *R. multiflora platyphylla*
Introduction: 1817
Earliest American citation: Kenrick, Boston, 1832

Description: "Greville's Superb Cluster, or Scarlet Multiflora, with flowers of various shades in the same cluster, a climber" (Brighton, Boston, 1841).
"Crimson, changing all shades to white" (Storrs & Harrison, Ohio, 1896).
Remarks: "A large plant will not unfrequently show more than a thousand flowers, all blooming in clusters and of several shades of color" (Parsons 1869). "A tender variety of no value" (Ellwanger 1910). There have been a number of imposters going by the name of 'Seven Sisters.' One that apparently made the rounds in Ohio and Pennsylvania has been identified as the 'Red Dorothy Perkins' or 'Excelsa'.
Historic commercial sources: 36

'Solfaterre'

Noisette
Synonyms: 'Augusta', 'Solfatare'
Introduction: Boyau, 1843
Earliest American citation: McIntosh, Ohio, 1845
Description: "Superb, bright pale yellow" (Bloomington Nursery, Illinois, 1859).
"Sulphur yellow, large and fine" (Atlanta Nurseries, Georgia, 1870).
Remarks: "Not very satisfactory for the north; for planting in greenhouses" (Templin, Ohio, 1904).
Historic commercial sources: 31

'Souvenir de la Malmaison'

Bourbon
Synonym: 'Queen of Beauty'
Introduction: Beluze, 1843
Earliest American citation: Lake Erie Nursery, Ohio, 1846
Description: "Pale flesh; large and double" (Atlanta Nurseries, Georgia, 1870).
Remarks: "It has been considered the finest Rose of its class for thirty years" (Good & Reese, Ohio, 1889).
Historic commercial sources: 34

'Souvenir d'un Ami'

Tea
Synonym: 'Queen Victoria'
Introduction: Belot-Defougere, 1846
Earliest American citation: Southern Nurseries, Mississippi, 1851
Description: "Rose and salmon, shaded" (Columbus Nursery, Ohio, 1860).
"White, shaded with pink" (Langdon, Alabama, 1881).

Rosa 'Souvenir de la Malmaison'. The Good & Reese Co., Springfield, Ohio, 1889.

Remarks: An excellent bedding rose; highly scented (Ellwanger 1910).

"This rose excited curiosity as well as admiration. We wonder how it acquired its unusual blessings of perfect features, form, texture, color, fragrance, beauty and strength of foliage and perfect hardiness. . . . Parsons says in his book, 'The Rose,' 'It is indeed the queen of the tea-scented roses and will rank the very first among them'" (Keays 1935).

Historic commercial sources: 27

'Sunset'

Tea

Introduction: P. Henderson, New York, 1883

Earliest American citation (other): Thompson, Kentucky, 1888

Description: "Rich golden amber, elegantly tinged and shaded with dark ruddy copper" (Jackson, Georgia, 1904).

Hanna Rion (1912) likened the color of Sunset rose to "topaz and ruby beauty."

Remarks: "I find it in habit and bloom identical with Perle des Jardins" (Smith 1885).

Historic commercial sources: 19

'Sydonie'

Hybrid Perpetual, Damask Perpetual

Synonym: 'Sidonie'

Introduction: Dorisy/Vibert, 1846

Earliest American citation: Rennie, Virginia, 1853

Description: "Blush, large and fine" (Bloomington Nursery, Illinois, 1859).

"Light pink large and full" (Columbus Nursery, Ohio, 1860).

Remarks: "A charming old variety, much esteemed, rose color; very large and full; a constant bloomer" (Long 1888).

Historic commercial sources: 17

'Tausendschön'

Hybrid Multiflora

Synonym: 'Thousand Beauties'

Introduction: Kiese/J. C. Schmidt, 1906

Earliest American citation: Childs, New York; New England Nurseries, Massachusetts, 1910

Description: "Almost thornless, the buds are cherry pink, opening to softer shades, all shades being found in a single cluster; has glossy light green foliage" (Fremont Nursery, Ohio, 1932).

Remarks: "The most sensational Climbing Rose yet introduced even barring Crimson Rambler. A single cluster of flowers is a bouquet in itself; hence the very fitting name, 'Thousand Beauties'" (Dingee & Conard, Pennsylvania, 1925).

Historic commercial sources: 21

'The Bride'

Tea

Introduction: 1885

Earliest American citation: Thompson, Kentucky, 1888

Description: "White rose" (Storrs & Harrison, Ohio, 1896).

Remarks: "A fine bunch of these buds, cut with long sprays of foliage, would grace any bride in her wedding robes. It is unsurpassed for purity of whiteness" (Good & Reese, Ohio, 1889).

Historic commercial sources: 29

'Triomphe du Luxembourg'

Tea

Introduction: Hardy/Sylvain-Pean, 1835

Earliest American citation: Winter, New York, 1844

Description: "Salmon buff, shaded with a deep rose; distinct and fine" (Columbus Nursery, Ohio, 1860).

Remarks: Recommended as an excellent bedding rose (Ellwanger 1910).

Historic commercial sources: 25

'Turner's Crimson Rambler'

Hybrid Multiflora

Synonym: 'Crimson Rambler'

Introduction: Prof. R. Smith/Turner, 1893

Earliest American citation: Storrs & Harrison, Ohio, 1896

Description: "A grand new hardy climbing rose with immense trusses of bright crimson flowers" (Storrs & Harrison, Ohio, 1896).

Remarks: Grows 15–20 ft. high. Early twentieth century writers lamented that often the Crimson Rambler was the only ornamentation of small town or rural houses. Horace McFarland (1923) disputed the value of 'Turner's Crimson Rambler': "Having long ago lost my devotion . . . first because it was so over planted as to become monotonous, and second because of its bad behavior in inviting mildew all the time."

Historic commercial sources: 47

'Ulrich Brunner fils'

Hybrid Perpetual

Synonym: 'Ulrich Brunner'

Introduction: Levet, 1881

Earliest American citation: Thompson, Kentucky, 1888

Description: "Cherry red" (Storrs & Harrison, Ohio, 1896).

Remarks: "A splendid Rose either for garden or forcing" (Iowa Seed, Des Moines, 1914).

Historic commercial sources: 26

'White Dorothy'

Hybrid Wichurana

Synonym: 'White Dorothy Perkins'

Introduction: Cant, 1908

Earliest American citation: Pilkington, Oregon, 1912

Description: "We believe it is a better rose in many respects than [Dorothy Perkins]. It bears double pure white flowers in immense panicles" (Archias, Missouri, 1917).

Remarks: "The vines are a sheet of white during blooming season" (Ernst, Ohio, 1926).

Historic commercial sources: 21

'White Maman Cochet'

Tea

Introduction: Cook, 1896

Earliest American citation: Templin, Ohio; Jackson, Georgia, 1904

Description: "Creamy white tinged with a soft blush" (Pilkington, Oregon, 1912).

Remarks: "Of all the roses that I have grown I know of none that will compare with the White Cochet. It is nearly hardy; with a little covering it will stand our winters [Illinois] and will give us more flowers and greater beauty than any other rose that I know of" (Dintleman 1910).

Historic commercial sources: 18

Rosa banksiae

Synonyms: Lady Banks Rose, White Lady Banks, Yellow Lady Banks

Introduction: 1796 (single white form)

Earliest American citation: Prince, New York, 1826

Description: Small white or yellow flowers—the double white is fragrant, like violets, but the double yellow reputedly is not.

Remarks: Yellow Lady Banks is now *Rosa banksiae* 'Lutea', introduced in 1824. "It is in the States south of this [Philadelphia] where it must be seen to be pronounced the most graceful, luxuriant, and beautiful of roses; there, it is a perfect evergreen, covering the ends, fronts, and in some instances, the entire dwelling of many of the inhabitants, who name it the Evergreen Multiflora" (Buist 1854).

White Lady Banks (syn. *R. banksiae banksiae*, *R. banksiae* 'Alba Plena') was introduced by Kerr in 1807.

Historic commercial sources: 21

Rosa eglanteria

Species Rose

Synonyms: *Rosa rubiginosa*, eglantine, sweetbrier, sweetbriar

Introduction: by 1551

Earliest American citation: George Washington, ca. 1786.

Description: "R. Rubiginosa is a beautiful Rose in its original condition [single flowers of pale to deep pink with apple-scented foliage], and there are many improved varieties. The Splendid, less fragrant, but with large crimson flowers. The Rose Angle [sic], very double, bright rose-colored flowers; the Celestial, very double and fragrant; the Carmine, semi-double red flowers" (Copeland 1867).

Remarks: "Whenever there is a hedge to be planted, it should have a few plants of the sweet brier interspersed; it bears clipping well, and even a hedge of itself would prove a garden ornament rarely equaled, being of lively green, and its many associations will make it always pleasing" (Buist 1854).

"This lovely ornament . . . is universally admired for the delicious fragrance of its foliage, and for nothing else" (*The American Rose Culturist* 1855).

"The sweet-brier, found wild in various parts of the world, is too well known to need further notice" (Parkman 1871a).

"I have never seen any since we left our Wisconsin home [for the Montana Territory], when I was fourteen years old, but we had two large bushes there in front of our sitting-room window, and on dewy mornings and evenings, the air was delicious with fragrance" (Mrs. F. A. R. 1886).

For regional invasiveness concerns regarding *Rosa eglanteria*, see Appendix D.

Historic commercial sources: 26

Rosa foetida 'Persiana'

Hybrid Foetida Persiana
Synonyms: 'Persian Yellow', 'Persian Double Yellow'
Introduction: Willock, 1837
Earliest American citation: Lake Erie Nursery, Ohio, 1846
Description: "Double full, deep golden yellow" (Storrs & Harrison, Ohio, 1896).
Remarks: The editor of the 1848 *The Horticulturist* had this to say about the Persian Yellow rose: "This is a truly charming addition to our collection of roses, large as the latter is. Indeed we should say that the smallest collection is scarcely complete without it. It is far superior to the *Harrison* [sic] in the form and shape of the flower, much more double, and a fine, clear, distinct, yellow in its color."

"We never gathered the yellow Roses, for two reasons: their frail petals dropped so quickly that they were valueless, and their spiny armament was too defensive for ordinary attack. It seemed to show that they were never meant to be picked" (Earle 1902).

Historic commercial sources: 35

Rosa ×*harisonii* 'Harison's Yellow'

Hybrid Foetida, Austrian Brier
Synonyms: 'Harrisonii', Yellow Rose of Texas
Introduction: Harison, New York, 1830
Earliest American citation (other): Hogg, New York, 1834
Description: "Small, bright yellow, an early and profuse bloomer" (Bloomington Nursery, Illinois, 1859).
Remarks: "Perhaps more useful as garden plants than for cut flowers" (Biltmore, North Carolina, 1907). Harison's Yel-

low rose reputedly was a popular companion to settlers moving to the western territories in North America.

McFarland (1923) described both 'Harison's Yellow' and the Persian yellow rose, "They are lank and ugly, and gradually become more and more unkempt, but nothing that I know gives the same rose pleasure that they do when, in early rose-time, their dainty, double, definitely yellow flowers open amid scented foliage. They should be planted so they are faced with dwarfer growing roses."

Historic commercial sources: 34

Rosa laevigata

Species Rose, Cherokee Rose
Synonyms: 'Blanc de Neige', Camellia Rose, 'Nivea'
Introduction: 1759
Earliest American citation: Thomas Jefferson, 1804
Description: "Snowy white" (Shepherd, California, 1891). "Both double and single" (California Nursery, 1894).
Remarks: Although it bore an Americanized common name, *Rosa laevigata* came originally from China. "It may be remarked, in passing, that the origin of the Cherokee rose on this continent is shrouded in mystery. It was found by Michaux in the South, but has never been found wild since his time. It is hardly believed to be a native rose, though by analogy with some other rare Southern plants, it might be. It has Asiatic relatives" (Legend of the Cherokee Rose 1882).

"One of the finest pillar roses in cultivation" (Cox, California, 1907).

Historic commercial sources: 17

Rosa rugosa

Species Rose
Synonyms: Japan rose, wrinkled-leaved rose, Russian rose, *Rosa rugueux*
Introduction: by 1799
Earliest American citation: M'Mahon, 1806
Description: "Fine large, crimson purple" (Atlanta Nurseries, Georgia, 1870). *Rosa rugosa* was available in several colors, including the white 'Alba' and the dark pink 'Rubra'.
Remarks: "The foliage is deep glossy green, entirely free from mildew and insect pests, the entire bushes having the appearance of flowering shrubs of exquisite shape and beauty" (Archias, Missouri, 1917).

Rosa rugosa has proved to be invasive in some areas of the United States. Please refer to Appendix D for specific regional information concerning invasive species.

Historic commercial sources: 24

APPENDIX A

All-American Ornamental Plants and Regional Plant Lists

GROWERS OFFERED MANY THOUSANDS of plants in the early years of our country—at least 25,000 different taxa by my count and certainly many more. Regardless of time or location, some plants kept appearing on availability lists. Eventually, I started paying attention to the trends and noted 103 plants that not only were available for all the time periods (1750–1799, 1800–1824, 1825–1849, 1850–1874, 1875–1899, 1900–1924, and 1925–1940) but also were listed at least once for each region. Growers offered these 103 plants in their trade lists continuously from the earliest years of written commercial record (1719) to the catalogs of the 1930s *and* each of these plants was listed at least one time, and often many times over, in each of these six regions of the United States: New England, Middle Atlantic, Southern, Great Lakes, Central and Great Plains, and Mountain and Western States. They compose my All-American plant list.

Included in the All-American plant list are thirty-three tree species, twenty-five perennials, eighteen shrubs, fifteen annuals, six bulbs, five vines, and the genus *Rosa*. There are forty-two native American species and sixty-one exotic plants—a testimony to the international knowledge of and trade in plants that has taken place for nearly 300 years.

These plants truly contributed to the fabric and foundation of American garden making. Included are plants of former fashion and design savvy like the Lombardy poplar; ornamental herbs such as lavender; stately native American trees like the tulip tree and white oak; traditional herbaceous favorites, for example, the hollyhock and Maltese cross; and oriental gems like the China pink.

It is not surprising to see plants like the purple lilac or the snowball viburnum on an All-American favorites list. Perhaps more surprising is the inclusion of shrubs like the pomegranate and mimosa or sensitive plant, which occupied greenhouses in the North and were planted out in the warmer South and Far West, and the singling out of the cucumber tree from among all the other lovely magnolias. On this list appear a number of genera that had many cultivars subject to the vagaries of availability and fashion, but the basic species were always present. Significant genera included the ever popular bulbs *Crocus*, *Tulipa*, and *Narcissus*; *Phlox*, whose named varieties were as ephemeral as bloodroot in the springtime; and, of course, *Rosa*, which in form, if not in specific details, has been a guest in American gardens since Governor Winthrop commented on its presence in seventeenth-century Massachusetts gardens.

THE ALL-AMERICAN ORNAMENTAL PLANTS

Abies balsamea . . . . balsam fir
Acer negundo . . . . box elder
Acer saccharinum . . . . silver maple
Acer saccharum . . . . sugar maple
Aesculus hippocastanum . . . . horse chestnut
Alcea rosea . . . . hollyhock
Amaranthus caudatus . . . . love-lies-bleeding
Amorpha fruticosa . . . . indigo shrub
Antirrhinum majus . . . . snapdragon
Aristolochia macrophylla . . . . Dutchman's pipe
Aurinia saxatilis . . . . golden alyssum
Betula populifolia . . . . American white birch
Callistephus chinensis . . . . Chinese aster
Calycanthus floridus . . . . Carolina allspice
Campanula medium . . . . Canterbury bells
Campsis radicans . . . . trumpet creeper
Castanea dentata . . . . American chestnut
Catalpa . . . . catalpa, bean tree
Celastrus scandens . . . . bittersweet
Cercis canadensis . . . . redbud
Chionanthus virginicus . . . . fringe tree
Chrysanthemum . . . . Chinese chrysanthemum
Consolida ajacis . . . . larkspur
Convallaria majalis . . . . lily-of-the-valley
Cornus florida . . . . dogwood
Cornus stolonifera . . . . red-twigged dogwood
Cotinus coggygria . . . . smoke bush
Crataegus laevigata . . . . English hawthorn
Crocus . . . . crocus
Dianthus barbatus . . . . sweet William
Dianthus caryophyllus . . . . carnation
Dianthus chinensis . . . . China pink
Dianthus deltoides . . . . maiden pink
Dianthus plumarius . . . . grass pink
Dictamnus albus . . . . gasplant
Echinacea purpurea . . . . purple coneflower
Erysimum cheiri . . . . wallflower
Fraxinus americana . . . . white ash
Gleditsia triacanthos . . . . honeylocust
Gomphrena globosa . . . . globe amaranth
Hedysarum coronarium . . . . French honeysuckle
Hemerocallis lilioasphodelus . . . . lemon lily
Hibiscus syriacus . . . . rose of Sharon
Hyacinthus orientalis . . . . hyacinth

Impatiens balsamina . . . . balsam
Juglans nigra . . . . black walnut
Juniperus virginiana . . . . red cedar
Laburnum anagyroides . . . . golden chain
Larix decidua . . . . European larch
Lathyrus latifolius . . . . perennial sweet pea
Lavandula angustifolia . . . . lavender
Lilium superbum . . . . superb lily
Liquidambar styraciflua . . . . sweet gum
Liriodendron tulipifera . . . . tulip tree
Lobelia cardinalis . . . . cardinal flower
Lonicera sempervirens . . . . . . scarlet trumpet honeysuckle
Lunaria annua . . . . honesty, money plant
Lychnis chalcedonica . . . . Maltese cross
Lychnis coronaria . . . . rose campion
Magnolia acuminata . . . . cucumber tree
Matthiola incana . . . . ten-weeks stock
Mesembryanthemum crystallinum . . . . ice plant
Mimosa pudica . . . . sensitive plant
Narcissus . . . . daffodil, jonquil
Pelargonium . . . . bedding geranium
Philadelphus coronarius . . . . mock orange
Phlox . . . . perennial phlox
Phlox subulata . . . . moss pink
Physocarpus opulifolius . . . . ninebark
Picea abies . . . . Norway spruce
Pinus strobus . . . . white pine
Pinus sylvestris . . . . Scotch pine
Platanus occidentalis . . . . American sycamore
Platycladus orientalis . . . . oriental arborvitae
Polianthes tuberosa . . . . tuberose
Populus deltoides . . . . cottonwood
Populus nigra 'Italica' . . . . Lombardy poplar
Primula auricula . . . . primrose
Prunus glandulosa . . . . . . dwarf double-flowering almond
Punica granatum . . . . pomegranate
Pyracantha coccinea . . . . evergreen thorn
Quercus alba . . . . white oak
Quercus rubra . . . . red oak
Reseda odorata . . . . sweet mignonette
Robinia hispida . . . . rose acacia
Robinia pseudoacacia . . . . yellow locust
Rosa . . . . rose
Salix babylonica . . . . weeping willow

Scabiosa atropurpurea . . . . mourning bride
Sorbus americana . . . . American mountain ash
Sorbus aucuparia . . . . European mountain ash
Symphoricarpos orbiculatus . . . . snowberry
Syringa ×*persica* . . . . Persian lilac
Syringa vulgaris . . . . lilac
Syringa vulgaris var. *alba* . . . . white lilac
Tagetes erecta . . . . African marigold

Tagetes patula . . . . French marigold
Thuja occidentalis . . . . American aborvitae
Tilia americana . . . . basswood
Tsuga canadensis . . . . hemlock
Tulipa . . . . tulip
Viburnum opulus 'Roseum' . . . . snowball
Viola tricolor . . . . pansy

The other lists in this appendix provide a sample of the plants that were commonly available in the nursery and seed catalogs for different regions in different eras. You will find plants appropriate to the gardens of New England in the 1830s, as well as those for Far West landscapes of the 1880s. These lists provide a place to start your investigation of the plants that were popular in your area in earlier times—the catalogs being only one part of the picture, as I have explained elsewhere in this book. I listed only the plants most frequently offered by nurseries. It would be wonderful if equal amounts of information were available from all time periods and regions. Obviously, this is not the case, so you will note some lists are based on fewer references than others, depending on the documentation that is available. Except where noted, the plants in these lists were common to at least half the period catalogs or advertisements to which I had access. Occasionally, a plant does not appear a certain number of times within one period, but is consistently available in a region over time. Those plants are indicated with an asterisk (*) and are included in the period where they appear to have the most prominence. Remember, these plant lists are only *representative* of the complete picture. For example, over 4000 taxa were offered in the catalogs of the Mountain and Western States and I have chosen only about 100 plants, again based on the frequency of their appearance in catalogs.

Within a region, each succeeding list can be used cumulatively with the ones preceding it; once a plant is known in an area, we assume that it stayed. The date next to the species name is the year for which I have an initial commercial cita-tion for *that region*. This year can be interpreted as the year by which the plant is known to have been cultivated in those states. Of course, it is possible, and in some cases probable, that these plants may have much earlier dates of actual intro-duction into a particular state or area. Since I am grouping the plants by *frequency of availability*, it is possible for a plant to have a first citation year that is earlier than the time period in which it appears. When that happens, it is your call, as the plant was obviously available in that part of the country earlier, but perhaps not *commonly* so. Another important consideration as you use these lists is that the regions are large and include, in most cases, a range of hardiness. For example, the tender palms or eucalyptus that were available and cultivated in California obviously are not appropriate for a Montana garden, although these plants appear together in the same regional lists. Some of the plants appear on the regional invasive plant lists in Appendix D. Be sure to check the plants on your list for possible problems with invasive-ness. For a plant list specific to a state, please use the infor-mation in Appendix B, Historic Commercial Plant Sources, to compile listings from specific catalogs.

Finally, many of these plants are featured in the plant encyclopedia or in chapter 3, Gardens and Geography, and additional information is available in those places. Other plants were not common enough across the country to be in the plant encyclopedia, but still had significance for a particular section of the country. Their inclusion in these lists provides additional valuable information to the garden historian.

ORNAMENTAL PLANTS CULTIVATED IN AMERICA BEFORE 1750

The years provided refer to citations in literature rather than commercial sources as in all other lists.

Achillea millefolium (1718)
Aconitum napellus (1631)
Alcea rosea (1631)
Anemone coronaria (1655)
Aquilegia vulgaris (1631)
Aster novae-angliae (1737)
Buxus sempervirens (1652)
Buxus sempervirens 'Suffruticosa' (1737)
Calendula officinalis (1631)
Callistephus chinensis (1735)
Cercis canadensis (1739)
Chionanthus virginicus (1735)
Cornus florida (1735)
Cornus florida f. *rubra* (1736)
Crataegus crus-galli (1734)
Dianthus caryophyllus (1672)
Digitalis purpurea f. *albiflora* (1737)
Erysimum cheiri (1631)
Fritillaria imperialis (1655)
Galanthus nivalis (1737)
Hedera helix (1748)
Hibiscus syriacus (1736)
Iris germanica (1672)
Iris germanica 'Florentina' (1737)
Juniperus virginiana (1735)
Kalmia latifolia (1734)
Laburnum anagyroides (1735)
Larix decidua (1735)
Lilium candidum (1654)
Lilium superbum (1738)
Liriodendron tulipifera (1737)
Lunaria annua (1672)
Magnolia acuminata (1736)
Magnolia virginiana (1736)
Matthiola incana (1631)
Narcissus (1737)
Nerine sarniensis (1736)
Paeonia (1737)
Papaver orientale (1741)
Papaver somniferum (1631)

Phlox (1737)
Phlox subulata (1745)
Polianthes tuberosa (1735)
Primula veris (1747)
Quercus virginiana (1742)
Ricinus communis (1737)
Rosa spp. (1654)
Syringa ×*persica* (1738)
Syringa vulgaris (ca. 1652)
Tanacetum parthenium (1672)
Taxodium distichum (1737)
Tulipa (1682)
Viola tricolor (1718)
Yucca filamentosa (1735)

NEW ENGLAND REGION

Connecticut, Maine, Massachusetts, New Hampshire, Rhode Island, Vermont

New England Region, 1750–1824

John Townley advertised these flower seeds in *The Boston Evening-Post*, 31 March 1760:

Alcea rosea
Amaranthus caudatus
Campanula medium
Centaurea cyanus
Consolida ajacis
Convolvulus tricolor
Dianthus barbatus
Dianthus caryophyllus
Dianthus chinensis
Dianthus plumarius
Echinops ritro
Erysimum cheiri
Gomphrena globosa
Helianthus spp.
Iberis spp.
Impatiens balsamina
Ipomoea purpurea
Lathyrus spp.
Lavatera spp.
Lupinus albus
Lupinus hirsutus
Matthiola incana
Nigella damascena
Omphalodes linifolia
Papaver somniferum 'Carnation-flowered'

Polygonum orientale or *Amaranthus hypochondriacus*
Primula ×*polyantha*
Scabiosa atropurpurea
Silene armeria
Tagetes erecta

New England Region, 1825–1849

Ornamental plants common to at least four of fourteen catalogs from Massachusetts and not included in a previous list for this region:

Abies balsamea (1832)
Acer platanoides (1832)
Acer saccharum (1832)
Aconitum napellus (1832)
Aesculus hippocastanum (1832)
Aesculus parviflora (1832)
Ailanthus altissima (1832)
Alcea rosea 'Nigra' (1834)
Antirrhinum majus (1834)
Apios americana (1834)
Aquilegia canadensis (1834)
Aquilegia sibirica (1835)
Aquilegia vulgaris (1834)
Aristolochia macrophylla (1832)
Asclepias incarnata (1832)
Asclepias tuberosa (1834)
Aster novae-angliae (1832)
Aurinia saxatilis (1834)
Baptisia australis (1834)
Belamcanda chinensis (1832)
Calycanthus floridus (1832)
Campanula pyramidalis (1834)
Campsis radicans (1832)
Catalpa spp. (1832)
Catananche caerulea (1834)
Centranthus ruber (1834)
Cercis canadensis (1832)
Chionanthus virginicus (1832)
Cladrastis kentukea (1832)
Clematis virginiana (1833)
Clematis vitalba (1832)
Clethra alnifolia (1832)
Cobaea scandens (1832)
Colutea arborescens (1832)
Convallaria majalis (1832)
Coreopsis lanceolata (1834)
Coreopsis verticillata (1834)
Cotinus coggygria (1832)
Crataegus laevigata (1832)
Dahlia (1832)
Daphne mezereum (1832)

Delphinium elatum (1832)
Delphinium exaltatum (1835)
Delphinium grandiflorum (1834)
Dianthus superbus (1834)
Dictamnus albus (1832)
Dictamnus albus var. *purpureus* (1835)
Digitalis ferruginea (1835)
Digitalis lutea (1834)
Digitalis purpurea (1832)
Digitalis purpurea f. *albiflora* (1832)
Echinacea purpurea (1834)
Echinops sphaerocephalus (1834)
Eupatorium coelestinum (1834)
Fagus grandifolia (1832)
Fagus sylvatica (1832)
Fagus sylvatica Atropurpurea Group (1832)
Filipendula rubra (1832)
Filipendula ulmaria (1834)
Filipendula vulgaris (1834)
Fraxinus americana (1832)
Fraxinus excelsior (1832)
Gentiana saponaria (1834)
Gerardia quercifolia (1834)
Geum chiloense (1835)
Ginkgo biloba (1832)
Gleditsia triacanthos (1832)
Hedysarum coronarium (1834)
Helianthus giganteus (1834)
Hesperis matronalis (1832)
Hibiscus militaris (1834)
Hibiscus moscheutos subsp. *palustris* (1834)
Hibiscus syriacus, single and double (1832)
Hosta plantaginea (1832)
Hosta ventricosa (1832)
Hyacinthus orientalis (1834)
Iris germanica 'Florentina' (1835)
Juniperus virginiana (1832)
Kalmia latifolia (1832)
Kerria japonica 'Pleniflora' (1832)
Koelreuteria paniculata (1832)
Laburnum anagyroides (1832)
Larix decidua (1832)
Larix laricina (1832)
Liatris scariosa (1834)
Lilium candidum (1832)
Lilium martagon (1832)
Linum perenne (1832)
Liriodendron tulipifera (1832)
Lobelia cardinalis (1832)
Lobelia fulgens (1832)

Lobelia siphilitica (1835)
*Lonicera flava (1832)
*Lonicera periclymenum
    'Belgica' (1832)
*Lonicera sempervirens (1832)
*Lonicera tatarica (1832)
Lupinus perennis (1834)
Lupinus polyphyllus (1834)
Lychnis chalcedonica (1832)
Lychnis flos-cuculi (1832)
Lychnis coronaria (1832)
Lythrum salicaria (1835)
*Maclura pomifera (1832)
*Magnolia acuminata (1832)
*Magnolia tripetala (1832)
Monarda didyma (1834)
Monarda fistulosa (1834)
*Narcissus (1834)
Oenothera biennis (1834)
Oenothera macrocarpa (1839)
Paeonia officinalis (1833)
Paeonia suffruticosa (1833)
Papaver orientale (1834)
Papaver orientale var.
    bracteatum (1834)
Penstemon barbatus (1841)
*Philadelphus coronarius (1832)
Phlox carolina (1834)
Phlox divaricata (1834)
Phlox maculata (1835)
Phlox maculata subsp.
    pyramidalis (1834)
Phlox paniculata (1835)
Phlox stolonifera (1834)
*Physocarpus opulifolius (1832)
Physostegia virginiana (1834)
*Picea abies (1832)
*Picea glauca (1832)
Polemonium caeruleum (1834)
Potentilla atrosanguinea (1834)
Potentilla nepalensis (1834)
Primula auricula (1833)
Primula veris (1834)
Pulsatilla vulgaris (1834)
*Rhododendron maximum
    (1832)
*Robinia hispida (1832)
*Rosa 'Maiden's Blush' (1832)
*Rosa 'Quatre Saisons' (1832)
*Rosa rubrifolia (1832)
*Rosa 'Tuscany' (1832)
*Rosa 'York and Lancaster'
    (1832)
Rudbeckia fulgida (1834)
Rudbeckia laciniata (1834)
*Salix alba subsp. vitellina (1832)
Salix babylonica (1832)

Senna marilandica (1832)
*Sorbus aucuparia (1832)
*Symphoricarpos albus (1833)
*Symphoricarpos orbiculatus
    (1832)
*Syringa ×persica (1832)
*Syringa vulgaris (1832)
*Syringa vulgaris var. alba
    (1832)
Tanacetum parthenium 'Flore
    Pleno' (1835)
*Tilia platyphyllos (1832)
Tradescantia virginiana (1832)
*Tsuga canadensis (1832)
Tulipa (1834)
Tulipa gesneriana (1834)
*Ulmus carpinifolia (1832)
*Ulmus glabra (1832)
*Ulmus procera (1832)
Veronicastrum virginicum (1832)
*Viburnum opulus 'Roseum'
    (1832)
*Vinca major (1832)
*Vinca minor (1832)
Viola odorata (1834)
Viola tricolor (1834)
Wisteria frutescens (1832)
*Wisteria sinensis (1832)
*Yucca filamentosa (1832)

New England Region, 1850–1874

Plants common to at least five of fourteen nursery catalogs and not included in a previous list for this region:

*Acer saccharinum (1833)
Achillea ptarmica (1845)
Adonis vernalis (1852)
Aquilegia glandulosa (1852)
Aquilegia skinneri (1852)
Armeria maritima (1832)
Aurinia saxatilis var. compactum
    (1862)
Bellis perennis (1841)
*Betula pendula (1833)
Campanula carpatica (1845)
Campanula latiloba (1845)
Campanula persicifolia (1835)
Campanula punctata (1852)
*Chaenomeles spp. (1832)
Chasmanthium latifolium
    (1859)
*Chrysanthemum (1832)
Delphinium formosum (1859)
Dicentra spectabilis (1853)

*Digitalis grandiflora (1834)
Digitalis purpurea 'Gloxiniiflora'
    Gloxinioides Group (1862)
Dodecatheon meadia (1845)
*Forsythia viridissima (1853)
Fritillaria imperialis (1835)
Gaura lindheimeri (1859)
Hemerocallis lilioasphodelus
    (1835)
Iberis sempervirens (1862)
Iris latifolia (1835)
Iris xiphium (1841)
*Lilium lancifolium (1832)
Lilium longiflorum (1841)
Lilium speciosum (1835)
Lychnis ×haageana (1862)
Lychnis viscaria (1851)
*Mahonia aquifolia (1853)
Myosotis palustris (1859)
Narcissus jonquilla (1836)
Oenothera biennis var.
    grandiflora (1862)
*Paeonia 'Humei' (1833)
*Paeonia lactiflora (1833)
*Paeonia tenuifolia (1833)
Penstemon digitalis (1841)
Penstemon gentianoides (1851)
Penstemon murrayanus (1862)
Phlox (1834)
*Pinus nigra (1841)
*Pinus strobus (1832)
*Pinus sylvestris (1841)
Platycodon grandiflorus (1833)
Stipa pennata (1836)
Tanacetum coccineum (1859)
*Thuja occidentalis (1833)
Veronica spicata (1841)

New England Region, 1875–1899

Plants common to at least seven of twenty nursery lists and not included in a previous list for this region:

Anemonella thalictroides (1859)
Aquilegia caerulea (1835)
Aquilegia chrysantha (1875)
*Betula pendula 'Laciniata'
    (1841)
*Betula populifolia (1841)
Callirhoe involucrata (1873)
*Canna indica (1833)
*Cerastium tomentosum (1862)
Cypripedium calceolus var.
    pubescens (1852)
*Deutzia gracilis (1861)

Drosera rotundifolia (1879)
*Epigaea repens (1857)
Erythronium americanum
    (1879)
Gentiana andrewsii (1862)
Gypsophila paniculata (1862)
Hepatica americana (1835)
*Ilex verticillata (1841)
*Juniperus communis
    'Hibernica' (1872)
*Kalmia angustifolia (1833)
Lavandula angustifolia (1859)
Liatris spicata (1841)
Lilium auratum (1866)
Lilium canadense (1835)
Lilium speciosum var. album
    (1852)
Lilium speciosum var. rubrum
    (1852)
Lilium superbum (1836)
*Macleaya cordata (1873)
Mitchella repens (1879)
Mitella diphylla (1879)
Nymphaea odorata (1875)
*Paeonia officinalis 'Rubra
    Plena' (1833)
Parnassia caroliniana (1879)
*Phlox subulata (1835)
*Picea pungens f. glauca (1881)
*Populus deltoides (1853)
*Populus nigra 'Italica' (1832)
*Prunus glandulosa (1832)
*Rhododendron calendulaceum
    (1832)
*Rhododendron catawbiense
    (1841)
*Rosa 'American Beauty' (1889)
*Rosa 'Baltimore Belle' (1853)
*Rosa 'Coquette des Alps'
    (1889)
*Rosa 'Fisher Holmes' (1889)
*Rosa 'Hermosa' (1853)
*Rosa 'John Hopper' (1889)
*Rosa 'La France' (1889)
*Rosa 'La Reine' (1853)
*Rosa 'Madame Plantier' (1853)
*Rosa 'Queen of the Prairies'
    (1853)
*Rosa 'Seven Sisters' (1832)
Sanguinaria canadensis (1835)
*Spiraea prunifolia (1853)
Tagetes patula (1867)
Tiarella cordifolia (1879)
Trillium cernuum (1879)
Trillium erectum (1841)
Trillium grandiflorum (1852)
*Viburnum opulus (1881)

Viola canadensis (1841)
Viola obliqua (1841)
Viola pedata (1841)
Viola pubescens (1841)
Weigela florida (1853)

New England Region, 1900–1924

Plants common to at least three of five nursery catalogs and not included in a previous list for this region:

Abies concolor (1910)
Achillea ptarmica (1841)
Anemone ×hybrida (1888)
Anemone ×hybrida 'Königin Charlotte' (1910)
Anthemis tinctoria (1889)
Berberis thunbergii (1910)
Campanula rotundifolia (1835)
Celastrus scandens (1832)
Clematis 'Henryi' (1889)
Clematis 'Jackmanii' (1889)
Clematis 'Madame Edouard André' (1901)
Clematis terniflora (1901)
Cornus florida (1832)
**Dianthus deltoides* (1836)
Forsythia suspensa var. *fortunei* (1901)
Gaillardia ×grandiflora (1910)
*Gladiolus (1881)
Hamamelis virginiana (1832)
Helenium autumnale (1834)
Heuchera sanguinea (1910)
Hibiscus 'Crimson Eye' (1894)
Hibiscus moscheutos (1836)
Hydrangea arborescens (1833)
Hydrangea paniculata 'Grandiflora' (1889)
Iris 'Queen of May' (1910)
Juniperus communis 'Hibernica' (1881)
*Kniphofia uvaria (1869)
Lathyrus odoratus (1867)
Leucanthemum ×superbum (1910)
Lilium lancifolium 'Flore Pleno' (1887)
Lonicera japonica 'Halliana' (1889)
*Lunaria annua (1835)
Malva moschata (1910)
Parthenocissus quinquefolia (1880)

Phlox carolina 'Miss Lingard' (1889)
*Phlox drummondii (1867)
Picea pungens 'Koster' (1910)
Rhododendron viscosum (1841)
Rhus typhina (1841)
Rosa 'Aglaia' (1901)
Rosa 'Alfred Colomb' (1889)
Rosa 'Anna De Diesbach' (1889)
Rosa 'Baronne Adolphe de Rothschild' (1889)
Rosa 'Dorothy Perkins' (1901)
Rosa eglanteria (1832)
Rosa 'Général Jacqueminot' (1889)
Rosa 'Madame Gabriel Luizet' (1889)
Rosa 'Madame Norbert Levavasseur' (1910)
Rosa 'Magna Charta' (1889)
Rosa 'Marshall Wilder' (1889)
Rosa 'Mrs. John Laing' (1889)
Rosa 'Paul Neyron' (1889)
Rosa rugosa (1910)
Rosa 'Turner's Crimson Rambler' (1901)
Rosa wichurana (1901)
Rudbeckia laciniata 'Hortensia' (1901)
Sedum spectabile (1887)
Solenostemon scutellarioides (1901)
Spiraea japonica 'Anthony Waterer' (1901)
Spiraea ×vanhouttei (1910)
Stokesia laevis (1889)
Syringa reticulata (1910)
Tropaeolum majus (1836)
*Ulmus americana (1841)
Valeriana officinalis (1851)
Veronica subsessilis (1887)

New England Region, 1925–1940

Plants common to at least three of five catalogs and not included in a previous list for this region:

Anemone coronaria (1834)
Arabis alpina (1915)
**Berberis thunbergii* 'Atropurpurea' (1917)
**Callistephus chinensis* (1836)
*Campanula medium 'Calycanthema' (1917)

**Cardiospermum helicacabum* (1836)
*Celosia argentea var. *cristata* (1836)
*Centaurea cyanus (1836)
Cosmos bipinnatus (1889)
Delphinium ×belladonna (1917)
**Eschscholzia californica* (1836)
**Euphorbia marginata* (1836)
**Gaillardia pulchella* (1867)
Gypsophila repens (1887)
**Helianthus annuus* (1836)
**Helichrysum bracteatum* (1867)
**Heliotropium arborescens* (1867)
**Humulus japonicus* 'Variegatus' (1917)
**Impatiens balsamina* (1836)
*Ipomoea alba (1836)
**Ipomoea quamoclit* (1836)
*Juniperus sabina (1841)
*Ligustrum ibota (1910)
*Lilium brownii (1866)
Lilium henryi (1914)
*Lilium pumilum (1866)
Lilium regale (1927)
**Limonium latifolium* (1862)
Lobelia erinus 'Crystal Palace' (1867)
Lobularia maritima (1836)
*Malus ioensis 'Plena' (1853)
**Mimulus moschatus* (1867)
Mirabilis jalapa (1836)
*Paeonia 'Festiva Maxima' (1852)
Papaver rhoeas (1915)
Parthenocissus tricuspidata (1889)
Petunia ×hybrida (1867)
Philadelphus coronarius 'Aureus' (1901)
Physalis francheti (1915)
*Pinus mugo (1872)
**Polianthes tuberosa* 'The Pearl' (1889)
**Portulaca grandiflora* (1867)
Pueraria montana var. *lobata* (1915)
Reseda odorata (1836)
**Rhodotypos scandens* (1910)
Ricinus communis 'Zanzibarensis' (1915)
Salpiglossis sinuata (1867)
Salvia farinacea (1915)
Salvia splendens (1833)
Sanvitalia procumbens 'Flore Pleno' (1915)

**Saponaria ocymoides* (1862)
Scabiosa caucasica (1841)
Schizanthus pinnatus (1867)
Tagetes tenuifolia 'Pumila' (1867)
Verbena ×hybrida (1867)
**Xeranthemum annuum* (1836)
Zinnia (1836)

MIDDLE ATLANTIC REGION

Delaware, Maryland, New Jersey, New York, Pennsylvania, Washington, D.C.

Middle Atlantic Region, 1770–1799

Plants common to at least three of six nursery catalogs, which offered mainly shrubs and trees.

Abies balsamea (1771)
Acer rubrum (1771)
Acer saccharum (1771)
Aesculus pavia (1783)
Betula lenta (1771)
Calycanthus floridus (1783)
Catalpa (1771)
Cornus florida (1771)
Corylus americana (1771)
Juniperus virginiana (1771)
Lindera benzoin (1771)
Liriodendron tulipifera (1771)
Myrica pensylvanica (1771)
Philadelphus coronarius (1771)
Picea mariana (1771)
Pinus strobus (1771)
Prunus caroliniana (1771)
Prunus glandulosa (1771)
Quercus alba (1771)
Quercus coccinea (1771)
Quercus velutina (1771)
Robinia pseudacorus (1771)
Sassafras albidum (1771)
Tsuga canadensis (1771)
Viburnum opulus 'Roseum' (1771)

Middle Atlantic Region, 1800–1824

Plants common to at least four of eight nursery catalogs and not included in a previous list for this region:

Anemonella thalictroides (1804)
Aquilegia canadensis (1804)
Aralia spinosa (1783)
Artemisia absinthium (1807)
Asarum canadense (1804)
Asclepias decumbens (1804)
Asclepias incarnata (1804)
Asclepias tuberosa (1783)
Asimina triloba (1783)
Aster novae-angliae (1804)
Aureolaria flava (1804)
Baptisia australis (1783)
Baptisia tinctoria (1783)
Celastrus scandens (1804)
Cercis canadensis (1804)
Chelone glabra (1783)
Chionanthus virginicus (1783)
Clethra alnifolia (1783)
Convallaria majalis (1807)
Coreopsis auriculata (1804)
Cypripedium acaule (1804)
Dianthus barbatus (1796)
Dianthus caryophyllus (1796)
Dodecatheon meadia (1783)
Echinacea purpurea (1783)
Gentiana saponaria (1804)
Geranium maculata (1804)
Geranium sanguineum (1807)
Gleditsia triacanthos (1783)
Hamamelis virginiana (1783)
Hemerocallis lilioasphodelus (1799)
Hibiscus moscheutos (1783)
Hibiscus moscheutos subsp. *palustris* (1804)
Hibiscus syriacus (1790)
Hyacinthus orientalis (1807)
Ilex opaca (1783)
Inula helenium (1807)
Iris versicolor (1804)
Iris virginica (1804)
Iris xiphium (1807)
Kalmia latifolia (1771)
Lathyrus latifolius (1796)
Liatris spicata (1804)
Lobelia cardinalis (1783)
Lobelia siphilitica (1804)
Lupinus perennis (1804)
Lychnis chalcedonica (1796)
Magnolia acuminata (1783)
Magnolia grandiflora (1783)
Magnolia tripetala (1783)
Magnolia virginiana (1783)
Mertensia virginica (1804)
Mimulus ringens (1804)

Monarda didyma (1783)
Monarda fistulosa (1804)
Paeonia 'Humei' (1810)
Paeonia lactiflora (1810)
Paeonia officinalis (1807)
Phlox paniculata (1783)
Phlox subulata (1804)
Physostegia virginiana (1804)
Platanus occidentalis (1783)
Podophyllum peltatum (1799)
Salvia officinalis (1807)
Sanguinaria canadensis (1804)
Sanguisorba canadensis (1804)
Sarracenia purpurea (1804)
Senna marilandica (1804)
Spigelia marilandica (1783)
Stachys byzantina (1807)
Taxodium distichum (1783)
Thuja occidentalis (1783)
Tilia americana (1783)
Tulipa (1810)
Veratrum viride (1804)
Veronicastrum virginicum (1804)
Viola pedata (1804)

Middle Atlantic Region, 1825–1849

Plants common to at least eight of fourteen lists and not included in a previous list for this region. These particular catalogs featured mainly herbaceous plants:

*Acer saccharinum (1783)
Aconitum napellus (1807)
*Aesculus hippocastanum (1792)
*Aesculus parviflora (1804)
Alcea rosea (1810)
*Amorpha fruticosa (1783)
Antirrhinum majus (1810)
Aquilegia vulgaris (1796)
Armeria maritima (1822)
Bergenia crassifolia (1822)
Campanula medium (1796)
Campanula persicifolia (1826)
Campanula pyramidalis (1826)
Centranthus ruber (1807)
*Cephalanthus occidentalis (1783)
Clematis recta (1826)
*Clethra alnifolia (1783)
*Colutea arborescens (1790)
*Daphne mezereum (1792)
Delphinium elatum (1810)
Delphinium formosum (1857)

Delphinium grandiflorum (1822)
*Dianthus plumarius (1807)
Dictamnus albus (1796)
Digitalis ferruginea (1811)
Digitalis lutea (1810)
Digitalis purpurea (1810)
*Diospyros virginiana (1783)
Echinacea purpurea (1783)
*Euonymus americanus (1783)
Eupatorium coelestinum (1804)
Filipendula rubra (1804)
Filipendula ulmaria (1822)
Filipendula vulgaris (1822)
*Fraxinus americana (1771)
*Gleditsia triacanthos (1783)
*Halesia carolina (1792)
Helianthus ×multiflorus (1804)
Hemerocallis fulva (1811)
Hesperis matronalis (1796)
Hibiscus militaris (1783)
Hosta plantaginea (1828)
Hosta ventricosa (1811)
*Hypericum kalmianum (1783)
*Ilex verticillata (1783)
Iris germanica 'Florentina' (1807)
Iris pumila (1807)
*Kalmia angustifolia (1783)
*Laburnum anagyroides (1790)
*Lilium superbum (1783)
Linum perenne (1796)
*Liquidambar styraciflua (1783)
Lychnis coronaria (1796)
Lythrum salicaria (1826)
Oenothera fruticosa subsp. *glauca* (1826)
Paeonia suffruticosa (1822)
Paeonia tenuifolia (1819)
Penstemon barbatus (1811)
Penstemon digitalis (1826)
*Philadelphia coronarius (1771)
Phlox carolina (1826)
Phlox divaricata (1804)
Phlox maculata (1804)
*Picea mariana (1771)
Polemonium caeruleum (1822)
Primula auricula (1810)
Primula ×polyantha (1822)
*Ptelea trifoliata (1783)
*Quercus velutina (1771)
Ranunculus acris 'Flore Pleno' (1822)
*Rhododendron maximum (1783)
*Robinia hispida (1783)
Rudbeckia laciniata (1804)
*Salix babylonica (1790)

Sedum telephium (1807)
*Staphylea trifolia (1783)
*Syringa vulgaris (1771)
*Syringa vulgaris var. *alba* (1771)
Tanacetum parthenium 'Flore Pleno' (1810)
Tradescantia virginiana (1818)
Viola odorata (1810)
Yucca filamentosa (1804)
Yucca gloriosa (1804)

Middle Atlantic Region, 1850–1874

Plants common to at least four of nine nursery catalogs and not included in a previous list for this region:

Abies alba (1790)
*Acer negundo (1783)
Achillea millefolium (1811)
Achillea ptarmica (1844)
Aconitum chinensis (1844)
Aconitum lycoctonum subsp. *lycoctonum* (1844)
Adonis vernalis (1834)
*Aesculus flava (1783)
Anemone hupehensis var. *japonica* (1857)
Aquilegia glandulosa (1844)
Aquilegia skinneri (1857)
*Aristolochia macrophylla (1783)
Arundo donax (1792)
Arundo donax 'Versicolor' (1826)
Astilbe japonica (1848)
Aurinia saxatilis (1796)
Bellis perennis (1807)
Campanula carpatica (1829)
Campanula trachelium (1822)
Ceratostigma plumbaginoides (1857)
*Chrysanthemum (1810)
Cladrastis kentukea (1844)
Clematis integrifolia (1826)
Colchicum autumnale (1820)
*Cotinus coggygria (1790)
Crocus (1819)
Delphinium barlowii (1844)
Dicentra spectabilis (1857)
Eryngium amethystinum (1831)
Erysimum cheiri (1796)
Filipendula ulmaria 'Multiplex' (1844)
*Fraxinus excelsior (1807)
Fritillaria imperialis (1807)

Fritillaria meleagris (1860)
Geranium pratense (1829)
Geum chiloense (1844)
Gillenia trifoliata (1804)
Gladiolus (1820)
*Gymnocladus dioica (1807)
Helleborus niger (1820)
Hemerocallis minor (1822)
Hosta sieboldiana (1844)
*Hydrangea macrophylla (1807)
*Ilex aquifolium (1819)
Iris 'La Pactole' (1857)
Iris pallida (1819)
Iris persica (1810)
*Kerria japonica 'Pleniflora' (1819)
*Larix decidua (1792)
*Larix laricina (1783)
Lilium brownii (1854)
Lilium bulbiferum (1844)
Lilium candidum (1807)
Lilium lancifolium (1827)
Lilium longiflorum (1844)
Lilium maculatum (1854)
Lilium martagon (1807)
Lilium speciosum (1854)
Lilium speciosum var. rubrum (1860)
Lilium ×testaceum (1860)
Limonium latifolium (1829)
Lupinus polyphyllus (1834)
Lychnis flos-cuculi (1829)
Lysimachia nummularia (1834)
Macleaya cordata (1829)
*Magnolia tripetala (1783)
Myosotis palustris (1854)
Narcissus (1807)
Narcissus jonquilla (1807)
Oenothera macrocarpa (1844)
Paeonia officinalis 'Rubra Plena' (1822)
Paeonia tenuifolia 'Flore Pleno' (1857)
Papaver orientale (1822)
Papaver orientale var. bracteatum (1829)
Paradisea liliastrum (1822)
Penstemon digitalis (1826)
Penstemon gentianoides (1844)
*Phalaris arundinacea var. picta (1826)
Picea abies (1771)
*Pinus sylvestris (1792)
Platycodon grandiflorus (1829)
*Populus nigra 'Italica' (1790)
Potentilla atrosanguinea (1834)
Potentilla ×hopwoodiana (1844)

*Prunus persica 'Plena' (1792)
Quercus robur (1807)
Rudbeckia hirta (1804)
Sedum aizoon (1822)
Sedum sieboldii (1844)
*Sorbus americana (1783)
*Sorbus aucuparia (1792)
Stachys byzantina (1807)
*Symphoricarpos albus (1807)
*Symphoricarpos orbiculatus (1783)
Taxus baccata 'Adpressa' (1857)
*Tilia platyphyllos (1810)
Tulipa 'Duc van Thol' (1820)
*Ulmus carpinifolia (1807)
Valeriana officinalis (1829)
Veronica gentianoides (1829)
Veronica spicata (1829)
Veronica spuria (1844)
Viola tricolor (1796)
*Wisteria sinensis (1834)
Yucca recurvifolia (1844)

Middle Atlantic Region, 1875–1899

Plants common to at least three of seven nursery catalogs and not included in a previous list for this region:

*Achillea filipendulina (1860)
*Adonis vernalis (1834)
Allium moly (1834)
*Aquilegia caerulea (1829)
*Aruncus dioicus (1807)
*Catananche caerulea (1796)
*Chaenomeles spp. (1834)
*Cobaea scandens (1827)
Coreopsis lanceolata (1804)
Cortaderia selloana (1865)
*Deutzia gracilis (1860)
*Forsythia viridissima (1859)
*Galanthus nivalis (1807)
Gypsophila paniculata (1865)
*Hedera helix (1807)
*Hydrangea macrophylla (1807)
Lilium auratum (1870)
*Lychnis ×haageana (1848)
*Magnolia denudata (1834)
*Magnolia ×soulangeana (1844)
Myosotis dissitiflora (1875)
*Ornithogalum umbellatum (1807)
*Parthenocissus quinquefolia (1804)
*Pilosella aurantiaca (1810)
*Polemonium reptans (1804)

Primula elatior (1822)
Primula veris (1811)
Ranunculus acontifolius (1822)
*Rhododendron ponticum (1807)
Saccharum ravennae (1870)
*Sedum album (1860)
*Sedum kamchatichum (1860)
*Sedum populifolium (1826)
*Spiraea prunifolia (1859)
*Sprekelia formosissima (1807)
Stipa pennata (1865)
*Taxus baccata 'Fastigiata' (1826)
Tricyrtis hirta (1875)
*Trillium erectum (1804)
*Trillium grandiflorum (1807)
*Uvularia grandiflora (1829)
Viola odorata 'Marie Louise' (1875)
*Weigela florida (1859)

Middle Atlantic Region, 1900–1924

Plants common to at least three of seven nursery catalogs and not included in a previous list for this region:

Anemone ×hybrida 'Whirlwind' (ca. 1905)
Anthemis tinctoria (1910)
Arabis alpina (1834)
Aristolochia macrophylla (1783)
Berberis thunbergii (1859)
*Buxus sempervirens (1807)
Clematis 'Henryi' (ca. 1905)
Clematis 'Jackmanii' (ca. 1905)
Clematis terniflora (ca. 1905)
Dahlia (1819)
Fagus sylvatica (1826)
Forsythia suspensa (1859)
Hydrangea paniculata 'Grandiflora' (1870)
Iberis sempervirens (1834)
Iris ensata (1870)
Juniperus communis 'Hibernica' (1870)
Ligustrum ovalifolium (1870)
Lonicera japonica 'Halliana' (1870)
Morus alba 'Pendula' (ca. 1905)
Paeonia 'Duchess de Nemours' (1860)
Paeonia 'Festiva Maxima' (1860)
Parthenocissus tricuspidata (1876)

Philadelphus coronarius 'Aureus' (ca. 1905)
*Platanus orientalis (1792)
Picea pungens f. glauca (ca. 1905)
Populus deltoides (1783)
Prunus cerasifera 'Pissardii' (1910)
Rosa 'Aglaia' (ca. 1905)
Rosa 'Alfred Colomb' (ca. 1905)
Rosa 'American Beauty' (ca. 1905)
Rosa 'Anna de Diesbach' (ca. 1905)
Rosa 'Baltimore Belle' (1860)
Rosa 'Clio' (ca. 1905)
Rosa 'Dorothy Perkins' (ca. 1905)
Rosa foetida 'Persiana' (1860)
Rosa 'Frau Karl Druschki' (ca. 1905)
Rosa 'Général Jacqueminot' (1860)
Rosa 'Gruss an Teplitz' (1910)
Rosa 'La France' (1876)
Rosa 'Madame Norbert Levavasseur' (ca. 1905)
Rosa 'Madame Plantier' (1844)
Rosa 'Magna Charta' (1910)
Rosa 'Margaret Dickson' (ca. 1905)
Rosa 'Mrs. John Laing' (ca. 1905)
Rosa 'Paul Neyron' (ca. 1905)
Rosa 'Prince Camille De Rohan' (1870)
Rosa 'Queen of the Prairies' (1860)
Rosa rugosa (ca. 1905)
Rosa 'Tausendschön' (1910)
Rosa 'Turner's Crimson Rambler' (ca. 1905)
Rosa 'Ulrich Brunner fils' (1910)
Rosa wichurana (ca. 1905)
Rudbeckia laciniata 'Hortensia' ('Golden Glow') (ca. 1905)
Scabiosa caucasica (1827)
Sedum spectabile (1882)
Spiraea japonica 'Anthony Waterer' (ca. 1905)
Spiraea thunbergii (1870)
Spiraea ×vanhouttei (ca. 1905)
Syringa vulgaris 'Charles X' (1844)
*Tagetes erecta (1807)
*Tagetes patula (1807)
Ulmus americana (1804)
Viburnum plicatum (1859)
*Zinnia (1810)

Middle Atlantic Region, 1925–1940

Plants common to at least three of five nursery catalogs and not included in a previous list for this region:

*Acer palmatum (1917)
Achillea ptarmica 'The Pearl' (double, 1860)
Anchusa azurea 'Dropmore' (1910)
Calendula officinalis (1807)
Callistephus chinensis (1810)
Campanula medium 'Calycanthema' (1910)
Centaurea cyanus (1807)
Centaurea montana (1910)
Chamaecyparis pisifera 'Plumosa' (1870)
Consolida ajacis (1810)
*Cornus florida f. rubra (1917)
Cosmos bipinnatus (1910)
Delphinium Belladonna Group (1917)
Delphinium ×bellamosum (1928)
Dianthus deltoides 'Brilliant' (1931)
Geum 'Lady Stratheden' (1931)
Geum 'Mrs. Bradshaw' (1924)
Gypsophila elegans (1928)
Gypsophila repens (1829)
Heuchera sanguinea (1910)
*Juniperus excelsa 'Stricta' (1934)
*Juniperus ×pfitzeriana (1934)
Lathyrus odoratus (1870)
Lavandula angustifolia (1807)
Leucanthemum ×superbum (1910)
Leucanthemum ×superbum 'Alaska' (1917)
Lilium speciosum var. album (1860)
Lonicera tatarica (1834)
Matthiola incana (1810)
Myosotis alpestris (1870)
Pachysandra terminalis (1917)
Paeonia 'Felix Crousse' (1917)
Papaver nudicaule (1844)
Papaver rhoeas (1910)
Petunia ×hybrida (1870)
Phlox carolina 'Miss Lingard' (1910)
Portulaca grandiflora (1870)
Rosa 'Étoile de France' (1917)
Rosa 'Los Angeles' (1924)
Rosa 'Madame Butterfly' (1924)
Rosa 'Madame Edouard Herriot' (1924)
Rosa 'Paul's Scarlet Climber' (1924)
Rosa 'Pink Killarney' (1931)
Rosa 'Red Radiance' (1924)
Rosa 'Talisman' (1931)
Spiraea ×billardii (1860)
Stokesia laevis (1875)
Tanacetum coccineum (1867)
Tropaeolum majus (1870)
Verbena ×hybrida (1860)
*Viburnum plicatum var. tomentosum (1917)
Viola cornuta (1882)

SOUTHERN REGION

Alabama, Arkansas, Florida, Georgia, Kentucky, Louisiana, Mississippi, North Carolina, South Carolina, Tennessee, Texas, Virginia, West Virginia

The first three southern garden plant lists are based on early newspaper advertisements with the exception of the Minton Collins broadside (Richmond, Virginia, 1793). I have chosen to list all plants from these publications and have not edited plants that appeared in an earlier list as I have done with most of the other plant lists in this appendix.

Combined list of garden plants that were advertised in six southern nursery lists and newspaper ads prior to 1800 (Richardson 1941; Chappell 2000):

Adonis aestivalis (1799)
Amaryllis belladonna (1792)
Amberboa (Centaurea) moschata (1799)
Anemone (1792)
Buxus sempervirens 'Suffruticosa' (1768)
Callistephus chinensis (1799)
Campanula medium (1799)
Convallaria majalis (1792)
Crocus (1792)
Dianthus barbatus (1799)
Erysimum cheiri (1792)
Helianthemum spp. (1793)
Hyacinthus orientalis (1765)
Iberis (1799)
Impatiens balsamina (1793)
Iris persica (1792)
Kochia scoparia (1799)
Lilium (1765)
Magnolia (1778)
Matthiola incana (1793)
Mimosa pudica (1799)
Narcissus (1754)
Narcissus tazetta (1799)
Papaver somniferum (1799)
Pelargonium (1793)
Polianthes tuberosa (1792)
Primula auricula (1799)
Primula ×polyantha (1799)
Ranunculus (1792)
Reseda odorata (1799)
Rosa 'Centifolia Muscosa' (1793)
Rosa cinnamomea (1793)
Rosa 'Maiden's Blush' (1793)
Scolymus hispanica (1799)
Scorpiurus vermiculata (1799)
Silene (1799)
Solidago (1799)
Tagetes erecta (1799)
Tagetes patula (1799)
Tulipa (1754)
Viola (1793)
Viola tricolor (1799)

Combined list of plants from two southern newspaper advertisements, John Bryant in *Charleston Times*, 13 Febuary 1808, and Robert Squibb, *Charleston Courier*, 1812:

Erica (1812)
Melia azedarach (1808)
Nerium oleander (1812)
Pelargonium (1808)
Rosa multiflora (1812)
Viburnum tinus (1812)

All ornamental plants included in advertisement in *The Virginian*, 16 February 1826, by Wm. Owen and G. L. Leckie, druggists and apothecaries, Lynchburg, Virginia:

Adonis aestivalis
Alcea rosea (double-flowered)
Amaranthus caudatus
Amaranthus tricolor
Amberboa moschata
Antirrhinum majus
Aquilegia vulgaris
Belamcanda chinensis
Calendula officinalis
Callistephus chinensis
Campanula medium
Canna indica
Cardiospermum helicacabum
Catananche caerulea
Celosia argentea var. cristata
Centaurea cyanus
Cerinthe major
Chenopodium capitatum
Chrysanthemum indicum (white)
Colutea arborescens
Consolida ajacis (double flowered)
Convolvulus tricolor
Coreopsis spp.
Crocus sativus (or possibly Carthamus tinctoria)
Cytisus scoparius
Dahlia
Dianthus barbatus
Dianthus caryophyllus
Dianthus chinensis
Dianthus deltoides
Dianthus plumarius
Digitalis purpurea
Ecballium elaterium
Erysimum cheiri
Erysimum cheiri 'Bloody Warrior'
Gomphrena globosa (purple)
Hedysarum coronarium
Helianthus annuus (double)
Hesperis matronalis
Hibiscus syriacus
Hibiscus trionum
Iberis umbellata or Iberis amara
Impatiens balsamina
Ipomoea ×multifida
Ipomoea purpurea

Ipomoea quamoclit
Lablab purpurea
Lathyrus odoratus cv.
Lathyrus odoratus 'Painted Lady'
Lavandula angustifolia
Lavatera spp.
Legousia speculum-veneris
Linum perenne
Lunaria annua
Lupinus hirsutus
Lupinus luteus
Lupinus perennis
Lychnis chalcedonica
Lychnis coronaria
Matthiola incana
Matthiola incana 'Annua'
Mesembryanthemum
  crystallinum
Mimosa pudica
Mirabilis jalapa
Momordica balsamina
Myrtus communis
Oenothera biennis
Papaver somniferum 'Carnation-
  flowered'
Papaver somniferum (double
  white)
Pelargonium spp.
Philadelphus coronarius
Physalis alkekengi
Pilosella aurantiaca
Polemonium caeruleum
Primula ×polyantha
Reseda odorata
Scabiosa atropurpurea
Scabiosa stellata
double purple jacobea (?)
Senna marilandica
Silene armeria
Solanum melongena
Star in the East (?)
Tagetes erecta
Tagetes patula
Thymus
Tragopogon pratensis
Ulex europaeus
Valeriana officinalis
Viola tricolor

Southern Region, 1850–1874

Plants common to at least six of sixteen nursery catalogs and not included in a previous list for this region:

Abies alba (1853)

Abies balsamea (1853)
Aesculus hippocastanum (1853)
Buxus sempervirens (1854)
Buxus sempervirens
  'Arborescens' (1853)
Calycanthus floridus (1853)
Cedrus deodora (1851)
Chaenomeles spp. (1853)
Chrysanthemum (1853)
Cotinus coggygria (1858)
Deutzia gracilis (1858)
Deutzia scabra (1853)
Euonymus japonicus (1853)
Forsythia viridissima (1856)
Gardenia augusta (1851)
Ginkgo biloba (1854)
Gymnocladus dioica (1854)
Hibiscus syriacus (1851)
Juniperus communis 'Hibernica'
  (1856)
Juniperus communis 'Suecica'
  (1853)
Laburnum anagyroides (1853)
Lagerstroemia indica (1853)
Magnolia acuminata (1854)
Magnolia denudata (1854)
Magnolia grandiflora (1853)
Magnolia liliiflora (1853)
Magnolia macrophylla (1854)
Mahonia aquifolia (1854)
Paeonia (1851)
Paulownia imperialis (1851)
Phlox (1851)
Picea abies (1853)
Picea glauca (1854)
Pinus strobus (1854)
Platycladus orientalis (1853)
Populus nigra 'Italica' (1858)
Prunus laurocerasus (1853)
Prunus persica 'Plena' (1854)
Pyracantha coccinea (1853)
Rosa 'Adam' (1853)
Rosa 'Baltimore Belle' (1851)
Rosa 'Baronne Prevost' (1851)
Rosa 'Bougere' (1851)
Rosa 'Caroline' (1851)
Rosa 'Chromatella' (1851)
Rosa 'Clara Sylvaine' (1851)
Rosa 'Comte Bobinski' (1856)
Rosa 'Cramoisi Supérieur'
  (1851)
Rosa 'Devoniensis' (1851)
Rosa 'Géant des Batailles' (1851)
Rosa 'Hermosa' (1851)
Rosa 'Lamarque' (1851)
Rosa 'La Reine' (1851)
Rosa 'Le Pactole' (1851)

Rosa 'Leveson Gower' (1851)
Rosa 'Louis Philippe' (1853)
Rosa 'Madame Bosanquet'
  (1851)
Rosa 'Madame Breon' (1853)
Rosa 'Madame Laffay' (1851)
Rosa 'Marquis de Boccella'
  (1853)
Rosa 'Ophire' (1851)
Rosa 'Pie IX' (1856)
Rosa 'Prince Albert' (1851)
Rosa 'Queen of the Prairies'
  (1851)
Rosa 'Safrano' (1851)
Rosa 'Solfaterre' (1851)
Rosa 'Souvenir de la Malmaison'
  (1851)
Rosa 'Souvenir d'un Ami'
  (1851)
Rosa 'Triumphe du
  Luxembourg' (1851)
Salix babylonica (1853)
Spiraea cantoniensis (1853)
Spiraea douglasii (1854)
Spiraea prunifolia (1853)
Syringa vulgaris (1853)
Syringa vulgaris var. alba (1853)
Taxodium distichum (1851)
Taxus baccata 'Fastigiata' (1851)
Thuja occidentalis (1851)
Thuja plicata (1853)
Tsuga canadensis (1853)
Verbena ×hybrida (1851)
Viburnum opulus 'Roseum'
  (1851)
Weigela florida (1854)
Wisteria sinensis (1853)

Southern Region, 1875–1899

Plants common to at least five of fourteen nursery catalogs and not included in a previous list for this region:

*Acer platanoides (1854)
Acer saccharinum (1853)
Caladium bicolor (1873)
Chilopsis linearis (1888)
Colocasia esculenta (1873)
Cortaderia selloana (1873)
*Cupressus funebris (1856)
*Eriobotrya japonica (1856)
*Fuchsia (1858)
*Heliotropium arborescens
  (1858)
*Jasminum nudiflorum (1858)

Juniperus virginiana (1851)
*Laurus nobilis (1856)
Ligustrum ovalifolium (1856)
*Ligustrum vulgare (1856)
*Lilium speciosum (1861)
Lonicera periclymenum 'Belgica'
  (1856)
Lonicera sempervirens (1851)
Melia azedarach
  'Umbraculiformis' (1881)
*Michelia figo (1858)
*Osmanthus fragrans (1856)
*Populus alba (1858)
*Prunus glandulosa (1858)
Punica granatum (1870)
Rosa 'Bon Silene' (1856)
Rosa 'Catherine Mermet' (1881)
Rosa 'Duchesse de Brabant'
  (1881)
Rosa 'Général Jacqueminot'
  (1859)
Rosa 'Homère' (1868)
Rosa 'Isabella Sprunt' (1870)
Rosa 'La France' (1888)
Rosa 'Madame Alfred Carrier'
  (1888)
Rosa 'Madame Charles Wood'
  (1888)
Rosa 'Maréchal Niel' (1868)
Rosa 'Marie Guillot' (1881)
Rosa 'Papa Gontier' (1888)
Rosa 'Paul Neyron' (1881)
Rosa 'Perle des Jardins' (1881)
Rosa 'Pink Daily' (1881)
Rosa 'The Bride' (1888)
Solenostemon scutellinoides
  (1873)
*Thea bohea (1856)
Thuja occidentalis 'Aurea' (1858)
Trachelospermum jasminoides
  (1871)

Southern Region, 1900–1924

Plants common to at least four of ten nursery catalogs and not included in a previous list for this region:

Abelia ×grandiflora (1906)
Acer negundo (1860)
Acer saccharum (1858)
Arundo donax 'Versicolor'
  (1881)
*Aucuba japonica (1851)
*Bellis perennis (1881)
*Camellia japonica (1853)

Campsis grandiflora (1859)
Catalpa speciosa (1906)
Celtis occidentalis (1903)
Cercis canadensis (1853)
Cinnamomum camphora (1894)
Clematis terniflora (1903)
Cobaea scandens (1873)
Convallaria majalis (1792)
Cornus florida (1903)
Firmiana simplex (1860)
Fraxinus americana (1854)
Gelsemium sempervirens (1860)
Gladiolus (1861)
Hedera helix (1858)
Hibiscus rosa-sinensis (1873)
Hydrangea macrophylla 'Thomas Hogg' (1888)
Hydrangea paniculata 'Grandiflora' (1881)
Ilex opaca (1851)
Jasminum sambac 'Grand Duke' (1888)
Koelreuteria paniculata (1858)
Lantana camara (1853)
Ligustrum amurense (1881)
Ligustrum ibota (1858)
Lilium auratum (1871)
Lilium speciosum var. *rubrum* (1861)
Liquidambar styraciflua (1898)
Liriodendron tulipifera (1858)
Lobularia maritima (1881)
Lonicera japonica 'Aureareticulata' (1870)
Lonicera japonica 'Halliana' (1870)
Magnolia ×soulangeana (1861)
Magnolia virginiana (1856)
Miscanthus sinensis 'Variegatus' (1898)
Miscanthus sinensis 'Zebrinus' (1888)
Nandina domestica (1856)
Parthenocissus quinquefolia (1858)
Parthenocissus tricuspidata (1871)
Petunia ×hybrida (1868)
Photinia serrulata (1856)
Pittosporum tobira (1845)
Platanus occidentalis (1895)
Platycladus orientalis 'Aurea Nana' (1906)
Poncirus trifoliata (1894)
Populus deltoides (1858)
Prunus cerasifera 'Pissardii' (1898)

Pueraria montana var. *lobata* (1907)
Quercus coccinea (1871)
Quercus palustris (1871)
Rhododendron indica (1853)
Robinia hispida (1853)
Rosa 'American Beauty' (1888)
Rosa 'Bridesmaid' (1895)
Rosa 'Climbing Bridesmaid' (1904)
Rosa 'Clotilde Soupert' (1898)
Rosa 'Dorothy Perkins' (1907)
Rosa 'Étoile de Lyon' (1888)
Rosa 'Frau Karl Druschki' (1907)
Rosa 'Gruss an Teplitz' (1904)
Rosa 'Kaiserin Auguste Viktoria' (1898)
Rosa 'Madame Caroline Testout' (1904)
Rosa 'Madame Norbert Levavasseur' (1906)
Rosa 'Magna Charta' (1881)
Rosa 'Maman Cochet' (1904)
Rosa 'Marie Lambert' (1904)
Rosa 'Mary Washington' (1898)
Rosa 'Mlle. Francisca Kruger' (1888)
Rosa 'Reine Marie Henriette' (1881)
Rosa 'Turner's Crimson Rambler' (1898)
Rosa 'White Maman Cochet' (1904)
Salvia splendens (1853)
Spiraea ×billardii (1871)
Spiraea japonica 'Anthony Waterer' (1906)
Spiraea ×vanhouttei (1906)
Thuja occidentalis 'Pyramidalis' (1853)
Ulmus americana (1854)
Viola tricolor (1799)
Vitex agnus-castus (1858)
Wisteria frutescens (1858)
Wisteria sinensis 'Alba' (1861)
Yucca filamentosa (1871)
Zinnia (1881)

Southern Region, 1925–1940

Plants common to at least three of six catalogs and not included in a previous list for this region:

Acroclinium roseum (1895)
Anthemis tinctoria (1907)

Aster novae-angliae (1903)
Aurinia saxatilis (1871)
Berberis thunbergii (1881)
Brachycome iberdifolia (1925)
Canna 'Roi Humbert' (1919)
Catharanthus roseus (1888)
Centaurea imperialis (1925)
Clematis 'Jackmanii' (1906)
Cosmos bipinnatus (1895)
Cosmos sulphureus 'Klondyke' (1928)
Crocosmia ×crocosmiiflora (1894)
Curcubita spp. (ornamental gourds) (1925)
Eschscholzia californica (1895)
Gypsophila elegans (1925)
Helichrysum bracteatum (1917)
Hippeastrum ×johnsonii (1853)
Iberis amara 'Hyacinth-Flowered White' (1928)
Lathyrus odoratus (1895)
Leucanthemum ×superbum (1907)
Leucanthemum ×superbum 'Alaska' (1928)
Linum grandiflorum 'Coccineum' (1925)
Lobelia erinus (1881)
Papaver rhoeas (1895)
Phaseolus coccineus (1925)
Phlox drummondii (1881)
Portulaca grandiflora (1881)
Ricinus communis (1881)
Salpiglossis sinuata (1925)
Schizanthus pinnatus (1925)
Symphoricarpos albus (1858)
Symphoricarpos orbiculatus (1858)
Tanacetum coccineum (1871)
Tanacetum parthenium (single and double, 1871)
Torenia fournieri (1881)
Tropaeolum majus (1881)
Tropaeolum peregrinum (1925)

GREAT LAKES REGION

Illinois, Indiana, Michigan, Minnesota, Ohio, Wisconsin

Great Lakes Region, 1835–1849

Plants common to at least three of six nursery catalogs:

Abies balsamea (1843)
Acer saccharinum (1843)
Aesculus glabra (1843)
Aesculus parviflora (1843)
Ailanthus altissima (1843)
Alcea rosea (1835)
Antirrhinum majus (1835)
Aquilegia canadensis (1835)
Artemisia abrotanum (1845)
Berberis vulgaris (1843)
Broussonetia papyrifera (1843)
Buxus sempervirens 'Suffruticosa' (1843)
Calycanthus floridus (1843)
Campanula medium (1835)
Campsis grandiflora (1843)
Campsis radicans (1845)
Catalpa bignonioides (1845)
Celastrus scandens (1843)
Cercis canadensis (1843)
Chionanthus virginicus (1845)
Chrysanthemum (1843)
Clematis flammula (1835)
Clematis virginiana (1835)
Clematis vitalba (1835)
Colutea arborescens (1843)
Convallaria majalis (1845)
Cotinus coggygria (1843)
Dahlia (1843)
Daphne mezereum (1845)
Delphinium elatum (1835)
Delphinium grandiflorum (1835)
Dianthus chinensis (1835)
Dianthus plumarius (1835)
Dianthus superbus (1835)
Dictamnus albus (1845)
Digitalis ferruginea (1835)
Digitalis grandiflora (1835)
Diospyros virginiana (1843)
Echinacea purpurea (1835)
Euonymus europaeus (1845)
Filipendula ulmaria (1845)
Gleditsia triacanthos (1843)

Halesia carolina (1845)
Hedera helix (1845)
Hesperis matronalis (1845)
Hibiscus syriacus (1843)
Hosta plantaginea (1845)
Hosta ventricosa (1845)
Hydrangea macrophylla (1843)
Jasminum officinale (1845)
Kerria japonica 'Pleniflora' (1843)
Laburnum anagyroides (1843)
Larix decidua (1845)
Larix laricina (1843)
Lathyrus latifolius (1843)
Ligustrum vulgare (1845)
Lindera benzoin (1843)
Liriodendron tulipifera (1843)
Lobelia cardinalis (1835)
Lonicera periclymenum 'Belgica' (1845)
Lonicera sempervirens (1843)
Lonicera tatarica (1843)
Lonicera xylosteum (1843)
Lupinus polyphyllus (1835)
Lychnis chalcedonica (1835)
Lychnis coronaria (1835)
Maclura pomifera (1843)
Magnolia acuminata (1843)
Magnolia virginiana (1845)
Paeonia suffruticosa (1845)
Papaver orientale (1845)
Parthenocissus quinquefolia (1845)
Periploca graeca (1845)
Philadelphus coronarius (1843)
Phlox (1835)
Phlox subulata (1845)
Physocarpus opulifolius (1843)
Physostegia virginiana (1835)
Picea abies (1845)
Pinus strobus (1843)
Platycladus orientalis (1843)
Polemonium caeruleum (1835)
Populus alba (1843)
Prunus glandulosa (1843)
Ribes aureum (1843)
Robinia hispida (1843)
Robinia pseudoacacia (1843)
Rosa 'Baltimore Belle' (1845)
Rosa 'Champneys' Pink Cluster' (1843)
Rosa 'Charles X' (1845)
Rosa 'Devoniensis' (1845)
Rosa 'George the Fourth' (1843)
Rosa ×*harisonii* 'Harison's Yellow' (1843)
Rosa 'Hermosa' (1845)
Rosa 'Lamarque' (1845)

Rosa 'Madame Hardy' (1843)
Rosa 'Seven Sisters' (1843)
Rosa 'Triomphe du Luxembourg' (1845)
Salix alba (1843)
Salix alba var. *vitellina* (1843)
Salix babylonica (1843)
Salix babylonica 'Crispa' (1843)
Salix viminalis (1843)
Shepherdia argentea (1843)
Sorbaria sorbifolia (1845)
Sorbus americana (1845)
Sorbus aucuparia (1845)
Symphoricarpos albus (1843)
Symphoricarpos orbiculatus (1843)
Syringa ×*chinensis* (1845)
Syringa ×*persica* (1843)
Syringa vulgaris (1843)
Syringa vulgaris var. *alba* (1843)
Tanacetum parthenium (1835)
Thuja occidentalis (1843)
Tsuga canadensis (1843)
Verbena ×*hybrida* (1845)
Viburnum opulus 'Roseum' (1843)
Vinca minor (1843)
Viola tricolor (1845)
Wisteria frutescens (1845)
Wisteria sinensis (1843)

Great Lakes Region, 1850–1874

Plants common to at least five of thirteen nursery catalogs and not included in a previous list for this region:

Achillea ptarmica (1845)
Astilbe japonica (1845)
Bellis perennis (1845)
Clematis recta (1846)
Crocus (1858)
Dianthus caryophyllus (1835)
Dicentra spectabilis (1858)
Filipendula vulgaris (1835)
Fritillaria imperialis (1843)
Hemerocallis fulva (1845)
Iberis sempervirens (1867)
Iris (1845)
Liatris spicata (1845)
Lilium candidum (1845)
Lilium lancifolium (1845)
Lilium speciosum (1859)
Lilium speciosum var. *roseum* (1859)
Lilium speciosum var. *rubrum* (1859)

Narcissus (1858)
Paeonia 'Humei' (1846)
Pinus nigra (1845)
Pinus sylvestris (1858)
Rosa 'Baronne Prevost' (1846)
Rosa foetida 'Persiana' (1846)
Rosa 'La Reine' (1845)
Rosa 'Queen of the Prairies' (1845)
Tanacetum parthenium 'Flore Pleno' (1845)
Tulipa (1845)
**Yucca filamentosa* (1845)

Great Lakes Region, 1875–1899

Plants common to at least four of thirteen catalogs and not included in a previous list for this region:

Ageratum houstonianum (1859)
Begonia (1859)
Caladium bicolor (1874)
Canna indica (1874)
Callistephus chinensis (1889)
Chaenomeles spp. (1843)
Colocasia esculenta (1874)
Consolida ajacis (1858)
Cymbalaria muralis (1874)
Delphinium formosum (1859)
Dianthus barbatus (1835)
Gladiolus (1843)
Heliotropium arborescens (1860)
Impatiens balsamina (1889)
Lathyrus odoratus (1889)
Lilium auratum (1872)
Lobularia maritima (1889)
Mesembryanthemum crystallinum (1877)
Mirabilis jalapa (1889)
Myosotis palustris (1867)
Petunia ×*hybrida* (1860)
Phlox drummondii (1889)
Polianthes tuberosa 'The Pearl' (1889)
Portulaca grandiflora (1889)
Reseda odorata (1889)
Salpiglossis sinuata (1889)
Salvia splendens (1846)
Scabiosa atropurpurea (1889)
Solenostemon scutelloides (1874)
Thunbergia alata (1889)
Verbena ×*hybrida* (1889)
Zantedeschia aethiopica (1874)
Zinnia (1889)

Great Lakes Region, 1900–1924

Plants common to at least five of ten nursery catalogs and not included in a previous list for this region:

*Acer platanoides (1858)
**Aristolochia macrophylla* (1845)
Betula pendula 'Laciniata' (1858)
Catalpa speciosa (1878)
Clematis 'Jackmanii' (1889)
Clematis terniflora (1896)
**Digitalis purpurea* (1835)
Hydrangea paniculata 'Grandiflora' (1877)
**Juniperus communis* 'Hibernica' (1894)
**Ligustrum ovalifolium* (1893)
*Maclura pomifera (1843)
*Paeonia 'Festiva Maxima' (1872)
Parthenocissus tricuspidata (1877)
**Populus deltoides* (1887)
Rosa 'Aglaia' (1901)
Rosa 'Dorothy Perkins' (1905)
Rosa 'Général Jacqueminot' (1874)
Rosa 'Gruss an Teplitz' (1904)
*Rosa 'Hermosa' (1845)
Rosa 'Maréchal Niel' (1874)
Rosa 'Mrs. John Laing' (1889)
Rosa 'Paul Neyron' (1877)
Rosa 'Perle des Jardins' (1889)
*Rosa 'Prince Camille Rohan' (1874)
*Rosa 'Seven Sisters' (1843)
Rosa 'Turner's Crimson Rambler' (1896)
Spiraea japonica 'Anthony Waterer' (1901)
Spiraea ×*vanhouttei* (1889)
Tilia americana (1845)
*Ulmus americana (1843)
Viburnum plicatum (1893)
Weigela florida (1858)

Great Lakes Region, 1925–1940

Plants common to at least four of five nursery catalogs and not included in a previous list for this region:

Anchusa azurea 'Dropmore' (1925)

Berberis thunbergii (1896)

Buddleia (1920)

Chamaecyparis pisifera (1894)

Chamaecyparis pisifera 'Plumosa Aurea' (1894)

Clematis 'Henryi' (1889)

Clematis 'Madame Edouard André' (ca. 1905)

Cornus paniculata (1925)

Delphinium Belladonna Group (1925)

Deutzia gracilis (1858)

Deutzia scabra 'Plena' (1901)

Gypsophila paniculata (1872)

Hydrangea arborescens 'Grandiflora' (1908)

Juniperus ×*pfitzeriana* (1925)

Kniphofia 'Pfitzeri' (1905)

Ligustrum amurense (1925)

Lonicera japonica 'Halliana' (1877)

Malus angustifolia (1845)

Malus ioensis 'Plena' (1845)

Morus alba 'Pendula' (1896)

Paeonia 'Edulis Superba' (1925)

Paeonia 'Felix Crousse' (1925)

Paeonia 'Karl Rosenfeld' (1925)

Paeonia 'Monsieur Jules Elie' (1925)

Paeonia officinalis 'Rubra Plena' (1896)

Philadelphus coronarius 'Aureus' (1896)

Populus nigra 'Italica' (1845)

Rosa 'American Beauty' (1920)

Rosa 'Dr. W. Van Fleet' (1920)

Rosa 'Excelsa' (1920)

Rosa 'Frau Karl Druschki' (ca. 1905)

Rosa 'Madame Caroline Testout' (1897)

Rosa 'Mrs. Aaron Ward' (1920)

Rosa 'Silver Moon' (1920)

Rosa 'Soleil d' Or' (1905)

Rosa 'Souvenir de Claudius Pernet' (1925)

Rosa 'Tausendschön' (1920)

Tamarix africanus (1858)

Tanacetum coccineum (1889)

Thuja occidentalis 'Globosa' (1878)

CENTRAL AND GREAT PLAINS REGION

Iowa, Kansas, Missouri, Nebraska, North Dakota, Oklahoma, South Dakota

Central and Great Plains Region, 1853–1874

Plants common to at least three of five nursery lists:

Abies balsamea (1860)

Abutilon pictum (1860)

Aloysia triphylla (1860)

Calycanthus floridus (1853)

Campsis radicans (1853)

Chaenomeles spp. (1853)

Cotinus coggygria (1853)

Dahlia (1853)

Deutzia scabra (1860)

Dicentra spectabilis (1860)

Hibiscus syriacus (1853)

Hosta plantaginea (1860)

Hosta ventricosa (1860)

Larix decidua (1860)

Lonicera periclymenum 'Belgica' (1860)

Lonicera sempervirens (1853)

Paeonia (1853)

Pelargonium graveolens (1860)

Pelargonium 'Nutmeg-scented' (1860)

Pelargonium tomentosum (1860)

Phlox (1853)

Picea abies (1860)

Pinus nigra (1860)

Pinus strobus (1853)

Pinus sylvestris (1860)

Populus nigra "Italica" (1860)

Prunus glandulosa (1853)

Rosa 'Baltimore Belle' (1869)

Rosa 'Bougere' (1860)

Rosa 'Géant des Batailles' (1860)

Rosa 'Général Jacqueminot' (1860)

Rosa 'George IV' (1853)

Rosa 'La Reine' (1860)

Rosa 'Louis Philippe' (1853)

Rosa 'Madame Laffay' (1860)

Rosa 'Queen of the Prairies' (1853)

Syringa vulgaris (1853)

Tanacetum parthenium (1860)

Thuja occidentalis (1853)

Tsuga canadensis (1860)

Verbena ×*hybrida* (1853)

Veronica gentianoides (1860)

Viburnum opulus 'Roseum' (1853)

Weigela florida (1860)

Wisteria sinensis (1860)

Yucca filamentosa (1860)

Central and Great Plains Region, 1875–1899

Plants common to at least four of nine nursery catalogs and not included in a previous list for this region:

Acer negundo (1884)

Acer platanoides (1860)

Acer saccharinum (1860)

Acer saccharum (1860)

*Ageratum houstonianum (1860)

*Alcea rosea (1871)

*Begonia (1871)

*Bellis perennis (1860)

Berberis vulgaris 'Atropurpurea' (1860)

Betula pendula (1884)

Betula pendula 'Laciniata' (1885)

*Callistephus chinensis (1871)

*Canna indica (1869)

Catalpa speciosa (1853)

Chaenomeles spp. (1853)

*Chrysanthemum (1860)

Clematis 'Jackmanii' (1885)

Dianthus barbatus (1871)

Dianthus caryophyllus (1869)

Forsythia viridissima (1860)

Fraxinus americana (1860)

Gladiolus (1869)

*Heliotropium arborescens (1860)

Juniperus communis 'Hibernica' (1871)

Juniperus virginiana (1860)

*Lantana camara (1860)

Liriodendron tulipifera (1871)

*Lobelia erinus (1871)

Lonicera tatarica (1860)

Morus alba var. *tatarica* (1884)

Parthenocissus quinquefolia (1860)

Petunia ×*hybrida* (1860)

Philadelphus coronarius (1860)

Polianthes tuberosa (1876)

*Portulaca grandiflora (1853)

Prunus glandulosa (1853)

Rosa 'Baltimore Belle' (1871)

Rosa 'Madame Plantier' (1860)

Rosa 'Queen of the Prairies' (1853)

Rosa 'Seven Sisters' (1860)

Salix caprea 'Pendula' (1885)

Salix ×*pendulina* (1886)

Sorbus aucuparia (1860)

Sorbus ×*thuringiaca* (1885)

Syringa ×*persica* (1876)

Syringa vulgaris var. *alba* (1860)

Tilia americana (1871)

Ulmus americana (1860)

Ulmus glabra 'Camperdowni' (1885)

*Viola tricolor (1860)

*Zinnia elegans (1875)

Central and Great Plains Region, 1900–1924

Plants common to at least five of nine catalogs and not included in a previous list for this region:

*Achillea ptarmica (1860)

*Amaranthus tricolor (1876)

*Antirrhinum majus (1860)

*Calendula officinalis (1875)

*Celastrus scandens (1860)

*Centaurea cineraria (1876)

*Centaurea cyanus (1875)

*Clematis terniflora (1899)

*Cobaea scandens (1875)

*Colocasia esculenta (1876)

*Consolida ajacis (1875)

*Convallaria majalis (1860)

*Delphinium formosum (1871)

*Deutzia gracilis (1871)

*Dianthus caryophyllus (1869)

*Dianthus chinensis (1875)

*Dianthus plumarius (1875)

Dicentra spectabilis (1860)

*Digitalis purpurea (1860)

Dioscorea batatas (1908)

*Eschscholzia californica (1875)

*Gomphrena globosa (1875)

*Helichrysum bracteatum (1875)

*Hemerocallis lilioasphodelus (1853)

Hydrangea paniculata 'Grandiflora' (1871)

*Ipomoea quamoclit (1875)

*Iris (1871)

*Juglans nigra (1886)

Lathyrus odoratus (1875)

Leucanthemum ×superbum (1908)

Lilium auratum (1869)

Lilium lancifolium (1853)

Lilium speciosum (1869)

Lilium speciosum var. *rubrum* (1869)

Linum perenne (1875)

Lonicera japonica 'Halliana' (1871)

Lychnis chalcedonica (1875)

Paeonia 'Festiva Maxima' (1869)

Papaver orientale (1875)

Picea pungens f. *glauca* (1899)

Populus alba (1853)

Populus nigra 'Italica' (1860)

Rosa 'American Beauty' (1908)

Rosa 'Gruss an Teplitz' (1908)

Solenostemon scutellinoides (1875)

Spiraea japonica 'Anthony Waterer' (1908)

Spiraea prunifolia (1860)

Spiraea ×vanhouttei (1908)

Tagetes erecta (1875)

Tagetes patula (1875)

Tropaeolum peregrinium (1875)

Central and Great Plains Region, 1925–1940

Plants common to at least three of five catalogs and not included in a previous list for this region:

Anredera cordifolia (1884)

Aquilegia caerulea (1914)

Berberis thunbergii (1918)

Brachycome iberdifolia (1884)

Canna 'Roi Humbert' (1914)

Caragana arborescens (1919)

Cardiospermum helicacabum (1875)

Catalpa bungei (1919)

Celosia argentea Childsii Group (1927)

Clematis 'Henryi' (1908)

Coreopsis lanceolata (1908)

Coreopsis tinctoria (1875)

Cornus stolonifera (1914)

Cosmos bipinnatus (1908)

Curcubita spp. and other ornamental gourds (1875)

Elaeagnus angustifolia (1887)

Gypsophila paniculata (1876)

Hydrangea arborescens (1914)

Impatiens balsamina (1884)

Ipomoea tricolor 'Heavenly Blue' (1927)

Iris 'Madame Chereau' (1914)

Kochia scoparia (1908)

Lathyrus latifolius (1875)

Lathyrus odoratus 'America' (1908)

Lilium lancifolium 'Flore Pleno' (1914)

Linum grandiflorum 'Rubrum' (1875)

Lobularia maritima 'Little Gem' (1908)

Lycium barbarum (1914)

Malus ioensis 'Plena' (1919)

Mesembryanthemum crystallinum (1876)

Mirabilis jalapa (1875)

Momordica balsamina (1875)

Myosotis palustris (1860)

Nigella damascena (1875)

Paeonia 'Edulis Superba' (1919)

Paeonia 'Felix Crousse' (1919)

Paeonia 'Karl Rosenfeld' (1919)

Paeonia 'Louis Van Houtte' (1921)

Papaver rhoeas (1908)

Papaver rhoeas 'American Legion' (1927)

Papaver somniferum (1875)

Parthenocissus tricuspidata (1876)

Petunia 'Rosy Morn' (1927)

Phaseolus coccineus (1884)

Philadelphus ×lemonei (1914)

Picea glauca 'Densata' (1899)

Platycodon grandiflorus (1860)

Populus deltoides (1887)

Prunus triloba (1871)

Reseda odorata (1875)

Rhus typhina 'Dissecta' (1921)

Ricinus communis (1875)

Robinia pseudoacacia (1884)

Rosa 'Dorothy Perkins' (1908)

Rosa 'F. J. Grootendorst' (1927)

Rosa 'Frau Karl Druschki' (1914)

Rosa 'Kaiserin Auguste Viktoria' (1908)

Rosa 'Madame Caroline Testout' (1919)

Rosa 'Madame Norbert Levavasseur' (1908)

Rosa 'Mrs. Aaron Ward' (1927)

Rosa 'Prince Camille de Rohan' (1914)

Rosa 'Tausendschön' (1914)

Rosa 'Turner's Crimson Rambler' (1908)

Rosa 'White Dorothy' (1914)

Rudbeckia laciniata 'Golden Glow' (1908)

Salix alba var. *vitellina* (1853)

Salix pentandra (1887)

Salvia splendens (1860)

Scabiosa atropurpurea (1876)

Schizanthus pinnatus (1875)

Spiraea ×billardii (1860)

Spiraea thunbergii (1876)

Symphoricarpos albus (1860)

Symphoricarpos orbiculatus (1860)

Tanacetum coccineum (1871)

Tropaeolum majus (1875)

Viburnum trilobum (1871)

Vinca minor (1871)

Wisteria sinensis 'Alba' (1908)

MOUNTAIN AND WESTERN STATES

Arizona, California, Colorado, Idaho, Montana, Nevada, New Mexico, Oregon, Utah, Washington, Wyoming

Mountain and Western States, 1870–1899

Plants common to at least four of eight nursery catalogs:

Abutilon (1873)

Acacia melanoxylon (1872)

Acacia molissima (1880)

Acer negundo (1873)

Agapanthus africanus (1874)

Agave (1874)

Albizia julibrissin (1880)

Aloysia triphylla (1880)

Calocedros decurrens (1874)

Camellia japonica (1891)

Campsis radicans (1873)

Canna indica (1873)

Chaenomeles spp. (1873)

Chamaecyparis lawsoniana (1874)

Chamaerops humilis (1880)

Chrysanthemum (1873)

Cinnamomum camphora (ca. 1875)

Colocasia esculenta (1880)

Cordyline australis (1880)

Cortaderia selloana (1873)

Cryptomeria japonica (1872)

Cupressus funebris (1872)

Cupressus macrocarpa (1874)

Dahlia (1873)

Dianthus caryophyllus (1873)

Dracaena (1880)

Eriobotrya japonica (1880)

Erythrina crista-galli (1873)

Eucalyptus globulus (ca. 1855)

Euonymus japonicus (1873)

Fraxinus americanus (1873)

Fuchsia (1880)

Ginkgo biloba (1873)

Gladiolus (1880)

Grevillea robusta (1880)

Hibiscus syriacus (1873)

Jasminum (1889)

Juniperus chinensis 'Hibernica' (1873)

Lagerstroemia indica (1880)

Lilium longiflorum (1873)

Lilium pardilinum (1874)

Liriodendron tulipifera (1873)

Magnolia acuminata (1874)

Magnolia grandiflora (1874)

Melia azedarach (1880)

Melia azedarach 'Umbraculiformis' (1892)

Nerium oleander (1873)

Passiflora caerulea (1873)

Pelargonium (1873)

Petunia ×hybrida (1873)

Phoenix dactylifera (1880)

Phormiun tenax (1872)

Phormium tenax 'Variegata' (1872)

Picea abies (1873)

Pinus ponderosa (1880)

Pinus radiata (1874)

Pittosporum (1880)

Platycladus orientalis (1873)

Platycladus orientalis 'Aurea' (1873)

Plumbago auriculata (1880)

Populus deltoides (1873)

Populus nigra 'Italica' (1873)

Prunus persica 'Plena' (1891)

Pseudotsuga menziesii (1880)

Punica granatum (1873)

Rosa 'Bougere' (1889)

Rosa 'Géant des Batailles' (1889)

Rosa 'Général Jacqueminot' (1889)

Rosa 'Homère' (1889)

Rosa laevigata (1889)

Rosa 'Marie Van Houtte' (1889)

Rosa 'Perle des Jardins' (1889)

Rosa 'Sunset' (1889)

Rosa 'The Bride' (1889)

Rosa 'Triomphe du Luxembourg' (1889)

Sabal palmetto (1874)

Salix alba (1873)

Salix alba var. *vitellina* (1873)

Schinus molle (1874)

Sciadopitys verticillata (1889)

Sequoiadendron giganteum (1874)

Serenoa repens (1874)

Solenostemon scutellinoides (1873)

Sorbus aucuparia (1880)

Syringa vulgaris var. *alba* (1880)

Taxus baccata (1889)

Thuja occidentalis (1873)

Thuja occidentalis 'Aurea' (1880)

Trachycarpus fortunei (1873)

Ulmus americana (1873)

Verbena ×*hybrida* (1873)

Viburnum opulus 'Roseum' (1873)

Viburnum tinus (1880)

Viola tricolor (1873)

Weigela florida (1873)

Wisteria sinensis (1880)

Wisteria sinensis 'Alba' (1889)

Yucca whipplei (1874)

Zantedeschia aethiopica (1873)

Mountain and Western States, 1900–1924

Ornamental plants common to at least five of nine catalogs and not included in a previous list for this region:

Ageratum houstonianum (1873)

Alcea rosea (1873)

Antirrhinum majus (1873)

Begonia (1891)

Bellis perennis (1873)

Calendula officinalis (1880)

Callistephus chinensis (1873)

**Calycanthus floridus* (1873)

*Canna indica (1873)

Centaurea cyanus (1907)

Clematis 'Jackmanii' (1880)

Consolida ajacis (1873)

**Convallaria majalis* (1873)

Coreopsis lanceolata (1891)

Cosmos bipinnatus (1891)

*Cycas revoluta (1892)

Dianthus barbatus (1873)

Digitalis purpurea (1873)

Erysimum cheiri (1873)

Eschscholzia californica (1874)

Gypsophila elegans (1907)

Gypsophila paniculata (1907)

**Heliotropium arborescens* (1873)

Impatiens balsamina (1873)

Ipomoea purpurea (1873)

Ipomoea quamoclit (1907)

Lantana camara (1880)

Lathyrus odoratus (1873)

Leucanthemum ×*superbum* (1890)

*Lilium auratum (1892)

*Lilium speciosum (1892)

*Lilium speciosum var. *rubrum* (1892)

Liriodendron tulipifera (1873)

Lobelia erinus (1873)

Lobularia maritima (1886)

Matthiola incana (1873)

**Mesembryanthemum crystallinum* (1880)

Mirabilis jalapa (1880)

Nigella damascena (1907)

Paeonia (1892)

Papaver nudicaule (1907)

Papaver orientale (1907)

Papaver rhoeas (1891)

Parthenocissus quinquefolia (1894)

Parthenocissus tricuspidata (1880)

**Philadelphus coronarius* (1894)

*Phlox (1873)

Phlox drummondii (1873)

**Polianthes tuberosa* (1880)

Portulaca grandiflora (1880)

Reseda odorata (1873)

Rosa 'American Beauty' (1889)

Rosa 'Kaiserin Auguste Viktoria' (1895)

Rosa 'La France' (1891)

Rosa 'Madame Caroline Testout' (1907)

*Rosa 'Papa Gontier' (1889)

Salpiglossis sinuatus (1873)

Salvia splendens (1891)

Scabiosa atropurpurea (1873)

*Spiraea ×*vanhouttei* (1894)

Syringa vulgaris (1880)

Tagetes erecta (1873)

Tanacetum parthenium (1894)

**Thuja occidentalis* (1873)

Tropaeolum majus (1873)

Zinnia (1873)

Mountain and Western States, 1925–1940

Plants common to at least four of seven nursery catalogs and not included in a previous list for this region:

**Acroclinium roseum* (1873)

**Amaranthus caudatus* (1873)

*Arctotis grandis (1907)

Aurinia saxatilis (1873)

Berberis thunbergii (1892)

Buddleia (1894)

Campanula medium (1873)

Celosia argentea Plumosa Group (1907)

Celosia argentea var. *cristata* (1907)

Coreopsis tinctoria (1891)

Curcubita spp., and other ornamental gourds (1873)

Delphinium Belladonna Group (1912)

**Helianthus annuus* (1908)

Helichrysum bracteatum (1891)

*Lablab purpureus (1873)

Limonium latifolium (1874)

Linum grandiflorum 'Coccineum' (1907)

*Lobelia erinus 'Crystal Palace' (1907)

**Myosotis alpestris* (1907)

Syringa ×*persica* (1889)

Tagetes patula (1880)

Tanacetum coccineum (1895)

*Thunbergia alata (1873)

APPENDIX B
Historic Commercial Plant Sources

THE FIRST SET OF TABLES in this appendix categorizes by region all commercial sources cited in the Encyclopedia of Heirloom Ornamental Plants. This section will give details to the serious garden researcher as to exactly who offered what in the old nursery and seed catalogs and advertisements. All references do not list the same types of plants, nor do all regions have the same number of resources. When dealing with historical topics, one has to use what one can find. Sometimes only a few pages of a catalog were available. Sometimes, a nursery had issued several different catalogs, but only one was extant, so only a portion of that nursery's plants are represented. Some of the citations are early newspaper advertisements and several are those reported by other researchers.

Under *Abbreviation* are the codes, indicating historic commercial sources, used in the plant tables. These codes are composed of initials particular to the source and the last three digits of the year of issue. The name, location, and year of the source are included. If an entry lacks a code and says *Ref*, that catalog was used solely for reference or for an illustration and its plants are not included in the appendix.

The types of plants offered in each document and the total number of taxa occupy the fifth and sixth columns. Under *Plants*, A stands for annuals; B, bulbs; P, perennials; R, roses; S, shrubs; T, trees; and V, vines.

The repository of the original material is listed under *Loc* wherever possible. In some cases, photocopies were used and their contributors are indicated. Secondary sources are included.

AT—photocopy, courtesy of Arthur Tucker, Delaware State College

CGL—Cherokee Garden Library, Atlanta, Georgia

CWRU—Case Western Reserve University, Cleveland, Ohio

DA—author's collection

GG—photocopy, courtesy of Greg Grant, Center, Texas

GS—photocopy, courtesy of George Stritikis, Homewood, Alabama

LHB—Liberty H. Bailey Hortorum, Cornell University, Ithaca, New York

LL—Lloyd Library, Cincinnati, Ohio

MOHS—*Missouri Horticultural Society Proceedings* 1887

MHS—Massachusetts Horticultural Society, Boston, Massachusetts

NAL—National Agricultural Library, Beltsville, Maryland

OHS—Ohio Historical Society, Columbus, Ohio

SGHS—Southern Garden History Society Plant List (Chappell 2000)

SK—photocopy, courtesy of Scott Kunst, Old House Gardens, Ann Arbor, Michigan

Smith—Smithsonian Institution, Washington, D.C.

TE—Trail End State Historic Site, Sheridan, Wyoming

UDel—University of Delaware, Newark, Delaware

UMn—Andersen Horticulture Library, University of Minnesota

UVA—University of Virginia, Charlottesville, Virginia; mf indicates microfilm of original document

In order to compile a more specific plant list for your location, first locate the tables that list catalogs for your region. For example, if you wish to compile a plant list for an 1889 Queen Anne–style house in St. Louis, go to the Central and Great Plains tables. Record all catalogs that offered plants in Missouri prior to 1889. Assume that once a plant has been introduced into an area it remains there, although that might not always be the case. Your list might include these references:

CS860	St. Louis Nursery, St. Louis, MO	1860
Bf869	Brookfield Nursery, Brookfield, MO	1869
PS875	Plant Seed Co., St. Louis, MO	1875
Mic876	Henry Michel & Co, St. Louis, MO	1876
PS884	Plant Seed Company, St. Louis, MO	1884
Kv887	Kirksville Nursery, Kirksville, MO	1887
Sk887	Stark Nurseries, Louisiana, MO	1887
Srx887	Sarcoxie Nurseries, Sarcoxie, MO	1887

Lengthy source lists do not result for every state and era, although each region has adequate representation. Remember also that after the construction of the transcontinental railway, transporting goods from one area to another was affordable. Start with those nurseries that were closest to your dwelling for your plant list, but keep in mind that plants may have come into that area via a variety of sources, including local and more distant nurseries, and could have been carried in by the inhabitants and shared among themselves.

Next, survey the tables of heirloom ornamental plants in this appendix and list those plants that indicate any of the eight sources. The result will be a list of trees, shrubs, and herbaceous plants that are historically and geographically appropriate for your landscape.

COMMERCIAL SOURCES CITED IN THE ENCYCLOPEDIA

NEW ENGLAND
Connecticut, Maine, Massachusetts, New Hampshire, Rhode Island, Vermont

pre-1800

Abbrev.	Nursery or Seed Company	City, State	Year	Plants	Taxa	Loc.
BG719	E. Davies, *Boston Gazette*, 29 Feb.–7 Mar. 1719	Boston, MA	1719	P	1	UVAmf
Bst760	J. Townley, *The Boston Evening-Post*, 31 Mar. 1760	Boston, MA	1760	ABPV	58	UVAmf

1800–1849

Abbrev.	Nursery or Seed Company	City, State	Year	Plants	Taxa	Loc.
Ken832	William Kenrick	Boston, MA	1832	ABPRSTV	527	LHB
Br833	Brighton Nursery	Boston, MA	1833	ABPRSTV	663	LHB
H834	Hovey & Co.	Boston, MA	1834	ABPV	132	MHS
H835	Hovey & Co.	Boston, MA	1835	ABPV	81	MHS
Ken835	William Kenrick	Boston, MA	1835	ABPV	225	LHB
Bt836	George C. Barrett	Boston, MA	1836	ABPSTV	574	LHB
H836	Hovey & Co.	Boston, MA	1836	BPV	81	MHS
Bk838	Joseph Breck & Co.	Boston, MA	1838	APV	61	NAL
H839	Hovey & Co.	Boston, MA	1839	ABPV	74	MHS
Br841	Brighton Nursery	Boston, MA	1841	ABPRSTV	1253	LHB
H844	Hovey & Co.	Boston, MA	1844	P	31	UDel
Bk845	Joseph Breck & Co.	Boston, MA	1845	P	134	LHB
H845	Hovey & Co.	Boston, MA	1845	P	38	MHS
H847	Hovey & Co.	Boston, MA	1847	BPV	57	?

1850–1874

Abbrev.	Nursery or Seed Company	City, State	Year	Plants	Taxa	Loc.
Bk851	Joseph Breck & Co.	Boston, MA	1851	ABPV	179	MHS
H852	Hovey & Co.	Boston, MA	1852	BPV	178	MHS
R853	H. S. Ramsdell	Thompson, CT	1853	BPRST	86	DA

Sac853	Saco Nurseries	Saco, ME	1853	PRSTV	140	NAL
OC857	Old Colony Nurseries	Plymouth, MA	1857	ABPSV	135	UDel
H859	Hovey & Co.	Boston, MA	1859	ABPV	226	MHS
OC861	Old Colony Nurseries	Plymouth, MA	1861	BPRST	91	?
H862	Hovey & Co.	Boston, MA	1862	ABPV	128	MHS
H863	Hovey & Co.	Boston, MA	1863	ABPV	130	MHS
H866	Hovey & Co.	Boston, MA	1866	BP	41	UDel
Wd867	Theodore C. H. Wendel	Boston, MA	1867	ABPSV	557	LHB
Bk869	Joseph Breck & Co.	Boston, MA	1869	P	89	UDel
Ref	Washburn & Co.	Boston, MA	1870			DA
Bk871	Joseph Breck & Co.	Boston, MA	1871	BPV	112	MHS
Ref	Benjamin Wells	Boston, MA	1871			UDel
H873	Hovey & Co.	Boston, MA	1873	BPV	118	UDel

1875–1899

Abbrev.	Nursery or Seed Company	City, State	Year	Plants	Taxa	Loc.
Bk875	Joseph Breck & Co.	Boston, MA	1875	PV	85	UDel
H875	Hovey & Co.	Boston, MA	1875	ABPV	144	CWRU
Mn875	Manning Nurseries	Reading, MA	1875	BP	48	CWRU
Bk878	Joseph Breck & Co.	Boston, MA	1878	BPV	112	MHS
G879	Edward Gillett	Southwick, MA	1879	BPSV	77	MHS
G880	Edward Gillett	Southwick, MA	1880	BPSTV	275	UDel
Bk881	Joseph Breck & Co.	Boston, MA	1881	BPV	114	MHS
Rd881	Reading Nursery	Reading, MA	1881	BPRSTV	93	DA
G883	Edward Gillett	Southwick, MA	1883	ABPS	177	MHS
G886	Edward Gillett	Southwick, MA	1886	BPSV	154	MHS
Mn887	Manning Nurseries	Reading, MA	1887	BPSV	258	MHS
H888	Hovey & Co.	Boston, MA	1888	ABPV	93	UDel
CA889	C. E. Allen	Brattleboro, VT	1889	ABPRSTV	1340	DA
Mn889	Manning Nurseries	Reading, MA	1889	BPSV	440	MHS
G890	Edward Gillett	Southwick, MA	1890	BPSV	197	MHS
Bk894	Joseph Breck & Co.	Boston, MA	1894	ABP	108	MHS
Ell894	Ellis Brothers	Keene, NH	1894	APV	32	Smith

1900–1924

Abbrev.	Nursery or Seed Company	City, State	Year	Plants	Taxa	Loc.
Du901	R. B. Dunning & Co.	Bangor, ME	1901	APRSV	108	DA
NE910	New England Nurseries	Bedford, MA	1910	BPRSTV	1084	DA
G914	Edward Gillett	Southwick, MA	1914	BPRSTV	573	DA
Gg915	J. J. H. Gregory & Son	Marblehead, MA	1915	ABPSV	255	DA
Bk917	Joseph Breck & Sons	Boston, MA	1917	ABPRSTV	1105	DA

1925–1940

Abbrev.	Nursery or Seed Company	City, State	Year	Plants	Taxa	Loc.
Fsk927	Fiske Seed Co.	Boston, MA	1927	BPSTV	419	DA
Gg928	J. J. H. Gregory & Son	Marblehead, MA	1928	ABPSV	247	DA
Hrd931	F. H. Horsford	Charlotte, VT	1931	ABPRSTV	752	DA
ASL937	Allen, Sterling & Lothrop	Portland, ME	1937	ABPV	122	DA
Bar939	W. E. Barrett	Providence, RI	1939	ABPSV	356	DA

MIDDLE ATLANTIC
Delaware, Maryland, New Jersey, New York, Pennsylvania, Washington, D.C.

1770–1799

Abbrev.	Nursery or Seed Company	City, State	Year	Plants	Taxa	Loc.
Pr771	William Prince	Flushing, NY	1771	PSTV	54	Hedrick 1988 (reprint)
JB783	Bartram Nursery	Philadelphia, PA	1783	ABPSTV	286	
Pr790	William Prince	Flushing, NY	1790	BRSTV	81	AT
JB792	Bartram Nursery	Philadelphia, PA	1792	PRSTV	90	NAL
GM796	Goldthwaite & Moore	Philadelphia, PA	1796	PV	28	UDel
Pr799	William Prince	Flushing, NY	1799	P	3	AT

1800–1824

Abbrev.	Nursery or Seed Company	City, State	Year	Plants	Taxa	Loc.
M804	Bernard M'Mahon	Philadelphia, PA	1804	ABPRSTV	638	LHB
JB807	Bartram Nursery	Philadelphia, PA	1807	ABPRSTV	458	NAL
WB810	William Booth	Baltimore, MD	1810	ABPRSTV	196	NAL
Ln811	D. & C. Landreth	Philadelphia, PA	1811	BPV	123	UDel
Pr818	William Prince	Flushing, NY	1818	ABPSV	188	NAL
Bld819	James Bloodgood & Co.	Flushing, NY	1819	BPRSTV	239	NAL
Pr820	William Prince	Flushing, NY	1820	BPV	154	SK
Pr822	William Prince	Flushing, NY	1822	ABPV	197	NAL, LHB
PM822	Prince & Mills	Flushing, NY	1822	BPV	29	NAL

1825–1849

Abbrev.	Nursery or Seed Company	City, State	Year	Plants	Taxa	Loc.
Ln826	D. & C. Landreth	Philadelphia, PA	1826	BPV	188	NAL
Pr826	William Prince	Flushing, NY	1826	ABPRSTV	1158	LHB
Ab827	Albany Nursery	Albany, NY	1827	BP	41	LHB
Tb827	G. Thorburn & Son	New York, NY	1827	ABPRSTV	235	NAL
Ln828	D. & C. Landreth	Philadelphia, PA	1828	BPV	214	CWRU
Pr829	William Prince	Flushing, NY	1829	ABPV	420	CWRU
Ab830	Albany Nursery	Albany, NY	1830	BP	39	LHB
Pr831	William Prince	Flushing, NY	1831	ABPV	452	LHB
TH834	Thomas Hogg	New York, NY	1834	ABPRSTV	394	LHB
Ab839	Albany Nursery	Albany, NY	1839	ABPV	86	LHB
Ref	William Prince	Flushing, NY	1841			DA
Bu844	Robert Buist	Philadelphia, PA	1844	BPV	150	NAL
Pr844	William Prince	Flushing, NY	1844	P	318	NAL
Wn844	Winter & Co.	Flushing, NY	1844	ABPRSTV	1268	LHB
Ln847	D. & C. Landreth	Philadelphia, PA	1847	PV	40	UDel
EB848	Ellwanger & Barry	Rochester, NY	1848	ABPV	174	LHB

1850–1874

Abbrev.	Nursery or Seed Company	City, State	Year	Plants	Taxa	Loc.
Pr854	William Prince	Flushing, NY	1854	BPV	158	UDel
Bu857	R. Buist	Philadelphia, PA	1857	BPV	103	MHS
Pr857	William Prince	Flushing, NY	1857	ABPSV	1234	MHS
Bu859	R. Buist	Philadelphia, PA	1859	BPSTV	536	NAL
Bu860	R. Buist	Philadelphia, PA	1860	BPV	92	MHS
EB860	Ellwanger & Barry	Rochester, NY	1860	ABPRSTV	1727	NAL

Pr860	William Prince	Flushing, NY	1860	BPV	302	LHB
EB862	Ellwanger & Barry	Rochester, NY	1862	BPV	306	NAL
Bu866	R. Buist	Philadelphia, PA	1866	BPV	106	MHS
EB867	Ellwanger & Barry	Rochester, NY	1867	ABPV	516	NAL
Ln868	D. Landreth & Sons	Philadelphia, PA	1868	PV	50	LHB
Ref	B. K. Bliss & Son	New York, NY	1869			DA
MM870	Moon Mahlon	Morrisville, PA	1870	BPRSTV	332	DA
OK870	M. O'Keefe, Son & Co.	Rochester, NY	1870	ABPV	604	DA
BB873	Briggs & Bros.	Rochester, NY	1873	BPV	425	DA
Ref	James Vick	Rochester, NY	1873			DA

1875–1899

Abbrev.	Nursery or Seed Company	City, State	Year	Plants	Taxa	Loc.
EB875	Ellwanger & Barry	Rochester, NY	1875	BPV	532	CWRU
Dr876	Henry A. Dreer	Philadelphia, PA	1876	ABPRSTV	1629	DA
Ln879	D. Landreth & Sons	Philadelphia, PA	1879	PV	38	LHB
JV881	James Vick	Rochester, NY	1881	R	34	DA
Ref	Dingee & Conard Co.	West Grove, PA	1882			DA
EB882	Ellwanger & Barry	Rochester, NY	1882	ABPV	249	LHB
Ln884	D. & C. Landreth	Philadelphia, PA	1884	PV	45	LHB
Ln889	D. Landreth & Sons	Philadelphia, PA	1889	BPV	47	DA
Ref	John Lewis Childs	Floral Park, NY	1894			DA
Ref	Green's Nursery Co.	Rochester, NY	1894			DA
AB895	A. Blanc	Philadelphia, PA	ca.1895	BPSTV	193	DA
Ref	Wm. Henry Maule	Philadelphia, PA	1897			DA
Ref	The Lovett Co.	Little Silver, NJ	1898			DA
Ref	Peter Henderson & Co.	New York, NY	1899			DA
Ref	James Vick	Rochester, NY	1899			DA

1900–1924

Abbrev.	Nursery or Seed Company	City, State	Year	Plants	Taxa	Loc.
Ref	Peter Henderson & Co.	New York, NY	1903			DA
HwC905	Hooker, Wyman, & Co.	Rochester, NY	ca.1905	BPRSTV	91	DA
Ric905	Rice Brothers	Geneva, NY	ca.1905	BPRSTV	34	DA
Ref	John Lewis Childs	Floral Park, NY	1907			DA
Ref	Henry A. Dreer	Philadelphia, PA	1908			DA
Ref	J. M. Thorburn	New York, NY	1908			DA
JC910	John Lewis Childs	Floral Park, NY	1910	ABPRSTV	191	DA
PH910	Peter Henderson & Co.	New York, NY	1910	ABPRSTV	1231	DA
Ref	John Lewis Childs	Floral Park, NY	1914			DA
Ref	Peter Henderson & Co.	New York, NY	1915			DA
EB917	Ellwanger & Barry	Rochester, NY	1917	PRSTV	1304	DA
Ref	Bertrand H. Farr	Wyomissing, PA	1920			DA
HN922	Harrison's Nurseries	Berlin, MD	1922	BPRSTV	141	DA
Dk924	William C. Duckham	Madison, NJ	1924	PRS	126	DA

1925–1940

Abbrev.	Nursery or Seed Company	City, State	Year	Plants	Taxa	Loc.
Ref	Dingee & Conard	West Grove, PA	1925			DA
Ref	Henry A. Dreer	Philadelphia, PA	1925			DA
Bol928	F. W. Bolgiano & Co.	Washington, DC	1928	ABPV	289	DA
Mch931	Henry F. Michell	Philadelphia, PA	1931	ABPRSV	794	DA
JHr934	Joseph Harris	Coldwater, NY	1934	ABPV	334	DA
My934	Maloney Bros. Nursery	Dansville, NY	1934	APRSTV	346	DA
Bun939	Bunting Nurseries, Inc.	Selbyville, DE	1939	PRSTV	166	DA

SOUTH

Alabama, Arkansas, Florida, Georgia, Kentucky, Louisiana, Mississippi, North Carolina, South Carolina, Tennessee, Texas, Virginia, West Virginia

1750–1799

Abbrev.	Advertisement or Seed Company	City, State	Year	Plants	Taxa	Loc.
TA754	Thomas Arnott, *South Carolina Gazette*, 19 Dec. 1754	Charleston, SC	1754	B	2	UVAmf
JW765	John Watson, *South Carolina Gazette*, 10 Nov. 1765	Charleston, SC	1765	B	6	UVAmf
PC768	Peter Crowells, Dec. 1786	Charleston, SC	1768	BPR	10	Richardson 1941
MC792	Minton Collins, *Virginia Gazette*, 5 Nov. 1792	Richmond, VA	1792	BP	11	SGHS
MC793	Minton Collins	Richmond, VA	1793	ABPR	12	AT
JS793	Joseph Simpson, *The Virginia Gazette*, 29 Mar. 1793	Petersburg, VA	1793	RT	10	UVAmf
GF799	George French, *The Virginia Herald*, 15 Jan. 1799	Fredericksburg, VA	1799	ABP	30	SGHS

1800–1849

Abbrev.	Advertisement	City, State	Year	Plants	Taxa	Loc.
JBy808	John Bryant, *Charleston Times*, 13 Feb. 1808	Charleston, SC	1808	AT	2	
RSq812	Robert Squibb, *Charleston Courier*	Charleston, SC	1812	RS	4	
OL826	Owens & Leckie, *The Virginian*, 16 Feb. 1826	Lynchburg, VA	1826	ABPSV	85	UVAmf

1850–1874

Abbrev.	Nursery or Seed Company	City, State	Year	Plants	Taxa	Loc.
SN851	Southern Nurseries	Washington, MS	1851	APRST	268	GG
JR853	Joseph Rennie	Richmond, VA	1853	ABPRSTV	153	UVA
LY854	Thomas Lindley	Fayetteville, NC	1854	ST	101	CGL
Pom856	Pomaria Nurseries	Pomaria, SC	1856	ARSTV	198	NAL
Brk858	P. J. Berckmans	Augusta, GA	1858	RSTV	227	NAL
VN858	C. C. Langdon, Vineland Nurseries	Langdon Station, AL	1858	R	12	GS
Sta858	Staunton Nurseries	Staunton, VA	1858	ABPRSTV	172	UVA
Brk859	P. J. Berckmans	Augusta, GA	1859	RSTV	269	CGL
Hop859	Hopewell Nursery	Fredericksburg, VA	1859	ARS	64	UVA
Aff860	Thomas Affleck	Brenham, TX	1860	ABPRSTV	102	GS
MN860	Montgomery Nurseries	Montgomery, AL	1860	BPRSTV	32	GS
Brk861	P. J. Berckmans	Augusta, GA	1861	ABPRSTV	541	NAL
TR868	B. Truett & Son	Nashville, TN	1868	ABPRSTV	185	CGL
ATN870	Atlanta Nurseries	Atlanta, GA	1870	RSTV	160	CGL
Dwr870	J. S. Downer & Son	Fairview, KY	1870	ARSTV	76	NAL
Den871	C. B. Denson	Pittsboro, NC	1871	ABPRSTV	448	NAL
Brk873	P. J. Berckmans	Augusta, GA	1873	ABPRSTV	223	CGL

1875–1899

Abbrev.	Nursery or Seed Company	City, State	Year	Plants	Taxa	Loc.
AP881	Arnold Puetz	Jacksonville, FL	1881	ABPRSTV	110	GG
Lg881	Langdon Nurseries	Mobile, AL	1881	ABPRSTV	553	GG

LR881	Louisville Rose Co.	Louisville, KY	1881	ABPRSV	646	DA
VB885	Virgin Branch Nurseries	Batesville, VA	1885	T	5	UVA
Tho888	Geo. Thompson & Sons	Louisville, KY	1888	ABPRSTV	700	DA
MV888	Mission Valley Nurseries	Victoria County, TX	1888	PRSTV	100	DA (reprint)
Pf888	Pearfield Nursery	Frelsburg, TX	1888	RSTV	23	GG
AEx894	American Exotic Nurseries	Seven Oaks, FL	1894	ABPRSTV	196	DA
JBk895	J. O. Barksdale	Red Hill, VA	1895	T	29	UVA
PP895	Pilot Point Nurseries	Pilot Point, TX	1895	ST	15	GG
Ull895	Ullathorne Seed Co.	Memphis, TN	1895	ABPV	91	CGL
Wm895	Waldheim Nursery	Boerne, TX	1895	RST	31	GG
Pf896	Pearfield Nursery	Frelsburg, TX	ca.1896	BPRST	30	GG
MV898	Mission Valley Nurseries	Victoria County, TX	1898	BPRSTV	110	GG
Rs898	Rosedale Nurseries	Brenham, TX	1898	RSTV	240	GG

1900–1924

Abbrev.	Nursery or Seed Company	City, State	Year	Plants	Taxa	Loc.
Hgh903	Highlands Nursery	Kawana, NC	1903	BPRSTV	573	DA
JK904	J. E. Jackson	Gainesville, GA	1904	ABPRSTV	419	CGL
RP904	Royal Palm Nurseries	Oneco, FL	1904	ABPRSTV	231	GG
Brk906	P. J. Berckmans	Augusta, GA	1906	BPRSTV	351	GG
BN907	Biltmore Nursery	Biltmore, NC	1907	ABPRSTV	1633	DA
Vd907	Valdesian Nurseries	Bostic, NC	1907	BPRSTV	53	DA
WY907	W. A. Yates	Brenham, TX	ca.1907	BPRSTV	195	GG
JD909	J. W. Dudley & Sons	Parkersburg, WV	1909	ABPRSV	64	DA
GSM914	Glen Saint Mary Nurseries	Glen St. Mary, FL	1914	ABPRSTV	170	DA
CoS917	Comal Springs Nursery	New Braunfels, TX	1917	ABPRSTV	254	GG
Oz919	Ozark Seed and Plant Co.	Nashville, AR	1919	BPRSTV	97	DA

1925–1940

Abbrev.	Nursery or Seed Company	City, State	Year	Plants	Taxa	Loc.
TM925	Tucker Mosby Seed Co.	Memphis, TN	1925	ABPRSTV	227	DA
Per927	Perfection Nurseries	Foley, AL	1927	ABPSTV	95	DA
Rt928	Reuter's Seed Co.	New Orleans, LA	1928	ABPV	141	CGL
Wyt931	Job P. Wyatt & Sons	Raleigh, NC	1931	ABPV	186	DA
Prk938	George W. Park Seed Co.	Greenwood, SC	1938	ABPRSTV	1722	DA
Kyo939	Kiyono Nurseries	Crichton, AL	1939	BPSTV	235	DA

GREAT LAKES
Illinois, Indiana, Michigan, Minnesota, Ohio, Wisconsin

1835–1849

Abbrev.	Nursery or Seed Company	City, State	Year	Plants	Taxa	Loc.
Pkt835	S. C. Parkhurst	Cincinnati, OH	1835	APSV	80	NAL
SG843	Spring Garden Nursery	Cincinnati, OH	1843	BPRSTV	293	NAL
Clv845	Cleveland Nursery	Cleveland, OH	1845	APRSTV	214	NAL
Mc845	McIntosh & Co.	Cleveland, OH	1845	ABPRSTV	638	OHS
LEN846	Lake Erie Nursery	Cleveland, OH	1846	ABPRSTV	253	NAL
Laz848	A. H. Lazell	Columbus, OH	1848	RSTV	41	OHS

1850–1874

Abbrev.	Nursery or Seed Company	City, State	Year	Plants	Taxa	Loc.
AlN858	Alton Nursery	Alton, IL	1858	ABPRSTV	152	NAL
PG858	Persimmon Grove Nursery	Princeton, IL	1858	ABPRSTV	138	NAL
Blo859	Bloomington Nursery	Bloomington, IL	1859	ABPRSTV	743	LHB
Col860	Columbus Nursery	Columbus, OH	1860	ABPRSTV	513	DA
T866	E. Y. Teas & Bros.	Richmond, IN	1866	BP	11	NAL
Tru866	William P. Truitt	Adams County, OH	1866	BT	8	OHS
Blo867	Bloomington Nursery	Bloomington, IL	1867	AP	85	NAL
Blo868	Bloomington Nursery	Bloomington, IL	1868	BP	128	LHB
Blo872	Bloomington Nursery	Bloomington, IL	1872	ABP	129	LHB
T872	E. Y. Teas & Bros	Richmond, IN	1872	BP	64	CWRU
Blo873	Bloomington Nursery	Bloomington, IL	1873	BP	89	CWRU
T873	E. Y. Teas & Bros	Richmond, IN	1873	BP	70	CWRU
SH874	Storrs, Harrison, & Co.	Painesville, OH	1874	ABPRSTV	946	DA

1875–1899

Abbrev.	Nursery or Seed Company	City, State	Year	Plants	Taxa	Loc.
Blo875	Bloomington Nursery	Bloomington, IL	1875	BPS	38	UDel
Col877	Columbus Nursery	Columbus, OH	1877	ABPRSTV	1106	DA
Wau878	Waukegan Nursery	Waukegon, IL	1878	ST	52	DA
Blo883	Bloomington Nursery	Bloomington, IL	1883	BPV	133	LHB
Blo886	Bloomington Nursery	Bloomington, IL	1886	BP	30	UDel
GR889	Good & Reese	Springfield, OH	1889	ABPRSTV	1265	DA
Liv889	A. W. Livingston Sons	Columbus, OH	1889	ABPV	188	DA
RE893	W. Reid	Bridgeport, OH	1893	PSTV	79	DA
SH894	Storrs, Harrison, & Co.	Painesville, OH	1894	ST	126	DA
SH896	Storrs, Harrison, & Co.	Painesville, OH	1896	ABPRSTV	1153	DA
Scf896	W. N. Scarff	New Carlisle, OH	1896	ABPV	20	DA
MCL898	Miss C. H. Lippincott	Minneapolis, MN	1898	ABPRSV	199	DA
Imy899	Imlay Florist	Zanesville, OH	1899	ABPRSV	171	DA

1900–1924

Abbrev.	Nursery or Seed Company	City, State	Year	Plants	Taxa	Loc.
CL901	Call's Nurseries	Perry, OH	1901	RSTV	128	DA
Scf901	W. N. Scarff	New Carlisle, OH	1901	R	12	DA
Crk904	Crookston Nurseries	Crookston, MN	1904	BPRST	26	DA
Ref	L. Templin & Sons	Calla, OH	1904			DA
Wag905	Wagner Park	Sidney, OH	1905	ABPRSTV	542	DA
LW905	Leo Weltz	Wilmington, OH	ca.1905	BPRSTV	51	DA
Ref	Good & Reese	Springfield, OH	1906			DA
SH908	Storrs, Harrison, & Co.	Painesville, OH	1908	ABPRSTV	1340	DA
Sz910	John A. Salzer	LaCrosse, WI	1910	ABPRSTV	492	DA
Ref	Storrs & Harrison	Painesville, OH	1914			DA
Ref	Vaughan's Seed Store	Chicago, IL	1914			DA
Ref	The Wing Seed Co.	Mechanicsburg, OH	1914			DA
Ch915	Champion Nurseries	Perry, OH	1915	PRSTV	105	DA
Bd919	Brand Nursery	Faribault, MN	1919	PS	366	DA
ACN920	Alexander Co. Nurseries	McClure, IL	1920	RS	60	DA

1925–1940

Abbrev.	Nursery or Seed Company	City, State	Year	Plants	Taxa	Loc.
SH925	Storrs, Harrison, & Co.	Painesville, OH	1925	ABPRSTV	982	DA
Er926	Ernst Nurseries	Eaton, OH	1926	ABPRSTV	431	DA
WA928	Whitten-Ackerman	Bridgman, MI	1928	BPRSTV	60	DA
Al930	Allen's Nurseries	Geneva, OH	1930	ABPRSTV	453	DA
Fr932	Fremont Nursery	Fremont, OH	1932	ABPRSTV	757	DA

CENTRAL AND GREAT PLAINS
Iowa, Kansas, Missouri, Nebraska, North Dakota, Oklahoma, South Dakota

1850–1874

Abbrev.	Nursery or Seed Company	City, State	Year	Plants	Taxa	Loc.
Dmk853	Denmark Nursery	Denmark, IA	1853	ABPRSTV	58	NAL
CS860	St. Louis Nursery	St. Louis, MO	1860	ABPRSTV	430	NAL
Dmk868	Denmark Nursery	Denmark, IA	1868	BPRSTV	33	NAL
Bf869	Brookfield Nursery	Brookfield, MO	1869	ABPRSTV	471	Smith
KN871	Kansas Home Nursery	Lawrence, KS	1871	T	5	NAL
SSN871	Sunnyside Nurseries	Clinton, IA	1871	ABPRSTV	205	NAL

1875–1899

Abbrev.	Nursery or Seed Company	City, State	Year	Plants	Taxa	Loc.
PS875	Plant Seed Co.	St. Louis, MO	1875	ABPSV	308	DA
Mic876	Henry Michel & Co.	St. Louis, MO	1876	ABPSTV	842	SK
PS884	Plant Seed Co.	St. Louis, MO	1884	ABPRSTV	293	DA
WsN885	Willis Nursery	Ottawa, KS	1885	BPRSTV	78	NAL
ShN886	Shenandoah Nursery	Shenandoah, IA	1886	BPRSTV	100	DA
Kv887	Kirksville Nursery	Kirksville, MO	1887	ST	18	MOHS
Sk887	Stark Nurseries	Louisiana, MO	1887	STV	26	MOHS
Sgfld887	Springfield Nursery	Missouri	1887	ST	19	MOHS
Srx887	Sarcoxie Nurseries	Sarcoxie, MO	1887	RST	21	MOHS
Ex888	Exeter & Geneva Nurseries	Geneva, NE	1888	BPRSTV	94	DA
ShN899	Shenandoah Nursery	Shenandoah, IA	1899	BPRSTV	99	DA

1900–1924

Abbrev.	Nursery or Seed Company	City, State	Year	Plants	Taxa	Loc.
Ref	Iowa Seed Co.	Des Moines, IA	1901			DA
GS908	Griswold Seed Co.	Lincoln, NE	1908	ABPRSV	411	DA
ISC914	Iowa Seed Co.	Des Moines, IA	1914	ABPRSTV	688	DA
Ref	Archias' Seed Co.	Sedalia, MO	1917			DA
Ref	Neosho Nurseries	Neosho, MO	1917			DA
Nb918	Nebraska Seed Co.	Omaha, NE	1918	ABPSV	256	DA
NN919	Northern Nursery Co.	Ipswich, SD	1919	RSTV	32	UMinn
SN919	Sonderegger Nurseries	Beatrice, NE	1919	BPSTV	336	DA
Fg920	Ferguson Seed Farms	Oklahoma City, OK	1920	ABPV	141	DA
Gy921	Gurney Seed & Nursery Co.	Yankton, SD	1921	BPRSTV	266	DA
BrdK922	Barteldes Seed Co.	Lawrence, KS	1922	ABPRSTV	204	DA
NW924	Northwest Nursery Co.	Valley City, ND	ca.1924	ST	38	UMinn

1925–1940

Abbrev.	Nursery or Seed Company	City, State	Year	Plants	Taxa	Loc.
HF927	Henry Field	Shenandoah, IA	1927	ABPRSTV	503	DA
EF927	Earl Ferris Nursery	Hampton, IA	ca.1927	ABPRSTV	211	DA
Gy927	Gurney Seed & Nursery Co.	Yankton, SD	1927	ABPRSTV	412	DA
FbN933	Fairbury Nurseries	Fairbury, NE	1933	ABPRSTV	132	DA
OW939	Oscar H. Will & Co.	Bismarck, ND	1939	ABPRSTV	413	DA

MOUNTAIN STATES AND WEST
Arizona, California, Colorado, Idaho, Montana, Nevada, New Mexico, Oregon, Utah, Washington, Wyoming

1850–1874

Abbrev.	Nursery or Seed Company	City, State	Year	Plants	Taxa	Loc.
Osb855	Wm. B. Osborne, Nurseryman, *The Star*	Los Angeles, CA	1855	RS	4	Padilla 1961
RTm873	R. J. Trumbull Nursery	Oakland, CA	1873	ABPRSTV	179	NAL
MS874	Miller & Sievers	San Francisco, CA	1874	ABPST	82	NAL

1875–1899

Abbrev.	Nursery or Seed Company	City, State	Year	Plants	Taxa	Loc.
SR880	Santa Rosa Nursery	Santa Rosa, CA	1880	ABPRSTV	442	LHB
DM887	D. M. Moore	Ogden, UT	1887	BPRSTV	46	NAL
BN889	A. F. Boardman	Auburn, CA	1889	ABPRSTV	218	LHB
TS891	Theodosia Burr Shepherd	Ventura, CA	1891	ABPRSTV	462	LHB
Bg892	H. H. Berger & Co.	San Francisco, CA	1892	ABPRSTV	341	LHB
Ca894	California Nursery	Niles, CA	1894	ABPRSTV	1196	LHB
FC895	Fancher Creek Nursery	Fresno, CA	ca.1895	ABPRSTV	456	LHB

1900–1924

Abbrev.	Nursery or Seed Company	City, State	Year	Plants	Taxa	Loc.
Tg904	A.G. Tillinghast	La Conner, WA	1904	ABPV	30	DA
Cx907	Cox Seed Co.	San Francisco, CA	1907	ABPRSTV	844	DA
Ash908	Ashby Nursery	Berkeley, CA	1908	ABPRSTV	325	DA
Ger911	Germain Seed Co.	Los Angeles, CA	1911	ABPRSTV	541	DA
Pk912	J.B. Pilkington	Portland, OR	1912	ABPRSTV	653	DA
Buf914	Buffum Pure Seed Co.	Worland, WY	1914	T	2	TE
Un916	Union Seed & Fuel Co.	Boise, ID	1916	ABPV	78	DA
Az921	Arizona Seed & Floral Co.	Phoenix, AZ	1921	ABPSV	161	DA
Brd922	Barteldes Seed Co.	Denver, CO	1922	ABPRSTV	204	DA
St923	State Nursery & Seed Co.	Helena, MT	1923	BPST	174	DA

1925–1940

Abbrev.	Nursery or Seed Company	City, State	Year	Plants	Taxa	Loc.
Az925	Arizona Seed & Floral Co.	Phoenix, AZ	1925	ABPRV	212	DA
SW925	Southwestern Seed & Nursery Co.	Santa Fe, NM	ca.1925	PRSTV	77	DA
PW926	Porter-Walton	Salt Lake City, UT	1926	ABPRSTV	696	DA
Un933	Union Seed & Fuel Co.	Boise, ID	1933	ABPV	98	DA
GJ936	Grand Junction Seed Co.	Grand Junction, CO	1936	ABPRSV	326	DA
PHd937	Paul J. Howard	Los Angeles, CA	1937	ABPRSTV	574	DA
Lb939	Lamb Nurseries	Spokane, WA	1939	ABPRSTV	732	DA

PLANT AVAILABILITY BY SOURCE AND REGION

These tables indicate the catalogs in which particular plant species appeared. The plants are arranged alphabetically. Sources are listed only for the main species in the encyclopedia. Varieties of each species are included in each table. Please remember that equal numbers of catalogs were not used in all regions; therefore availability is not comparable between regions.

Abies balsamea (balsam fir)

New England	Ken832, Br833, Bt836, Br841, OC861, LC872, Rd881, NE910, G914, Bk917
Middle Atlantic	Pr771, JB783, Pr790, JB792, M804, Bld819, Pr826, Tb827, TH834, Wn844, Bu859, EB860, MM870, EB917, HN922, Bun939
South	JR853, LY854, Brk858, Sta858, Aff860, Dwr870, Den871, Hgh903, BN907
Great Lakes	SG843, Clv845, Mc845, LEN846, AlN858, PG858, Blo859, En859, Col860, Tru866, Wau878, SS887, SH894, CL901, Crk904, Wag905, SH908, Sz910, Ch915, SH925, Er926, Fr932
Central/Plains	Dmk853, CS860, Dmk868, KN871, SSN871, PS884, ShN886, Kv887, Ex888, ShN899, EF927
Mountain/West	Ca894, Cx907, PK912

Acer negundo (box elder)

New England	Br833, Br841, Sac853, NE910
Middle Atlantic	JB783, M804, Pr826, TH834, Wn844, Bu859, EB860, HWC905, EB917, HN922, My934
South	Aff860, MV888, MV898, Hgh903, Brk906, BN907, CoS917
Great Lakes	LEN846, PG858, Col860, SH894, Crk904, SH908, Sz910, SH925, Al930, Fr932
Central/Plains	PS884, ShN886, Sgfld887, Ex888, ShN899, NN919, SN919, Gy921, BrdK922, NW924, Gy927, OW939
Mountain/West	RTm873, MS874, DM887, Ca894, FC895, PK912, Brd922, PW926

Acer platanoides (Norway maple)

New England	Ken832, Br833, Br841, OC861, Rd881, NE910, Bk917, Fsk927, Hrd931
Middle Atlantic	JB792, Pr826, Wn844, Bu859, EB860, HWC905, EB917, HN922, My934, Bun939
South	LY854, Sta858, Aff860, Den871, JBk895, Brk906, BN907, Oz919
Great Lakes	PG858, Col860, SH894, SH896, LW905, Wag905, Ch915, SH925, Er926, Al930, Fr932
Central/Plains	CS860, PS884, Sk887, ShN899, SSN871, SN919, EF927, Gy927
Mountain/West	DM887, Ca894, FC895, Cx907, Ger911, PK912, PW926

Acer saccharinum (silver maple)

New England	Br833, Br841, Sac853, LC872, NE910, Bk917, Fsk927, Hrd931
Middle Atlantic	JB783, M804, JB807, WB810, TH834, Wn844, Bu859, EB860, HWC905, Ric905, HN922, My934
South	JR853, LY854, Sta858, Brk861, Den871, VB885, MV888, AEx894, JBk895, PP895, JK904, Brk906, BN907, Vd907, WY907, GSM914
Great Lakes	SG843, Clv845, Mc845, LEN846, AlN858, PG858, Blo859, Col860, Wau878, SH894, SH896, CL901, Crk904, SH908, Ch915, SH925, Er926, WA928, Al930, Fr932
Central/Plains	CS860, SSN871, PS884, WsN885, ShN886, Sgfld887, Ex888, ShN899, NN919, SN919, Gy921, BrdK922, NW924, EF927, Gy927, FbN933
Mountain/West	Rtm873, Ca894, FC895, Cx907, Ger911, PK912, Brd922, SW925, PW926

Acer saccharum (sugar maple)

New England	Ken832, Br833, Br841, LC872, Rd881, NE910, Bk917, Fsk927, Hrd931
Middle Atlantic	Pr771, JB783, Pr790, JB792, M804, WB810, Bld819, Pr826, Tb827, Wn844, Bu859, EB860, EB917, HN922, My934
South	Sta858, Aff860, TR868, Den871, JBk895, Hgh903, Brk906, BN907, Vd907, Oz919
Great Lakes	SG843, LEN846, AlN858, PG858, Col860, SH894, CL901, LW905, Ch915, SH925, Al930, Fr932
Central/Plains	CS860, SSN871, WsN885, ShN886, Sgfld887, ShN899, SN919, Gy921, BrdK922, EF927, Gy927, FbN933
Mountain/West	Rtm873, Ca894, FC895, Brd922, PW926

Achillea ptarmica (sneezewort)

New England	Bk845, Bk851, H852, Sac853, OC857, H859, Mn887, Mn889, Bk894, Ell894, NE910, G914, Gg915, Bk917, Fsk927, Gg928, Hrd931, ASL937, Bar939

Middle Atlantic	Bu844, Pr844, EB848, Pr854, Bu857, Pr857, Bu859, Bu860, EB860, EB862, Bu866, EB867, EB875, EB882, PH910, EB917, Dk924, Mch931, My934
South	Den871, JK904, BN907, Pk938
Great Lakes	Mc845, LEN846, Blo859, Blo867, Blo868, Blo872, Blo873, Col877, Blo883, GR889, SH896, Wag905, SH908, Sz910, SH925, Er926, Fr932
Central/Plains	CS860, SSN871, Mic876, ISC914, SN919, Gy921, EF927, Gy927, HF927, OW939
Mountain/West	PK912, SW925, PW926, PHd937

Aconitum napellus (monkshood)

New England	Ken832, H834, H835, Ken835, H836, H839, Br841, Bk845, Bk851, H852, Sac853, OC857, H859, H862, H863, H873, H875, H888, CA889, Bk894, NE910, Gg915, Bk917, Fsk927, Gg928, Hrd931, ASL937, Bar939
Middle Atlantic	JB807, Ln826, Ln828, Pr829, Ab830, Pr831, TH834, Ab839, Bu844, EB848, Pr854, Bu857, Pr857, EB860, Pr860, EB862, Bu866, EB867, Ln868, EB875, Ln879, Ln889, PH910, Mch931
South	Den871, BN907, Pk938
Great Lakes	Mc845, Blo859, Blo867, Blo868, Blo872, Blo883, Er926, Fr932
Central/Plains	CS860
Mountain/West	Lb939

Aesculus hippocastanum (horse chestnut)

New England	Ken832, Br833, Bt836, Br841, R853, Sac853, Rd881, NE910, Bk917
Middle Atlantic	JB792, JB807, WB810, Bld819, Pr826, TH834, Wn844, Bu859, EB860, HWC905, EB917, HN922, My934
South	JR853, Ly854, Brk858, Sta858, Brk861, Dwr870, Den871, JBk895, BN907
Great Lakes	Mc845, LEN846, AlN858, Blo859, Col860, SH894, CL901, SH908, Ch915, SH925, Er926, Fr932
Central/Plains	CS860, SSN871, WsN885, Sgfld887, Ex888, SN919, Gy921
Mountain/West	Rtm873, Ca894, FC895, Cx907, PK912, PW926

Agapanthus africanus (blue Nile lily)

New England	Br833, NE910
Middle Atlantic	Pr820, Pr857, DR876, AB895
South	JR853
Great Lakes	Blo859, Col877, GR889, Tem904
Central/Plains	Mic876
Mountain/West	MS874, SR880, TS891, Ca894, FC895, Cx907, Ash908, Ger911, PW926, PHd937

Ageratum houstonianum (ageratum)

New England	Bt836, Wd867, CA889, Gg915, Bk917, ASL937, Bar939
Middle Atlantic	Pr857, EB860, OK870, DR876, PH910, Bol928, JHr934
South	TR868, Brk873, AP881, LR881, Tho888, AEx894, Ull895, JD909, Wyt931, Pk938
Great Lakes	Blo859, SH874, Col877, GR889, Liv889, SH896, MCL898, Imy899, Tem904, Wag905, SH908, Sz910
Central/Plains	CS860, SSN871, PS875, Mic876, PS884, GS908, ISC914, Nb918, Fg920, BrdK922, EF927, Gy927, OW939
Mountain/West	Rtm873, Cx907, Ash908, Ger911, Un916, Az921, Brd922, Az925, PW926, Un933, GJ936, PHd937, Lb939

Ailanthus altissima (tree-of-heaven)

New England	Ken832, Br833, Br841, NE910, Hrd931
Middle Atlantic	Pr826, TH834, Wn844, Bu859, EB860, EB917
South	TR868, BN907, Pk938
Great Lakes	SG843, Clv845, Mc845, LEN846, Laz848, Col860, Sz910, SH925
Central/Plains	Dmk853, CS860, PS884, Ex888, HF927
Mountain/West	SR880, Ca894, FC895, PW926

Akebia quinata (akebia)

New England	CA889, Bk917
Middle Atlantic	Bu859, MM870, DR876, EB917
South	Den871, Brk873, Lg881, Rs898, Brk906, BN907, WY907, Pk938
Great Lakes	Col877, GR889, Wag905, SH908, SH925
Central/Plains	SSN871, Mic876, ISC914, SN919
Mountain/West	TS891, Ca894, FC895, Cx907, PK912

Alcea rosea (hollyhock)

New England	Bst760, Ken832, H834, H835, Ken835, Bt836, H836, Bk838, H839, Br841, H844, H845, H847, Bk851, H852, H859, H862, H863, H866, Wd867, Bk869, Bk871, H873, Bk875, H875, Mn875, Bk878, Bk881, H888, CA889, Mn889, Bk894, Ell894, NE910, Gg915, Bk917, Gg928, ASL937, Bar939
Middle Atlantic	WB810, Ln811, Ln826, Ab827, Ln828, Pr829, Pr831, TH834, Ab839, Wn844, Bu857, Pr857, Bu859, EB860, Bu866, EB867, Ln868, OK870, EB875, DR876, Ln879, EB882, Ln884, PH910, EB917, Dk924, Bol928, Mch931, JHr934, My934
South	OL826, Ull895, CoS917, TM925, Rt928, Wyt931, Pk938

Great Lakes	Pkt835, Clv845, Mc845, LEN846, PG858, Blo872, Blo873, Blo875, GR889, Liv889, Scf896, SH896, MCL898, Imy899, Wag905, SH908, Sz910, SH925, Er926, Al930, Fr932
Central/Plains	SSN871, Mic876, PS884, GS908, ISC914, Nb918, SN919, Fg920, Gy921, BrdK922, EF927, Gy927, HF927, FbN933, OW939
Mountain/West	Rtm873, SR880, TS891, Ca894, Cx907, Ger911, PK912, Un916, Az921, Brd922, St923, Az925, PW926, Un933, GJ936, PHd937, Lb939

Amaranthus caudatus (love-lies-bleeding)

New England	Bst760, Bt836, Wd867, CA889, Bk917
Middle Atlantic	WB810, OK870, DR876, PH910, Bol928
South	OL826, Ull895, Wyt931, Pk938
Great Lakes	GR889
Central/Plains	PS875, Mic876, PS884, ISC914, Nb918, BrdK922, HF927
Mountain/West	RTm873, SR880, Cx907, Ger911, Az921, Brd922, Az925, GJ936, PHd937

Amaranthus tricolor (Joseph's coat)

New England	Bt836, Wd867, CA889, Gg915, Bk917, Bar939
Middle Atlantic	JB807, WB910, OK870, DR876, PH910, Bol928
South	OL826, Brk873, AP881, Ull895, Wyt931, Pk938
Great Lakes	GR889, Liv889, SH896, Imy899
Central/Plains	PS875, Mic876, PS884, ISC914, Nb918, BrdK922, Gy927, HF927
Mountain/West	RTm873, Cx907, Ger911, Brd922, GJ936

Amorpha fruticosa (bastard indigo)

New England	Br833, Br841, NE910
Middle Atlantic	JB783, JB792, M804, JB807, Pr826, Tb827, TH834, Wn844, Bu859, EB860, MM870, EB917, HN922
South	Brk858, Sta858, Den871, Hgh903, BN907, Pk938
Great Lakes	Clv845, Mc845, Al930, Fr932
Central/Plains	CS860, SN919, OW939
Mountain/West	SR880, Ca894, PK912

Anemone (Japanese anemone)

New England	H888, CA889, Mn889, Bk894, Ell894, NE910, Gg915, Bk917, Fsk927, Hrd931
Middle Atlantic	Pr857, EB860, EB862, BB873, HWC905, PH910, EB917, Mch931, My934
South	Brk873, BN907, Pk938
Great Lakes	SH874, GR889, SH896, SH908, SH925, Fr932
Central/Plains	ISC914, SN919
Mountain/West	TS891, Ca894, Cx907, Ash908, PK912, PHd937, Lb939

Anemone coronaria (wind flower)

New England	H834, H835, H836, H859, H862, H863, H873, H875, Bk917, Fsk927, ASL937, Bar939
Middle Atlantic	WB810, Pr820, Ln828, Ln889, JC910, PH910, Mch931
South	TM925, Pk938
Great Lakes	SH908
Central/Plains	none
Mountain/West	RTm873, Ger911

Anredera cordifolia (Madeira vine)

New England	CA889, Bk917
Middle Atlantic	PH910, Bol928
South	Lg881, Tho888
Great Lakes	LEN846, SH874, Col877, Liv889, Imy899, SH908, Er926
Central/Plains	PS884, GS908, ISC914, Nb918, SN919, Fg920, BrdK922, HF927, FbN933, OW939
Mountain/West	Rtm873, SR880, Cx907, Brd922, Az925

Antirrhinum majus (snapdragon)

New England	Bst760, H834, Ken835, Bt836, Bk838, H839, Br841, H847, Bk851, OC857, H859, H863, H866, Wd867, Bk871, H873, H875, Bk878, Bk881, H888, CA889, Gg915, Bk917, Gg928, ASL937, Bar939
Middle Atlantic	WB810, Ab827, Pr829, Ab830, Pr831, TH834, Ab839, Bu844, Wn844, EB848, Bu857, Pr857, Bu859, EB860, EB862, EB867, OK870, EB875, DR876, Ln884, PH910, Bol928, Mch931, JHr934, My934
South	OL826, JR853, Den871, LR881, Ull895, CoS917, TM925, Wyt931, Pk938,
Great Lakes	Pkt835, Clv845, Mc845, Blo868, Blo872, Blo873, Blo875, GR889, Liv889, SH896, Imy899, Wag905, Sh908, Sz910, SH925, Er926, Al930
Central/Plains	CS860, SSN871, PS875, Mic876, PS884, GS908, ISC914, Nb918, Fg920, BrdK922, EF927, Gy927, HF927, OW939
Mountain/West	Rtm873, SR880, Cx907, Ger911, PK912, Az921, Brd922, Az925, PW926, Un933, GJ936, Lb939

Apios americana (potato bean)

New England	H834, H835, H836, Br841, H859, G886, G890, G892, G914
Middle Atlantic	JB783, M804, Ln811, Pr818, Ln826, Tb827, Ln828, Pr831, Pr857, Pr860, AB895, PH910
South	none
Great Lakes	Pkt835, GR889, Liv889, Sz910
Central/Plains	ISC914
Mountain/West	none

Aquilegia canadensis (American columbine)

New England	H834, Ken835, Bt836, Bk838, Br841, Bk851, OC857, H859, H862, H863, Bk871, Bk878, G879, Bk881, G883, G886, Mn889, G890, G892, NE910, G914, Bk917, Hrd931
Middle Atlantic	M804, JB807, Ln811, Pr818, Pr822, Ln826, Pr826, Ln828, Pr829, Pr831, TH834, Bu844, Pr844, Wn844, EB848, Bu857, Pr857, Bu859, Bu860, Bu866, EB917, Mch931
South	MS874, Hgh903, BN907, Pk938
Great Lakes	Pkt835, Clv845, Mc845, LEN846, Al930
Central/Plains	Gy921, OW939
Mountain/West	PW926

Aquilegia vulgaris (European columbine)

New England	H834, H835, Ken835, Bt836, H836, Bk838, H839, Br841, H844, Bk845, H845, H847, H852, H859, H862, H863, Wd867, Bk869, Bk871, H873, Bk875, H875, Bk878, CA889, Mn889, NE910, G914
Middle Atlantic	JB807, Pr826, Ab827, Pr829, Pr831, TH834, Ab839, Ln847, Pr857, OK870, DR876
South	OL826, BN907, Pk938
Great Lakes	Pkt835, Clv845, GR889, SH896, SH908
Central/Plains	Mic876, PS884, SN919
Mountain/West	none

Aristolochia macrophylla (Dutchman's pipe)

New England	Ken832, Br833, Br841, CA889, NE910, Gg915, Bk917, Fsk927, Hrd931, Bar939
Middle Atlantic	JB783, JB792, M804, JB807, Pr826, Tb827, Wn844, Bu859, EB860, DR876, HWC905, PH910, EB917, HN922, My934
South	BN907, Pk938
Great Lakes	Clv845, LEN846, PG858, GR889, SH896, Wag905, SH908, SH925, Er926, WA928, Al930, Fr932
Central/Plains	SSN871, Mic876, PS884, ISC914, SN919, HF927, FbN933
Mountain/West	Ca894, FC895, Cx907, Ger911, PK912, Lb939

Armeria maritima (sea thrift)

New England	Ken832, Ken835, Br841, Bk851, H852, H859, H862, H863, Mn889, Bk894, NE910, G914, Bk917, Hrd931
Middle Atlantic	Pr822, Pr826, Ab827, Pr829, Ab830, Pr831, TH834, Ab839, Pr844, EB848, Pr854, Pr857, EB860, EB862, EB882, PH910, EB917, Mch931, JHr934, My934
South	BN907, Pk938
Great Lakes	Clv845, Blo873, GR889, Liv889, MCL898, Al930, Fr932

Central/Plains	ISC914, SSN871
Mountain/West	Ash908, Ca894, Cx907, Ger911, PHd937, Lb939

Asclepias tuberosa (butterfly weed)

New England	H834, H835, Ken835, Bt836, Bk838, Br841, H852, OC857, H859, H862, H863, H873, H875, G883, G886, Mn887, H888, Mn889, G890, G892, NE910, G914, Bk917, Hrd931
Middle Atlantic	JB783, M804, JB807, Pr818, Pr820, Pr822, Ln826, Pr826, Ab827, Tb827, Ln828, Pr829, Ab830, Pr831, TH834, Ab839, Pr844, Wn844, Ln847, EB848, Pr857, EB867, EB875, EB882, PH910, EB917, Mch931
South	Hgh903, BN907, Pk938
Great Lakes	Pkt835, Mc845, SH896, Wag905, SH908, SH925, Er926, Fr932
Central/Plains	Mic876
Mountain/West	Lb939

Aster novae-angliae (Michaelmas daisy)

New England	Ken832, H834, Ken835, Br841, Bk845, Bk851, H852, H859, Mn887, Mn889, G890, G892, Bk894, NE910, G914, Bk917, Fsk927, Hrd931, ASL937
Middle Atlantic	M804, JB807, Ln811, Pr818, Pr826, Pr829, Pr831, Pr854, Pr857, EB867, EB875, EB882, PH910, EB917, JHr934
South	Hgh903, BN907, Wyt931
Great Lakes	SH908, Er926
Central/Plains	ISC914, SN919, FbN933
Mountain/West	Ger911, SW925, PW926, Phd937

Aurinia saxatilis (gold alyssum)

New England	H834, H835, H836, H839, H847, H859, Bk869, Bk871, Bk875, H875, Bk878, Bk881, H888, CA889, Mn889, Bk894, Gg915, Gg928, ASL937, Bar939
Middle Atlantic	GM796, WB810, TH834, Bu844, Bu859, Bu860, Ln865, Bu866, Ln868, OK870, Ln879, Ln884, Ln889, DR876, PH910, EB917, Mch931, JHr934
South	Den871, Wyt931, Pk938
Great Lakes	Blo872, WAG905, Sz910, SH925, Al930, Fr932
Central/Plains	ISC914, BrdK922, HF927
Mountain/West	RTm873, Ger911, Brd922, SW925, PW926, GJ936, Phd937, Lb939

Baptisia australis (false indigo)

New England	Ken832, H834, H835, Bt836, H836, Bk838, H839, Br841, H847, Bk851, OC857, H859, H862, H863, H873, H875, Mn875, G883, Mn887, H888, Mn889, Bk894, NE910, Bk917, Hrd931
Middle Atlantic	JB783, M804, JB807, Pr818, Pr826, Tb827, Pr829, Pr831, TH834, Pr844, Wn844, EB848, Pr854, Bu857, Pr857, Bu859, Bu860, EB862, Bu866, EB867, EB875, EB882, PH910, EB917, Mch931, My934
South	Den871, Hgh903, BN907, Pk938
Great Lakes	Pkt835, Blo867, Blo868, Blo883, Sz910, Er926, Fr932
Central/Plains	none
Mountain/West	SW925, Lb939

Begonia spp. (begonia)

New England	CA889, Gg915, Bk917, Bar939
Middle Atlantic	AB895, JC910, PH910, Mch931, JHr934
South	TR868, Brk873, AP881, LR881, Tho888, AEx894, JK904, Oz919, Per927
Great Lakes	Blo859, SH874, Col877, GR889, Liv889, SH896, MCL898, Imy899, Tem904, SH908, Sz910, Al930
Central/Plains	SSN871, PS875, Mic876, PS884, ISC914, Nb918, Fg920, BrdK922, OW939
Mountain/West	TS891, Cx907, Ash908, Ger911, Un916, Brd922, St923, PHd937, Lb939

Bellis perennis (English daisy)

New England	Br841, Bk851, H852, OC857, H859, H862, H863, Wd867, H869, Bk871, H873, Bk875, H875, Mn875, Bk878, Bk881, CA889, Mn889, NE910, Gg915, Bk917, Gg928, ASL937, Bar939
Middle Atlantic	JB807, WB810, Pr822, Pr829, Pr831, TH834, Pr844, Pr857, Bu860, EB860, EB862, Bu866, Ln868, OK870, EB875, DR876, EB882, Ln889, PH910, EB917, Dk924, Bol928, Mch931, JHr934
South	LR881, Tho888, Ull895, BN907, TM925, Wyt931, Pk938
Great Lakes	Clv845, Blo859, Blo867, Blo868, Blo872, Blo873, Blo883, GR889, MCL898, Imy899, SH908, Er926, Al930
Central/Plains	CS860, PS875, Mic876, PS884, GS908, ISC914, Nb918, Fg920, BrdK922, Gy927
Mountain/West	Rtm873, SR880, Ca894, Cx907, Ger911, Un916, Az921, Brd922, Az925, SW925, Un933, GJ936, PHd937

Berberis thunbergii (Japanese barberry)

New England	NE910, G914, Bk917, Fsk927, Hrd931
Middle Atlantic	Bu859, HWC905, PH910, EB917, HN922, My934, Bun939
South	Hgh903, Brk906, BN907, TM925, Pk938
Great Lakes	SH896, Wag905, SH908, Ch915, Bd919, SH925, Er926, WA928, Fr932
Central/Plains	Nb918, SN919, Gy921, BrdK922, EF927, Gy927, HF927, FbN933, OW939
Mountain/West	Bg892, PK912, Brd922, SW925, PW926, GJ936, PHd937, Lb939

Berberis vulgaris 'Atropurpurea' (purple common barberry)

New England	Sac853, OC861, CA889, NE910, G914
Middle Atlantic	Bu859, EB860, MM870, PH910, EB917
South	Pom856, Brk861, TR868, Den871, BN907, Pk938
Great Lakes	AlN858, Blo859, Col860, Col877, SH896, Wag905, SH908, Ch915, ACN920
Central/Plains	CS860, SSN871, ShN886, Sk887, Ex888, ShN899, Nb918, SN919
Mountain/West	DM887, Ca894, FC895, Cx907, PK912

Betula pendula (European white birch)

New England	Br833, Br841, Sac853, OC861, LC872, NE910, Bk917, Hrd931
Middle Atlantic	Bld819, Pr826, Wn844, Bu859, EB860, EB917
South	Sta858, Den871, JBk895, BN907, Pk938
Great Lakes	Blo859, Col860, Wau878, SH896, SH908, SH925
Central/Plains	PS884, ShN886, Sgfld887, Sk887, Srx887, ShN899, SN919, NW924
Mountain/West	SR880, Ca894, FC895, Cx907, Ash908, PW926, PHd937

Buxus sempervirens (common box)

New England	Br841, OC861, NE910, Bk917
Middle Atlantic	JB807, WB810, Bld819, Pr826, EB917, HN922, My934, Bun939
South	LY854, Pom856, Brk858, Brk861, ATN870, Dwr870, Den871, Rs898, Brk906, BN907, WY907, TM925, Pk938, Kyo939
Great Lakes	LEN846, Col860, Wag905, SH925, Er926, Fr932
Central/Plains	CS860
Mountain/West	Bn889, Ca894, Ger911, PK912, PW926, Lb939

Buxus sempervirens 'Suffruticosa' (dwarf edging box)

New England	Ken832, Br833, Br841, NE910
Middle Atlantic	WB810, TH834, Wn844, Bu859, EB917, HN922, Bun939

South — LY854, Aff860, MN860, TR868, ATN870, Dwr870, Lg881, Brk906, BN907

Great Lakes — SG843, Clv845, Mc845, Col860, SH894, Wag905, SH908

Central/Plains — none

Mountain/West — Ca894, FC895, Cx907, PK912

Caladium (ornamental-leaved caladium)

New England — CA889

Middle Atlantic — DR876, AB895, Bol928, Mch931

South — Brk873, AP881, Lg881, LR881, Tho888, AEx894, JD909, JK904, Brk906, Per927, Rt928

Great Lakes — SH874, Col877, GR889, Liv889, SH896, Imy899, Wag905, Tem904, SH908, Sz910, Er926, Al930, Fr932

Central/Plains — SSN871, Mic876, PS884, GS908, Nb918, Fg920

Mountain/West — SR880, TS891, Ca894, Az925, PW926

Calendula officinalis (pot marigold)

New England — Gg915, Bk917, Gg928, ASL937, Bar939

Middle Atlantic — JB807, PH910, Bol928, Mch931, JHr934, MY934

South — OL826, Wyt931, Pk938

Great Lakes — GR889, Liv889, MCL898, Imy899, SH908, Sz910, Al930

Central/Plains — PS875, Mic876, GS908, ISC914, Fg920, BrdK922, EF927, Gy927, HF927, OW939

Mountain/West — SR880, Cx907, Ger911, Un916, Az921, Brd922, Az925, PW926, Un933, GJ936, PHd937

Callistephus chinensis (China aster)

New England — Bt836, Wd867, Gg915, Bk917, Gg928, ASL937, Bar939

Middle Atlantic — WB810, OK870, DR876, PH910, Bol928, JHr934, My934

South — GF799, OL826, LR881, JD909, TM925, Wyt931, Pk938

Great Lakes — GR889, Liv889, Scf896, MCL898, Imy899, SH908, Sz910, Er926, Al930

Central/Plains — SSN871, PS875, Mic876, PS884, GS908, ISC914, Nb918, Fg920, EF927, Gy927, HF927, OW939

Mountain/West — RTm873, SR880, TS891, Tg904, Cx907, Ger911, Un916, Az921, Az925, PW926, Un933, GJ936, PHd937, Lb939

Calycanthus floridus (sweet shrub)

New England — Ken832, Br833, Br841, Sac853, OC861, Rd881, CA889, NE910, Bk917, Fsk927

Middle Atlantic — JB783, Pr790, JB792, M804, JB807, JB792, M804, JB807, WB810, Bld819, Pr826, TH834,

Wn844, Bu859, EB860, DR876, PH910, EB917, HN922, My934

South — JR853, Sta858, MN860, ATN860, Dwr870, Den871, Lg881, Hgh903, Brk906, BN907, GSM914, Oz919, TM925, Pk938

Great Lakes — SG843, Mc845, LEN846, AlN858, Blo859, Col860, GR889, RE893, SH896, CL901, LW905, Wag905, SH908, Sz910, Ch915, SH925, Er926, Al930, Fr932

Central/Plains — Dmk853, CS860, SSN871, Mic8786, WsN885, ShN886, Ex888, ShN899, ISC914, SN919, BrdK922, HF927

Mountain/West — Rtm873, DM887, Ca894, FC895, Cx907, Ger911, PK912, Brd922, PW926, PHd937, Lb939

Camellia japonica (camellia)

New England — Br833

Middle Atlantic — JB807, DR876, PH910

South — JR853, Brk661, Brk873, Lg881, AEx894, MV898, Brk906, BN907, GSM914, Per927, Kyo939

Great Lakes — Clv845, Blo859, SH874, GR889, Tem904

Central/Plains — Bf869, SSN871, PS875, Mic876, PS884

Mountain/West — TS891, Bg892, Ca894, FC895, Cx907, Ash908, Ger911, PK912, PHd937

Campanula carpatica (Carpathian bellflower)

New England — Bk845, Bk851, Sac853, OC857, H859, H863, Wd867, Bk871, H873, H875, Bk878, Bk881, Mn887, H888, Mn889, Bk894, NE910, G914, Bk917, Fsk927, Hrd931

Middle Atlantic — Pr829, Pr831, Bu844, Wn844, EB848, Bu857, Pr857, Bu859, EB862, EB867, OK870, EB875, PH910, EB917, Dk924, Mch931, My934

South — BN907, Pk938

Great Lakes — LEN846, Blo859, Blo867, Blo868, Blo873, Blo883, SH896, Wag905, SH908, SH925, Fr932

Central/Plains — SSN871, PS875, HF927

Mountain/West — Cx907, Ger911, PK912, PHd937, Lb939

Campanula medium (Canterbury bells)

New England — Bst760, Ken832, H834, Ken835, Bt836, Bk838, H839, Br841, Bk851, H859, H862, H863, Wd867, Bk869, Bk871, H873, Bk875, H875, Bk878, Bk881, H888, CA889, Bk894, NE910, G914, Gg915, Bk917, Gg928, Hrd931, ASL937, Bar939

Middle Atlantic — GM796, WB810, Ab827, Pr829, Ab830, Pr831, TH834, Ab839, Ln847, EB848, Pr857, OK870, DR876, Ln884, Ln889, PH910, Dk924, TM925, Bol928, JHr934, My934

South — GF799, Ull895, Wyt931, Pk938

Great Lakes	Pkt835, Clv845, Mc845, Blo872, Blo875, GR889, Liv889, SH896, MCL898, Imy899, SH908, Sz910, SH925, Al930, Fr932
Central/Plains	PS875, Mic876, PS884, GS908, ISC914, Nb918, SN919, Fg920, EF927, Gy927, HF927, FbN933, OW939
Mountain/West	Rtm873, Cx907, PK912, Un916, Az921, Az925, SW925, PW926, Un933, GJ936, PHd937, Lb939

Campanula pyramidalis (chimney bellflower)

New England	H834, Ken835, H839, Br841, H844, H845, H847, Bk851,H862, H863, Wd867, Bk869, Bk871, H873, Bk875, H875, Bk878, Bk881, H888, Mn889, NE910, Bk917
Middle Atlantic	Pr826, Ln828, Pr829, Pr831, TH834, Ab839, Wn844, Ln847, EB848, Bu857, Pr857, Bu859, Bu860, Ln868, OK870, EB875, DR876, Ln879, Ln884, Ln889, PH910, Dk924, Mch931, JHr934
South	BN907
Great Lakes	Clv845, Mc845, Blo872, Blo873, GR889, SH908, SH925
Central/Plains	Mic876
Mountain/West	Cx907, Ger911, PW926, Lb939

Campsis grandiflora (Chinese trumpet creeper)

New England	Ken832, Br833, Br841, Rd881, CA889
Middle Atlantic	Pr826, TH834, Wn844, Bu859, EB860, MM870, DR876, PH910
South	JR853, Sta858, Brk859, Brk861, Lg881, Rs898, Hgh903, Brk906, BN907, CoS917
Great Lakes	SG843, Clv845, Mc845, LEN846, AlN858, Col860, Col877, Wag905
Central/Plains	Mic876
Mountain/West	FC895, Cx907, Pk912

Campsis radicans (trumpet creeper)

New England	Ken832, Br833, Bt836, Br841, NE910, Bk917, Fsk927, Hrd931
Middle Atlantic	JB783, M804, JB807, WB810, Pr826, Tb827, TH834, Wn844, Bu859, EB860, MM870, DR876, EB917, Bun939
South	Sta858, Lg881, Hgh903, BN907, GSM914, Pk938
Great Lakes	Clv845, Mc845, LEN846, Blo859, RE893, SH896, SH908, SH925
Central/Plains	Dmk853, CS860, SSN871, Mic876, WsN885, ShN886, Ex888, ShN899, GS908, ISC914, SN919, Gy921, BrdK922, Gy927, HF927
Mountain/West	Rtm873, SR880, DM887, Bn889, Ca894, FC895, Cx907, Ger911, Brd922, PW926

Canna indica (Indian shot)

New England	Br833, Bt836, Wd867, CA889, Bk917, Hrd931, Bar939
Middle Atlantic	JB807, OK870, AB895, HWC905, PH910, Mch931
South	OL826, Lg881, LR881, Tho888, AEx894, MV898, JD909, CoS917, Oz919, TM925, Per927, Rt928, Pk938, Wyt931
Great Lakes	SH874, COL877, GR889, Liv889, Scf896, MCL898, Tem904, LW905, SH908, Sz910, Er926, Fr932
Central/Plains	Bf869, SSN871, PS875, Mic876, PS884, GS908, ISC914, Nb918, SN919, Fg920, Gy921, BrdK922, Gy927, HF927, FbN933, OW939
Mountain/West	Rtm873, SR880, TS891, FC895, Cx907, Ger911, Un916, Az921, Brd922, Az925, PW926, Un933, GJ936, PHd937

Cardiospermom helicacabum (balloon vine)

New England	Bt836, CA889, Gg915, Bk917, Gg928, Bar939
Middle Atlantic	JB807, Tb827, OK870, DR876, PH910, Bol928
South	OL826, Ull895, Wyt931, Pk938
Great Lakes	GR889, SH896, Imy899, Sz910
Central/Plains	PS875, Mic876, PS884, GS908, ISC914, Fg920, Gy927, HF927
Mountain/West	Cx907, Ger911, Az921, Az925, PW926, GJ936

Castanea dentata (American chestnut)

New England	Rd881
Middle Atlantic	JB783, M804, JB807, Bld819, Tb827, EB917
South	LV854, Den871, JBk895, Hgh903, Brk906, BN907
Great Lakes	SG843, LEN846, PG858, Blo859, SH896, CL901, Er926, Fr932
Central/Plains	CS860, Sgfld887, Ex888, ShN899, Gy921, BrdK922
Mountain/West	Cx907, Brd922

Catalpa

New England	Ken832, Br833, Bt836, Br841, Sac853, OC861, NE910, Bk917
Middle Atlantic	Pr771, JB783, Pr790, M804, WB810, Bld819, Pr826, Tb827, TH834, Wn844, Bu859, EB860, MM870, HWC905, EB917, My934
South	Sta858, Aff860, MV888, Wm895, MV898, Rs898, Hgh903, Brk906, BN907, WY907, GSM914, Oz919, Pk938
Great Lakes	SG843, Clv845, Mc845, Len846, Laz848, AlN858, PG858, Blo859, Col860, Wau878, RE893, SH894, CL901, Wag905, SH908, Sz910, Ch915, SH925, Er926, Al930, Fr932

| Central/Plains | Dmk853, CS860, PS884, WsN885, ShN886, Sgfld887, Sk887, Ex888, ShN899, SN919, Gy921, EF927, Gy927, FbN933 |
| Mountain/West | RTm873, SR880, Ca894, FC895, Cx907, Ger911, PK912, PHd937 |

Cedrus deodora (Deodar cedar)

New England	none
Middle Atlantic	Bu859, EB860, MM870, DR876
South	SN851, JR853, Ly854, Pom856, Brk858, Sta858, Brk861, ATN870, Den871, Rs898, Brk906, BN907, WY907, GSM914, Kyo939
Great Lakes	Col860
Central/Plains	none
Mountain/West	Bg892, Ca894, FC895, Cx907, Ger911, PK912, PHd937

Celastrus scandens (American bittersweet)

New England	Ken832, Br841, NE910, G914, Bk917, Fsk927, Hrd931
Middle Atlantic	JB783, M804, JB807, WB810, Bld819, Pr826, Tb827, Wn844, EB860, PH910, EB917, My934, Bun939
South	Hgh903, BN907, Pk938
Great Lakes	SG843, Clv845, LEN846, SH925, Er926, Al930
Central/Plains	CS860, ShN886, ShN899, ISC914, NN919, SN919, Gy921, EF927, HF927, FbN933, OW939
Mountain/West	SR880, PK912, PW926, Lb939

Celosia argentea var. *cristata* (crested cockscomb)

New England	Bt836, Wd867, CA889, Bk917, Gg928, Bar939
Middle Atlantic	OK870, DR876, PH910, Bol928, JHr934
South	OL826, Ull925, CoS917, Wyt931, Pk938
Great Lakes	SH896, MCL898, Imy899, SH908, Sz910, Al930
Central/Plains	PS875, Mic876, PS884, ISC914, Nb918, BrdK922, EF927, HF917, OW939
Mountain/West	Cx907, Ger911, Az925, PW926, Un933, GJ936, PHd937

Centaurea cyanus (bachelor's buttons)

New England	Bst760, Bt836, CA889, Gg915, Bk917, Gg928, ASL937, Bar939
Middle Atlantic	JB807, DR876, PH910, Bol928, Mch931, JHr934, My934
South	OL826, Ull895, CoS917, TM925, Wyt931, Pk938
Great Lakes	Liv889, MCL898, Imy899, SH908, Sz910, SH925, Er926

| Central/Plains | PS875, Mic876, PS884, GS908, ISC914, Nb918, Fg920, BrdK922, EF927, Gy927, HF927, OW939 |
| Mountain/West | Cx907, Ash908, Ger911, PK912, Un916, Az921, Brd922, Az925, PW926, Un933, GJ936, PHd937 |

Centranthus ruber (red valerian)

New England	H834, H835, Ken835, H836, H839, Br841, Bk851, Sac853, OC857, H859, H862, H863, Bk869, Bk871, H873, Bk875, H875, Mn875, Bk878, Bk881, Mn887, H888, Mn889, NE910
Middle Atlantic	JB807, Pr822, Pr826, Tb827, Pr829, Pr831, TH834, Bu844, Pr844, EB848, Bu857, Pr857, Bu859, Bu860, EB860, EB862, Bu866, EB867, EB875, DR876, EB882, Ln889, PH910, EB917, Mch931, My934
South	none
Great Lakes	Mc845, SH925, Fr932
Central/Plains	Mic876
Mountain/West	PHd937, Lb939

Cercis canadensis (redbud)

New England	Ken832, Br833, Br841, Sac853, OC861, G880, NE910, G914, Bk917
Middle Atlantic	JB783, M804, JB807, WB810, Bld819, Pr826, Wn844, Bu859, EB860, MM870, PH910, EB917, My934
South	JR853, Rs898, Hgh903, Brk906, BN907, WY907, GSM914, CoS917, TM925, Pk938
Great Lakes	SG843, Clv845, Mc845, LEN846, PG858, Blo859, Col860, RE893, SH894, SH908, Er926, Fr932, WA928
Central/Plains	ShN886, ShN899, HF927
Mountain/West	Bn889, Ca894, FC895, Cx907, PK912, PW926, PHd937

Chaenomeles spp. (flowering quince)

New England	Ken832, Br841, R853, Sac853, OC861, Rd881, CA889, NE910, Bk917, Hrd931
Middle Atlantic	TH834, Bu859, EB860, DR876, HWC905, PH910, EB917, HN922
South	JR853, Pom856, Brk858, Dwr870, ATN870, Den871, Lg881, MV888, Pf888, PP895, MV898, Rs898, Brk906, BN907, TM925, Pk938, Kyo939
Great Lakes	Mc845, LEN846, AlN858, PG858, Blo859, Col860, Col877, GR889, RE893, SH896, CL901, Wag905, SH908, SH925, Er926, WA928, Al930, Fr932
Central/Plains	Dmk853, CS860, SSN871, Mic876, WsN885, ShN886, Kv887, Ex888, ShN899, SN919, HF927, FbN933

Mountain/West | Rtn873, Bn889, Bg892, Ca894, FC895, Cx907, Ash908, Pk912, PW926, PHd937, Lb939

Chamaecyparis pisifera (retinospora)

New England | NE910, Bk917, Hrd931
Middle Atlantic | MM870, DR876, EB917, HN922, My934, Bun939
South | Den871, Lg881, Rs898, Brk906, BN907, Kyo939
Great Lakes | SH894, CL901, Wag905, SH908, SH925, Er926, Al930, Fr932
Central/Plains | none
Mountain/West | TS891, Bg892, PK912

Chionanthus virginicus (fringe tree)

New England | Ken832, Br833, Br841, Sac853, Rd881, CA889, NE910, Bk917
Middle Atlantic | JB873, M804, JB807, WB810, Bld819, Pr826, TH834, Wn844, Bu859, EB860, MM870, DR876, PH910, EB917
South | Sta858, Dwr870, Den871, Lg881, Hgh903, Brk906, BN907, Pk938
Great Lakes | SG843, Mc845, LEN846, En859, Col860, Col877, GR889, RE893, SH896, CL901, LW905, Wag905, SH908, Ch915
Central/Plains | WsN885, Shn886, Ex888, SN919
Mountain/West | PK912, PHd937

Chrysanthemum

New England | Ken832, Ken835, OC857, OC861, Wd867, CA889, Du901, NE910, Gg915, Bk917, Fsk927, Gg928, Hrd931, ASL937
Middle Atlantic | WB810, Bld819, Pr857, EB860, OK870, DR876, PH910, Bol928, JHr934, My934
South | OL826, JR853, Pom856, Hop859, MN860, Brk861, Dwr870, Brk873, Lg881, LR881, Ull895, Brk906, BN907, Vd907, JD909, TM925, Per927, Pk938
Great Lakes | SG843, Clv845, Mc845, PG858, Blo859, Col870, SH874, Col877, GR889, Liv889, SH896, MCL898, Imy899, Tem904, Wag905, SH908, Sz910, Er926, Al930, Fr932
Central/Plains | CS860, SSN871, PS875, Mic876, PS884, GS908, ISC914, Nb918, SN919, Fg920, BrdK922, HF927
Mountain/West | RTm873, SR880, Bn889, TS891, Ca894, FC895, Cx907, Ash908, Ger911, Un916, Brd922, St923, Az925, Un933, GJ936, Lb939

Clarkia (farewell to spring, godetia)

New England | Bt836, Wd867, CA889, Gg915, Bk917, Gg928, ASL937, Bar939

Middle Atlantic | OK870, DR876, PH910, Bol928, JHr934
South | Ull895, TM895, Wyt931, Pk938
Great Lakes | GR889, Liv889, SH896, MCL898, Imy899, SH908, Sz910
Central/Plains | PS875, Mic876, PS884, GS908, ISC914, Fg920, BrdK922, Gy927, OW939
Mountain/West | RTm873, MS874, SR880, Cx907, Ash908, Ger911, Az921, Brd922, Az925, PW926, GJ936, PHd937, Lb939

Clematis flammula (virgin's bower)

New England | Bt836, Br841, CA889, Bk917
Middle Atlantic | Tb827, Wn844, Bu859, EB860, DR876, PH910
South | Sta858, ATN870, BN907, TM925
Great Lakes | Pkt835, Mc845, LEN846, SH874, GR889, SH896
Central/Plains | CS860, SSN871, WsN885
Mountain/West | RTm873, Ca894, FC895, Cx907, Ger911

Clematis 'Jackmanii' (Jackman's clematis)

New England | CA889, Du901, NE910, Bk917
Middle Atlantic | DR876, HWC905, PH910, EB917, My934, Bun939
South | Tho888, Brk906, BN907, TM925, Pk938
Great Lakes | GR889, Liv889, SH896, CL901, LW905, Wag905, SH908, Sz910, Ch915, SH925, Er926, WA928, Al930, Fr932
Central/Plains | WsN885, Ex888, ShN899, GS908, ISC914, NN919, SN919, Gy921, BrdK922, EF927, Gy927, HF927, FbN933, OW939
Mountain/West | SR880, DM887, Ca894, FC895, Ash908, Cx907, Ger911, PK912, Brd922, SW925, PW926, Lb939

Clematis terniflora (sweet autumn clematis)

New England | Du901, NE910, G914, Bk917, Fsk927, Gg928, Hrd931
Middle Atlantic | HWC905, PH910, EB917, HN922, Bol928, My934, Mch931, Bun939
South | Hgh903, Brk906, BN907, WY907, CoS917, Oz919, Pk938
Great Lakes | SH896, CL901, Wag905, SH908, Sz910, Ch915, SH925, Er926, Al930, Fr932
Central/Plains | ShN899, GS908, ISC914, SN919, Gy921, EF927, Gy927, HF927, FbN933
Mountain/West | Cx907, Ash908, PK912, PW926

Clematis virginiana (Virginia clematis)

New England | Br833, Bt836, Br841, G880, CA889, NE910, G914, Bk917, Hrd931
Middle Atlantic | JB783, M804, JB807, Pr826, Tb827, Wn844, Bu859, EB860, EB917

South   Hgh903, BN907
Great Lakes   Pkt835, Clv845, LEN846, GR889, SH896,
                       CL901
Central/Plains   CS860
Mountain/West   none

Clethra alnifolia (summersweet)

New England   Ken832, Br833, Br841, Sac853, Rd881,
                       NE910, G914, Hrd931
Middle Atlantic   JB783, JB792, M804, JB807, WB810, Bld819,
                       Pr826, Tb827, Wn844, Bu859, MM870,
                       PH910, EB917, HN922, My934
South   Sta858, Den871, Hgh903, BN907, Pk938
Great Lakes   LEN846, Blo859, SH896, SH925, Er926,
                       Fr932
Central/Plains   ISC914
Mountain/West   none

Cobaea scandens (cup-and-saucer vine)

New England   Ken832, Br833, Bt836, Wd867, CA889,
                       Gg915, Bk917, Gg928, Bar939
Middle Atlantic   Tb827, MM870, OK870, DR876, PH910,
                       Bol928, JHr934
South   Brk873, LR881, Tho888, Ull895, JK904,
                       JD909, TM925, Wyt931, Pk938
Great Lakes   SH874, GR889, MCL898, Imy899, SH896,
                       SH908, Sz910
Central/Plains   PS875, Mic876, PS884, GS908, ISC914,
                       Nb918, Gy927, HF927, OW939
Mountain/West   TS891, Cx907, Ash908, Ger911, Az921,
                       Az925, PW926

Colocasia esculenta (elephant ears)

New England   CA889, Bk917
Middle Atlantic   DR876, AB895, PH910, Bol928
South   Brk873, AP881, Lg881, LR881, Tho888,
                       AEx894, JK904, Brk906, JD909, CoS917,
                       Per927, Rt928, Wyt931
Great Lakes   SH874, Col877, GR889, Liv889, Imy899,
                       Tem904, Wag905, SH908, Sz910, Er926,
                       Al930, Fr932
Central/Plains   Mic876, PS884, GS908, ISC914, Nb918,
                       SN919, Fg920, Gy921, BrdK922, HF927,
                       FbN933
Mountain/West   SR880, TS891, Ca894, FC895, Ger911,
                       Brd922, PW926

Colutea arborescens (bladder senna)

New England   Ken832, Br833, Br841, Sac853, OC861,
                       NE910
Middle Atlantic   Pr790, JB792, JB807, WB810, Bld819, Pr826,
                       TH834, Wn844, EB860, MM870, EB917
South   OL826, Den871, Lg881, BN907, Pk938

Great Lakes   SG843, Clv845, Mc845, LEN846, Col860,
                       Fr932
Central/Plains   CS860, SSN871
Mountain/West   Lb939

Consolida ajacis (larkspur)

New England   Bst760, Bt836, Wd867, CA889, Gg915,
                       Bk917, Gg928, ASL937, Bar939
Middle Atlantic   WB810, OK870, DR876, PH910, Bol928,
                       Mch931, JHr934, My934
South   GF799, OL826, Ull895, CoS917, Rt928,
                       Wyt931, Pk938
Great Lakes   PG858, GR889, Liv889, SH896, MCL898,
                       Imy899, SH908
Central/Plains   PS875, Mic876, PS884, GS908, ISC914,
                       Fg920, BrdK922, EF927, HF927, OW939
Mountain/West   RTm873, Cx907, Ash908, Ger911, Nb918,
                       Az921, Brd922, Az925, PW926, Un933,
                       GJ936, PHd937

Convallaria majalis (lily-of-the-valley)

New England   Ken832, H834, Ken835, Br841, Bk845,
                       Bk851, H852, Sac853, OC857, H859, H866,
                       Mn875, G883, G886, Mn887, CA889,
                       Mn889, G890, G892, Ell894, NE910, G914,
                       Gg915, Fsk927, Hrd931
Middle Atlantic   JB807, WB810, Ln811, Bld819, PM822,
                       Pr822, Ln826, Pr826, Ln828, Pr829, Pr831,
                       TH834, Pr844, Wn844, EB848, Pr854, Pr857,
                       EB860, Pr860, EB862, EB867, BB873, EB875,
                       DR876, EB882, JC910, PH910, EB917,
                       Mch931
South   MC792, MC793, Den871, AP881, Hgh903,
                       BN907, Oz919, TM925, Pk938
Great Lakes   Clv845, Mc845, LEN846, Blo859, Blo867,
                       Blo868, Blo872, T872, Blo873, T873, Blo875,
                       Col877, Blo883, Blo886, GR889, SH896,
                       Crk904, SH908, Sz910
Central/Plains   CS860, Mic876, GS908, ISC914, Gy921,
                       BrdK922, HF927, OW939
Mountain/West   RTm873, DM887, Ca894, FC895, PK912,
                       Un916, Brd922, PW926, Lb939

Coreopsis lanceolata (lance-leaf coreopsis)

New England   H834, Ken835, Br841, Bk845, Bk851, H852,
                       OC857, H859, H862, H863, Mn887, Mn889,
                       G890, G892, Bk894, Ell894, NE910, G914,
                       Gg915, Bk917, Gg928, Hrd931
Middle Atlantic   M804, Pr829, Pr831, TH834, Wn844, EB867,
                       EB875, EB882, PH910, EB917, Mch931
South   Hgh903, BN907, Pk938
Great Lakes   Mc845, LEN846, SH896, SH908, Sz910,
                       SH925, Er926, Al930

| Central/Plains | GS908, ISC914, Nb918, BrdK922, Gy927, HF927 |
| Mountain/West | TS891, Cx907, Ash908, Ger911, PK912, Brd922, PW926, PHd937 |

Coreopsis tinctoria (calliopsis)

New England	Bt836, Wd867, CA889, Bk917, Bar939
Middle Atlantic	OK870, DR876, PH910, Bol928, JHr934
South	Ull895
Great Lakes	GR889, SH896, MCL898, Sz910, Er926
Central/Plains	PS875, Mic876, PS884, GS908, Nb918, Fg920, Gy927, HF927, OW939
Mountain/West	TS891, Ash908, Ger911, Un916, PW926, Un933, GJ936, Lb939

Cornus florida (dogwood)

New England	Ken832, Br833, Br841, NE910, G914, Bk917
Middle Atlantic	Pr771, JB783, Pr790, M804, JB807, Bld819, Pr826, Tb827, Wn844, Bu859, EB860, PH910, EB917, HN922, My934, Bun939
South	Hgh903, Brk906, BN907, TM925, GSM914, Pk938
Great Lakes	SG843, LEN846, RE893, SH894, SH896, Wag905, SH908, SH925, Al930, Fr932
Central/Plains	CS860, Srx887, ISC914, SN919
Mountain/West	PK912

Cornus stolonifera (red-twigged dogwood)

New England	Br833, Br841, NE910, G914, Hrd931
Middle Atlantic	JB783, M804, WB810, Pr826, EB860, MM870, EB917, HN922, My934
South	Hgh903, BN907, TM925, Per927
Great Lakes	SG843, Blo859, SH925, Fr932
Central/Plains	ISC914, Gy921, EF927, OW939
Mountain/West	Ca894, Cx907, PK912

Cortaderia selloana (pampas grass)

New England	H862, H863, Wd867, H873, H875, H888, CA889, Bk917, Bar939
Middle Atlantic	Ln868, OK870, DR876, Ln879, EB882, Ln884
South	Brk873, AP881, Lg881, MV888, Pf896, MV898, RP904, Brk906, BN907, WY907, GSM914, CoS917, Per927, Kyo939
Great Lakes	Blo868, Blo872, Blo873, SH874, Col877, GR889
Central/Plains	PS875, Mic876, PS884
Mountain/West	RTm873, SR880, Bn889, Ca894, FC895, Cx907, Ger911, PK912

Cosmos bipinnatus (cosmos)

| New England | CA889, Gg915, Bk917, Gg928, ASL937, Bar939 |

Middle Atlantic	PH910, Bol928, JHr934, My934
South	Ull895, JD909, TM925, Rt928, Wyt931, Pk938
Great Lakes	SH896, MCL898, Imy899, SH908, Sz910, Er926, Al930
Central/Plains	GS908, ISC914, Nb918, Fg920, BrdK922, Gy927, HF927, OW939
Mountain/West	TS891, Bg892, Cx907, Ash908, Un916, Az921, Brd922, Az925, PW926, Un933, GJ936, PHd937, Lb939

Cotinus coggygria (smoke bush)

New England	Ken832, Br833, Br844, R853, Rd881, CA889, NE910, Bk917
Middle Atlantic	Pr790, JB807, Bld819, Pr826, TH834, Wn844, Bu859, EB860, MM870, DR876, My934
South	Brk858, Sta858, Aff860, Brk861, Dwr870, Den871, Lg881, MV888, Brk906, BN907, Pk938
Great Lakes	SG843, Clv845, Mc845, LEN846, AlN858, PG858, Blo859, Col860, GR889, RE893, SH896, CL901, LW905, Wag905, Ch915
Central/Plains	Dmk853, CS860, Dmk868, Wsn885, ShN886, Sk887, Ex888, ShN899, ISC914, SN919
Mountain/West	Bn889, Ca894, FC895, Cx907, PK912, PW926

Crataegus laevigata (English hawthorn)

New England	Ken832, Br833, Br841, Sac853, OC861, CA889, NE910, Bk917, Fsk927
Middle Atlantic	Pr790, JB807, Bld819, Pr826, TH834, Wn844, Bu859, EB860, EB917, My934
South	JR853, Sta858, Aff860, Den871, BN907, Pk938
Great Lakes	Mc845, LEN846, SH894, LW905, SH908, Ch915, SH925, Al930, Fr932
Central/Plains	PS884, ISC914, SN919
Mountain/West	SR880, Ca894, FC895, Cx907, Ash908, PK912, PW926

Crinum spp. (southern lily)

New England	Pr820, EB860, AB895, PH910
Middle Atlantic	none
South	Aff860, Brk873, AP881, AEx894, RP904, Per927
Great Lakes	SH895
Central/Plains	Mic876
Mountain/West	TS891, Bg892, Ca894

Crocus

| New England | H847, H862, H863, H866, Bk871, Bk878, Bk881, Rd881, Mn887, G892, NE910, Fsk927 |
| Middle Atlantic | Bld819, Pr820, Ln828, Bu844, Wn844, Bu857, EB860, Pr860, EB862, BB873, EB882, HWC905, Ric905, JC910, Mch931 |

South	MC792, MC793, Den871, JD909, Oz919
Great Lakes	AlN858, PG858, Blo859, T872, Blo873, T873, Blo883, SH925
Central/Plains	GS908, ISC914, HF927
Mountain/West	RTm873, Az921, St923

Dahlia

New England	Ken832, Br833, Bt836, OC861, Wd867, CA889, Gg915, Bk917, Gg928, Bar939
Middle Atlantic	Bld819, OK870, DR876, Ric905, PH910, HN922, Bol928, JHr934
South	OL826, SN851, Sta858, Brk861, TR868, Brk873, Lg881, LR881, Tho888, Ull895, Vd907, JD909, CoS917, Oz919, TM925, Rt928, Wyt931, Pk938
Great Lakes	SG843, Mc845, LEN846, AlN858, PG858, Tru866, SH874, Col877, GR889, Liv889, SH896, MCL898, Imy899, Crk904, Tem904, Wag905, SH908, Sz910, Er926, WA928, Al930, Fr932
Central/Plains	Dmk853, CS860, Dmk868, Bf869, SSN871, PS875, Mic876, PS884, Ex888, GS908, ISC914, Nb918, SN919, Fg920, Gy921, BrdK922, EF927, Gy927, HF927, OW939
Mountain/West	RTm873, SR880, TS891, Ca894, FC895, Cx907, Ash908, Ger911, Un916, Az921, Brd922, Az925, Un933, PW926, PHd937

Daphne mezereon (February daphne)

New England	Ken832, Br833, Br841, R853, Sac853, Rd881, Hrd931
Middle Atlantic	JB792, JB807, WB810, Bld819, Pr826, TH834, Wn844, Bu859, EB860, EB917
South	Sta858, Den871, BN907, Pk938
Great Lakes	Clv845, Mc845, LEN846, Col860
Central/Plains	none
Mountain/West	none

Delphinium elatum (bee larkspur)

New England	Ken832, H834, H835, Ken835, Bt836, H836, Bk838, H839, Br841, H844, Bk845, H845, H847, Bk851, H859, Bk869, Bk871, H873, Bk875, H875, Bk878, Bk881, Bk894, Gg915, Bk917, Gg928
Middle Atlantic	WB810, Pr822, Pr826, Ab827, Tb827, Pr829, Ab830, Pr831, TH834, Pr844, Wn844, Pr854, Pr857, EB862, EB867, Ln868, OK870, EB875, Ln879, EB882, Ln884, Ln889, PH910
South	none
Great Lakes	Pkt835, Clv845, Mc845, LEN846, Blo872
Central/Plains	ISC914
Mountain/West	RTm873, Ger911, GJ936

Delphinium grandiflorum (great-flowered delphinium)

New England	H834, H835, Ken835, Bt836, H836, Bk838, H839, Br841, Bk845, H847, Bk851, H859, Wd867, Bk869, Bk871, Bk875, H875, Bk878, Bk881, Mn889, G914, Gg915, Bk917, Gg928, Hrd931, ASL937
Middle Atlantic	Pr822, Pr826, Tb827, Pr829, Ab830, Pr831, TH834, Ab839, Bu844, Pr844, Wn844, Ln847, EB848, Pr854, Bu857, Pr857, Bu859, Bu860, EB860, EB862, EB867, Ln868, OK870, EB875, DR876, Ln879, Ln884, Ln889, PH910, EB917, Bol928, Mch931
South	BN907, Pk938
Great Lakes	Pkt835, Mc845, LEN846, Blo867, Blo868, Blo872, Blo883, WAG905, Al930, Fr932
Central/Plains	PS875, Mic876, SN919, Gy927
Mountain/West	PK912, PW926, Lb939

Deutzia gracilis (slender deutzia)

New England	OC861, CA889, Du901, NE910, Bk917, Fsk927, Hrd931
Middle Atlantic	Bu859, EB860, MM870, DR876, PH910, EB917, HN922, My934, Bun939
South	Pom856, Brk858, Sta858, Brk861, Dwr870, Den871, Lg881, Rs898, Brk906, BN907
Great Lakes	AlN858, Blo859, Col860, Col877, GR889, RE893, SH896, CL901, Wag905, SH908, SH925, Er926, Al930, Fr932
Central/Plains	CS860, SSN871, Mic876, ISC914, Gy921, BrdK922, Gy927
Mountain/West	Bg892, Ca894, Cx907, Brd922, PW926

Dianthus barbatus (sweet William)

New England	Bst760, H834, H835, Ken835, Bt836, H836, Bk838, H839, Br841, H844, Bk845, H845, H847, H852, H859, H862, H863, H866, Wd867, Bk869, Bk871, Bk875, H875, Mn875, Bk878, Bk881, Mn887, H888, CA889, Mn889, Bk894, G914, Gg915, Bk917, Gg928, Hrd931, ASL937, Bar939
Middle Atlantic	GM796, JB807, WB810, Ln811, PM822, Pr822, Ln826, Pr826, Tb827, Ln828, Pr829, Ab830, Pr831, TH834, Ab839, Bu844, Pr844, Wn844, EB848, Bu857, Pr857, Bu859, Bu860, EB860, EB862, Bu866, Ln868, OK870, EB875, DR876, Ln879, Ln884, Ln889, PH910, EB917, Dk924, Bol928, Mch931, JHr934, My934
South	GF799, OL826, Den871, Ull895, BN907, CoS917, TM925, Rt928, Wyt931, Pk938
Great Lakes	Pkt835, Clv845, PG858, Blo872, Blo873, SH874, Blo875, Blo883, GR889, Liv889, SH896, MCL898, Wag905, Imy899, SH908, Sz910, SH925, Er926, Al930, Fr932

Central/Plains	CS860, SSN871, PS875, Mic876, PS884, GS908, ISC914, Nb918, SN919, BrdK922, EF927, Gy927, HF927, OW939
Mountain/West	RTm873, SR880, Cx907, Ash908, Ger911, PK912, Un916, Az921, Brd922, PW926, Un933, GJ936, Lb939

Dianthus caryophyllus (carnation)

New England	BG719, Bst760, Ken832, H834, Ken835, Bt836, H836, H839, Br841, H844, H845, H847, H852, OC857, H859, H862, H863, H866, Wd867, H873, H875, H888, CA889, Ell894, Gg915, Bk917, Gg928, Bar939
Middle Atlantic	GM796, JB807, WB810, Ln811, Bld819, PM822, Ln826, Pr826, Tb827, Ln828, Ab830, Pr831, Pr844, Wn844, Ln847, Bu857, Pr857, Bu859, EB860, Bu866, EB867, Ln868, OK870, EB875, DR876, Ln879, Ln884, Ln889, PH910, Mch931, JHr934
South	OL826, Brk873, LR881, Ull895, JD909, CoS917, TM925, Rt928, Wyt931, Pk938
Great Lakes	Pkt835, SG843, AlN858, Blo859, Blo868, Blo872, Blo873, SH874, Col877, GR889, Liv889, Scf896, SH896, MCL898, Imy899, Tem904, Wag905, SH908, Sz910, Er926, Al930, Fr932
Central/Plains	Bf869, SSN871, PS875, Mic876, PS884, GS908, ISC914, Nb918, Fg920, Gy927, HF927, FbN933, OW939
Mountain/West	RTm873, SR880, TS891, Ca894, FC895, Tg904, Cx907, Ger911, PK912, Un916, Az921, Az925, SW925, PW926, Un933, PHd937, Lb939

Dianthus chinensis (China pink)

New England	Bst760, Ken832, Bt836, Br841, H859, H862, H863, Wd867, H875, CA889, Gg915, Bk917, Gg928, Bar939
Middle Atlantic	JB807, WB810, Pr826, Tb827, Pr829, Pr831, TH834, Ab839, EB848, Pr857, EB860, OK870, DR876, PH910, Bol928, Jhr934
South	OL826, Ull895, BN907, CoS917, TM925, Rt923, Wyt931
Great Lakes	Pkt835, Clv845, LEN846, PG858, Blo867, Blo872, GR889, Liv889, MCL898, Imy899, SH908, Al930
Central/Plains	PS775, Mic876, PS884, GS908, ISC914, Nb918, Fg920, Gy927, OW939
Mountain/West	RTm873, SR880, Cx907, Ger911, PW926, GJ936

Dianthus plumarius (grass pink)

New England	Bst760, H834, Bk838, Br841, H847, H859, Bk869, Bk871, Bk875, Bk878, Bk881, Mn887, CA889, Mn889, Bk894, G914, Bk917, Gg928, Hrd931, Bar939
Middle Atlantic	JB807, Ln826, Tb827, Ln828, TH834, Pr844, Wn844, Ln847, Pr854, Pr857, EB860, EB863, Bu866, Ln868, OK870, DR876, PH910, Dk924, Bol928, Mch931, JHr934, My934
South	OL826, Den871, BN907, CoS917, Pk938
Great Lakes	Pkt835, SG843, Clv845, PG858, Blo859, Blo867, Blo883, GR889, Liv889, MCL898, SH908, Sz910, Er926, Al930, Fr932
Central/Plains	PS875, Mic876, PS884, GS908, ISC914, SN919, BrdK922, Gy927, HF927, OW939
Mountain/West	Ger911, Brd922, PW926, PHd937, Lb939

Dicentra spectabilis (bleeding heart)

New England	Sac853, OC857, H859, Bk871, H873, H875, Mn875, Bk878, Bk881, Rd881, Mn887, CA889, Mn889, G890, G892, Bk894, Ell894, NE910, G914, Bk917, Fsk927, Hrd931
Middle Atlantic	Pr857, EB860, Pr860, EB862, Bu866, EB867, OK870, BB873, EB875, DR876, EB882, JC910, EB917, Bol928, Mch931, My934
South	Den871, Tho888, BN907, Pk938
Great Lakes	PG858, Blo859, Col860, T866, Blo867, Blo868, Blo872, T872, Blo873, T873, Blo875, Col877, Blo883, Liv889, SH896, Crk904, SH908, Sz910, SH925, Er926, Al930, Fr932
Central/Plains	CS860, Dmk868, SSN871, Mic876, ShN886, ShN899, GS908, ISC914, Nb918, SN919, Gy921, Gy927, HF927, FbN933, OW939
Mountain/West	RTm873, Ca894, PK912, PW926, Lb939

Dictamnus albus (gasplant)

New England	Ken832, H839, Br841, H844, Bk845, H845, H847, H852, Sac853, H859, H862, H863, Bk869, Bk871, H873, Bk875, H875, Bk878, Bk881, Mn887, H888, Mn889, Bk894, Gg915, Bk917, Fsk927, Hrd931, Gg928, Bar939
Middle Atlantic	GM796, JB807, Pr822, Pr826, Pr829, Pr831, Ab839, Bu844, Pr844, Wn844, EB848, Bu857, Pr857, Bu859, Bu860, EB860, EB862, Bu866, EB867, Ln868, EB875, EB882, Ln889, PH910, EB917, Mch931
South	Den871, BN907, Pk938
Great Lakes	Clv845, Mc845, LEN846, Blo859, Blo867, Blo868, Blo872, Blo883, SH896, Wag905, SH908, Er926, Fr932
Central/Plains	Bf869, SSN871
Mountain/West	Ger911, Lb939

Digitalis purpurea (foxglove)

New England	Ken832, H834, H835, Ken835, H836, Bt836, Bk838, H839, Br841, Bk845, H847, Bk851, H852, H859, H862, H863, Bk869, Bk871, H873, Bk875, H875, Mn875, Bk878, Bk881, CA889, Mn889, Bk894, Ell894, Gg915, Bk917, Gg928, Hrd931, ASL937, Bar939
Middle Atlantic	WB810, Ln811, Pr822, Ln826, Tb827, Ln828, Ab830, TH834, Ab839, Bu844, Pr844, Wn844, Ln847, EB848, Pr854, Bu857, Pr857, Bu859, Bu866, EB867, Ln868, OK870, EB875, DR876, Ln879, Ln884, Ln889, PH910, EB917, Dk924, JHr934, My934
South	OL826, Ull895, BN907, TM925, Wyt931, Pk938
Great Lakes	Pkt835, LEN846, Blo872, GR889, Imy899, SH908, Sz910, SH925, Er926, Al930, Fr932
Central/Plains	CS860, PS875, PS884, GS908, ISC914, Nb918, SN919, Fg920, BrdK922, HF927, OW939
Mountain/West	RTm873, Cx907, Ash908, PK912, Az921, Brd922, PW926, GJ936, PHd937

Dioscorea batatas (cinnamon vine)

New England	CA889, Bk917
Middle Atlantic	Pr857, PH910, Bol928
South	Wyt931
Great Lakes	GR889, LIV889, Scf896, SH896, Tem904, SH908, Sz910
Central/Plains	GS908, ISC914, Nb918, SN919, Gy921, BrdK922, Gy927, HF927
Mountain/West	Brd922, PW926

Dodecatheon meadia (shooting star, pride of Ohio)

New England	Bk845, H852, OC857, H859, H862, H863, Bk869, Bk871, H873, Bk875, H875, Bk881, G883, G886, Mn889, G890, G892, G914, Bk917, Hrd931
Middle Atlantic	JB783, M804, JB807, WB810, Pr818, Pr822, Ln826, Ln828, Pr829, Pr831, TH834, Bu844, Pr844, Wn844, EB848, Pr854, Bu857, Pr857, Bu859, Bu860, EB860, Pr860, EB862, Bu866, EB867, OK870, EB875, PH910
South	Den871, Hgh903, BN907
Great Lakes	none
Central/Plains	Bf869
Mountain/West	Ger911, Lb939

Echinacea purpurea (purple coneflower)

New England	H834, H835, Ken835, Bt836, H836, Bk838, H839, Br841, Bk845, Bk851, H852, H859, H862, H863, G883, G886, Mn887, Mn889, NE910, Bk917, Hrd931, Bar939

Middle Atlantic	JB783, M804, JB807, Pr818, Pr822, Ln826, Pr826, Tb827, Ln828, Pr829, Pr831, TH834, Pr844, Wn844, EB848, Pr854, Pr857, EB862, Bu866, EB867, EB875, PH910, Dk924, Mch931, JHr934, My934
South	Den871, Hgh903, BN907, TM925, Pk938
Great Lakes	Pkt835, Clv845, Mc845, LEN846, Wag905, SH908, Er926, Fr932
Central/Plains	OW939
Mountain/West	PK912, PW926, PHd937, Lb939

Eriobotrya japonica (medlar, loquat)

New England	none
Middle Atlantic	Bu859
South	JS793, Pom856, Aff860, Brk861, AP881, Lg881, AEx894, Rs898, BN907, WY907, Kyo939
Great Lakes	none
Central/Plains	none
Mountain/West	SR880, Bn889, Ca894, FC895, Cx907

Erysimum cheiri (wallflower)

New England	Bst760, H834, Bt836, H836, Bk838, H839, H859, H862, H863, Wd867, Bk871, H873, Bk875, H875, H888, CA889, Bk917, Gg928, ASL937, Bar939
Middle Atlantic	GM796, WB810, Tb827, Pr831, Ln847, Bu857, Pr857, Bu859, Bu860, Ln868, OK870, DR876, Ln879, Ln884, PH910, Bol928, Mch931
South	MC792, GF799, OL826, Ull895, Rt928, Wyt931, Pk938
Great Lakes	Pkt835, Blo872, SH896, MCL898, Imy899, SH908, Sz910, Al930
Central/Plains	SSN871, Mic876, PS884, GS908, ISC914, Fg920, BrdK922, EF927
Mountain/West	RTm873, Tg904, Cx907, Ash908, Ger911, Pk912, Un916, Az921, Brd922, Az925, PW926, Un933, PHd937

Eschscholzia californica (California poppy)

New England	Bt836, Wd867, CA889, Gg915, Bk917, Gg928, ASL937, Bar939
Middle Atlantic	OK870, DR876, PH910, Bol928, JHr934
South	Ull895, TM925, Wyt931, Pk938
Great Lakes	GR889, SH896, MCL898, Imy899, SH908, Sz910, Er926
Central/Plains	PS875, Mic876, PS884, GS908, Nb918, Fg920, BrdK922, GY927, HF927, OW939
Mountain/West	MS874, SR880, Bg892, Cx907, Ger911, Un916, Az921, Brd922, PW926, Un933, OW939

Eucalyptus globulus (blue gum)

New England	Bk917
Middle Atlantic	none
South	none
Great Lakes	none
Central/Plains	PS884
Mountain/West	RTm873, MS874, SR880, Bn889, Bg892, Ca894, FC895, Cx907, Ash908, Ger911, PHd937

Euonymus americanus (strawberry tree)

New England	Br833, Br841, R853, G880
Middle Atlantic	JB783, JB792, M804, JB807, Bld819, Pr826, TH834, Wn844, Bu859, EB860
South	Sta858, Brk858, Aff860, Hgh903, BN907, Pk938
Great Lakes	Clv845, AlN858, Col860, RE893, SH894, CL901, SH908, Fr932
Central/Plains	CS860, SSN8781, Gy921, Gy927
Mountain/West	PW926

Fagus sylvatica (European beech)

New England	Ken832, Br833, Br841, OC861, LC872, NE910, Bk917
Middle Atlantic	Pr826, Wn844, Pars857, Bu859, EB860, HWC905, EB917, HN922
South	JR853, Brk858, Sta858, Brk861, Den871, BN907
Great Lakes	Mc845, LEN846, Col860, RE893, SH894, SH896, SH908, Sz910, Ch915, SH925
Central/Plains	PS884
Mountain/West	Ca894, FC895, Cx907, PK912

Filipendula vulgaris (dropwort)

New England	H834, Ken835, Bt836, Br841, Bk845, H852, Sac853, OC857, H859, Mn887, Mn889, G914
Middle Atlantic	Pr822, Ln826, Pr826, Ln828, Pr829, Pr831, TH834, Bu844, Pr844, Wn844, EB848, Pr857, Bu859, Bu860, EB862, Bu866, EB867, EB875, EB882, EB917,
South	Den871, BN907
Great Lakes	Pkt835, LEN846, Blo859, Blo867, Blo868, Blo872, T872, T873, Blo883, Wag905, Fr932
Central/Plains	SSN871
Mountain/West	Lb939

Forsythia viridissima (golden bell)

New England	Sac853, OC861, CA889, NE910, G914
Middle Atlantic	Bu859, EB860, MM870, DR876, PH910, EB917, HN922, My934

South	Pom856, Brk858, Sta858, Aff860, Brk861, ATN870, Dwr870, Den871, Lg881, Rs898, Brk906, BN907, WY907, Per927, Pk938
Great Lakes	PG858, Blo859, Col860, Col877, GR889, SH896, Wag905, SH908, ACN920, SH925, Er926, Fr932
Central/Plains	CS860, SSN871, WsN885, ShN886, ShN899, ISC914, Nb918, SN919, EF927
Mountain/West	DM887, Ca894, FC895, PK912

Fraxinus americana (American ash)

New England	Ken832, Br833, Br841, OC861, NE910, Bk917, Fsk927
Middle Atlantic	Pr771, JB783, WB810, Bld819, Pr826, Tb827, Wn844, Bu859, EB860, MM870, EB917
South	Ly854, Sta858, Den871, MV898, Hgh903, Brk906, BN907, CoS917
Great Lakes	Clv845, LEN846, Col860, Wau878, RE893, SH894, Crk904, Sz910, SH925, Al930
Central/Plains	CS860, PS884, WsN885, ShN886, Srx887, Ex888, ShN899, BrdK922, Gy921, Gy927, FbN933
Mountain/West	RTm873, SR880, DM887, Ca894, FC895, Cx907, Ger911, Brd922, PW926

Fritillaria imperialis (crown imperial)

New England	Ken835, Bt836, H847, Bk851, H862, H863, H866, Bk871, Mn875, Bk878, Bk881, NE910
Middle Atlantic	JB807, Bld819, Pr820, Tb827, Ln828, Ab830, Ab839, Pr860, EB860, EB862, EB867, BB873, EB875, EB882, Mch931
South	Brk861, Den871
Great Lakes	SG843, PG858, Blo859, T872, Blo873, Blo883, T873
Central/Plains	none
Mountain/West	Lb939

Galanthus nivalis (snowdrop)

New England	H847, Bk851, H862, H863, Mn875, NE910, Fsk927
Middle Atlantic	JB807, Pr820, Ln828, EB860, Pr860, BB873, EB875, EB882
South	none
Great Lakes	Blo859, Blo883, SH925
Central/Plains	GS908, ISC914
Mountain/West	RTm873

Gardenia augusta (gardenia)

New England	Br833, CA889
Middle Atlantic	PH910

South   SN851, Pom856, Brk858, Aff860, MN860, Brk861, ATN870, Lg881, MV888, Pf888, AEx894, Pf896, MV898, Rs898, JK904, Brk906, BN907, CoS917, TM925, Per927, Pk938, Kyo939

Great Lakes   SH874, GR889, SH896, SH908

Central/Plains   Mic876, ISC914

Mountain/West   SR880, Bg892, PHd937

Gelsemium sempervirens (Carolina jasmine)

New England   G880

Middle Atlantic   JB783, M804, Bld819, Pr826, Tb827, Bu859

South   MN860, Brk873, AP881, Lg881, AEx894, Hgh903, RP904, Brk906, BN907, GSM914, Pk938, Kyo939

Great Lakes   none

Central/Plains   none

Mountain/West   PHd937

Gladiolus (sword lily)

New England   Rd881, CA889, Gg915, Gg928, Hrd931, Bar939

Middle Atlantic   Pr820, Wn844, Pr857, EB860, MM870, OK970, DR876, AB895, HWC905, Ric905, PH910, HN922, Bol928, Mch931

South   Brk861, Den871, Brk873, Lg881, LR881, Tho888, AEx894, JD909, CoS917, Oz919, Rt928, Wyt931

Great Lakes   SG843, Blo859, SH874, Col877, GR889, Liv889, Scf896, SH896, Crk904, Tem904, LW905, Wag905, SH908, Sz910, Er926, WA928, Al930, Fr932

Central/Plains   Bf869, SSN871, Mic876, PS884, WsN885, Ex888, ISC914, Nb918, SN919, Fg920, Gy921, BrdK922, EF927, HF927, FbN933, OW939

Mountain/West   SR880, TS891, Ca894, FC895, Tg904, Cx907, Ash908, Brd922, Az925, PW926, Un933, GJ936

Gleditsia triacanthos (honey locust)

New England   Ken832, Br833, Br841, OC861, LC872, NE910

Middle Atlantic   JB783, Pr790, M804, JB807, WB810, Bld819, Tb827, Ken832, Br833, TH834, Br841, Wn844, Bu859, EB860, MM870, EB917, HN922

South   Sta858, Brk861, BN907, Pk938

Great Lakes   SG843, Clv845, LEN846, Wau878, CL901, SH908, Sz910, SH925

Central/Plains   PS884, Ex888, ShN899, SN919, Gy921, EF927, Gy927

Mountain/West   SR880, Ca894, FC895, Ger911, PK912

Gomphrena globosa (globe amaranth)

New England   Bst760, Bt836, Wd867, CA889, Gg915, Bk917, Gg928, ASL937, Bar939

Middle Atlantic   JB807, OK870, DR876, PH910, Jhr934

South   OL826, Ull895, Wyt931, Pk938

Great Lakes   GR889, Liv889, MCL898, Imy899, Sz910

Central/Plains   PS875, Mic876, PS884, GS908, ISC914, BrdK922, Gy927

Mountain/West   RTm873, Cx907, Ger911, Brd922, Az925, PW926, PHd937

Gourds, ornamental

New England   Bt836, Wd867, Ca889, Bk917, Bar939

Middle Atlantic   OK870, DR876, Bol928, PH910

South   Pk938

Great Lakes   Liv889, SH896, MCL898, Imy899, SH908, Sz910

Central/Plains   Mic876, PS884, GS908, ISC914, Nb918, Fg920, BrdK922, OW939

Mountain/West   SR880, Cx907, Ger911, Az921, Brd922, Az925, Un933, GJ936, PHd937, Lb939

Gypsophila elegans (annual baby's breath)

New England   Wd867, Bk917, Gg928, ASL937, Bar939

Middle Atlantic   Bol928, Mch931, JHr934

South   TM925, Wyt931, Pk938

Great Lakes   Liv889, MCL898, SH908, Sz910

Central/Plains   PS884, GS908, ISC914, Fg920, BrdK922, EF927, Gy927, OW939

Mountain/West   Cx907, Ash908, Ger911, Un916, Az921, Brd922, Un933, PHd937

Gypsophila paniculata (baby's breath)

New England   H862, H863, H873, H875, Mn887, H888, CA889, Mn889, Bk894, NE910, G914, Gg915, Bk917, Fsk927, Gg928, Hrd931, ASL937, Bar939

Middle Atlantic   Ln868, DR876, Ln884, EB882, PH910, EB917, Dk924, Mch931, JHr934, My934

South   BN907, Wyt931, Pk938

Great Lakes   Blo872, Blo873, Wag905, SH908, SH925, Er926, Al930, Fr932

Central/Plains   Mic876, GS908, ISC914, Nb918, BrdK922, HF927, FbN933, OW939

Mountain/West   Cx907, Ger911, PK912, Un916, Brd922, St923, PW926, GJ936, PHd937, Lb939

Hedera helix (English ivy)

New England   Br833, Br841, Rd881, CA889, Bk917

Middle Atlantic   JB807, WB810, Bld819, Pr826, TH834, Wn844, Bu859, DR876, PH910, JHr934, My934, Bun939

South	Sta858, ATN870, Den871, Tho888, AEx894, Rs898, BN907, Vd907, JD909, WY907, Per927, Pk938, Kyo939
Great Lakes	Clv845, Mc845, LEN846, PG858, Blo859, SH874, Col877, Imy899, CL901, Tem904, Wag905, SH925, Al930
Central/Plains	CS860, Mic876, OW939
Mountain/West	SR880, TS891, Cx907, Ash908, Ger911, PK912, PW926, PHd937

Helichrysum bracteatum (strawflower)

New England	Wd867, CA889, Gg915, Bk917, Gg928, ASL937, Bar939
Middle Atlantic	OK870, DR876, PH910, Bol928
South	CoS917, Rt923, Wyt931, Pk938
Great Lakes	Liv889, SH896, MCL898, SH908, Sz910, Er926, Al930
Central/Plains	PS875, Mic876, PS884, ISC914, Nb918, BrdK922, EF927, Gy927, HF927, OW939
Mountain/West	TS891, Tg904, Cx907, Ger911, Brd922, Az925, PW926, GJ936, PHd937

Heliotropium arborescens (heliotrope)

New England	Wd867, CA889, Gg915, Bk917, ASL937, Bar939
Middle Atlantic	M804, JB807, EB860, PH910, Bol928, JHr934
South	Sta858, Hop859, Brk861, Brk873, AP881, Tho888, JD909, TM925, Wyt931
Great Lakes	AlN858, Col860, SH874, Col877, GR889, Liv889, SH896, MCL898, Imy899, Tem904, SH908, Sz910
Central/Plains	CS860, SSN871, PS875, Mic876, PS884, GS908, ISC914, Nb918, Fg920, BrdK922, Gy927, HF927, OW939
Mountain/West	RTm873, Bn889, TS891, Cx907, Ger911, Un916, Brd922, PW926, GJ936, PHd937

Hemerocallis lilioasphodelus (lemon lily)

New England	Ken835, Br841, Bk845, Bk851, H852, R853, Sac853, OC857, H859, H873, Mn887, Mn889, G892, Bk894, G914, Bk917, Hrd931
Middle Atlantic	Pr799, Ln811, Pr820, PM822, Pr822, Ln826, Pr826, Ln828, Pr829, Pr831, TH834, Pr844, Wn844, EB848, Pr854, Pr857, AB895, PH910, EB917
South	Den871, BN907, CoS917, Rt928
Great Lakes	Clv845, LEN846, PG858, Blo859, SH896, Wag905, SH908, SH925, Fr932
Central/Plains	Dmk853, CS860, Mic876, GS908, ISC914, SN919, Gy921, BrdK922, HF927, FbN933
Mountain/West	Ca894, Ash908, PK912, Brd922, SW925, PW926, PHd937, Lb939

Hesperis matronalis (dame's rocket)

New England	Ken832, H834, H835, Ken835, Bt836, H836, Bk838, H839, Br841, H844, Bk845, H845, H847, Bk851, H852, H859, H863, Bk869, Bk875, H875, Bk878, CA889, Mn889, Ell894, NE910, Bk917, Gg928, ASL937, Bar939
Middle Atlantic	GM796, WB810, Ln811, Pr822, Ln826, Pr826, Tb827, Ln828, Pr829, Pr831, Pr844, Wn844, Ln847, EB848, Pr854, Pr857, EB867, Ln868, OK870, EB875, DR876, EB882, PH910, Bol928, Mch931
South	OL826, TM925, Pk938
Great Lakes	Pkt835, Clv845, LEN846, Blo872, Blo873, Blo875, GR889
Central/Plains	Dmk853, PS875, Mic876, PS884, GS908
Mountain/West	RTm873, Ger911, GJ936

Hibiscus moscheutos (swamp rose mallow)

New England	Bt836, G883, G886, Mn887, Mn889, G890, G892, NE910, G914, Bk917, Fsk927, Hrd931
Middle Atlantic	JB783, M804, JB807, Ln811, Pr818, Pr822, Ln826, Pr826, Ln828, Pr829, Pr831, TH834, Wn844, Ln847, Pr857, Pr844, EB848, Pr854, EB862, Bu866, EB867, EB875, EB917, Mch931
South	Hgh903, BN907, Pk938
Great Lakes	Pkt835, LEN846, Wag905, SH908
Central/Plains	SN919
Mountain/West	none

Hibiscus syriacus (althea, rose of Sharon)

New England	Ken832, Br833, Br841, R853, Sac853, OC861, Rd881, NE910, Bk917
Middle Atlantic	Pr790, M804, JB807, WB810, Bld819, Tb827, TH834, Wn844, Bu859, EB860, MM870, DR8786, HWC905, Ric905, PH910, EB917, HN922, Bun939
South	OL826, SN851, JR853, Brk858, MN860, Brk861, ATN870, Dwr870, Den871, Lg881, MV888, Pf888, PP895, Wm895, Pf896, MV898, Rs898, Brk906, BN907, WY907, GSM914, CoS917, Oz919, TM925, Per927, Pk938
Great Lakes	SG843, Clv845, Mc845, LEN846, Laz848, PG858, Blo859, Col860, Col877, GR889, RE893, SH894, SH896, CL901, Wag905, LW905, SH908, Ch915, ACN920, SH925, Er926, WA928, Al930, Fr932
Central/Plains	Dmk853, CS860, SSN871, WsN885, ShN886, Sk887, Ex888, ShN899, ISC914, SN919, BrdK922, Gy927, HF927, FbN933
Mountain/West	RTm873, DM887, Bg892, Ca894, FC895, Cx907, PK912, Brd922, PW926

Hippeastrum ×*johnsonii* (St. Joseph's lily)

New England	CA889, Bk917
Middle Atlantic	EB860, DR876, AB895
South	JR853, TM925, Per927, Rt928
Great Lakes	GR889, Liv889, SH896, Imy899, Wag905, SH908
Central/Plains	SSN871, GS908, ISC914
Mountain/West	TS891, Ca894, FC895

Hosta plantaginea (plantain lily)

New England	Ken832, Ken835, Br841, Bk845, Bk851, OC857, Mn875, Mn887, CA889, Mn889, Bk894, Bk917, Hrd931
Middle Atlantic	DR876, Ln828, Pr829, Pr831, TH834, Ab839, Bu844, EB848, Wn844, Pr854, Bu857, Pr857, Bu859, Bu860, EB860, EB862, Bu866, EB867, EB875, EB882, EB917, PH910
South	Den871, BN907
Great Lakes	Clv845, Mc845, LEN846, Blo859, Blo867, Blo868, Blo872, T872, Blo873, T873, Blo875, Col877, Blo883, Blo886, GR889, SH896
Central/Plains	CS860, Bf869, SSN871, Mic876, GS908, ISC914, SN919, HF927
Mountain/West	Lb939

Hosta ventricosa (blue day lily)

New England	Ken832, Ken835, Br841, Bk845, Bk851, OC857, Mn875, Mn887, Mn889, Bk917
Middle Atlantic	Ln811, Pr820, Pr822, Ln826, Pr826, Ln828, Pr829, Pr831, TH834, Ab839, Bu844, Pr844, Wn844, EB848, Pr854, Bu857, Pr857, Bu859, Bu860, EB860, EB862, Bu866, EB867, EB875, DR876, EB882, EB917
South	BN907, Pk938
Great Lakes	Clv845, Mc845, LEN846, PG858, Blo867, Blo868, Blo872, T872, Blo873, T873, Blo875, Blo883, Blo886, Wag905, Fr932
Central/Plains	CS860, Bf869, SSN871, Mic876
Mountain/West	Lb939

Hyacinthus orientalis (hyacinth)

New England	H834, Ken835, Bt836, H847, Bk851, H862, H863, H866, Bk871, Mn875, Bk878, Bk881, Rd881, NE910, Fsk927
Middle Atlantic	JB807, Ln811, Bld819, Pr820, PM822, Ln826, Ln828, Bu844, Wn844, Bu857, Pr857, EB860, Pr860, EB862, EB867, BB873, EB875, EB882, HWC905, JC910, Mch931
South	JW765, MC792, MC793, GF799, SN851, MN860, Brk861, Den871, LR881, JD909, CoS917, Oz919
Great Lakes	SG843, Mc845, AlN858, PG858, Blo859, T872, Blo873, T873, Blo883, GR889, SH896, LW905, Wag905, SH925

Central/Plains	Bf869, SSN871, GS908, ISC914, HF927
Mountain/West	RTm873, FC895, Az921, St923

Hydrangea macrophylla (changeable hydrangea)

New England	Ken832, Br833, Br841, CA889
Middle Atlantic	JB807, Bld819, Pr826, TH834, Wn844, Bu859, EB860, MM870, DR876, Mch931
South	Sta858, Brk861, Brk873, Lg881, AEx894, Rs898, JK904, BN907
Great Lakes	SG843, Clv845, Mc845, Blo859, SH874, Col877, GR889, SH896, Tem904, SH908
Central/Plains	none
Mountain/West	Ca894, FC895, Cx907, Ash908, Ger911, PHd937

Hydrangea paniculata 'Grandiflora' (peegee hydrangea)

New England	CA889, Du901, NE910, G914, Bk917, Hrd931
Middle Atlantic	MM870, DR876, HWC905, Ric905, PH910, EB917, HN922, My934, Bun939
South	Lg881, Tho888, Rs898, JK904, Brk906, BN907, WY907, Vd907, GSM914, Oz919
Great Lakes	Col877, GR889, RE893, SH896, CL901, LW905, SH908, Ch915, Bd919, ACN920, SH925, Er926, WA928, Al930, Fr932
Central/Plains	SSN871, Mic876, ShN886, ShN899, GS908, ISC914, Nb918, SN919, Gy921, EF927, Gy927, HF927
Mountain/West	Ca894, FC895, Cx907, PK912, PW926, GJ936

Iberis sempervirens (candytuft)

New England	Bst760, H862, H863, Bk871, H873, Bk875, H875, Bk878, Bk881, Mn887, H888, Mn889, Bk894, NE910, G914, Bk917, ASL937, Hrd931
Middle Atlantic	TH834, EB875, EB882, JC910, PH910, EB917, Mch931, JHr934
South	Den871, Brk873, BN907, Wyt931, Pk938
Great Lakes	Blo867, Blo868, Blo872, Blo873, SH874, Blo875, Blo883, GR889, SH896, Wag905, SH908, SH925, Fr932
Central/Plains	Mic876, ISC914, HF927
Mountain/West	Ca894, PW926, GJ936, Lb939

Ilex opaca (American holly)

New England	Ken832, Br833, Br841
Middle Atlantic	JB783, M804, JB807, WB810, Bld819, Pr826, Tb827, Wn844, Bu859, Bun939
South	SN851, Sta858, ATN870, AEx894, Hgh903, Brk906, BN907, GSM914, Per927, Kyo939
Great Lakes	SG843
Central/Plains	none
Mountain/West	none

Impatiens balsamina (balsam)

New England	Bst760, Bt836, CA889, Gg915, Bk917, ASL937, Bar939
Middle Atlantic	JB807, WB810, OK870, DR876, PH910, Bol928, JHr934
South	MC793, GF799, OL826, AP881, LR881, Ull895, CoS917, Rt923, Wyt931, Pk938
Great Lakes	GR889, Liv889, Scf896, SH896, MCL898, Imy899, SH908, Sz910, Al930
Central/Plains	PS875, PS884, GS908, ISC914, Nb918, Fg920, BrdK922, GY927, HF927, OW939
Mountain/West	RTm873, SR880, TS891, Tg904, Cx907, Ger911, Un916, Az921, Brd922, Az925, PW926, Un933, PHd937

Ipomoea purpurea (morning glory)

New England	Bst760, Wd867, CA889, Gg915, Bk917, Gg928
Middle Atlantic	JB783, Pr818, OK870, DR876, PH910
South	OL826, Ull895, TM925, Wyt931, Pk938
Great Lakes	Liv889, MCL898, SH908, Sz910, Al930
Central/Plains	PS875, Mic876, PS884, GS908, BrdK922, EF927
Mountain/West	RTm873, SR880, Tg904, Cx907, Ash908, Az921, Brd922, Az925, PW926, Un933

Ipomoea quamoclit (cypress vine)

New England	Bt836, Wd867, CA889, Gg915, Bk917, Gg928, Bar939
Middle Atlantic	JB807, WB810, OK870, DR876, PH910
South	OL826, AP881, LR881, Ull895, CoS917, TM925, Wyt931, Pk938
Great Lakes	GR889, Liv889, Imy899, SH908, Sz910
Central/Plains	PS875, Mic876, PS884, GS908, ISC914, Nb918, Fg920, BrdK922, Gy927, HF927
Mountain/West	Cx907, Ger911, Un916, Az921, Brd922, Az925, PW926, GJ936

Iris ensata (Japanese iris)

New England	H873, H875, Mn887, H888, CA889, Mn889, G892, NE910, Bk917, Hrd931
Middle Atlantic	MM870, BB873, AB895, HWC905, JC910, PH910, EB917, JHr934, My934
South	Brk906, Pk938
Great Lakes	Blo886, GR889, SH896, Wag905, SH925, Fr932
Central/Plains	ISC914, SN919, Gy921, BrdK922, Gy927
Mountain/West	Bg892, Cx907, PK912, Brd922, PHd937

Iris germanica (bearded iris)

New England	Ken832, Ken835, Bt836, Br841, Bk845, H847, Bk851, OC857, H863, H866, Bk871, H875, Bk878, Bk881, Mn887, Mn889, G890, G892, G914, Hrd931
Middle Atlantic	M804, Ln811, Bld819, Pr820, PM822, Ln826, Pr826, Ab827, Ln828, Pr829, Ab830, Pr831, TH834, Ab839, Bu844, EB848, Pr854, Bu857, Pr857, Bu859, Pr860, EB867, BB873, EB875, EB882, EB917, HN922, Dk924, Mch931, My934
South	Den871, BN907, Oz919
Great Lakes	Clv845, LEN846, Blo859, Blo867, Blo868, T872, Blo873, T873, Blo883, Blo886, LW905, Bd919, SH925, Er926
Central/Plains	SSN871, Gy921, BrdK922, Gy927, HF927, FbN933
Mountain/West	RTm873, MS874, SR880, DM887, Brd922, St923, PHd937, Lb939

Iris xiphium (Spanish iris)

New England	Br841, H847, Bk851, H862, H863, H866, Bk871, Bk878, Bk881, G892
Middle Atlantic	JB807, WB810, Pr820, PM822, Pr826, Pr829, Pr831, TH834, Pr857, EB860, Pr860, EB862, EB867, BB873, EB875, AB895, JC910, Mch931
South	Den871
Great Lakes	Blo859, Blo883, SH925
Central/Plains	none
Mountain/West	RTm873

Jasminum officinale (jasmine)

New England	Ken832, Br833, Br841
Middle Atlantic	Pr826, TH834, Wn844, Bu859, EB860, DR876, PH910
South	ATN870, Lg881, RP904, BN907, CoS917
Great Lakes	Mc845, LEN846, Laz848, SH874, Col877
Central/Plains	Mic876
Mountain/West	Ca894, FC895, Cx907, PK912, PHd937

Juglans nigra (black walnut)

New England	R853
Middle Atlantic	JB783, Pr790, M804, JB807, Bld819, Tb827, EB917
South	Den871, Brk906, BN907, Vd907
Great Lakes	LEN846, Fr932
Central/Plains	ShN886, Ex888, ShN899, NN919, SN919, Gy921, NW924, EF927, FbN933, OW939
Mountain/West	Ca894, FC895, Cx907, Ger911

Juniperus communis 'Hibernica' (Irish juniper)

New England	LC872, Rd881, NE910, G914, Bk917, Hrd931
Middle Atlantic	Bu859, EB860, MM870, HWC905, EB917, HN922, My934, Bun939
South	Pom856, Brk858, Sta858, Brk861, ATN870, Dwr870, Den871, VB885, JBk895, Brk906, BN907, Vd907, CoS917, Oz919, TM925, Per927
Great Lakes	SH894, CL901, LW905, SH908, Ch915, SH925, Er926, Al930
Central/Plains	SSN871, Mic876, WsN885, ShN886, ShN899, BrdK922
Mountain/West	RTm873, Bn889, Ca894, FC895, PK912, Brd922, PW926

Juniperus virginiana (red cedar)

New England	Ken832, Br833, Br841, OC861, NE910, G914, Bk917, Fsk927, Hrd931
Middle Atlantic	Pr771, JB783, Pr790, M804, JB807, WB810, Bld819, Pr826, Tb827, Wn844, Bu859, EB860, EB917, HN922
South	JS793, SN851, LY854, Aff860, TR868, ATN870, Lg881, MV888, PP895, Wm895, Pf896, MV898, Hgh903, BN907, WY907, GSM914
Great Lakes	SG843, LEN846, Blo859, En859, Col860, Wau878, SH894, CL901, SH908, SH925, Fr932
Central/Plains	Dmk853, CS860, ShN886, PS884, ShN899, Kv887, Sk887, WsN885, Ex888, SN919, BrdK922, NW924, EF927, Gy927, FbN933
Mountain/West	Rtm873, FC895, Ger911, PK912, Brd922, PHd937

Kalmia latifolia (mountain laurel)

New England	Ken832, Br833, Br841, G880, Rd881, NE910, G914, Bk914, Bk917, Hrd931
Middle Atlantic	Pr771, JB783, M804, JB907, WB810, Bld819, Pr826, Tb827, Wn844, Bu859, EB860, EB817, HN922
South	Dwr870, Den871, Hgh903, Brk906, BN907, Per927, Pk938
Great Lakes	Mc845, LEN846, SH896, WAG905, Fr932
Central/Plains	none
Mountain/West	PK912

Kerria japonica 'Pleniflora' (corchorus, kerria)

New England	Ken832, Br833, Br844, R853, NE910, G914, Bk917, Fsk927
Middle Atlantic	Bld819, Pr826, TH834, Wn844, Bu859, EB860, MM870, PH910, EB917, My934
South	Sta858, ATN870, Den871, Lg881, Brk906, BN907
Great Lakes	SG843, Clv845, Mc845, LEN846, Laz848, Col860, SH896, Wag905, SH908, Er926, Al930
Central/Plains	SSN871, ISC914, SN919
Mountain/West	SR880, Ca894, Ash908, Pk912, Lb939

Koelreuteria paniculata (golden raintree)

New England	Ken832, Br833, Br841, Sac853, OC861, NE910
Middle Atlantic	Pr826, TH834, Wn844, Bu859, EB860, MM870, EB917, My934
South	Brk858, Sta858, Brk861, Dwr870, Den871, Lg881, Brk906, BN907, CoS917, Pk938
Great Lakes	Mc845, Blo859, Fr932
Central/Plains	CS860
Mountain/West	SR880, Ca894, FC895, Cx907, PK912, PHd937

Lablab purpureus (purple hyacinth bean)

New England	Bt836, CA889, Bk917, Bar939
Middle Atlantic	OK870, DR876, PH910, Bol928, JHr934
South	OL826, Ull895, TM925, Wyt931, Pk938
Great Lakes	GR889, Liv889, MCL898, SH908, Sz910
Central/Plains	PS875, Mic876, PS884, GS908, ISC914, Nb918, BrdK922, HF927
Mountain/West	RTm873, Cx907, Ger911, Az921, Brd922, Az925, Un933, GJ936

Laburnum anagyroides (golden chain)

New England	Ken832, Br833, Bt836, R853, OC861, Bk917
Middle Atlantic	Pr790, JB792, JB807, WB810, Bld819, Pr826, Tb827, TH834, Wn844, Bu859, EB860, MM870, DR876, EB917, HN922
South	JR853, LY854, Sta858, Aff860, Brk861, Den871, BN907, Pk938
Great Lakes	SG843, Clv845, Mc845, LEN846, AlN858, PG858, Col860, Wag905
Central/Plains	CS860
Mountain/West	RTm873, FC895, Cx907, PK912, PW926

Lagerstroemia indica (crepe myrtle)

New England	none
Middle Atlantic	JB807, Bu859, MM870, HN922, Bun939
South	JR853, Aff860, MN860, ATN870, Dwr870, Den871, Brk873, Lg881, MV888, Pf888, Tho888, AEx894, PP895, Wm895, Pf896, MV898, Rs898, RP904, Brk906, BN907, WY907, GSM914, CoS917, TM925, Per927, Pk938, Kyo939
Great Lakes	Mc845, SH874, Col877, GR889
Central/Plains	Mic876
Mountain/West	SR880, Bg892, Ca894, FC895, Cx907, Ger911, PHd937

Lantana camara (shrub verbena)

New England	Gg915, Gg928, Bar939
Middle Atlantic	M804, EB860, DR876, PH910, Bol928
South	JR853, Brk873, LR881, Tho888, JK904, JD909, Per927
Great Lakes	AlN858, Blo859, Col860, SH874, Col877, GR889, SH896, MCL898, SZ910
Central/Plains	CS860, SN871, PS875, Mic876, PS884, ISC914, Fg920, BrdK922, HF927
Mountain/West	SR880, FC895, Cx907, Ash908, Ger911, Un916, Az921, Brd922, Az925, GJ936, PHd937

Larix decidua (larch)

New England	Ken832, Br833, Br841, R853, Sac853, OC861, LC872, Rd881, Bk917
Middle Atlantic	JB792, JB807, Bld819, Pr826, Bu859, EB860, MM870, EB917
South	LY854, Sta858, Dwr870, Den871, BN907
Great Lakes	Clv845, Mc845, LEN846, AlN858, PG858, Blo859, Col860, Wau878, SH894, SH896, SH908, Sz910, Fr932
Central/Plains	CS860, Dmk868, SSN871, PS884, ShN886, Sgfld887, Srx887, ShN899, NW924
Mountain/West	SR880, Ca894, Cx907, PK912

Lathyrus latifolius (perennial sweet pea)

New England	Bst760, Ken832, H834, H835, Ken835, Bt836, H836, Bk838, H839, Br841, H844, H845, H847, Bk851, H852, OC857, H862, H863, Bk869, Bk871, H873, Bk875, H875, Bk878, Bk881, Mn887, H888, CA889, Mn889, Ell894, Bk917, Hrd931, ASL937, Bar939
Middle Atlantic	GM796, JB807, WB810, PM822, Pr822, Pr826, Tb827, Pr829, Pr831, TH834, Ab839, Bu844, Pr844, Wn844, Ln847, EB848, Pr854, Bu857, Pr857, Bu859, Bu860, EB862, Ln865, Bu866, EB867, Ln868, OK870, EB875, DR876, Ln879, EB882, Ln884, Ln889, PH910, Mch931, JHr934, My934
South	BN907, Wyt931, Pk938
Great Lakes	Pkt835, Mc845, LEN846, Blo883, Liv889, SH896, MCL898, Wag905, SH908, Sz910, SH925, Er926, Fr932
Central/Plains	PS875, Mic876, PS884, GS908, ISC914, HF927, Gy927
Mountain/West	SR880, Cx907, Ger911, PW926, GJ936, Lb939

Lathyrus odoratus (annual sweet pea)

New England	Wd867, CA889, Du901, Gg915, Bk917, Gg928, ASL937, Bar939
Middle Atlantic	OK870, DR876, PH910, Bol928, Mch931, JHr934, My934
South	OL826, Ull895, JD909, CoS917, TM925, Rt928, Wyt931, Pk938

Great Lakes	GR889, Liv889, Scf896, SH896, MCL898, Imy899, SH908, Sz910, SH925, Er926, Al930
Central/Plains	PS875, Mic876, PS884, GS908, ISC914, Nb918, Fg920, BrdK922, EF927, Gy927, OW939
Mountain/West	RTm873, SR880, Tg904, Cx907, Ash908, Ger911, Un916, Az921, Brd922, Az925, PW926, Un933, PHd937

Leucanthemum ×superbum (Shasta daisy)

New England	NE910, G914, Gg915, Bk917, Fsk927, ASL937, Bar939
Middle Atlantic	PH910, EB917, Mch931, JHr934, My934
South	BN907, CoS917, TM925, Wyt931
Great Lakes	Wag905, SH908, Sz910, Er926, Al930
Central/Plains	GS908, ISC914, Nb918, SN919, Fg920, Gy921, BrdK922, EF927, Gy927, HF927
Mountain/West	Cx907, Ash908, Ger911, PK912, Az921, Brd922, St923, Az925, PW926, GJ936, PHd937, Lb939

Liatris spicata (gayfeather)

New England	H834, Br841, H859, H873, H875, G883, G886, Mn887, Mn889, G890, G892, Hrd931, Bar939
Middle Atlantic	M804, JB807, Ln811, Pr818, Pr820, Ln826, Ln828, Pr829, Pr831, Ab839, Pr844, Wn844, EB848, Pr857, EB860, EB862, EB867, EB875, EB882, JHr934
South	Den871, Hgh903, Pk938
Great Lakes	Mc845, Blo859, Blo867, Blo868, Blo872, Blo873, Blo875, Blo883, Er926
Central/Plains	OW939
Mountain/West	none

Ligustrum ovalifolium (California privet)

New England	NE910, Bk917, Fsk927
Middle Atlantic	MM870, Ric905, PH910, EB917, HN922
South	Pom856, Lg881, MV888, Pf888, PP895
Great Lakes	RE893, SH896, SH908, Sz910, Ch915
Central/Plains	Ex888, ShN899, SN919, BrdK922
Mountain/West	Ca894, Cx907, Brd922, PW926

Ligustrum vulgare (common privet)

New England	Ken832, Br841, LC872, NE910, G914
Middle Atlantic	WB810, Pr826, TH834, Wn844, Bu859, MM870, EB917
South	Pom856, Sta858, Dwr870, ATN870, Den871, Lg881, Rs898, BN907
Great Lakes	Clv845, Mc845, LEN846, Laz848, Blo859, Col860, ACN920, SH925, Fr932
Central/Plains	Dmk853, CS860, ShN886, FbN933
Mountain/West	RTm873, Ca894, PW926

Lilium auratum (gold-band lily)

New England	H866, Bk871, H873, H875, Mn875, Bk878, Bk881, Mn887, H888, CA889, Mn889, G890, G892, NE910, G914, Gg915, Bk917, Fsk927, Hrd931, Bar939
Middle Atlantic	EB867, OK870, BB873, EB875, DR876, EB882, Ric905, JC910, PH910, Mch931, JHr934
South	Den871, Brk873, Lg881, AEx894, BN907, Oz919, TM925, Pk938
Great Lakes	Blo868, Blo872, T872, Blo873, T873, Blo875, Col877, Blo886, GR889, Liv889, SH896, Imy899, SH908, SH925, Al930, Fr932
Central/Plains	Bf869, SSN871, WsN885, GS908, ISC914, Nb918, SN919, Gy921, HF927, FbN933
Mountain/West	Bg892, Ca894, FC895, Cx907, PK912, St923, PW926

Lilium canadense (Canadian martagon)

New England	Ken835, Bk851, H859, H866, G879, G883, G886, Mn887, CA889, Mn889, G890, G892, G914, Bk917, Fsk927, Hrd931
Middle Atlantic	M804, Pr820, Ln826, Ab827, Ln828, Ab830, TH834, Ab839, Pr854, Pr860, BB873, JC910, Mch931, JHr934
South	Hg903, BN907, Den871
Great Lakes	none
Central/Plains	none
Mountain/West	none

Lilium candidum (Madonna lily)

New England	Ken832, Ken835, Bt836, Br841, H852, H859, H866, Bk871, Mn875, Bk878, Bk881, Mn887, CA889, Mn889, G892, NE910, G914, Fsk927, Hrd931
Middle Atlantic	JB807, Bld819, Pr820, Ln826, Ln828, Ab839, Bu844, Wn844, Pr854, EB860, Pr860, Bu866, EB867, BB873, EB875, EB882, JC910, Mch931, JHr934
South	Den871, AEx894, BN907, Oz919
Great Lakes	Mc845, Col877, GR889, Imy899, Blo859, T866, Blo868, Blo872, T872, Blo873, T873, Blo886, SH925, Fr932
Central/Plains	Bf869, SSN871, WsN885, GS908, ISC914, SN919
Mountain/West	RTm873, Ca894, PK912, St923, Lb939

Lilium lancifolium (tiger lily)

New England	Ken832, Ken835, Br841, Bk851, H852, H859, H866, Mn875, Mn887, CA889, Mn889, G890, G892, NE910
Middle Atlantic	Ab827, Ln828, Bu844, Pr854, Bu866, MM870, BB873, EB875, EB882, Ab830, JHr934
South	Den871, AEx894, BN907, Oz919
Great Lakes	Mc845, PG858, Blo859, Blo868, Blo872, T872, Blo873, T873, Blo875, Col877, Liv889, Blo886
Central/Plains	Dmk853, SSN871, ShN886, ShN899, ISC914, HF927, Gy921, OW939,
Mountain/West	DM887, FC895, Cx907, PK912, PW926, Lb939

Lilium martagon (martagon lily)

New England	Ken832, Ken835, Bt836, Br841, Bk851, H852, H859, H866, Bk871, Bk878, Bk881, Mn887, Mn889, G890, G892, Hrd931
Middle Atlantic	JB807, Bld819, Pr820, TH834, Pr854, EB860, Pr860, BB873, EB875, JHr934
South	Pk938
Great Lakes	Blo859, Blo872, Blo873
Central/Plains	none
Mountain/West	none

Lilium pumilum (coral lily)

New England	H866, H873, H875, Mn887, CA889, Mn889, G890, G892, NE910, G914, Hrd931, Bar939
Middle Atlantic	Pr854, EB860, Pr860, Ric905, JC910, Mch931, JHr934
South	none
Great Lakes	GR889, LIV889
Central/Plains	GS908, ISC914, OW939
Mountain/West	Lb939

Lilium speciosum (Japan lily, rubrum lily)

New England	H852, H859, H866, H873, H875, Mn875, Rd881, Mn887, CA889, Mn889, Bk871, Bk878, Bk881, G890, G892, NE910, G914, Gg915, Bk917, Fsk927, Hrd931, Bar939
Middle Atlantic	Pr854, EB860, Pr860, Bu866, EB867, OK870, BB873, EB875, DR876, EB882, JC910, PH910, Mch931, JHr934
South	Den871, Brk873, Brk861, Lg881, AEx894, Oz919, TM925
Great Lakes	Blo859, T866, Blo868, Blo872, T872, Blo873, T873, Blo875, Col877, Blo886, GR889, Liv889, SH896, LW905, SH908, SH925, Al930, Fr932
Central/Plains	Bf869, SSN871, WsN885, GS908, ISC914, Nb918, SN919, Gy921, HF927, FbN933
Mountain/West	Bg892, Ca894, FC895, Cx907, PK912, St923, PW926

Lilium superbum (superb lily)

New England	Bt836, Br841, H852, H859, H866, Mn887, Mn889, Bk851, G883, G886, CA889, G890, G892, NE910, G914, Bk917, Fsk927, Hrd931
Middle Atlantic	JB783, M804, Pr818, Ln826, Ln828, Ab830, Ab839, Bu844, Pr854, Bu866, EB867, BB873, EB875, JC910, Mch931
South	Den871, Hgh903, BN907
Great Lakes	T873, SH896, SH908, Al930
Central/Plains	Bf869, GS908
Mountain/West	RTm873

Lilium ×testaceum (Nankeen lily)

New England	H866, Bk871, Bk878, Bk881, Mn887, CA889, Hrd931
Middle Atlantic	EB860, EB862, EB867, OK870, BB873, EB875, JC910
South	Den871
Great Lakes	Blo872, T872, Blo873, T873, Blo875, Col877
Central/Plains	Bf869
Mountain/West	none

Linum perenne (perennial flax)

New England	Ken832, H834, H835, Ken835, Bt836, H836, Bk838, H839, Br841, Bk871, H873, H875, Mn887, H888, Mn889, Bk917, Hrd931, ASL937, Bar939
Middle Atlantic	GM796, Pr822, Ab827, Tb827, Pr829, Ab830, Pr831, TH834, Ab839, Pr844, Wn844, Pr857, EB860, EB862, EB867, EB875, OK870, EB882, PH910, EB917, Mch931, JHr934, My934
South	OL826, Wyt931, Pk938
Great Lakes	Pkt835, Blo859, Blo872, Blo873, Blo875, Blo883, SH908, Er926, Al930, Fr932
Central/Plains	Bf869, PS875, Mic876, PS884, ISC914, HF927, OW939
Mountain/West	Ash908, PW926, Lb939

Liquidambar styraciflua (sweet gum)

New England	Ken832, Br833, Br841
Middle Atlantic	JB783, Pr790, M804, JB807, Bld819, Pr826, Tb827, Wn844, EB860, EB917
South	Rs898, Hgh903, Brk906, BN907, WY907, GSM914, Pk938
Great Lakes	Blo859, RE893, SH894, Fr932
Central/Plains	Sgfld887, Srx887
Mountain/West	PK912, PHd937

Liriodendron tulipifera (tulip tree)

New England	Ken832, Br833, Br841, Sac853, OC861, G880, Rd881, NE910, Bk917

Middle Atlantic	JB783, Pr771, Pr790, M804, WB810, Bld819, Pr826, Tb827, TH834, Wn844, Bu859, EB860, EB917, HN922, My934
South	Sta858, Den871, Lg881, Rs898, Hgh903, Brk906, BN907, WY907, Per927, Pk938
Great Lakes	SG843, Clv845, LEN846, AlN858, PG858, Blo859, Col860, Wau878, SH894, LW905, Ch915, Er926, Al930, Fr932
Central/Plains	SSN871, WsN885, ShN886, Sk887, Srx887, ShN899, BrdK922, FbN933
Mountain/West	RTm873, SR880, Ca894, FC895, Cx907, PK912, Brd922, PW926

Lobelia cardinalis (cardinal flower)

New England	Ken832, H834, H835, Ken835, H836, Bk838, Bt836, H839, Br841, H844, Bk845, H847, Bk851, H852, OC857, H859, Wd867, Bk869, Bk871, H873, Bk875, H875, Bk878, G879, Bk881, G883, G886, Mn887, H888, Mn889, G890, G892, Bk894, NE910, G914, Gg915, Bk917, Hrd931, Bar939
Middle Atlantic	JB783, M804, JB807, WB810, Ln811, Pr818, Pr822, Ln826, Pr826, Ab827, Tb827, Ln828, Pr829, Pr831, TH834, Ab839, Pr844, Wn844, Ln847, EB848, Pr854, Bu857, Pr857, Bu859, Bu866, Ln868, OK870, DR876, Ln889, PH910, EB917, Mch931, My934
South	Hgh903, Wyt931, Pk938
Great Lakes	Pkt835, Mc845, LEN846, Blo872, SH908, SH925, Al930, Fr932
Central/Plains	SSN871, SN919, HF927
Mountain/West	Cx907, Ger911, PK912, PW926, PHd937, Lb939

Lobelia erinus (edging lobelia)

New England	Wd867, CA889, Gg915, Bk917, Gg928, ASL937, Bar939
Middle Atlantic	OK870, DR876, PH910, Bol928, JHr934
South	AP881, LR881, Tho888, Ull895, TM925, Wyt931, Pk938
Great Lakes	SH874, Col877, GR889, Liv889, MCL898, Imy899, SH908, Sz910
Central/Plains	SSN871, PS875, Mic876, PS884, GS908, ISC914, Nb918, Fg920, BrdK922, EF927
Mountain/West	RTm873, FC895, Cx907, Ash908, Ger911, Un916, Az921, Brd922, Az925, PW926, Un933, PHd937

Lobularia maritima (sweet alyssum)

New England	Bt836, Wd867, CA889, Gg915, Bk917, Gg928, ASL937, Bar939
Middle Atlantic	WB810, OK870, DR876, PH910, Bol928, JHr934

South	AP881, LR881, Ull895, JK904, JD909, TM925, Rt928, Wyt931, Pk938
Great Lakes	GR889, Liv889, SH896, MCL898, Imy899, Wag905, SH908, Sz910, SH925, Al930
Central/Plains	PS875, Mic876, GS908, ISC914, Nb918, Fg920, BrdK922, EF927, Gy927, HR927, OW939
Mountain/West	Tg904, Cx907, Ash908, Ger911, Un916, Az921, Brd922, Az925, PW926, Un933, GJ936, PHd937, Lb939

Lonicera flava (yellow trumpet honeysuckle)

New England	Ken832, Br833, Br841, Sac853, G880, Rd881
Middle Atlantic	Pr826, TH834, Wn844, DR876, HWC905
South	JR853, Pom856, Brk861, ATN870, Den871, Lg881, Hgh903, BN907
Great Lakes	SG843, LEN846, PG858, Blo859, Col860, GR889
Central/Plains	CS860, SSN871, WsN885, ShN886, BrdK922
Mountain/West	Ca894, Brd922

Lonicera japonica 'A"="Aureareticulata' (gold-netted honeysuckle)

New England	none
Middle Atlantic	PH910, EB917
South	ATN870, Den871, Lg881, Tho888, AEx894, Rs898, Brk906, BN907, Vd907, WY907
Great Lakes	RE893, SH896, SH908, SH925
Central/Plains	Dmk868, Mic876
Mountain/West	Ca894, Cx907, Ger911

Lonicera japonica 'Halliana' (Hall's Japan honeysuckle)

New England	CA889, Du901, NE910, Bk917, Fsk927
Middle Atlantic	MM870, DR876, HWC905, Ric905, PH910, EB917, My934, Bun939
South	Den871, Lg881, MV888, AEx894, Hgh903, RP904, BN907, WY907, CoS917, TM925
Great Lakes	Col877, GR889, RE893, SH896, Wag905, Ch915, SH925, Er926, WA928, Al930
Central/Plains	SSN871, ShN886, Sk887, GS908, ISC914, SN919, Gy921, BrdK922, Gy927, HF927, FbN933
Mountain/West	DM887, Cx907, Ger911, PK912, Brd922, Az925, PW926, PHd937

Lonicera periclymenum 'Belgica' (Belgian honeysuckle)

New England	Ken832, Br833, Br841, Sac853, NE910, Bk917
Middle Atlantic	Pr790, TH834, Wn844, Bu859, EB860, DR876, EB917
South	Pom856, Brk858, Sta858, Brk861, ATN870, Lg881, MV888, Tho888, AEx894, MV898, Rs898, Brk906, BN907, WY907

Great Lakes	Clv845, Mc845, LEN846, GR889, SH908, SH925
Central/Plains	CS860, Dmk868, SSN871, WsN885, BrdK922
Mountain/West	Ca894, Cx907, PK912, Brd922

Lonicera sempervirens (scarlet honeysuckle)

New England	Ken832, Br833, Br841, Sac853, Rd881, Du901, NE910, Bk917
Middle Atlantic	JB783, M804, JB807, WB810, Pr826, TH834, Wn844, Pars857, EB860, HWC905, EB917
South	JR853, Sta858, Brk861, ATN870, Den871, Lg881, MV888, AEx894, Rs898, MV898, Hgh903, Brk906, BN907, WY907, GSM914, CoS917
Great Lakes	SG843, Clv845, Mc845, LEN846, Laz848, AlN858, PG858, Blo859, Col860, GR889, RE893, SH896, CL901, SH925, Fr932
Central/Plains	Dmk853, CS860, Dmk868, SSN871, ShN886, GS908, NN919, Gy921, Gy927, EF927, HF927
Mountain/West	SR880, DM887, Lb939

Lonicera tatarica (bush honeysuckle)

New England	Ken832, Br833, Br841, R853, Sac853, OC861, Rd881, CA889, Du901, NE910, Bk917, Fsk927, Hrd931
Middle Atlantic	Pr826, TH834, Wn844, Bu859, EB860, EB917, HN922, My934, Bun939
South	JR853, Pom856, Den871, BN907, CoS917, Pk938
Great Lakes	SG843, Clv845, Mc845, LEN846, PG858, Blo859, Col860, Col877, GR889, RE893, SH896, Crk904, Wag905, SH908
Central/Plains	CS860, Dmk868, WsN885, ShN886, Ex888, ShN899, GS908, ISC914, SN919, Gy921, EF927, Gy927
Mountain/West	DM887, Ca894, Cx907, Ger911, PK912, PW926, Lb939

Lupinus polyphyllus (lupine)

New England	H834, Ken835, Bt836, Bk838, H839, H844, Bk845, H845, H847, Bk851, H852, H859, H862, H863, Bk871, H873, H875, Bk878, Bk881, H888, Mn889, Bk894, NE910, Bk917, Hrd931, Bar939
Middle Atlantic	TH834, Ab839, Pr844, Wn844, EB848, Pr854, Pr857, EB860, Ln865, Ln868, Ln884, PH910, Dk924, Mch931
South	Pk938
Great Lakes	Pkt835, Mc845, LEN846, Blo872, Wag905
Central/Plains	none
Mountain/West	SR880, PK912

Lychnis chalcedonica (Maltese cross)

New England	Ken832, H834, H835, Ken835, Bt836, H836, Bk838, H839, Br841, H844, Bk845, H847, Bk851, H852, Sac853, OC857, H859, H862, H863, Wd867, Bk871, H873, Bk875, H875, Bk878, Bk881, Mn887, H888, CA889, Mn889, Bk894, NE910, G914, Bk917, Hrd931, ASL937
Middle Atlantic	GM796, JB807, Ln811, Bld819, PM822, Pr822, Ln826, Pr826, Ab827, Tb827, Ln828, Pr829, Ab830, Pr831, TH834, Ab839, Bu844, Pr844, Wn844, Ln847, EB848, Pr854, Bu857, Pr857, Bu859, Bu860, EB860, EB862, Bu866, EB867, Ln868, OK870, EB875, DR876, Ln879, EB882, Ln884, Ln889, PH910, EB917, Dk924, Bol928, Mch931, JHr934, My934
South	OL826, Den871, BN907, Pk938
Great Lakes	Pkt835, Clv845, Mc845, LEN846, Blo859, Blo867, Blo868, Blo872, T872, Blo873, T873, Blo875, Blo883, Blo886, GR889, Liv889, SH896, Wag905, SH908, Sz910, SH925, Er926
Central/Plains	CS860, SSN871, PS875, Mic876, PS884, GS908, ISC914, Gy927, HF927
Mountain/West	RTm873, Cx907, Ger911, PK912, St923, PW926, Lb939

Lychnis coronaria (rose campion)

New England	Ken832, H834, Ken835, Bt836, H836, Bk838, H839, Br841, Bk845, H852, H859, H862, H863, H873, H875, H888, Mn889, Bk894, Gg915, Bk917, Gg928, Hrd931, ASL937
Middle Atlantic	GM796, WB810, Ln811, Pr822, Ln826, Ln828, Pr829, Pr831, Pr844, Wn844, Ln847, EB848, Pr854, Pr857, Ln868, OK870, Ln879, Ln889, NE910, PH910, Mch931, My934
South	Pk938
Great Lakes	Pkt835, Clv845, Mc845, LEN846, SH908, SH925, Er926, Fr932
Central/Plains	PS875, Mic876, PS884, BrdK922
Mountain/West	RTm873, SR880, Brd922, PW926, Lb939

Lychnis flos-cuculi (ragged robin)

New England	Ken832, H8334, Ken835, Br841, Bk845, H847, Bk851, H852, SAC853, OC857, H859, Bk894, Ell894, G914, Bk917, Hrd931, Hy934
Middle Atlantic	Pr829, Pr831, TH834, Ab839, Bu844, Pr844, Wn844, EB848, Pr854, Bu857, Pr857, Bu859, Bu860, EB860, EB862, Bu866, EB867, EB875
South	Den871, Pk938
Great Lakes	Mc845, LEN846, Blo859, Blo867, Blo872
Central/Plains	Bf867, Mic876
Mountain/West	none

Maclura pomifera (Osage orange)

New England	Ken832, Br833, Br841, OC861, LC872
Middle Atlantic	Pr826, TH834, Wn844, Bu859, EB917
South	LY854, Sta858, Brk861, TR868, Den871, Lg881, Pk938
Great Lakes	SG843, Mc845, LEN846, Blo859, CL901, SH908, Sz910, Ch915
Central/Plains	Dmk853, PS884, Ex888, ShN899, SN919
Mountain/West	SR880, Ger911

Magnolia acuminata (cucumber tree)

New England	Ken832, Br833, Br841, Sac853, G880, Rd881, NE910
Middle Atlantic	JB783, JB792, M804, JB807, WB810, Bld819, Pr826, Tb827, Wn844, Bu859, EB860, EB917
South	LY854, Brk858, Sta858, Brk861, TR868, Dwr870, Den871, Lg881, Hgh903, BN907, Pk938
Great Lakes	SG843, Clv845, Mc845, LEN846, AlN858, PG858, Blo859, Col860, SH894, SH896, CL901, SH908, Ch915, Al930
Central/Plains	SN919
Mountain/West	MS874, SR880, Ca894, FC895, PK912

Magnolia grandiflora (southern magnolia)

New England	none
Middle Atlantic	JB783, M804, JB807, WB810, Bld819, Pr826, Tb827, Wn844, Bu859, MM870, HN922
South	SN851, JR853, Ly854, Pom856, Brk858, Aff860, Brk861, ATN870, Dwr870, Den871, Brk873, AP881, Lg881, MV888, Pf888, AEx894, PP895, Wm895, Pf896, MV898, Rs898, Hgh903, JK904, Brk906, BN907, Vd907, WY907, GSM914, CoS917, Per927, Pk938, Kyo939
Great Lakes	Col877
Central/Plains	Mic876, PS884
Mountain/West	MS874, Bn889, TS891, Ca894, FC895, Cx907, Ash908, Ger911, PK912, PHd937

Magnolia ×soulangeana (saucer magnolia)

New England	Bk917
Middle Atlantic	Wn844, Bu859, EB860, DR876, EB917, My934
South	Brk861, Dwr870, Den871, Lg881, Brk906, BN907, Pk938, Kyo939
Great Lakes	Mc845, LEN846, Col860, SH894, SH896, CL901, Wag905, Ch915, Fr932
Central/Plains	none
Mountain/West	Ca894, PK912, PHd937

Magnolia virginiana (sweet bay magnolia)

New England	Ken832, Br833, Br841
Middle Atlantic	JB783, JB792, M804, JB807, WB810, Bld819, Pr826, Tb827, TH834, Wn844
South	Pom856, Sta858, Dwr870, Lg881, Lg881, AEx894, Hgh903, BN907, Kyo939
Great Lakes	Clv845, Mc845, LEN846, Col860, SH925, Fr932
Central/Plains	none
Mountain/West	MS874

Mahonia aquifolia (Oregon grape holly)

New England	Sac853, OC861, Rd881, NE910, Bk917
Middle Atlantic	Bu859, EB860, MM870, EB917
South	Ly854, Pom856, Brk858, Sta858, Brk861, Dwr870, Den871, Hgh903, Brk906, BN907, Pk938
Great Lakes	Mc845, LEN846, PG858, Blo859, Col860, SH894, Wag905, SH908, Er926, Fr932
Central/Plains	CS860
Mountain/West	Ca894, FC895, PK912

Malus ioensis var. *plena* (Bechtel's double crab)

New England	Sac853, NE910, Bk917, Fsk927, Hrd931
Middle Atlantic	HWC905, EB917, My934
South	BN907, Oz919
Great Lakes	Clv845, LEN846, LW905, SH908, SH925, Er926, WA928, Al930, Fr932
Central/Plains	SN919, Gy921, EF927, Gy927, HF927, FbN933
Mountain/West	Cx907, Ash908, PK912, PW926, PHd937, Lb939

Matthiola incana (stock)

New England	Bst760, Bt836, Wd867, CA889, Gg915, Bk917, ASL937, Bar939
Middle Atlantic	WB810, OK870, DR876, PH910, Bol928, Mch931, JHr934, My934
South	MC793, GF799, OL826, Ull895, TM925, Wyt931
Great Lakes	Liv889, SH896, MCL898, Imy899, SH908, Sz910, Al930
Central/Plains	PS875, Mic876, PS884, ISC914, Nb918, BrdK922, EF927, Gy927, OW939
Mountain/West	RTm873, SR880, TS891, Tg904, Cx907, Ger911, Un916, Az921, Brd922, Az925, PW926, Un933, GJ936, Lb939

Melia azedarach (chinaberry)

New England	Br841, Br833
Middle Atlantic	Pr790, JB807, WB810, Pr826, Bld819

South	JS793, JB808, Lg881, MV888, Pf888, AEx894, Wm895, MV898, Rs898, Brk906, BN907, Vd907, WY907, GSM914, CoS917, TM925, Per927
Great Lakes	Mc845
Central/Plains	Srx887
Mountain/West	SR880, Bg892, Ca894, FC895, Cx907, Ger911, PHd937

Mesembryanthemum crystallinum (ice plant)

New England	Bt836, Wd867, CA889, Bk917, Bar939
Middle Atlantic	WB810, OK870, DR876, PH910
South	OL826, Tho888, Ull895, TM925, Pk938
Great Lakes	Col877, GR889, Liv889, SH896, MCL898, Imy899, SH908, Sz910
Central/Plains	Mic876, PS884, GS908, ISC914, Gy927, HF927, OW939
Mountain/West	SR880, TS891, FC895, Cx907, Ash908, GJ936, PHd937

Mirabilis jalapa (four-o'clock)

New England	Bt836, Wd867, CA889, Gg915, Bk917, Gg928, ASL937, Bar939
Middle Atlantic	WB810, OK870, DR876, PH910, Bol928, JHr934
South	OL826, Ull895, TM895, Wyt931, Pk938
Great Lakes	GR889, Liv889, SH896, MCL898, Imy899, SH908, Er926, Al930
Central/Plains	PS875, PS884, GS908, ISC914, Nb918, Fg920, BrdK922, Gy927, HF927, OW939
Mountain/West	SR880, Cx907, Ger911, Un916, Az921, Brd922, Az925, PW926, Un933, GJ936, PHd937

Momordica balsamina (balsam apple)

New England	Bt836, Wd867
Middle Atlantic	PH910, Bol928
South	OL826, Ull895, TM925, Wyt931, Pk938
Great Lakes	GR889, Liv889, SH896, SH908
Central/Plains	PS875, Mic876, PS884, GS908, ISC914, Nb918, Fg920, BrdK922, Gy927, HF927
Mountain/West	Cx907, Ger911, Az921, Brd922, Az925

Monarda didyma (beebalm)

New England	H834, H835, Ken835, Bt836, H836, H839, Br841, Bk845, Bk851, OC857, H859, G880, G883, Mn887, Mn889, G892, Ell894, NE910, G914, Bk917, Hrd931
Middle Atlantic	JB783, M804, JB807, WB810, Ln811, Pr822, Ln826, Ab827, Pr826, Tb827, Ln828, Pr829, Ab830, Pr831, TH834, Ab839, Bu844, Pr844, Wn844, EB848, Pr854, Bu857, Pr857, Bu859, Bu860, Bu866, EB882, EB917, My934

South	BN907, Hgh903, Pk938
Great Lakes	Pkt835, Er926
Central/Plains	ISC914, HF927, FbN933
Mountain/West	none

Myosotis species (forget-me-not)

New England	OC857, H859, H862, H863, Bk869, H873, Bk875, H875, Mn875, H888, CA889, Bk894, Ell894, NE910, Gg915, Bk917, Gg928, ASL937, Bar939
Middle Atlantic	Pr854, Bu857, Pr857, Bu859, Bu860, EB860, EB862, Ln865, Bu866, EB867, Ln868, OK870, EB875, DR876, Ln879, EB882, Ln884, Ln889, PH910, Dk924, Bol928, Mch931, JHr934, My934
South	LR881, Tho888, BN907, TM925, Wyt931, Pk938
Great Lakes	Blo867, Blo868, Blo872, Col877, Blo883, Blo886, GR889, Liv889, SH896, Wag905, SH908, SH925, Er926, Al930, Fr932
Central/Plains	CS860, PS875, Mic876, PS884, GS908, ISC914, Nb918, Fg920, EF927, HF927, OW939
Mountain/West	Tg904, Cx907, Ger911, PK912, Un916, Az921, Az925, PW926, Un933, GJ936, PHd937

Narcissus (jonquil, daffodil)

New England	H834, Bt836, H847, Bk851, H862, H863, H866, Bk871, Mn875, Bk878, Bk881, G892, NE910
Middle Atlantic	JB807, Bld819, Pr820, Bu844, EB848, Bu857, Pr857, Bu859, Bu860, EB860, Pr860, EB862, EB867, BB873, EB875, JC910, Mch931
South	TA754, JW765, MC792, GF799, Brk861, Den871, Lg881, JD909, CoS917, Oz919
Great Lakes	AlN858, PG858, Blo859, T872, Blo873, T873, Blo883, SH925
Central/Plains	Bf869, GS908, ISC914, HF927
Mountain/West	RTm873, Az921

Nerium oleander (oleander)

New England	Br833
Middle Atlantic	Pr790, JB807, Tb827, DR876
South	RSq812, JR853, Pom856, Brk858, Brk861, Brk873, Lg881, LR881, AEx894, Rs898, JK904, RP904, Brk906, BN907, WY907, GSM914, Per927
Great Lakes	Blo859, SH874, Col877, GR889, Tem904, Sz910
Central/Plains	Bf869, SSN871, Mic876, ISC914
Mountain/West	RTm873, MS874, SR880, Bn889, Ca894, FC895, Cx907, Ger911, PHd937

Oenothera macrocarpa (Ozark sundrops)

New England	Ken839, H844, Bk845, H845, Bk851, H852, H859, H863, Bk869, Bk871, H873, Bk875, H875, Bk878, Bk881, Mn887, Mn889, Bk894, NE910, G914, Hrd931, ASL937
Middle Atlantic	Pr844, Wn844, Bu857, Pr857, Bu859, Bu860, EB860, Bu866, EB867, OK870, EB875, Mch931
South	Pk938
Great Lakes	Blo867, Blo868, Blo872, Blo883, SH908, SH925
Central/Plains	Bf869, OW939
Mountain/West	Lb939

Ornithogalum umbellatum (white star-of-Bethlehem)

New England	Bst760, Bt836, Mn887, Mn889, NE910
Middle Atlantic	JB807, Pr818, Pr820, Ln828, PR860, EB867, EB875, EB882
South	none
Great Lakes	PG858, Blo883
Central/Plains	Bf869, ISC914
Mountain/West	Lb939

Osmanthus fragrans (sweet olive)

New England	none
Middle Atlantic	none
South	Pom856, Brk858, Aff860, Brk861, Den871, Lg881, AEx894, MV898, Rs898, Brk906, BN907, WY907, Kyo939
Great Lakes	none
Central/Plains	Mic876
Mountain/West	Bg892, Ca894, Cx907, PHd937

Paeonia (peony)

New England	Ken835, Bt836, H839, Br841, Bk845, Bk851, Sac853, OC857, H859, Mn875, Rd881, Mn887, Mn889, Bk894, Bk917, Fsk927, Hrd931
Middle Atlantic	Ln811, Bld819, Pr820, PM822, Ln826, Pr826, Ab827, Tb827, Ln828, Pr829, Ab830, Pr831, TH834, Ab839, Bu844, EB848, Bu857, Pr857, Bu859, Pr860, Bu866, EB867, OK870, BB873, EB875, EB882, HWC905, JC910, PH910, EB917, HN922, My934
South	SN851, JR853, Sta858, Aff860, Brk861, TR868, Den871, LR881, Brk906, BN907, JD909, Oz919, Pk938
Great Lakes	Clv845, LEN846, Blo859, Col860, T866, Blo872, T872, Blo873, T873, Blo883, Blo886, SH896, Crk904, LW905, Wag905, SH908, Sz910, Bd919, Er926, Al930, Fr932

Central/Plains	Dmk853, CS860, Dmk868, Bf869, SSN871, Mic876, WsN885, ShN886, Ex888, ShN899, GS908, SN919, Gy921, BrdK922, Gy927, HF927
Mountain/West	DM887, Bg892, Ca894, Cx907, Brd922, St923, Lb939

Papaver orientale (oriental poppy)

New England	H834, H835, Ken835, H836, H839, Br841, H845, H847, Bk851, H852, Sac853, H859, Wd867, Bk869, Bk871, H873, Bk875, Bk878, Bk881, Mn887, H888, CA889, Mn889, Bk894, NE910, G914, Gg915, Bk917, Gg928, Hrd931, ASL937, Bar939
Middle Atlantic	Pr822, Pr826, Pr829, Pr831, TH834, Pr844, Wn844, EB848, Pr854, Pr857, EB860, EB862, EB867, Ln868, OK870, EB875, EB882, HWC905, PH910, EB917, Dk924, Bol928, Mch931, JHr934, My934
South	BN907, Pk938
Great Lakes	Clv845, Mc845, LEN846, Blo867, Blo868, Blo872, Blo873, Col877, SH896, Imy899, Wag905, SH908, Sz910, Er926, SH925, Al930, Fr932
Central/Plains	PS875, Mic876, PS884, GS908, ISC914, Nb918, SN919, BrdK922, Gy927, HF927, FbN933, OW939
Mountain/West	Cx907, Ash908, Ger911, PK912, Un916, Brd922, St923, SW925, PW926, Un933, PHd937, Lb939

Papaver somniferum and *P. rhoeas* (annual poppy)

New England	Bst760, Bt836, Wd867, CA889, Gg915, Bk917, Gg928, ASL937, Bar939
Middle Atlantic	JB807, OK870, DR876, PH910, Bol928, Jhr934, My934
South	GF799, OL826, Ull895, TM895, Wyt931, Pk938
Great Lakes	GR889, Liv889, Scf896, SH896, MCL898, Imy899, SH908, Sz910, Er926
Central/Plains	Mic876, PS884, GS908, ISC914, Nb918, Fg920, BrdK922, EF927, Gy927, HF927, OW939
Mountain/West	SR880, TS891, Cx907, Ger911, Un916, Az921, Brd922, Az925, PW926, Un933, GJ936

Parthenocissus quinquefolia (Virginia creeper)

New England	Ken832, G880, Rd881, CA889, NE910, G914, Bk917, Fsk927, Hrd931
Middle Atlantic	M804, JB807, WB810, Wn844, Bu859, EB860, MM870, DR876, HWC905, PH910, EB917, HN922

South	Sta858, Den871, Lg881, Hgh903, BN907, WY907, CoS917, TM925
Great Lakes	Clv845, Mc845, LEN846, Col877, GR889, Liv889, RE893, SH896, CL901, SH908, Sz910, SH925, Er926
Central/Plains	CS860, Mic876, WsN885, ShN886, Ex888, ShN899, ISC914, NN919, SN919, Gy921, BrdK922, EF927, Gy927, HF927, FbN933, OW939
Mountain/West	Ca894, FC895, Cx907, Ash908, Ger911, PK912, Brd922, Az925, SW925, PW926, PHd937

Parthenocissus tricuspidata (Boston ivy)

New England	CA889, NE910, Bk917, Fsk927, Hrd931, ASL937, Bar939
Middle Atlantic	DR876, HWC905, PH910, EB917, HN922, Mch931, My934, Bun939
South	Den871, Brk906, BN907, WY907, CoS917
Great Lakes	Col877, GR889, Liv889, RE893, CL901, Wag905, SH908, Sz910, Ch915, SH925, Er926, WA928, Al930, Fr932
Central/Plains	Mic876, Ex888, ISC914, SN919, Gy921, BrdK922, EF927, Gy927, HF927, FbN933
Mountain/West	SR880, Ca894, FC895, Cx907, Ash908, Ger911, PK912, Brd922, PW926, GJ936, PHd937

Passiflora caerulea (passion vine)

New England	Br833, Bk917
Middle Atlantic	JB807, Wn844, PH910
South	Tho888, BN907, TM925
Great Lakes	GR889, Liv889, Imy899, SH896, Tem904, SH908
Central/Plains	PS884, GS908, ISC914, BrdK922
Mountain/West	RTm873, SR880, TS891, Ca894, FC895, Cx907, Ger911, Brd922, PW926

Paulownia imperialis (empress tree)

New England	Sac853
Middle Atlantic	Bu859, EB860
South	SN851, JR853, Brk858, Sta858, Aff860, Brk861, ATN870, Den871, Lg881, Brk906, BN907, Pk938
Great Lakes	Mc845, LEN846, Col860, SH925
Central/Plains	none
Mountain/West	SR880, Ca894, FC895, Cx907, Ger911, PK912

Pelargonium spp. (bedding geranium)

New England	Br833, Wd867, CA889, Gg915, Bk917, Gg928
Middle Atlantic	MC793, Tb827, EB860, DR876, PH910, Bol928, Mch931

South	Jby808, SN851, JR853, Sta858, Hop859, MN860, Brk861, TR868, Brk873, AP881, LR881, Tho888, Jk904, JD909, TM925
Great Lakes	Clv845, Blo859, Col860, SH874, Col877, GR889, SH896, MCL898, Imy899, Tem904, SH908, Sz910
Central/Plains	Dmk853, CS860, Bf869, SSN871, PS875, Mic876, PS884, GS908, ISC914, Nb918, Fg920, Gy927, HF927, OW939
Mountain/West	RTm873, SR880, Ca894, FC895, Cx907, Ash908, Az921, St923, Az925, Un933, GJ936, PHd937

Penstemon barbatus (scarlet penstemon)

New England	Br841, Bk845, H847, Bk851, H852, Sac853, H859H862, H863, H873, H875, Mn887, H888, Mn889, Bk894, Bk917, Hrd931, ASL937, Bar939
Middle Atlantic	Ln811, Ln826, Pr826, Ln828, Pr829, Pr831, TH834, Bu844, Pr844, Wn844, EB848, Bu857, Bu859, Bu860, EB860, EB862, Ln865, EB867, Ln868, EB875, Ln879, EB882, EB917
South	none
Great Lakes	Mc845, Blo859, Blo867, Blo868, Blo872, Blo883, SH908
Central/Plains	Bf869
Mountain/West	RTm873, Lb939

Periploca graeca (silk vine)

New England	Ken832, Br833, Br841
Middle Atlantic	JB792, M804, Pr826, Wn844, Bu859, EB860, DR876, EB917
South	Brk906, BN907
Great Lakes	Clv845, LEN846, Laz848, Col860, SH908
Central/Plains	ShN886, ShN899, ISC914
Mountain/West	Ca894, Cx907, PK912

Petunia ×*hybrida* (petunia)

New England	Wd867, CA889, Gg928, ASL937, Bar939
Middle Atlantic	OK870, DR876, Bol928, JHr934, My934
South	TR868, Brk873, LR881, Tho888, Ull895, JD909, TM925, Per927, Rt928, Wyt931
Great Lakes	Col860, SH874, Col877, GR889, Liv889, SH896, MCL898, Imy899, Wag905, SH908, Sz910, Er926, Al930
Central/Plains	CS860, PS875, Mic876, PS884, GS908, Nb918, Fg920, HF927, OW939
Mountain/West	SR880, TS891, Tg904, Cx907, Ash908, Az921, PW926, Un933, GJ936, PHd937

Philadelphus coronarius (mock orange)

New England	Ken832, Br833, Br841, Sac853, OC861, Rd881, CA889, Du901, NE910, Bk917, Fsk927, Hrd931
Middle Atlantic	Pr771, Pr790, JB792, WB810, Bld819, TH834, Wn844, Bu859, EB860, MM870, DR876, HWC905, PH910, EB917, HN922, My934, Bun939
South	Sta858, MN860, Brk861, TR868, Den871, Lg881, Brk906, BN907, WY907, CoS917, Oz919, TM925, Per927, Pk938
Great Lakes	SG843, Clv845, Mc845, Laz848, LEN846, AlN858, PG858, Blo859, En859, Col860, Col877, GR889, RE893, SH896, CL901, Wag905, LW905, SH908, Sz910, Bd919, SH925, Er926, WA928, Fr932
Central/Plains	CS860, Mic876, WsN885, ShN886, Sk887, Ex888, ShN899, GS908, SN919, Gy921, BrdK922, EF927, Gy927, HF927, FbN933
Mountain/West	Osb855, Bn889, Ca894, FC895, Cx907, Ash908, PK912, Brd922, SW925, PW926, GJ936, PHd937

Phlox

New England	Ken832, H834, H835, Ken835, Bt836, H836, Bk838, H839, Br841, Bk845, H845, H847, Bk851, H852, Sac853, OC857, H859, OC861, H862, H863, Wd867, Bk869, Bk871, Bk875, H875, Bk878, Bk881, G883, G886, Mn887, H888, Mn889, G890, G892, Bk894, Ell894, NE910, Fsk927, Hrd931, ASL937
Middle Atlantic	JB783, M804, JB807, Ln811, Ln826, Ab827, Tb827, Ln828, Pr829, Pr831, TH834, Ab839, Bu844, Pr844, Wn844, Ln847, EB848, Pr854, Bu857, Pr857, Bu859, Bu860, EB860, EB862, Bu866, EB867, EB875, DR876, EB882, Ln884, Ln889, Ric905, JC910, PH910, EB917, JHr934, Mch931, My934
South	SN851, JR853, Aff860, Brk861, Den871, Brk873, Lg881, BN907, JD909, Rt928, Wyt931, Pk938
Great Lakes	Pkt835, Clv845, Mc845, LEN846, PG858, Blo859, Col860, Blo868, Blo872, T872, Blo873, T873, SH874, Blo875, Col877, Blo883, Blo886, GR889, Liv889, SH896, MCL898, Crk904, Wag905, SH908, Sz910, SH925, Er926, Al930, Fr932
Central/Plains	Dmk853, CS860, Dmk868, Bf869, SSN871, PS875, Mic876, GS908, ISC914, SN919, Gy921, BrdK922, EF927, Gy927, HF927, FbN933, OW939
Mountain/West	SR880, Ca894, FC895, Cx907, Ger911, PK912, Brd922, St923, SW925, GJ936, PHd937, Lb939

Phlox drummondii (Drummond's phlox)

New England	Wd867, CA889, Gg915, Bk917, Gg928, ASL937, Bar939
Middle Atlantic	OK870, DR876, PH910, Bol928, JHr934
South	AP881, LR881, CoS917, TM925, Rt928, Wyt931, Pk938
Great Lakes	GR889, Liv889, Scf896, SH896, MCL898, Imy899, SH908, Sz910, Er926, Al930
Central/Plains	PS875, Mic876, PS884, GS908, ISC914, Nb918, Fg920, BrdK922, EF927, Gy927, HF927, OW939
Mountain/West	RTm873, SR880, Tg904, Cx907, Ger911, Un916, Az921, Brd922, Az925, PW926, Un933, GJ936, PHd937

Phlox subulata (creeping phlox)

New England	Ken835, Br841, Bk845, Bk851, H859, G883, G886, Mn887, Mn889, G890, G892, NE910, G914, Bk917, Hrd931
Middle Atlantic	M804, JB807, Ln811, Pr822, Ln826, Pr826, Ab827, Ln828, Pr829, Pr831, TH834, Ab839, Bu844, Wn844, EB848, Pr854, Pr857, EB867, EB875, EB882, EB917, Mch931, My934
South	Hgh903, BN907
Great Lakes	Clv845, Mc845, LEN846, SH896, SH908
Central/Plains	ISC914, SN919, Gy921, Gy927, HF927
Mountain/West	SW925, GJ936, Lb939

Physostegia virginiana (obedient plant)

New England	H834, H835, Ken835, Bt836, H836, Bk838, Br841, Bk845, Bk851, H852, H859, G880, G883, NE910, G914, Bk917, Hrd931, ASL937
Middle Atlantic	M804, Ln811, Pr818, Pr844, Ln826, Pr826, Tb827, Ln828, Pr829, Pr831, TH834, Bu844, Pr854, Bu857, Pr857, Bu859, Bu860, EB862, EB867, EB875, PH910, EB917, Mch931, JHr934, My934
South	Hgh903, BN907, Pk938
Great Lakes	Pkt835, Mc845, LEN846, Blo868, SH908, SH925, Er926, Fr932
Central/Plains	Bf869, SN919
Mountain/West	PW926, PHd937, Lb939

Picea abies (Norway spruce)

New England	Ken832, Br833, Br841, R853, Sac853, OC861, LC872, Rd881, NE910, G914, Bk917, Fsk927, Hrd931
Middle Atlantic	Pr771, JB807, Pr826, Wn844, Bu859, EB860, MM870, HWC905, EB917, HN922, My934, Bun939

South	JR853, LY854, Pom856, Brk858, Sta858, Aff860, Brk861, TR868, ATN870, Dwr870, Den871, Lg881, VB885, JBk895, Hgh903, Brk906, BN907, Vd907, TM925, Pk938
Great Lakes	Clv845, Mc845, LEN846, AlN858, PG858, Blo859, En859, Col860, Tru866, Wau878, SH894, CL901, Crk904, Wag905, SH908, Sz910, Ch915, SH925, Er926, Al930
Central/Plains	CS860, Dmk868, SSN871, Mic876, PS884, WsN885, ShN886, Kv887, Srx887, Ex888, ShN899, SN919, BrdK922, EF927, FbN933
Mountain/West	RTm873, SR880, DM887, Ca894, FC895, PK912, Brd922, PW926

Picea glauca (white spruce)

New England	Ken832, Br833, Br841, LC872, Rd881, NE910, Bk917, Fsk927, Hrd931
Middle Atlantic	Bld819, Pr826, Tb827, Bu859, EB860, MM870, EB917
South	LY854, Sta858, Brk861, ATN870, Dwr870, Den871, Hgh903, BN907
Great Lakes	Mc845, PG858, En859, Wau878, SH894, Crk904, Sz910, SH925
Central/Plains	PS884, ShN886, Kv887, ShN899, EF927
Mountain/West	FC895

Picea pungens (Colorado spruce)

New England	Rd881, NE910, G914, Fsk927, Hrd931
Middle Atlantic	HWC905, Ric905, EB917, HN922, My934
South	Hgh903, BN907, Oz919, Pk938
Great Lakes	SH894, SH908, SH925, Er926, Al930
Central/Plains	ShN899, NN919, SN919, Gy921, BrdK922, NW924, EF927, Gy927, OW939
Mountain/West	PK912, Brd922, PW926, PHd937

Pinus nigra (Austrian pine)

New England	Br841, OC861, LC872, Rd881, NE910, Bk917, Fsk927, Hrd931
Middle Atlantic	JB807, Bu859, EB860, MM870, EB917, HN922, Bun939
South	JR853, Brk861, Dwr870, Lg881, BN907
Great Lakes	Clv845, AlN858, PG858, En859, Blo859, Col860, Wau878, SH894, CL901, SH908, Sz910, Ch915, SH925, Er926
Central/Plains	CS860, Dmk858, SSN871, Mic876, PS884, WsN885, ShN886, Ex888, ShN899, SN919, Gy921, FbN933
Mountain/West	RTm873, DM887, Ca894, FC895, PK912

Pinus strobus (white pine)

New England	Ken832, Br841, OC861, LC872, NE910, G914, Bk917
Middle Atlantic	Pr771, JB783, Pr790, JB792, M804, JB807, Bld819, Pr826, Tb827, Wn844, Bu859, EB860, MM870, EB917, HN922
South	LY854, Brk858, Sta858, Brk861, TR868, ATN870, Dwr870, Hgh903, BN907
Great Lakes	SG843, Mc845, LEN846, AlN858, PG858, Blo859, En859, Col860, Wau878, SS887, SH894, CL901, SH908, Ch915, SH925, Er926
Central/Plains	Dmk853, CS860, Dmk868, KN871, PS884, WsN885, ShN886, Kv887, Srx887, Sk887, ShN899, EF927
Mountain/West	Ca894, Ger911, PK912

Pinus sylvestris (Scotch pine)

New England	Br841, OC861, LC872, NE910, Hrd931
Middle Atlantic	JB792, JB807, Pr826, Wn844, Bu859, EB860, MM870, EB917, HN922, My934
South	Sta858, Brk861, TR868, Dwr870, BN907
Great Lakes	AlN858, PG858, Blo859, En859, Col860, Tru866, Wau878, SH894, CL901, SH908, Sz910, Ch915, SH925, Er926
Central/Plains	CS860, Dmk868, SSN871, Mic876, PS884, WsN885, ShN886, Kv887, Sk887, Srx887, Ex888, ShN899, SN919, Gy921, NW924, EF927, Gy927, OW939
Mountain/West	DM887, FC895, Cx907

Pittosporum tobira (Japanese pittosporum)

New England	none
Middle Atlantic	none
South	Pom856, Brk858, Brk861, Den871, Lg881, AEx894, MV898, Rs898, RP904, Brk906, BN907, WY907, CoS917, Per927, Kyo939
Great Lakes	none
Central/Plains	none
Mountain/West	SR880, Ca894, FC895, Cx907, PHd937

Platanus occidentalis (American sycamore)

New England	Ken832, Br833, Br841
Middle Atlantic	JB783, Pr790, M804, JB807, WB810, Bld819, Pr826, Tb827, Wn844, Bu859, EB860
South	JS793, Wm895, Rs898, MV898, BN907, WY907, GSM914, CoS917, Pk938
Great Lakes	SG843, Clv845
Central/Plains	CS860, ShN886, Ex888, SN919, BrdK922
Mountain/West	Ger911, PK912, Brd922

Platycladus orientalis (oriental arborvitae)

New England	Ken832, Br841, R853, OC861
Middle Atlantic	JB792, JB807, WB810, Pr826, TH834, Wn844, Bu859, EB860, HN922, Bun939
South	SN851, JR853, LY854, Brk858, Sta858, Aff860, Brk861, TR868, ATN870, Den871, Lg881, AEx894, PP895, Wm895, MV898, Rs898, BN907, WY907, CoS917, TM925, Per927
Great Lakes	SG843, Mc845, LEN846, AlN858, Blo859, Col860, SH925, Fr932
Central/Plains	PS884, SN919
Mountain/West	RTm873, SR880, Bn889, FC895, Ger911, PHd937, Lb939

Platycodon grandiflorus (balloon flower)

New England	H834, Br841, Sac853, H859, H862, H863, Wd867, Bk871, Bk875, Bk878, Bk881, Mn887, H888, CA889, Mn889, Bk894, Ell894, NE910, Gg915, Bk917, Gg928, Hrd931, ASL937, Bar939
Middle Atlantic	Pr829, Pr831, TH834, Bu844, Pr844, Wn844, EB848, Pr854, Bu857, Pr857, Bu859, EB860, EB862, EB867, Ln868, OK870, EB875, Ln879, EB882, Ln884, Ln889, PH910, EB917, Dk924, Mch931, JHr934
South	Den871, BN907, TM925
Great Lakes	Clv845, Mc845, Blo859, Blo867, Blo868, Blo872, SH896, Wag905, SH908, Sz910, SH925, Al930, Fr932
Central/Plains	CS860, SSN871, ISC914, SN919, Gy927, HF927, OW939
Mountain/West	PK912, PW926, PHd937, Lb939

Polemonium caeruleum (Jacob's ladder)

New England	H834, Bt836, Bk838, Br841, Bk845, Bk851, H852, OC857, H859, H862, H863, Bk871, H873, H875, Mn887, Mn889, NE910, Bk917, Hrd931, Bar939
Middle Atlantic	Pr822, Pr826, Tb827, Pr829, Pr831, TH834, Bu844, Pr844, EB848, Pr854, Pr857, EB860, EB862, EB867, EB875, EB882, PH910, EB917, JHr934
South	OL826, Den871, BN907, Pk938
Great Lakes	Pkt835, Clv845, LEN846, Blo867, Blo868, Blo883, Wag905, SH908, Fr932
Central/Plains	Bf869
Mountain/West	PW926

Polianthes tuberosa (tuberose)

New England	H834, Bt836, CA889, Bk917, Gg928, Bar939
Middle Atlantic	Pr790, Pr818, Bld819, Pr820, Wn844, OK870, DR876, PH910, Bol928

South | MC792, MC793, GF799, Aff860, Den871, Brk873, AP881, Lg881, LR881, AEx894, JK904, WY907, JD909, CoS917, Per927, Rt928, Wyt931

Great Lakes | Mc845, LEN846, PG858, Blo859, SH874, Col877, GR889, Liv889, Scf896, SH896, SH908, Sz910, Er926

Central/Plains | Mic876, PS884, WsN885, Ex888, GS908, ISC914, Fg920, Gy921, BrdK922, HF927, FbN933

Mountain/West | RTm873, SR880, Ca894, FC895, Cx907, Az921, Brd922, Az925, PW926, PHd937

Populus alba (white poplar)

New England | Ken832, Br833, Br841, NE910, Bk917

Middle Atlantic | Pr826, TH834, Wn844, Bu859, EB917

South | Brk858, Sta858, Aff860, Den871, Lg881, MV888, MV898, Rs898, BN907

Great Lakes | SG843, Clv845, Mc845, LEN846, Laz848, Blo859, En859, Col860, SH894, SH896

Central/Plains | Dmk853, CS860, Ex888, NN919, SN919, Gy921, NW924, Gy927, OW939

Mountain/West | Ca894, FC895, PW926

Populus deltoides (cottonwood)

New England | Sac853, Rd881, NE910, Bk917

Middle Atlantic | JB783, WB810, Pr826, Ric905, HWC905, EB917, HN922, My934

South | Sta858, Jbk895, Hgh903, Brk906, BN907, Vd907, WY907, GSM914, Oz919, Per927

Great Lakes | SS887, SH894, SH896, CL901, Crk904, SH908, Ch915, SH925, Er926, Al930, Fr932

Central/Plains | Ex888, ShN899, NN919, SN919, Gy921, BrdK922, EF927, Gy927, FbN933, OW939

Mountain/West | RTm873, SR880, DM887, Ca894, FC895, Cx907, Ger911, PK912, Brd922

Populus nigra 'Italica' (Lombardy poplar)

New England | Ken832, Br833, Rd881, NE910, Bk917, Hrd931

Middle Atlantic | Pr790, WB810, Bld819, Pr826, TH834, Wn844, Bu859, EB860, HWC905, EB917, HN922, My934, Bun939

South | Brk858, Aff860, Brk861, TR868, Den871, ATN870, Lg881, MV888, PP895, MV898, Brk906, BN907, WY907, GSM914

Great Lakes | Clv845, Blo859, Col860, SH894, Wag905, SH908, Ch915, SH925, Er926, Fr932, Al930

Central/Plains | CS860, Dmk868, SSN871, ShN886, Sk887, ShN899, SN919, Gy921, BrdK922, EF927, Gy927

Mountain/West | RTm873, SR880, DM887, Ca894, FC895, Cx907, PK912, Brd922, SW925, PHd937

Portulaca grandiflora (moss rose)

New England | Wd867, Gg915, Bk917, Gg928, ASL937

Middle Atlantic | OK870, DR876, PH910, Bol928, JHr934, My934

South | LR881, Ull895, TM895, Rt928, Wyt931, Pk938

Great Lakes | GR889, Liv889, Scf896, SH896, MCL898, Imy899, SH908, Er926, Al930

Central/Plains | Dmk853, PS875, Mic876, PS884, GS908, ISC914, Nb918, Fg920, BrdK922, EF927, HF927, OW939

Mountain/West | SR880, Tg904, Cx907, Ger911, Un916, Az921, Brd922, Az925, PW926, Un933, GJ936, PHd937

Primula veris (primrose)

New England | H834, H835, Bt836, Bk838, Bk845, Bk851, Wd867, Bk875, H875, Bk878, Bk881, Mn889, Bk894, NE910, Bk917, Hrd931

Middle Atlantic | Ln811, Pr822, Ln826, Tb827, Ln828, Pr831, Bu844, Ln847, EB848, Pr854, Pr857, Ln868, DR876, EB882, Ln884, Ln889, PH910, EB917, Bol928, Mch931, JHr934, My934

South | Pk938

Great Lakes | LEN846, Wag905, SH908, Sz910

Central/Plains | PS875, Mic876, Nb918, Gy927

Mountain/West | PK912, GJ936, Lb939

Prunus glandulosa (dwarf flowering almond)

New England | Ken832, Br841, R853, Sac853, Rd881, CA889, Hrd931, FbN933

Middle Atlantic | Pr790, JB792, JB807, Bld819, TH834, Wn844, Bu859, EB860, MM870, EB917, Bun939

South | Sta858, MN860, TR868, ATN870, Den871, Lg881, Rs898, Brk906, BN907, Oz919, TM925

Great Lakes | SG843, Clv845, Mc845, LEN846, Laz848, AlN858, PG858, Blo859, Col860, CL901, SH908, SH925, WA928, Al930, Fr932

Central/Plains | Dmk853, CS860, Dmk868, SSN871, WsN885, ShN886, Ex888, ShN899, ISC914, SN919, BrdK922, EF927, Gy927, HF927, OW939

Mountain/West | RTm873, Ca894, Bn889, Brd922, SW925, PW926, PHd937, Lb939

Prunus persica 'Plena' (double-flowering peach)

New England | Ken832, Br841, NE910

Middle Atlantic | JB792, JB807, WB810, Th834, Bu859, EB860, DR876, EB917, HN922, Bun939

South | SN851, LY854, Brk858, Sta858, MN860, ATN870, Den871, Lg881, BN907, WY907

Great Lakes | Clv845, LEN846, AlN858, Col860, SH925

Central/Plains | none
Mountain/West | TS891, Bg892, Ca894, FC895, Cx907, PHd937

Pseudotsuga menziesii (Douglas fir)

New England | NE910, Hrd931
Middle Atlantic | Bu859, EB860, EB917, HN922
South | Brk861, ATN870, Den871, Hgh903, BN907
Great Lakes | Wau878, SH896, Wag905, SH908, SH925, Al930
Central/Plains | SN919, NW924, EF927
Mountain/West | SR880, Bg892, Ca894, FC895, Cx907

Pueraria montana var. *lobata* (kudzu)

New England | Gg915, Bk917, Gg928, Bar939
Middle Atlantic | PH910, Bol928
South | BN907, CoS917, Oz919, TM925, Pk938
Great Lakes | SH908, Er926, WA928
Central/Plains | ISC914, SN919, Fg920, Gy921, BrdK922, Gy927, FbN933
Mountain/West | Ger911, PK912, Az921, Brd922, Az925, PW926, GJ936

Quercus alba (white oak)

New England | Br841, NE910
Middle Atlantic | Pr771, JB783, Pr790, M804, JB807, Pr826, Tb827, Wn844, EB917
South | Den871, Hgh903, BN907
Great Lakes | Wau878
Central/Plains | Gy927
Mountain/West | FC895

Quercus palustris (pin oak)

New England | NE910, Bk917, Fsk927
Middle Atlantic | Pr790, M804, JB807, Tb827, Wn844, EB917, HN922, Bun939
South | Den871, Hgh903, Brk906, BN907, WY907, GSM914
Great Lakes | Wag905, SH925, Fr932
Central/Plains | SN919, EF927, FbN933
Mountain/West | Cx907, PK912

Quercus rubra (red oak)

New England | Br833, Br841, NE910, Fsk927
Middle Atlantic | JB783, M804, JB807, Pr826, Tb827, Wn844, Bu859, EB917, HN922, My934
South | Hgh903, BN907
Great Lakes | LEN846, Wau878, SH894, Wag905, SH925, Er926
Central/Plains | SN919, Gy921, Gy927
Mountain/West | Cx907

Reseda odorata (mignonette)

New England | Bt836, Wd867, Gg915, Bk917, Gg928, ASL937, Bar939
Middle Atlantic | JB807, WB810, Tb827, OK870, DR876, PH910, Mch931, JHr934
South | GF799, OL826, AP881, LR881, TM925, Wyt931, Pk938
Great Lakes | GR889, Liv889, Scf896, SH896, MCL898, Imy899, SH908, Sz910, Al930
Central/Plains | PS875, Mic876, PS884, GS908, ISC914, Nb918, Fg920, BrdK922, EF927, Gy927, HF927
Mountain/West | RTm873, SR880, TS891, Tg904, Cx907, Ash908, Ger911, Az921, Brd922, Az925, PW926, GJ936, PHd937

Rhododendron spp.

New England | Ken832, Bt836, Br841, G880, CA889, NE910, G914, Bk917
Middle Atlantic | Pr790, WB810, Bld819, Wn844, Bu859, EB860, DR8786, HWC905, PH910, EB917, HN922, Mch931
South | JR853, Brk858, Brk861, Den871, Brk873, LR881, AEx894, Hgh903, Brk906, BN907, JD909, Per927, Kyo939
Great Lakes | Mc845, PG858, Blo859, Col860, SH874, SH896, Cl901, LW905, Wag905, SH908, Sz910, Ch915, Al930, Fr932
Central/Plains | Mic876, ShN899
Mountain/West | Ca894, TS891, Cx907, PK912, PHd937

Rhododendron calendulaceum (flame azalea)

New England | Ken832, Br841, G880, NE910, G914
Middle Atlantic | Wn844, Bu859
South | Hgh903, Brk906, BN907
Great Lakes | Al930
Central/Plains | none
Mountain/West | none

Rhododendron catawbiense (Catawba rhododendron)

New England | Br841, G880, Rd881, NE910, G914, Bk917, Hrd931
Middle Atlantic | Wn844, Bu859, EB860
South | Den871, Hgh903, Brk906, BN907
Great Lakes | CL901, Wag905, Al930, Fr932
Central/Plains | SSN871
Mountain/West | none

Rhododendron indicum (Chinese azalea)

New England | Br833, Br841
Middle Atlantic | Mch931

South   JR853, Brk858, Brk861, Lg881, AEx894, Brk906, BN907, Per927, Kyo939
Great Lakes   Blo859, SH874, GR889, Tem904, SH908
Central/Plains   SSN871, Mic876
Mountain/West   Cx907, Ash908

Rhododendron maximum (rose bay)

New England   Ken832, Br833, Br841, NE910, G914, Hrd931
Middle Atlantic   JB783, JB792, M804, JB807, Pr826, TH834, Wn844, Bu859
South   JR853, Hgh903, BN907
Great Lakes   Mc845, LEN846, GR889, Wag905, Fr932
Central/Plains   none
Mountain/West   none

Ricinus communis (castor bean)

New England   Bst760, ASL937, Bar939
Middle Atlantic   JB807, WB810, OK870, PH910, Bol928, JHr934
South   LR881, Ull895, TM895, Wyt931, Pk938
Great Lakes   Liv889, SH896, MCL898, Imy899, Wag905
Central/Plains   PS8785, PS884, GS908, ISC914, Nb918, Gy927, OW939
Mountain/West   TS891, Cx907, Ger911, Un916, Az921, Az925, PW926, Un933

Robinia hispida (rose acacia)

New England   Ken832, Br833, Br841, Sac853, NE910
Middle Atlantic   JB783, Pr790, M804, JB807, Bld819, Pr826, TH834, Wn844, Bu859, EB860, PH910, EB917
South   JR853, Sta858, Aff860, Lg881, Hgh903, Brk906, BN907, Oz919
Great Lakes   SG843, Clv845, Mc845, Blo859, SH925
Central/Plains   Dmk853, CS860, Ex888, ISC914, SN919, FbN933
Mountain/West   RTm873, Ca894, PK912, Lb939

Robinia pseudoacacia (black locust)

New England   Ken832, Br833, Br841, NE910
Middle Atlantic   Pr771, JB783, Pr790, M804, JB807, WB810, Bld819, Tb827, Wn844, Pr826, Bu859, EB860, MM870, EB917, My934
South   PP895, Hgh903, Brk906, BN907, Pk938
Great Lakes   SG843, Clv845, Mc845, LEN846, Col860, Wau878, SH908, Sz910, SH925
Central/Plains   PS884, Ex888, ShN899, SN919, Gy921, Gy927, HF927, FbN933
Mountain/West   SR880, Ca894, FC895, Cx907, Ger911, PK912, Buf914, PW926

Rosa (rose)

New England   Ken832, Br833, Br841, R853, Sac853, OC861, CA889, Du901, NE910, G914, Bk917, Hrd931
Middle Atlantic   Pr790, JB792, JB807, WB810, Bld819, Pr826, TH834, Wn844, EB860, MM870, DR876, JV881, HWC905, Ric905, PH910, EB917, HN922, My934, Bun939
South   JS793, MC793, JR853, Sta858, VN858, Brk859, Hop859, Aff860, MN860, Brk861, TR868, ATN870, Dwr870, Den871, Brk873, AP881, Lg881, LR881, MV888, Tho888, AEx894, Wm895, Pf896, MV898, Rs898, JK904, Brk906, BN907, Vd907, WY907, JD909, GSM914, CoS917, Oz919, TM925, Pk938
Great Lakes   SG843, Clv845, Mc845, LEN846, Laz848, AlN858, Blo859, En859, Col860, SH874, Col877, GR889, SH896, Imy899, CL901, Scf901, Crk904, Tem904, LW905, Wag905, SH908, Sz910, Ch915, ACN920, SH925, Er926, WA928, Al930, Fr932
Central/Plains   Dmk853, CS860, Dmk868, Bf869, SSN871, PS884, WsN885, ShN886, DM887, Ex888, GS908, ISC914, SN919, Gy921, BrdK922, EF927, Gy927, HF927, FbN933
Mountain/West   Osb855, RTm873, SR880, Bn889, TS891, Ca894, FC895, Cx907, Ash908, Ger911, PK912, Brd922, Az925, SW925, PW926, GJ936, PHd937, Lb939

Rosa 'Adam'

New England   CA889
Middle Atlantic   none
South   SN851, JR853, Brk858, Brk859, Brk861, TR868, LR881, Tho888, Rs898, JK904
Great Lakes   SH874, COL877, GR889
Central/Plains   CS860
Mountain/West   Bn889, TS891

Rosa 'Aglaia'

New England   Du901, NE910, G914, Bk917
Middle Atlantic   HWC905, PH910, EB917
South   MV898, Rs898, BN907
Great Lakes   CL901, Scf901, LW905, SH908, Sz910, Ch915, Er926
Central/Plains   ShN899, GS908, ISC914, SN919, Gy921, Gy927
Mountain/West   Cx907, Ash908

Rosa 'Alfred Colomb'

New England	CA889, Du901, NE910, Bk917
Middle Atlantic	MM870, HWC905, PH910, EB917
South	LR881, Tho888, Brk906, BN907, GSM914
Great Lakes	SH874, GR889, SH896, Wag905, SH908, Ch915, Al930
Central/Plains	GS908, Gy921
Mountain/West	Ca894, FC895

Rosa 'American Beauty'

New England	CA889, Du901, NE910
Middle Atlantic	HWC905, PH910, EB917, Bun939
South	Tho888, MV898, Rs898, BN907, WY907, CoS917, Oz919, TM925
Great Lakes	GR889, SH896, CL901, LW905, Wag905, Sz910, Er926, Fr932
Central/Plains	GS908, ISC914, SN919, Gy921, BrdK922, Gy927, HF927, FbN933
Mountain/West	Bn889, Ca894, FC895, Cx907, Ash908, Ger911, PK912, Brd922, Az925, SW925, GJ936

Rosa 'American Beauty, Climbing'

New England	none
Middle Atlantic	EB917, My934, Bun939
South	CoS917, TM925
Great Lakes	ACN920, SH925, Er926, WA928, Al930, Fr932
Central/Plains	ISC914, Sn919, HF927
Mountain/West	Az925, PW926, GJ936

Rosa 'Anna De Diesbach'

New England	CA889, Du901, NE910, G914, Bk917, Hrd931
Middle Atlantic	MM870, HWC905, PH910, EB917, HN922
South	Brk861, ATN870, LR881, Tho888, Brk906, BN907, GSM914
Great Lakes	SH874, Col877, GR889, SH896, Wag905, SH908, Ch915, SH925, Al930
Central/Plains	GS908, ISC914, Gy921, HF927
Mountain/West	Ca894, Cx907, Ash908, PK912, Az925

Rosa 'Appoline'

New England	CA889
Middle Atlantic	EB860, MM870, DR876
South	Pom856, Brk859, Brk861, TR868, Lg881, LR881, Tho888, Rs898, BN907, GSM914
Great Lakes	Blo859, Col860, SH874, Col877, GR889
Central/Plains	SSN871
Mountain/West	FC895

Rosa 'Archiduc Charles'

New England	CA889
Middle Atlantic	Wn844, EB860, DR876
South	JR853, Brk858, Brk859, Brk861, TR868, AP881, Lg881, LR881, JK904
Great Lakes	Mc845, LEN846, Blo859, Col860, Col877, GR889
Central/Plains	CS860, SSN871
Mountain/West	none

Rosa 'Augusta Mie'

New England	CA889
Middle Atlantic	EB860, MM870
South	Pom856, Brk861, TR868, ATN870, Lg881, LR881
Great Lakes	AlN858, PG858, Col860, SH874, Col877, GR889
Central/Plains	CS860, SSN871
Mountain/West	Ca894

Rosa 'Baltimore Belle'

New England	R853, Sac853, CA889, Du901, NE910, G914
Middle Atlantic	EB860, MM870, DR876, HWC905, PH910, EB917
South	SN851, Brk858, Brk859, Hop859, Brk861, ATN870, LR881, Tho888, MV898, Rs898, BN907
Great Lakes	Clv845, Mc845, LEN846, AlN858, Blo859, Col860, SH874, Col877, GR889, SH896, Wag905, CL901, Scf901, SH908, Sz910, Ch915, Fr932
Central/Plains	SSN871, Bf869, SSN871, WsN885, ShN886, Srx887, Ex888, ShN899, ISC914, SN919, HF927
Mountain/West	Ca894, FC895

Rosa banksiae

New England	Ken832, Br833, Br841
Middle Atlantic	Pr826, EB860
South	SN851, Brk858, Brk859, Brk861, Lg881, LR881, Tho888, CoS917
Great Lakes	PG858, Blo859
Central/Plains	none
Mountain/West	Ca894, FC895, Cx907, Ash908, Ger911, Az925

Rosa 'Baron de Bonstetten'

New England	CA889, Du901, NE910
Middle Atlantic	PH910, EB917
South	LR881, Brk906
Great Lakes	SH896, SH908, Ch915, Al930
Central/Plains	ISC914
Mountain/West	Bn889, Ca894, FC895, Cx907, PK912

Rosa 'Baroness Rothschild'

New England	CA889, NE910, G914, Bk917
Middle Atlantic	MM870, DR876, PH910, EB917
South	Lg881, LR881, Tho888
Great Lakes	SH874, GR889, Wag905
Central/Plains	none
Mountain/West	Ca894, FC895, PK912

Rosa 'Baronne Prevost'

New England	Sac853, CA889
Middle Atlantic	EB860, MM870
South	SN851, JR853, Hop859, Pom856, Brk858, Brk859, Brk861, TR868, ATN870, Lg881, LR881, Rs898, WY907
Great Lakes	LEN846, AlN858, PG858, Blo859, Col860, SH874, Col877
Central/Plains	CS860
Mountain/West	Ca894

Rosa 'Bon Silène'

New England	CA889
Middle Atlantic	DR876, JV881, PH910
South	Brk858, Brk859, Brk861, TR868, Lg881, LR881, Tho888, AEx894, Rs898, MV898, JK904, BN907, Vd907, WY907, GSM914, CoS917
Great Lakes	Mc845, SH874, Col877, GR889, SH896, SH908
Central/Plains	ISC914
Mountain/West	Bn889, Ca894, Cx907

Rosa 'Bougere'

New England	CA889
Middle Atlantic	Wn844, EB860, DR876
South	SN851, JR853, Brk858, Brk859, Hop859, Brk861, TR868, Lg881, LR881, Tho888, Wm895, JK904, GSM914
Great Lakes	Clv845, Mc845, Blo859, Col860, SH874, Col877, GR889
Central/Plains	CS860, Bf869, SSN871
Mountain/West	Bn889, TS891, Ca894, FC895

Rosa 'Caroline'

New England	none
Middle Atlantic	EB860, JV881
South	JR853, Pom856, Brk858, Brk859, Hop859, Brk861, TR868, Lg881
Great Lakes	Clv845, Mc845, Blo859, SH874
Central/Plains	CS860, Bf869
Mountain/West	none

Rosa 'Caroline de Sansal'

New England	none
Middle Atlantic	EB860
South	Pom856, Brk858, Brk859, Brk861, TR868, Lg881, LR881, Rs898, WY907
Great Lakes	AlN858, Blo859, Col860, SH874, Col877
Central/Plains	CS860, Bf869
Mountain/West	none

Rosa 'Catherine Mermet'

New England	CA889
Middle Atlantic	Ric905
South	Lg881, LR881, Tho888, Pf896, MV898, Rs898, JK904, WY907, GSM914, CoS917
Great Lakes	GR889, SH896, CL901, SH908, Sz910
Central/Plains	GS908
Mountain/West	Bn889, TS891, Ca894, Cx907, Ash908, Ger911

Rosa 'Chromatella'

New England	CA889
Middle Atlantic	EB860, MM870, DR876
South	SN851, JR853, Pom856, Brk858, VN858, Brk859, Hop859, Brk861, TR868, ATN870, Lg881, LR881, MV888, Tho888, AEx894, Rs898, JK904, WY907, GSM914, CoS917
Great Lakes	Clv845, Mc845, Col860, SH874, Col877, GR889, SH896, SH908
Central/Plains	none
Mountain/West	TS891, Ca894, FC895, Cx907, Ger911

Rosa 'Clotilde Soupert'

New England	Bk917
Middle Atlantic	PH910, EB917
South	Rs898, JK904, Brk906, BN907, WY907, GSM914, CoS917
Great Lakes	SH896, Wag905, SH908, Sz910
Central/Plains	GS908, ISC914, HF927
Mountain/West	Ca894

Rosa 'Comtesse de Murinais'

New England	R853, CA889
Middle Atlantic	EB860, DR876, EB917
South	Brk858, Brk859, Brk861, LR881, Tho888, Rs898
Great Lakes	AlN858, Col860, Col877, GR889, SH896, SH908, SH925
Central/Plains	CS860, WsN885
Mountain/West	Ca894, FC895

Rosa 'Coquette des Alpes'

New England	CA889, Du901, NE910
Middle Atlantic	DR876, HWC905, EB917
South	Lg881, Tho888
Great Lakes	Col877, GR889, SH896, CL901, SH908, Sz910
Central/Plains	WsN885, GS908, ISC914, Gy927
Mountain/West	Ca894, FC895

Rosa 'Cramoisi Supérieur'

New England	Sac853, CA889
Middle Atlantic	Wn844, EB860, DR876, JV881, PH910
South	SN851, JR853, Pom856, Brk859, Hop859, Brk861, TR868, ATN870, AP881, Lg881, LR881, Rs898, WY907, GSM914
Great Lakes	Clv845, Mc845, Blo859, Col860, SH874, Col877, GR889, SH896, Tem904, Sz910
Central/Plains	SSN871
Mountain/West	Bn889, Ca894, Cx907, Ash908

Rosa 'Crested Moss'

New England	Br841, R853, NE910, G914
Middle Atlantic	Wn844, EB860, DR876, EB917
South	SN851, LR881, Rs898, BN907, TM925
Great Lakes	Clv845, Mc845, AlN858, Col860, SH874, CL901, Scf901, LW905, Ch915, Er926
Central/Plains	CS860, SSN871, ISC914
Mountain/West	Cx907

Rosa 'Devoniensis'

New England	Sac853
Middle Atlantic	Wn844, EB860, DR876, PH910
South	SN851, JR853, Brk858, Brk859, Hop859, Brk861, TR868, ATN870, AP881, Lg881, LR881, AEx894, Rs898, JK904, BN907, GSM914
Great Lakes	Clv845, Mc845, LEN846, Blo859, Col860, SH874, Col877, GR889, SH896
Central/Plains	none
Mountain/West	Ca894, FC895, WY907, Ash908

Rosa 'Dorothy Perkins'

New England	Du901, NE910, G914, Bk917, Hrd931
Middle Atlantic	HWC905, Ric905, PH910, EB917, My934, Bun939
South	BN907, JD909, CoS917, Oz919, TM925
Great Lakes	LW905, Wag905, SH908, Sz910, Ch915, ACN920, SH925, WA928, Al930, Fr932
Central/Plains	GS908, ISC914, SN919, Gy921, EF927, Gy927, HF927, FbN933
Mountain/West	Ger911, PK912, Az925, PW926, GJ936

Rosa 'Duchesse de Brabant'

New England	CA889
Middle Atlantic	JV881, PH910
South	AP881, Lg881, LR881, Tho888, Wm895, Rs898, JK904, Brk906, WY907 GSM914
Great Lakes	Col877, GR889, SH896, Wag905, SH908
Central/Plains	SSN871, ISC914
Mountain/West	Bn889, Ca894, Cx907, Ash908

Rosa 'Étoile de Lyon'

New England	CA889
Middle Atlantic	none
South	MV888, Tho888, Pf896, Rs898, JK904, Brk906, BN907, WY907, GSM914, CoS917, TM925
Great Lakes	GR889, SH896, SH908
Central/Plains	GS908
Mountain/West	Bn889, FC895, Cx907, Ger911, PK912, Az925

Rosa 'Excelsa'

New England	Bk917, Hrd931
Middle Atlantic	EB917, My934, Bun939
South	TM925
Great Lakes	ACN920, SH925, Er926, WA928, Al930, Fr932
Central/Plains	SN919, Gy921, BrdK922, Gy927, HF927
Mountain/West	Brd922, SW925

Rosa 'Frau Karl Druschki'

New England	NE910, Bk917, Hrd931
Middle Atlantic	Ric905, PH910, EB917, HN922, Dk924, My934, Bun939
South	BN907, WY907, JD909, GSM914, CoS917, Oz919
Great Lakes	LW905, SH908, Sz910, Ch915, SH925, Er926, WA928, Al930, Fr932
Central/Plains	GS908, ISC914, Gy921, EF927, Gy927, HF927
Mountain/West	PK912, Az925, SW925, PW926

Rosa 'Géant des Batailles'

New England	Sac853
Middle Atlantic	EB860, DR876
South	SN851, JR853, Pom856, Brk858, VN858, Brk859, Brk861, TR868, ATN870, LR881, Tho888, Rs898, BN907, WY907, GSM914
Great Lakes	PG858, Blo859, Col860, SH874, Col877, GR889
Central/Plains	CS860, Bf869, SSN871, WsN885
Mountain/West	Bn889, TS891, Ca894, FC895

Rosa 'Général Jacqueminot'

New England	CA889, Du901, NE910, G914, Bk917, Hrd931
Middle Atlantic	EB860, MM870, DR876, HWC905, PH910, EB917, HN922, Bun939
South	Brk859, Hop859, Brk861, TR868, ATN870, Lg881, LR881, MV888, Tho888, AEx894, MV898, Rs898, JK904, Brk906, BN907, Vd907, GSM914, Oz919, TM925
Great Lakes	SH874, Col877, GR889, SH896, CL901, LW905, Wag905, SH908, Sz910, Ch915, SH925, Er926, WA928, Al930
Central/Plains	CS860, Bf869, SSN871, WsN885, GS908, ISC914, SN919, EF927, Gy927, HF927
Mountain/West	DM887, Bn889, TS891, Ca894, FC895, Cx907, Ash908, Ger911, PK912, Az925

Rosa 'General Washington'

New England	CA889, Du901
Middle Atlantic	MM870, DR876
South	TR868, ATN870, Lg881, LR881, Tho888, Oz919
Great Lakes	SH874, Col877, GR889, SH896, CL901
Central/Plains	Bf869, SSN871, WsN885, Ex888, ISC914
Mountain/West	DM887, Bn889, Ca894, FC895

Rosa 'Gloire de Dijon'

New England	CA889, Bk917
Middle Atlantic	EB860, DR876, JV881, PH910
South	Pom856, Hop859, Brk861, TR868, ATN870, LR881, Tho888, AEx894, BN907
Great Lakes	SH874, Col877, GR889
Central/Plains	Bf869
Mountain/West	Bn889, Ca894, Cx907

Rosa 'Gloire des Mousseux'

New England	CA889
Middle Atlantic	EB860, DR876
South	LR881, MV888, Pf888, Rs898
Great Lakes	Blo859, Col860, SH874, GR889, CL901, Scf901
Central/Plains	WsN885, ShN899
Mountain/West	Bn889, Ca894, Cx907

Rosa 'Gruss An Teplitz'

New England	NE910, Bk917
Middle Atlantic	PH910, EB917, Dk924, Mch931, My934, Bun939
South	JK904, GSM914, CoS917, Oz919, TM925
Great Lakes	Tem904, Wag905, SH908, Sz910, ACN920, SH925, Er926, WA928, Al930, Fr932

Central/Plains	ISC914, GS908, SN919, Gy921, Brd922, EF927, Gy927, HF927
Mountain/West	Ash908, Ger911, PK912, Brd922, Az925, SW925, PW926, GJ936

Rosa 'Hermosa'

New England	Sac853, CA889, Bk917
Middle Atlantic	Wn844, EB860, DR876, JV881, PH910
South	SN851, JR853, Brk858, Brk859, Hop859, TR868, Brk861, ATN870, Lg881, LR881, Tho888, AEx894, MV898, JK904, BN907, WY907, JD909
Great Lakes	Clv845, Mc845, LEN846, Blo859, Col860, SH874, Col877, GR889, SH896, Tem904, Wag905, SH908, Sz910
Central/Plains	CS860, SSN871, GS908, ISC914, HF927
Mountain/West	Ca894

Rosa 'Homère'

New England	CA889
Middle Atlantic	MM870, DR876
South	R868, Lg881, LR881, Tho888, AEx894, Rs898
Great Lakes	SH874, Col877, GR889
Central/Plains	SSN871
Mountain/West	Bn889, TS891, Ca894, FC895

Rosa 'Isabella Sprunt'

New England	CA889
Middle Atlantic	MM870, DR876, JV881, PH910
South	ATN870, AP881, Lg881, LR881, Tho888, AEx894, MV898, Rs898, JK904, WY907, GSM914
Great Lakes	Col877, GR889, Tem904, Sz910
Central/Plains	SSN871
Mountain/West	TS891, Ca894, FC895, Cx907

Rosa 'John Hopper'

New England	CA889, NE910, Bk917
Middle Atlantic	PH910, EB917
South	TR868, ATN870, Lg881, LR881, Tho888, Rs898, Brk906, BN907, Oz919
Great Lakes	SH874, Col877, GR889, SH908, Sz910, SH925
Central/Plains	SSN871, WsN885, GS908, ISC914
Mountain/West	DM887, Bn889, Ca894, FC895, Cx907

Rosa 'Jules Margottin'

New England	CA889, NE910
Middle Atlantic	EB860, MM870
South	Brk859, Hop859, Brk861, TR868, ATN870, Lg881, LR881, Tho888

Great Lakes	PG858, Col860, SH874, Col877, GR889, CL901
Central/Plains	CS860, Gy927
Mountain/West	Bn889

Rosa 'Kaiserin Auguste Viktoria'

New England	Bk917
Middle Atlantic	PH910, EB917, My934, Bun939
South	Rs898, JK904, Brk906, BN907, Vd907, WY907, CoS917, TM925
Great Lakes	SH896, Wag905, SH908, Al930, Fr932
Central/Plains	GS908, SN919, BrdK922, EF927, Gy927, HF927
Mountain/West	FC895, Cx907, Ash908, Ger911, PK912, Brd922, Az925, PW926, GJ936

Rosa 'Killarney'

New England	NE910, Bk917
Middle Atlantic	PH910, EB917
South	WY907, JD909, CoS917, TM925
Great Lakes	Sz910, SH925, Fr932
Central/Plains	GS908, ISC914, SN919, BrdK922, Gy927
Mountain/West	Cx907, PK912, Brd922, PW926

Rosa 'La France'

New England	CA889, G914, Bk917
Middle Atlantic	DR876, HWC905, PH910, EB917
South	Tho888, AEx894, Wm895, Pf896, MV898, Rs898, JK904, BN907, WY907, CoS917, TM925
Great Lakes	Col877, GR889, SH896, Wag905, SH908, ACN920, Fr932
Central/Plains	GS908, ISC914, Gy921, BrdK922, HF927
Mountain/West	TS891, Ca894, FC895, Cx907, Ash908, Ger911, PK912, Brd922, Az925, PW926

Rosa 'La Reine'

New England	Sac853, CA889, G914
Middle Atlantic	EB860, MM870, DR876
South	SN851, JR853, Brk858, VN858, Brk859, Hop859, Brk861, TR868, ATN870, Lg881, LR881, MV888, Tho888, Rs898
Great Lakes	Mc845, LEN846, AlN858, PG858, Blo859, Col860, SH874, Col877, GR889, Wag905
Central/Plains	CS860, Bf869, SSN871, ISC914
Mountain/West	Bn889, Ca894, FC895

Rosa 'Lamarque'

New England	CA889
Middle Atlantic	Wn844, EB860, DR876, JV881, PH910

South	SN851, JR853, Pom856, Brk858, VN858, Brk859, Hop859, Brk861, TR868, ATN870, Lg881, LR881, Tho888, AEx894, MV898, Rs898, JK904, BN907, WY907, GSM914, CoS917
Great Lakes	Clv845, Mc845, LEN846, Blo859, Col860, SH874, Col877, GR889, SH896, Tem904, Wag905, SH908
Central/Plains	CS860, SSN871
Mountain/West	Bn889, Ca894, FC895, Cx907, Ger911

Rosa 'Le Pactole'

New England	CA889
Middle Atlantic	EB860, DR876, Tho888
South	SN851, JR853, Brk858, Brk859, Hop859, Brk861, TR868, Lg881, LR881, Rs898, JK904
Great Lakes	Clv845, Mc845, Blo859, Col860, SH874, Col877, GR889, SH896, Tem904
Central/Plains	SSN871
Mountain/West	FC895

Rosa 'Louis Philippe'

New England	CA889
Middle Atlantic	Wn844, DR876
South	JR853, Pom856, Brk858, Brk859, Hop859, Brk861, TR868, Lg881, LR881, MV888, Tho888, AEx894, Rs898, JK904, WY907, GSM914
Great Lakes	Mc845, Blo859, Col860, SH874, Col877, GR889, Sz910
Central/Plains	Dmk853, CS860, SSN871
Mountain/West	Bn889, Ash908

Rosa 'Luxemborg'

New England	R853, CA889
Middle Atlantic	Wn844, EB860, MM870
South	Brk858, VN858, Brk859, Brk861, ATN870, Tho888
Great Lakes	Mc845, AlN858, PG858, Blo859, Col860, SH874, SH896, CL901, SH908
Central/Plains	CS860, Bf869, WsN885, EF927
Mountain/West	Ca894

Rosa 'Madame Bravy'

New England	CA889
Middle Atlantic	EB860, DR876, JV881, PH910
South	Brk859, Hop859, Brk861, TR868, ATN870, Lg881, LR881, Tho888, RS898
Great Lakes	Blo859, Col860, SH874, Col877, GR889
Central/Plains	SSN871
Mountain/West	TS891, FC895

Rosa 'Madame Caroline Testout'

New England	Bk917
Middle Atlantic	EB917, Dk924, Mch931, Bun939
South	JK904, BN907, WY907, CoS917, Oz919
Great Lakes	SH897, Wag905, SH925, Er926, WA928, Fr932
Central/Plains	EF927, HF927, SN919, Gy921, BrdK922, Gy927
Mountain/West	Cx907, Ash908, Ger911, PK912, Brd922, Az925, PW926

Rosa 'Madame Charles Wood'

New England	NE910
Middle Atlantic	MM870
South	Tho888, Pf888, AEx894, Pf896, Rs898, BN907, WY907, CoS917
Great Lakes	SH874, Col877, GR889, SH896, Wag905
Central/Plains	SSN871, ISC914
Mountain/West	Ca894, FC895

Rosa 'Madame Gabriel Luizet'

New England	Ca889, Du901, NE910, Bk917
Middle Atlantic	PH910, EB917
South	BN907, Oz919
Great Lakes	GR889, Wag905, SH925, Fr932
Central/Plains	GS908
Mountain/West	Ca894, FC895, Cx907

Rosa 'Madame Laffay'

New England	R853, Sac853
Middle Atlantic	EB860, MM870
South	SN851, JR853, Brk859, Hop859, Brk861, TR868
Great Lakes	Clv845, Mc845, AlN858, Blo859, Col860, SH874
Central/Plains	CS860, Bf869, SSN871
Mountain/West	none

Rosa 'Madame Norbert Levavasseur'

New England	NE910, G914, Bk917, Hrd931
Middle Atlantic	HWC905, Ric905, JC910, PH910, EB917, Mch931
South	Brk906, BN907, Vd907, WY907, JD909, GSM914, CoS917, Oz919
Great Lakes	SH908, Sz910, SH925, Er926, Al930
Central/Plains	GS908, ISC914, SN919, Gy927, HF927, FbN933, OW939
Mountain/West	Ger911, PK912, PW926

Rosa 'Madame Plantier'

New England	Sac853, Rd881, CA889, NE910, G914, Bk917
Middle Atlantic	Wn844, EB860, MM870, DR876, HWC905, PH910, EB917
South	Pom856, Lg881, LR881, Tho888, Rs898, BN907, Oz919
Great Lakes	Blo859, Col877, GR889, SH896, CL901, SH908, Sz910
Central/Plains	CS860, SSN871, WsN885, ShN886, Ex888, ShN899, GS908, ISC914, SN919, Gy921, EF927, Gy927
Mountain/West	Bn889, FC895, Lb939

Rosa 'Magna Charta'

New England	CA889, Du901, NE910, Bk917, Hrd931
Middle Atlantic	PH910, EB917, HN922, Mch931, Bun939
South	LR881, MV888, Tho888, BN907, JD909, GSM914, Oz919
Great Lakes	GR889, SH896, Wag905, SH908, Sz910, SH925, Al930, Fr932
Central/Plains	GS908, ISC914, Gy921, EF927, HF927
Mountain/West	Ca894, Cx907, Ash908, Ger911, SW925

Rosa 'Maman Cochet'

New England	Bk917
Middle Atlantic	PH910, EB917
South	JK904, BN907, JD909, Vd907, GSM914, CoS917, TM925
Great Lakes	SH896, Tem904, Wag905, SH908, Sz910, Er926
Central/Plains	GS908, ISC914, SN919
Mountain/West	Cx907, Ash908, Ger911, PK912, Az925, PW926

Rosa 'Maréchal Neil'

New England	CA889
Middle Atlantic	MM870, DR876, JV881, PH910
South	TR868, ATN870, AP881, Lg881, LR881, MV888, Pf888, Tho888, AEx894, Wm895, Pf896, MV898, Rs898, JK904, BN907, Vd907, WY907, GSM914, CoS917
Great Lakes	SH874, Col877, GR889, SH896, CL901, Tem904, Wag905, SH908, Sz910
Central/Plains	SSN871, ISC914
Mountain/West	Bn889, Ca894, FC895, Cx907, Ash908, PK912, Az925

Rosa 'Marie Guillot'

New England	CA889
Middle Atlantic	JV881, PH910
South	LR881, Pf888, Tho888, AEx894, Rs898, JK904, BN907, WY907, GSM914, CoS917

Great Lakes	SH896, Tem904, SH908
Central/Plains	GS908
Mountain/West	Bn889, Ca894

Rosa 'Marie van Houtte'

New England	CA889
Middle Atlantic	DR876, PH910
South	LR881, Tho888, Rs898, JK904, WY907, GSM914, CoS917
Great Lakes	GR889, SH896, Tem904, SH908
Central/Plains	ISC914
Mountain/West	Bn889, TS891, Ca894, FC895, Cx907, Ash908, Ger911, PK912

Rosa 'Marshall P. Wilder'

New England	CA889, Du901, NE910, Bk917
Middle Atlantic	PH910, EB917, My934
South	Rs898, BN907, GSM914, Oz919
Great Lakes	GR889, SH896, CL901, Wag905, SH908, Ch915, SH925, Fr932
Central/Plains	none
Mountain/West	TS891, Ca894, FC895, Cx907

Rosa 'Meteor'

New England	CA889
Middle Atlantic	none
South	Tho888, Wm895, MV898, Rs898, JK904, BN907, CoS917
Great Lakes	GR889, SH896, Tem904, SH908
Central/Plains	GS908, ISC914
Mountain/West	TS891, Ca894, Ash908, Ger911, Az925

Rosa 'Mistress Bosanquet'

New England	Sac853
Middle Atlantic	Wn844, EB860, DR876
South	SN851, JR853, Pom856, Brk858, Brk859, Hop859, Brk861, TR868, LR881, Tho888
Great Lakes	Mc845, Blo859, Col860, SH874, Col877, GR889
Central/Plains	CS860
Mountain/West	Ca894

Rosa 'Mrs. Aaron Ward'

New England	Bk917
Middle Atlantic	PH910, Dk924, Bun939
South	CoS917
Great Lakes	ACN920, Er926, Fr932, SH925, Al930, WA928
Central/Plains	EF927, Gy927, HF927
Mountain/West	PK912, PW926

Rosa 'Mrs. John Laing'

New England	CA889, NE910, G914, Bk917, Hrd931
Middle Atlantic	HWC905, PH910, EB917, HN922, My934, Bun939
South	Rs898, BN907, Oz919
Great Lakes	GR889, SH896, CL901, Wag905, SH908, Sz910, Ch915, SH925, Er926, Al930, Fr932
Central/Plains	GS908, ISC914
Mountain/West	Bn889, Ca894, Cx907, Ash908, PK912, PW926

Rosa 'Niphetos'

New England	CA889
Middle Atlantic	EB860, JV881
South	SN851, Brk858, Brk859, Brk861, LR881, Tho888, AEx894, Rs898
Great Lakes	Mc845, GR889, SH896
Central/Plains	none
Mountain/West	Bn889, TS891, Ca894, Cx907

Rosa 'Ophirie'

New England	none
Middle Atlantic	EB860, DR876
South	SN851, JR853, Pom856, Brk858, Brk859, Hop859, Brk861, TR868, Lg881, LR881
Great Lakes	Mc845, Col860, SH874, Col877
Central/Plains	none
Mountain/West	Ash908

Rosa 'Papa Gontier'

New England	CA889
Middle Atlantic	Ric905
South	Tho888, AEx894, Wm895, MV898, Rs898, JK904, BN907, Vd907, WY907, GSM914
Great Lakes	GR889, SH896, CL901, SH908
Central/Plains	GS908
Mountain/West	Bn889, Ca894, FC895, Cx907, Ash908, Ger911, PK912, Az925, PW926

Rosa 'Paul Neyron'

New England	CA889, NE910, G914, Bk917, Hrd931
Middle Atlantic	DR876, HWC905, PH910, EB917, HN922, Bun939
South	Lg881, LR881, MV888, Tho888, AEx894, Pf896, MV898, Rs898, JK904, BN907, GSM914, Oz919, TM925, WY907, CoS917
Great Lakes	Col877, GR889, SH896, CL901, LW905, Wag905, SH908, Sz910, Ch915, SH925, Er926, WA928, Al930, Fr932

Central/Plains	GS908, ISC914, SN919, Gy921, EF927, Gy927, HF927
Mountain/West	DM887, TS891, Ca894, FC895, Cx907, Ash908, Ger911, PK912, Az925, PW926

Rosa 'Perle des Jardin'

New England	CA889
Middle Atlantic	PH910
South	LR881, MV888, Pf888, Tho888, Wm895, MV898, Rs898, JK904, BN907,WY907, CoS917
Great Lakes	GR889, SH896, CL901, Tem904, Wag905, SH908, Sz910
Central/Plains	GS908
Mountain/West	Bn889, TS891, Ca894, FC895, Cx907, Ash908, Ger911, PK912

Rosa 'Pie IX'

New England	none
Middle Atlantic	EB860, MM870
South	Pom856, Brk858, VN858, Brk859, Hop859, Brk861, TR868, Lg881, LR881
Great Lakes	AlN858, Blo859, Col860, SH874, Col877
Central/Plains	CS860, Ex888
Mountain/West	none

Rosa 'Prince Albert'

New England	Sac853
Middle Atlantic	EB860
South	SN851, JR853, Brk858, Brk859, Hop859, Brk861, TR868, Lg881, LR881, MV888
Great Lakes	Mc845, AlN858, Blo859, Col860, SH874
Central/Plains	CS860
Mountain/West	none

Rosa 'Prince Camille De Rohan'

New England	CA889, NE910, Hrd931
Middle Atlantic	MM870, HWC905, PH910, EB917, My934
South	TR868, Lg881, LR881, MV888, Rs898, BN907, Oz919
Great Lakes	SH874, Col877, GR889, SH896, LW905, Wag905, SH908, Ch915, SH925, Fr932
Central/Plains	GS908, ISC914, SN919, Gy921, Gy927, HF927
Mountain/West	Ca894, FC895, Cx907, Ash908, Ger911, PK912, PW926

Rosa 'Princess Adélaïde'

New England	R853, Du901
Middle Atlantic	EB860, MM870, DR876, EB917
South	SN851, LR881, Rs898

Great Lakes	Blo859, Col860, SH874, Col877, GR889, SH896, SH908
Central/Plains	CS860, GS908
Mountain/West	Bn889, Ca894

Rosa 'Quatre Saisons Blanc Mousseux'

New England	CA889
Middle Atlantic	Wn844, EB860
South	SN851, Brk858, Brk859, ATN870, Lg881, LR881, Tho888, Rs898, BN907
Great Lakes	AlN858, Blo859, Col860, SH874, Col877, CL901, Scf901, SH908
Central/Plains	ShN899
Mountain/West	FC895

Rosa 'Queen of the Prairies'

New England	R853, Sac853, CA889, Du901, NE910
Middle Atlantic	EB860, MM870, DR876, HWC905, PH910, EB917
South	SN851, Brk858, Brk859, Hop859, Brk861, ATN870, Lg881, LR881, MV888, Rs898, BN907, Oz919
Great Lakes	Clv845, Mc845, AlN858, PG858, Blo859, Col860, SH874, Col877, GR889, SH896, CL901, Scf901, Crk904, Wag905, SH908, Sz910, Ch915, Fr932
Central/Plains	Dmk853, CS860, Bf869, SSN871, WsN885, ShN886, Srx887, Ex888, ShN899, GS908, ISC914, Gy921, Gy927, FbN933
Mountain/West	DM887, Ca894, FC895

Rosa 'Reine Marie Henriette'

New England	CA889
Middle Atlantic	PH910
South	LR881, MV888, Tho888, Rs898, JK904, BN907, WY907, GSM914, CoS917
Great Lakes	GR889, SH896, Tem904
Central/Plains	none
Mountain/West	Bn889, TS891, Ca894, Cx907, Ash908, Ger911, PK912

Rosa 'Safrano'

New England	CA889
Middle Atlantic	DR876, JV881, PH910
South	SN851, JR853, Pom856, Brk858, Brk859, Brk861, TR868, ATN870, AP881, Lg881, LR881, Tho888, AEx894, Rs898, JK904, BN907, WY907, GSM914, CoS917
Great Lakes	Blo859, Col860, Col877, GR889, SH896, SH908, Sz910
Central/Plains	CS860, SSN871
Mountain/West	TS891, Ca894, FC895, Cx907, Ash908, Ger911

Rosa 'Salet'

New England	CA889, NE910
Middle Atlantic	EB860, DR876, EB917
South	Brk859, Brk861, ATN870, Lg881, LR881, MV888, BN907, Oz919
Great Lakes	Blo859, Col860, SH874, Col877, CL901
Central/Plains	SSN871, WsN885, SN919
Mountain/West	Ca894

Rosa 'Sanguinea'

New England	Br833, CA889
Middle Atlantic	Wn844, EB860, DR876, JV881
South	Hop859, LR881, Lg881, Rs898
Great Lakes	Mc845, Col860, SH874, Col877, Tem904
Central/Plains	Dmk853
Mountain/West	none

Rosa 'Seven Sisters'

New England	Ken832, Br841, CA889, Du901
Middle Atlantic	Wn844, EB860, DR876, My934
South	SN851, LR881, MV888, Tho888, Rs898
Great Lakes	SG843, Clv845, Mc845, SH874, GR889, SH896, CL901, Wag905, SH908, Ch915, Fr932
Central/Plains	CS860, Bf869, WsN885, ShN886, Ex888, ShN899, ISC914, SN919, HF927
Mountain/West	Ca894, FC895, SW925

Rosa 'Solfatarre'

New England	Sac853, CA889
Middle Atlantic	EB860, MM870, DR876
South	SN851, Pom856, Brk858, VN858, Brk859, Hop859, Brk861, TR868, ATN870, Lg881, LR881, Rs898, JK904, GSM914
Great Lakes	Mc845, LEN846, Blo859, Col860, SH874, Col877, GR889, SH896, Tem904
Central/Plains	CS860
Mountain/West	Bn889, Ca894

Rosa 'Souvenir de la Malmaison'

New England	Sac853
Middle Atlantic	EB860, MM870, DR876
South	SN851, JR853, Brk858, VN858, Brk859, Hop859, Brk861, TR868, ATN870, Lg881, LR881, Tho888, AEx894, MV898, Rs898, BN907, WY907
Great Lakes	LEN846, PG858, Blo859, Col860, SH874, Col877, GR889, SH896, SH908
Central/Plains	SSN871, GS908
Mountain/West	Ca894, FC895

Rosa 'Souvenir d'un Ami'

New England	CA889
Middle Atlantic	EB860, DR876, PH910
South	SN851, JR853, Pom856, Brk858, Brk859, Brk861, TR868, Lg881, LR881, Tho888, AEx894
Great Lakes	Blo859, SH874, Col877, GR889, SH896, SH908, Ch915
Central/Plains	CS860
Mountain/West	Bn889, TS891, Ca894, FC895

Rosa 'Sunset'

New England	CA889
Middle Atlantic	PH910
South	Tho888, AEx894, MV898, JK904, Vd907, CoS917
Great Lakes	GR889, SH896
Central/Plains	ISC914
Mountain/West	Bn889, TS891, Ca894, FC895, Cx907, Ash908, Ger911, PK912

Rosa 'Sydonie'

New England	none
Middle Atlantic	EB860, MM870
South	JR853, Pom856, Brk858, Brk859, Brk861, Lg881, LR881, MV888, Rs898
Great Lakes	AlN858, Blo859, Col860, SH874, Col877
Central/Plains	CS860
Mountain/West	none

Rosa 'Tausendschön'

New England	NE910, Bk917
Middle Atlantic	JC910, PH910, EB917
South	CoS917, TM925
Great Lakes	ACN920, SH925, Er926, Al930, Fr932
Central/Plains	ISC914, SN919, BrdK922, EF927, Gy927, HF927
Mountain/West	PK912, Brd922, SW925

Rosa 'The Bride'

New England	CA889
Middle Atlantic	Ric905, PH910
South	Tho888, AEx894, Wm895, Pf896, MV898, Rs898, JK904, BN907, Vd907, WY907, GSM914, CoS917
Great Lakes	GR889, SH896, Wag905, SH908, Sz910
Central/Plains	ISC914
Mountain/West	Bn889, TS891, Ca894, FC895, Cx907, Ash908, Ger911, Az925

Rosa 'Triomphe du Luxembourg'

New England	none
Middle Atlantic	Wn844, EB860, DR876
South	SN851, JR853, Brk858, Brk859, Hop859, Brk861, TR868, LR881, Tho888
Great Lakes	Clv845, Mc845, LEN846, Blo859, Col860, Col877, GR889
Central/Plains	CS860
Mountain/West	Bn889, TS891, Ca894, FC895, Cx907

Rosa 'Turner's Crimson Rambler'

New England	Du901, NE910, G914, Bk917
Middle Atlantic	HWC905, Ric905, JC910, PH910, EB917, Bun939
South	MV898, Rs898, BN907, Vd907, JD909, GSM914, Oz919, TM925, CoS917
Great Lakes	SH896, CL901, Scf901, LW905, Wag905, SH908, Sz910, Ch915, SH925, Er926, WA928, Al930, Fr932
Central/Plains	ShN899, GS908, ISC914, Gy921, EF927, Gy927, HF927, FbN933, OW939
Mountain/West	Cx907, Ash908, Ger911, PK912, Az925, SW925

Rosa 'Ulrich Brunner fils'

New England	NE910, Bk917, Hrd931
Middle Atlantic	PH910, EB917, HN922, Bun939
South	Tho888, BN907, JD909, Oz919
Great Lakes	SH896, Wag905, SH908, Sz910, Ch915, Fr932
Central/Plains	ISC914, SN919, Gy921, HF927
Mountain/West	Ca894, Cx907, Ash908, Ger911, PK912

Rosa 'White Dorothy'

New England	Bk917, Hrd931
Middle Atlantic	EB917, My934
South	CoS917, SW925
Great Lakes	Ch915, ACN920, SH925, Fr932
Central/Plains	ISC914, SN919, Gy921, BrdK922, EF927, Gy927, HF927, FbN933
Mountain/West	PK912, Brd922, SW925

Rosa 'White Maman Cochet'

New England	Bk917
Middle Atlantic	PH910, EB917
South	JK904, WY907, JD909, GSM914, CoS917, TM925
Great Lakes	Tem904, Wag905, SH908, Er926
Central/Plains	ISC914, SN919
Mountain/West	Cx907, PK912, PW926

Rosa eglanteria (sweetbriar)

New England	Ken832, Br841, NE910, G914, Bk917
Middle Atlantic	WB810, Bld819, Pr826, Tb827, TH834, Wn844, DR876, PH910, EB917
South	Hgh903, BN907, Pk938
Great Lakes	SG843, Blo859, SH896, SH908
Central/Plains	ISC914, Gy927, HF927
Mountain/West	TS891, Ca894

Rosa foetida 'Persiana'

New England	R853, Sac853, CA889, NE910, Bk917, Hrd931
Middle Atlantic	EB860, HWC905, PH910, EB917
South	SN851, Brk858, Brk859, Brk861, BN907, Oz919
Great Lakes	LEN846, AlN858, PG858, Blo859, Col860, SH874, SH896, Ch915, SH925, Er926, Fr932
Central/Plains	CS860, WsN885, SN919, Gy921, Gy927
Mountain/West	Ca894, FC895, PK912

Rosa ×*harisonii* 'Harison's Yellow'

New England	Br841, R853, Sac853, Hrd931
Middle Atlantic	TH834, Wn844, EB860, HWC905, EB917
South	SN851, LR881, BN907, Oz919
Great Lakes	SG843, Clv845, Mc845, LEN846, AlN858, PG858, Blo859, Col860, SH874, Crk904, Ch915, SH925
Central/Plains	Dmk853, CS860, Ex888, ISC914, Gy921, Gy927, OW939
Mountain/West	Ca894, Lb939

Rose laevigata (Cherokee rose)

New England	Ken832, Br833
Middle Atlantic	Pr826
South	SN851, Aff860, Tho888, RP904, BN907, GSM914
Great Lakes	none
Central/Plains	none
Mountain/West	Bn889, TS891, Ca894, FC895, Cx907, Ash908, Ger911, Az925

Rosa rugosa (Japan rose)

New England	NE910, G914, Bk917, Hrd931
Middle Atlantic	HWC905, PH910, EB917
South	ATN870, Hgh903, BN907, Pk938
Great Lakes	SH896, SH908, SH925, Er926
Central/Plains	NN919, Gy921, EF927, FbN933
Mountain/West	TS891, Bg892, Ca894, PK912, PW926

Rudbeckia laciniata (coneflower, golden glow)

New England	H834, H835, Ken835, Bt836, H836, H839, Br841, H844, H845, H847, H859, H862, H863, H873, H875, Du901, NE910, G914, Hrd931
Middle Atlantic	M804, Pr818, Pr822, Ln826, Pr826, Tb827, Ln828, Pr829, Pr831, Pr844, Wn844, Pr854, Pr857, HWC905, Ric905, JC910, PH910, EB917
South	BN907, Per927, Wyt931
Great Lakes	Pkt835, Wag905, SH908, Sz910, SH925, Er926, Fr932
Central/Plains	HF927, GS908, Nb918, SN919, Gy921, BrdK922, Gy927, FbN933, OW939
Mountain/West	Cx907, PK912, Brd922, PW926, GJ936, Phd937

Salix babylonica (weeping willow)

New England	Ken832, Br833, Bt836, Br841, R853, Sac853, OC861, Rd881
Middle Atlantic	Pr790, JB807, WB810, Bld819, Pr826, TH834, Wn844, Bu859, EB860, MM870, EB917, My934
South	JS793, JR853, LY854, Brk858, Sta858, Aff860, Brk861, ATN870, Dwr870, Den871, PP895, MV898, Brk906, BN907, Vd907, GSM914, CoS917, Per927
Great Lakes	SG843, Mc845, LEN846, Laz848, Blo859, En859, Col860, SH894, SH908, SH925, Er926, Fr932
Central/Plains	Dmk853, CS860, WsN885, Sk887, Ex888
Mountain/West	FC895, Cx907, PK912, SW925, PW926, PHd937

Salpiglossis sinuata (painted tongue)

New England	Wd867, CA889, Gg915, Bk917, Gg928, ASL937, Bar939
Middle Atlantic	OK870, DR876, PH910, Bol928, JHr934
South	TM925, Wyt931, Pk938
Great Lakes	GR889, Liv889, SH896, MCL898, Imy899, SH908, Sz910, Al930
Central/Plains	PS875, Mic876, PS884, GS908, ISC914, Fg920, BrdK922, Gy927, HF927, OW939
Mountain/West	RTm873, Tg904, Cx907, Ash908, Ger911, Un916, Az921, Brd922, Az925, PW926, Un933, GJ936, PHd937

Salvia splendens (scarlet sage)

New England	Br833, CA889, Gg915, Bk917, Gg928, ASL937, Bar939
Middle Atlantic	OK870, DR876, PH910, Bol928, JHr934

South	JR853, Brk873, AP881, Tho888, AEx894, Ull895, JK904, CoS917, TM925, Per927, Rt928, Wyt931, Pk938
Great Lakes	LEN846, Col877, GR889, Liv889, SH896, MCL898, Imy899, Wag905, SH908, Al930
Central/Plains	CS860, SSN871, PS875, Mic876, GS908, ISC914, Nb918, Fg920, BrdK922, EF927, Gy927, OW939
Mountain/West	TS891, Cx907, Ger911, Un916, Az921, Brd922, Az925, PW926, Un933, GJ936, PHd937, Lb939

Scabiosa atropurpurea (mourning bride)

New England	Bst760, Bt836, Wd867, CA889, Gg915, Bk917, Gg928, ASL937, Bar939
Middle Atlantic	JB807, OK870, DR876, PH910, Bol928
South	OL826, CoS917, TM925, Rt928, Wyt931
Great Lakes	GR889, Liv889, SH896, MCL898, Imy899, SH908, Sz910, Al930
Central/Plains	PS875, Mic876, PS884, GS908, Nb918, Fg920, BrdK922, EF927, OW939
Mountain/West	RTm873, Cx907, Ger911, Un916, Az921, Brd922, Az925, PW926, GJ936, PHd937, Lb939

Schizanthus pinnatus (butterfly flower)

New England	Bt836, Wd867, CA889, Gg915, Bk917, Gg928, ASL937, Bar939
Middle Atlantic	OK870, DR876, PH910, Mch931, JHr934
South	TM925, Wyt931, Pk938
Great Lakes	GR889, Liv889, MCL898, SH908, Al930
Central/Plains	PS875, PS884, GS908, ISC914, BrdK922, OW939
Mountain/West	RTm873, Cx907, Ger911, Brd922, Az925, PW926, GJ936

Senna marilandica (Maryland cassia)

New England	Ken832, H834, H835, Ken835, Bt836, H836, H839, Br841, H844, H845, H847, H859, H862, H863, G883, G886, Mn887, Mn889, G890, G892, NE910, G914
Middle Atlantic	M804, JB807, WB810, Ln811, Pr818, Bld819, PM822, Pr822, Ln826, Pr826, Tb827, Ln828, Pr829, Pr831, TH834, Ab839, Pr844, Pr854, Pr857, Bu857, Bu859, Bu860, EB862, EB882
South	OL826, Hgh903
Great Lakes	Pkt835, Er926, Fr932
Central/Plains	none
Mountain/West	Lb939

Solenostemon scutellarioides (coleus)

New England	Du901, Gg915, Bk917, Gg928, ASL937, Bar939
Middle Atlantic	DR876, PH910, Bol928, JHr934
South	TR868, Brk873, AP881, LR881, Tho888, AEx894, Ull895, JK904, JD909, Per927, Wyt931
Great Lakes	SH874, Col877, GR889, SH896, MCL898, Imy899, Tem904, Wag905, SH908, Sz910, Al930
Central/Plains	PS875, Mic876, PS884, GS908, ISC914, Fg920, BrdK922, Gy927, HF927, OW939
Mountain/West	RTm873, SR880, TS891, FC895, Cx907, Ger911, Brd922, GJ936, PHd937

Sorbus aucuparia (European mountain ash)

New England	Ken832, Br833, Br841, R853, Sac853, OC861, NE910, Bk917, Fsk927, Hrd931
Middle Atlantic	JB792, JB807, Bld819, Pr826, TH834, Wn844, Bu859, EB860, MM870, EB917, My934
South	JR853, LY854, Sta858, Aff860, JBk895, BN907, Pk938
Great Lakes	Clv845, Mc845, LEN846, Laz848, AlN858, PG858, Blo859, En859, Col860, Wau878, SH894, SH896, CL901, Crk904, LW905, Wag905, SH908, SH925, Al930, Fr932
Central/Plains	CS860, Dmk868, WsN885, ShN886, Sgfld887, ShN899, SN919, NW924, EF927, OW939
Mountain/West	SR880, DM887, Bn889, Ca894, FC895, Cx907, PK912, PW926

Spiraea japonica 'Anthony Waterer'

New England	Du901, NE910, G914, Bk917, Fsk927, Hrd931
Middle Atlantic	HWC905, PH910, EB917, HN922, My934, Bun939
South	Brk906, BN907, WY907, CoS917, Kyo939
Great Lakes	Cl901, LW905, Wag905, SH908, Ch915, SH925, Er926, Al930, Fr932
Central/Plains	GS908, Isc914, SN919, Gy921, BrdK922, EF927, Gy927, HF927, FbN933
Mountain/West	Cx907, Ger911, PK912, Brd922, PW926, Lb939

Spiraea prunifolia (bridal wreath)

New England	Sac853, CA889, Du901, NE910, Bk917, Fsk927, Hrd931
Middle Atlantic	Bu859, EB860, MM870, DR876, HWC905, EB917, My934

South	JR853, LY854, Pom856, Brk858, Sta858, Brk861, TR868, ATN870, Den871, Lg881, MV888, MV898, Rs898, Brk906, BN907, WY907
Great Lakes	AlN858, Blo859, Col877, GR889, RE893, SH896, Wag905, Bd919, SH925, Er926, Fr932
Central/Plains	CS860, SSN871, Mic876, Sk887, ISC914, SN919, Gy921, Gy927, HF927
Mountain/West	DM887, Bg892, Ca894, Cx907, PK912, SW925, PW926, Lb939

Spiraea ×vanhouttei (Vanhoutte's spirea)

New England	NE910, G914, Bk917, Fsk927, Hrd931
Middle Atlantic	HWC905, Ric905, PH910, EB918, My934, Bun939
South	Hgh903, Brk906, BN907, WY907, GSM914, CoS917, Oz919, Per927
Great Lakes	GR889, RE893, SH896, CL901, LW905, Wag905, SH908, Sz910, Ch915, Bd919, ACN920, SH925, Er926, WA928, Al930, Fr932
Central/Plains	GS908, ISC914, Nb918, NN919, SN919, BrdK922, Gy921, EF927, Gy927, HF927, FbN933, OW939
Mountain/West	Ca894, FC895, Ger911, PK912, Brd922, SW925, PW926, GJ936, Lb939

Sprekelia formosissima (Jacobean lily)

New England	CA889, Bk917
Middle Atlantic	JB807, Pr818, Pr820, Wn844, EB860, OK870, DR876, AB895, Mch931
South	JR853, Den871, Brk873, AP881, Lg881, TM925
Great Lakes	GR889, Liv889, Imy899, SH896, SH908
Central/Plains	SSN871, Mic876, ISC914
Mountain/West	TS891, Ca894

Symphoricarpos albus (snowberry)

New England	Ken832, Br833, Br841, R853, Rd881, CA889, NE910, G914, Bk917, Fsk927, Hrd931
Middle Atlantic	JB807, Bld819, Tb827, TH834, Wn844, Bu859, EB860, MM870, EB917, HN922, My934, Bun939
South	Brk858, Brk861, Den871, Hgh903, BN907, TM925, Pk938
Great Lakes	SG843, Clv845, Mc845, LEN846, Laz848, Blo859, Wag905, Bd919, SH925, Er926, Al930, Fr932
Central/Plains	CS860, ShN886, Kv887, ISC914, SN919, Gy921, EF927, Gy927, HF927
Mountain/West	SR880, Ash908, PK912, SW926, PW926, PHd937

Symphoricarpos orbiculatus (coralberry)

New England	Ken832, Br833, Br841, Sac853, OC861, NE910, G914, Hrd931
Middle Atlantic	JB783, JB792, M804, Tb827, Wn844, Bu859, EB860, EB917, HN922, My934, Bun939
South	Sta858, Brk861, Den871, Lg881, Hgh903, BN907, TM925, Pk938
Great Lakes	SG843, Clv845, Mc845, LEN846, Laz848, Wag905, Bd919, SH925, Er926, Al930, Fr932
Central/Plains	CS860, ShN899, ISC914, SN919, Gy921, EF927, Gy927, FbN933
Mountain/West	FC895, PK912, SW925, PW926

Syringa ×persica (Persian lilac)

New England	Ken832, Br833, Br841, R853, Sac853, NE910, Fsk927
Middle Atlantic	JB792, WB810, Bld819, Pr826, TH834, Wn844, Bu859, EB860, EB917
South	JR853, Sta858, Dwr870, Den871, Rs898, BN907, CoS917, Oz919
Great Lakes	SG843, Clv845, Mc845, LEN846, PG858, Blo859, Col860, SH896, Wag905, SH908, Sz910, SH925, WA928, Al930, Fr932
Central/Plains	Mic876, ShN886, ShN899, ISC914, SN919, Gy921, EF927, HF927, FbN933, OW939
Mountain/West	DM887, Bn889, Ca894, FC895, Ger911, SW925, PW926, GJ936, PHd937, Lb939

Syringa vulgaris (lilac)

New England	Ken832, Br833, Br841, Rd881, NE910, G914, Bk917, Fsk927, Hrd931
Middle Atlantic	Pr771, Pr790, JB807, WB810, Bld819, Pr826, TH834, Wn844, Bu859, EB860, DR876, EB917, HN922, My934
South	JR853, Brk858, Sta858, Aff860, MN860, Brk861, Dwr871, Wm895, Pf896, Rs898, BN907, CoS917, Oz919, TM925, Pk938
Great Lakes	SG843, Clv845, Mc845, LEN846, Laz848, PG858, Blo859, Col860, Col870, GR889, RE893, SH896, CL901, Crk904, LW905, Wag905, SH908, Ch915, Bd919, ACN920, SH925, Er926, WA928, Al930, Fr932
Central/Plains	Dmk853, CS860, Dmk868, Mic876, WsN885, ShN886, Ex888, ShN899, ISC914, NN919, SN919, Gy921, BrdK922, EF927, Gy927, HF927, FbN933, OW939
Mountain/West	Osb855, SR880, DM887, Bn889, Ca894, Cx907, Ash908, Ger911, PK912, Brd922, St923, SW925, Lb939

Tagetes erecta (African marigold)

New England	Bst760, Bt836, Wd867, CA889, Gg915, Bk917, Gg928, ASL937, Bar939
Middle Atlantic	JB807, OK870, DR876, PH910, Bol928, JHr934, My934
South	GF799, OL826, Ull895, Rt928, Wyt931
Great Lakes	GR889, Liv889, SH896, MCL898, SH908, Sz910, Al930
Central/Plains	PS875, Mic876, PS884, GS908, Nb918, Fg920, BrdK922, EF927, OW939
Mountain/West	RTm873, SR880, Tg904, Cx907, Ger911, Un916, Az921, Brd922, Az925, PW926, Un933, GJ936, PHd937

Tagetes patula (French marigold)

New England	Wd867, CA889, Gg915, Bk917, Gg928, ASL937
Middle Atlantic	JB807, OK870, DR876, PH910, Bol928, JHr934, My934
South	GF799, OL826, TM895, Ull895, Rt928, Wyt931, Pk938
Great Lakes	GR889, Liv889, MCL898, Imy899, SH908, Sz910, Al930
Central/Plains	PS875, Mic876, PS884, GS908, Nb918, Fg920, BrdK922, OW939
Mountain/West	SR880, Ger911, Un916, Az921, Brd922, Az925, PW926, Un933, GJ936, PHd937

Tanacetum parthenium (feverfew)

New England	Ken835, Bt836, Bk838, Br841, Bk845, Bk851, H852, OC857, H859, Wd867, H873, H875, Mn875, Bk878, CA889, Bk917, Gg928
Middle Atlantic	WB810, Pr822, Pr826, Ab827, Pr829, Ab830, Pr831, Ab839, Pr844, Wn844, EB848, Pr854, Pr857, EB860, OK870, DR876, Ln879, Ln884, Ln889, Ph910, Bol928, Mch931, JHr934
South	Den871, Brk873, Tho888, JD909, TM925, Wyt931, Pk938
Great Lakes	PKt835, Clv845, Mc845, PG858, Blo859, Blo867, Blo868, Blo872, SH874, Col877, Blo883, GR889, SH896, MCL898, Imy899, Wag905, SH908, Sz910
Central/Plains	CS860, Bf869, SSN871, PS875, Mic876, PS884, GS908, Nb918, Fg920, BrdK922, EF927, Gy927, HF927
Mountain/West	Ca894, FC895, Cx907, Ash908, Ger911, Un916, Brd922, Un933, Lb939

Thuja occidentalis (American arborvitae)

New England	Br833, Br841, R853, LC872, Rd881, NE910, Bk917, Fsk927, Hrd931

Middle Atlantic	JB783, JB792, M804, JB807, WB810, Bld819, Pr826, Tb827, Wn844, Bu859, EB860, MM870, HWC905, EB917, HN922, My934, Bun939
South	SN851, LY854, Pom856, Brk858, Sta858, Brk861, TR868, ATN870, Dwr870, Den871, Lg881, JBk895, Hgh903, Brk906, BN907, Vd907, Oz919, TM925, Pk938
Great Lakes	SG843, Mc845, LEN846, AlN858, PG858, Blo859, En859, Col860, Tru866, Wau878, SH894, CL901, LW905, Wag905, SH908, Sz910, Ch915, SH925, Er926, Al930, Fr932
Central/Plains	Dmk853, CS860, Dmk868, KN871, Mic876, PS884, WsN885, ShN886, Kv887, Sk887, Srx887, Ex888, ShN899, SN919, Gy921, BrdK922, NW924, EF927
Mountain/West	Rtm873, Bn889, Ca894, FC895, Ger911, Brd922, PW926, PHd937, Lb939

Thunbergia alata (black-eyed Susan vine)

New England	Br833, Bt836, Wd867, CA889, Bk917, Bar939
Middle Atlantic	OK870, DR876, PH910, Bol928, JHr934
South	LR881, Pk938
Great Lakes	GR889, Liv889, SH896, MCL898, Imy899, SH908, Sz910, Al930
Central/Plains	PS875, Mic876, PS884, ISC914, Nb918, BrdK922, Gy927
Mountain/West	RTm873, Cx907, Ger911, Un916, Brd922, Un933, GJ936

Tilia americana (basswood)

New England	Br833, Br841, Rd881, NE910, Bk917, Fsk927
Middle Atlantic	JB783, Pr790, M804, JB807, WB810, Bld819, Pr826, Wn844, Bu859, EB860, MM870, EB917, HN922
South	Ly854, Sta858, Den871, JBk895, Hgh903, Brk906, BN907, Pk938
Great Lakes	SG843, Clv845, RE893, SH894, LW905, Wag905, Sz910, Ch915, SH925, Er926, Al930, Fr932
Central/Plains	SSN871, WsN885, ShN886, Ex888, ShN899, SN919, Gy921, Gy927, FbN933, OW939
Mountain/West	FC895, Ca894, Cx907, Ash908, PW926

Tilia platyphyllos (European linden)

New England	Ken832, Br833, Br841, R853, Sac853, OC861, Rd881, Bk917, Fsk927
Middle Atlantic	WB810, Bld819, Pr826, TH834, Wn844, Bu859, EB860, EB917, HN922
South	LY854, Sta858, Dwr870, Den871, JBk895, Brk906, BN907
Great Lakes	Clv845, Blo859, Col860, RE893, SH894, SH896, Wag905, SH908, Ch915, SH925, Fr932

Central/Plains	SSN871, PS884, Sk887
Mountain/West	Ca894, FC895, PK912, PW926

Tradescantia virginiana (spiderwort)

New England	Ken832, H834, Ken835, Br841, Bk845, Bk851, H852, OC857, H859, H862, H863, G880, G883, G886, Mn887, Mn889, G890, G892, NE910, G914
Middle Atlantic	Pr818, Pr822, Pr826, Ab827, Pr829, Ab830, Pr831, TH834, Ab839, Bu844, Pr844, Wn844, EB848, Pr857, EB860, EB862, EB867, EB875, EB882, PH910, EB917
South	Den871, Hgh903, BN907, Pk938
Great Lakes	Clv845, Mc845
Central/Plains	OW939
Mountain/West	Lb939

Tropaeolum majus (nasturtium)

New England	Bt836, Wd867, CA889, Du901, Gg915, Bk917, Gg928, ASL937, Bar939
Middle Atlantic	OK870, DR876, PH910, Bol928, JHr934, My934
South	LR881, Ull895, TM895, Rt928, Wyt931, Pk938
Great Lakes	GR889, Liv889, SH896, MCL898, Al930
Central/Plains	PS875, Mic876, PS884, ISC914, Fg920, BrdK922, EF927, Gy927, HF927, OW939
Mountain/West	RTm873, SR880, Tg904, Cx907, Ger911, Un916, Az921, PW926, Un933, GJ936, PHd937

Tropaeolum peregrinium (canary vine)

New England	Wd867, CA889, Gg915, Bk917, Gg928, Bar939
Middle Atlantic	OK870, DR876, PH910, Bol928
South	TM925, Wyt931, Pk938
Great Lakes	GR889, Liv889, SH896, MCL898, SH908, Sz910
Central/Plains	PS875, Mic876, PS884, GS908, ISC914, Fg920, BrdK922, HF927, OW939
Mountain/West	RTm873, Cx907, Ger911, Az921, Brd922, Az925, PW926, GJ936

Tsuga canadensis (Canadian hemlock)

New England	Ken832, Br833, Br841, OC861, LC872, Rd881, NE910, G914, Bk917, Fsk927
Middle Atlantic	Pr771, JB783, Pr790, WB810, Bld819, Pr826, Tb827, Wn844, Bu859, EB860, MM870, EB917, HN922, Bun939
South	JR853, LY854, Brk858, Sta858, Brk861, TR868, ATN870, Den871, Lg881, Hgh903, BN907

Great Lakes — SG843, Clv845, LEN846, Blo859, En859, Col860, Wau878, SS887, SH894, CL901, Wag905, SH908, Sz910, SH925, Er926

Central/Plains — CS860, Dmk868, KN871, SSN871, PS884, ShN886, EF927

Mountain/West — Ca894

Tulipa (tulip)

New England — Bst760, H834, Bt836, H847, Bk851, H862, H863, H866, Bk871, Mn875, Bk878, Bk881, Rd881, G892, NE910, Fsk927

Middle Atlantic — WB810, Bld819, Pr820, PM822, Ab830, Ab839, Bu844, Pr857, EB860, Pr860, EB862, EB867, BB873, EB875, EB882, Crk904, HWC905, Ric905, JC910, Mch931

South — TA754, JW765, MC792, MC793, Brk861, Den871, LR881, JD909, CoS917, Oz919

Great Lakes — Mc845, AlN858, PG858, Blo859, T872, Blo873, T873, Blo883, LW905, SH925, Al930

Central/Plains — Bf869, SSN871, WsN885, ISC914, HF927

Mountain/West — RTm873, Az921, St923

Ulmus americana (American elm)

New England — Ken832, Br841, OC861, LC872, NE910, Bk917, Fsk927, Hrd931

Middle Atlantic — M804, JB807, WB810, Wn844, Bu859, EB860, HWC905, Ric905, EB917, HN922, My934, Bun939

South — LY854, Sta858, Brk861, Den871, Hgh903, Brk906, BN907, GSM914, CoS917, Oz919, TM925

Great Lakes — SG843, LEN846, Blo859, En859, Col860, Wau878, RE893, SH894, CL901, Wag905, SH908, Sz910, SH925, Er926, Al930, Fr932

Central/Plains — CS860, WsN885, ShN886, Srx887, Ex888, ShN899, NN919, SN919, Gy921, BrdK922, NW924, HF927, FbN933, OW939

Mountain/West — RTm873, SR880, DM887, Ca894, FC895, Cx907, Ger911, PK912, Brd922, SW925, PW926

Verbena ×*hybrida* (verbena)

New England — Wd867, CA889, Gg915, Bk917, Gg928, ASL937, Bar939

Middle Atlantic — EB860, OK870, DR876, PH910, Bol928, JHr934, My934

South — SN851, Sta858, Hop859, Aff860, Brk861, TR868, Brk873, AP881, Lg881, LR881, Tho888, JD909, CoS917, TM925, Per927, Rt928, Wyt931, Pk938

Great Lakes — Clv845, Mc845, LEN846, AlN858, PG858, Col860, SH874, Col877, GR889, Liv889, Scf896, SH896, MCL898, Imy899, Sz910, Al930

Central/Plains — Dmk853, CS860, Bf869, SSN871, PS875, Mic876, PS884, GS908, ISC914, Nb918, Fg920, BrdK922, EF927, GY927, HF927, OW939

Mountain/West — RTm873, SR880, Bn889, Ca894, FC895, Tg904, Cx907, Ger911, Un916, Az921, Brd922, PW926, Un933, GJ936, PHd937, Lb939

Viburnum opulus 'Roseum' (snowball)

New England — Ken832, Br833, Br841, R853, Sac853, Rd881, CA889, NE910, G914, Fsk927, Hrd931

Middle Atlantic — Pr771, Pr790, JB792, JB807, WB810, Bld819, Pr826, TH834, Wn844, Bu859, EB860, DR876, EB917, HN922, My934, Bun939

South — JR853, Brk858, Sta858, Aff860, Brk861, TR868, ATN870, Dwr870, Den871, Brk906, BN907, Vd907, Oz919, TM925, Pk938

Great Lakes — SG843, Clv845, Mc845, LEN846, Laz848, PG858, Blo859, En859, Col860, Col877, GR889, RE893, SH896, CL901, Crk904, Wag905, SH908, Bd919, SH925, Er926, WA928, Al930, Fr932

Central/Plains — Dmk853, CS860, Dmk868, SSN871, Mic876, WsN885, ShN886, Sk887, Srx887, Ex888, ShN899, ISC914, SN919, Gy921, BrdK922, EF927, Gy927, HF927, FbN933, OW939

Mountain/West — Osb855, Rtm873, SR880, DM887, Bn889, Ca894, FC895, Cx907, Ash908, Ger911, PK912, Brd922, SW925, PW926, Lb939

Vinca major (large periwinkle)

New England — Ken832, Br833, Br841, OC857, CA889, OC857

Middle Atlantic — JB807, Pr826, Wn844, Pr857, EB860

South — Lg881, Rs898, JK904, Brk906, BN907

Great Lakes — Clv845, Mc845, GR889, Wag905

Central/Plains — SSN871, Mic876

Mountain/West — SR880, FC895

Vinca minor (creeping myrtle)

New England — Ken832, Br833, Br841, OC857, NE910, G914

Middle Atlantic — JB807, WB810, Bld819, Pr826, Wn844, Pr857, EB860

South — Den871, Brk873, Lg881, Hgh903, BN907

Great Lakes — SG843, Clv845, Mc845, Wag905

Central/Plains — SSN871, Mic876, SN919, Gy927, HF927

Mountain/West — Ca894, PW926, GJ936, Lb939

Viola odorata (sweet violet)

New England — H834, H835, Ken835, H836, H839, Br841, Bk845, Bk851, H852, OC857, Wd867, G914, Gg915, Bk917, Gg928, ASL937, Bar939

Middle Atlantic | JB807, Ln811, Pr822, Ln826, Pr826, Ln828, Pr829, Pr831, Ab839, Bu844, Pr844, Wn844, EB848, Bu857, Pr857, Bu859, EB860, EB862, Bu866, EB867, Ln868, DR876, Ln879, EB882, Ln884, Ln889, PH910

South | Aff860, Lg881, JD909, Pk938

Great Lakes | Clv845, Scf896, SH896

Central/Plains | CS860, PS875, Mic876, PS884, ISC914, Nb918, SN919, BrdK922, Gy927

Mountain/West | Cx907, Ger911, Az921, Brd922, Az925, GJ936

Viola tricolor (pansy)

New England | H834, Ken835, Bt836, Br841, Bk845, H847, Bk851, OC857, H863, Wd867, H873, H875, Mn875, H888, CA889, Mn889, Ell894, Gg915, Bk917, Gg928, ASL937, Bar939

Middle Atlantic | GM796, Pr822, Pr829, Pr831, TH834, Wn844, Ln847, EB848, Bu857, Pr857, Bu859, Bu860, EB860, EB862, Bu866, EB867, Ln868, OK870, EB875, DR876, Ln879, EB882, Ln884, PH910, JC910, Bol928, Mch931, JHr934, My934

South | GF799, OL826, Brk873, AP881, LR881, Ull895, JK904, JD909, CoS917, TM925, Per927, Rt928, Wyt931, Pk938

Great Lakes | Clv845, Mc845, LEN846, PG858, Blo859, Col860, Blo872, SH874, Col877, GR889, SH896, Liv889, Scf896, MCL898, Imy899, Tem904, SH908, Sz910, Er926

Central/Plains | CS860, SSN871, PS875, Mic876, PS884, ISC914, Fg920, BrdK922, EF927, Gy927, HF927, FbN933, OW939

Mountain/West | RTm873, SR880, Bn889, TS891, Ca894, FC895, Tg904, Cx907, Ash908, Ger911, Un916, Az921, Brd922, Az925, PW926, Un933, GJ936, PHd937, Lb939

Weigela florida (old-fashioned weigela)

New England | Sac853, Rd881, CA889, Du901, Bk917, Fsk927, Hrd931

Middle Atlantic | Bu859, EB860, MM870, DR876, PH910, EB917, HN922, My934, Bun939

South | Ly854, Pom856, Brk858, Sta858, Brk861, TR868, ATN870, Dwr870, Den871, Lg881, Rs898, BN907, Oz919, TM925, Per927

Great Lakes | AlN858, PG858, Blo859, Col860, GR889, RE893, SH896, CL901, Wag905, SH908, Sz910, Ch915, Bd919, ACN920, SH925, Er926, WA928, Al930, Fr932

Central/Plains | CS860, Dmk868, SSN871, WsN885, ShN886, Ex888, ShN899, GS908, ISC914, SN919, Gy921, BrdK922, EF927, HF927, FbN933

Mountain/West | RTm853, SR880, DM887, Bn889, Ca894, FC895, Cx907, PK912, Brd922, PW926, PHd937, Lb939

Wisteria frutescens (American glycine)

New England | Ken832, Br833, Hy834, Br841

Middle Atlantic | Pr790, JB792, M804, WB810, Wn844, TH834, Wn844, Bu859, EB860, DR876

South | Sta858, Aff860, Den871, AEx894, Rs898, Hgh903, RP904, Brk906, BN907

Great Lakes | Clv845, Laz848, Blo859, Col860

Central/Plains | CS860, Mic876, ShN899, HF927

Mountain/West | none

Wisteria sinensis (Chinese wisteria)

New England | Ken832, Br833, Br841, Rd881, CA889, Du901, NE910, Bk917, Fsk927, Hrd931

Middle Atlantic | TH834, Wn844, Bu859, EB860, DR876, HWC905, PH910, EB917, HN922, Bol928, My934, Bun939

South | JR853, Pom856, Brk858, Sta858, MN860, Brk861, ATN870, Dwr870, Den871, Lg881, MV888, AEx894, MV898, Rs898, Brk906, BN907, WY907, GSM914, CoS917, Oz919, TM925, Per927, Pk938

Great Lakes | SG843, Clv845, Mc845, LEN846, AlN858, PG858, Col877, GR889, RE893, SH896, CL901, Wag905, Sz910, Ch915, ATN920, SH925, Er926, WA928, Al930, Fr932

Central/Plains | Dmk853, CS860, SSN871, WsN885, ISC914, BrdK922, EF927, Ex888, GS908, SN919, Gy921, Gy927, FbN933

Mountain/West | SR880, DM887, Bn889, Bg892, Ca894, FC895, Cx907, Ash908, Ger911, PK912, Brd922, Az925, PW926, PHd937

Yucca filamentosa (thready yucca)

New England | Ken832, Ken835, Br841, Bk851, H852, H859, Mn875, Rd881, CA889, Mn889, Bk894, NE910, G914, Bk917

Middle Atlantic | M804, JB807, Pr818, Ln826, Pr826, Ln828, Pr829, Pr831, TH834, Bu844, Pr844, Wn844, EB848, Bu857, Pr857, Bu859, EB860, EB862, Bu866, EB867, MM870, EB875, DR876, HWC905, PH910, EB917, Mch931, My934

South | Den871, AEx894, Hgh903, RP904, BN907, GSM914, Pk938

Great Lakes | Mc845, LEN846, T866, Blo868, T872, T873, Col877, SH896, Wag905, SH908, SH925, Er926, Fr932

Central/Plains | CS860, Dmk868, SSN871, Mic876, ShN886, ShN899, ISC914, SN919, Gy921, EF927, Gy927, HF927, FbN933

Mountain/West | SR880, Ca894, FC895, PW926, Lb939

Zantedeschia aethiopica (calla lily)

New England	CA889, NE910, Fsk927
Middle Atlantic	JC910, Mch931
South	Brk861, LR881, Tho888, AEx894, JK904, JD909, Rt928
Great Lakes	Blo859, SH874, Col877, GR889, Liv889, SH896, Imy899, Tem904, SH908, Wag905, Sz910, SH925
Central/Plains	Bf869, Mic876, PS884, GS908, ISC914, SN919, BrdK922
Mountain/West	RTm873, SR880, TS891, Bg892, Ca894, FC895, Ash908, Az921, Brd922, Az925, PW926

Zinnia elegans

New England	Bt836, Wd867, Gg915, Bk917, Gg928, ASL937, Bar939
Middle Atlantic	WB810, OK870, Pr818, Bol928, PH910, JHr934, My934
South	AP881, LR881, CoS917, TM925, Rt928
Great Lakes	SH896, GR889, Liv889, MCL898, Imy899, SH908, Sz910, Er926, Al930
Central/Plains	PS875, Mic876, PS884, GS908, ISC914, Nb918, Fg920, BrdK922, EF927, Gy927, OW939
Mountain/West	RTm873, SR880, Cx907, Ger911, Un916, Az921, Brd922, Az925, PW926, Un933, GJ936, PHd937

APPENDIX C

Contemporary Sources for Heirloom Plants

IN ADDITION TO THESE FINE SPECIALTY nurseries and seed houses, you find heirloom plants in many places, including your local garden centers and nurseries as well as the large mail order companies. Be on the lookout for "straight" species or native plants. Search out the old cultivars and hybrids too. These are rapidly disappearing and deserve a place in modern gardens. Beware of companies that claim to sell "heirlooms" and then produce a modern—for example, an inappropriately dwarf or scentless—variety. Choose open-pollinated seeds when available. Don't forget to check out what is growing in your own neighborhood—in older gardens, cemeteries, and even in the culverts. You just might discover an old-time treasure.

These firms were in operation at the time of this writing, January 2003. Most require a nominal fee, usually $3.00, for a printed catalog and many also do business over the Internet.

HEIRLOOM SPECIALISTS

Heritage Flower Farm
33725 County Road L
Mukwonago, Wisconsin 53149
(262) 662-0804
www.heritageflowerfarm.com
Boutique nursery growing perennials, vines, and a few unusual shrubs cultivated in gardens at least a century ago.

Mountain Brook Primroses; Mountain Brook Consulting
373 Elbow Pond Road
Andover, New Hampshire 03216
(603) 735-5828
www.mtnbrook.com
Old and new primroses, auriculas, and violas. Twenty years of experience in the restoration of historic landscapes and re-creation of period gardens.
202, 203, 232, 233

Old House Gardens—Heirloom Bulbs
536 Third Street
Ann Arbor, Michigan 48103
(734) 995-1486
www.oldhousegardens.com
America's only mail-order source devoted entirely to preserving and promoting heirloom flower bulbs—daffodils, dahlias, and much more—from the 1200s to the 1950s, many of them available nowhere else.
241, 243, 244, 246, 247, 248, 249, 250, 251, 253, 254, 258, 259, 260, 261, 262, 264, 265, 266

Old Sturbridge Village
1 Old Sturbridge Village Road
Sturbridge, Massachusetts 01566
(508) 347-3362
www.osv.org

Perennial Pleasures Nursery of Vermont
P.O. Box 147, 63 Brickhouse Road
East Hardwick, Vermont 05836
(802) 472-5104
www.antiqueplants.com
Wide selection of old-time annuals, herbs, and perennials.

Petals from the Past
16034 County Road 29
Jemison, Alabama 35085
(205) 646-0069
www.petalsfromthepast.com
Cottage garden perennials, herbs, and old roses, as well as heirloom fruits and vegetables.

Select Seeds: Antique Flowers
180 Stickney Hill Road
Union, Connecticut 06076-4617
(860) 684-9310
www.selectseeds.com
Specializes in antique flowers.

Thomas Jefferson Center for Historic Plants at Monticello
P.O. Box 316
Charlottesville, Virginia 22901
(800) 243-1743
www.twinleaf.org
269, 276

OLD ROSES

The Antique Rose Emporium
G. Mike Shoup
9300 Lueckemeyer Road
Brenham, Texas 77833
(979) 836-5548; (800) 441-0002
www.wearerroses.com
278, 283, 285, 286

Ashdown Roses
P.O. Box 308
Landrum, South Carolina 29356
(864) 468-4900
www.ashdownroses.com

Pickering Nurseries
670 Kingston Road
Pickering, Ontario L1V 1A6, Canada
(905) 839-2111; fax (905) 839-4807
www.pickeringnurseries.com

The Roseraie at Bayfields
P.O. Box R
Waldoboro, Maine 04572-0919
(207) 832-6330
www.roseraie.com

Vintage Gardens Antique Roses
2833 Old Gravenstein Highway South
Sebastopol, California 95472
(707) 829-2035
www.vintagegardens.com

SEEDS

See also heirloom specialists (above): Old Sturbridge Village Select Seeds: Antique Flowers Thomas Jefferson Center for Historic Plants at Monticello

Baker Creek Heirloom Seeds
2278 Baker Creek Road
Mansfield, Missouri 65704
(417) 924-8917
www.rareseeds.com

Chiltern Seeds
Bortree Stile, Ulverston
Cumbria, England LA12 7PB
www.edirectory.co.uk/chilternseeds
Extensive seed list; international.

The Flower and Herb Exchange
3076 North Winn Road
Decorah, Iowa 52101
(563) 382-5990
www.seedsavers.org

Fragrant Garden Nursery
P. O. Box 4246
Brookings, Oregon 97415
(541) 412-8840
www.fragrantgarden.com
Antique sweet peas.
146, 147

J. L. Hudson Seedsman
Star Route 2, Box 337
La Honda, California 94020
www.jlhudsonseeds.net

Mikamoki Seeds
17846 Buckingham
Logan, Ohio 43138
www.mikamoki.com
Flowers, herbs, and vegetables.

Southern Exposure Seed Exchange
P.O. Box 460
Mineral, Virginia 23117
www.southernexposure.com
"Saving the past for the future."

BULBS

*See also heirloom specialists (above):
Old House Gardens—Heirloom Bulbs*

B&D Lilies
330 "P" Street
Port Townsend, Washington 98368
(360) 765-4342; fax (360) 765-4074
www.bdlilies.com

Brent and Becky's Bulbs
7463 Heath Trail
Gloucester, Virginia 23061
(877) 661-2852
www.brentandbeckybulbs.com
248, 256, 266

McClure & Zimmerman
335 South High Street
Randolph, Wisconsin 53956
(800) 883-6998
www.mzbulb.com

HERBACEOUS PLANTS

*See also heirloom specialists (above): Heritage Flower Farm
Mountain Brook Primroses, Perennial Pleasures Nursery of
Vermont, Petals from the Past, Thomas Jefferson Center for
Historic Plants at Monticello*

Bluestone Perennials
7211 Middle Ridge Road
Madison, Ohio 44057
(800) 852-5243
www.bluestoneperennials.com
Old varieties of *Campanula* and *Anemone*, among other
plant selections.

Canyon Creek Nursery
3527 Dry Creek Road
Oroville, California 95965
(530) 533-2166
www.canyoncreeknursery.com
Old varieties of *Dianthus* and *Viola*.

Companion Plants
7247 Coolville Ridge Road
Athens, Ohio 45701
(740) 592-4643
www.companionplants.com
Emphasis on herbs; also perennials and natives.

Flower Scent Gardens
14820 Moine Road
Doylestown, Ohio 44230-5946
(330) 658-5946
www.flowerscentgardens.com
Fragrant heliotrope and mignonette among other
aromatic offerings.

Klehm's Song Sparrow Perennial Farm
13101 East Rye Road
Avalon, Wisconsin 53505
(800) 553-3715
www.songsparrow.com
Antique peonies, herbaceous and tree.
<page no.>

Plant Delights Nursery, Inc.
9241 Sauls Road
Raleigh, North Carolina 27603
(919) 772-4794
www.plantdelights.com
Selected old-time varieties share space with the best of the
new plants.

Prairie Nursery
P.O. Box 306
Westfield, Wisconsin 53964
(800) 476-9453
www.prairienursery.com
Nursery-propagated native plants.

Well-Sweep Herb Farm
205 Mount Bethel Road
Port Murray, New Jersey 07865
(908) 852-5390
www.wellsweep.com

HEMEROCALLIS (DAYLILIES)

Moonshadow Gardens
5463 Spotslee Circle
Mechanicsville, Virginia 23111-4216
(804) 746-8160
Daylilies representing every decade since the 1890s.

The Perennial Patch
6713 Wade Stedman Road
Wade, North Carolina 28395
(910) 483-2838
www.GardenEureka.com/PEREN
Over 200 pre-1960 daylilies.

IRIS

Adamgrove
31642 Wieneke Branch Road
California, Missouri 65018
adamgrove@socket.net
(573) 796-3829 (e-mail preferable)

Superstition Iris Gardens
2536 Old Highway
Cathey's Valley, California 95306
(209) 966-6277

Winterberry Gardens
1225 Reynolds Road
Cross Junction, Virginia 22625
(540) 888-4447

TREES, SHRUBS, AND VINES

Completely Clematis Specialty Nursery
217 Argilla Road
Ipswich, Massachusetts 01938-2617
(978) 356-3197
www.clematisnursery.com
Species and heirloom cultivars of *Clematis*.

forestfarm
990 Tetherow Road
Williams, Oregon 97544-9599
(541) 846-6963
www.forestfarm.com

Green Nurseries and Landscape
415 North Greeno Road
Fairhope, Alabama 36532-3033
(334) 928-8469
Old camellia cultivars.
110, 111

Roslyn Nursery
211 Burrs Lane
Dix Hills, New York 11746
(631) 643-9347
www.roslynnursery.com
A few heirloom *Rhododendron*, among other treats.

Woodlanders
1128 Colleton Avenue
Aiken, South Carolina 29801
(803) 648-7522
www.woodlanders.net
Southeast natives.

TROPICALS

Color Farm
1604 West Richway Drive
Albert Lea, Minnesota 56007
www.colorfarm.com
Coleus specialist—a few old varieties.

Glass House Works
Church Street, P.O. Box 97
Stewart, Ohio 45778-0097
(740) 662-2142
www.glasshouseworks.com

Logee's Greenhouses, Ltd.
141 North Street
Danielson, Connecticut 06239
(888) 330-8038
www.logees.com
Antique pelargoniums and begonias, as well as other tender species.

PLANT SOURCE DATABASES

Andersen Horticultural Library
P.O. Box 39
Chanhassen, Minnesota 55317-0039
www.plantinfo.umn.edu
Annual subscription required to access database of plants and American sources.

RHS Plant Finder
The Royal Horticultural Society
80 Vincent Square
London SW1P 2PE
www.rhs.org.uk
Publishes book of UK sources annually; maintains database for general use.

APPENDIX D

Invasive Heirloom Ornamental Plants

HEIRLOOM ORNAMENTAL PLANTS vary by more than their habit, flower color, or leaf structure. They also bring to the garden different degrees of vigor or even aggressiveness. Many times, a plant brought to this country from another—an exotic—was placed in a more secure environment without the predators, pests, or diseases that it might have struggled against in its native habitat. The result is that many exotics are particularly successful in American soil. The same situation can also be true even if the move was just across this country, with plants native to one section becoming invasive in another American ecosystem.

Executive Order 13112 (William J. Clinton, 3 February 1999) defines an "invasive species" as a species that is nonnative (or alien) to the ecosystem under consideration and "whose introduction causes or is likely to cause economic or environmental harm or harm to human health." Governmental agencies on the local, state, and regional levels are responsible for identifying plants that conform to this definition for their areas and sometimes rank them according to varying degrees of invasiveness. It goes without saying that anytime we bring a plant into cultivation we must learn all its habits in our own particular environment. In the past, the aggressive tendencies of some plants were not recognized until decades after their introduction. In other cases, invasiveness was immediately identified and caution was counseled in early gardening literature, such as for the star-of-Bethlehem (*Ornithogalum umbellatum*).

This book includes a number of heirloom plants that have different degrees of invasiveness when introduced into cultivation. The list does not claim to represent *all* heirloom plant species that might be on an "invasive-plant watch list." These plants have been rated on a numerical scale, particular to this book alone, that attempts to synthesize the state and regional lists, as of early 2003, of invasive and potentially invasive ornamental plants. The status of individual plants should be considered fluid and easily changed for better or worse. Additional plants might also be appropriately added to this list as more information is collected and observations are analyzed. For more information, please consult with your state's natural resources department or the following Web sites:

www.invasivespecies.gov
http://plants.usda.gov

KEY

Habit   T, tree; S, shrub; V, vine; P, perennial (or biennial); A, annual; B, bulb; R, rose

N   native to the United States

Ex   exotic

REGIONS

NE   Connecticut, Maine, Massachusetts, New Hampshire, Rhode Island, Vermont

MA   Delaware, Maryland, New Jersey, New York, Pennsylvania, Washington, D.C.

SO   Alabama, Arkansas, Florida, Georgia, Kentucky, Louisiana, Mississippi, North Carolina, South Carolina, Tennessee, Texas, Virginia, West Virginia

GL   Illinois, Indiana, Michigan, Minnesota, Ohio, Wisconsin

C/GP Iowa, Kansas, Missouri, Nebraska, North Dakota, Oklahoma, South Dakota

MtW Arizona, California, Colorado, Idaho, Montana, Nevada, New Mexico, Oregon, Utah, Washington, Wyoming

RANKING

1. Plant identified as a "noxious weed," "severe threat," or "highly invasive" in at least one state within the region.
2. Plant identified as invasive to varying degrees, depending on locality. Consult with your local authorities and proceed with caution.
3. Potentially invasive "species of concern."

POTENTIALLY INVASIVE HEIRLOOM ORNAMENTAL PLANTS

Plant	Habit	N/Ex	NE	MA	SO	GL	C/GP	MtW
Acer palmatum, Japanese maple	T/S	Ex	3					
Acer platanoides, Norway maple	T	Ex	1	1	2	2	3	
Acer pseudoplatanus, European sycamore maple	T	Ex	3	1				
Ailanthus altissima, tree of heaven	T	Ex	1	1	1	2		2
Akebia quinata, chocolate vine	V	Ex	3	2	2			
Albizia julibrissin, silk tree	T	Ex		2	1			
Alcea rosea, hollyhock	P	Ex					3	
Amorpha fruticosa, false indigo	S	N	2					1
Arundo donax, giant reed	P	Ex			2			2
Asparagus densiflorus, asparagus fern	A	Ex			1			
Belamcanda chinensis, blackberry lily	P	Ex				2		
Berberis thunbergii, Japanese barberry	S	Ex	1	1	2		3	
Berberis vulgaris, common barberry	S	Ex	1					
Betula pendula, European birch	T	Ex					3	

POTENTIALLY INVASIVE HEIRLOOM ORNAMENTAL PLANTS

Plant	Habit	N/Ex	NE	MA	SO	GL	C/GP	MtW
Broussonettia papyrifera, paper mulberry	T	Ex		3	2			
Buddleia davidii, butterfly bush	S	Ex		3				
Caragana arborescens, Siberian pea shrub	S	Ex	3					
Cardiospermum halicacabum, love-in-a-puff	V	N			1			
Catalpa	T	N		3				
Celastrus orbiculatus, oriental bittersweet	V	Ex	1	3	1	1		
Centaurea cyanus, cornflower	A	Ex	3		3		3	
Cinnamomum camphora, camphor tree	T	Ex			1			
Clematis terniflora, sweet autumn clematis	V	Ex	3	3	2			
Colocasia esculenta, taro, elephant ears	B	Ex			1			
Convallaria majalis, lily-of-the-valley	P	Ex	3					
Cornus sericea, red-twig dogwood	S	N	2					
Cytisus scoparius, Scotch broom	S	Ex	3	3				1
Elaeagnus angustifolia, Russian olive	T	Ex	1	3	2		3	1
Euonymus alatus, winged euonymus	S	Ex	1	2	1	2		
Euonymus europaeus, European euonymus	T/S	Ex					3	
Euonymus fortunei, winter creeper	V	Ex	2	3	1	2		
Filipendula ulmaria, meadowsweet	P	Ex	3					
Gypsophila paniculata, baby's breath	P	Ex	3					1
Hedera helix, English ivy	V	Ex	3	2	2		3	
Hemerocallis fulva, orange daylily	P	Ex	3	2	3		3	
Hesperis matronalis, dame's rocket	P	Ex	2	2	1	2	3	1
Hibiscus trionum, bladder ketmia	P	Ex				1	3	1
Hieracium aurantiacum, orange hawkweed	P	Ex	3					
Humulus japonicus, Japanese hops	V	Ex	3	2	2		3	
Ipomoea alba, moon flower	V	Ex						1
Ipomoea batatas, sweet potato vine	V	Ex	3	3	2			1

POTENTIALLY INVASIVE HEIRLOOM ORNAMENTAL PLANTS

Plant	Habit	N/Ex	NE	MA	SO	GL	C/GP	MtW
Ipomoea ×multifida, cardinal climber	V	Ex						1
Ipomoea purpurea, morning glory	V	Ex			2			1
Ipomoea quamoclit, cypress vine	V	Ex						1
Ipomoea tricolor, morning glory	V	Ex						1
Iris cristata, crested iris	P	N						1
Iris ensata, Japanese iris	P	Ex						1
Iris germanica, German iris	P	Ex						1
Iris pallida, bearded iris	P	Ex						1
Iris pseudacorus, yellow flag	P	Ex	1	2	3		3	1
Iris pumila, dwarf iris	P	Ex						1
Iris sibirica, Siberian iris	P	Ex						1
Iris xiphium, Spanish iris	B	Ex						1
Juniperus virginiana, red cedar	T/S	N	2					
Kochia scoparia, burning bush	A	Ex	3			1	3	1
Lantana camara, shrubby verbena	S	Ex			1			
Lathyrus latifolius, perennial sweet pea	V	Ex	3				3	
Leucojum aestivum, summer snowflake	B	Ex	3					
Ligustrum japonicum, Japanese privet	S	Ex			2			
Ligustrum obtusifolium, California privet	S	Ex	1	2	2			
Ligustrum vulgare, common privet	S	Ex	2	2	1	2	3	
Linum perenne, perennial flax	P	Ex					3	
Livistona chinensis, Chinese fan palm	T	Ex			2			
Lonicera fragrantissima, breath-of-spring	S	Ex			1			
Lonicera japonica, Japanese honeysuckle	V	Ex	1	1	1	1	3	
Lonicera tatarica, tatarian honeysuckle	S	Ex	1	2				
Lunaria annua, money plant	P (Bi)	Ex	3					
Lychnis flos-cuculi, ragged robin	P	Ex	3					
Lysimachia nummularia, creeping Jenny	P	Ex	2	2	2		3	

POTENTIALLY INVASIVE HEIRLOOM ORNAMENTAL PLANTS

Plant	Habit	N/Ex	NE	MA	SO	GL	C/GP	MtW
Lythrum salicaria, loosestrife	P	Ex	1	1	1	1	1	1
Maclura pomifera, Osage orange	S	N	2	3		2	3	
Melia azedarach, chinaberry	T	Ex			1			
Miscanthus sinensis, Japanese silver grass	P	Ex	3		1			
Morus alba, white mulberry	T	Ex	3	2	2	2	3	
Myosotis scorpioides, forget-me-not	P	Ex	3	2				
Nandina domestica, sacred bamboo	S	Ex			1			
Narcissus poeticus, poet's narcissus	B	Ex					3	
Narcissus pseudonarcissus, Lent lily	B	Ex					3	
Ornithogalum umbellatum, star-of-Bethlehem	B	Ex	3	3	2	2	3	
Pachysandra terminalis, pachysandra	V	Ex	3					
Papaver somniferum, opium poppy (cultivation is illegal in most states)	A	Ex			1			
Parthenocissus tricuspidata, Boston ivy	V	Ex					3	
Paulownia tomentosa, princess tree	T	Ex	2	2	2			
Penstemon digitalis, beardtongue	P	N	3					
Phalaris arundinacea, canary grass	P	N	2			1	1	
Philadelphus coronarius, mock orange	S	Ex					3	
Physocarpus opulifolius, ninebark	S	N	2					
Picea abies, Norway spruce	T	Ex		3			3	
Picea glauca, white spruce	T	N		3			3	
Pinus nigra, Austrian pine	T	Ex		3			3	
Pinus sylvestris, Scotch pine	T	Ex		3				
Poncirus trifoliata, hardy orange	T	Ex		3				
Populus alba, white poplar	T	N	2	2	2			
Populus tremuloides, quaking aspen	T	N	2					
Ptychosperma elegans, Alexander palm	T	Ex			2			
Pueraria montana var. *lobata*, kudzu	V	Ex	2	1	1	2	1	1
Quercus robur, English oak	T	Ex	3	3				
Rhus glabra, smooth sumach	S	N	2					
Ricinus communis, castor bean	A	Ex			2			
Robinia hispida, rose acacia	S	N	3				3	

POTENTIALLY INVASIVE HEIRLOOM ORNAMENTAL PLANTS

Plant	Habit	N/Ex	NE	MA	SO	GL	C/GP	MtW
Robinia pseudoacacia, black locust	T	N	2	2		2		
Rosa eglanteria, eglantine rose	R	Ex	3					
Rosa multiflora, multiflora rose	R	Ex	1	1	1	1	1	
Rosa rugosa, Japanese rose	R	Ex	3	1				
Rudbeckia hirta, black-eyed Susan	A	N	3	2				
Saccharum ravennae, ravenna grass	P	Ex						2
Salix alba, white willow	T	Ex	3	3				
Salix alba var. *vitellina*, golden willow	T	Ex					3	
Salix babylonica, weeping willow	T	Ex	3					
Sedum acre, stonecrop	P	Ex	3					
Sorbus aucuparia, European mountain ash	T	Ex	3					
Spiraea japonica, Japanese spirea	S	Ex		3	2			
Symphoricarpos orbiculatus, coralberry	S	N		3				
Syringa vulgaris, common lilac	S	Ex					3	
Tamarix spp., tamarisk	S	Ex		3	2		3	1
Thymus serpyllum, thyme	P	Ex	3					
Ulex europaeus, European gorse	S	Ex						2
Valeriana officinalis, garden heliotrope	P	Ex	2					
Viburnum lantana, wayfaring tree	S	Ex	3					
Viburnum opulus var. *opulus*, European highbush cranberry	S	Ex	3			2		
Viburnum plicatum, Japanese snowball	S	Ex	3					
Vinca major, large periwinkle	V	Ex		3	2			
Vinca minor, creeping myrtle	V	Ex	2	2	2	2	3	
Wisteria floribunda, Japanese wisteria	V	Ex	3	2	2			
Wisteria sinensis, Chinese wisteria	V	Ex		2	1			

BIBLIOGRAPHY

A. A. E., Mrs. 1878. Gardening in Wyoming Territory. *Vick's Monthly Magazine* 1 (6): 171.

A. C. 1868. Notes on the hardiness of some trees and shrubs. *The Gardener's Monthly* 10 (7): 206.

A. C. F. 1885. The home. *Vick's Monthly Magazine* 8 (9): 265–266.

Adams, Denise W. 1998. *Hardy Herbaceous Plants in Nineteenth-Century Northeastern United States Gardens and Landscapes*. 2 vols. Ph.D. dissertation. The Ohio State University.

Aeberli, William, and Margaret Becket. 1982. Joseph Harris—captain of the Rochester seed industry. *The University of Rochester Library Bulletin* 35: 69–83.

The African lily. 1887. *American Agriculturist* 46 (3): 119.

The Akebia in fruit. 1869. *American Agriculturist* 28 (1): 19.

Akebia quinata. 1868. *The Gardener's Monthly* 10 (5): 149.

Albro, Mary D. 1936. *Pioneer Rose Trail*. Unpublished manuscript.

Allen, C. L. 1894. Mignonette. *American Gardening* 15 (16): 294.

———. 1902. *Bulbs and Tuberous-Rooted Plants*. New York: Orange Judd.

Allen, Lewis F. 1856. Ornamental trees—the Lombardy poplar. *The Horticulturist* 6 (1): 16–18.

An Amateur [Hogg, T.]. 1847a. Half a dozen rare herbaceous plants. *The Horticulturist* 2 (2): 72–74.

———. 1847b. The petunia and its culture. *The Horticulturist* 2 (3): 111.

———. 1848. Selection of the best hardy shrubs. *The Horticulturist* 2 (11): 509–513.

———. 1850. On the gladiolus or corn flag. *The Horticulturist* 4 (10): 464–466.

The American Rose Culturist. 1855. New York: C. M. Saxton.

Anderson, Edgar. 1952. *Plants, Man, and Life*. Boston: Little, Brown.

Annuals and their cultivation. 1853. *The Horticulturist* 3 (4, 5): 157–165; 207–213.

Answers to correspondents: white and scarlet mignonette. 1883. *The Ladies' Floral Cabinet* 12 (1): 47.

Armitage, Allan M. 2001. *Armitage's Manual of Annuals, Biennials, and Half-Hardy Perennials*. Portland, Oregon: Timber Press.

Arnold, C. M. 1882. Wild gardens. *Vick's Monthly Magazine* 5 (4): 101–102.

Artistic color combinations with perennial flowers. 1905. *The Garden Magazine* 1 (3): 132.

Ash, Thomas. 1682. *Carolina; or, A Description of the Present State of That Country*. London, W.C.

Ashe, Thomas. 1809. *Travels in America, performed in 1806*. London: Richard Phillips.

"Aunt Fanny." 1883. The farmer's door-yard. *Vick's Monthly Magazine* 5 (5): 143.

B. 1888. Old-fashioned Carolina gardens. *The American Garden* 9 (7): 262–263.

Bailey, Liberty H. 1891. *Annals of Horticulture in North America for the Year 1890*. New York: Orange Judd.

———. 1893. *Annals of Horticulture in North America for the Year 1892*. New York: Rural Publishing.

———. 1906a. *Cyclopedia of American Horticulture*. 5th ed. 4 vols. New York: Macmillan.

———. 1906b. *The Survival of the Unlike*. 5th ed. New York: Macmillan.

———. 1935. *The Standard Cyclopedia of Horticulture*. 3 vols. New York: Macmillan.

Bailey, Liberty H., ed. 1903. *How to Make a Flower Garden*. New York: Doubleday, Page.

Bailey, Liberty H., and Ethel Z. Bailey. 1976. *Hortus Third*. Rev. ed. New York: Macmillan.

Baker, Bernice. 1894. Anemone Whirlwind in the cemetery. *The Mayflower* 13 (5): 262.

The balloon-vine or heartseed. 1872. *American Agriculturist* 31 (3): 101.

Barnard, Samuel, ed. 1888. *Annual Reports of the Nebraska State Horticultural Society, 1887 and 1888*. Lincoln, Nebraska: Journal Company.

Barnes, William H., ed. 1899. *Transactions of the Kansas State Horticultural Society*. Topeka: J. S. Parks.

Barnett, Della. Personal communication with author. 11 February 2003.

Barry, Patrick. 1850. Drooping trees. *The Horticulturist* 5 (3): 123–126.

———. 1854. The Dielytra spectabilis. *The Horticulturist* 4 (7): 300–302.

———. 1872. The maples. *The Horticulturist* 27 (312): 161–164.

Becar, Noel. 1848. Notes on the culture of the camellia. *The Horticulturist* 3 (6): 269–272.

Beecher, Henry W. 1859. *Plain and Pleasant Talk about Fruits, Flowers and Farming*. New York: Derby & Jackson.

Beers, Julia R. 1895. Gossip with the Mayflower for '95. *The Mayflower* 12 (8): 211–213.

Bement, C. N. 1860. Wild flowers—their cultivation, etc. *The Horticulturist* 15: 564.

Bennett, Ida D. 1903. *The Flower Garden: A Handbook of Practical Garden Lore*. New York: McClure, Phillips.

Berkeley, Edmund, and Dorothy S. Berkeley. 1969. *Dr. Alexander Garden of Charles Town*. Chapel Hill: University of North Carolina Press.

Berkeley, Edmund, and Dorothy S. Berkeley, eds. 1992. *The Correspondence of John Bartram*. Gainesville: University of Florida.

Beston, Henry. 1935. *Herbs and the Earth*. Garden City: Doubleday, Doran.

Betts, Edwin M., ed. 1981. *Thomas Jefferson's Garden Book, 1766–1824*. Philadelphia: American Philosophical Society.

Betts, Edwin M., and Hazlehurst B. Perkins. Revised by Peter J. Hatch. 1986. *Thomas Jefferson's Flower Garden at Monticello*. Charlottesville: University Press of Virginia.

Birnbaum, Charles A., ed. 1996. *Guidelines for the Treatment of Cultural Landscapes*. Washington, D.C.: National Park Service.

——— 1999. *Protecting Cultural Landscapes: Planning Treatment and Management of Historic Landscapes*. Preservation Briefs #36. Washington, D.C.: National Park Service.

Birnbaum, Charles A., and Robin Karson, eds. 2000. *Pioneers of American Landscape Design*. New York: McGraw-Hill.

A bit of the sub-tropical. 1872. *American Agriculturist* 31 (1): 24.

Blanchan, Neltje. 1913. *The American Flower Garden*. New York: Doubleday, Page.

Blauvelt, Isaac. 1878. Garden on the house top. *Vick's Monthly Magazine* 1 (1): 22.

Blitch, Riley M. 1997. Vernacular gardens of rural Florida. *Magnolia* 13 (2): 1–4, 8.

Bloom, Alan. 1991. *Alan Bloom's Hardy Perennials*. London: B. T. Batsford.

Bourne, Herman. 1833. *Flores Poetici, The Florist's Manual*. Reprint, Guilford, Connecticut: Opus Publications, 1988.

Brackenbridge, William D. 1847. The Cloth of Gold rose. *The Horticulturist* 2 (1): 35–36.

Bradford, William. 1654. Some Observations. In *William Bradford, The Collected Verse*, edited by Michael Runyan, 1974. St. Paul, Minnesota: John Colet Press.

Breck, Joseph. 1846a. A chapter on phloxes. *The Horticulturist* 1 (3): 122–127.

———. 1846b. On the cultivation of the lily tribe. *The Horticulturist* 1 (2): 66–70.

————. 1851. *The Flower-Garden or Breck's Book of Flowers*. Boston: John P. Jewett.

————. 1858. *The Flower-Garden*. New York: A. O. Moore.

Bresloff, Philip C. 1915. Redeeming a city lot back yard. *The Garden Magazine* 22 (4): 119.

Brickell, John. 1737. *The Natural History of North-Carolina*. Dublin: Printed by James Carson for the author.

Bridgeman, Thomas. 1840. *The Florist's Guide*. New York: T. Bridgeman.

————. 1857. *The Young Gardener's Assistant*. New York: C. M. Saxton.

Britton, Nathaniel L., and Addison Brown. 1896. *An Illustrated Flora of the United States, Canada and the British Possessions*. 3 vols. New York: Charles Scribner's Sons.

Brown, Simon, ed. 1857. April—Flowers and flower gardens. *New England Farmer* 9 (4): 153–154.

Brown, Thomas. 1993. *A List of California Nurseries and Their Catalogues: 1850–1900*. Self-published.

Browne, D. J. 1846. *The Trees of America*. New York: Harper & Brothers.

Buckingham, James. 1840. *The Eastern and Western States of America*. 2 vols. London: Fisher, Son, & Co.

Buckley, S. P. 1847. Notes on indigenous trees and shrubs. *The Horticulturist* 1 (12): 557–561.

Buist, Robert. 1839. *The American Flower Garden Directory*. Philadelphia: E. L. Carey & A. Hart.

————. 1854. *The Rose Manual*. Philadelphia: A. Hart and Lippincott, Grambo, & Co.

————. 1868. Gardens and grounds of J. W. Gordon, Esq., Cleveland, Ohio. *The Gardener's Monthly* 10 (4): 113–114.

Burkholder, C. L. 1926. Attractive vines for the home. *Better Homes and Gardens* 4 (9): 68.

California gardens and homes. 1876. *The Ladies' Floral Cabinet* 5 (54): 88.

California gleanings. 1886. *Vick's Monthly Magazine* 9 (3): 87.

Cannas. 1884. *The Ladies' Floral Cabinet* 12 (3): 72–73.

Canney, J. W. 1921. Discussion on ornamental shrubs and trees. In *Eighteenth Annual Report of the South Dakota State Horticultural Society*, edited by N. E. Hansen. Pierre, South Dakota: Hipple Printing: 57–58.

Capstick, William. 1882. The Marechal Niel rose. *The Gardener's Monthly* 24 (288): 360.

Carpet bedding. 1881. *Vick's Monthly Magazine* 4 (4): 120–122.

C. F. 1885. The home. *Vick's Monthly Magazine* 8 (9): 265–266.

Chamberlain, Montague. 1916. The story of the modern gladiolus. *The Garden Magazine* 23 (4): 229–231.

Chappell, Gordon W., ed. 2000. *Southern Garden History Society: Southern Plant Lists*. Unpublished manuscript.

The chestnut as an ornamental tree. 1869. *American Agriculturist* 28 (9): 340.

Childs, John L. 1893. *The Gladiolus, Its History, Species and Cultivation*. New York: Mayflower Press.

Chorlton, William. 1849. The culture of the dahlia. *The Horticulturist* 4 (5): 210.

Church, Ella R. 1884. *The Home Garden*. New York: D. Appleton.

C. L. 1879. Climate of Nevada. *Vick's Monthly Magazine* 2 (7): 204–205.

Clematis Jackmanii. 1883. *Vick's Monthly Magazine* 6 (5): 132.

Cloud, Dorothy. 1927. *The Culture of Perennials*. New York: Dodd, Mead.

Coats, Alice. 1956. *Flowers and Their Histories*. New York: Pitman Publishing.

————. 1992. *Garden Shrubs and Their Histories*. New York: Simon and Schuster.

Cobbett, William. 1821. *The American Gardener or A Treatise on the Situation, Soil, Fencing and Laying-out of Gardens*. London: C. Clement.

Cochran, James R. 1995. *Gardens of Historic Charleston*. Columbia: University of South Carolina Press.

Colby, Fred M. 1884. The gardens of our grandmothers. *The Ladies' Floral Cabinet* 12 (7): 222–223.

Color arrangements. 1875. *The Horticulturist* 30 (351): 273.

The Complete Florist. 1844. Philadelphia: Lea and Blanchard.

Comstock, J. L. 1850. On the beauty of our indigenous plants. *The Horticulturist* 4 (10): 454–455.

Cooke, Ian. 2001. *The Gardener's Guide to Growing Cannas*. Portland, Oregon: Timber Press.

Cope, Caleb. 1851. First flowering of the *Victoria regia* in the United States. *The Horticulturist* 6: 459–460.

Copeland, Robert M. 1867. *Country Life: A Handbook of Agriculture, Horticulture, and Landscape Gardening*. New York: Orange Judd.

Cowles, Mrs. E. D. 1921. Creating a home out of a bit of pasture. In *Eighteenth Annual Report of the South Dakota State Horticultural Society*, edited by N. E. Hansen. Pierre, South Dakota: Hipple Printing: 76–77.

Cranefield, F., ed. 1912. *Annual Report of the Wisconsin State Horticultural Society for the Year 1912*. Madison: Democrat Printing.

Crawford, Matthew. 1911. *The Gladiolus*. Chicago: Vaughan's Seed Store.

Cridland, Robert B. 1926. *Practical Landscape Gardening*. 2nd ed. New York: A. T. De La Mare.

Cultivation of the phlox. 1846. *The Magazine of Horticulture* 12 (3): 100–103.

Darling, Ada. 1883. White day lilies. *Vick's Monthly Magazine* 6 (4): 170–171.

Darlington, E. D. 1909. Nasturtium—the best flower for the million. *The Garden Magazine* 9 (1): 15–17.

Darlington, William. 1849. *Memorials of John Bartram and Humphrey Marshall*. Philadelphia. Reprint, New York: Hafner, 1967.

Davies, Richard. 1850. Landscape gardening. *Western Horticultural Review* 1 (1): 19–20.

The day lilies—funkias. 1887. *American Agriculturist* 46 (8): 347.

de Bray, Lys. 1986. *Manual of Old-Fashioned Shrubs*. Somerset, England: Oxford Illustrated Press.

de Forest, Elizabeth. 1982. *The Gardens and Grounds at Mt. Vernon*. Mt. Vernon, Virginia: The Mount Vernon Ladies' Association of the Union.

Denton, Daniel. 1670. *A Brief Description of New-York*. London: Printed for John Hancock.

Design for a flower garden. 1855. *Magazine of Horticulture* 21: 330–332.

de Vos, Francis. 1967. Early plant introductions from China and Japan. *Plants and Gardens* 23 (3): 46–49.

Dickerson, Brent C. 1992. *The Old Rose Advisor*. Portland, Oregon: Timber Press.

Dintlemann, L. F. 1910. Beautifying home grounds. In *Transactions of the Illinois State Horticultural Society for the Year 1909*. Springfield: Illinois State Horticultural Society: 463–467.

Dirr, Michael A. 1998. *Manual of Woody Landscape Plants*. 5th ed. Champaign, Illinois: Stipes Publishing.

———. 2002. *Dirr's Trees and Shrubs for Warm Climates*. Portland, Oregon: Timber Press.

Disease of hollyhock. 1871. *Gardener's Monthly* 13: 55.

Dobson, Beverly R., and Peter Schneider. 2002. *Combined Rose List 2002*. Mantua, Ohio: Peter Schneider.

Dobyns, Winifred S. 1931. *California Gardens*. New York: Macmillan.

Downing, Andrew J. 1844 (1842). *Cottage Residences*. 2nd ed. New York: Wiley & Putnam.

———. 1853. *Rural Essays*. New York: George P. Putnam.

———. 1859 (1841). *A Treatise on the Theory and Practice of Landscape Gardening*. 6th ed. New York: A.O. Moore.

Downing, Andrew J., ed. 1847a. New or hardy shrubs. *The Horticulturist* 1 (9): 418–420.

———. 1847b. Two trees worth planting. *The Horticulturist* 2 (6): 270.

———. 1849a. Domestic notices: Yorkville nursery— Thomas Hogg & Son. *The Horticulturist* 4 (1): 44.

———. 1849b. On the drapery of cottages and gardens. *The Horticulturist* 3 (8): 353–359.

———. 1851a. The neglected American plants. *The Horticulturist* 6 (5): 201–203.

———. 1851b. Notices of new plants. *The Horticulturist* 6 (7): 325.

Doyle, Martin. 1835. *The Flower Garden*. New York: Moore & Payne.

Duchscherer, Paul, and Douglas Keister. 1999. *Outside the Bungalow*. New York: Penguin Studio.

Duffy, Sherman R. 1909. Personal experiences: a solution of the perennial poppy problem. *The Garden Magazine* 10 (2): 50.

———. 1916. My experiences with some of the newer daffodils. *The Garden Magazine* 24 (12): 50–51.

Dunbar, John. 1906. All the barberries worth growing. *The Garden Magazine* 4 (3): 122–124.

Durand, L. 1857. Grounds for farm houses. *The Horticulturist* 7 (5): 225–226.

Earle, Alice M. 1901. *Old Time Gardens*. New York: Macmillan.

———. 1902. *Sun-Dials and Roses of Yesterday*. New York: Macmillan.

E. B. R., Mrs. 1857. Wild flowers. *New England Farmer* 9 (4): 175.

Eddison, Sydney. 1992. *A Passion for Daylilies*. New York: Henry Holt.

Editor's letter-box. 1871. *Tilton's Journal of Horticulture* 9 (11): 349–352.

Egan, W. C. 1911. Larkspurs that really flourish. *The Garden Magazine* 12 (6): 267–268.

Egleston, Nathaniel H. 1878. *Villages and Village Life with Hints for Their Improvement*. New York: Harper & Brothers.

Elder, Walter. 1850. *The Cottage Garden of America*. Philadelphia: Moss and Brother.

———. 1861a. The culture of trees for shelter to buildings. *The Gardener's Monthly* 3 (3): 140.

———. 1861b. Trees and shrubbery. *The Gardener's Monthly* 3 (10): 322–323.

———. 1863. Despise not the small things. *The Gardener's Monthly* 4 (4): 78.

———. 1870. Essay on bedding plants. *The Gardener's Monthly* 12 (4): 107.

Eliot, Charles. 1891. Two studies for house plantings. *Garden and Forest* 4 (165): 184.

Elliott, F. R. 1868. *Popular Deciduous and Evergreen Trees and Shrubs for Planting in Parks, Gardens, Cemeteries, Etc.* New York: Francis W. Woodward.

———. 1881. *Hand Book of Practical Landscape Gardening*. New York: D. M. Dewey.

Elliott, J. Wilkinson. 1902. *A Plea for Hardy Plants*. New York: Doubleday, Page.

Ellwanger, George. 1889. *The Garden's Story*. New York: D. Appleton.

Ellwanger, H. B. 1910. *The Rose*. New York: Dodd, Mead.

Elwes's snowdrop is blooming in suburban gardens. 1890. *Garden and Forest* 3 (99): 36.

Ely, Helena R. 1903. *A Woman's Hardy Garden*. New York: Macmillan.

———. 1917. *Another Hardy Garden Book*. New York: Macmillan.

Emmet, Alan. 1996. *So Fine A Prospect: Historic New England Gardens*. Hanover, New Hampshire: University Press of New England.

E. S. S. 1878. A beautiful flower. *Vick's Monthly Magazine* 1 (5): 143.

Falconer, William. 1876. Hardy herbaceous plants for July. *The Gardener's Monthly* 18 (September): 261.

F. A. R., Mrs. 1886. The sweet brier. *Vick's Monthly Magazine* 9 (10): 307.

Faris, John T. 1932. *Old Gardens in and About Philadelphia and Those Who Made Them*. Indianapolis: Bobbs-Merrill.

Favretti, Rudy F., and Gordon P. DeWolf. 1972. *Colonial Gardens*. Barre, Massachusetts: Barre Publishers.

Favretti, Rudy J., and Joy P. Favretti. 1978. *Landscapes and Gardens for Historic Buildings*. Nashville, Tennessee: American Association for State and Local History.

———. 1990. *For Every House a Garden*. Hanover, New Hampshire: University Press of New England.

Fearnley-Whittingstall, Jane. 1999. *Peonies: The Imperial Flower*. London: Weidenfeld & Nicolson.

February, 1880. 1880. *Vick's Monthly Magazine* 3 (1): 33–36.

Fessenden, Thomas. 1857. *The New American Gardener*. 30th ed. New York: C.M. Saxton.

A few words for herbaceous plants. 1856. *The Magazine of Horticulture* 12 (8): 345–349.

Fiala, Fr. John L. 1988. *Lilacs, The Genus Syringa*. Portland, Oregon: Timber Press.

Finch, Bill. Personal communication with author. 1 November 2002.

First Biennial Report of the Oregon State Board of Horticulture. 1891. Portland, Oregon: A. Anderson.

Flagg, Wilson. 1856a. The lime and the locust. *The Magazine of Horticulture* 22 (12): 562–566.

———. 1856b. Our American firs and spruces. *The Magazine of Horticulture* 22 (5): 238–246.

———. 1856c. Our native pines. *The Magazine of Horticulture* 22 (2): 86–93.

———. 1857. On the planting of trees: New England. *The Horticulturist* 9 (9): 436–437.

Floramant. 1882. The oleander. *The Gardener's Monthly and Horticulturist* 24 (278): 43–44.

Flower garden and pleasure ground seasonable hints. 1879. *The Gardener's Monthly* 21 (4).

Fogg, Lawrence D. 1900. The aster—culture and varieties. *How to Grow Flowers.* 7 (6): 10.

Forget-me-nots. 1867. *Tilton's Journal of Horticulture*: 336.

The forsythia as a pillar plant. 1891. *Garden and Forest* 4 (156): 74.

Foster, Suel. 1872. Our native ornamental trees. *The Horticulturist* 27 (11): 327.

Four new spiraeas. 1856. *The Magazine of Horticulture* 22 (1): 38–41.

Fox, Helen M. 1928. *Garden Cinderellas: How to Grow Lilies in the Garden.* New York: Macmillan.

French, Henry F. 1857. Hedges. *New England Farmer* 9 (3): 120.

Fuld, Maurice. 1909. Dahlias for everybody's garden. *The Garden Magazine* 9 (4): 232–234.

Fuller, Andrew, ed. 1868. *Woodward's Record of Horticulture II.* New York: Francis W. Woodward.

Galle, Fred C. 1987. *Azaleas.* Portland, Oregon: Timber Press.

Gardiner, John, and David Hepburn. 1804. *The American Gardener.* Washington: Samuel H. Smith.

Genders, Roy. 1983. *The Cottage Garden and the Old-Fashioned Flowers.* London: Pelham Books.

Gilmer, Maureen. 1995. *Redwoods and Roses: The Gardening Heritage of California and the Old West.* Dallas, Texas: Taylor.

Gold, T. S. 1850. Flowers for the million. *The Horticulturist* 4 (9): 419–421.

The gold-banded lily. 1882. *Vick's Monthly Magazine* 5 (2): 56.

Goodman, L. A. 1887. Summer meeting at Louisiana. In *Twenty-Ninth Annual Report of the State Horticultural Society of the State of Missouri, 1886.* Jefferson City, Missouri: 32–78.

Goodsell, N., ed. 1832. Horticulture. *The Genesee Farmer* 2 (18): 144.

Gosse, Philip H. 1859. *Letters from Alabama.* Reprint, Tuscaloosa: University of Alabama Press, 1993.

Gray, J. B. 1854. Evergreen trees. *The Horticulturist* 4 (8): 360–362.

Greely, Rose. 1922. Planting around the city house. *The House Beautiful* 52 (2): 128–129, 160.

Green, Roland. 1828. *A Treatise on the Cultivation of Ornamental Flowers.* Boston: Russell & Thorburn.

Greenleaf, Mrs. 1878. Beauty in Nevada. *Vick's Monthly Magazine* 1 (2): 60–61.

Griffiths, Mark. 1994. *Index of Garden Plants.* Portland, Oregon: Timber Press.

Gurney, George W. 1921. Flowering shrubs and perennials. In *Eighteenth Annual Report of the South Dakota State Horticultural Society,* edited by N. E. Hansen. Pierre, South Dakota: Hipple Printing.

Guthrie, Jane. 1902. The story of an old garden. *Harper's Monthly Magazine*: 980–986.

"H." 1882. My home in Florida. *Vick's Monthly Magazine* 5 (7): 217.

Hale, Anne G. 1868. Domestic economy; or, how to make the home pleasant. *New England Farmer* 2 n.s. (5): 245–251.

Hampden, Mary. 1922. *Bulb Gardening.* New York: Charles Scribner's Sons.

Hansen, N. E., ed. 1921. *Eighteenth Annual Report of the South Dakota State Horticultural Society.* Pierre, South Dakota: Hipple Printing.

Hardiness of rhododendrons. 1895. *American Gardening* 16 (40): 214.

Harding, Mrs. Edward. 1917. *The Book of the Peony.* Philadelphia: J. B. Lippincott.

Hardy climbers: the Wistaria. 1884. *The Ladies' Floral Cabinet* 12 (3): 78–79.

Hardy herbaceous plants, part III. 1884. *The Ladies' Floral Cabinet* 13 (8): 248–250.

The hardy hydrangea as a decorative plant. 1891. *Garden and Forest* 4 (150): 7–8.

Hardy vines and creepers. 1884. *The Ladies' Floral Cabinet* 13 (1): 14–16.

Hatfield, T. D. 1888. Bedding plants for spring. *Garden and Forest* 1 (June): 210.

Havens, Henry B. 1885. The classes of roses. *The Gardener's Monthly* 27 (316): 99–100.

Haworth-Booth, Michael. 1950. *The Hydrangeas.* London: The Garden Book Club.

Hedges in the south. 1870. *The Gardener's Monthly* 12 (9): 276.

Hedrick, Ulysses P. 1988. *A History of Horticulture in America to 1860 with an Addendum of Books Published from 1861–1920 by Elisabeth Woodburn*. Portland, Oregon: Timber Press.

Hemlock hedges. 1870. *The Gardener's Monthly* 12 (2): 52.

Henderson, Charles. 1901. *Henderson's Picturesque Gardens and Ornamental Gardening Illustrated*. New York: Peter Henderson.

Henderson, Peter. 1875. *Gardening for Pleasure*. New York: Orange Judd.

———. 1890. *Henderson's Handbook of Plants*. New York: Peter Henderson.

———. 1909. *Practical Floriculture*. New York: Orange Judd.

Hill, Amelia L. 1923. *Garden Portrait*. New York: Robert M. McBride.

Hill, W. E. 1890. Wild flowers under cultivation. *Garden and Forest* 3 (113): 204.

Hints for May. Flower-garden and pleasure-ground. 1863. *The Gardener's Monthly* 5 (5): 129–130.

Historical Atlas Map of Santa Clara County, California. 1876. Reprint, San Jose, California: Smith & McKay Printing, 1973.

Hitchcock, Susan L. 1998. *The Colonial Revival Gardens of Hubert Bond Owens*. Master's thesis. Athens, Georgia: The University of Georgia.

Hoffman, M. H. A., H. J. van de Laar, et al. 2000. *Naamlijst Van Vaste Planten* (List of Names of Perennials). Boskoop, The Netherlands: Boomteelt Praktijkonderzoek.

———. 2000. *Naamlijst Van Houtige Gewassen* (List of Names of Woody Plants). Boskoop, The Netherlands: Boomteelt Praktijkonderzoek.

The hollyhock. 1863. *The Gardener's Monthly* 5 (9): 270–271.

The hollyhock–cover illustration. 1894. *American Gardening* 15 (16): 356.

Hoopes, Josiah. 1872a. How to plant a rural home. *The Horticulturist* 27 (6): 164–167.

———. 1872b. The planting of dooryards and small grounds with ornamental trees, shrubs, and evergreens. *The Horticulturist* 27 (2): 40–43.

———. 1874. Ornamental vines. *The Horticulturist* 29 (337): 193–195.

Hovey, Charles M., ed. 1841. Residence of A. J. Downing, Botanical Gardens and Nurseries, Newburgh, New York. *The Magazine of Horticulture* 7 (11): 403, 409.

———. 1846. New varieties of chrysanthemums. *The Magazine of Horticulture* 12 (6): 213–216.

———. 1856. Our ornamental trees. *The Magazine of Horticulture* 22 (3): 138–141.

Hovey, John C. 1871. Lilium excelsum. *Tilton's Journal of Horticulture and Florist's Companion* 9 (11): 322–323.

How to beautify our home grounds. 1894. *American Gardening* 15 (14): 157–158.

Hume, H. Harold. 1929. *Gardening in the Lower South*. New York: Macmillan.

———. 1951. *Camellias: Kinds and Culture*. New York: Macmillan.

Hunt, Rachel M. M. 1953. *William Penn, Horticulturist*. Pittsburgh: University of Pittsburgh.

Hybrid Scotch pink. 1884. *The Ladies' Floral Cabinet* 12 (6): 175.

Hydrangeas for lawn decoration. 1894. *American Gardening* 15 (15): 265.

Imlay, G. (Gilbert). 1793. *A Description of the Western Territory of North America*. Dublin: William Jones.

Irvin, Hillary. 1995. Through the allees, the French influence. In *The Southern Heirloom Garden*, edited by Welch and Grant. Dallas, Texas: Taylor.

Jack, J. G. 1894. The earliest flowering shrubs. *Garden and Forest* 7 (317): 112–113.

Jacobson, Arthur L. 1992. *Purpleleaf Plums*. Portland, Oregon: Timber Press.

———. 1996. *North American Landscape Trees*. Berkeley: Ten Speed Press.

January, 1886. 1886. *Vick's Monthly Magazine* 9 (1): 1–4.

J. B. 1881. The herbaceous border. *Vick's Monthly Magazine* 4 (10): 314.

J. D. H., Mrs. 1878. Making a home in Texas. *Vick's Monthly Magazine* 1 (1): 11.

J. E. J. 1883. Window boxes of flowers. *The Ladies' Floral Cabinet* 12 (6): 176.

Johnson, Edward. 1654. *A History of New-England*. London: Printed for Nath. Brooke.

Johnson, George W. 1865. *The Cottage Gardeners' Dictionary*. London: Henry G. Bohn.

Johnson, Leonard H. 1927. *Foundation Planting*. New York: A. T. De La Mare.

Johnson, Louisa M. 1856. *Every Lady Her Own Flower Gardener*. New York: C. M. Saxton.

Josselyn, John. 1672. *New England Rarities Discovered*. London: G. Widdowes.

Karson, Robin. 1995. *The Muses of Gwinn*. New York: Sagapress.

Keays, Mrs. Frederick Love. 1935. *Old Roses*. New York: Macmillan.

Keeler, Harriet. 1900. *Our Native Trees*. New York: Charles Scribner's Sons.

———. 1903. *Our Northern Shrubs*. New York: Charles Scribner's Sons.

———. 1910. *Our Garden Flowers*. New York: Charles Scribner's Sons.

Kellaway, Herbert J. 1915. *How to Lay Out Suburban Home Grounds*. New York: John Wiley & Sons.

Kenrick, William. 1841. *The New American Orchardist*. Boston: Otis, Broaders.

Kern, G. M. 1855. *Practical Landscape Gardening*. Cincinnati, Ohio: Moore, Wilstach, Keys.

Kilmarnock weeping willow. 1861. *The Gardener's Monthly* 3 (10): 309.

King, Margaret R. 1889. *Memoirs of the Life of Mrs. Sarah Peter*. 2 vols. Cincinnati: Robert Clarke.

King, Mrs. Francis (Louisa Y. King). 1915. *The Well-Considered Garden*. New York: Charles Scribner's Sons.

———. 1921. *The Little Garden*. Boston: Atlantic Monthly Press.

———. 1923. *Variety in the Little Garden*. Boston: Atlantic Monthly Press.

———. 1925. *Chronicles of the Garden*. New York: Charles Scribner's Sons.

Kirby, A. M. 1909. *Daffodils, Narcissus and How to Grow Them*. New York: Doubleday, Page.

Kirtland, Jared P. 1845. *An Address Delivered Before the Oberlin Agricultural and Horticultural Society, October 1, 1845*. Oberlin: James M. Fitch.

Knapke, Luke, ed. 1987. *Liwwät Böke, 1807–1882: Pioneer*. Minster, Ohio: Minster Historical Society.

Köhlein, Fritz. 1987. *Iris*. Portland, Oregon: Timber Press.

Kulp, William O. 1879. Flower beds—bedding plants and their arrangement. In *Transactions: Iowa Horticultural Society, 1879*. 1880. N. p: 480–483.

Lancifolium lily. Rubrum. 1879. *Vick's Monthly Magazine* 2 (8): 230.

Larkspurs in a Chicago garden. 1911. *The Garden Magazine* 12 (6): 269.

Latrobe, Charles J. 1835. *The Rambler in North America, 1832–1833*. New York: Harper & Brothers.

Laurie, Alex, and D. C. Kiplinger. 1947. *Garden and Greenhouse Chrysanthemums*. New York: A. T. De La Mare.

Lawns and lawn trees. 1878. *Vick's Monthly Magazine* 1 (3): 69–71.

Lawson, John. 1718. *The History of Carolina*. London: Printed for T. Warner.

Lea, Thomas G. 1844. Floral calendar of native plants. *Western Farmer* 4 (4–5): 211–213, 235–238.

Leach, David G. 1961. *Rhododendrons of the World*. New York: Charles Scribner's Sons.

Legend of the Cherokee rose. 1882. *The Gardener's Monthly* 24 (285): 282.

Leighton, Ann. 1986a. *American Gardens in the Eighteenth Century "For Use and Delight."* Amherst: The University of Massachusetts Press.

———. 1986b. *Early American Gardens "For Meate or Medicine."* Amherst: The University of Massachusetts Press.

———. 1987. *American Gardens of the Nineteenth Century "For Comfort and Affluence."* Amherst: The University of Massachusetts Press.

L. E. L. 1879. Mountains of Oregon. *Vick's Monthly Magazine* 2 (5): 136–137.

Lelievre, Jacques-Felix. 1838. *New Louisiana Gardener*. Translated by Sally Kittredge Reeves. Reprint, Baton Rouge: Louisiana State University, 2001.

Lenox, W. 1849. The effects in landscape of various common trees. *The Horticulturist* 3 (12): 555–557.

Lewis, Peter, and Margaret Lynch. 1989. *Campanulas*. Portland, Oregon: Timber Press.

Lilium Martagon. 1884. *The Ladies' Floral Cabinet* 12 (3): 69–71.

Lockwood, Alice G. B. 1933–1934. *Gardens of Colony and State*. 2 vols. New York: Charles Scribner's Sons.

Long, Elias. 1888. *The Home Florist*. Springfield, Ohio: Charles A. Reeser.

———. 1893. *Ornamental Gardening for Americans*. New York: Orange Judd.

Loudon, John C. 1838. *An Encyclopedia of Gardening*. London: Longman, Rees, Orme, Brown, Green, and Longman.

Lummis, W. D. F. 1879. The lawn and the flower garden. In *Transactions: Iowa Horticultural Society*. N. p.: 201–206.

Luney, Elisabeth. 1897. The Clematis. *The Mayflower* 13 (5): 269.

Maccubin, Robert P., and Peter Martin. 1986. *British and American Gardens in the Eighteenth Century*. Williamsburg, Virginia: Colonial Williamsburg Foundation.

Mackintosh, R. S. 1936. More beautiful country homes. *The Minnesota Horticulturist* 64 (9): 168.

Macoboy, Stirling. 1997. *Illustrated Encyclopedia of Camellias*. Portland, Oregon: Timber Press.

MacPherson, J. 1885. A well-kept garden. *Vick's Monthly Magazine* 8 (8): 231.

Major, H. F. 1909. Landscape gardening in a suburban community. In *Transactions of the Illinois State Horticultural Society for the Year 1908*. Springfield, Illinois: Illinois State Horticultural Society: 282–287.

Manda, W. A. 1887. Plants new or little known. *The American Garden* 8 (12): 382.

Manks, Dorothy. 1967. Origins of American horticulture. *Plants and Gardens* 23 (3): 4–11.

Manning, J. Woodward. 1931. *The Plant Buyers Index*. Reading, Massachusetts: J. W. & E. G. Manning.

Manning, Warren. 1883. Herbaceous plants. *The Ladies' Floral Cabinet* 12 (3): 75.

———. 1884a. Our native lilies. *The Ladies' Floral Cabinet* 13 (8): 246–247.

———. 1884b. Our native shrubs. *The Ladies' Floral Cabinet* 13 (2): 40–41.

———. 1886. Hardy perennials for beds. *Vick's Monthly Magazine* 9 (3): 76–77.

Marryat, Frederick. 1839. *A Diary in America with Remarks on Its Institutions*. Philadelphia: n.p.

Marshall, William E. 1928. *Consider the Lilies*. New York: A. T. De La Mare.

Martin, Peter. 1991. *The Pleasure Gardens of Virginia from Jamestown to Jefferson*. Princeton, New Jersey: Princeton University Press.

Massey, W. F. 1893. Sterculio platanifolia and umbrella China-tree. *American Gardening* 14 (1): 45.

Mattiers, E. A. 1880. About zinnias. *Vick's Monthly Magazine* 3 (3): 77.

Mauncy, Albert. 1992. *The Houses of St. Augustine 1565–1821*. Gainesville: University Press of Florida.

Maynard, Samuel T. 1903. *Landscape Gardening*. New York: John Wiley & Sons.

McAlester, Virginia, and Lee McAlester. 1996. *A Field Guide to American Houses*. New York: Alfred A. Knopf.

McCurdy, Robert M. 1927. *Garden Flowers*. New York: Doubleday, Page.

McFarland, J. Horace. 1923. *The Rose in America*. New York: Macmillan.

———. 1938. *Roses of the World in Color*. New York: Houghton Mifflin.

McKinney, Ella P. 1927. *Iris in the Little Garden*. Boston: Little, Brown.

M'Mahon, Bernard. 1806. *The American Gardener's Calendar*. Reprint, Philadelphia: B. Graves, n.d.

Meager, Leonard. 1670. *The English Gardener*. London: Printed for P. Parker.

Meehan, Thomas. 1854. A new shade tree. *The Horticulturist* 4 (1): 14–15.

———. 1857. Shrubs with ornamental berries. *The Horticulturist* 7 (6, 7, 8): 265–268, 308–310, 355–357.

———. 1870 The rhododendron. *The Gardener's Monthly* 12 (6): 175–177.

———. 1871. Disease of hollyhock. *The Gardener's Monthly* 13: 55.

———. 1878–1879. *The Native Flowers and Ferns of the United States*. 2 vols. Boston: L. Prang.

Meyers, Amy R., and Margaret B. Pritchard. 1998. *Empire's Nature, Mark Catesby's New World Vision*. Chapel Hill: University of North Carolina Press.

Miellez, A. 1861. Rhododendrons. *The Gardener's Monthly* 3 (8, 12): 239, 361–362.

Miller, Wilhelm. 1909a. English effects with hardy climbers. *The Garden Magazine* 10 (3): 126–129.

———. 1909b. English effects with long-lived bulbs. *The Garden Magazine* 9 (6): 343–347.

———. 1909c. What America can teach England about shrubs. *The Garden Magazine* 9 (2): 75–78.

Mitchell, Sydney. 1934. Potted plants for patios. *Sunset* 72 (5): 10–11.

M. K. 1851. The ailanthus and its calumniators. *Western Horticultural Review* 2 (2): 66–67.

Moberly, Susan O. 1899. The bed of annuals. *The Mayflower* 15 (4): 172.

Morse, Lester L., ed. 1917. *Field Notes on Sweet Peas*. San Francisco: C. C. Morse.

Nehrling, H. 1894. Exotic trees and shrubs for Florida gardens—IV. *Garden and Forest* 7 (316): 102–103.

Neill, Patrick. 1851. *The Fruit, Flower and Kitchen Garden* (*Adapted to the United States*). Philadelphia: Henry Carey Baird.

Neosho Nurseries. 1917. *How to Beautify Your Home Grounds*. Neosho, Missouri: Neosho Nurseries.

New and rare plants. Retinospora plumosa. 1870. *The Gardener's Monthly* 12 (11): 345.

Newcomb, Peggy C. 1985. *Popular Annuals of Eastern North America: 1865–1914*. Washington, D.C.: Dumbarton Oaks.

New or rare plants. 1885. *The Gardener's Monthly* 27 (320): 229.

New or rare plants, Anemone Japonica Honorine Jobert. 1863. *The Gardener's Monthly* 5 (11): 345.

Notes from the pines: a tropical effect. 1887. *American Agriculturist* 46 (2): 52.

Notes on the evergreen ivy. 1849. *The Horticulturist* 4 (6): 252–255.

N. T. T. 1856. Little things: or a walk in my garden . . . no. 6. *New England Farmer* 8 (3): 142–143.

Nuttall, Thomas. 1842. *The North American Sylva*. 3 vols. Philadelphia: J. Dobson.

Oakley, Isabella. 1886. Winter flowers about San Francisco Bay. *Vick's Monthly Magazine* 9 (3): 72–75.

Oberholtzer, George W. 1879. Report on laying out, fencing, and planting of farms and yards. In *Transactions: Iowa Horticultural Society*. N. p.: 329–333.

An Observer. 1854. What to plant, and how to plant. *The Horticulturist* 4 n.s. (3): 112–115.

An oddly formed begonia. 1884. *Vick's Monthly Magazine* 7 (10): 308.

Old-fashioned flowers. 1882. *Vick's Monthly Magazine* 5 (December): 360–362.

An Old Florist. 1861. The Indian or Chinese Azalea: its introduction, cultivation, propagation and description of the best sorts, new and old. *The Gardener's Monthly* 3 (9, 10, 11): 263–264, 301–302, 335–337.

An Old Gardener. 1822. *The Practical American Gardener*. Baltimore: Fielding Lucas, Jr.

———. 1881. Bulbs in the house. *Vick's Monthly Magazine* 4 (7): 201–203.

"Olive." 1899. Salpiglossis. *The Mayflower* 15 (4): 175.

Olmsted, Frederick L. 1860. *A Journey in the Back Country*. Reprint, Williamstown, Massachusetts: Corner House Publishers, 1972.

———. 1888. Plan for a small homestead. *Garden and Forest* 1 (5): 111.

Olmsted, Frederick L., Frederick V. Coville, and Harlan P. Kelsey, eds. 1924. *Standardized Plant Names*. Salem, Massachusetts: American Joint Committee on Horticultural Nomenclature.

Olney, L. D. 1878. Flower gardening in Oregon. *Vick's Monthly Magazine* 1 (1): 15.

An ornamented cottage. 1856. *New England Farmer* 8 (5): 224–225.

Ortloff, H. Stuart. 1931. *Perennial Gardens*. New York: Macmillan.

Padilla, Victoria. 1961. *Southern California Gardens*. Los Angeles: University of California Press.

Paeonies. 1879. *Vick's Monthly Magazine* 2 (4): 105–106.

Pankhurst, Alex. 1992. *Who Does Your Garden Grow?* Colchester, England: Earl's Eye Publishing.

Parish, G. B. 1890. Californian palms. *Garden and Forest* 3 (99): 48.

Parkman, Francis. 1871a. *The Book of Roses*. Boston: J. E. Tilton.

———. 1871b. Double purple wistaria. *Tilton's Journal of Horticulture* 9 (2): 47.

———. 1871c. Lilium tenuifolium. *Tilton's Journal of Horticulture* 9 (April): 104–105.

Parnell, Charles. 1880a. Balsam apple. *Vick's Monthly Magazine* 3 (11): 348.

———. 1880b. Coboea scandens. *Vick's Monthly Magazine* 3 (9): 279–280.

————. 1881. Birthwort. *Vick's Monthly Magazine* 4 (2): 41–42.

————. 1882a. Dielytra spectabilis. *Vick's Monthly Magazine* 5 (7): 203.

————. 1882b. The red Japan anemone. *Vick's Monthly Magazine* 5 (2): 40–41.

————. 1883. The begonia. *The Ladies' Floral Cabinet* 12 (3): 71–73.

Parsons, Samuel. 1869. *Parsons on the Rose.* New York: Orange Judd.

————. 1882. Rarer ornamental trees and ornamental gardening. *The Gardener's Monthly* 24 (227): 2–5.

————. 1891. *Landscape Gardening.* New York: G. P. Putnam's Sons.

Paulsen, J. W. 1846. Plants in bloom, in the garden of C. L. Bell, Esq., in the vicinity of New Orleans, in November, 1845. *The Magazine of Horticulture* 12 (1): 22–24.

Peck, J. M. 1837. *A New Guide for Emigrants to the West.* Boston: Gould, Kendall & Lincoln.

Pedley, W. K., and R. Pedley. 1974. *Coleus: A Guide to Cultivation and Identification.* Edinburgh: John Bartholomew & Son.

Perrett, Antoinette. 1922. A rose and purple garden in July. *The House Beautiful* 52 (1): 21, 72.

Phillips, George A. 1933. *Delphiniums: Their History and Cultivation.* New York: Macmillan.

Picton, Paul. 1999. *The Gardener's Guide to Growing Asters.* Portland, Oregon: Timber Press.

Plank, E. N. 1894. Botanical notes from Texas—XXIII. *Garden and Forest* 7 (340): 342–343.

Prince, William R. 1846. *Prince's Manual of Roses.* Reprint, New York: Earl M. Coleman, 1979.

Prunus pissardi. 1885. *The Gardener's Monthly* 27 (8): 229.

Putnam, B. L. 1894. A plea for wild flowers. *Garden and Forest* 7 (317): 118.

Rainwater, Hattie, ed. 1933. *Garden History of Georgia, 1733–1933.* Atlanta, Georgia: Peachtree Garden Club.

Ramsey, Leonidas W., and Charles H. Lawrence. 1931. *Garden Pools: Large and Small.* New York: Macmillan.

Rand, Edward S. 1876. *Popular Flowers and How to Cultivate Them.* New York: Hurd and Houghton.

R. B. S. 1880. The oleander in Galveston. *Vick's Monthly Magazine* 3 (4): 136.

Read, Robert W., ed. 2001. *Nehrling's Early Florida Gardens.* Gainesville: University Press of Florida.

Rehder, Alfred. 1940. *Manual of Cultivated Trees & Shrubs Hardy in North America.* Reprint, Portland, Oregon: Dioscorides Press, 1990.

Report of the Commissioner of Agriculture for the Year 1869. 1870. Washington, D.C.: Government Printing Office.

Rexford, Eben E. 1886. Flowers for special effect. *Vick's Monthly Magazine* 9 (4): 101.

————. 1890. *Home Floriculture.* Rochester: James Vick Seedsman.

————. 1900. Hardy border plants. *How to Grow Flowers* 7 (6): 8–9.

————. 1912. *Amateur Gardencraft.* Philadelphia: J. B. Lippincott.

Rice, Mrs. S. T. 1879. Holland bulbs in the south. *Vick's Monthly Magazine* 2 (5): 151.

Richardson, Emma B. 1941. *The Heyward-Washington House Garden.* Charleston Museum Leaflet No. 15. Charleston, South Carolina: The Charleston Museum.

Richardson, James. 1854. Evergreen trees—the American holly. *The Horticulturist* 4 (5): 205–208.

Ries, Victor. 1936. *The Home Flower Garden.* Bulletin 99. Agricultural Extension Service. The Ohio State University.

Rion, Hanna. 1912. *Let's Make a Flower Garden.* New York: McBride, Nast.

Rion, Mary C. 1860. *Ladies' Southern Florist.* Reprint, Columbia: University of South Carolina Press, 2001.

Robbins, Mary. 1892. *The Rescue of an Old Place.* Boston: Houghton, Mifflin.

Robinson, Solon. 1845a. Notes of travel in the southwest—no. VI. *The Cultivator* 2 (9): 271–273.

————. 1845b. Notes of travel in the west. *The Cultivator* 2 (3): 92–94.

————. 1845c. Notes of travel in the west—no. II. *The Cultivator* 2 (4): 124–126.

Robinson, William. 1870. *The Wild Garden.* Reprint, London: Century Hutchinson, 1986.

Rogers, Allan. 1995. *Peonies.* Reprint, Portland, Oregon: Timber Press, 2000.

The rose acacia. 1887. *American Agriculturist* 46 (7): 306.

R. S. B. 1894. Home ground arrangements. *American Gardening* 15 (12): 212.

Rudbeckia "Childs' Golden Glow." 1895. *The Mayflower* 11 (12): 361.

Russell, J. W. 1837. Observations on the cultivation of Rhododendron maximum. *The Magazine of Horticulture* 3 (9): 330–331.

Sargent, Charles S., ed. 1890. Two American honeysuckles. *Garden and Forest* 3 (112): 187.

————. 1891a. The Douglas fir. *Garden and Forest* 4 (166): 205–206.

————. 1891b. The sugar maple. *Garden and Forest* 4 (164): 170.

————. 1894a. New or little-known plants: the fringe trees. *Garden and Forest* 7 (338): 325–326.

————. 1894b. North American thorns. *Garden and Forest* 7 (335): 292–293.

————. 1894c. The pride of China tree. *Garden and Forest* 7 (315): 92.

————. 1894d. The white ash. *Garden and Forest* 7 (346): 402.

————. 1895. Old-fashioned gardens. *Garden and Forest* 8 (July): 281–282.

Sargent, Henry W. 1854. The newer deciduous trees and shrubs. *The Horticulturist* 4 (7): 303–305.

Sarudy, Barbara W. 1992. South Carolina seed merchants and nurserymen before 1820. *Magnolia, Bulletin of the Southern Garden History Society* 8 (3): 6–10.

————. 1998. *Gardens and Gardening in the Chesapeake, 1700–1805.* Baltimore: Johns Hopkins University Press.

Saul, John. 1857. Evergreens *The Horticulturist* 7 (5): 220–223.

Saunders, William. 1855. Designs for improving country residences. *The Horticulturist* 5 n.s. (9): 403–405.

Sayers, Edward. 1837. The farm house garden. *The Horticultural Register* 3 (10): 362.

————. 1839. *The American Flower Garden Companion.* Boston: Weeks, Jordan.

Schmid, Wolfram G. 1991. *The Genus Hosta.* Portland, Oregon: Timber Press.

Scott, Frank J. 1870. *The Art of Beautifying Suburban Home Grounds of Small Extent.* New York: D. Appleton.

Scott, William H. 1853. A few hints on farmers' houses. *The Horticulturist* 3 (6): 269–272.

Scruggs, Mrs. Gross R., ed. 1931. *Gardening in the Southwest.* Dallas, Texas: Southwest Press.

Seasonable hints. 1886. *The Gardener's Monthly* 28 (10): 289.

Seavey, Fanny. 1893. Horticulture at the World's Fair. *American Gardening* 14 (6): 328–331.

Second Biennial Report of the Montana State Board of Horticulture, 1901–1902. 1902. Helena, Montana: Independent Publishing.

Sedgwick, Mabel Cabot. 1907. *The Garden Month by Month.* Garden City, New York: Garden City Publishing.

A select list of ornamental shrubs, vines, & c. 1857. *The Horticulturist* 7 (4): 172–173.

Shaffer, E. T. H. 1939. *Carolina Gardens.* Raleigh: The University of North Carolina Press.

Shelton, Louise. 1931. *Continuous Bloom in America.* New York: Charles Scribner's Sons.

Sherlock, Chesla C. 1922. *Bulb Gardening.* Des Moines, Iowa: Fruit, Garden and Home.

Shinn, Charles H. 1894. Some trees at Rancho Chico. *Garden and Forest* 7 (339): 332.

Shurtleff, Arthur A. 1899. Some old New England flower gardens. *New England Magazine* 21 (December): 422–424.

Simonds, O. C. 1909. Wild flowers. In *Transactions of the Illinois State Horticultural Society for the Year 1908.* Springfield, Illinois: Illinois State Horticultural Society: 77–79.

————. 1931. *Landscape-Gardening.* New York: Macmillan.

Slade, Daniel D. 1895. *The Evolution of Horticulture in New England.* New York: Putnam's Sons.

Smith, A. J. 1912. Lilies. In *Annual Report of the Wisconsin State Horticultural Society for the Year 1912*, edited by F. Cranefield. Madison: Democrat Printing Co: 7–10.

Smith, F. F. 1885. Flowering of the Sunset rose. *The Gardener's Monthly* 27 (318): 170.

Snowdrops and snowflakes. 1885. *Vick's Monthly Magazine* 8 (3): 68–70.

Some plants little grown. 1888. *The American Garden* 9 (4): 146.

Spencer, Darrell. 1997. *The Gardens of Salem: The Landscape History of a Moravian Town in North Carolina*. Winston-Salem, North Carolina: Old Salem.

Spencer, James H. 1910. The best vines for the coldest sections. *The Garden Magazine* 10 (6): 272–273.

Spurrier, John. 1793. *Practical Farmer*. Wilmington, Delaware: Brynburg & Andrews.

Stearn, William T. 1986. Historical survey of the naming of cultivated plants. *Acta Horticulturae* 182: 19.

Steele, Fletcher. 1925. *Design in the Little Garden*. Boston: Atlantic Monthly Press.

Still, Steven M. 1994. *Manual of Herbaceous Ornamental Plants*. 4th ed. Champaign, Illinois: Stipes.

Strang, Elizabeth L. 1915. Planting bulbs for spring bloom. *The Garden Magazine* 22 (3): 73–76.

Streatfield, David C. 1994. *California Gardens: Creating a New Eden*. New York: Abbeville Press.

Stritikus, George. 1992. Azaleas in the antebellum landscape. *Magnolia* 9 (1): 12.

Stritikus, George R., and Melanie Johns. 1996. A nurseryman evaluates southern gardens of the 1850s. *Magnolia* 12 (4): 1–4; 8–9.

Swem, E. G. 1957. *Brothers of the Spade: Correspondence of Peter Collinson, of London and of John Custis, of Williamsburg, Virginia, 1734–1746*. Barre, Massachusetts: Barre Gazette.

Swett, Naomi, and Adolph Meyer. 1928. Landscaping plans and upkeep. *House & Garden* 53 (6): 80, 150, 158.

Symons-Jeune, B. H. B. 1934. *Phlox, a Flower Monograph*. London: The Garden Book Club.

T. 1847. Lawns and shade trees. *The Cultivator* 4 (9): 275–276.

Tabor, Grace. 1912. *Making the Grounds Attractive with Shrubbery*. New York: McBride, Nast.

———. 1916. *The Landscape Gardening Book*. New York: Robert M. McBride.

———. 1925. *Old-Fashioned Gardening*. New York: Robert M. McBride.

Tabor, I. G. 1906. A planting plan for a deep-bayed border. *The Garden Magazine* 4 (1): 16–17.

Taylor, Frederic W. 1893. *Annual Report of the State Horticultural Society, Nebraska, 1893*. Lincoln, Nebraska: Published by the State.

Taylor, Norman. 1915. A hundred native perennials for the wild garden. *The Garden Magazine* 21 (4): 214–215.

Teschemacher, James E. (J. E. T.) 1835. On artificial rock-work. *The Horticultural Register* 1: 457–458.

Thomas, John J. 1846. Grouping flowers—a suggestion. *The Horticulturist* 1 (3): 120–122.

———. 1855a. Perennials for lawns. *Illustrated Annual Register of Rural Affairs for 1855–6–7*. Vol. l. Reprint, 1886: 299.

———. 1855b. Artificial rock-work. *Illustrated Annual Register of Rural Affairs for 1855–6–7*. Vol. 1. Reprint, 1886: 301.

———. 1858. Supports for climbers. *Rural Affairs*. New York: Luther Tucker: 42–44.

Treatment of shrubbery in small gardens. 1863. *The Gardener's Monthly* 5 (7): 206–207.

Trees for rural cemeteries. 1854. *The Horticulturist* 4 n.s. (4): 153–158.

A trip to Cuba and the southern states, no. 10. 1858. *The Horticulturist* 8 (3): 126–127.

Trumbull, E. E. 1916. A summer with some of the new gladioli. *The Garden Magazine* 23 (4): 232.

T. S. H. 1869. A journey to New Mexico—III. *The Cultivator & Country Gentleman* 23 (835): 42.

Tucker, Luther. 1848. Rural architecture—Hope Cottage. *The Cultivator* 5 (1): 9–10.

Tucker, Luther, and John J. Thomas, eds. 1869. Ornamental trees. *The Cultivator & Country Gentleman* 24 (861): 56.

Ulrich, Laurel T. 1991. *A Midwife's Tale*. New York: Vintage Books.

USDA, NRCS. 2002. The PLANTS Database, Version 3.5 (http://plants.usda.gov). National Plant Data Center, Baton Rouge, Louisiana.

Valk, William W. 1847. Remarks on roses. *The Horticulturist* 1 (7): 307–309.

———. 1848. The Wistaria Sinensis. *The Horticulturist* 3 (2): 63–66.

van de Laar, H. J., and P. C. de Jong. 2000. *Naamlijst Van Houtige Gewassen* (*List of Names of Woody Plants*). Boskoop, The Netherlands: Boomteelt Praktijkonderzoek.

van der Donck, Adrian. 1655. *Beschryvinge Van Nieuw-Nederlant* (Description of the New Netherlands) [non vide].

Van Rensselaer, Mrs. Schuyler. 1900. *Art Out-Of-Doors.* New York: Charles Scribner's Sons.

Vick, James, ed. 1878a. Annual climbers. *Vick's Monthly Magazine* 1 (6): 195–198.

———. 1878b. The carnation and its culture. *Vick's Monthly Magazine* 1 (2): 44–45.

———. 1878c. A few fine plants. *Vick's Monthly Magazine* 1 (12): 356–357.

———. 1878d. Fine petunias. *Vick's Monthly Magazine* 1 (8): 246.

———. 1878e. Flowers and flower-beds. *Vick's Monthly Magazine* 1 (2): 39–41.

———. 1878f. The hollyhock. *Vick's Monthly Magazine* 1 (5): 185.

———. 1878g. Honeysuckles. *Vick's Monthly Magazine* 1 (9): 261.

———. 1878h. The tuberose. *Vick's Monthly Magazine* 1 (3): 86–87.

———. 1878i. The phlox and the pansy. *Vick's Monthly Magazine* 1 (1): 7.

———. 1879a. Ornamental gourds. *Vick's Monthly Magazine* 2 (1): 5–6.

———. 1879b. The petunia. *Vick's Monthly Magazine* 2 (5): 135.

———. 1879c. The rocket larkspur. *Vick's Monthly Magazine* 2 (5): 135.

———. 1881a. Hedges and hedge plants. *Vick's Monthly Magazine* 4 (2): 36–38.

———. 1881b. Virginia creeper. *Vick's Monthly Magazine* 4 (9): 275–278.

———. 1882a. April 1882. *Vick's Monthly Magazine* 5 (4): 92–100.

———. 1882b. Flowering shrubs. *Vick's Monthly Magazine* 5 (8): 227–230.

———. 1882c. A late summer shrub. *Vick's Monthly Magazine* 5 (9): 259–260.

———. 1883a. The Chinese snowball. *Vick's Monthly Magazine* 6 (10): 294.

———. 1883b. Clematis and its uses. *Vick's Monthly Magazine* 6 (11): 324.

———. 1883c. Double Acroclinium. *Vick's Monthly Magazine* 6 (1): 4.

———. 1883d. A handsome grass. *Vick's Monthly Magazine* 6 (4): 102.

———. 1883e. The pelargoniums. *Vick's Monthly Magazine* 6 (7): 194–202.

———. 1884. Golden mock orange. *Vick's Monthly Magazine* 7 (10): 291–292.

Visits to country places—no. 6 around New York. 1857. *The Horticulturist* 7 (1): 22–24.

Visits to country places—no. 9 around Baltimore. 1857. *The Horticulturist* 7 (5): 206–208.

Vobeyda, Mrs. F. E. 1938. Hardy lilies for Minnesota. *The Minnesota Horticulturist* 66 (6): 105, 109.

W. A. R. 1882. Rose, Etoile de Lyon. *The Gardener's Monthly* 24 (281): 134.

Warburton, Bee, ed. 1978. *The World of Irises.* Wichita, Kansas: The American Iris Society.

Warder, John A. 1858. *Hedges and Evergreens.* New York: A. O. Moore.

Warner, Anna B. 1872. *Gardening by Myself.* Reprint, West Point, New York: The Constitution Island Association, 1924.

Watson, Alexander. 1859. *The American Home Garden.* New York: Harper & Brothers.

Watts, May T. 1957. *Reading the Landscape: An Adventure in Ecology.* Reprint, New York: Macmillan, 1968.

Waugh, Frank A. 1905. All the foxgloves worth cultivating. *The Garden Magazine* 1 (1): 15–16.

———. 1928. *Book of Landscape Gardening.* New York: Orange Judd.

W. C. M. 1886. Plants for Nebraska. *Vick's Monthly Magazine* 9 (11): 343.

Webster, Helen N. 1939. *Herbs.* Boston: Hale, Cushman & Flint.

Weidenmann, Jacob. 1870. *Beautifying Country Homes.* Reprint, Watkins Glen, New York: American Life Foundation, 1978.

Welch, William C. 1989. *Perennial Garden Color: Perennials, Cottage Gardens, Old Roses, and Companion Plants.* Dallas, Texas: Taylor.

Welch, William C., and Greg Grant. 1995. *The Southern Heirloom Garden.* Dallas, Texas: Taylor.

W. H. C. 1868. Vines for a stump. *The Gardener's Monthly* 10 (4): 183.

Wheeler, E. D. 1899. Forestry. In *Transactions of the Kansas State Horticultural Society, 1898*. Topeka: J. S. Parks: 96–101.

White, Edward. 1930. *The Chrysanthemum and Its Culture*. New York: Orange Judd.

Wickson, E. J. 1915. *California Flowers, Shrubs, Trees and Vines*. San Francisco: Pacific Rural Press.

Wilcox, R. S. 1938. Hardier roses. *The Minnesota Horticulturist* 66 (5): 84–84, 88.

Wilder, Louise. 1918. *Colour in My Garden*. New York: Doubleday, Page.

———. 1937. *The Garden in Color*. New York: Macmillan.

Wilder, Marshall P. 1847. The new Japan lilies. *The Horticulturist* 2 (1): 31–34.

———. 1871. Tree paeonies. *Tilton's Journal of Horticulture* 9 (July): 193–196.

Williams, Henry, ed. 1872. Woodward's gardens, San Francisco, California. *The Horticulturist* 27 (12): 356–361.

Williams, H. T. 1870. Climbing plants as helps to home adornment. *The Gardener's Monthly* 3 n.s. (12): 361–365.

Wilson, Ernest H. 1915a. The best of the hardy climbing shrubs. *The Garden Magazine* 21 (2): 31–35.

———. 1915b. The story of the modern rose. *The Garden Magazine* 21 (5): 253–256.

———. 1916. Hardy rhododendrons. *The Garden Magazine* 23 (5): 288–292.

———. 1920. The romance of our trees: the horsechestnut. *The Garden Magazine* 30 (7): 267–271.

———. 1932. *Aristocrats of the Garden*. 2 vols. Boston: Stratford.

Wilson, Helen Van Pelt. 1946. *Geraniums: Pelargoniums for Windows and Gardens*. New York: M. Barrows.

Wilson, James. 1849. A notice of the double Japan Spirea. *The Horticulturist* 3 (8): 377.

Wister, John C. 1930. *Bulbs for American Gardens*. Boston: Stratford.

Withers, Ann E. 1878. What was done in Missouri. *Vick's Monthly Magazine* 1 (3): 77.

Wood, Alphonso. 1851. *A Class-Book of Botany*. Claremont, New Hampshire: Manufacturing Co.

Wood, William. 1634. *New England Prospect*. Reprint, Boston: E. M. Boynton, 1898.

Wooding, J. 1885. Cottage gardening at Upland, Delaware Co., Pa. *The Gardener's Monthly* 27 (322): 293–294.

Wright, Richardson. 1924. *The Practical Book of Outdoor Flowers*. Philadelphia: J. B. Lippincott.

Wright, Walter. 1911. *Popular Garden Flowers*. New York: Doubleday, Page.

Wyman, Donald. 1969. *Shrubs and Vines for American Gardens*. New York: Macmillan.

———. 1990. *Trees for American Gardens*. New York: Macmillan.

The zebra-striped Eulalia. 1876. *American Agriculturist*. 35 (12): 460.

INDEX

[*Crocus*]
'Giant Yellow'. See *Crocus ×luteus* 'Mammoth Yellow'
'King of the Blues', 246
×luteus 'Mammoth Yellow', **246**. See also *Rosa* 'Chromatella'
'Golden Yellow'. See *C. ×luteus* 'Mammoth Yellow'
susianus. See *C. angustifolius*
vernus 'Purpureus Grandiflorus', 246
crown imperial. See *Fritillaria imperialis*
cuckoo flower. See *Lychnis flos-cuculi*
cucumber tree. See *Magnolia acuminata*
Culver's root. See *Veronicastrum virginicum*
Cupressus lawsoniana. See *Chamaecyparis lawsoniana*
cup and saucer vine. See *Cobaea scandens*
cups-and-saucers. See *Campanula medium*
Curcurbita
argyrosperma, 142
pepo var. *ovifera*, 142
currant, Missouri. See *Ribes aureum*
cycad. See *Cycas revoluta*
Cycas revoluta, 41, **88**, 209
Cydonia
japonica. See *Chaenomeles speciosa*
maulei. See *Chaenomeles japonica*
Cymbopogon citratus, 42
cypress. See *Chamaecyparis*
golden Sawara. See *Chamaecyparis pisifera* 'Plumosa Aurea'
Golden thread-leaf Japan. See *Chamaecyparis pisifera* 'Filifera Aurea'
Hinoki. See *Chamaecyparis obtusa*
Japan. See *Chamaecyparis pisifera*
Lawson's. See *Chamaecyparis lawsoniana*
Plumed Sawara. See *Chamaecyparis pisifera* 'Plumosa'
Sawara. See *Chamaecyparis pisifera*

Thread-branched Japan. See *Chamaecyparis pisifera* 'Filifera'
Veitch's silver. See *Chamaecyparis pisifera* 'Squarrosa'
Cypripedium, 60, 161, 235
Cytissus laburnum. See *Laburnum anagyroides*

daffodil. See *Narcissus*
hoop petticoat. See *Narcissus bulbocodium*
pink trumpet. See *Narcissus* 'Mrs. R. O. Backhouse'
wild. See *Narcissus pseudonarcissus*
dahlia, hardy. See *Helianthus*
Dahlia, 39, 50, 57, 236, 237, 238, 246, 247
'Bonny Blue', 247
'Jane Cowl', 247
'Jersey's Beauty', **247**
'Kaiser Wilhelm', **247**
'Thomas A. Edison', 247
'Tommy Keith', 247
'Union Jack', 247
'Yellow Gem', 247
daisy. See *Bellis*; *Leucanthemum*; *Rudbeckia*; *Tanacetum*
Belgian. See *Bellis perennis*
English. See *Bellis perennis*
moonpenny. See *Leucanthemum ×superbum*
mountain. See *Bellis perennis*
painted. See *Tanacetum coccineum*
Persian. See *Tanacetum coccineum*
Shasta. See *Leucanthemum ×superbum*
yellow. See *Rudbeckia hirta*
damask violet. See *Hesperis matronalis*
dame's violet. See *Hesperis matronalis*
Daphne, 30
cneorum, 114
mezereon, 114, 236
Darlingtonia californica, 161
daylily. See *Hemerocallis*
blue. See *Hosta ventricosa*
crown. See *Hemerocallis fulva* 'Flore Pleno'
custard. See *Hemerocallis lilioasphodelus*
Japan. See *Hosta plantaginea*

Siberian grass-leaved. See *Hemerocallis minor*
tawny. See *Hemerocallis fulva*
white. See *Hosta plantaginea*
Delaware, 38
delphinium, Chinese. See *Delphinium grandiflorum*
Delphinium
ajacis. See *Consolida ajacis*
alpinum. See *D. elatum*
×belladonna. See *D.* Belladonna Group
Belladonna Group, 177, 179
×bellamosum, 179
Blackmore & Langdon Hybrids, 179
chinense. See *D. grandiflorum*
'Cliveden Beauty' (Belladonna Group), 179
consolida. See *Consolida ajacis*
elatum, 30, 179
exaltatum, 178
formosum, 178
grandiflorum, 162, 178
grandiflorum 'Album', 178
grandiflorum 'Blue Butterfly', 179
intermedium. See *D. elatum*
sinense. See *D. grandiflorum*
Wrexham Hybrids, 179
deutzia. See *Deutzia*
dwarf. See *Deutzia gracilis*
fuzzy. See *Deutzia scabra*
Lemoine. See *Deutzia ×lemoinei*
rough-leaved. See *Deutzia scabra*
slender-branched. See *Deutzia gracilis*
Deutzia, 29, 53, 57, **114**, 255
gracilis, 114
×lemoinei, 107, 114
scabra, 114
scabra 'Pride of Rochester', 114
devil's darning needles. See *Clematis virginiana*
Dianthus, 30, 42, 47, 51, 52, 156, 201, 236
barbatus, 37, 38, 53, 158, 159, 162, **179, 208**, 214, 218, 263
barbatus 'Holburn Glory', 179
barbatus 'Newport Pink', 179
barbatus 'Nigricans' (Nigrescens Group), 179
'Bat's Double Red', 180

caryophyllus, 36, 52, **217**. See also *Matthiola incana*
caryophyllus 'Grenadin', 217
chinensis, 51, 57, 210, 217, 218. See also *Ipomoea quamoclit*
chinensis 'Heddewigii', 218
deltoides, 159
deltoides 'Brilliant', 180
'Essex Witch', 180
'Her Majesty', 180
hortensis. See *D. plumarius*
'Inchmery', 180
'Lady Granville', 180
'Margaret Curtis', 180
montanus, 160
'Mrs. Sinkins', 180
plumarius, 159, 179, 180
'Rose de Mai', **180**
'Spring Beauty', 180
superbus, 180
Dicentra, 39, 163
cucullaria, 52
eximia, 180
formosa, 180
spectabilis, 53, 162, 180
spectabilis 'Alba', 180
Dictamnus
albus, 105, 162, 173, 181
albus var. *purpureus*, 173, **181**
Dielytra spectabilis. See *Dicentra spectabilis*
Diervilla florida. See *Weigela florida*
Digitalis
ambigua. See *D. grandiflora*
aurea. See *D. grandiflora*
ferruginea, 182
grandiflora, 178, 182
lutea, **182**
orientalis. See *D. grandiflora*
purpurea, 32, 50, 156, 163, 174, **181**, 195, 255, 263
purpurea 'Alba'. See *D. purpurea* f. *albiflora*
purpurea f. *albiflora*, 182
purpurea 'Gloxiniiflora' (Gloxinioides Group), 182
Dioscorea batatas, **142**
Ditremexa marilandica. See *Senna marilandica*
dittany, white. See *Dictamnus albus*
Dodecatheon meadia, 171, 182
dogberry. See *Cornus sanguinea*
dogwood
bloody. See *Cornus sanguinea*; *C. stolonifera*

woodbine. See *Clematis*;
    Lonicera
woolflower. See *Celosia argentea*
    (Childsii Group)
Wyoming, 54, **56**

Xeranthemum, 219
Xylosteum tartaricum. See
    Lonicera tatarica

yahoo. See *Euonymus atropur-*
    pureus

yellow wood. See *Cladrastis ken-*
    tukea
yew. See *Taxus*
yew, upright Japanese. See *Taxus*
    cuspidata
Yucca, 22, 156, 177, 210
    aloifolia, 102, 206
    angustifolia, 206
    filamentosa, 48, 51, 52, 163,
        206
    gloriosa, 206

Zantedeschia
    aethiopica, 48, 54, 238, 254,
        267
    albomaculata, **267**
zebra grass. See *Miscanthus*
    sinensis 'Zebrinus'
Zelkova serrata, 101
Zephyranthes atamasca, 252, 254
Zinnia, 31, 32, 43, 51, 57, 198,
        199, 201, 210, 212
    elegans, **233**, 234
    elegans 'Cactus', **234**
    elegans 'California Giants',
        234

elegans 'Lilliput', 234
haageana, 234
multiflora. See *Z. peruviana*
pauciflora. See *Z. peruviana*
peruviana, 234